Turner Publishing Company
Publishers of America's History
P.O. Box 3101
Paducah, Kentucky 42002-3101

Co-published by
Mark A. Thompson, Associate Publisher

Pre-Press work by M.T. Publishing Company, Inc.
Graphic Designers: Elizabeth A. Dennis and John L. Mathias

Copyright © 2001
Sons of the Republic of Texas

This book or any part thereof may not be reproduced without the written consent of the Sons of the Republic of Texas and the Publishers.

The materials were compiled and produced using available information; Turner Publishing Company, M.T. Publishing Company, Inc., and the Sons of the Republic of Texas regret they cannot assume liability for errors or omissions.

Library of Congress
Control Number 00-134402

ISBN: 978-1-68162-232-3

Contents

Sons of the Republic of Texas History _____ 5

The Republic of Texas _____ 6

The Sons Of The Republic Of Texas _____ 11

Knights Of The Order Of San Jacinto _____ 23

Sons of the Republic of Texas Biographies _____ 27

Index _____ 182

Publisher's Note

It is with great pleasure that we introduce this new volume on The Sons of the Republic of Texas, and we hope all will enjoy our newest title that chronicles the history of this organization and the settlement of what is now the State of Texas.

We extend our gratitude to The Sons of the Republic of Texas for their cooperation in producing this book. Special thanks to O. Scott Dunbar, KSJ for his assistance in getting this publication underway. Also we wish to thank Melinda Williams for her assistance in seeing this project through to its completion.

Finally, we are indeted to hundreds of The Sons of the Republic of Texas members who took the time to submit their biographies for inclusion in this historic book.

Dave Turner, President
Mark A. Thompson, Associate Publisher

Sons of the Republic of Texas History

The Republic of Texas

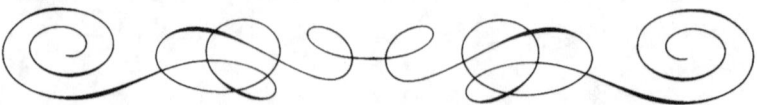

Joe E. Ericson, KSJ

Texas historians frequently assert that the Republic of Texas was born April 21, 1836 as a consequence of the Texian's victory at the Battle of San Jacinto. More than three hundred years of European penetration and settlement, however, along with over a century of Spanish and Mexican rule preceded that decisive event in the history of Texas.

From 1519 when Alverez de Pineda spent forty days at the mouth of the Rio Grande until 1659 when the Spanish began founding missions along the Rio Bravo (Rio Grande), explorers such as Cabeza de Vaca, Francisco de Coronado, and Hernando de Soto traversed the region now know as Texas, and the Spanish perfected their claim to the area. These early adventurers sought new lands for their king, a strait linking the Atlantic and Pacific Oceans, caches of precious metal and gems to enrich themselves and their king, and prestige for the Spanish crown.

After 1680 they were followed by a series of missionary expeditions aimed at Christianizing the native inhabitants of the region who had lived there for centuries. Early efforts such as the founding of Corpus Christi de la Isleta (1680), San Francisco de los Tejas (1690), and Nuestra Padre San Franscisco de los Tejas (1716) failed as a result of neglect by vice regal authorities and the growing hostility of Indians themselves.

After a lapse of some fifty years, in 1756, the Spanish launched a general program of expansion of effort in Texas prompted by a combination of external and internal forces. Learning in 1687 of Robert Cavalier, Sieur de la Salle's activities in and along the Texas coast, the foundation of New Orleans in 1718 by Jean Baptiste Le Moyne, Sieur de Bienville, and the creation of a French trading post at Natchitoches in northern Louisiana in 1713-1714 by Louis Juchereau de St. Denis alerted the Spanish authorities to the threat of French encroachment from their possessions east of Texas.

Increasing Indian hostility in the early years of the Eighteenth Century demonstrated the necessity of presidios (forts garrisoned with professional soldiers) and permanent settlements to guarantee successful Spanish missionary efforts. By 1716 six new missions were founded, five of them extending along a line from the Neches River to Los Adaes. Presidios were established on the Neches and by 1718 at San Antonio de Béxar on the San Antonio River. As late as 1769, virtually all of Spain's efforts at expansion in Texas had ended in failure.

Moreover, as an outgrowth of the Seven Years' War (1756-1763), Spain acquired possession of Louisiana, placing the more aggressive Anglo-Americans on her northeast border rather than the less enterprising French. Along with other external threats to and increasing internal troubles within, this situation prompted the Spanish crown to adopt new policies for its Texas colony. After 1769, all missions and presidios except San Antonio and La Bahía (Goliad) were to be abandoned; settlers from eastern portions of the colony were ordered to remove to San Antonio de Béxar to strengthen its defense; and new Indian policies that called for extermination of the Apaches in Texas.

In the summer of 1773, more than 500 Spanish settlers in eastern Texas, including those at Los Ais,

Los Adaes, and Nacogdoches, were forced to leave their homes and proceed westward to San Antonio. The following year, a group of them under the leadership of Antonio Gil Y'Barbo were allowed to leave and establish a pueblo at Bucareli on the Trinity River. A combination of floods and Indian raids caused these colonists to abandon Bucareli in 1779 and move eastward to Nacogdoches.

Conditions in Texas remained reasonably stable thereafter until 1800 when Napoleon Bonaparte persuaded the Spanish monarch to return Louisiana to French control. Three years later, the French emperor antagonized the Spanish and presented them with a new and more serious external threat by selling Louisiana to the United States. Texas was once again on the border sharing a boundary with the land-hungry Anglo-Americans east of the Sabine River.

Spanish authorities then adopted the new policies aimed at preserving their sovereignty over Texas. Garrisons were increased in number and in manpower; loyal Spanish citizens were encouraged to colonize the region; and the boundaries of Texas were closed to Anglo-American intruders.

Spanish attempts to close her western borders to Anglo-American settlement coupled with the urge for westward expansion among those Americans brought on a series of filibustering expeditions between 1800 and 1821. The Philip Nolan expedition of 1800-1801, the Gutiérrez-McGee expedition of 1812-1813, and the James Long expedition of 1819-1821 were effectively suppressed, and the successful Mexican Revolution of 1821 brought to an end this flurry of filibustering activity.

On the eve of Mexican independence after approximately three hundred years of Spanish rule, there were only three small settlements in Texas: San Antonio with some 2,500 inhabitants, including its garrison troops; La Bahía (Goliad) with 618 inhabitants, including garrison forces; and Nacogdoches with 660 inhabitants. This, then, was the Texas the new Mexican government had inherited.

In an attempt to induce settlers to immigrate, as early as 1806 the Spanish had offered inducements to persons in Louisiana to cross the Sabine River into their Texas colony. Potential settlers from Louisiana provided they were Catholic and were not Africans or mulattoes were encouraged to settle along the banks of the Guadalupe River, at San Antonio, or at La Bahía, but not at Nacogdoches where they would be a source of trouble involving those who remained in Louisiana. By 1809, however, this permission was withdrawn and the door to foreign immigrants again closed.

Despite Spanish attempts to forestall foreign immigration, from 1803 to 1821, scores – perhaps hundreds – of persons, some Spanish subjects, others not, crossed back and forth freely from Louisiana into Texas. Most ultimately returned to Louisiana but many remained in Texas around Nacogdoches and San Augustine in eastern Texas, while others stayed around San Antonio and along the Guadalupe River in central parts of the territory.

After 1821, the Mexican government feeling that it was absolutely necessary to populate the province took the bold and ultimately fatal experiment of permitting, even encouraging, foreign immigration in Texas. Thus, in 1823, a federal colonization law confirmed an application by Stephen F. Austin for an empresario's contract, a contract originally negotiated by his father Moses Austin. This, Austin's first contract, authorized him to settle 300 families. All such immigrants were required to profess the Roman Catholic religion and furnish satisfactory evidence of their morality and good habits.

Immigrant families who qualified could claim one league (4,428 acres) and one labor (177 acres) of land. Austin's early colonists generally selected the rich bottom lands along the Brazos and Colorado Rivers, but some settled over the entire territory between the San Jacinto and Lavaca Rivers and between the Gulf of Mexico and the San Antonio to Nacogdoches road (El Camino Real). By 1831 the colony numbered 5,665 persons, probably including slaves since they were not separately enumerated.

To encourage immigration, in 1824 the details of colonization were passed down to the states of the Mexican federation. The Mexican Federal Constitution (1824) having consolidated the provinces of Coahuila and Texas as one of the new states of that union thus delegated the responsibility for further colonization in Texas to its legislature. A state colonization law was enacted in 1825 at Saltillo. The new law required prospective settlers to furnish satisfactory evidence of their Catholic beliefs, their morality, and their good habits. They were then permitted to settle as individual families or groups of families recruited by an empresario. Families were granted a league of land which they were required to cultivate or occupy within six years. Empresarios were rewarded with as much as five leagues for each hundred families they recruited up to a maximum of 800. Single men were given only one-fourth as much land as heads of families but were given a full grant when they married.

Only six weeks after the law became effective, empresario grants had been awarded to Robert Leftwich, Green DeWitt, Frost Thorn, and Haden Edwards. In 1826 and 1827, additional grants were given to eleven empresarios, including a second grant to Stephen F. Austin, calling for settlement of some 8,000 families. None of these contract numbers was entirely fulfilled, in some cases not a single family was recruited.

Before and after the passage of the law of 1825, Anglo-Americans began streaming into Texas, many without permission. Population of the Province of Texas was estimated by the Spanish authorities at less than 3,000 persons. By 1834, however, the population had reached more than 24,000, most of the increase in the form of Anglo-American immigrants. A survey of the province conducted by Mexican officials in 1827 revealed that the power and influence of the government was waning rapidly in East Texas and that the influx of Anglo-Americans was increasing steadily. Alarmed, the Federal Congress in 1830 enacted legislation banning further immigration from nations bordering on the Republic of Mexico.

The Mexican government felt the prohibition was necessary to save Texas as a part of its republic. Anglo-American settlers, however, saw it as a direct blow at them and detrimental to the future of Texas. They believed that without further immigration from the United States the region would never realize its vast potential. They never ceased to agitate for its repeal, and in 1833 Anglo-American immigration was again permitted and new empresario contracts awarded.

As the numbers of Anglo-Americans in Texas escalated the stage was set for a conflict between men of vastly different cultures. Dissimilar ideas concerning government, religion, and society were most significant between the two ethnic groups. Added to these was the inherent European distaste, shared by most Americans, for the racial composition of the Mexican nation, dominated as it was by mestizos (persons of mixed Spanish and native American blood).

A series of actions by Mexican authorities beginning in 1831 led inexorably to the uprising of 1836. Initially, the federal government sent a collector to Texas in 1831 to enforce its customs laws and also additional soldiers to assist Mexican officials in enforcing the nation's laws. Officers charged with these duties were inept and overbearing. Anglo-Americans especially resented the presence and conduct of Mexican troops who often were imperious dons or rag-tag dark skinned men recruited from the lowest ranks of Mexican society.

These actions led to a minor insurrection at Anahuac in 1832 which ended almost without bloodshed. The Battle of Nacogdoches later in the year resulted in clearing East Texas of Mexican military forces. Thus, the 1832 uprising proved eminently successful. Mexican troops were withdrawn and customs duties suspended. Within a few weeks, however, colonists at San Felipe issued a call for a convention to meet with them to discuss grievances and adopt a constructive program.

Resolutions adopted by this group of delegates included requests for land titles to be issued to settlers in East Texas, for exemption from customs duties for three years, for land to be set aside for school purposes, and for investigation of and defense against the Cherokee Indians in East Texas. These modest proposals, for some unknown reason, were never presented to the requisite Mexican authorities.

The Consultation of 1832 also created committees of safety and correspondence in each locality. An important outgrowth of this action was a call for a second convention to meet at San Felipe the following year. The Convention of 1833 reiterated the request made the previous year, and strongly urged the repeal of all anti-immigration laws and separate statehood for Texas. Anticipating approval of their request for separation from Coahuila, the Convention also drafted an American-style constitution for Texas and asked the Mexican Federal Congress to approve it.

Stephen F. Austin was sent to Mexico City to seek approval of all requests including statehood. After months of inactivity, Mexican officials arrested Austin and cast him into prison, where his attorneys Peter W. Grayson and Spencer H. Jack found him and obtained his release on bail. Austin was not able to gain amnesty and leave Mexico City until mid-summer 1835.

The first violent action leading directly too the Texas Revolution the next year grew out of an attempt in January 1835 by the Mexican government to enforce collection of customs duties at Anahuac and Galveston. Misunderstandings between colonists and Mexican officials escalated thereafter, and culminated in an order by President Antonio Lopez de Santa Anna in September 1835 that colonists surrender their arms. Engagements between colonists and Mexican troops at San Patricio, Gonzales, and San Antonio soon followed. Despite continued efforts by Texians to effect some sort of agreement that would allow them to obtain separate statehood and a measure of self-government American style, events inexorably pushed them toward a declaration of independence.

Learning of armed resistance by Texas colonists, General Santa Anna determined to enforce his decrees and bring about the unconditional surrender of the Texians in residence. General Martin Perfecto de Cos immediately began moving troops into Texas and establishing his headquarters at San Antonio. By October 24, 1835, San Antonio was under siege. The Siege of Béxar culminated in the surrender of more than 1100 troops to the Texians under the leadership of Colonel Frank Johnson and Colonel Ben Milam.

About March 1, 1836, however, a scouting party of some 150 Texians, remnants of a projected attack on Matamoros, was destroyed almost to a man near San Patricio by Mexican cavalry under the command of General Jose Urrea. Later that month, the Mexican general encountered Colonel James W. Fannin's command near Goliad, attacked, and brought about the surrender of the Texian forces. March 27, Palm Sunday, the prisoners were massacred and their bodies buried in mass graves.

Meanwhile, General Santa Anna at the head of an army of 6,000 men entered Texas to subdue the Texians. His advanced forces reached San Antonio February 23, 1836 and immediately lay siege to colonial forces there who elected to defend the walls of the Alamo. The morning of March 6, Santa Anna's troops took the place by storm, killing most of its defenders. His strategy called for him to sweep eastward bringing havoc to all resistance.

While these events were unfolding in the west, a convention of fifty-nine delegates assembled at Washington-on-the-Brazos. Meeting from March 1 through March 17, this body prepared the Texas Declaration of Independence, established a provisional government, placed delegate Sam Houston in command of the Texas Army, and drafted a constitution for the Republic of Texas for approval by the people of the new nation.

News of the Goliad massacre, the fall of the Alamo, Santa Anna's eastward movement, and the steady retreat to the east of Houston's army combined to produce a panic causing settlers to abandon their homes and most of their possessions and flee toward the Sabine River and safety. Known as the Runaway Scrape, it quickly depopulated large areas of the territory. The provisional government fled eastward as well.

With Houston and his forces in retreat and Santa Anna's steady march to the east, the stage was set for one of most important battles in world history. By April 20, the Texians were camped near Lynch's Ferry where Buffalo Bayou joins the San Jacinto River. At that time Santa Anna with some 1,200 Mexican troops came up and camped nearby. An indecisive minor engagement between advanced units took place that day, but on the afternoon of April 21, the Texas army advanced across the prairie separating them from the Mexicans, took them by surprise, and inflicted a resounding defeat. In some eighteen minutes, the Texians killed some 630 of their enemies and took an additional 730 prisoners. Only nine Texans died and only thirty-four were wounded.

The following day Santa Anna was captured and was induced to order all Mexican forces to cease fighting and fall back beyond San Antonio and Victoria. The Mexican president agreed to help secure the permanent independence of Texas and to fix the boundary at the Rio Grande on the south.

Although the Republic of Texas could now claim a precarious existence as a nation, many persons in the new republic and in the United States assumed that it would not long remain independent but soon become a part of the United States. In September 1836 Texas citizens elected a set of national officers, but at the same time they voted overwhelming approval of union with states in the American federation. Sam Houston, hero of the Battle of San Jacinto, was easily elected the Republic's first president, while Mirabeau B. Lamar was elected his vice president.

During Houston's first administration (1836-1838) the working framework of government was created and put in motion, diplomatic recognition by some of the world's powers attained, and problems of national defense and public finance addressed. Moreover, facing the same necessity of attracting desirable permanent settlers, The Congress of the Republic launched a comprehensive land grant system. Containing only some 40,000 non-Indian inhabitants at the outset of its birth, the republic could not hope to defend itself against threats from other nations and from hostile Indian depredations.

Generous land grants of up to a league and labor were offered veterans of the Texas Revolution, and additional amounts of land granted to permanently disabled veterans, to those who participated in the Battle of San Jacinto, and to heirs of the men who died at the Alamo, Goliad, and Matamoros. Empresario contracts similar to those awarded by the Mexican government were also instituted but this practice was discontinued by 1844. In addition, the Texas Congress in 1838 enacted the first homestead legislation in America. It permitted persons to preempt as much as 320 acres at only fifty cents an acre and protected the homestead from seizure for debt.

Texas land could thus be acquired in larger amounts and for less fees than that offered from the public domain of the United States. As a consequence, during the life of the Republic hundreds of thousands of Americans crossed the Sabine River to settle in Texas. At the same time immigration from Europe was actively encouraged. Thousands of eager settlers primarily from Germany, France, and England became Texas residents, and Mexican immigration continued to swell the population of south and southwest parts of the Republic.

National defense policies were focused almost entirely upon the rumors of an imminent invasion from south of the Rio Grande, although internal discord in Mexico forestalled such an encroachment. President Houston's Indian policy centered on two tactics: keeping Texas troops out of Indian territory and entering into treaties of friendship that protected their claims to their lands.

Public finance was perhaps the nation's greatest immediate problem. Despite a modest tariff schedule, a general property tax, poll taxes, business taxes, and land fees, the treasury remained almost without funds. At the same time, public expenditures amounted to more than $2,000,000 annually. To cover the deficit, the government resorted to seeking foreign loans and printing paper money that quickly depreciated.

The national constitution prohibited Houston from seeking immediate re-election, and by a near unanimous vote he was succeeded by Mirabeau B. Lamar (1838-1841). The administration of the Republic's second president saw the capitol moved to the frontier town of Austin. Lamar soon reversed Houston's Indian policy and under his direction aggressive military operations launched the bloodiest Indian wars Texas had experienced. The Cherokee Indians in East Texas were attacked and driven off their land and out of Texas, and repeated forays against the Comanches resulted in practically eliminating Indian raids.

The financial affairs of the young nation worsened. Taxes were difficult to collect and brought only small returns to the treasury; expenditures exceeded revenues by more than $3,000,000 during Lamar's presidency; a $5,000,000 loan sought in the United States was not subscribed; and the government again resorted to printing paper money which again rapidly depreciated.

In the realm of foreign affairs the Lamar government had successfully gained recognition of the independence of Texas by France, the Netherlands, Great Britain, and Belgium added to the prior recognition by the United States. Attempts to arrive at an understanding with Mexico were repeated rebuffed, and annexation to the United States was not accomplished.

Lamar's three-year term was followed by a second Houston administration (1841-1844). The election of the popular war-time leader brought about a return to economy in expenditures, peace with the Indians, and avoidance of a revival of the war with Mexico. Expenditures were reduced to a total of some $500,000 for the three years of Houston's term; currency laws were repealed and the amount of paper money sharply reduced; the military forces of the nation were reduced to a few companies of Rangers. Despite these stringent measures, Texas money continued to depreciate and the nation's debt to increase steadily.

Under the General's direction, treaties with Indian tribes were again negotiated and trading posts established at a number of locations. These and other non-aggressive actions produced a period of relative freedom from Indian wars until the time of annexation.

President Houston resisted the popular demand for war with Mexico and exerted great effort to secure peace and recognition of the nation's independence. Revival of the movement to annex Texas to the United States, however, brought to an end any agreement with Mexico.

The basic policies of Houston's two administrations were continued by the nation's fourth president, Dr. Anson Jones (1844-1846). At the same time, events in the United States signaled a change in that nation's attitude toward the annexation of Texas. The election of 1844 saw a pro-Texas candidate, James K. Polk, gain a narrow victory. Outgoing president John Tyler, reading Polk's election as a mandate on the Texas question, again placed the question of annexation before Congress.

Early in 1845, after consultations among President Tyler, President-elect Polk, and Congressional leaders, an annexation bill was enacted by Congress. It provided for the admission of Texas as a full state, if it passed its own acceptance measure before January 1, 1846, Texas to retain ownership of all its public lands, permission of the new state to divide into four more states, and banning slavery north of 36 degrees, 30 minutes. The President was empowered to made minor adjustments if they proved necessary.

President Anson Jones acted promptly calling for a convention to approve the offer of annexation. In July 1845, the delegates voted to join the union with only one dissenting vote, and it set to work immediately on a proposed state constitution to submit to Congress and the voters of Texas. That constitution and annexation were approved by a vote of some 4,000 to 200 October 13, 1845.

Congress promptly accepted the proposed constitution, and on December 29, 1845, President James K. Polk signed the measure making Texas an American state. In a brief but moving ceremony, on February 19, 1846, the last president of the Republic of Texas presided over the lowering of the Texas flag and handed over his authority to Pinckney Henderson, the state's first governor. As the Texas flag came down, Anson Jones concluded his farewell address with these words: "The Republic of Texas is no more."

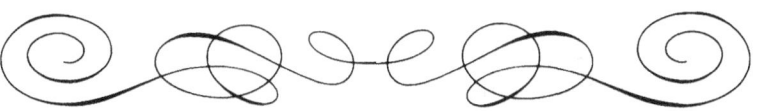

The Sons Of The Republic Of Texas

The history of the Sons of the Republic of Texas stretches back one hundred years. F. M. O. Fenn, who lived at Richmond, was one of the early members of the present organization. He organized the original society of the Sons of the Republic. Fenn had his original certificate of membership, signed at Houston on April 21, 1893, by W. A. Craddock, president, and P. Briscoe, secretary. He also had his original membership badge of Deaf Smith Chapter (#1), Sons of the Republic, organized at Richmond, April 10, 1893.

According to Fenn, several sons and grandsons of veterans living at Richmond discussed the organization of a society to be composed of male descendants of veterans of the Texas Republic, and on April 10, 1893, a meeting of the organizers was held, and a call issued for a meeting at Fenn's office on April 11 of all sons and grandsons of veterans of the Texas Revolution. A report of the organization appeared in the *Galveston News* under Richmond dateline of April 12, 1893.

The sons and grandsons of veterans of the Texas Revolution met yesterday at the office of F. M. O. Fenn and organized Deaf Smith Chapter. The following members were enrolled: S. J. Winston, J. H. P. Davis, F. M. O. Fenn, S. P. Walter, James William and C. R. Scott, Thos. Fulcher, W. M. and Robert Darst, Sam and Robert Hodges, W. Robinson, Bush Pleasants, Alex and Rufus McNabb, Mayfield Damon, Dr. Dillard, J. J. Fenn and Oscar Scott.

The following officers were elected: S. J. Winston, president; J. H. P. Davis, first vice president; F. M. O. Fenn, second vice president; James H. Scott, third vice president; Thos. Fulcher, secretary; W. M. Darst, assistant secretary; Dr. J. L. Dillard, treasurer; R. H. Darst, historian general.

This chapter will meet in the city of Houston on the 19th instant and participate in the celebration of the 21st.

The Richmond Sons of the Republic came to Houston on April 19, and on April 20, 1893, a state organization of Sons of the Republic of Texas was perfected with W. A. Craddock of Brenham as state president and P. Briscoe of Houston as secretary.

The original Sons of the Republic seems to have been quite active for a number of years, and accompanied the surviving veterans to their annual reunions. Fenn had the badge of the encampment at Lampasas.

A photostat of the above mentioned clipping and membership certificate is now filed in the minute book of San Jacinto Chapter (#1) for the year 1938 as a permanent record. The original certificate, together with a ribbon or badge which reads "Deaf Smith Chapter (#1), Sons of the Republic of Texas — 1836 — Richmond, Texas, April 10, 1893" is now in the archives of the San Jacinto Museum of Texas History at the San Jacinto Battleground, having been placed there in 1939 by the Sons of the Republic of Texas.

F. M. O. Fenn

F. M. O. Fenn, the moving spirit of the original Sons of the Republic of Texas, was one of the distinguished citizens of his native Fort Bend County. He was a son of John R. Fenn, who with his father came to Texas as Austin colonists. John R. Fenn served in General Houston's army in the Revolution but had the misfortune of being captured by Colonel Almonte's Mexican division a few days prior to the Battle of San Jacinto. John Fenn contrived his escape from the Mexicans shortly after the Battle of San Jacinto and became a leading citizen of Fort Bend County. Following the Woll invasion, John Fenn joined the volunteers under General Somervell, and marched with them to the Rio Grande, but obeyed orders of President Houston and did not cross the Rio Grande with the Mier Expedition. During the Civil War he served in the Confederate Army. He died in 1904.

From *TEXAS UNDER MANY FLAGS* the following is taken:

> *Francis Marion Otis Fenn was liberally educated, attending Roanoke College at Salem, Virginia, and the University of Virginia. He has long been famous as an orator and campaign speaker. He was awarded a medal for oratory at Roanoke College in 1879 and was also a medalist at the University of Virginia. He began the practice of law in Houston, where he remained until 1888...He had a prominent part in the political uprising in Fort Bend County, which brought about a rule for rotation in public office. He held public office in Fort Bend County for more than twenty years, but never sought public office nor solicited a vote in his behalf.*

The thought of perpetuating the ideals of the Texas Veterans was widespread, for about 1915-17, Hon. Hobart Huson of Refugio attempted to organize a group called "The Sons of the Texas Revolution." Among the charter members were Albert Sidney Burleson, Carlos Bee, Robert J. Kleberg, Gland Kuykendall, Thomas Y. Banks, Thomas J. Lancaster, Jose Antonio Navarro and Frank S. Huson. However, because of his youth and World War I, it was not perfected. The records of this group were also turned over to the present incorporated organization.

Under the title of "Neglected Anniversaries," the *Houston Chronicle* in March, 1917, published the following timely editorial:

> *Houston celebrated the second day of March in only a very formal and perfunctory way.*
>
> *That the banks closed cannot be placed to the credit of the people, because that was but obedience to statute law, and with the exception of the very creditable banquet given by the engineering department of the city, at which the menu cards were gems of the draftsman's art and in complete harmony with the sentiment associated with the day, there was no observance of the day by due and formal ceremony.*
>
> *Since then, another memorable anniversary has come and gone absolutely without notice. Yet it was the eighty-first anniversary of a day whereon the standard of human valor was, by a little band of Texans, lifted to a height never before reached in all the world's history, where it has stood unchallenged until this day.*
>
> *The Chronicle believes both the 2nd of March, a double anniversary, that of the birth of Sam Houston and of the signing of the Declaration of Texas Independence, and the 6th of March, that of the fall of the Alamo, should be unfailingly observed by the people of Texas.*
>
> *"The mind instinctively associates with great men, the date and place of their birth and associates with great events the day on which such events transpired.*
>
> *Tested by the only true standard—that of achievement—Sam Houston was one of the great men of this nation.*
>
> *Not only was his career unmatched in uniqueness, but from his achievements flowed far reaching results, and the importance and value of what he did will be made more and more manifest with the passing of time.*
>
> *The Declaration of Independence was in the light of the environment of the 58 men who signed it a most momentous deliverance. Nothing greater in the way of a statement of the convictions and purposes of the representatives of any people has been set in type or graven with a pen since July 4, 1776, and the anniversary of that event should never go by unnoticed.*
>
> *As was fitly graven on the monument erected many years ago in honor of the heroes of the Alamo, they are 'enrolled in the host of Leonidas and the mighty dead.' They taught mankind 'the lesson of*

earth's loftiest martyrdom,' and reflected on Texas a glory as fadeless as the stars.

To keep alive the memory of deeds such as these is more than a privilege. It is a duty which the people of Texas cannot neglect without reflecting upon their own patriotism and state pride.

It was the realization of such gross neglect of our great State holidays as set forth in this editorial that prompted 22 patriotic citizens of Houston to sign a call for the reorganization of "The Sons of the Republic of Texas for Harris County," which would have as its objective "To promote the celebration of March 2nd (Independence Day) and April 21st (San Jacinto Day) and to perpetuate the hallowed memory of the sacrifices made at the Alamo on March 6th and at Goliad on March 27th by having proper celebrations and exercises, each year, of such character as will arouse and keep alive the patriotic sentiments and feeling of the people of Texas." This call, as published in the *Houston Chronicle* of March 2, 1922, follows:

The undersigned urgently request to meet with them at the University Club on the afternoon of Wednesday, March 15th, at 5 o'clock, all the men, residents of Harris County, whose ancestors performed some service, military or civil, for Texas during the period between 1820 and January 1, 1846.

According to contemporary newspaper accounts, the call for organization was signed by the following men: Lewis R. Bryan, Charles E. Ashe, O. M. Kendall, Franklin Williams, George A. Hill, Sidney H. Huston, Milton Howe, Jacob F. Wolters, Andrew J. Houston Williams, W. E. Kendall, A. M. John, August De Zavala, Lewis R. Bryan, Jr., Royston Williams, Guy M. Bryan, Clarence Kendall and E. T. Branch.

Of these sponsors, seven served as president, and each year since organization, one or more served in some official capacity.

After two preliminary meetings were held, officers for the first year were elected at a meeting held at the University Club on the evening of March 30, 1922: Col. Andrew Jackson Houston, son of General Sam Houston, president; Judge Lewis R. Bryan, nephew of Stephen F. Austin and son of Moses Austin Bryan, a soldier of San Jacinto, first vice president; Judge Charles E. Ashe, grandson of President Anson Jones, second vice president; Odin M. Kendall, grandson of General Sidney Sherman, secretary; Harvey Dumble, grandson of Honorable William Harrison King, an early mayor of Houston, treasurer; and Judge A. C. Allen, a member of the Allen family that founded the City of Houston, and Judge L. B. Moody, grandson of Dr. Thomas Mitchell, a Houston physician and Main Street druggist in 1838-39, as executive committeemen.

The *Houston Post* in its issue of April 1, 1922, recognized the newly formed society in the following commendatory editorial:

A cordial welcome is due Texas' latest patriotic organization, the Sons of the Republic of Texas, composed of the male descendants of the founders of the Republic and the early builders of Texas. There's a wide field of usefulness for the new organization, and the character of the men composing its membership insures that some valuable services will be rendered the State.

Texas has a history of incomparable richness among the States. As the greatness of the State becomes more evident, the significance of the work of the early Texas patriots is better realized. They grow in heroic stature as they recede into the past. They take their places alongside those who established the American Republic itself.

There is need for the memory of those patriots and their achievements to be kept alive. The principles for which they fought need to be held up before Texans today. The inspiration that comes from a knowledge and understanding of the spirit and achievements of the founders of the Texas Republic will develop a nobler citizenship today. The throngs of new citizens settling in Texas should know Texas history and catch the spirit of its makers.

It is highly desirable that a State patriotism be cultivated. Being a State settled rapidly with people from all parts of the country, this side of Texas life has not been highly developed as it has been in some of the older States. More attention should be given to developing popular pride and love for State, and the Sons of the Republic of Texas are especially fitted to preserve and present Texas history in its true light and to inspire the proper love for the State among the new generation.

Those who are eligible to membership in the society may justly feel proud of the distinction. They are to be congratulated.

But the honor carries with it the responsibility of helping to perpetuate the ideals of government cherished by their forefathers, that the present day Texans may be imbued with the same heroic spirit that possessed the pioneers. It is gratifying to see the worthy descendants of those men assuming this responsibility. Organized and working together they can exercise an influence that will profoundly affect for good the life of the State.

During the first year, 1922, dues were paid by thirty-five members, and, perhaps, these should be designated as Charter Members. In 1932 the names on the membership roll numbered 81, showing geographical the following distribution: Houston 63; Austin 3; Alvin 1; Angleton 1; Beaumont 1; Boston, MA, 1; Comanche 1; Galveston 1; Fort Bragg, NC, 2; San Angelo 1; San Antonio 1; Eagle Lake 1; La Porte 1; Wharton 1; De Walt 1; Goose Creek 1, and two honorary members in Houston.

Every organization in its inception has one or two enthusiastic sponsors who are really responsible for its creation. This brief historical sketch would not be complete without a word as to the real founders of the Sons of the Republic of Texas. The *Houston Post* of March 3, 1922, says: "Mr. Kendall (Odin M.) is father of the idea of organizing the Sons of the Republic of Texas and was instrumental in getting a sufficient number interested to form an organization." An inspection of available correspondence files shows that Judge Lewis R. Bryan was also extremely active in the organization of the project and its development through the years. (A perusal of the charter members of the 1893 Sons of the Republic shows twelve of the original members to have been members of the present incorporated organization.)

That our organization has done well its task of encouraging a proper observance of Texas Independence Day and San Jacinto Day, locally, is amply shown when one compares the news columns printed prior to and after the formation of the Sons of the Republic of Texas. Observance of these anniversaries were sometimes mentioned with a bare statement that the Court House and City Hall would be closed; since 1922, however, these events have had generous publicity with such headlines as "Thousands Trek to Hallowed San Jacinto Grounds to Honor Heroes," "San Jacinto Battleground Overflows With Patriots," "30,000 Texans Pay Tribute to San Jacinto Dead," and "Texas Day Speaker Scores Neglect of Historical Landmarks."

Immediately after organization, a committee composed of A. Y. Austin, Franklin Williams, W. E. Kendall, Frank M. Gossett and Fletcher M. Jones was named to arrange the celebration of San Jacinto Day. The *Houston Post* of April 22, 1922, said: "Thousands gathered to commemorate the 86th anniversary of the Battle of San Jacinto upon the Battle Ground where the independence of Texas was achieved. Col. A. J. Houston presided and told of the objects of the Sons of the Republic of Texas. Honorable Clarence R. Wharton, prominent attorney and Texas historian, made the principal address.

In 1923, the Sons of the Republic of Texas, in cooperation with the Houston Chamber of Commerce, staged what was perhaps the most heavily attended celebration of San Jacinto Day ever held. President L. R. Bryan introduced the speakers of the day, they being Hon. Pat M. Neff, governor of Texas, Hon. E. Lee Trinkle, governor of Virginia, and Gen. Julian S. Carr of North Carolina. Gen. Jacob F. Wolters read General Houston's report of the Battle of San Jacinto. The entire membership of the Texas Senate and House of Representatives were honored guests; the Governor's salute was fired by a detachment of Coast Artillery from Fort Crockett and music was furnished by the Texaco and Humble Oil and Refining Company's bands. Newspaper estimates of the attendance varied from 25,000 to 40,000.

Another outstanding program was rendered in 1924, when Hon. Eugene H. Blount, a member of the Texas Legislature and descendant of a pioneer Texas family, spoke, as recorded by the *Houston Post Dispatch*: "Amid the trailing moss of the majestic trees of the Battle Ground of San Jacinto Texans from the wide expanse of the State paused Wednesday afternoon to pay homage to those heroes of 90 years ago who have inscribed an immortal page on the world's history. It was estimated that a crowd of 25,000 came to this shrine of the Lone Star Republic and State, braving the impending rain to pay that respect which springs from the heart for those who have fought in the name of their country's freedom."

In 1925, Judge L. B. Moody presided and Hon. Clarence R. Wharton made the address and governor E. Lee Trinkle of Virginia, for the second time was a speaker on a San Jacinto Day program. Other distinguished visitors were governor W. A. Brandon of Alabama, governor Miriam A. Ferguson of Texas and former governor James E. Ferguson of Texas. Newspaper reports gave 30,000 as the estimated attendance. In 1925 Judge L. B. Moody inaugurated the custom of having a March 2nd noon day luncheon jointly with the Daughters of the Republic of Texas in commemoration of Texas Independence Day. Perhaps the most notable results to come from these Independence Day programs was the inauguration of the San Jacinto Memorial Tree project suggested by Hon. Ross S. Sterling, later governor of Texas, at the March 2nd dinner in 1929.

On May 1, 1929, in accordance with Sterling's suggestion for planting a live oak tree in memory of each soldier who fought at San Jacinto, to be planted along Texas State Highway No. 4-21-'36, otherwise known as the Battle Ground Road, Houston Williams, then president, appointed a committee to secure funds for the planting of this memorial and the placing of a permanent marker bearing the names of these soldiers. This was the beginning of the real effort which ultimately led to the erection of the San Jacinto Monument.

Prior to 1931, all programs with the exception of the one at the Rice Hotel had been held at the camp site of the Texan Army in the San Jacinto Battlefield Park. In 1931 a change of location was made and the celebration was described by the *Houston Post Dispatch* as follows:

> At a fork in the sleepy San Jacinto—where its waters meet the tranquil Buffalo Bayou—three thousand Texans, awed by nature's beauty, stood in silent reverence Tuesday afternoon and paid homage to their heroes.
>
> From the muddy branches of the Brazos, the red clay banks of the Colorado, the silent forests that line the placid Trinity and the vast lands that border the drowsy Rio Grande they came—to honor San Jacinto's warriors.
>
> Beneath somber skies, in the shadow of the giant moss hung oak where Santa Anna surrendered to Sam Houston on that memorable day 95 years ago, they gathered, to tread the hallowed field.
>
> The gently rolling hills, on which the decisive 18 minute battle was fought, were dotted with the Lone Star States's native sons, as the message from their drive, planted in honor of each of the Texans, that posterity might know that Texas, after nearly a century, does not forget their valor.
>
> Brilliant for its simplicity, the ceremony marking the birth of Texas liberty at its cradle, inspired the spectators and filled them with profound patriotism.
>
> The sheltering branches of great gray oaks, campsite of General Santa Anna and the Mexican Army, was the scene of the ninety-fifth anniversary ceremony.
>
> Beneath a whispering canopy, speakers told the story of the swift conflict which freed Texas from Mexican thralldom."

In the absence of Governor Sterling, former governor W. P. Hobby dedicated the three hundred sixty live oaks that had been planted along the Battle Ground Road in memory of the soldiers who fought at San Jacinto; a replica of the San Jacinto Battle Flag was presented by Mrs. Lucy Craig, daughter of Gen. Sidney Sherman; and the First School Band of Houston played the San Jacinto Battle song, "Come to the Bower." United States Senator Tom Connally told in a masterly way the story of the Battle. In 1934, the following Charter was issued by the State of Texas:

The Sons of the Republic of Texas Charter

THE STATE OF TEXAS,
County of Harris.

Know All Men by These Presents:
That we, R. B. Morris, J. C. McVea and Frank M. Gossett, all citizens of Harris County, Texas, under and by virtue of the laws of the State of Texas, do hereby form and incorporate ourselves into a voluntary association under the terms and conditions hereinafter set out, as follows:

ONE: The name and style of this association shall be THE SONS OF THE REPUBLIC OF TEXAS.

TWO: Its object shall be:

1. To perpetuate the memory and spirit of the men and women who have achieved and maintained the independence of Texas.

2. To encourage historical research into the earliest records of Texas; to foster the preservation of documents and relics, and to encourage the publication of records of individual service of soldiers and patriots of the Republic of Texas.

3. To promote the observance of Texas Independence Day (March Second) and San Jacinto Day (April Twenty-first); to commemorate the undaunted courage of the colonists in the battle of Gonzales, The Lexington of Texas, (October Second); and to perpetuate the hallowed memories of the sacrifices made at the Alamo (March Sixth) and at Goliad (March Twenty-seventh), by holding proper celebrations and exercises each year of such character as will arouse and keep alive the patriotic sentiments and feelings of the people of Texas.

THREE: This association may acquire by purchase, grant, gift or otherwise, real estate associated with historic events of Texas; and personal property, such as books, manuscripts and other historical records and relics of the Texas Revolution and the days of the Republic; mark, improve and maintain historic sites and the burial places of Texas patriots.

FOUR: The business of this association shall be transacted in the City of Houston, and at such other places in the State of Texas as this association, by its subordinate chapters, may from time to time designate.

FIVE: The time for which this association shall exist is fifty years.

SIX: There shall be seven directors called the Executive Committee, and the following are those appointed for the first year, and until their successors are elected and qualified:

> Charles E. Ashe, Houston, Texas
> C. E. Gilbert, Houston, Texas
> L. A. Daffan Gilmer, Houston, Texas
> Frank M. Gossett, Houston, Texas
> J. C. McVea, Houston, Texas
> L. B. Moody, Houston, Texas
> R. B. Morris, Houston, Texas

SEVEN: The association has no capital stock and owns no other goods, chattels, lands, rights or credits.

IN WITNESS WHEREOF, we have hereunto signed our names this the 2nd day of October, 1934.

> R. B. Morris,
> J. C. McVea,
> Frank M. Gossett.

County of Harris.

Before me, the undersigned authority, on this day personally appeared R. B. Morris, J. C. McVea and Frank M. Gossett, known to me to be the persons whose names are subscribed to the foregoing instrument, and each acknowledged to me that he executed the same for the purposes and consideration therein expressed. Given under my hand and seal of office on this the 16th day of October, 1934.

> L. C. Colbert
> Notary Public in and for
> Harris County, Texas

THE STATE OF TEXAS
DEPARTMENT OF STATE

I, W. W. Heath, Secretary of State, of the State of Texas, do hereby certify that the foregoing is a true and correct copy of the charter of THE SONS OF THE REPUBLIC OF TEXAS, with the endorsement thereon, as now appears of record in this department.

In Testimony Whereof, I have hereunto signed my name officially and caused to be impressed hereon the Seal of State at my office in the City of Austin, this 20th day of October, A. D., 1934.

> W. W. Heath (SEAL)
> Secretary of State.

With the approach of and during the Texas Centennial of 1936, the Sons of the Republic of Texas were active on both state and local levels. Prominent among the members was the late Louis Wiltz Kemp, SRT president, who was chairman of the Historical Advisory Committee which resulted in the marking of hundreds of Texas' veterans graves and other historical sites.

That a towering monument was ultimately erected on that glorious battlefield is due in part to the efforts of the Sons of the Republic of Texas, among other groups, and due mainly to one of our honorary members, the late Jesse Holman Jones. This monument stands before all the world as a testimony to the valor of brave men who value freedom above security.

A committee was appointed by San Jacinto Chapter president J. Perry Moore, which led to the founding of the San Jacinto Museum of History. Another of our members, the late George A. Hill, Jr., contributed the contents of one wing, and many others contributed items which are still on permanent display.

Through the years, the chapters and individual members of the Sons of the Republic of Texas in each locality, in San Antonio, in Dallas, in Austin, etc., have contributed to the development of our Texas heritage, and in educating our youth to emulate the spirit of the men and women who established and maintained the Republic of Texas.

During his lifetime, Hill created an essay contest in memory of his father, a San Jacinto veteran, James Monroe Hill. In recent years the organization conducted a state-wide oratorical contest open to juniors and seniors in high schools stimulating the interest of our youth in the deeds of heroism of these early Texans.

In the late 1930s, the late Houston Wade discovered a letter from Sam Houston to William Dangerfield wherein he spoke of an order of "Knights of the Order of San Jacinto—as a reward for the worthy," the badge of which order would be a green sash. This order was revived in 1941 by the Sons of the Republic of Texas, to be bestowed on those who had performed outstanding service in the cause of Texas Heritage, and many prominent Americans have since been inducted.

The San Jacinto observance increased each year, and in 1948 when the Battleship Texas was berthed there, Admiral Chester W. Nimitz and several prominent Texans were invested as "Knights of the Order of San Jacinto" before a crowd of thousands.

A permanent member of the SRT serves on the Battleship Texas Commission, and the San Jacinto State Park Commission is also composed of members of the SRT and one member of the DRT.

In 1954 the late Senator Joseph McCarthy drew a crowd of many thousands to the historic site in commemoration of those soldiers who fought against the totalitarianism of that day.

The Sons of the Republic of Texas were also instrumental in having an Archives and Library Building erected by the State of Texas. Within weeks after Governor Price Daniel took office, a committee composed of Joseph F. Blanton, Houston, president, SRT; Joseph Wearden, Victoria, past president, SRT; Mrs. Barclay Megarity, Waco, president, DRT, and executive secretary, SRT; Frank E. Tritico, Houston, secretary-treasurer, SRT; Very Reverend Anton J. Frank, Houston, chaplain, SRT; George W. Hill, Austin, past historian, SRT (although not on the committee was invited to be present by the chairman), visited him in his office and outlined an eight-point program concerning the location of the state archives and recommended a permanent building. Mr. Wearden was the chairman, as the program had begun during his term of office. He had plans of the Tennessee State Archives Building and others. Both Mrs. Wearden and Governor Daniel had suggested that the name be the "Archives and Library Building."

After the meeting this committee waited on attorney general Will Wilson, who wrote the legislation making it a felony to vandalize a state marker. Among the other points approved by the governor were the required teaching of a year of Texas History in state supported schools and the giving of statutory standing to the Texas State Historical Survey Commission.

On April 21, 1958 Governor Price Daniel, principal speaker at San Jacinto Day ceremonies, reactivated the Texas Navy as a patriotic group and as an arm of the Civil Defense of the State of Texas and issued the first two commissions as admirals in the newly reactivated Navy to Lloyd Gregory, chairman of the Battleship Texas Commission and Frank E. Tritico, president of the San Jacinto Chapter. He asked that an annual review of the Texas Navy be held each year at the San Jacinto Day celebration.

Endeavoring to perpetuate the memory and spirit of those pioneers who established and maintained the Republic of Texas, Mr. Summerfield G. Roberts of Dallas, through the Sons of the Republic of Texas, annually contributed a prize of $1,000 known as the "Summerfield G. Roberts Award" to the author of the best book portraying these ideals and spirit.

In 1959, the San Jacinto Chapter donated the site of the home of President David G. Burnet to Harris County as a memorial to that great Texan and for the use of the citizens of East Harris County, designating it "Burnet Park."

In 1959 the San Jacinto Chapter SRT contributed $4,000 to the erection of the magnificent entrance gates at the San Jacinto Battleground put up by the San Jacinto State Park Commission composed of W. N. Blanton, Sr., Houston; William T. Kendall, Houston; and Fred Hartman of Baytown. The chapter also presented a translite of the Battle of San Jacinto to the Sam Houston Museum at Huntsville.

Greenwood Stoneham Chapter (#15) of Navasota has helped with the park at Washington-on-the-Brazos and cooperated in the Texas Independence Day Organization in the observation of Texas Independence Day and in locating a museum there.

Other chapters have aided in local restoration projects such as the Noble Home, etc., or in erecting local museums.

In the fall of 1961, under president Frank E. Tritico, the Sons of the Republic of Texas published *A Brief History of the Texas Navy* by Admiral Samuel Murray Robinson, U.S.N. Retired. A copy of this publication was mailed to each senior and junior high school, both public and private, in Texas and to all universities and colleges, as a supplemental chapter in the teaching of Texas history.

In October 1961, a monument was erected and dedicated in the State Cemetery to the late Senator Andrew Jackson Houston, son of General Sam Houston and first president of the present incorporated organization.

Through the efforts of George Charlton of Tomball, the site of the town of "New Kentucky" was donated by the Champion Paper Company and was dedicated by the Sons as a park for the citizens of West Harris County.

The SRT petitioned the Congress of the United States to spare from sale in the San Jacinto Ordinance Depot, the site of the home and grave of Lorenzo de Zavala, first Vice President of the Republic of Texas.

In 1961, the Sons aided in obtaining an appropriation for the new wing of the Sam Houston Museum at Huntsville as they had done under Roderick J. Watts, previously obtaining funds for the wing dedicated March 2, 1959.

The culmination of a project begun by president Tritico, the dedication of Padre Island as a National Park, was effected through work by the Sons and other groups.

The Sons, in cooperation with the Trustees of the San Jacinto Museum of History and the San Jacinto State Park Commission, helped to obtain an appropriation from the Legislature to repair the San Jacinto Monument. The SRT has long had an interest in the San Jacinto Monument for it was planned, erected, financed and dedicated through the efforts and at the instigation of the Sons. For that reason the San Jacinto State Park Commission has always been composed of two members of the SRT and one of the DRT. After hurricane Carla the San Jacinto Chapter donated $3,000, as did the San Jacinto Museum of History with a similar appropriation from the Governor's emergency fund, so that the roof might be repaired and the Museum opened in time for San Jacinto Day 1962.

April 10, 1962, marked the dedication of the Texas Archives and Library Building at which C. Stanley Banks presided as chairman of the Library Commission. Those present of the original committee who planned with Gov. Price Daniel January 27, 1957 were Mrs. Joseph Wearden of Victoria (whose husband had initiated the project in 1955); Mrs. Barclay Megarity, past president, DRT; SRT president Frank E. Tritico, and the Very Rev. Anton J. Frank.

Also in April, the Henderson Yoakum Chapter (#21) sponsored a replica of a blacksmith shop at the Sam Houston Shrine in Huntsville.

Through the generosity of Dr. Herbert P. Gambrell, five hundred copies of his first edition of *Anson Jones, the Last President of Texas* were distributed to libraries outside the state.

At the 1965 Annual Meeting of the Sam Houston Memorial Association Louis Lenz, KSJ, presented to the Sons of the Republic of Texas, in President Kemper Williams presence, Sam Houston's Knight Templar Masonic Sword. It had been discovered by the late Houston Wade and used to invest all Knights of the Order of San Jacinto since its reorganization by the SRT. The sword is kept in a display case at the Sam Houston Museum in Huntsville.

The year 1966 saw the restoration of the Presidio La Bahia at Goliad through the generosity of our late honorary member, Mrs. Kathryn Stoner O'Connor with member Raiford L. Stripling, KSJ, as architect. A section of the old calabozo was set aside for use by the SRT. Later, during the presidency of Brownson Malsch, the old mission fortress was visited by the Spanish ambassador Jaime Arguelles at the invitation of the Sons. In Houston, the "Clock of Texas," one of the two glockenspiels in the United States, was dedicated. It depicted animated scenes from each of the six national periods of Texas history and played authentic music of each period three times a day. Frank E. Tritico was historian designer and Dale Clark of California, the builder.

During the HemisFair, both the Sons and Knights took part and had days dedicated to them. That same year (1968) saw the establishment of the "La Bahia Awards" by Mrs. O'Connor, at the suggestion of Compatriot Stripling. The award has been presented annually "to promote research, suitable presentation and appropriate dissemination of historical data relative to Texas heritage...influence upon Texas culture of Spanish Colonial heritage in laws, customs, language, religion, architecture, art, and other related fields." The Presidio La Bahia Awards are presented to the winners in person at Presidio La Bahia, near Goliad, on the first weekend in December.

Many members assisted in plans for the State Park at Washington-on-the-Brazos. Stripling erected a replica of Independence Hall and Harvin C. Moore was architect for the "Star of the Republic Museum" to which many Sons have made contributions. The Sons furnished an exhibit on Sam Houston and the Knights of the Order of San Jacinto. The Sons also assisted the San Felipe State Park Association in rebuilding the replica of Austin's cabin which had been destroyed.

During the presidency of Brownson Malsch, Mrs. O'Connor set up plans and funding for a Spanish Texas Microfilm Center which was approved by the Sons at the annual meeting in Houston on April 18, 1970. The Center is a continuing, long range project organized by the Sons of the Republic of Texas. Its purpose is to establish a collection of research materials on microfilm for the study of the Hispanic influence on Texas culture. It will fill a great and growing need for a single source through which scholars may secure for study microfilm copies of the incredibly vast legacy of documents, letters, reports, etc. covering three hundred years of the direct Spanish influence in Texas. The Spanish Texas Microfilm Center is housed at the University of Texas at San Antonio Library.

Through Andrew Moses Lester, the Sons presented a bust of David Crockett to the Alamo which was placed in the Long Barracks Museum.

In 1973 another bust of honorary member Dwight D. Eisenhower was placed in his birthplace in Denison.

Through the generosity of George R. Brown, KSJ, and the Brown Foundation under the chairmanship of Ben Blanton and Frank Tritico, a "Lone Star Pavilion" was placed in Burnet Woods Park in Cincinnati, Ohio, along with a plaque commemorating the event and replicas of the "Twin Sisters" cannon donated by honorary member Thomas H. Shartle. Identical replicas and plaques were dedicated in 1974 at the San Jacinto Battleground on San Jacinto Day and in Ohio in August to commemorate the gift of cannon from the citizens of Cincinnati to Sam Houston's army which contributed to the Texans victory at San Jacinto.

The SRT Texas History Essay Contest was founded in 1974 by the Brown Foundation, as a contest to be conducted for graduating seniors in all public and private high schools in the State of Texas on a subject exploring the spirit of the early frontier during the Republic of Texas. Prizes are awarded each year to the winners of the three best essays in appropriate ceremonies at the Battleground during the observance of San Jacinto Day. Prizes totaled $2,000 each year and the Brown Foundation funded the contest through 1980. Since 1980 the contest has been funded by Robert F. Ritchie, KSJ; D. Gordon Wiley, KSJ; Harry G. Seeligson, KSJ; Nadine Seeligson (Mrs. Harry G.); Jesse R. Milam, KSJ; Pattie Milam (Mrs. Jesse R., Jr.); and Bell Helicopter Textron Humanities Fund of Fort Worth. Since 1989, annual prizes have varied between $4,000 and $8,000. Total annual prizes from 1974 through 1994 total $66,000 dollars.

The year 1974 saw the microfilming of the SRT membership files which were placed in the Presidio. Through the efforts of the historian of the San Jacinto Chapter, the City Council of Houston named the high bridge (Loop 610) over the Ship Channel, the General Sidney Sherman Bridge.

The Adolphus N. Sterne Chapter (#19) of Nacogdoches was reactivated in 1975 by Ford Simpson, and an outstanding investiture of Knights took place in the House of Representatives in the Texas State Capitol under the historic San Jacinto Battle flag.

During the Bicentennial year, both chapters and the general organization took part in observing our nation's birthday. The resources of the Microfilm Center were used by Gerald Doyle in gathering an outstanding exhibit of "Three Hundred Years of Calligraphy on the Spanish Borderlands" which was exhibited at the Beaumont Art Museum, the San Jacinto Museum of History, and the Midland Art Museum. In December, the exhibit was awarded the first prize in the La Bahia Awards. Through the efforts of Spain's consul general in Texas, the Honorable Eric I. Martel, one of Spain's Bicentennial gifts were replicas of the uniforms and arms of the grenadiers who served with Count Don Bernardo Galvez during the American Revolution. The first uniformed company, called "Los Granaderos de Galvez" was under the command of vice president general Barrera of San Antonio.

In recognition of her many contributions to preserving, propagating and presenting our Spanish heritage, culture and values to the people of the state of Texas, the late Mrs. Kathryn Stoner O'Connor, honorary member, 1977, at the Presidio La Bahia in Goliad, King Juan Carlos conferred upon her the dignity of Dame Grand Cross of the Order of Isabel La Catolica. The dignity of Grand Cross is held today by twenty heads of state in the world, and this was the first Grand Cross to be conferred in the United States.

In November, 1978, the Granaderos de Galvez, led by president general Charles E. Barrera, past president general Frank E. Tritico, honorary member Eric I. Martel, Spanish Texas Microfilm Center director Carmen Perry, and others toured Spain and met with King Juan Carlos at the Palace de la Zarzuela. They presented the King many gifts relating to Texas, outstanding among which was a resolution passed unanimously by the U.S. House of Representatives in recognition of the great contribution of Spanish Captain General Bernardo de Galvez to the independence of the United States. Tritico explained the concept of the Spanish Texas Microfilm Center to the King, and Miss Perry presented him with copies of documents. The name of the Sons of the Republic of Texas and its activities are now well known in Spain.

Work continues on indexing the books and documents in the Kathryn Stoner O'Connor Collection which is housed at the University of Texas in San Antonio. President general Larry W. Hays negotiated the agreement between the SRT and the board of regents of the University of Texas System whereby title to the collection remains in the Sons, but it is on indefinite loan to the University of Texas at San Antonio. When completed, the collection will be valued at more than a million dollars and will be a great source of material to researchers of the Spanish Colonial influence on Texas.

During president general Hayes' administration, three new chapters were added to the roster: George Bell Madeley Chapter (#30) in Conroe; George Washington Hill Chapter (#31) in Corsicana; and Jean B. Bavoux Chapter (#32) in Clear Lake City. Membership in all chapters continued to increase, evidencing a renewed interest in the preservation of our history and heritage.

Robert F. Ritchie, KSJ, of Dallas was elected president general at the annual meeting in Bryan in 1981 and turned his attention to the finances of the SRT. He requested voluntary contributions from the membership when the finances reached a low ebb and later raised the annual dues to cover expenses of the growing organization. He also served as the SRT representative on the Battleship Texas Commission.

Judge Joseph J. Fisher, KSJ, assumed the reins of leadership in 1982 at the annual meeting in Beaumont. Judge Fisher was largely responsible for the reactivation of the Col. Alexander Horton Chapter (#20) in San Augustine which rose from a membership of three to almost two hundred. He was tireless in his efforts and traveled throughout the state on behalf of the SRT. Through his efforts and those of Ernest Smith, the Marshall Chapter (#18) was reactivated and seedlings for several new East Texas chapters were planted. Judge Fisher wanted to make sure the SRT would have a prominent position in the observance of the Texas Sesquicentennial, so he appointed an SRT Sesquicentennial Committee and gave the committee a number of ideas and leadership to assure SRT participation.

Judge Fisher enhanced the publicity concerning the Presidio La Bahia Awards, the Summerfield G. Roberts Award and the scholarship awards, more than doubling the number of entries of each. Chairman Frank E. Tritico announced the additional gift of the O'Connor Foundation of $25,000 to continue the Presidio La Bahia Awards.

During Judge Fisher's administration Carmen Perry retired as director of the Spanish Texas Microfilm Center and was replaced by Isabel de Pedro Solis.

President General Joseph G. Ginn, KSJ, was elected in Clear Lake City where he was instrumental in organizing the Jean B. Bavoux Chapter. He continued the recruitment of new members and the organization of new chapters. He inaugurated the William Mayfield Chapter (#34) of Brenham and Washington Counties. He doubled the size of the Sesquicentennial Committee, enlarging both the geographic representation and the inclusion of several prominent honorary members. The committee met in Austin under his leadership and undertook several projects of statewide scope. As president general of the SRT he had the distinction of welcoming H.R.H. Princess Anne of Great Britain to the San Jacinto Battleground on behalf of the first families of Texas. With chairman Frank E. Tritico he laid plans for a nationwide celebration of San Jacinto Day, 1986.

President General Ginn's second term began with a most successful Annual Meeting in San Antonio on March 31, 1984. Early in this term a book bearing the title "Spanish Explorers of the Southwest" was distributed to all junior and senior high schools in Texas, public and private. Distribution was made possible by a grant from the SRT Sesquicentennial Committee to the Texas Historical Association.

Joe Ginn, KSJ, along with other SRT members appeared before the Texas Senate sponsoring a bill to make April 21, 1986, the official State Sesquicentennial Holiday. This bill, originated by president general Ginn, passed both the Texas House and Senate by unanimous vote and was signed into law by governor Mark White in early 1985.

President General Abe San Miguel assumed office on April 13, 1985, at the Annual Meeting in Marshall. On August 17, 1985 he journeyed to Bay City to issue the charter to and install officers of the new Matagorda Chapter (#35).

Sesquicentennial Year programs were begun in various parts of the state with president general San Miguel in attendance at many of the celebrations. The SRT Annual Meeting was held in Houston on April 19-20, 1986. The highlight of this weekend was the San Jacinto Day Activities at the Battleground on Monday, April 21, 1986. Members of the SRT and Knights of the Order of San Jacinto joined with other state and national dignitaries in celebrating this Great Day.

Vice president of the United States George Bush was inducted into the Sons of the Republic of Texas as a distinguished honorary member at the SRT annual meeting held at the River Oaks Country Club in Houston on April 19, 1986. After vice president Bush was presented his membership medal and certificate, he addressed the large audience attending the banquet at the annual meeting.

The San Jacinto Monument platform was center stage for the Official Texas Sesquicentennial Program held April 21, 1986. The Knights of the Order of San Jacinto were seated on the platform with vice president George Bush and Texas governor Mark White. Speakers included Sen. Barbara Jordan, Russell Kendall, Sam Houston, IV, KSJ, and Mrs. Grady Rash, president general of the DRT.

President General Joe E. Ericson, KSJ, announced in 1986 SRT membership exceeded 1,500 and was spread across the United States and into many foreign lands. A record number of 246 new members was admitted during the Sesquicentennial Year. Two new SRT chapters were chartered on December 7, 1986: the Ephraim M. Daggett Chapter (#36) of Fort Worth and the Albert Sidney Johnston Chapter (#37) of Cedar Park (near Austin).

The SRT Sesquicentennial Committee, represented by past president general Joe Ginn, KSJ, assisted in the planting of an Oak tree on the spot where Santa Anna surrendered to Sam Houston. The surrender was reenacted and televised to the Capitol in Austin via satellite.

Two official Historical Markers were placed by the SRT Sesquicentennial Committee. One, honoring Dr. Ashbell Smith, was placed in Baytown through the generosity of Dr. Drew Williams. A second Historical Marker was placed in Sam Houston Park commemorating the founding of the Sons of the Republic of Texas in Houston April 20, 1893, and the refounding in Houston March 2, 1922.

The 1986 SRT Sesquicentennial Yearbook including biographical sketches of the Knights of San Jacinto was published and distributed to all members.

The new Sam Houston Chapter (#38) in Katy was chartered in 1987.

Summerfield G. Roberts, KSJ, founded and funded the award named after him. Mrs. Annie Lee Warren Roberts, widow of the late S. G. Roberts, chose to continue the award from year to year following her husband's death. In 1987 Mrs. Roberts very generously funded the Summerfield G. Roberts Award permanently through an endowment gift. The cash award of two thousand five hundred dollars ($2,500) goes each year for the best creative writing on Texas History subjects which best portray the spirit, character, strength and deeds of men and women during the years of the Republic.

The constitution and bylaws were revised in 1987 and published in *THE TEXIAN*.

The General Office of the SRT was moved in 1987 from Crosby to 5942 Abrams Road, Suite 222, Dallas, Texas 75231 with Mrs. Maydee J. Scurlock employed as Executive Secretary. Full records of members in all chapters were entered on computer records in the new office.

In 1988, all SRT membership applications and associated materials from 1974 through June 1, 1988, were microfilmed. Records prior to 1974 were microfilmed in 1974. One set of the microfilms was placed in the library of the University of Texas at San Antonio with the other SRT records, and other sets were donated by SRT chapters to local public libraries in Dallas, Houston, Fort Worth, San Augustine and elsewhere. A printed INDEX by member and ancestor was completed and made available for purchase by chapters or members.

New members received into the SRT in 1988-89 while Stephen J. Hay, Jr., KSJ, was president general totaled 217 according to historian general Charles L. Billings, KSJ.

Two heroes of the Alamo, William Barret Travis and James Butler Bonham, were honored in impressive ceremonies held in Edgefield, SC, on August 19, 1989 when a seven-foot granite monument was unveiled near the site of the Travis Homestead with about three hundred persons attending. The Texas delegation attending the ceremonies included L. Charles Billings, KSJ, historian general, SRT, with his wife, Peggy; Sam Addelsey of the *Dallas Morning News*, and Gary James of KPRC-TV Channel 2 Houston. The Texas delegation, accompanied by U.S. senator Strom Thurmond, toured the Bonham Home which is being restored by the Sons of the Republic of Texas, old Edgefield Archives and the Saluda Historical Society. All events were covered by TV Channel 2 and were featured on "The Eyes of Texas" on Oct. 14, 1989.

The newly created Anson Jones Chapter (#39) held its charter meeting in Abilene on January 18, 1990. The charter was presented to the new chapter by Stephen J. Hay, Jr., KSJ, president general.

An organizational meeting for the James Butler Bonham Chapter (#40) was held January 14, 1990, in the home of Joseph G. Ginn, KSJ. Membership in the chapter is drawn from Bexar, Comal and Guadalupe Counties.

In 1990 president general Sam Houston IV, KSJ, announced that membership in the SRT stood at over two thousand.

Records in the general office of the Sons of the Republic of Texas revealed in 1990 that there were ten members of the SRT who had been members for fifty years or more. On May 6, 1990, the fifty-year members included: Gameswell D. Gantt, Jr., Del Rio; Col. William Edward Lobit, Galveston; August E. Myers, Richmond; James Lawrence Wood, Refugio; and William K. Craig, KSJ, Raymond M. Hill, Jubal R. Parten and John Schumacher, all of Houston; J. Henry Doscher, Jr., Abilene; and Samuel Partlow, Liberty.

SRT's microfilm library of member's names and their ancestors was expanded by seven new rolls of film in 1990, making a total of 37 rolls of film on member's application papers.

A crowd of about ten thousand people gathered at Washington-on-the-Brazos on March 2, 1991, to help celebrate the 155th birthday of Texas. Sam Houston IV, great grandson of General Sam Houston, led the crowds in citing the Toast to Texas using pure Texas spring water. Houston was the current president general of the Sons of the Republic of Texas and a Knight of the Order of San Jacinto. A huge birthday cake was enjoyed by the visitors to the historic site.

Three new chapters were chartered in 1992: the John S. "Rip" Ford Chapter (#41) in Odessa, the Samuel Givens Evetts Chapter (#42) in Benbrook, and the Maj. James P. Campbell Chapter (#43) in Manvel.

Historian general Madison Wright reported that 199 new members had been approved in 1991-1992. The San Jacinto Foundation donated funds in 1992 to buy the General Office a much needed new computer and printer. In 1992 the Executive Committee approved a numbering system whereby each member of the SRT was assigned a membership number for the first time.

A shortened form of membership application was approved to be used for male relatives of DRT members and SRT members who joined between September 19, 1992 and March 2, 1993, the 200th Anniversary of Sam Houston's birth. Members who joined using this shortened form are called the "Sam Houston Class." A total of 332 new members joined under this program.

So successful was the use of the short form by relatives of DRT and SRT members in joining the "Sam Houston Class" of the SRT, that the short form was approved for use from April 3, 1993 to March 2, 1994 to honor another Texas hero by offering the "Stephen F. Austin Class."

Another historic marker was unveiled on January 28, 1993, at the hallowed ground where the Battle of San Jacinto was fought to gain independence for the Republic of Texas. Officers and members of the Knights of the Order of San Jacinto gathered at San Jacinto State Park, near the sun dial, to unveil a marker in commemoration of the 150th anniversary of the founding of the Order of San Jacinto on January 28, 1843, by Sam Houston, president of the Republic of Texas.

In founding the order President Houston notified the Republic's Ambassador to England, Ashbel Smith, that he was the first knight of the new order "with a green sash as his badge of distinction, among the medals, ribbons and sashes worn by European diplomats."

The Knights of the Order of San Jacinto was re-established by the Sons of the Republic of Texas in 1941. Since 1941 there have been a total of 144 Texans named to the impressive list who have been knighted with Gen. Sam Houston's dress sword in annual ceremonies held each year by SRT members. Forty-seven are living and twelve of these have served as past knight commanders.

Among the Knight honorees over the years has been one U.S. vice president (John Nance Garner), U.S. senators, Texas governors, university presidents, judges from all levels of the judiciary, admirals and generals of the armed services, ambassadors, and two newspaper columnists.

Two new chapters were chartered in 1993: the El Paso Chapter (#44) in El Paso and the Ranger John Beeman Chapter (#45) in Mesquite.

Joseph G. Ginn, KSJ, chairman of the Presidio La Bahia Committee, reported that the 25th Anniversary Program of the Presidio La Bahia Awards was held at Goliad on December 5 and 6, 1992, with a Spanish History Symposium on the afternoon of December 5, a banquet for a hundred people that night, and a Mass on Sunday morning celebrated by Bishop Fellhauer of Victoria.

In 1993, the William B. Travis Chapter presented a set of the SRT microfilms to the San Antonio Public Library, and the SRT presented a set of the microfilms to the DRT to be placed in the Alamo Library.

The rules for the annual SRT Texas History Essay Contest, which had been limited to high school seniors in Texas, were changed for the 1994 contest to include also high school seniors residing outside of Texas.

In April, 1994, L. Charles Billings, KSJ, was elected President General and served for two years. More than 670 new member applications were aproved in 1994 by Historian General Walter Nass.

Three new chapters were chartered in 1994 and 1995: Ashbel Smith Chapter (#46) in Baytown, Davy Crockett Chapter (#47) in Granbury, and the John O. Meusebach Chapter (#48) in Fredericksburg.

The SRT Headquarters Office was moved in 1996 from Dallas, TX, to 1717 Eighth Street, Bay City, TX 77414.

In 1996, the Annual Meeting was in League City near Houston, hosted by the San Jacinto Chapter #1.

One new chapter was chartered in 1996: Gateway to Texas Chapter (#49) in Shelby County.

Membership in the SRT in 1996 included 3,391 active members, as well as 53 Honorary Members and 424 Junior Members. Three hundred and sixty-two applications were approved in 1996 by Historian General Scott Dunbar.

In 1997, the Annual Meeting was held in Bay City, hosted by the Matagorda Chapter #35, and gave many members an opportunity to visit the new headquarters office.

President General LaVon Tindall, KSJ, (1996,1997) reported six new chapters chartered in 1997, including Prince Carl of Solms-Braunfels Chapter (#50) in New Braunfels, Andrew Kent Chapter (#51) in New Mexico, Piney Woods Chapter (#52) in Tyler, Monument Hill Chapter (#53) in La Grange, Noah Smithwick Chapter (#54) in Burnet, and Henry Awalt Chapter (#55) in Fairfield. During his tenure, President General Tindall held the first two Chapter President's Workshops, in San Marcos and New Braunfels, respectively. The Workshops provided orientation, information, and suggestions to Chapter Presidents. The first Chapter Handbook was also compiled and printed to give the presidents a better understanding of the SRT organization and specific ideas for chapters.

In 1997, the SRT went on the Internet with a web page: www.srttexas.org, and with the General Office e-mail address: srttexas@srttexas.org.

The SRT Spanish-Texas Microfilm Center Collection at the University of Texas, San Antonio, was appraised in 1997, and the collection was valued at $521,565 dollars.

Under President General Tindall's tenure, the Educator of the Year Award was established and first awarded at the Annual Meeting in Nacogdoches in April of 1998. This meeting was hosted by the Gateway to Texas Ch. #49, the Alexander Horton Ch. #20, and the Adolphus Sterne Ch. #19.

The High School Essay Fund was established in 1997 with a generous donation by Honorary Member Billy Price. This fund was supplemented by a generous bequest in 1998 of $40,000 from the estate of Past President General Robert F. Ritchie, KSJ.

The Permanent Building Fund was established thanks to revenue from mineral rights bequeathed to the SRT from deceased Past President H. Sellers Rogers. The fund was supplemented by donations of the SRT membership, under the direction of the Long-Range Planning Committee.

The history of the Sons of the Republic of Texas began one hundred years ago and the spirit of their patriotic forebears continues in the breasts of their sons today. Those pioneers purchased their freedom not in gold but in blood, and their sons have fought in every war since. It would be impossible to recount the many heroic deeds of their sons, or to enumerate all of their efforts on behalf of Texas heritage. This brief history does not purport to tell the whole story of the Sons of the Republic of Texas, but is only an outline to demonstrate its members' interest in our Texas heritage from the earliest beginning to the present day.

President General O. Scott Dunbar (1998, 2000) reports one new chapter chartered the Angelina Chapter (#56).

Under President General Dunbar's tenure, in 1998 the SRT choose a new loose-leaf format for printing the 1998 Yearbook (edited by LaVon Tindall, KSJ). 1998 also saw a new editor for *The Texian;* Kevin J. Dunbar took over from Sam Malone, KSJ who was editor for 12 years. In 1998 the Executive Committee adopted to start each meeting for those attending to announce the name of his ancestor, this is called the Honor Roll. The 1999 Annual Meeting was held in Houston and the 2000 Annual Meeting was held in Collage Station. The 2000 Investiture of Knights was conducted in the rotunda of the George H. Bush Presidential Library on the campus of Texas A&M University. In 1998 the SRT started planting the official Stephen F. Austin Oak Trees on all Courthouse lawn in Texas. In 1998 the SRT Reflections Program to document the SRT history started. In 1998 the SRT and the KSJ official flags were produced with the help of Rogers McLane, KSJ. In 1999 the SRT initiated a new award which is called Lifetime Achievement Award. William T. Kendall, KSJ received this award in 1999 and Gordon Wiley, KSJ received this award in 2000. In 1999 the Black Powder Brigade started enrolling members and at the December1999 Presidio La Bahia meeting all charter members of the Black Powder Brigade were sworn in as Colonels in a commissioning ceremony. The Black Powder Brigade started it's tradition as official escort to the President General and Knights of San Jacinto. The December 1999 La Bahia program was the last one chaired after 15 years by retiring chairman Joseph G. Ginn, KSJ. In 1999 and 2000 all members of the SRT started assembling information on his ancestor to be printed in the Ancestor Album due for publication 2001.

Knights Of The Order Of San Jacinto

The Republic of Texas was a struggling young nation with very few liquid assets and lots of debt when Sam Houston began his second term in the office of President.

The situation had grown ever more dire and in 1842 President Houston hastily dispatched to Europe the astute Doctor, Soldier, and Statesman of the Republic, Ashbel Smith, to obtain full recognition and additional credits for the Republic. Houston chose Smith as the Texas Representative to the Court of St. James and to the Royal Court in Paris because of Smith's extensive knowledge of and acquaintanances in both of these important European Capitols. The appointment also acknowledged the outstanding services rendered to the Republic by Ashbel Smith.

Since the beginning of his second term Sam Houston had been planning an award to outstanding members of the Republic's military and political bodies who had faithfully served Texas under very trying circumstances. Recalling all the pomp and circumstances of life in Washington, D.C., especially that of representatives of foreign nations, Houston realized that our representative to European Courts needed some sign of office that would put him on an equal level with his European peers.

In a letter dated January 28, 1843 (*see letter on right*) Sam Houston announced the organization of the Knights of the Order of San Jacinto with the first two members being Ashbel Smith and William Daingerfield. Houston instructed Daingerfield to advise Smith that he was to assume the title "Sir Knight" and that the Ensign of the Order was to be a Green Ribbon worn over the left breast. It has been said that Houston chose the color green in commemoration of his Springtime (April 21) victory over Santa Anna at the Battle of San Jacinto. Unfortunately after Texas became a state in 1846 and the heroes of the Republic began to fade away, the Order fell into disarray.

In 1941 The Sons of the Republic of Texas reestablished the Order to honor those Texans who have performed outstanding service to or have made a sacrifice beyond the bounds of duty on behalf of the State of Texas or have by their talents contributed to the development of the heritage of Texas. A maximum of only three regular or honorary SRT members may be elected to the Order in any one year. Since its reestablishment in 1941 there have been one hundred fifty seven (157) men invested as Knights, forty three (43) of whom survive as of June 15, 2000.

The current Knights have come from all walks of life, including a Vice President of the United States, United States Senators and Representatives, a Secretary of Commerce, Supreme Court Justices, many prominent Judges and Lawyers, Physicians, Educators, Historians, business men, military officers, and all Past Presidents General of The Sons of the Republic of Texas.

MARCH 2, 1836
FEBRUARY 19, 1846

Washington

28th Jany 1843

Dear Daingerfield,

I have finished a sort of semi-official letter, to give you authority to do right about the notes. I must have little fellows. They will save us, and put down the greatest of wits. I do not wish anyone to know that they are to come until they are out.

I regretted previous to your departure that I had so little time to converse with you alone. I had ten thousand things to say to you, about your trip to Europe, and other things which are unsaid. No matter. I hope we will meet again, and when I can, I will write to you. You will to me I hope! I intend to make-to (sic) make more leisure, than I have enjoyed of late. I hope you will attend particularly to the subject of my <u>Portrait</u>, and consult with my friend Christi about the matter. I did wrong to speak of it in my semi-official letter to you, but when I wrote it I did not think that I would have time to scribble you this note.

I pray you on your arrival at Washington, to commend me to Mr. Van Zandi, and in England or France to Colonel Ashbel Smith, and announce to him, that <u>he</u>, as will (sic) as <u>yourself</u> is a Knight of the order of San Jacinto, and the Ensign of the order, is a Green Ribbon, in the left breast, or Button hole of the coat opposite the heart.

This I have right to create, and as I am a friend to "Order," I surely have a right to start an order, and thus to create some reward for the <u>worthy</u>, as we have no cash to encourage Gentlemen in preserving creating (sic) order. If you don't like the thing in this shape, you can, when you see Smith if you wish it, when you see his uniform (if it is not Green) wear the Ribbon as a part of the uniform and if it is Green, then wear a blue or Red Ribbon. Tis quite late and I must close my note. Stop, Captain Chrisman called to see about the horses. What will you have done with them – Tell me if I can serve you. I may wish to buy them. I will take them at valuation, if all mine are not drown'd in the overflow, as I fear they are.

Mr. H — is not well, but can sit up. Tis pleased to commend me to Judge Eve, and Capt. Elliot.

Salute all friends! God grant you His choicest blessings.

Truly Thine
Ever
Houston

Daingerfield
*   in haste*

Knights of the Order of San Jacinto

Name	Year
George Alfred Hill, Jr. *	1941
Louis Wiltz Kemp	1942
Eugene Campbell Barker	1944
George Bannerman Dealey	1944
William E. Howard	1944
William Earl Kendall	1944
John Crane McVea	1944
Charles Edward Gilbert, Jr. *	1945
Chester William Nimitz	1945
Harry Pennington *	1945
John Martin Spellman	1945
William Fulton Tarver	1945
Witham Bartholomew Bates	1952
Hugh Roy Cullen *	1952
Surnmerfield Griffith Roberts	1952
Valin Ridge Woodward *	1952
Randall Eugene Briscoe	1953
Hobart Huson III *	1953
Odin Menard Kendall	1953
Jesse Holman Jones	1953
John M. Moore, Jr.	1953
Robert Buckner Morris	1953
George Dubose Sears	1953
Charles R. Tips *	1953
Franklin Williams	1953
William Neal Blanton *	1955
William Theodore Kendall *	1955
Lewis Randolph Bryan, Jr.	1956
Paine Lee Bush *	1956
Price Daniel	1956
Andrew Dilworth *	1956
Anton J. Frank	1956
Walter B. McKinney	1956
Temple Houston Morrow *	1956
A. Frank Smith, Jr.	1956
Joseph Wearden	1957
C. Stanley Banks *	1958
Roderick John Watts	1958
A. Garland Adair	1959
Joseph Francis Blanton *	1959
Francis Gevirer Guittard *	1959
Houston Wade	1959
George Rufus Brown *	1960
Herman Brown	1960
Herbert Pickens Gambrell *	1960
Karl St. John Hoblitzelle	1960
Samuel Murray Robinson	1960
Louis Lenz	1961
H. Sellers Rogers	1961
Edgar Eggleston Townes	1961
John Nance Garner	1962
Frank Mulder Gossett	1962
Paul Randolph Stalnaker	1962
Frank Edward Tritico *	1962
George Lester Charlton	1963
John Spence Hornbuckle	1963
James William Sartwelle	1963
Clifford B. Jones	1964
Allan Shivers	1964
Joseph Lynn Clark	1965
Pat Ireland Nixon	1965
Edward Muegge Schiwetz	1965
Ed Arnold	1966
Dorsey Bardard Hardeman II *	1966
Harvin Cooper Moore, Jr. *	1966
Warren S. Bellows	1967
Edward Aubrey Clark *	1967
Will Edward A. Odom *	1967
Kemper Williams *	1967
James Milton Day	1968
George Plunkett Red	1968
Raiford Leak Stripling *	1968
James Sladen Maverick *	1969
Philip James Montalbo	1969
Lloyd J. Gregory	1970
Harry G. Seeligson *	1970
William Neal Blanton, Jr.	1971
Alexander Herbemont Fraser *	1971
John Milton Brownson Malsch *	1971
James Lanier Britton	1972
Joseph Jefferson Fisher *	1972
John Ben Shepperd	1972
Malcolm Dallas McLean	1973
William H. Oberste	1973
R. Henderson Shuffler	1973
Sam Long	1974
Walter Nold Mathis	1974
Donald Gordon Wiley *	1974
John Ward Beretta	1975
Tom Talmage Main, Jr. *	1975
Rupert N. Richardson	1975
Fred Holmsley Moore	1976
Peter Boyd Wells, Jr.	1976
Paul Eaton Wise *	1976
Carlos Edwardo Barrera	1977
George A. Butler, Jr.	1977
James Evetts Haley	1977
William Partlow Daniel	1978
Sidney Sherman Kendall	1978
Eric I. Martel	1978
Robert Field Ritchie *	1979
Ralph W. Steen	1979
J. Lon Tinkle	1979
Joseph George Ginn *	1980
George Edward Madeley	1980
Dorman H. Winfrey	1990
Thomas J. Drury	1981
Larry Weldon Hays	1981
Frank Russell Kendall	1981
William Kendall Craig	1982
Theodore R. Fehrenbach	1982
Joseph Milton Nance	1982
Ray Miller	1983
Dennis O'Connor	1983
Tom O'Connor	1983
Arch Bruce Marshall	1984
Ernest Frederick Smith *	1984
Robert E. Stripling	1984
L. Tuffly Ellis	1985
Sam Houston IV *	1985
Jack R. Maguire *	1985
Roger N. Conger	1986
Abe San Miguel, Jr.	1986
Paul Gervais Bell	1987
Holland McCombs	1987
Ralph W. Yarborough	1987
Joe Ellis Ericson *	1988
Robert Taylor Huebner	1988
Samuel Stewart Malone *	1988
Raleigh Douglas Huebner	1989
William Smythe Shepherd *	1989
Lloyd Charles Billings	1990
Stephen John Hay, Jr. *	1990
Ralph Ray Wallace III	1990
Harris Masterson	1991
Jesse Rush Milam, Jr. *	1991
Ron Stone	1991
Reagan Cartwright	1992
Ben H. Procter	1992
Frank Everson Vandiver	1992
Joe B. Frantz	1993
Walter Elzie O'Neal	1993
George W. Strake, Jr.	1993
Curren Rogers McLane *	1994
Lee Canfield Ritchie	1994
Gifford Elmore White	1994
Gilbert Carvajal	1995
Homer Townsend Love, Jr.	1995
Robert A. Gammage	1996
LaVon Tindall	1996
Doyle H. Willis	1996
Henry A. Guerra, Jr.	1997
Joseph M. Clark, Jr.	1998
Madison B. Wright, Jr.	1998
Chas. P. Briggs III	2000
Scott Dunbar	2000
Andrew J. Houston	2000

* Past Knight Commanders

Officers Of Knights Of The Order Of San Jacinto
2000 - 2001

L. Charles Billings, KSJ	Knight Commander
Ben H. Procter, KSJ	First Deputy Knight Commander
LaVon Tindall, KSJ	Second Deputy Knight Commander
Madison B. Wright Jr., KSJ	Third Deputy Knight Commander
Joseph G. Ginn, KSJ *	Knight Secretary
Sam Houston IV, KSJ *	Knight Treasurer
Joe Ellis Ericson, KSJ *	Knight Chaplain
F. Russell Kendall, KSJ	Immediate Past Knight Commander

Sons of the Republic of Texas Biographies

JAMES LEMUEL ALLEN

James Lemuel Allen was born in Kentucky to Samuel and May (Lamme) Allen, natives of Virginia and Kentucky, respectively. He was the grandson of the Virginian, Richard Allen, and great-grandson of Rev. John Allen, a native of Massachusetts. He was also a cousin of General Ethan Allen of Revolutionary fame.

Young James was a student at Marion College in Missouri when he and other students volunteered for military service in Texas. He was assigned to serve with Travis in San Antonio. He joined the troops at the Alamo in early spring of 1836, and on March 5, he and another young soldier, Galba Fuqua, were being considered as couriers. Col. Travis must send someone to Goliad in a last effort to get Col. Fannin to send reinforcements. Travis had grown fond of these two young men and found it difficult to choose between the two of them. Bonham stepped forward, picked up a stick and broke it into two unequal parts, saying, "The long stick is Allen and the short is Fuqua." Travis drew the long stick and Allen rode out on March 5, the day before the siege.

He later served with "Deaf" Smith as a scout. He missed the Battle of San Jacinto, but was instrumental in burning bridges behind the Mexican lines, thus cutting off their means of retreat. He also served under Captain Bell in the Indian Battle of Corpus Christi, July 1845.

Allen settled in Indianola, where he served as County Judge, town Mayor and later as Justice of the Peace.

In 1849, he married Frederica Mensching, and together they reared seven children. At the beginning of the Civil War, he was serving as tax assessor/collector. When the Union troops arrived at Indianola, he was captured and held on Saluria Island. He soon escaped by swimming underwater and dragging an object to serve as a target for the enemy's gunboat fire.

In 1867, he and his family moved to Dewitt County where he owned a farm of 260 acres. He was a member of the Baptist Church and a Mason.

Allen was a highly respected citizen who kept well-posted on current issues of the day and was outspoken on what he believed to be for the best.

He died April 25, 1901, at his home five miles west of Yoakum, TX. *Submitted by William K. Knox (GGGS) #6441*

MARTIN ALLEN

Martin Allen was born Nov. 28, 1780, in Kentucky. He married Elizabeth Vice, Sept. 27, 1804. They had ten children: Miles N., Anna C., Mary G., James Bud, Elizabeth, Martin Jackson, Nancy, Sally Ann (Sarah), Benjamin, and Caroline Eliza.

In 1812, Martin joined the Gutierrez-Magee Expedition. His father, Benjamin Allen, was killed at the Battle of Medina, south of San Antonio in 1813. Martin was in Arkansas Territory in1817, and by 1821 he and his family were living in Allen's Settlement, named in his honor, Natchitoches Parish, La. At this time he joined Stephen F. Austin to become one of the "Old 300" original colonists. In Texas by Dec. 1821, he planted a garden, built a cabin, and became one of the first settlers on Peach Creek on the Colorado River. He then went back to Louisiana for his family, but because of his wife's illness sent his two oldest sons — Miles N. and James Bud — to plant a crop and claim his land. He was granted one sitio of land in present Wharton County in July 1824, and one labor of land in present Austin County. He and his entire family were in Texas by 1826, and appear on the first Texas census.

Martin Allen was captain of a volunteer company fighting Tonkawa Indians, signed the loyalty resolution to Mexico in 1827, and opposed the Fredonian Rebellion. He was made a road supervisor in 1830, and was granted the right to operate a ferry across Buffalo Bayou near Harrisburg. He was a regidor of the ayuntamiento in San Felipe, was a Captain in the Civil Militia, and was appointed Justice of the Peace.

The Martin Allen family operated a "public house" for many years, having moved to Austin County on land granted to Miles N. Allen, his son who died very young. Wm. Barret Travis handled many legal matters for him, and was a frequent guest and visitor. This property was called Eight Mile Point on Allen's Creek (Eight Mile Creek), and was on the well-traveled road from San Felipe to the coast of Texas. Martin served in the Texas War for Independence, and gave much in goods and service to help Texas win its freedom from Mexico. In a petition for land for service he wrote, "I often furnished Horses Guns Ammunition and Provisions to Young Men who were not in a situation to furnish themselves." He also wrote, "Your petitioner lives on the publickest road in the country."

Martin Allen died at his home at Eight Mile Point in Austin County in 1837, leaving an estate of 8,600 acres, animals, wagons, and slaves. His wife Elizabeth died in 1843, and both are buried in the Allen-Johnston Cemetery on Allen's Creek. At least five generations of the Martin and Elizabeth Allen family were born and lived on this same property, just 8 miles south of San Felipe de Austin.

A Texas State Historical Marker was dedicated in 1993 to the memory of Martin Allen, and to his service and accomplishments in early Texas history. It is on State Highway 36, four miles north of Wallis, eight miles south of Sealy, just across the road and the railroad from the Martin Allen original property.

Martin Allen descendants and members of the Sons of the Republic of Texas: Walter E. Belt, Jr. #4955, Lucas Paul Coleman #5145S, George Howard Coleman #5146S, Clarence Hugh Woliver, Jr.#4991, David Allen Woliver #5318S, Walter Hugh Woliver #5319S, *Submitted by* Katherine Allen Harrison , The Daughters of the Republic of Texas #7112, Descendants of Stephen F. Austin's "Old 300."

JAMES A. ALLISON

My great-great-grandfather was James A. Allison (b. 1810), who, along with his father, brothers and their families left Hardeman County, TN, for Texas in 1833 in oxen-drawn wagons, and arrived in Texas by March 1835. James and brother, William, fought in the Texas Revolution. Thereafter, they and their other brother, Elihu, received First Class Headright land grants. In 1847,

James Allison *Robert Ray Allison*

James and Elihu sold their land and purchased property on the San Gabriel River in Williamson County. James soon had to defend his property, as two Mexican land grantees had sold the same property to another family, thus igniting a long-lasting land war. The courts eventually ruled in James' favor. James was a farmer/stock-raiser, and made numerous cattle drives. The Allisons gave land for the Allison-Friendship church, school and cemetery. James (and brother, Elihu), age 51, enlisted in the Militia for the Confederacy. Their sons were also Confederate soldiers, during which James' son, Elihu 11, died of illness. James and wife, Delilah, died in 1874 and were buried in the Allison-Friendship Cemetery. In 1970s, the Army Corps of Engineers, preparing to dam the San Gabriel River, moved the cemetery to Granger. James and his entire family, like other pioneers, endured enormous hardships and were Republic of Texas heroes. *Submitted by Robert Ray Allison #3748*

CARL CONRAD AMSLER

Carl Conrad Amsler and wife, Mary, came to Austin's Colony in July 1834, from Switzerland. He traveled up the Brazos River and settled on spring-fed lands near the present-day Bellville, Texas. He helped found the town of Cat Springs, not far from San Felipe de Austin. He erected a log cabin and began farming.

Karl Conrad *Catsprings monument*

In the autumn of 1835 while working in the fields, he received the call that reinforcements were needed in the Texas Army, as he recalled in an interview years later. After setting out, he met Stephen F. Austin and Col. William Pettus, whom he knew well, at Gonzales. On the morning of December 5, 1835, when Benjamin Milam called for volunteers to storm the town of San Antonio de Bexar, Carl Amsler stepped forward. The Texians succeeded in driving the Mexicans from San Antonio and were thereby able to occupy the Alamo for its ill-fated demise yet glorious memorial in March, 1836. In the interim, Carl Amsler enlisted for the Matamoros Expedition, meant to take the struggle for liberty deep into Mexico. Near Mission Refugio, Carl Amsler fell ill and was given an honorable discharge by Captain Thomas Pearson. The expedition went on to suffer disaster at the hands of Mexican troops.

Allowed to recuperate by Mexican rancheros who befriended him, Carl Amsler regained his strength and started back home. He met a "sociable old gentleman" near Goliad who appeared at his campfire. "Deaf" Erastus Smith gave Amsler his last two dollars after hearing his story. He took Amsler to the Texian camp where he retold his story to Col. James W. Fannin. He continued his travel east back to his homestead where he found most Anglos fleeing the colonial settlements. In his travel, he recounted finding settlers who had been scalped by Indians just prior to his arrival. Amsler still had not crossed east of the Brazos, but one night an Indian raid claimed the lives of some friends. The settlers realized they faced danger from both Indians and Mexican troops.

With his wife now pregnant, Amsler moved east until after the Texian victory at San Jacinto. Mary Amsler gave birth to Charles Amsler Jr. in the year of Texas Independence, 1836.

I, William Cathriner, am the great-great-grandson of Charles Amsler, and share my pride with many other descendants. *Submitted by William Cathriner, August 12, 1999. 4023 Branard Houston, Texas 77027 San Jacinto Chapter 1*

ELIPHALET LESTER ARNOLD

Eliphalet Lester Arnold and his wife, Clarissa H. Cone, were born and raised in Middlesex County, Connecticut. Before 1841, they moved from East Haddam, Connecticut, to Montgomery, Texas, with three of their children. There he joined his brother, Dr. Epaphras J. Arnold, a physician, who had already moved from Connecticut to New Orleans, and from New Orleans via Galveston (by ship in 1837) to Montgomery in Montgomery County, Texas. Dr. Arnold built an unusual house in Montgomery in the late 1840s in Connecticut style, which is still standing, and is currently being used for the City Hall.

Eliphalet Arnold indicated his profession in the 1850 U.S. Census as a smith, and in 1860 as a miller. His wife's will indicated that she and her husband owned a saw mill. Two of their children, Maria Clarissa Arnold and Ann A. Arnold were born in Montgomery, Texas.

Maria Clarissa Arnold was born in Montgomery, Texas, on February 28, 1843. She was called Clara. She attended the Chappell Hill Female College in Chappell Hill, Texas, and was graduated the class of 1860. *Submitted by Thomas S. McCall #3015*

LINO AROCHA

Lino Arocha was a direct descendent of Francisco Arocha and Juana Curbelo, who arrived at San Antonio de Bexar on march 9, 1731 with fifteen other Canary islands families who were sent to New Spain by King Phillip V.

During the Texas Revolution against Mexico, Lino's brother Antonio Cruz Arocha, campaigned with Juan N. Seguin's Ninth Company of Texas Volunteers at the Alamo and San Jacinto. Lino maintained their Rancho de San Rafael, at times defending the families and livestock from depredations by Indians and malcontents who roamed the area.

In 1835 the Spanish Viceroy issued an order for the Army to kill every third male member of Spanish families who had rebelled against the crown. Some family members fled to Louisiana, others to south Texas. Lino remained, and according to Republic of Texas records, he and Encarnacion Urrutia were issued marriage license number 73. They were married on May 6, 1841, and raised seven children near Calaveras, Texas.

Lino was born in 1810 to Miguel and Josefa Arocha, and he died in 1889. My great-great-grandfather is buried near Floresville, Texas. Some of his descendants still farm and ranch on portions of the original Spanish land grant. Robert J. Guzman #6385

EDUARDO ARRIOLA

Eduardo Arriola, my great-great-grandfather, was born in Nacogdoches, Texas, in 1785. He was the son of Joseph Antonio Arriola, b. 1766, and Ana Maria Jacoba Equis. Eduardo's grandfather was Joseph Marcelino de Arriola, b. 1736, in Monterrey, Nuevo Leon, Mexico, and was married to Juana Maria Palacios. They came to Texas in 1767, lived for a short while in Bexar, and then moved to Nacogdoches. Joseph Marcelino de Arriola was killed by the Indians near the Colorado River in 1788 during a trip to Bexar, possibly as a soldier. The original Arriola Rancho was located about a mile or so northeast of present-day Nacogdoches, on the old historic Highway 21 at La Nana Creek.

Eduardo married Candelaria Simes, daughter of Richard Simes of Bristol, England, and Maria de la Concepcion Perez, native of Bexar. Eduardo was awarded a league of land in present-day Hardin County. Then, before 1832, he was awarded another league of land in present-day Madison County, bordering on the Grimes County line, and was recorded as one of the first settlers in that area. Eduardo and his brothers-in-law, Ignatius Simes and Antonio Rios built a fort for protection against the Indians. When one of the family would hear of Indians in the area, that person would ring a bell to alert everyone to hasten into the fort for safety.

The old La Bahia Road cut through Eduardo's league, and this Arriola Rancho was used as a stopover for travelers on their way to Washington-on-the-Brazos. Visitors included Sam Houston, Thomas J. Rusk, William Travis, David Crockett and others.

Eduardo was a staunch supporter of Texas independence. He and four of his sons served under Capt. Elisha Clapp in the very early Texas Ranger days, and were discharged on December 19, 1842. He also served in the Somervell Campaign in 1842. Again, Eduardo and four of his sons are listed on the Gillaspie Monument in the Huntsville Cemetery as soldiers fighting for Texas independence.

The children of Eduardo and Candelaria were: Juan Jose, b. 1809; Jose Delores b. 1810; Maria Olalla Delilah, b. 1811; Francisco de Jesus, b. 1814; Massemore, b. 1816; Juan Pablo (John), b. 1818; Jose Teodoro, b. 1820; Jose Ylario (Eli) b. 1824; M. Gregorio (Gray) b. 1827; Masseneto, b. 1833; and Mary, b.1837.

Eduardo's son, Gregorio (Gray) Arriola also became a Texas Ranger and served under Big Foot Wallace at Fort Lincoln and Fort Inge. Ret. DPS Lt. *Submitted by Kenneth Ariola*

HENRY AWALT

Henry Awalt was born about 1804 in North Carolina, the grandson of a Revolutionary War veteran, Michael Abraham. Henry moved with his family to Franklin County, Tennessee, about 1819 and married Mary Reed. Two of their five children were born in Tennessee.

Records show the family of four appearing next in Nacogdoches, Texas, in 1835.

As a colonist in Impresario David G. Burnett's colony, Henry Awalt petitioned for and received one league of land from the Mexican government on October 11, 1835. His military service in the Army of the Republic of Texas dated from July 4, 1836 to September 12, 1836. The 4,605-acre tract he received was located around present-day Stewards Mill, about 5 miles north of Fairfield, Freestone County, Texas.

For his military service under Capt. Hamilton's Company of Infantry, Henry received 320 acres of bounty land on November 14, 1837. The land certificate was later transferred to Henry's brother-in-law, William B. Reed.

A final parcel, one labor, was received by Henry from the Republic of Texas Board of Land Commissioners, Nacogdoches, on July 24, 1838. The tract is located near present-day Henderson in Rusk, County.

Proof of Henry Awalt's service and residence in the Republic of Texas is as follows: petitioned for Colonization May 23, 1835, and subsequent title of possession was dated October 11, 1835; discharge dated September 12, 1836, for service in the Army of the Republic of Texas and Bounty Land Certificate for said service.

Henry chose to settle permanently on the Freestone County league, where he and Mary raised their five children and engaged in a variety of agricultural pursuits. Family history maintains that Henry lived in Freestone County in the late 1820s, prior to making his 1835 application for the land. This confirms the presence of the Awalt family in Freestone County for some 180 years at this writing, unto today's seventh generation. Three great-great-granddaughters — Christine Watson-Marsters, Cloace Ferguson-McGill and Pamala Jacobs-Day, still enjoy ownership of land in the Henry Awalt league.

The date of Henry Awalt's death is unknown but estimated to be about 1876. Sadly, his final resting place is open to speculation. It is believed that he and his wife Mary Reed are buried somewhere on the league of land Children of Henry and Mary Reed Awalt were:

(1) Isaac Reed Awalt, born about 1830, died about 1878. (2) George W. Awalt, born about 1832, was a school teacher in Freestone County, Texas, in 1870s. (3) Jessie C. Awalt, born 3-17-1835, just two months before his father, Henry, made application in Nacogdoches to be admitted to colonist status. Jessie died 12-13-1904. (4) PernElla Awalt, born about 1840, married Reverend W.G. Caperton; other children of W.G. and PernElla are not known, but Mary Reed Awalt's will names a granddaughter, M.W. Caperton. (4) Lemuel H. Awalt, born about 1842. The only information on Lemuel is his Confederate service record, the last record being a receipt roll dated October 1862, in Marshall, Texas (5) Albert Awalt, was the youngest child. Family history is that Albert was killed in a horse race.

Mary Reed Awalt's father, the Reverend Isaac Reed, was founder of the Old North Church in Nacogdoches, Texas. He built the church at his own expense and served as pastor from 1838-1847. May 3, 1937 an official State Historical Marker was placed under the tree where Isaac stood to preach one of the first Protestant sermons ever preached in Texas. A historical marker stands at the gravesite of Isaac in the Reed family cemetery near Clayton, Panola County, Texas. Isaac Reed bought a league of land (4,428 acres) from Manuel Antonio Romero, in Panola County, Texas, and made his home there. Subsequently, in company with his son-in-law, Henry Awalt, he made application and was granted a tract of land further west in what is now Freestone County Texas — the west perimeter of the present-day site of the town of Fairfield, Texas

The Henry Awalt Chapter No. 55, Sons of the Republic of Texas, was organized by Scott Watson Marsters, Sr. #6010, who was subsequently elected first president of the chapter. Scott is a great-great-great-great-grandson of Henry Awalt.

The Charter Award Ceremony for Chapter No. 55 Sons of the Republic of Texas was held March 28, 1998, in Fairfield, Freestone County, Texas. Master of Ceremonies was Past President General Lavon Tindall, KSJ, and guest speaker, Past President General Sam Houston, IV, KSJ.

WILLIAM GORDON BACHMAN

William Gordon Bachman was born in Georgia September 20, 1822, to John Bachman and his first wife, Mary Catherine Barbara Benecke. He was the youngest of their 11 children (4 brothers and 6 sisters). He came to Texas in 1842 and signed up with the Texas Army to repel Mexican General Rafael Vasquez in the spring of 1842. General Vasquez was defeated. He was paid for his service until 1853, by which time he had married Caroline Green and had two children, Ann Bachman and Lorenzo Bachman. In July 1853, William Gordon Bachman bought 320 acres from N.W. Bush in Austin County, Texas. In 1861, he was raised a Master Mason in Post Oak Island Lodge 181, in which he had several offices. December 5, 1882, William Gordon Bachman died, and was buried in the Ridgeway Cemetery, three miles west of Paige, Texas. *Submitted by Clark P. Wright and Madison B. Wright, Jr., KSJ*

DAVID RILEY BANTA

David Riley Banta, whom I claim as my Republic of Texas forebear, came to the Republic of Texas with his parents, Isaac and Eliza (Barker) Banta, in 1840. David was born in Indiana on April 17, 1829. He died at Voca, Texas, in the home of his daughter, Belle (Banta) Liverman (my grandmother) on May 13, 1917.

I remember him well. He sported a long, gray beard, drove a one-horse buggy and had a goatskin lap robe. Apparently homeless and living on his Confederate pension, he had a large family of children with whom he divided his time.

Prior to his death, and living in the home of his daughter, Alice, he was writing his memoirs when the home burned. Too late in his years, he never attempted to rewrite his memoirs.

My line of descent would read:

David Riley Banta married Margaret Jane Keith, who preceded him in death by many years.

His daughter, Belle, born 2-6-1869 and died 3-28-1963, married William Newton Liverman.

Belle's daughter, Lillian (my mother), born 9-14-1890 and died 11-26-1966, married on 1-26-1908 my father, Thomas Edward Spiller, known as Ed.

And I, Wayne Spiller, born March 2, 1911, married Nell Flournoy on June 23, 1935. *Submitted by Wayne Spiller*

JESSE BARKER

Jesse Barker was born in Perquimans County, North Carolina, in 1791 and moved to Missouri where he married Malinda Weeks.

At the request of his brother in 1827, he and his family brought a herd of horses to Texas and joined Austin's 4th Colony. In the 4th Colony census, it shows Jesse and his wife Melinda and four children and states that he "took the oath."

They lived around Austin's headquarters and he was engaged in frontier service against the Indians. In 1829, he and his family, his brother Lemon and his family, along with Billy Barton, Ruben Hornsby, a Mr. Wales, and two or three others came up and started a settlement at Bastrop.

Jesse died February 6, 1846 at Bastrop County, Republic of Texas

Jesse's son — Calvin Barker — was on the first Grand Jury

Jesse's grandson - whose father was Eleazor Block Barker — was the famous Texas Ranger — Dudley Snyder "Dud" Barker.

Part of the family finally settled in Williamson County, Texas, where many of his ancestors still live. *Submitted by Patrick Garry Gran - #4550*

DR. GEORGE WASHINGTON BARNETT

The tale of George Washington Barnett, son of Margaret and William Barnett, born 12 Dec 1793, Lancaster Co., SC. William Barnett was sheriff of Lancaster District. George Barnett moved to Williamson Co., TN, where he practiced medicine and married, 06 July 1820, Eliza Patton. By Jan 1, 1834 he moved from Mississippi to Washington-on-the-Brazos and practiced medicine in Austin's Colony.

In 1835, a company of Volunteers was raised in Washington with George W. Barnett as lieutenant. This company marched to Gonzales and then to San Antonio, where they were under fire December 5-10, 1835. General Martin Perfecto d Cos surrendered on December 10th.

In the elections held in Texas on Feb 1, 1836, George W. Barnett was elected as a delegate from Washington-on-the-Brazos. After adjournment of the convention, Dr. Barnett joined the Army. When General Houston decided to retreat, he gave permission to seek a place of safety for the families. Dr. Barnett and the families began their "Runaway Scrape." In an affidavit by Dr. Barnett on May 24, 1837, he stated that about April 18, 1836, he was in the town of Harrisburg. The Battle of San Jacinto was fought April 21, 1836 close by.

Eliza Patton Barnett was born 03 July 1802 in TN, died 21 Nov 1872 in Gonzales, TX. He died October 8/9 1848 in Gonzales Co., after escaping from an Indian raid when he went hunting. Evidence showed he had made a strong effort to defend himself. The body was interred in the old cemetery in Gonzales. In 1936, the Commissioner of Control, for Texas Centennial Celebrations erected a monument in George W.'s honor. When the Texas Star Museum was built at Washington-on-the-Brazos, a monument was placed with his name on it too. For his service in the Siege of Bexar, he received Bounty Certificate #320 acres in Gonzales; later he was granted 640 acres. He signed the Texas Declaration of Independence, on this document, as GW Barnett.

Granddaughter Ella Barnett, donated a cherry-wood drop leaf table to The Alamo and great-grandson's widow, Mrs. John Ruckman Barnett, donated photos, in one frame, of grandchildren Robert Lee, George Walker and Ella Barnett, including great-grandson, John Ruckman Barnett, who was grandson of William Lockridge Barnett and Elizabeth Celina Walker. Wm. L. was born 03 Jan 1830, d 30 Aug 1896, mrd. 28 Nov 1855 Elizabeth, who was b 23 Dec 1826, d 02 Apr 1920.

Issue:

Ella Barnett, b 16 Feb 1859, d 14 Jan 1944 in San Antonio.

John G. Barnett

George Walker Barnett, b 16 Aug 1868, d 22 Nov 1948

Robert Lee Barnett, b 29 Sept 1865, d 07 Jan 1942, mrd. Mary Jane Ruckman, b 10 Oct 1872, m 16 Jan 1900, d 15 Dec 1915, issue: William Lockridge Barnett II, b 14 Sept 1900, d 18 Apr 1976 d.s.p Margaret Lizzie Barnett Hensley, b 27 Sept 1906, d 14 Mar 1993 John Ruckman Barnett, b 18 Aug 1910, d 03 Aug 1960, mrd. 01 June 1939 Issue: Lee "Judy" Seitzler, b 01 June 1915

John Ruckman Barnett, Jr., b 05 Oct 1940, had: Diana Jeanne Barnett, John Ruckman Barnett III Robert Lee Barnett III Jerrold Lee Barnett, b 27 May 1947 had: Jerrold Lee Barnett, Jr. William Dickson Barnett, b 24 Sept 1950, had: William Dickson, Jr., Daniel James Barnett. *Submitted by Mrs. John Ruckman Barnett*

BERTHOLD BARTH

Berthold Barth was born to Joseph Wilhelm August Barth and Magdalena Meyer in November 1818 in Offenberg, in the valley of the Black Forest, Baden state.

Berthhold Barth

He arrived in Galveston, Texas, December 30, 1843, on the ship The Jean Key at the age of 25, with other Henry Castro colonists. He settled in and with the other colonist named the town of Castroville, Texas. He later moved to San Antonio, Texas. On November 12, 1845, he enlisted in the U.S. Army, under Brig. Gen. John E. Wool in Howe's Co. 2nd U.S. Dragoons. He fought in Mexico at Presidio, La Nava, San Fernando, Santa Rosa, Monclova and Parras. He participated in the capture of Vera Cruz under Major General Winfield Scott and at Cerro Gordo and Churubusco on the march to Mexico City. He received an honorable discharge on November 13, 1850 at Ft. Graham, Navarro County, Texas.

He married on September 11, 1855, to Wilhelmine Elizabeth Vogelsang in San Antonio, to which 10 children were born.

On March 13, 1862 at the age of 43, he enlisted in the Confederate Army, Samuel G. Newton's Co. 3rd Texas Volunteer Infantry. He received an honorable discharge in San Antonio on July 16, 1862 by reason of disability and being overage under the Conscript Act.

He died January 28, 1891, and was buried in the San Antonio National Cemetery.

Documentation is in the Texas Archives and the National Archives and in the San Antonio, Bexar County Courthouse. Berthold Barth was my great-grandfather. *Submitted by Albert Daniel Barth #2960*

JOHN ALLEN BARTON, JR.

Born in Temple, Texas, November 14, 1929, to John Allen Barton and Edna Gist Barton. Attended Salado Public Schools, Baylor University and Baylor University College of Dentistry.

Upon graduating from Baylor Dental, entered the dental internship program offered by the United States Air Force at Brooke Army Medical Center. Was married to Patricia Lawshe in 1955 in San Antonio and later became the father of three daughters.

One of the highlights of my Air Force career was being stationed in Washington, D.C., 7 years, which were in dental research at the National Institute of Standards and Technology.

I remained in the Air Force until 1976, and retired with the rank of Colonel, and have resided on the family farm at Bell Plains, which is located just east of Salado.

JEAN BENJAMIN BAVOUX

Jean was born in Auxere, France, in 1810. He was the son of Jean Claude Bavoux, a Napoleonic War veteran, and Margueritte Fraussereau. Jean served in the Royal French army of King Louis Philippe.

Jean married Marie Catherine Victoire Amette in Paris in 1831. From this marriage two children were born: Jean Baptiste born in Paris in 1833 and Ambrosine Desiree born in Paris in 1835.

Jean arrived in Galveston in October, 1841, followed by his wife and two children in June, 1842. In 1846, he was issued a Headright Certificate for 640 acres in Denton County, Texas, but remained in Galveston with his family, residing in the family home at 2621 Broadway until his death in 1847. He and his wife are both buried in the Old Catholic Cemetery on 40th and Broadway in Galveston.

Jean was a cabinetmaker by profession and produced fine furniture for the many new homes built in Galveston during the Republic of Texas period.

His son, Jean Baptiste, remained in Galveston and became prominent in business and the arts. He was a founding member and officer of the Societe Francaise de Biefaisance et d' Assistance Mutuelle in 1860. Jean Baptiste served in DeBray's Texas Cavalry during the Civil War, participating in the battles of Galveston, Mansfield, LA, and the Red River Campaign.

Joseph G. Ginn, KSJ #1609
Joseph G. Ginn, Jr. #1692
Dylan Gravenor Ginn #3803
Ian Patrick Ginn #4747
Robert John Ginn #2982
Marcus Junemann #3636
Charles Bavoux Partin #3866
Frank Herman Bavoux #3757

JOSIAH H. BELL

Josiah H. Bell, born August 22, 1791 in Chester District, South Carolina; son of John and Elizabeth Hughes Bell. After an apprenticeship in Nashville with his uncles, tailors and hatters by trade, he sought his fortune with his friend Moses Austin. They mined, traded with Indians and sold merchandise and bargained with the French and Spanish governments, which served them well as later pioneers in Texas. Bell married Mary Evaline McKenzie on December 1, 1818 in Christian County, Kentucky. The newlyweds settled in Natchitoches, Louisiana, where they lived until Moses Austin convinced Bell to join him in founding a colony in Texas.

James H. Bell

Bell and his family crossed the Sabine on April 22, 1821, thus preceding Stephen F. Austin into Texas. The Bell family became one of the first of the "Old Three Hundred" families settling in Austin's First Colony. Bell became Stephen F. Austin's trusted advisor, and was left in charge of the colony while Austin was in Mexico City to secure his land grants. Austin wrote of him as a man "having particular merit over the rest, as having a fine and well-established reputation for probity, calmness and intelligence, judgment and virtue."

Josiah settled for a short time near Washington, then descended down the Brazos "about five miles below La Bahia Road" at a spot which became known as "Bell's Landing" (now Columbia). For a short time in 1836, it seems to have been used as the capital, with President Houston occupying a small house in the Bell yard. Bell and his lovely wife provided accommodations for President Houston and other distinguished public men and foreign dignitaries, until Bell's death on May 17, 1838.

Three children lived to perpetuate Josiah's family in Texas: Elizabeth Lucinda, Thadeus C. and James Hall Bell. The undersigned are descendants of James Hall Bell (b. January 21, 1825), a distinguished lawyer who served on the Texas Supreme Court from 1858-1864. He was married to Catherine Elizabeth Townsend on December 1, 1847 in Houston. He died in Austin, Texas, on March 13, 1892, survived by his wife and six children. His son, Barclay Townsend (b. Oct. 30, 1852 in Columbia), married Lillian Grafton Alsworth (b. March 2, 1855 in Columbia) on May 5, 1874. Barclay and Lillian traveled by covered wagon to settle in the Panhandle of Texas. In later years, they lived in the home of their daughter, Emily Townsend Bell and E.S. Ireland in Hereford, Texas, where Barclay died July 29, 1930, and Lillian died at the age of 98 on May 17, 1953. Our mother and grandmother, Elizabeth Ireland Bonesio (Ms. Charlie Holt) (DRT #19764), daughter of E.S. and Emily Ireland, still resides in Hereford, as do her twin siblings, Richard Ireland and Rachael Henslee.

Woodrow Michael Bonesio #6147 William Michael Bonesio #6148.

JOSIAH HUGHES BELL

Josiah Hughes Bell and his young wife, the former Mary McKenzie of Kentucky, arrived in 1821 on the Brazos in the vicinity of Old Washington. It was to this distinguished future citizen of Barazoria County that Austin entrusted affairs of the colony during his trip to Mexico City, first as sindico (constable) and afterward as alcalde (judge) in 1822.

He established two of Brazoria County's earliest towns, one of them destined to become the first capital of the Republic of Texas called Columbia (known now and since the 1840s as West Columbia). He set about making a "landing" on the Brazos just below Varner's Creek. Here he erected docks, sheds and rooms for storing freight. The colonists were quick to dub the place "Bell's Landing."

Josiah Hughes Bell (one of the "Old 300") received land grants from Mexico under the terms of Austin's first contract with the Mexican government, 1824-1828.

He was born 22 August 1791 in Chester County, South Carolina, and died 30 May 1838 in Columbus, Texas. Children of Bell are Elizabeth Lucinda Bell; Thaddeus Constantine Bell; and James Hall Bell.

Elizabeth Lucinda Bell married Dr. James Wilson Copes on 4 April 1839. Dr. James Wilson Copes died on 8 October 1863.
Submitted by John Carson Copes III #4351

HIRAM BENNETT

Hiram Bennett was born 26 May 1796 in Georgia to William Bennett and an unknown mother, both of South Carolina.

In 1820, he married Theodosia Dobbs, born 1805 in Georgia, daughter of Lodowick Dobbs, born 1759, died 3 Jun 1814, and Sarah Adams, born 1767, died 1838.

An active member of the community in Franklin County, Georgia, Hiram was a landowner, served as a deputy sheriff and as a Justice of the Peace and for several years in the Georgia Militia.

Hiram Bennett *Hiram and Sarah Bennett*

The first of the couple's four children were born in Georgia:
James Madison 20 July 1821 Delilah C.   1823.
William Hardy 30 April 1825.
Elisha William 7 December 1828.

The family was in Cobb County, Georgia, when Sarah Ann was born 12 Jan 1831. There were several other Bennetts in the county, so they may have been visiting relatives.

After their son, Lewis Clark was born 7 Jan 1833, also in Georgia, Hiram, sold his land and moved the family to Alabama where his father, William, was living with his second wife, Sarah E., and their children:
Pleasant 14 Mar 1809
Georgia William Anderson   ca 1810 Jackson County, Alabama
Lucinda ca 1821 Jackson County, Alabama
R.A. ca 1823 Jackson County, Alabama
Unknown child ca 1827 Jackson County, Alabama
It was in Jackson County, Alabama, where three more children were born to Hiram and Docia:
Elijah David   12 Mar 1835
Lidia Jane   31 Mar 1836
Josiah Leath   26 Jan 1839

Before the 1840 census, Hiram took his family to Randolph County, Arkansas, where their last daughter, Mary Jane was born 23 Nov 1842.

In 1845, Hiram, Theodosia and seven of their children came to Texas as members of the Peters Colony. He was entitled to 640 acres of land, and is recorded under claim No. 76, Vol. 2. Theodosia died shortly after the family's arrival in Dallas County.

Hiram married for the second time in 1846, in Dallas County, to Sarah Dougan, born 27 Nov 1827 in Randolph County, Arkansas. Their seven children were:

John Calhoun	21 Oct 1847
Solomon Monroe	25 Dec 1849
Emily Elizabeth	30 Apr 1852
Enoch Noah	4 Nov 1854
Martha Naomi	5 may 1957
Alphus Lane	28 Jan 1861
Alfred Stephenson	28 Jan 1861

In Texas, Hiram was also an active member of his community, serving as Constable, Justice of the Peace and being involved in the establishment of the first school in the area.

During the Civil War, seven sons and at least two grandsons served their country.

Though Hiram and Sarah returned to Arkansas for a time, they were in Dallas County, Texas, when Hiram died 21 July 1888 at age 92. He is buried in the Bennett Family Cemetery, which is now a part of Laurel Oaks Cemetery in Mesquite, Texas. His wife, Sarah, died 27 Apr 1915 in Mesquite, Texas. My grandfather was John Calhoun Bennett. My great-grandfather was Hiram Bennett.

STEPHEN AND MARY BREAZEAL BENNETT

Stephen Bennett (1789-1874), and his wife, Mary Ann "Polly" Breazeal (1798-1877), with their twelve children, led a wagon train of about 100 settlers from Alabama to Texas in 1840. The Bennetts settled in Washington County, were burned out by Indians, and eventually settled in Gonzalez (now Lavaca) County. Stephen Bennett became a successful farmer and esteemed citizen. The Bennett children left their mark on Lavaca County as prominent trail-driving cattlemen, physicians, soldiers, county officials, teachers and Freemasons.

Stephen Bennett, a veteran of the War of 1812, was born in (now) Anderson County, South Carolina. He was the son of Elisha Bennett, a Revolutionary War soldier, and grandson of Archibald Todd, a Revolutionary War patriot.

Polly Breazeal was born in South Carolina, the granddaughter of William Griffin, a Revolutionary War North Carolina Regular soldier who served 84 months.

Stephen and Polly were married in South Carolina after his return from military service. They moved soon after to Alabama and lived there until their emigration to Texas. Both are buried in Bennett Cemetery on their old homestead in Lavaca County near the village of Sweet Home.

Submitted by Stephen Bennett Berry, (SRT #6825), a 4th great-grandson of Stephen Bennett.

RANDY RAY BILLINGSLEY

Captain Jesse Billingsley was born in Saguska Valley, Warren County, Tennessee, October 10, 1810. He was the fourth child of Jeptha and Marion Randolph Billingsley. The family moved to Coopers County, Missouri, in 1817, and later moved back to Tennessee around 1828 and settled in Gibson County near his admired close friend David Crockett. Jesse came to Texas on May 5th 1835, and received a Headright Certificate Number 130 for 1/3rd league of land as a single man, and settled near Cedar Creek in Bastrop County. He served in a Ranger Company under Coleman and received a Bounty Land Certificate #3442 for 320 acres for service from November 17th to December 17th 1835.

He received a Bounty Land Certificate #3054 for 320 acres of land for service with the Mina Volunteers, which was Company C in the Texas Army, from February 28th to June 1st 1836. He received Certificate #3 for one league of land for his disability of his left hand from a gunshot wound received in the Battle of San Jacinto. He received Certificate #404 for 640 acres of land for his service in the Battle of San Jacinto. He received Bounty Land Certificate #3055 for 320 acres of land and #3056 for 320 acres of land for his service in a Ranger Company from July 1st to October 1st 1836.

After the Siege of Bexar in December 1835, the Mina Volunteers were disbanded and Coleman resigned. Due to the continued problems in Texas, the Mina Volunteers reorganized on February 28th at Edward Burleson's home, and Jesse Billingsley was elected Captain. They reached Gonzales on March 1st and awaited reinforcements of Sherman and others. General Houston arrived on March 11th and the Mina Volun-

Captain Jesse Billingsley at age 26, circa 1836.

teers were placed under the command of Colonel Edward Burleson of the First Regiment. Here the orders were given to abandon Gonzales in the middle of the night, which would mean leaving behind all the provisions the citizens of Bastrop had given the Mina Volunteers.

Jesse strongly objected to this order, so General Houston came to him and assured him they would only move a few miles to a place more convenient for fighting and the next morning they could return for what they had left behind. Instead, they marched all night until next morning and were angered to hear the noise of exploding barrels of powder in the burning of their supplies at Gonzales. What angered them more were the viewing of women and children fleeing in terror due to their defenders leaving them unprotected in the middle of the night, which is remembered as the "Runaway Scrape."

Captain Jesse Billingsley at age 47, circa 1857.

After making camp at San Jacinto on the 20th of April, Colonel Sherman and about 70 of his men from his 2nd Regiment came under heavy fire from Santa Anna's army while they were out a few hundred yards from the camp. Jesse, not receiving any orders to aid Sherman, voluntarily led out his command and was followed by the entire 1st Regiment under command of its gallant leader, Colonel Burleson. Jesse and the others ignored orders from General Houston to countermarch and continued to support Sherman, telling Houston he could countermarch himself. Not receiving any support from the 2nd Regiment, due to Houston holding them back, they were forced to return to camp for general council. That evening, the officers entered into a solemn engagement to fight the next day, general or no general. The next day Jesse led his men into battle with the famous battle cry "Remember the Alamo, remember Fannin and Goliad." That day Jesse was wounded in the left hand from a gunshot leaving it crippled for life. Jesse's company had the most wounded of any company with a total of 14.

Jesse disbanded the Mina Volunteers in Mina June 1st 1836 and was issued Bounty Certificate #3054 for 320 acres for the time served, and Donation Certificate #101 for 640 acres for serving in the Battle of San Jacinto. He later joined a company of Rangers commanded by John C. Hunt on July 1st 1836 and served to October 1st 1836, and received Bounty Certificate # 3056 for 320 acres for time served.

Jesse, while serving in the army, was elected as the Representative of Mina and served in the First Congress from October 3, 1836 to June 13, 1837. While serving in Columbia, Jesse wore buckskins he had taken from an Indian and slept on a blanket on the Capitol floor, where he became known as the "Capitol watch dog." He was again elected on October 4, 1837, by a vote of 13 to 11 over Leander Cunningham, by the House of Representatives after a protest by Jesse over an illegal election. Jesse served his term through May 24, 1838.

Randy Billingsley, great grandson of Captain Jesse Billingsley

Prior to and after the Battle of San Jacinto, Jesse was active in defending Texas from the Indians and Mexico. He was in the Battle of Concepcion on October 28, 1835, where his friend Richard Andrews was killed. He was along with Burleson, Bowie, Johnson and Rusk at the "Grass Fight" in November 26, 1835. He was also at the Siege of Bexar on December 1835, where they swore to drive the Mexicans "from the border of Texas or leave our Bones to bleach on the plains of San Antonio."

Jesse, along with his old friend Burleson, fought at Brushy Creek February 25,1839, where Burleson's brother Jacob and Ed Blakey, John Walters and James Gilleland were killed by Comanche Indians. Jesse was again with Burleson along with Micah Andrews at the pursuit and battle known as the "Cordova Fight" in March of 1839, where Dr. Fentress, after killing an Indian, cut his head off to study in his practice when he got back to town. He was again with Dr. Fentress and Burleson at the "Battle of Plum Creek" on August 11, 1840 where Burleson captured the "Duty Roan" after killing the Indian riding it. He was also involved in the "Woll Campaign" in September 1842, along with Mayfield, Caldwell, Captain Jack Hays, Captain William Eastland and Burleson. Prior to Burleson's arrival, there was one instance near the Hondo River, where Billingsley recognizing want of harmony among the commanding officers, asked the soldiers, "Boys, do you want to fight?" The men answered with a loud "Yes." He then said, "Follow me," and led a considerable force very near the Mexican infantry and drew them up into a line of battle, when Colonel Caldwell of superior authority rode up and asked Billingsley, "Where are you going?" He replied, "To fight." Caldwell angrily commanded "Countermarch those men back to ranks!" Hearing this incident — along with Mayfield's at the "Dawson Massacre" — angered Burleson when he arrived to take command, and caused bitterness between him and Mayfield and Caldwell through the years.

Jesse was also at the "Battle of Salado" where Corodova, under the command of Adrian Woll, was killed, which ended the united work of the Mexicans and Indians against the Republic of Texas in 1842.

He and Burleson were chosen by the Mayor and Alderman of Bastrop to present a proposal to Congress to consider Bastrop the permanent seat of government, the "Capitol" on May 5th, 1838.

In 1838, he led an expedition from June 2 to July 6 surveying the land along the Pedernales and Llano rivers. He reported on land suitable for pasture and cultivating, with access to water and minerals with a mention of the size of the "Enchanted Rock."

He was commissioned by President Lamar to assist inspecting the records of the Board of Land Commissions in the counties west of the Brazos River for false claims. In doing so, he and Borden made a few enemies and were poisoned with adaberry pie and became very sick, but recovered to continue serving Texas.

On December 24, 1846 he was commissioned Colonel of the Second Regiment, Second Brigade, Fourth Division of Militia by Governor J. Pinkney Henderson and attested to by the Secretary of State, David G. Burnet. Although he was commissioned as Colonel, he preferred for his men to continue to call him "Captain."

He married Eliza Ann Winnans, the daughter of Francis and Julia Ann Whitaker Winans, on January 15, 1847. She was born in Illinois December 29, 1827, and moved to Texas with her parents in 1838. He and Eliza had three children, Jeptha Preston, born October 23, 1848, and Francis Marion, born 1850, and Miriam Ellen, born November 23, 1852.

He was elected to the House of Representatives in 1853 and re-elected in 1859, and represented Bastrop County in the Fifth and Eighth Legislature. In 1859, Jesse beat out C.C. McGinnis for a Texas House "Floating" District. Jesse fought to help pass the "Homestead Exemption Act" to prevent people from loosing their farm and ranch properties due to non-payment of debts.

Jesse was called upon to give his account of the actions taken preceding and at the Battle of San Jacinto, which was published in the Galveston Tri Weekly News September 19, 1857. This article caused other soldiers to step forward and give like accounts, which were documented in the "Texas Almanac."

State Capitol in Austin Texas. L-R: Randall Ray Billingsley- first son of Randy Billingsley, Tyler Tristan Billingsley- grandson of Randy Billingsley, Randy Ray Billingsley- first son of Randolph Billingsley, Randolph Jeptha Billingsley- father of Randy Billingsley and first son of Reuben Randolph Billingsley.

This caused a public debate, which pressured Sam Houston into giving his speech to the Senate February 28, 1859, in which he brought charges against Sidney Sherman and Dr. Labadie. Jesse and others were called to defend Sherman's honor against such charges, which were documented in the following Texas Almanacs.

Jesse, as well as Sam Houston, opposed secession and the Confederacy, which cost him re-election and the loss of friendship of those whom he had considered his friends. His opposition to slavery — and being shunned for teaching his father's slaves to read and write and teaching them blacksmith skills to better prepare them for the on coming "Reconstruction" — endangered him and his family. There were many slave owners who did not agree with his viewpoints and news reporters who were quick to publish news of this nature that would help sell their papers, one being the Bastrop Advertiser.

Although Bastrop County voted in the majority against secession, 335 for and 352 against, the statewide count was for secession and joined the Confederacy on March 23, 1861.

Jesse moved his family to McDade, Texas and settled into farming. He came out once more in 1874, to speak on behalf of a black soldier named Maxlin "Mack" Smith to see that Mack received his pension for fighting in the Battle of San Jacinto.

Jesse died on his farm in McDade October 1, 1880, and was buried at his request in his front yard by the grave of his faithful white horse "Gopher." His body was exhumed in 1929 and placed in the State Cemetery in Austin due to the gallant efforts of Mr. L.W. Kemp. Jesse's gravesite is placed on Republic Hill, section 1, row K, plot 24 in front of and to the right of "The Father of Texas" Stephen F. Austin, and now near another Texas hero Bob Bullock.

The State erected a granite marker in 1936 in Jesse's honor, stating his services to Texas as a country and a State. The 79th Liberty Ship was built by the Houston Shipbuilding Corporation and christened in 1943 with the name "Jesse Billingsley," paying tribute to his service to Texas. Jesse was remembered by the men who fought with him in their service to Texas as a spirited "take-charge, figure-it-out, can-do" type of man, which was needed to tame the country at this period. They were always proud to be called "Billingsley's Men."

This article was proudly submitted by great-great-grandson Randy Ray Billingsley, a direct descendant of Captain Jesse Billingsley. My father, Randolph Jeptha Billingsley, born February 15, 1925, was the first son of Reuben Randolph Billingsley, born February 16, 1893, who was the sixth child of Jeptha Preston Billingsley, born October 29, 1848, who was the first son of Captain Jesse Billingsley,

As my profession, I am the President of International Longshoreman's Association Local 28, located in Pasadena, Texas. I took office in this position in 1994 and was re-elected and started my second term in 1996, but may not be in this position upon printing of this book due to re-elections in October of 1999. I have been in the longshore industry since December 1, 1972, and hope to retire December 2001. I am a member of the San Jacinto Descendants San Jacinto Chapter of Houston, a member of the Sons of the Republic of Texas San Jacinto Chapter of Houston, and dual member of the Sam Houston Chapter of Houston. I am a member of the Texas Army and a member of the "Black Powder Brigade" in association with the Sons of the Republic of Texas.

I own a small cannon, which I have tagged with the name "Little Sister," which I use in the "Black Powder Brigade" to entertain the young children and adults in our various events we participate in to educate people on the proud history of our state of Texas. I am a proud Native Texan and have purchased the "Native Texan" birth certificate, which I show everyone who enters my home. I also purchased the "Native Texan" birth certificates for the late Bob Bullock and his wife, my distant cousin, Jan Bullock, for Christmas of 1997.

I have two sons, Randall and Preston, and two grandsons, Tyler and Joshua and one granddaughter, Amber to carry on the Billingsley history at this time, but hope to have more in the future – grandkids, that is.

State Capitol in Austin Texas L-R: Randy Ray Billingsley born 1-23-51, Connie Lynn Billingsley born 7-25-51, Mrs. Jan Bullock- wife of Lt. Gov. Bob Bullock holding Amber, Lynn Billingsley born 7-25-97, Monica Billingsley- daughter in law, Preston Billingsley born 2-26-77, second son of Randy and Connie.

I have given a lot of information on Captain Jesse in this article and wish to thank my Aunt Lila Smith, who is the lady responsible for getting me started in the research. Another lady I must thank would be the driving force that pushes me to continue our research together, my cousin Rosalind Brinkley, the "Billingsley Rose." I have a "Billingsley Rose" china set I have collected for my wife of thirty years, Connie Lynn Cude Billingsley. This collection was also started by my Aunt Lila showing me her collection with the Billingsley name on it, which fascinated me

Rosalind Brinkley and her husband Gary; Lila Smith and her daughter Marion Beckham; my parents; my wife Connie; my youngest son Preston and his wife Monica and my baby granddaughter Amber; and Melton and Bell Billingsley — along with Littons, Oatmans and other descendants — have attended historical luncheons at the State Capitol upon the invitation of Bob and Jan Bullock. The purpose of these luncheons was to exchange and view historical information on each others' ancestors. At separate luncheons, we were presented with gifts from Bob and Jan for attending. Among these gifts of gratitude were two gavels, one for the luncheon of August 20, 1997 and one for the luncheon of March 10, 1998. These gifts will be proudly displayed and forever cherished in remembrance of those who gave them.

Rosalind Brinkley and I went to the Capitol on April 20, 1999, to have H.R. 669 passed in the House of Representatives by Representative Zbranek, and S.R. 671 passed in the Senate by Senator Bernsen. The legislation credits Captain Jesse Billingsley as the first man to proclaim the famous battle cry, "Remember the Alamo!" We were honored to receive copies of each bill, along with photos of the event. Along with us for support were my wife Connie, Rosalind's husband Gary, my parents, my oldest son Randall and my grandson Tyler, Lila Smith and her daughter

Marion Beckham, and members of the "Black Powder Brigade."

I have many sources that have helped to document this information, which I will list as follows:

Individuals:
Randolph and Lula Belle Billingsley - parents
Connie Lynn Billingsley - wife
Lila Smith and her daughter Marion Beckham
Rosalind Brinkley and her husband Gary
Melton and Bell Billingsley
Bob and Jan Bullock
Mr. Ira Lott
Mr. Galen Greaser - General Land Office
Mr. Kenneth Kesselus - author
Mr. James M. Day - author
Others I may have failed to mention (librarians, assistants, museum employees etc.)

Documents – locations:
The Billingsley Papers - University of Texas at Austin
Washington on the Brazos Museum - Washington (Navasota, Texas)
Sam Houston Regional Library and Research Center – Liberty, Texas
Texas State Library – Austin, Texas
Clayton Genealogical Library – Houston, Texas
Austin Memorial Library – Cleveland, Texas
Rosenberg Library – Galveston, Texas
Texas General Land Office – Austin, Texas
Bureau of Vital Statistics – Austin, Texas
Genealogy Collection Texas State Library – Austin, Texas
Archives & Information Services Division – Austin, Texas
Bastrop County Courthouse – Bastrop, Texas
Southwest Micro Publishing Inc. - El Paso, Texas

Newspapers:
Galveston Tri -Weekly News - September 19, 1857
Bastrop Advertiser - July 26, 1873
Elgin Courier - 1929 and August 1932
Books and other publications:
Billingsley Book - Harry Alexander Davis
Edward Burleson Texas Frontier Leader - Jenkins and Kesselus
Texas Iliad - Steven L. Hardin & Gary S. Zaboly
Texas Almanac 1857-1873 - James M. Day
Sayersville Historical Association Bulletin No. 8 Fall1988
Recollections of Early Texas – (The Memoirs of John Holland Jenkins)
The Papers of the Texas Revolution 1835-1836 by John Holland Jenkins
The Izard County Historian (Dolph Arkansas) by Lindley
The Texas State Handbook
Heroes of San Jacinto - Sam Houston Dixon and L.W. Kemp
Bastrop County Before Statehood - Ken Kesselus
History of Bastrop 1846-1865 - Ken Kesselus
Reminiscences of 50 Years in Texas - John J. Linn
Indian Depredations in Texas - J.W. Wilbarger
History of Early Fayette County - Weyland and Wade
General Land Office Muster Roll Book of San Jacinto
Biographies of Leading Texans
TexasAlbum, Eighth Legislature
Annals of Travis County - Brown
A Pictorial History of Texas - Homer S. Thrall
Indian Papers of Texas and the Southwest - D.H. Winfrey
Texas Encyclopedia - Thomas W. Cutrer
Texas History Carved in Stone
History of Texas - John Henry Brown
Frontier Times - May 1939
Bandera Texas – J. Marvin Hunter
Maps of Texas 1527-1900 - James M. Day
History of Texas - Clarence R. Wharton
A Reappraisal of the Mexican Commander of Anahuac - Margaret Swett Henson
History of the Revolution in Texas - Newell
I'll Die Before I'll Run – C.L. Sonnichsen
The Life of Sam Houston – J.C. Darby 1855
Three Roads to the Alamo - William C. Davis
Births Dates in Direct Line Descendants:
Jesse Billingsley - 10/10/1810
Jeptha Preston Billingsley - 10/23/1848
Reuben Randolph Billingsley - 2/16/1893
Randolph Jeptha Billingsley - 2/15/1925
Randy Ray Billingsley - 1/23/1951, first son of Randolph Billingsley
Randall Ray Billingsley - 10/4/1969, first son of Randy Billingsley
Preston Lee Billingsley - 2/26/77, second son of Randy Billingsley
Tyler Tristan Billingsley - 7/17/95, son of Randall Billingsley
Amber Lynn Billingsley - 7/25/97, daughter of Preston Billingsley
Joshua Preston Billingsley - 8/20/1999, son of Preston Billingsley

JOHN BILLINGS

John Billings, son of Peter Billings, was born in 1803 in DeKalb County, Tennessee. He and his wife, Jane Zumwalt Billings, took their young family to the Republic of Texas in 1840. Also migrating to Texas at that time were John's brothers, James and Gibson, and sisters Elizabeth, Elsa Mae and Rebecca.

In 1850 John bought 167 acres of land from M.G. Dikes for $100. The land was described as near Sandy Creek on the west side of the Guadalupe River seventeen miles from the town of Gonzales.

John signed a petition to the Legislature of the Republic of Texas, asking that the County of Lavaca be formed. This item is in the State of Texas Archives.

During the next thirty years, John bought and sold several pieces of land. Then in 1870, he deeded to his sons, John Jr. and William MacDonald, all of his land in Gonzales County with the stipulation that the sons "promise to support and maintain me during my natural life." He died in 1872 and was buried in the Union-Sample Cemetery, as was his wife Jane who died in 1873.

Children of John and Jane were: Jasper (1824 Tennessee - 1870), married circa 1847 Emily Rackley (1824 Tennessee - 1914); William MacDonald (1832 Tennessee - 1903), married in 1856 in Gonzales County; Martha Caroline Ritchie (1840 Louisiana - 1880); John Jr. (1836 Tennessee); James, Otis; Nancy (1829 Tennessee - 1906), married in 1846 in Texas Edmond C. Burton (1830 – pre-1870); Amanda Jane (1840 Tennessee - 1916), married first in 1855 George Culver Tennelle (1825 Missouri - 1874) and married second James M. Brockius (1830-1903), and was buried in the Billings Cemetery; and Harriett, married first James H. Henson in 1864, and second Jasper Beene (1834 Alabama) in 1866.

DANIEL BIRD

Daniel Bird, my paternal great-great-grandfather, was born 23 January 1809 in Telfair County, Georgia, to Abraham and Sarah Bird.

Abraham Bird was born 1 January 1771 in Effingham County, Georgia. He served as Justice of the Peace and Court Clerk in Telfair County, Georgia, and held similar positions later when he lived in Marengo County, Alabama; he also owned land and farmed.

Daniel married Minerva Goodbread on 25 January 1831; they continued to live in Marengo County, Alabama, until 1834, when Daniel and Minerva with their three children, and her parents Phillip R. and Nancy Goodbread with their children, came to Texas.

At that time, Texas was part of the state of Coahuila, Mexico. Daniel bought a league of land (4423.4 acres) in East Texas, certified by "State of Coahuila and Texas Precinct of Viesca." They lived there about four years.

In 1838, Daniel received a league and a labor (177.1 acres) of land, being a First Class Headright given to married men arriving in Texas before 2 March 1836; a Patent, signed by Anson Jones, President of the Republic of Texas, was issued later. Daniel claimed this land in what is now Wilson County.

He farmed and ranched on it for 40 years. Some of his descendants still own some of this land.

Papers on file in the Records Division of the General Land Office in Austin prove that Daniel was granted other lands for service in the Texas Army. He also served in the Texas Militia during the Civil War.

Daniel's wife, Minerva, died 22 September 1867. She and other members of the Bird family are buried in the Bird Cemetery, located on one acre of the Headright, a few miles northeast of Stockdale in Wilson County.

On 7 December 1871, Daniel married Clarinda Jane Kimble Barnes, a widow. She was the daughter of Lt. George C. Kimble, who had marched with 32 men from Gonzales to the Alamo and was killed there.

Later, Daniel and his wife moved to a ranch in Kimble County on land that was given to her for her father's service in the Texas Revolution.

Daniel died 7 January 1885 in Junction and is buried in the public cemetery there. He was the father of twelve children: Ten born to Minerva, and two born to Clarinda.

Daniel was the true pioneer: Born in Georgia, growing up in Alabama, moving ever westward to Texas — first Montgomery County, then Bexar and Wilson County for forty years, and finally on to Kimble County for his last days. When he first settled on his Headright land in 1838, he was said to be the first Anglo settler on the Ecleto and his nearest neighbor was fifteen miles away. He seemed to have been a mover, joiner, server, doer. His record shows that he did his full share in all of the activities taking place around him. He was a Mason. He was the good neighbor.

Daniel lived in Texas under four of its six flags: Mexico, when Texas was part of the state of Coahuila; Republic of Texas; United States; and Confederacy.

Nine of my ancestors were in Texas before and during the Republic of Texas. They are: my great-great-great-grandparents, Daniel and Elizabeth Davidson Davis and Phillip R. Goodbread; my great-great-grandparents, Daniel and Minerva Bird and Zachariah and Rosanna Davis; and my great-grandparents William Gaines and Mary Ann Davis Bird.

I am Criag W. Smith, born 7 December 1913 in Stockdale, Wilson County, Texas. I am the son of Jesse Gaines Smith; he is the son of Elizabeth Minerva Bird Smith; she is the daughter of William Gaines Bird; he is the son of Daniel Bird.

I am a member of the Prince Carl of Solms-Braunfels Chapter of the Sons of the Republic of Texas.

CAPTAIN JOHN BIRD (1795 - 1839)

John Bird, along with his wife, Sarah Denton, their four children and several other families, moved from Tennessee to Texas in 1830. Arriving in Stephen F. Austin's Colony in June of 1830, the family initially settled near San Felipe, the capital of the colony. In October of 1831, Bird was granted a league of land near the Brazos River in present-day Burleson County.

During the early years in Texas, Bird, a veteran of the War of 1812, was active in protecting the settlers from Indian attacks, and organized some of the first companies that "ranged" the frontier. Later know as Texas Rangers, these companies helped to secure the land for the colonists. As tensions with the federal government in Mexico grew worse, Bird joined the Texian volunteers and served as a Captain throughout the Texas Revolution from Mexico.

In 1835, Bird commanded a company of volunteers at the Siege of Bexar. He participated in General Austin's Councils of War. On November 8th, 1835, a company under Bird's command engaged the Morales Calvary near San Antonio. During the skirmish, five Mexican soldiers were killed and several were wounded. Bird's company reported one man wounded. Bird subsequently served under Edward Burleson during the campaign that defeated the Mexican General Cos and took control of a mission known as the Alamo.

In March 1836, a desperate plea for help came from William Barret Travis, commander of the Texans remaining at the Alamo. Captain Bird organized a company of approximately 80 men at San Felipe and marched toward San Antonio. Near Gonzales, Bird received word from a messenger that the Alamo and all of the men in it had fallen at the hands of General Antonio Lopez de Santa Anna. Bird's company soon encountered the main body of the Texian Army under the command of General Sam Houston. Bird and his company joined Houston's army and served as Houston's rear guard.

Throughout Houston's retreat, Bird's company assisted settlers, primarily the women and children, who were fleeing the oncoming Mexican army. This event in Texas history, known as the "Runaway Scrape," was a time of great panic and fear among the colonists. Bird's company was involved in several minor skirmishes with Santa Anna's army and provided valuable intelligence to General Houston during the time the rag-tag group of volunteers was being organized into an army. At the Battle of San Jacinto, most of Bird's company were on assorted duties, including protecting the remaining settlers from continued Indian attacks and guarding supplies at Harrisburg.

After Texas independence was won, Bird continued to serve the new Republic with distinction. On May 26, 1839, Bird was killed in a battle that has come to be known as "Bird's Victory." Bird's company of 34 Rangers encountered over 240 Indians near the present-day city of Temple. The company retreated to a small ravine, now known as Bird's Creek, and successfully fought off wave after wave of attacking Indians. During one of the attacks,

Bird took an arrow to the chest. He died urging his men to "fight on like heroes." *Submitted by Ron Patterson, #5521*

JAMES BLAIR

James Blair came to Texas from Belleville, Illinois, in October, 1837 at the age of 37. He was born May 18, 1800, and died October 22, 1878. After his first wife, Martha, died, he married Nancy Brantley. From these unions he raised 10 children in Red River County, Texas. Prior to coming to Texas, he served as a lieutenant with Captain Abraham Lincoln in the Black Hawk Indian War of Illinois in 1832. James also served as a captain under General Tarrant in quelling various Indian uprisings in East Texas in 1841. He was a farmer and Indian fighter.

In 1850, James rode a horse by himself back to Illinois and brought his four grandchildren back to Texas after the death of his daughter and her husband. In 1855, he was awarded additional land in Texas for his service in the Black Hawk War.

His sons served in the Civil War in the 2nd Regiment-Texas Partisan, which later was merged with the 34th Texas Cavalry.

James was the great-great-great-grandfather of Jerral Duane Blair of Fort Worth, and the great-great-great-great-grandfather of Dr. Kevin Duane Blair of New Braunfels. *Submitted by Jerral Duane Blair #4693 Dr. Submitted by Kevin Duane Blair #6380J*

RANSOM GYWNN BLANTON

RG (he always went by his initials) was born to William and Elizabeth Blanton (both originally from Virginia) in 1814 in South Carolina. In the early 1830s, he, his mother, and several siblings moved to Harris County, Georgia. After their mercantile business in West Point failed, RG and his brothers, William and John, rode to Texas, just 8 months after the Battle of San Jacinto.

When the three brothers crossed the Sabine River, it was late and they were hungry. They saw smoke rising from the mud chimney of a house a short distance away, and trotted up to see if they could get a bite to eat. They were greatly surprised to discover that it was the home of their sister, Sarah Ann ("Annie"), who had married John Milton Tidwell and had moved to Texas some time earlier.

(On July 2, 1840, a raiding party of Kichai Indians murdered John Tidwell and took Annie and her children captive. After about a week of difficult travel, these Indians sold Annie and her children to some Delaware Indians, who took them to the Chickasaw nation, but treated them kindly. After a few more days of captivity, Annie heard of her brother [Richard] in Arkansas and wrote to him. He promptly came to their relief, paid their ransom, and took her and the children to live with him.)

RG worked for the Allen brothers, helping to survey the new town of Houston, and working as a contractor building new houses there. He and his brother, John, also served as Texas Rangers in Captain William Bicknell's Company. (John later joined the ill-fated Mier Expedition, was captured, and died in Mexico.) RG was also a farmer and rancher in various other counties in Texas, where he served as a Justice of the Peace, county commissioner, and tax collector. He died October 14, 1881, in Hutto, Texas.

RG married Sara Ann Veazey on January 9, 1845, in San Felipe, Austin County, Republic of Texas, and they had twelve children, among whom was **Benjamin Franklin Blanton** Ben was born in Colorado County, Texas, on February 2, 1855. Among other endeavors, he was a trail driver, first going on the Chisholm Trail when he was only 15 years of age. He rode the Trail twice more, the last time in 1878. In the course of his cattle drives and his scout work for the Texas Central Railroad, he had to fight both Indians and Mexican bandits (in which latter encounter he was shot in the shoulder and nearly died). Ben was a charter member of the National Frontiersmen's Association, and was chairman of its commission to mark the Chisholm Trail. He died on September 4, 1938, at the home of one of his sons (Robert) in Paris, Texas.

Ben married first Hattie Deal (who died in 1882) and then Lou Jane Neal, and had six children, among whom was **William Neal Blanton, Sr.** Bill was born on July 17, 1890, in Moody, Texas. He was a singularly active and effective individual. He was the head of 6 Chambers of Commerce in both Louisiana and Texas, becoming vice president and general manager of the Houston Chamber in 1929. He left that Chamber in 1951, stayed in Houston, and became president of the Blanton Drilling Company and chairman of the Medical Center National Bank.

L-R: W.N. Blanton Sr. and Benjamin J. Blanton

Among many other accomplishments, he helped to found St. Luke's United Methodist Church and was the first chairman of its administrative board. He was vice chairman of the Houston Port Commission; a director of the Houston Symphony Society; a member of the Methodist Hospital board for over 20 years; a trustee of the Boy Scouts of America (receiving its Silver Beaver Award); a member of the SAR; and a Mason, Shriner, and Rotarian for fifty years.

He was particularly interested in Texas history, and was instrumental in obtaining the funding to build the San Jacinto monument. Bill served as chairman of the San Jacinto Battleground Commission and was a longtime member of the SRT, being elected a Knight of San Jacinto in 1955, and serving as Knight Commander. He died in Houston on November 27, 1967.

Bill married first Vivian Tressider (who died in 1923) and then Louise Gorton Wynn, and had seven sons, who are **William Neal Blanton, Jr.** Judge Blanton was born on December 24, 1915, in Waco, Texas. He graduated from Rice University and the University of Texas School of Law. He served in World War II, first as a coastal artillery officer and later in the Second Armored Division, where he was military governor of Landkreiss Newmarkt, Germany.

He was a partner in the Houston law firm of Butler, Binion, Rice, Cook & Knapp, and was active in local Democratic politics. He was a delegate to the 1960 Democratic convention and was later twice elected chairman of the Harris County Democratic Executive Committee. He became Judge of the 11th Civil District

Court of Harris County in 1968, and was the first recipient of the Joe Greenhill Outstanding Trial Judge of Texas Award. He was never opposed for re-election and retired in 1988.

Judge Blanton is a Rotarian and a former director of the Houston Rotary Club. He is a longtime member and former chancellor of the SAR, receiving the George Washington Distinguished Service Award by the Paul Carrington Chapter of the SAR in 1995. He is a charter member of St. Luke's United Methodist Church and has been a member and vice chairman of its administrative board. He is a lifelong member of the SRT, serving as president of the San Jacinto Chapter and vice-president of the SRT, and was elected a Knight of San Jacinto in 1971.

He married Elizabeth Putnam and has three children (Jane, William, and Thomas.) Judge Blanton died November 9, 2000.

BENJAMIN FRANKLIN BLANTON

Ben was born April 9,1918, in Waco, Texas. He graduated from Rice University and served in World War II as a naval aviation officer, receiving a Bronze Star and a Purple Heart. He was a reporter for The Houston Post and was editor and publisher of the Brenham Banner Press. Ben served on the Chambers of Commerce in Sherman, Baton Rouge, and Wichita Falls, and was director of public relations for Rice University. He was chairman of the San Jacinto Battleground Advisory Board and a longtime member of the SRT. He died in Houston on February 27, 1974.

Ben married Carolyn Porter Wells and had two daughters (Beverly and Marilyn).

JOSEPH FRANCIS BLANTON

Joe was born on September 6, 1920, in Waxahachie, Texas. He graduated from Texas A&M and served in World War II in the Navy, where he commanded a subchaser.

He founded Blanton's Flowers in Houston in 1948 (retiring from the floral business in 1981), and served as a director of the FTD and as president of Houston Allied Florists.

Joe is a past president of the Rotary Club of River Oaks and of the Executives Association of Houston. He is a charter member of St. Luke's United Methodist Church, and has served on its administrative board and as president of the Hines Baker Bible Class. He is a Master Mason, and a longtime member of the SAR, serving as president of the Paul Carrington Chapter and receiving the SAR's Silver Good Citizenship Award and the Patriot's Medal. He was president general of the SRT in 1956, elected a Knight of San Jacinto in 1959, and served as Knight Commander.

Joe married Ruth Evelyn Edwards and has two sons (Fred and Mark).

ROBERT WYNN BLANTON

Wynn was born July 25, 1926, in Longview, Texas. He served in World War II in the Merchant Marine and the Army, and accidentally drowned at Galveston on May 30, 1949, while a sophomore at SMU.

JACK SAWTELLE BLANTON

Jack was born in Shreveport, Louisiana, on December 7, 1927. He graduated from the University of Texas at Austin — where he was the Southwest Conference Tennis champion — and from the University of Texas School of Law. He is a past president of the UT Ex-Students Association, and recipient of both the UT Distinguished Alumnus Award and of the Santa Rita Award. He is a member of the UT Development Board, and a former member and past chairman of the Board of Regents of the University of Texas System. He is on the council of overseers of the Jesse J. Jones Graduate School of Administration at Rice University, and has received honorary doctorates from St. Thomas University and Centenary College.

Jack was president, chairman of the board and CEO of Scurlock Oil Company and is president of Eddy Refining Company, as well as chairman of the board of trustees of Houston Endowment. He is a past president of the Mid-Continent Oil & Gas Association and of the Texas Mid-Continent Oil & Gas Association, a former director of the American Petroleum Institute; a director, member of the executive committee, and past chairman of the Greater Houston Partnership; and past president of The Houston Club. He is a member and former vice chairman of the board of trustees of the Methodist Health Care System; a director of the Texas Medical Center; and a former member of the board of managers of the Harris County Hospital District. He is also a director of the National Wildflower Research Center.

Jack is a member and past president of the Texas Philosophical Society; a former chairman of the Governor's Task Force on Private Sector Initiatives; a past president of the Southeast Texas Chapter of the Young Presidents Organization; and a member and past chairman of the administrative board of St. Luke's United Methodist Church.

Jack was inducted into the Texas Philanthropy Hall of Fame in 1998, in which year he also received the Joseph Jaworski Leadership Award from the American Leadership Forum. He was elected to the Texas Business Hall of Fame, and received the Distinguished Service Award from the Texas Mid-Continent Oil & Gas Association. The Paul Carrington Chapter of the SAR gave him the George Washington Distinguished Service Award in 1993.

Jack married Laura Lee Scurlock, and has three children (Elizabeth, Jack, and Eddy).

PAUL GORTON BLANTON

Paul was born November 11, 1930, in Houston, Texas. He graduated from Duke University and from Yale Divinity School, received his Masters in Sacred Theology from Perkins School of Theology, and his Ph.D. from Claremont Graduate School. He was director of the Methodist Student Foundation at Texas Woman's University, SMU, and Northwestern University. He was on the faculty at Southwestern University. He was with the Texas Department of Human Resources, helping senior citizens, when he died on January 19, 1989, in Wimberly, Texas, after an automobile accident.

Paul married first Patricia Ann Kenny, then Joy Lee Fisher, and lastly Andrea Lea McLaughlin, and had three children (Elizabeth [Lesa], Paul, and Samuel).

JAMES NEAL BLANTON

Neal was born on July 17, 1934, in Houston, Texas, and graduated from the University of Texas at Austin. He served with the Chambers of Commerce in Lake Charles and Hillsboro, and has been with the U.S. Department of Commerce in Austin and the U.S. Small Business Administration in Houston.

Neal married first Christine Satel, then Susan Wilda Bizzell, and has four children (James, John, Catherine, and Kate).

HARVEY (HENRY) BOGGS

Harvey (Henry) Boggs was born in 1802 in Clark County, Kentucky, the son of Charles Boggs and Ann Scobee. He grew up there and married Phebe Ligett, the daughter of John Ligett and Salley Daniley, on 3 Dec 1821.

About 1840, looking for better land to farm, Harvey, Phebe and six children (Sarah Ann, John William, Eliza Jane, Thomas Boone, Elizabeth, and Stephen S.) departed Kentucky for Monroe County, Missouri.

In 1844/1845 Harvey saw information that appeared on Peters Colony in Texas, telling how every married man could have a splendid tract of choice land by merely going and taking possession.

On 24 Nov 1845 a wagon train made up of five families from Missouri arrived at Cross Timbers (Whitesboro), Texas. Harvey and his now nine children (James W., Phoebe Angeline, and Lucy Allen) had arrived in Texas. In 1846, he paid the $1.00 poll tax in Grayson County, Texas. On 27 Dec 1848, he was designated an Associate Justice (Commissioner of the Court) for Cooke County, Texas.

During August and September 1849, he was on a committee to establish a road from Liberty (Gainesville) to the east county line.

As the head of a household, he was entitled to receive 640 acres of land.

General land office records state that on 28 Oct 1850, he was issued Certificate #1294. Fannin Third Class Headright #1193 was patented for 640 acres of land southeast of current Gainesville, Texas. The land was surveyed on 10 May 1852.

No exact date has been established when Harvey died, but it was before 21 Aug 1857. This was when Samuel Lindsey, the husband of Elizabeth Boggs, petitioned the Cooke County court to show cause, if any, why Phebe Boggs, the guardian of the estate of Harvey Boggs, shouldn't hand over the separate property of Elizabeth Boggs Lindsey.

No place of burial has been found yet, but it may have been Prairie Grove Cemetery. The cemetery is badly neglected and overgrown in a stand of trees behind the abandoned Prairie Grove Church. Many gravestones have been damaged by cattle roaming the area.

Phebe Boggs died February 1888, in Picketsville (Breckenridge), Texas, and is buried there. She had been living with the family of her son, James W. Boggs. *Submitted by Gerald P. Strong #5040 - 4th Great-grandson*

GARRETT E. BOONE

Garrett E. Boone was born in England in 1810, although the family apparently migrated to Curacao, West Indies. He was a sailor on a ship that wrecked in Matagorda Bay in the summer of 1832. He told his rescuer, F. W. Grasmeyer, that he was a native of Curacao.

After the shipwreck, he and another man salvaged goods from the ship and took them to San Antonio where they were sold. As they were leaving, they were arrested, tried, fined, and sentenced to die. As they were awaiting their fate, a Mexican girl came to them at night, released them, and gave them mules, saddles, money and supplies, as well as a small gold collar button each. If they were stopped by anyone, they were to show the buttons as proof that they had already paid their "tribute" to the authorities. The men then traveled to Bastrop County. (The collar button given to Garrett Boone in 1832 is in the possession of Robert M. Newton in 1999.)

In an affidavit many years later, F.W. Grasmeyer stated that Boone lived with him and worked for him in Bastrop County several years and that Boone "left my house ... about 1st March 1836 and was in the Battle of San Jacinto."

The new Republic was offering land as an inducement for new settlers, and Boone received 1,476 acres, choosing land in Bastrop County. San Jacinto veterans received 640 acres and he chose land in Fayette and Lee counties. He also received two other certificates for land, which he sold.

Tax rolls of Fayette County in 1837 and 1838 show Garrett Boone operating a store and saloon near Warda. He bought lots around the town square in LaGrange and the 1839 tax roll indicates he is living there. Family legend says he operated the first grocery store there.

Garrett Boone married Nancy Ann Fletcher in 1839. They began having their family with one child being born in 1839, Henry in 1840, Mary Virginia in 1842, Alfred in 1844, Sarah in 1848 and John in 1849.

In 1846, Boone again volunteered for military service when border disputes flared between Texas and Mexico.

News of the gold rush in California reached Texas and many men from the LaGrange area left on 1 May 1849. Several notes in a journal referred to "G.E. Boom." After mining about a year, the others returned home. A close friend told Nancy Boone that he had seen her husband get on the ship to return home, but he never saw him after that. His fate is still a mystery.

(Note: "Gerrit E. Boom" is the way he signed his name on deeds and other documents, indicating Dutch ancestry. However, after 1850, this began to be written "Garrett E. Boone" by others.) *Submitted by Robert M. Newton, Great-Grandson #6727*

DR. JAMES WILLIS BOOTH, JR.

Dr. Booth was born June 21, 1927 in Longview, Texas to James Willis Booth and Gladys Adams Booth, members of pioneer Longview families. He was a Navy pilot in World War II. He attended Longview schools, was graduated from SMU with a BBA degree and from Baylor University Dental College in 1955 with honors. He did post-graduate training at the University of Madrid in Spain, as well as the University of Brussels dental school, Brussels, Belgium and the University of Cologne, Cologne, Germany. He maintained his orthodontic practice in Longview until his retirement in 1997. Dr. Booth was member of the Cherokee Kiwanis Club, a past president of the Exchange Club, a member of the Texas and American Dental Associations, Gregg and Harrison County Dental Societies, American Association of Orthodontics, and the Southwest society of Orthodontics. He is a charter member of the Orthodontic Alumni Association of Baylor University College of Dentistry.

Dr. Booth is a member of the First Presbyterian Church of Longview, where he has served as a deacon. He is a member of Longview Masonic Lodge 404, 32nd-degree member of the Dallas Consistory of the Scottish Rite, a Noble of the Sharon Shrine Temple, Tyler, Texas. He is also a charter member of the Sons of the American Revolution, East Texas Chapter.

Dr. Booth has continued his interest in aviation throughout his life. He and his wife, also a pilot, have enjoyed many trips by air to different parts of the U.S. He has been a member of the Aircraft Owners and Pilots Association (AOPA) for over twenty years.

Dr. James Willis Booth, Jr.

His most notable hobby is photography. He was taking movies when he was fourteen, and then later progressed to different media, as times changed.

In 1948, he married Kathryn Elizabeth Adamson, daughter of Gilbert Charles Adamson and Kathryn Bates Adamson. Kathryn is active in the First Presbyterian Church where she is an elder and a Sunday school teacher. She has also served as moderator for the Women of the Church. She is a long-time member of the Shakespeare Club, PTA, the Junior League of Longview, the Green Thumb Garden Club and the Junior Literary Club, having served as president of each.

Dr. and Mrs. Booth were blessed with four children: Cynthia Elizabeth, James Willis III, Susan Ann, and William Morris Booth.

JAMES WILLIS BOOTH III

James was born March 1, 1951, Florence Nightingale Hospital, Dallas, Texas, to James Willis Booth, Jr., and Kathryn Adamson Booth. He attended Longview schools and completed high school in Boonville, Missouri, graduating from Kemper Military School in 1969. In 1973, he was graduated from Southwestern University, Georgetown, Texas, with a BA in mathematics. In 1975, he received a degree in electrical engineering from the University of Texas, Austin, Texas. In 1988, he was awarded an MBA from the University of Texas, Austin, graduating with honors. He is a member of the Texas Society of Professional Engineers.

James Willis Booth III   *Marker for Col. John Hamilton McNairy*

During his early years he became a member of the children of the American Revolution, and later became a charter member of the Sons of the American Revolution, East Texas Chapter.

He is married to Brenda Dawn Smith, daughter of Robert Turner Smith and Doris Spoonemore Smith of Pampa, Texas. Jim and Brenda and were blessed with two children: James Garrett Booth and Lauren McKinley Booth.

They are members of the Riverbend Church, Austin, Texas.

ROBERT E. BOOTH

Robert E. Booth — born in Gregg County, Texas, in 1954 and son of Talmadge Early Booth of Gregg County, Texas — is an architect with HKS Inc. on Dallas, Texas. Robert has been with HKS for 23 years. He is an owner of the firm, which is one of the largest architectural firms in the United States. He has participated in over 100 commercial projects throughout the U.S. and the world. His endeavors for HKS have taken him throughout Asia, Eastern Europe, Africa, and the Middle East.

Robert has two children, James Stuart Early Booth, born 1982, and Peyton Lee Booth, born in 1984.

Robert's great-great-great-grandfather is Col. John Hamilton McNairy, born in Guildford County, N.C., in 1804. He moved to Shelby County, TX in 1837. He married twice and was the father of 11 children. First wife was Sallie Leatherman, b TN, d MS, in 1836 on the way to Texas. He married his second wife Susan (Susanah) Runnels, b TN, 1824, in Shelby County, TX in 1841. She was the daughter of Henry Runnels and Margaret (Peggy) Smith who came from TN to TX in 1837.

Col. McNairy was one of the two Regulators who, at the request of Gen. Sam Houston, signed the peace treaty for the regulators to end the Regulator-Moderator War in 1844. Col. McNairy bought acreage in 1847 in the Coffeeville, Harrison County, Upshur County area (formerly all part of Shelby County). He moved there in 1847.

He was instrumental in getting Upshur County created and was elected the first State Representative from Upshur County in 1848. He was one of two State Representatives for Harrison County prior to Upshur County being formed out of Harrison County. He died at Coffeeville January 7, 1853. A State Historical Marker is located at his grave in the Old Coffeeville Cemetery, Upshur County, Texas.

Col. McNairy's paternal grandfather was Francis McNairy, patriot, of Guilford County, NC. John Hamilton McNairy is named after his maternal grandfather, Gen. John Hamilton, Revolutionary War, Battle of Guilford Courthouse, NC.

STUART LEE BOOTH

Stuart Lee Booth was on born on May 2, 1957 in Longview, Texas. His parents, Talmadge Early Booth and Frances Birdwell Booth, raised their family in Longview. Lee graduated from Longview High School in 1976 and then attended Sam Houston State University, where he majored in business administration.

The Stuart Lee Booth Family

In 1982, Lee returned to Longview where he joined his father at the Booth Insurance Agency. He purchased the agency in 1994.

He married Hollie Sue Grantom in 1982. They have two children: Adam Lee Booth and Dillon Talmadge Booth. Adam and Dillon are the fifth generation born in East Texas.

Lee has served as past president of both the Independent Insurance Agents of Longview and the Kiwanis Club of Longview. He has also been an active board member in the Longview Children's Association and with the United Way Admissions.

Lee is currently president-elect for the East Texas Chapter of the Sons of the American Revolution (SAR). He is also a member of the Sons of the Republic of Texas, Sons of Confederate Veterans, and General Society of War of 1812.

Lee entered into the Sons of the Republic of Texas under the lineage of Col. John Hamilton McNairy, who moved to Shelby County, Texas, in 1837. For additional information on Col. McNairy, see the ancestor biography supplied by Talmadge Booth.

TALMADGE EARLY BOOTH

Talmadge Booth was born December 16, 1929, in Longview, Texas. His father, James Willis Booth, and mother, Gladys Laressa Adams Booth, were members of pioneer families of Gregg County.

In 1950, Talmadge graduated from Southern Methodist University, Cox School of Business. He established the Booth Insurance Agency in June, 1950. He was awarded the Chartered Property Casualty Underwriter (CPCU) designation in 1963. He sold the agency to his son, Stuart Lee Booth, in March 1994. He married Frances Jo Birdwell in 1951. They had four children: Victoria Lynn Bingham, Robert Early Booth, Stuart Lee Booth, and Leanne Elizabeth McCarty. Frances Jo died in 1981.

Talmadge married Frances Monigold Liston** in 1983. She has one son, Thomas (Pat) Liston.
Talmadge Early Booth:
Military:
Marine Air Corps Reserve 1948-50
Navy Air Corps Reserve 1950-54
Activities and organizations:
Organizer/past president - Independent Insurance Agents, Men's Garden Club, and Exchange Club, Longview, Texas
Organizer - Greenwood Cemetery Association – president, 26 years to present date
Member - First United Methodist Church - served on administrative board
Past director - Longview Chamber of Commerce
Fraternal organizations - Kappa Alpha, SMU; Masonic Lodge
Charter member - Gregg County Historical Museum, Longview Beautification Association
Chairman - Parks Board (National Gold Medal award)
Hereditary organizations:
Sons of the Republic of Texas
Sons of Confederate Veterans
General Society of War of 1812
Organizer/ first president - East Texas Chapter, Sons of the American Revolution (SAR). Patriot Medal by the Texas Society of SAR
Florence Kendall Award, highest medal for membership recruiting, by National SAR
Hereditary Register of the United States of America 1973

FRANCES LISTON BOOTH

Native of Marshall, Texas - parents: Leonard and Genevieve Langley Monigold.
Valedictorian - Marshall High School 1952
Attended North Texas University.
Duchess to the Holiday in Dixie Festival
Married A. Eugene Liston in 1955. He died in 1979.
Activities and organizations:
Member - First United Methodist Church, Thelma Morgan Sunday School Class, Friendship Bible Study Club
Daughters of the American Revolution
United Daughters of the Confederacy (granddaughter of Confederate veteran.)
Past president - Shakespeare Club, Junior Literary Club of Longview, Magnolia Garden Club.
Author - "Keeper of the Candles," a series of family Christmas remembrances
Since their marriage in 1983, Frances and Talmadge have enjoyed travel and ballroom dancing.

JONES BOSTON

Jones Boston was a gristmiller. He was born ca. 1780, in the border region of North and South Carolina. A long odyssey carried him from early manhood in Smith County, Tennessee, to Lauderdale County, Alabama, and finally to the Republic of Texas, where he died August 4, 1840.

Jones Boston was accompanied to Texas by his wife, Nancy Ann, two maiden daughters, and nine Negro slaves. He settled near Montgomery, Texas, where he won Third Class Headright Certificate #230 from Washington County in December 1839. Six married daughters, and two sons, remained behind in Alabama.

Jones Boston and his wife both died suddenly in the summer of 1840, likely victims of the fever epidemic then sweeping South Texas. His daughter, Ruth, married John Marshall Wade the following November. Wade, founder of The Montgomery Patriot newspaper, was also notable for firing the "twin sisters" cannons during the Battle of San Jacinto.

Jones Boston's youngest son, Hugh, came from Alabama to lead a ten-year struggle to settle his father's affairs. Details appear in "Estate Papers of Jones Boston" by Hollis B. Boston, Jr., [Baltimore: Gateway Press 1995] found in major Texas libraries.

Submitted by Col. H.B. Boston, Jr., SRT 94695, and third great-grandson of Jones Boston

JESSE B. BOWMAN

Jesse B. Bowman perished in the Battle of the Alamo in March of 1836. Answering the Alamo's roll call on February 23, 1836, in

Bexar, Texas, Bowman was listed as a private and permanent volunteer. He was placed under the command of James Bowie, whose men consisted of elements of Captain John Chenoweth's 34th Infantry and Captain Burk's 4th Infantry, also known as the Mobile Grays.

On March 6, 1836, Jesse B. Bowman, along with approximately 187 other Texas patriots, lost their lives during the fall of the Alamo. The bodies of the defenders were burned by Mexican soldiers under General Santa Anna.

A Texas State Historical Marker near Jonesboro in River County, Texas.

Alamo Monument with Jesse B. Bowman listed.

Jesse B. Bowman's name appears on the Alamo Cenotaph, erected in 1936, as well as on a plaque inside the Alamo. In 1856, Texas built a monument to the memory of the heroes from the stones of the ruined Alamo walls, and placed it inside the first stone State Capitol at Austin. It included the name, "J.B. Bowman." The monument was destroyed by a fire, which razed the Capitol in 1881. In 1888 when a new Alamo monument was placed on the Capitol grounds, the name "J.B. Bournan" was erroneously chiseled on the monument. The state corrected the error in 1990.

Family history places the birth of Jesse B. Bowman in Rutherford County, Tennessee, about 1785. He and his family also lived in Illinois around 1811-14; in Posey County, Indiana, around 1814-20; in Ouchita County, Arkansas, in 1824; and in Hempstead County, Arkansas. In 1833, he moved across the Red River into Texas, settling in Red River County and qualifying for a First Class Headright Certificate granting him a league and labor of land.

Jesse B. Bowman's son, Joseph T., also served the Republic of Texas. He enrolled in the San Augustine volunteers on April 30, 1836, serving under Capt. Jno. M. Bradley, until July 30, 1836. He also served briefly in the Republic of Texas Militia in 1838 with Captain T.H. Tarrant's company.

Texas historical monuments to Jesse B. Bowman and his son, Joseph T. Bowman, are found in Clarksville, Texas, and near Grapeland, Texas.

In 1997, Jesse B. Bowman's great-great-great-grandson, Bob Bowman of Lufkin, Texas, (#6901AH) authored a book, "Search for an Alamo Soldier," on the life of his Alamo ancestor and the Bowman family.

NELSON A. BOX

Nelson A. Box was born in 1808 in Franklin County, Tenn., a son of Stephen F. Box and Keziah Box (or nee Helms Albright). He emigrated from Tennessee to Blount Co., Ala., then to Texas in 1834. He married Elizabeth Garner and they had several children, including Amanda.

After coming to Texas, Nelson Box enlisted in the Army of the Republic and fought at the Battle of San Jacinto in Captain Hayden Arnold's Company. Stephen F. Box his father and his family arrived in Texas November 1834, and settled about 12 miles east of Crockett, Texas. They constructed a fort out of large stakes buried in the ground for protection. They kept their wagons and other belongings in the fort and they lived in the fort for some time. This fort is on several maps as "Box's Fort."

Stephen F. Box had an active political life in each state that he lived. He and his sons were instrumental in the formation of a new county on the east side of the Trinity River from Robbins Ferry to the Neches River. They petitioned the Texas Congress on April 22nd, 1837, for it to be named after General Sam Houston, and therefore Houston County was formed.

Nelson Box died about 1849 and was buried in Box-Beeson Cemetery near Crockett, Texas.

My great-grandfather, W.W. Stallings, moved to Texas in 1867 after serving in the Confederate Army (the Army of Northern Virginia), being captured at the Battle of the Wilderness, and being confined at Elmira Prison. After moving to Texas, he met and married Amanda Box who was the daughter of Nelson Box.

Leighton Stallones
Austin Chapter 6920AH

CHARLES NEWTON BRIGANCE

Charles Newton Brigance, the son of David Brigance, was born at his parents' home on Station Camp Creek, eight miles west of Gallatin, Tennessee, on September 4, 1790. A Tennessee soldier in the War of 1812, he is on the muster roll of a company of mounted militia under Captain John W. Byrn, Col. John Alcorn's Regiment, from 24 Nov to 10 Dec 1813. Charles Newton ("CN") was in Troop 26 on the Natchez Expedition. He was pensioned for service in the War of 1812. In the United States House of Representatives in 1884, Mr. Charles Stewart introduced bill H.R. 5605 increasing CN's pension.

CN married Frances M. Dyer on 5 Jan 1816. They lived on the homestead established by his father until they left for Texas in 1838. In 1840, CN was listed on the census of the Republic of Texas, page 108, in Montgomery County (this part partitioned to form Grimes County in 1846). CN appears on the census in Grimes County until 1880.

After the death of his wife, CN never remarried. He lived in Anderson until the mid-1850s, and then moved to Roan's Prairie to live with his son, Harvey. He died on May 27, 1885. *Submitted by John Farrar Grissom #3808*

WILLIAM MARTIN BRITTAIN

Elder William Martin Brittain's gravestone lists his birth as 1774 in Surrey County, North Carolina, and his death as 16 September 1850 in Hamilton, Shelby, Texas. He is buried in what was known as Brittain Cemetery, now known as Hamilton Cemetery, located south of Center, Shelby, Texas. A State of Texas Historical Marker at gravesite reads:

Elder William Brittain and Rosanna Wright Brittain, North Carolina native William Brittain, 1774-1850. Became a preacher in his home state at the age of 25. In 1802 he married Rosanna Wright 1784-1856, the daughter of Revolutionary War veteran John Wright III. Inspired by missionary possibilities in the frontier regions to the West, William and Rosanna Brittain left North Carolina in 1824. After living in Alabama and Arkansas, they migrated to the Republic of Texas in 1837 and constructed a log cabin at this site. One room of the structure served as a classroom and church sanctuary for the pioneer settlers of the Sabine River steamboat port of Hamilton, later known as East Hamilton. A pioneer leader of the Baptist faith in East Texas, Elder Brittain was instrumental in the formation of several Shelby County congregations, including the Hamilton Church in 1846, originally aligned with the Predestinarian movement of Daniel Parker. He later joined Missionary Baptist of the Sabine Association and served as moderator of the organization in 1847. East Hamilton declined with the end of steamboat traffic. All that remains is this cemetery, the site of the Brittain's early home and chapel."

An affidavit filed in 1885 by D. Brittain (a son) states that his father, Wm. Brittain, immigrated to Texas in January 1837, subsequently receiving a land grant for 1280 acres, 640 of which was in Upshur County and later sold. On April 28, 1839, Sam Houston, William Kerr and four others organized the town site of Hamilton, the location of Elder Brittain's original home site, school and Baptist church. This area became headquarters for the infamous "Regulator-Moderator War." Troops had to be sent in to stop what was fast becoming a rebellion. Brent M. Brittain #3180, Doyle T. Brittain #6512, George J. Brittain #6283, James R. Brittain #2965, John W. Brittain #3181, Martin E. Brittain #6456, Melvin H. Brittain #6539, Michael Brittain #6284, Paul G. Brittain #6510, Perry G. Brittain #6857, Will R. Fuqua III #6285J

GILBERT BROOKS (1807-1893)

Gilbert Brooks was born in Haddam, Middlesex, Connecticut, on March 13, 1807. He came to Texas in 1831 on the schooner Call bringing sawmill equipment to Lynchburg with his partner, David Burnet. The ship ran aground in a storm in Galveston Bay and equipment was lost overboard. The boiler was recovered and floated to Lynchburg where a sawmill was built that was in operation until it burned in 1845.

Gilbert Brooks served in the Army of the Republic of Texas. His pension claim indicates he was a private in Colonel James Morgan's Company. Before the Battle of San Jacinto his father-in-law, Dr. Harvey Whiting — who lived on the east side of the Goose Creek — secured some of President Burnet's property to safety and rowed over to General Santa Anna's camp and negotiated for the safety of several sick females in his house. He treated the wounded of both sides. Dr. Whiting provided the Texas Army and Navy with boots, shoes, and beef. The Republic of Texas granted him title to his land.

Meanwhile, according to family history and documented in the September 29, 1951, edition of The Houston Press, General Houston ordered Brooks to escort President Burnet to safety in Galveston. The state papers were left behind, buried under the roots of a magnolia tree on the bank of a gully off the Goose Creek near the current location of Bicentennial Park in Baytown. Gilbert Brooks, his wife, Jane, and David Burnet went to Galveston in a skiff as the boat tacked near land, a detachment of Mexican cavalry rode up, dismounted, and leveled their rifles at the party on the boat. Jane Brooks then stood between the Mexican soldiers and the men on the boat. The Mexican soldiers did not fire.

Gilbert Brooks was one of the founders of the Cedar Bayou Masonic Lodge and the Cedar Bayou Methodist Church. It was reported that Sam Houston attended the dedication of the church building. After the death of Jane Whiting Brooks and his second wife, Gilbert Brooks married Jane's younger sister, Melissa. Their daughter, Jane, married Frederick William Martin who immigrated from Huemme Kreis, Holgusmar, Germany, in 1871. In a story in The Houston Post-Dispatch dated December 11 1924, Jane Martin described her father as having fought in four wars in early Texas history and her ancestors as dating all the way back to the pilgrims who came over on the Mayflower in 1620.

Collin and Marvin Martin were two of Frederick and Jane Martin's sons. Frederick William Martin (#6320) is the son of Marvin Martin. Frederick William Martin, Jr., (#6318) and John Dale Martin (#6319) are sons of Frederick William Martin.

Wayne Thomas Young (#5126S) is the grandson of Collin Martin. Jacob Frank Young (#5127s) and Trey Thomas Young (#5128S) are sons of Wayne Thomas Young.

ELKANAH BRUSH

Elkanah Brush of Massachusetts was the son of Gilbert Brush and Jennie Hunt, married December 13, 1781, in Ridgebury, CT. Elkanah married Sarah Duncan Farnham, and with their daughter, Catherine, and their two sons, Bradford and Gilbert Russell, moved from New York to Texas in 1834. Elkanah and his two sons received Headrights in the Power and Hewetson Colony in Refugio County in October of that same year. Sarah, their fourth child, who later married William Thomas Loftin of Grimes County, was born February 11, 1836, in their home on the Sarco River.

Tombstone of Sarah Duncan Brush, wife.

Elkanah was a member of Captain Ira J. Westover's party, which took possession of Fort Lipantitlan in November 1835. He also participated in the Siege of Bexar under Captain Phillip Dimmitt on December 11, 1835. On December 20, 1835, he signed the Goliad Declaration of Independence. On October 3, 1836, he took his seat as Representative from Refugio with the First Congress of Texas, which convened in Columbia.

Between 1840 and 1850, his family moved to Richmond, Fort Bend County, where he was listed as a farmer and stock-raiser. His wife, who is buried in the historical Morton Cemetery of Richmond, died December 2, 1850, at age 56. She was the daughter of John Farnham, Jr. and Sarissa Chapin.

Elkanah died in Grimes County circa 1854 when he was approximately 60 years of age.

MAJOR BENJAMIN FRANKLIN BRYANT

Major Benjamin Franklin Bryant was born March 15, 1800 in Wilkes County, Georgia, to Nathan Bryant and Rebecca Little. On December 10, 1820, he married Roxanna Price from Martin County, North Carolina. On September 4, 1834, he left Georgia for Texas with his wife and children, Jesse, Mary Francis, Barney and Jane Elizabeth. They crossed the Sabine at Gaines Ferry on November 10th and built a cabin on Polygoch Creek, two miles east of Milam in present-day Shelby County about fifteen miles east of San Augustine.

Benjamin Franklin Bryant was over six feet tall with black hair and side whiskers. When the Texas Revolution began, he responded to Sam Houston's call and recruited a company of forty-two volunteers who elected him captain. The company, mounted on Texas ponies and armed with long rifles, rode west to join the Texas Army. Families fleeing the enemy blocked the road with their belongings. Frightened people in "The Runaway Scrape," told of the fall of the Alamo and execution of Fannin's command at Goliad. On March 31, 1836, the company joined Sam Houston's main army at Bernardo, the plantation home of Jared E. Groces on the Brazos River. Captain Bryant was appointed commander of the Seventh Company, Second Regiment of Texian Volunteers under Sidney Sherman at the Battle of San Jacinto.

Texas Historical Marker

With Texas Independence, the Bryant Family settled in frontier Milam County on Little River, and at the request of Sam Houston, established a private fort known as Bryant Station. State archives records show that in 1842, Sam Houston, President of the Republic of Texas, appointed Major Bryant Indian Agent for the Lipan Apache and Tonkawa Indian Tribes. The Bryant family operated a pioneer trading post and fort that protected settlers from Indian attacks. On trails leading west, Bryant Station became a stopping point for stagecoaches and wagon trains going west.

In Bounty and Donation Land Grants of Texas, 1835-1888, Benjamin Bryant received Donation Certificate #314 for 640 acres from the Secretary of War on June 9, 1838 for service at the Battle of San Jacinto. An additional 640 acres in Coryell County were patented to him on February 8, 1846 for services as an Indian Agent.

Major Bryant's service as Frontiersman, Indian Fighter, and Peacemaker who signed treaties with Indian Tribes is well documented in letters between he and Sam Houston. The following books also offer vivid accounts of Indian battles: *Indian Depredations in Texas* by Wilbarger, *Battlefields of Texas* by Bill Groneman, *They Rode for The Lone Star* by Thomas W. Knowles and *Ghost Towns of Texas* by T. Lindsay Baker. The most documented battle took place on January 16, 1839 four miles north of Marlin in present day Falls County. After Indians led by Chief Jose Maria killed a group of women and children in the Morgan Massacre, Major Bryant commanded forty-eight settlers in the battle in which Major Bryant was wounded with five other settlers. Ten settlers were killed and the Indians lost about the same number. In later years, Chief Jose Maria visited Bryant at Bryant Station where they smoked a peace pipe. A Texas Historical Marker identifying the "Indian Battlefield" stands on State Highway 6, four miles north of Marlin in Falls County.

According to state archive records, on December 30, 1849, Benjamin Bryant and fifteen other citizens of Milam County, including his son, Jesse, filed a petition to create Falls County to include the Falls of the Brazos River. The petition stated that "This territory is very remote from the County Seat and inhabitants are put to great inconvenience." The citizens later voted that Marlin would become the County Seat. The Congress of the Republic of Texas later appointed Major Bryant Commissioner of Burleson County.

The first cabin built by Benjamin Bryant has been preserved in the town of Hemphill, Texas where his name was placed on a memorial honoring San Jacinto Veterans who lived in Sabine County. His name is also on the San Jacinto Monument and a Texas Historical Marker near Buckholts to remember Bryant Station. "Pioneer Village of Milam County Established as an Indian Trading Post by Major Benjamin F. Bryant, Frontiersman who had Commanded a Company in the Battle of San Jacinto. Appointed Indian Agent in 1842 by Sam Houston, President of the Republic of Texas. Little River Crossing on Trail and Stage Routes. U.S. Post Office, 1848-1874."

Between the 1830's and 1870's, Bryant Station consisted of homes, stores, a Masonic Lodge, blacksmith shops, schools, churches, and a Post Office which catapulted the village into prominence as a commercial center in central Texas. After the Civil War, the Santa Fe Railroad was built near Buckholts. This, along with other changes, contributed to the loss of Bryant Station as a commercial center in the area. All that remains is the Bryant Cemetery, making it one of the ghost towns of Texas.

On March 24, 1857, Major Bryant died, followed by his wife, Roxanna, who died on November 10, 1871. Roxanna was buried alongside her husband in the Bryant Cemetery. On March 10, 1931, the State of Texas reinterred the remains of Mr. and Mrs. Bryant on Republic Hill in the State Cemetery. Governor Pat Neff delivered a tribute speech to them in a joint session of the House and Senate at the State Capitol in Austin, Texas.

Great-great-grandson, E. Denton Bryant, Jr. # 2966, San Jacinto Chapter # 1, The Sons of the Republic of Texas.

E. DENTON BRYANT, JR.

E. Denton Bryant, Jr., was born on December 2, 1935 in Galveston, Texas, Galveston County. He is a direct descendant of Major Benjamin Franklin Bryant, who recruited and commanded the Seventh Company, Second Regiment under Sidney Sherman at the Battle of San Jacinto on April 21, 1836. After Texas Independence, Major Bryant founded a private fort at Bryant Station on Little River and was appointed Indian Agent for the Lipan Apache and Tonkawa Indian tribes by Sam Houston, President of the Republic of Texas. In addition to being a frontiersman, Indian fighter and peacemaker, Major Bryant, with fifteen other Milam County citizens, petitioned the Legislature of the Republic of Texas to form Falls County on December 30, 1849.

Denton Bryant is the son of Elmer Denton Bryant, Sr. and Azalea Alister Bryant, who moved to California during his early childhood and later returned to Texas to make their home in the Central Texas town of Chilton. He attended and graduated from Chilton Junior High School and was co-captain of the football team.

In the early 1950s, the family moved to Richardson, Texas, north of Dallas. Denton graduated from Richardson High School, where he excelled in football and track. He won All-District Team selection three years and was a member of two District Championship football teams and a Regional Championship relay track team.

Denton Bryant began his career with the Dr. Pepper company in Dallas, Texas, before entering Baylor University in Waco, Texas. He played Baylor freshman football until injuries cut short his athletic career. He graduated from Baylor University in 1960 with a Bachelor of Arts degree in behavioral science. He also attended Baylor Law School for six months prior to entering the United States Navy. While at Baylor, Denton served as an officer of the pre-law club and The Taurus Social Fraternity.

E. Denton Bryant, Jr.

While on active duty in the U.S. Navy and stationed in Norfolk, Virginia, he served in the Personnel Office of the Atlantic Fleet, which played an important role during the Berlin and Cuban Crises. After honorable discharge from the Navy in 1966, he pursued post-graduate studies in management at Texas Christian University. Pursuing a career in industrial training and education, he served as a Director of Engineering Cooperative Education in the aerospace industry and later as a Director of Management Development in the health care industry.

On April 19, 1969, he married Jo Ann Kitterer. They have two daughters, Dee Ann, born July 16, 1970, in Dallas, Texas, and Donna Lyn, born May 19, 1972, in Corpus Christi, Texas.

After serving as a vice president of personnel development in the food industry, Denton entered the energy industry as a corporate training director in Houston, Texas. In 1990, he retired from Texas Eastern Products Pipeline Co. after a 17-year career with Texas Eastern Companies. In 1989, Denton Bryant founded Training Enterprises Inc., a Texas corporation which provides human resources development consulting services. Since that time he has held positions as a corporate training director in the industrial gas industry and the safety equipment distribution industry, where he re-established a corporate university recognized by the Texas State Board of Public Accountancy.

He currently provides corporate training consulting on a contract basis for companies in northwest Harris County through the Center for Business and Economic Development of Tomball College. Denton has organized two Toastmasters Clubs and served as president. He later became area governor in downtown Houston. He has been elected and served as a director of the Northwest Park Municipal Utility District for over twenty-five years, and currently holds the position of investment officer and assistant secretary.

Denton Bryant is an endowed member of Edwin J. Kiest Masonic Lodge in Dallas Texas, a 32nd degree Scottish Rite Mason and a member of Arabia Shrine Temple in Houston, Texas. He is active in the Tomball Shrine Club and a member of the Tomball American Legion Post # 0127. He is an associate member of the George Bush Presidential Library and a member of the San Jacinto Museum of History. He also holds life memberships in the Baylor University Alumni Association, the Texas Navy, the San Jacinto Descendants and the Sons of the Republic of Texas.

Denton also serves on community committees such as the Small Business Development Council of North Harris Montgomery Community College District and the Economic Development Committee of the Cy-Fair Chamber of Commerce.

Professional memberships include the American Society for Training and Development and the American Management Association.

He is the immediate past-president general of the San Jacinto Descendants (1997-1999) and has served as treasurer general, president-elect and Houston Chapter president. He is dedicated to service in the Sons of the Republic of Texas and has served as district representative for the San Jacinto District, secretary, second vice president and first vice president of the San Jacinto Chapter #1. He enjoys speaking to groups such as Rotary Clubs, schools and Chambers of Commerce about Texas history. Hobbies include Texas history, golf, sailing, and collecting classic automobiles. Special interests include the Black Powder Brigade of the SRT where he serves as a commissioned colonel. He resides in Houston with his wife Jo Ann.

JESSE BRYANT

Jesse Bryant was born September 10, 1821 in Wilkes County, Georgia to Benjamin Franklin Bryant and Roxanna Price Bryant. He was their first child. On September 4, 1834, Benjamin F. Bryant left Georgia for Texas with his wife and family. They crossed the Sabine at Gaines Ferry on November 10th. They built a cabin and settled on Polygoch Creek, two miles east of Milam, in the present county of Shelby and about fifteen miles east of San Augustine.

Jesse Bryant

When the Texas Revolution began, Jesse's father, Benjamin, heeding Sam Houston's call for volunteers, recruited the Sabine Volunteers and was elected captain. His company joined Sam Houston's main army at Bernardo on March 31, 1836, at the plantation home of Jared E. Groces on the Brazos River. Captain Bryant commanded the Seventh Company Second Regiment under Sidney Sherman at the battle of San Jacinto. Jesse, the oldest son at fourteen years of age, remained at the Bryant homestead.

After the victory at San Jacinto and Texas Independence, the family moved to frontier Milam County on Little River and built a private fort known as Bryant Station at the behest of Sam Houston. According to state archives, in 1842, Sam Houston, President of the Republic of Texas, appointed Major Benjamin Bryant Indian Agent for the Lipan Apache and Tonkawa Indian tribes. The Bryant family operated a pioneer trading post and fort which became a village protecting settlers from Indian attacks. It was a stopping point for stagecoaches and supply wagon trains moving westward.

Jesse Bryant began farming on the Bryant Plantation in the fertile bottomlands of Little River and first married Mary I. Williams, daughter of John and Rebecca Williams. They were married on July 24, 1842 in Milam County, Texas. To this union were born seven children: Sarah E., William P., John Gilbert, Ann E., James William, Cathalena and Cordelia. The marriage ended in divorce and Mary moved to California taking the twin daughters with her.

Next, in November 1853, Jesse married Harriet N. Anderson, daughter of James Anderson. Harriet died in 1855. They had one son, Henry Clay.

The next year, 1856, Jesse married Harriet's sister, Eliza Anderson. From this marriage were born five sons and two daughters.

Jesse's father, Major Benjamin Bryant, died at Bryant Station, Texas on March 24, 1857 and was buried in Bryant Station Cemetery.

According to records in the Masonic Grand Lodge Library and Museum of Texas, Jesse was a very active Master Mason in the following Masonic Lodges: Bryant Station, Davilla, Ft. Richardson, Jacksboro, Texas; Granbury, Texas; Floyd City, Silverton, and Lockney in the Texas Panhandle.

According to a 1904 newspaper article Jesse wrote: "As many of the old timers are writing, I thought I would write also. I was born September 10, 1821 in Wilkes County, Georgia, so if I live until the 10th of next September, I will be 83 years old. I left Georgia in June 1834, landed in Texas in July of the same year, so next July will be 70 years since I came to Texas. We settled first in Sabine County, Texas. While there, my father was in the war of Texas Revolution under Sam Houston. He was in the Battle of San Jacinto. In 1837, we moved to Tenoxtitlan on the Brazos, which was then on the frontier. In 1840 we moved to Milam County on Little River, forty miles from any house. I served as a Texas Ranger under Captain Ross. I was in the commissary service during the Civil War. In 1877, I moved to Hood County and lived there 14 years. In 1891, I moved to Floyd County on the plains."

Confederate Pension application dated 1901, Lockney, Floyd County, Texas, a sworn statement says that Jesse served as Quartermaster in the beef department, CSA. He enlisted in the service of CSA at Belton, Texas, in July 1862 and drove and delivered beeves for the Confederacy. He was in the service about 2 years under Captain White, Captain Watts and D.R. Chamberlain.

On September 21, 1862, the families of Bryant Station wrote this letter: "We, whose names are here signed, believe the services of Jesse Bryant will be more beneficial to the country by remaining at home on detailed services to attend to the soldier families in his neighborhood, than they could possibly be in the Confederate Army. Therefore, we respectfully request that he be detailed in the services above mentioned."

According to Floyd County records, Jesse Bryant died on August 15, 1904 of intestinal fever at the age of 82 and is buried in the Lockney Cemetery in Lockney, Texas.

In August, 1995, The Daughters of the Republic of Texas placed a medallion marker on his grave honoring Jesse Bryant as Citizen of The Republic of Texas, 1836-1845. Great-grandson, Denton Bryant # 2966, San Jacinto Chapter # 1, The Sons of the Republic of Texas

DAVID BURKET

David Burket was born February 22, 1798 in what is now Howard County, Missouri. He married Mary Ann Zumwalt in 1818 in St. Charles, Missouri. They lived in Missouri as neighbors of the Daniel Boone family, and named a son after Daniel's son, Nathan Boone.

The Burkets — David, Mary Ann and four children — left Missouri, and with the Zumwalts and several families came by schooner down the Mississippi to New Orleans. They landed near Indianola on June 16, 1830. As Nathan Boone Burket remarked in "Early Days in Texas": "We soon sighted hundreds of deer and other wild animals." "Then a wagon train of some six in number came from Gonzales to haul us and our supplies to the colony, which was about ninety miles to the northwest."

David Burkett Historical Marker

David received a land grant from the Mexican government for 4,428 acres. The family remained near Gonzales until 1836, when the invading army of Santa Anna caused all the people to flee for their lives and Gonzales was burned to keep Santa Anna from taking it. This is referred to as "The Runaway Scrape," and David Burket and Adam Zumwalt were in charge of the families fleeing east.

David Burket had much more to worry about than Santa Anna's army. An Indian's arrow struck David about two years before his death. Many believed that this was the cause of his death on December 7, 1845. He was my great-great-grandfather. Samuel V. Haynes

AARON BURLESON

Aaron Burleson was born the youngest son of Captain James Burleson on October 10, 1815, near Decatur, Alabama. He came to Texas in 1827 after serving with General Andrew Jackson at the Battle of New Orleans. He was the brother of noted Indian fighter General Edward Burleson and was frequently with him on his expeditions against the Indians. Aaron fought under General Burleson at the capture of the Mexican army in San Antonio and at the Battle of San Jacinto. It is reported by one of his descendants that "in the picture of the surrender of Santa Anna in the capital building, he is the man holding a rope."

In 1838, he returned to Tennessee and married Minerva J. Seaton. He then returned to Texas. He and his wife settled at the mouth of Walnut Creek in Travis County. She died there in 1855, but not before they had eleven children (five of whom died at birth or in early infancy). In 1856, Aaron married Jane Tannehill. They also had eleven children (five also died at birth or in early infancy).

Aaron settled east of Austin in later years and died suddenly on January 13, 1885. He is buried with both of his wives in Rogers Hill Cemetery. *Submitted by Paul Blanton Covert #4696*

ALLEN DALE BURRESS

Allen Dale Burress was born in Fleming County, Kentucky, in 1808. He was the son of Benjamin and Elizabeth (Betsy) Mahan Burress. The family moved to Phillips County, Arkansas, in 1821.

He married Eveline Strong in St. Francis County, Arkansas, on Jan. 23, 1834.

Their children were Erastus Strong Burress, Louisa Jane Burress, Laura Virginia Burress, Matilda Josephine Burress, Helen Bar Burress, William Dobson Burress and John A. Burress.

Allen Dale and Eveline Burress migrated from St. Francis County, Arkansas, to Texas in 1841. The deed records of Harrison County, Marshall, Texas, show that on April 2, 1843, the purchase of 1,076 acres was made from Peter Whetson. The land was located near the present town site of Marshall, Texas.

Various other sales of and purchases of land and city property were made by Allen D. Burress and Eveline Burress between 1843 and 1860, and are on record in the office of the county clerk, Harrison County, Marshall, Texas.

Allen Dale Burress

Allen D. Burress was prominent in the political and civic affairs of Harrison County. He was interested in the county and city educational institutions. He was a member of a group of citizens that obtained approval of the state Legislature to establish the Republican Academy in Harrison County, March 16, 1848.

He was elected to the state Legislature in 1855 and served during the regular session Nov. 5, 1855 - Feb. 4, 1856 and the call session July 7 - Sept. 1, 1856.

Allen Burress owned a saw mill, blacksmith shop and a grist mill. His saw mill sawed the lumber for many of the early business houses and homes built in Marshall. He built his plantation home known as Steam Mill Place about one-and-a-half miles north of Marshall.

Eveline Burress died Aug. 6, 1850. She left seven children, the youngest not quite three months old. After the death of Eveline Burress, Allen D. Burress married Nancy Hatley of Marshall, Texas, on Feb. 5, 1852. Nancy Hatley Burress died in childbirth Dec. 3, 1852, after ten months of marriage. The baby died at birth.

On March 7, 1854, Allen D. Burress married Ruth Hopkins at Port Caddo near Marshall, Texas. Their children were Carter A. Burress and Elam D. Burress. Ruth Hopkins Burress died June 26, 1868.

Allen D. Burress died June 18, 1860. His death occurred under unusual circumstances. He died suddenly at Sulphur Springs, Hopkins County, Texas. An account of his death was published in The Texas Republican, Marshall, Texas, June 30, 1860. The paper states as follows: "In company with two gentlemen, he stopped at Sulphur Springs to get water. Here his companions, who were proceeding in another direction, left him. An hour or so later, some of the citizens found him in a dying and speechless condition."

The newspaper account states that he died of "general congestion or congestion of the brain." He is buried in Sulphur Springs, Texas. Otto Luron Frazer

BENJAMIN BURRIS

Benjamin Burris was the son of Elizabeth and John Burris. Benjamin Burris lived in Archers Fork, Ohio, in 1818. His wife was Susan Riggs. Eleven children were born to them in Archers Fork. Benjamin was a lumberman, stock raiser and trader. He made trips to New Orleans and also traveled to Scotland to have a 33rd Degree Masonic Degree conferred upon him.

In the fall of 1839, Benjamin Burris cut lumber for a house, loaded it on a boat with his family and sailed down the Ohio and Mississippi rivers, eventually landing at Galveston, Texas. Two more children were born in Texas. One of the landmarks on Galveston Island before the "flood" was the location of the Burris Home.

Benjamin Burris' home in Galveston was located somewhere in the vicinity of the present Galveston Airport. Benjamin became an important Galvestonian and citizen of the Republic of Texas. Benjamin and wife, Susan, both died about 1856. Both were buried on his farm near their Galveston home. Benjamin Burris is the great-great-grandfather of Bill G. Arnold, #3170, Sons of the Republic of Texas. *Submitted by Bill G. Arnold # 3170*

JOHN BUSBY

John Busby left the East Coast with Daniel Boone, settling in Missouri. John Busby married Rosanna McCall in August, 1807, in St. Charles, MO. They had one son, William S. Busby, born 8 January 1809.

William Busby arrived at Nacogdoches, Texas, on 10 May 1830 as a single 21-year-old male, according to Gifford White's book, "1830 Citizens of Texas." William stated he was from "LA," which was the Louisiana Territory at that time. William received a Spanish Land Grant from the State of Texas as a colonist in Joseph Vehlein's colony on 13 April 1835. The land grant was located in Montgomery County (present-day San Jacinto County). The land grant is available in Spanish and English.

On 25 December 1833, William married Harriet Perdum Brown, of Mississippi, the daughter of Masena and Tolman Brown. In 1836, William Busby was listed on the muster roll of the Texas Revolution in Captain Franklin Hardin's Company. He later moved to Houston, Harris County, Texas, and several children were born to them there, one being John Rankin Busby, the great-grandfather of Bille Franklin Busby and the great-great-grandfather of Russell Clyde Busby.

By 1851, William was on the tax rolls of DeWitt County, where he lived until his death in 1859. He is buried at Clinton, Texas, the county seat of DeWitt County at that time. *Submitted by Bille Franklin Busby, # 3479 Russell Clyde Busby, #3480*

CLAUDIUS BUSTER

Claudius Buster was born 21 Jan 1816, in Somerset, KY, to William Woods Buster, Jr. and Margaret Vaughan. In 1836, he and his father moved to Texas. Claudius married Sarah Harris Garrett 14 Sept 1847 in Washington Co., Texas. Claudius died 27 Dec 1889 (buried in Prairie Lea Cemetery, Brenham, Washington Co., Texas).

Claudius was a fighting Irishman, refined in the use of sword and firearms, Shakespeare reader, chess player, cultured and graceful person, blessed with a strong sense of humor, farmer, soldier, and patriot.

Private Claudius served in the Texas Volunteers under Capt. Thomas Green with Commandeer Mark Lewis from 20 March 1841 to 04 June 1841 on a campaign against the Comanche Indians.

In the Vascus, Woll, Somervell Campaigns and Mier Expedition, Claudius furnished his own arms, horse, and equipment. He was enrolled as second lieutenant on 17 Oct 1842, and promoted 18 Dec 1842 to captain. After his return home from prison in Perote, Mexico, Claudius was given a deputy clerkship in the county clerk's office, was twice elected Chief Justice of Washington County, engaged in farming, and accumulated property.

Claudius enlisted in the Civil War as Captain of Company C, Elmore's Regiment, 20th Texas Infantry, participating in the capture of Galveston 1 Jan 1863. He came home from the Civil War entirely broke, taking a job as "deepo" agent in Brenham for the few years it took to clear his land titles. Claudius is my great-great-grandfather. Kenneth Edward Estes #4539 Moses Austin Chapter #12

CAPTAIN ROBERT JAMES CALDER

Robert James Calder was born in Baltimore, Maryland, July 17, 1810, the son of James H. Calder and Jane E. Caldwell. His father died when he was three years old, and he was raised by his mother and a maternal uncle, Major James P. Caldwell. The family moved to Christian County, Kentucky, when Calder was nine years old, and in 1832 they left for Texas, arriving in the Brazoria District of the Mexican state of Coahuila Texas on April 16 of that year. The fight over a Mexican at Velasco Fort began on May 1, 1832, and Calder was put on duty until the surrender of the fort. In 1835, Calder fought in the Battle of Concepcion, and then accompanied Fannin on a recruiting expedition. The general council appointed him third lieutenant of artillery.

Calder commanded Company K of Burleson's Regiment at the Battle of San Jacinto. The battle not only established a new republic, but also removed Mexico as the only foreign barrier to the settlement of the American West.

On April 23, 1836, Sam Houston detailed Calder and Benjamin C. Franklin to carry dispatches to President Burnet at Galveston Island announcing the glorious victory at San Jacinto and the capture of Santa Anna. They started in a leaky skiff on the morning of the 23rd, took no provisions, and about sundown of the fourth day neared Galveston. They were hauled aboard the Texian ship Invincible, and then aboard the Independence. Thirteen guns were fired and the great news spread from vessel to vessel and then to land. The story of Calder's mission to Galveston is recorded in "A Pictorial History of Texas," pp. 519-522, Homer Thrall, St. Louis, Mo., Thompson & Co., 1879.

Calder was granted Bounty Certificate no. 1225 for 640 acres of land for serving in the Texas Army from March 1 to October 10. 1836. President Burnet appointed Calder Marshal of Texas in 1836; his duties were to take charge of shipwrecks and prizes. Calder was elected the first sheriff of Brazoria County in February 1837, and held that office for six years. He was elected mayor of Brazoria in 1838 and Chief Justice and Probate Judge of Brazoria County in 1844 and in 1846, but resigned in 1846 to move Richmond, Texas, which offered better educational opportunities for his children. He was elected mayor of Richmond, Texas in 1859, and served as Chief Justice and Probate Judge of Fort Bend County, Texas, from 1866 to April 1869. Calder then retired from public life and practiced law at Richmond. He voted for Annexation of Texas to the United States, and later for secession from the Union.

In 1832, Calder married Mary Walker Douglass, daughter of Samuel C. Douglass and Phoebe Cresswell of Richmond County, GA. They had six surviving children. Robert James Calder, Jr., born 1840, a second lieutenant CSA, in Terry's Rangers was killed in the Battle of Moss Creek, Tennessee, on January 12, 1864. Jane Eliza, born 1843, married W.C. Davidson. Zemula Walker Calder, born 1845, never married. Anna Maria, born 1847, married J.C. Williams. Samuel Douglas Calder, born 1849, married Loretta Lamar, daughter of former President Mirabeau B. Lamar. James P. Calder, born 1851, married Sallie Weston, daughter of John M. Weston and Louisa Chambers; they had a daughter, Mary Walker Calder, who married Benjamin Botts Rice, both of whom are grandparents of the author of this article.

The last public act of Captain Calder was the unveiling of the monument on Galveston Island, erected to the memory of those killed in the Battle of San Jacinto. The monument was later moved to the San Jacinto battlefield. Calder died August 28, 1885, the last of the surviving of the captains at San Jacinto. Calder and his wife are buried in Morton Cemetery, Richmond, Texas. In 1929, the state of Texas erected a monument to Calder and his wife on their gravesite.

Sources: "The Heroes of San Jacinto," pp. 269-172, Sam Houston Dixon and Louis W. Kemp, 1932; "A History of Texas and Texans," Vol. V, p. 2651, Frank W. Johnson, Eugene Barker, Ph.D, Ed., 1914; "The Handbook of Texas," Vol. 1, p. 267, Walter Prescot Webb, ed., 1952; "History of Fort Bend County," Clarence Wharton, 1939, pp. 144-146; "The Papers of the Texas Revolution 1835-1836," pp. 98-88, Jenkins, Presdial Press, Austin, 1973; "A Promiscuous Breed," pp. 1041, B. Rice Aston, Houston, 1995. B. Rice Aston

JOHN CAMPBELL

John Campbell was born 8 April 1817, probably in Lafayette County of the Arkansas Territory. He was the son of Joseph Campbell, Jr., and Rachel Orton. His father brought him to Texas on 22 March 1827 when the family settled in Green DeWitt's colony, receiving a parcel of land on the San Marcos River in Guadalupe County. In March 1836, at the age of 19, John Campbell joined a company of volunteers commanded by Captain Gipson Kuykendall. His unit served at the Battle of San Jacinto with orders to tend to the sick and the baggage at Harrisburg, serving as the rear guard to the main battle force. He was discharged on 1 October 1836 and received a land grant in Austin County for his military service.

John Campbell

After the war, John married Eleanor Whitley on March 25, 1826, and lived at Washington-on-the-Brazos from 1841-45. While there he was commissioned by the last president of the Republic of Texas, Dr. Anson Jones, to build his home. He moved back to Austin County where he operated a store and farmed at Travis, Texas. Around 1880 John and Eleanor moved to Brenham, Texas, where he operated a store until the time of his death on 6 May 1888. He is buried near Kenney, Austin County.

The biography was prepared by Samuel W. Hopkins, Jr., who is the great, great, grandson of John Campbell. Sam Hopkins is member 6483 of the Sons of The Republic of Texas, Chapter 52.

THOMAS CAPPS

Thomas Capps was born in North Carolina in about 1777. It is known that Thomas Capps lived in Tennessee for a number of years. A Thomas Capps paid taxes in Sullivan County, Tennessee, in 1812. It is believed Thomas Capps married Mary Canole in Sullivan County; however, the courthouse there was a fire victim of the Union Army in 1863.

Thomas Capps was living in Monroe County, Mississippi, by 1820. The homestead established by him on the Buttahatchis River, approximately four miles south of the present-day Greenwood Springs, Monroe County, was one of the original "Buttahatchise Settlements."

Thomas Capps was granted a conditional 640 acres of land August 2, 1841, in Robertson County, Texas. "The Texas Heritage," Vol. 2, 3rd-class immigrants between January 10, 1837 and January 1, 1840, lists Diamond Capps in Johnson County, Elcanah Capps in Henderson County, and Thomas Capps in Navarro County.

Thomas Capps is not listed in the 1850 Texas census. His wife, Mary Canole, at age 60, and daughter, Mariller, at age 15, are listed as living with his son, Harvy, at age 27. Also, listed living with Harvy are his wife, Catharine, at age 20; D.P. Riggell, at age 22; and Elcanah Capps, at age 24.

When the 640 acres granted by the April 10, 1851, unconditional land patent in Navarro County was sold on October 27, 1854, Mary Capps, Diamon Capps, Dermelia Bolton, Harvy Capps and Elcanah Capps were list as the heirs of Thomas Capps. Mariller Capps, a minor, was not listed.

Mariller Capps married James N. Wheeler in Robertson County, Texas, on December 28, 1854. Their only surviving child was Christopher Columbus Wheeler. The widow Mariller Capps married Granville W. Rose in Robertson County on February 3, 1862. They had Dieliew Rose, Annie Rose, and John Thomas Rose. Ken Leach 6870 Carlos Monroe Leach, Jr.

WILLIAM REDWINE CARNES

William Redwine Carnes, son of Wells and Linna Carnes, was born in Alabama. He married Elvira Brewer on January 10, 1837, in Hinds County, Mississippi. He moved to Nacogdoches County, Texas by 1839, where he received a land grant of 640 acres. William Redwine was a Methodist preacher. He helped establish the Old Pine Grove Methodist Church, where he and Elvira are both buried. Tombstones give birth and death dates of July 4, 1813- March 10, 1894 for William, and June 10, 1823 - July 20, 1899 for Elvira. William served in the Texas mounted rangers in 1840.

Children: Jasper N., Felix S., Rev. William Franklin, Louisa J., George Washington, Mary Elizabeth, Octavia Ann, Irving L., Harriet A., Melissa A., Aurelia "Ora" E. Submitted by: James H. Stokes, Jr. #2839

WILLIAM CARR

William Carr was born April 13, 1800, in St. Martin's Parish, Louisiana, and died March 17, 1874, Jefferson County, Texas. He married Nancy Ann Lee (date of birth unknown died 1849 in Jefferson County, Texas,) in St. Martin's Parish, Louisiana, on Aug. 16, 1816.

William Carr came to Jefferson County, Texas, with Austin's third colony in 1827. At the time of his arrival in Texas he had three children.

With the approaching Mexican Army, William participated in the "Runaway Scrape" by moving his family to the east side of the Sabine River. With victory at San Jacinto, he returned his family to Jefferson County.

In 1836, William Carr received payment for the use of a horse for the Army and in 1846, he received land grant for one league and one labor of land in Jefferson County.

The following document is from St. Martinville, La.: #242 Estate of Joseph Carr

On this sixteenth day of August in the year of our Lord one thousand eight hundred and sixteen, Before me Paul Briant, Judge of the Parish of St. Martin, Personally appeared James McLaughlin Husband of Lucie Carr, the daughter of Joseph Carr, and William Carr son of the said Joseph Carr deceased who declared and confessed that they have received of Nancy White formerly the wife of the said Joseph Carr now the wife of George Burrell, the sum of two hundred and thirty dollars each, in full for the portion of the estate of the said Joseph Carr in community with the said Nancy White, coming to them that is to say, to the aforesaid Lucie Carr, wife of the said Jas. McLaughlin and to the said William Carr.

In witness whereof the aforesaid James McLaughlin and William Carr have hereunto set their hands in presence of the undersigned witnesses and me the Judge aforesaid, the day and year above written. William Harris, witnesses James McLaughlin Jacob Clements William Carr Note: William Carr was sixteen years old and this was his wedding day Submitted by: John Thomas Lawhon # 4589 Great-great-great-grandson of William Carr

SALLY JANE CARSON

Sally Jane Carson was the only child of John Patterson Carson and Jane E. Kennedy (m.5/25/1844 in Brazoria). Born in January 1845 at Columbia, Brazoria County, her maternal grandmother was Sally (Sarah) Lewis (born N.C. 1791, died Brazoria 1852). Her mother was Jane E. Kennedy who died in 1856. At age eleven she was orphaned when her father was killed on Christmas Eve of the same year at Wharton. She lived at the boarding house of her

Sallie Jane Carson

grandmother, Catherine Jane Patterson Carson Borden, and her guardian (2/9/1857 until 4/30/1866 when she became twenty- one) was her uncle by marriage, Ammon Underwood, who had married her father's sister, Rachel, in January 1839. Grandmother Catherine died 1875.

At age thirteen (1858) Sally entered Bradford Academy, Bradford, Massachusetts as a piano student which she always taught after graduation in 1865.

Sally Jane Carson married four times. First was Josiah Bell Copes in 1867 at Columbia. When that failed she went to relatives in her grandmother's Louisiana starting place, Harrisonburg (Catahoula Parish). January 9, 1872 she married Lemuel Gipson Duke, Sr. and had Hazel S. Duke July 16, 1882 who bore St.Clair LaVerne Wier January 11, 1910 who fathered Joseph St. Clair Wier October 4, 1957 who had Jerry St. Clair Wier April 2, 1996. Last husbands were P.F. Claunch and Louis H. Karstendiek. Seven of her eight children lived to adulthood.

In 1885 she relocated to New Orleans; she died in 1922.

WILLIAM C. CARSON

William C. Carson, great-great-great-grandfather of Joseph St. Clair Wier, took his family of seven overland in 1824 from Harrisonburg, Louisiana, where the family of his wife, Catherine Jane (b. about 1798 — d. 1875) Patterson, had located after originating in Nova Scotia, to the San Bernard River in Brazoria County. (William, born about 1788, was the son of Robert Carson and a McClenon.) From Delaware to Louisiana, by way of Indiana, he now was among Austin's "Old 300" in Brazoria County, receiving 4,428 acres. When William died about 1829, Catherine moved the family to Columbia, where she operated a boarding house now known as the Ammon Underwood Museum. With sons in the army at the time of the "Runaway Scrape," Catherine fled with daughter, Rachel, to Richmond. With bullets flying overhead, Catherine helped to load the wagons as Mexicans fired at the refugees. On April 24, 1842, she married Gail Borden, Sr.

One son, John Patterson Carson, was a member of Captain Lockhart's company of "spies." He received 1/3 of a league of land for having arrived in Brazoria prior to 1835, and 320 acres for military service. (The certificate was signed by Albert Sidney Johnston, Secretary of War, 1839.) He was a member of the Columbia minutemen organized to deter continued Mexican hostility. Joseph St. Clair Wier #6307 Jerry St. Clair Wier #6460

JOHN CARUTHERS

John Caruthers, great-grandfather of this compiler, appears in the General Land Office of Texas file, Montgomery 247, as proving "according to law, that he arrived in this country in February 1830," a married man. John was one of five brothers who came to Texas at about this time. Two fought at San Jacinto, one guarded the baggage at Harrisburg, and one fell with Fannin at Goliad.

John was the fourth of twelve children born to Samuel Caruthers and Sarah Vaughn. Samuel was born in South Carolina, the son of Revolutionary War veteran John Caruthers. Samuel married Sarah on March 2, 1802, in Christian County, Kentucky where he farmed and engaged in land speculation in Illinois. John later said he was born in Ohio. The family moved to what is now Arkansas in about 1811, where John grew up in Lawrence and Independence counties.

John married Frances Murphy on October 28, 1827, and after the birth of a son, Samuel, on August 13. 1828, (grandfather of this compiler), they set out for Texas in early 1830. A second son, William, who later migrated to California, was born in Louisiana on 22 January 1830. John and Frances eventually had 14 children, 12 living to adulthood. The last was born when Frances was 44.

John and Frances settled in what later became Washington, then Montgomery, then Walker County. The Mexican government deeded to him a league of land on November 13, 1834, on the waters of the south branch of Harmon Creek. John is said to have been a surveyor and to have built an early Montgomery County cotton gin.

Out of state when San Jacinto occurred, John enlisted in Captain Pearson's Company of Cavalry, June 30, 1836, to September 30, 1836. Bounty Warrant 7077, patented September 7, 1846, awarded him 320 acres on Cummins Creek, a branch on the Trinity River. Montgomery County's 1840 "census" shows him possessed of 2,214 acres, 2 slaves, 10 horses, 40 cattle, and one brass clock.

After 1845, John moved his family to Tehuacana, Limestone County. He is often confused with another John Caruthers who lived in adjacent Hill County, then part of Navarro County. Historical information on that individual is known to appear in "A Historical Atlas of Texas," (Pool, 1975), "The State of Texas Federal Population Schedules of 1850," for Navarro County, "The Handbook of Texas" (Webb, 1976), and land records of Hill County.

While living in Limestone County, John participated in the so-called 1852 Hedgecoxe War, opposing a land company's receiving state land to sell to Peters Colony settlers. He and four other non-colonists called a meeting in Springfield to adopt a resolution calculated to arouse the people against the company. John died August 14, 1856, and Frances on October 3, 1857, at Tehuacana, where they are buried.

JAMES CATE

James Cate was born August 29, 1818, to Robert Cate and Isabella Carter of White County, Tennessee. He came by way of Missouri and entered Peters colony Texas in 1845. He received 640 acres as Texas Land Grant, Dallas County, near Cedar Springs. In 1847 he married Elvira Fay Minter, born Nov. 7, 1829, in Tennessee, who came with her family from Illinois. They settled in Grapevine, Texas, Tarrant County. They had twelve children. One was John Bellamy, our great-grandfather, of Bosque County. Others continued to live in Tarrant and Dallas counties. James is listed in "1845 Biographical History of Texas, Tarrant and Parker Counties," published by Lewis Publishing Co., Chicago, as an early settler and one of the leading families.

Both James and Elvira died in 1908, and were buried in the Cate family plot in Minter's Chapel Cemetery near Grapevine. Minter's Chapel was an early Methodist Church organized about 1853 by Rev. Green Minter, Elvira's father, and built on land donated by James and Elvira. Minter's Chapel Cemetery is one of several small graveyards located within the Dallas-Fort Worth Airport on the northwestern fringe. A new Minter's Chapel Methodist Church was later built on other property in Tarrant County. John Arthur Alvarez II #2958 Paul Cate Alvarez #5092 Life members San Jacinto Chapter, Houston, Texas Paul Cate Alvarez II #6922 Life member Moses Austin Chapter, Austin, Texas

JAMES CELLUM

James Cellum, a member of Captain William Kimbro's company, enlisted as a private in the Texas Army from April 1, 1836, to July 24, 1836, and was discharged per Certificate 2027 issued by the Secretary of War. A combination of spelling, handwriting and name pronunciation changed his birth name from Helm to Cellum, and caused Cellum to be misinterpreted as Clelens.

Cellum was born as James Helm (apparently pronounced hel-um) in Franklin County, Virginia, on June 11, 1815. He came to Texas in 1832, and settled in Nacogdoches, where he met and married Tennessee-born Emily Scott. Their original marriage certificate, in Spanish and performed by the Alcalde of Nacogdoches, notes James' name with a flowery H, which could be seen as either K or C preceding "ellum" — thus a name is born, and Helm becomes Cellum. Early historians had the name spelled as Clelens, and for years this spelling was the one shown in documents at San Jacinto. Research by several professional genealogists, spurred on by Col. F.A. Rogers, USAF (Ret.), a direct descendent, led to official acceptance of the spelling and name Cellum as the actual participant.

James Cellum was granted 320 acres of land in Llano County for his service, and was additionally granted 25 labors of land in Harrison County, which became the family homestead. He farmed here for many years, and was also a charter member of Marshal Masonic Lodge #22. After the War Between the States, he moved to a farm in Red River County, Texas, where he farmed until his passing on July 23, 1875. He was buried in the Gilliam Cemetery near Annona.

Frank A. Rogers, John L. Rogers, Adam E. Rogers, DeWitt Nelson, Spencer Jones

DAVIS CHANDLER

Davis Chandler (Clement Davis Chandler), born 1798 in South Carolina, married Priscilla (Prissa) Marshall, born Feb. 5, 1805, in Kentucky. From Washington County, Arkansas, Davis and Priscilla, along with Lewis and Louisa (9 months), came to Stephen F. Austin's Colony in Texas and took the oath to Mexico on Jan. 5, 1829, per Austin's Register of Families, Family #175. The Chandlers lived in the Austin County area during the early 1830s, where Davis Chandler received a Mexican title to 4,428.4 acres of land on March 10, 1831.

Davis Chandler was a member of Captain Cleveland's Millcreek Volunteers on July 1, 1836. The Chandlers moved to the Round Rock, Williamson County area, in the late 1830s. Davis's son, Lewis, was appointed Estate Administrator on Aug, 24, 1845. A Chandler School was in use from the early 1850s through 1911. There is now a Chandler Creek, a Chandler Creek Street, a Chandler Road and a Chandler Creek Housing Addition.

Priscilla's father John Marshall, was born on Oct. 10, 1781, on a quarantined ship in Long Island, New York, while his parents were immigrating from Ireland to America and on to South Carolina. John married Leah Ann Davis, born Sept. 6, 1785, in Lauren District, South Carolina, on March 8, 1802, in Christian County, Kentucky. John and Leah came to the Stephen F. Austin Colony in Texas from Washington County, Arkansas, Family #351, and took the oath to Mexico on May 5, 1830. The names of Prissa's brothers — Samuel, John, Joseph, Hugh and Elias — are on the San Jacinto Monument.

Louisa Chandler, born March 27, 1828, in Washington County, Arkansas, married John G. McKinzie on Feb. 23, 1864, in Comanche County, Texas, a second marriage for both. John was born March, 20, 1821 in Tennessee. Louisa's first husband and John's father, Charles, and brother, Kenneth, were killed by the Indians in Comanche County during the early 1860s. Louisa and John are buried in Live Oak Cemetery in Bell County, Texas.

Davis Chandler McKinzie, son of Louisa and John, was born on April 14, 1866, in Comanche County, Texas, and married Corinne Maude Cox in Bosque County, Texas, on May 22, 1917. Corinne was born on Feb. 24, 1889 in McLennan County, Texas.

Maxine Statie McKinzie, DRT #17379, daughter of Davis and Corinne, was born on May 11, 1924, in Coryell County, Texas, and married Truman Welborn on Nov. 15, 1947, in Tarrant County, Texas. Truman was born on Nov. 7, 1918, in Bryan County, Oklahoma. Their children are: Dennis Reagan, SRT #4856; Jan McKenzie, DRT #18333; and Mark Gregory, SRT #4857. Dennis Reagan Welborn #4856 Mark Gregory Welborn #4857

ROBERT WOODING CHAPPELL

Robert Wooding Chappell, He was called "Wooding" and he was born on May 14, 1782 in Halifax, Virginia. He came to Washington County, Texas in 1838 with his 85 year old mother and his three sons. He brought his pack of bear hounds and was a mighty hunter. He is credited with killing the last buffalo in Washington County in 1850.

R.W. Chappell

In 1841, he built a one room log cabin school for his children on his Washington County Plantation. He even imported a New England teacher to educate them.

Chappell Hill, Texas was named for him and two universities were established there, Chappell Hill female college in 1852 and Soule University in 1856. In 1875, Soule University was consolidated with Southwestern University in Georgetown.

Robert Wooding Chappell left the Washington County area because the influx of settlers coming in to Washington County threatened his hunting grounds.

His great, great, great, great granddaughter, Helen Elizabeth Chappell Williams, still lives on the original Chappell land near Chappell Hill. Mrs. Williams has three sons, John Robert Dixon, Chappell Evans Dixon, and Don Scott Dixon who are charter members of the William Mayfield Chapter #34 of the Sons of the Republic of Texas located in Washington County, Texas.

LEWIS LUNSFORD CHILES

Lewis Lunsford Chiles was born, according to the records, in 1811, to Dabney and Mary Chiles in Caroline County, Virginia. His ancestor, Walter Chiles, was an early settler (1638) of Jamestown, Virginia, and was elected speaker of the Virginia House of Burgess. Walter was a successful planter and owner of a merchant ship named "The Fame of Virginia." Lewis' mother and father died when he was in his early years, and he was raised by his aunt and uncle. At age 18, he left his birthplace and moved to Tennessee to live with some other members of the Chiles family. This is where he made contact with Sam Houston and learned about Texas.

In 1834, he moved to Texas and subsequently became a minuteman, and then part of the Texas Army and served with Captain William Patton's command under General Houston. He fought at the Battle of San Jacinto, and his name is inscribed in the marble wall inside the monument.

Grave marker of Lewis Lunsford Chiles 1811 to 1864

Raymond Dickens, Jr.

For his service in the Texas Army, he was granted land warrants in what is now Burleson and Milam counties. He is the founder of the town of Caldwell, Texas, and established the first general merchandise store there. In 1842 Lewis married Elizabeth Hitchcock, whose brother, Andrew Jackson Hitchcock, was with Colonel Fannin at Goliad when they were captured, and Hitchcock was one of the fortunate few to escape during the massacre.

Lewis and his wife raised a large family in a house he built about three blocks from the courthouse and accumulated over 10,000 acres of land on which he grew cotton. He was against secession at first, but changed his position when his son, James, joined the Confederate Army in 1861. During the Civil War, he donated much of his cotton to the cause of the Confederacy. The 1860 United States Census shows him to be the wealthiest man in Burleson County. His oldest son, James, died at Vicksburg in 1863.

Lewis Lunsford Chiles died on May 29, 1864, and is buried in the Old City Cemetery where the state of Texas erected a marker at his gravesite. Elizabeth was buried in the Old City Cemetery in Caldwell on June 9, 1877.

Chiles was the great-great-grandfather of the writer, Raymond A. Dickens, Jr., an attorney, who has two married children: Raymond Dickens, III, and Kathryn Dickens Scott. I am fortunate to be the owner of the musket used by Chiles at the Battle of San Jacinto, which somehow was obtained by my grandmother and given to me by her.

LOUIS PENA CHIRINO

Louis Pena Chirino (1820-1890), born of unknown parents in Mexico (1) is listed (2) as Louis Pena, a youth of 10 years aggregated with the Encarnation Chirino family in the Nacogdoches District. According to family legend Sr. Chirino observed Louis in the company of Indians passing through the Nacogdoches vicinity. Upon recognizing Louis to be of Spanish ancestry and apparently a captive, he purchased him from

Jesus S. (Jesse) Pena. Son of Louis P. Chirino and grandfather of Dr. Ben F. Edwards, Jr.

the Indians and raised him as an adopted son, hence the name Chirino attached to his name (3).

In November 1845, Louis married Maria Gregoria Y'Barbo, daughter of Anastacio Y'Barbo and Manuela Maria Sanches, and the great-granddaughter of Gil Y'Barbo. Fifteen children were born to Louis and Gregoria, the last being in 1875.

In 1860, Louis bought and made his home on 100 acres of farmland southwest of Nacogdoches in the Moral community. Louis served the Confederacy (4) as a member of Company A, 1st Battalion, 3rd Brigade, Texas State Troops. In the 1880s, he was a member of the Nacogdoches County school board and a provider of land for a parochial school.

Louis died in December 1890, and his wife sometime after 1900. Louis Pena Chirino is the great-grandfather of Dr. Ben F. Edwards, Jr., #6773

(1) The 1850 Census of Free Inhabitants of Nacogdoches County, Texas

(2) Gifford White, "1830 Citizens of Texas," Eakin Press, Austin, p118

(3) Affidavit by H.D. Ward, County Clerk, Nacogdoches County, and Jesus (Jesse) Pena, June 27, 1942

(4) Carolyn Reeves Ericson, "The People of Nacogdoches County in the Civil War"

ELISHA CLAPP

Elisha Clapp — an Indian and Mexican fighter, a Cavalry officer in the Battle of San Jacinto, a petitioner for the creation of Houston County, and a founder and trustee of Trinity College in Alabama, Houston County — was born in Tennessee in 1803.

His parents were Adam and Ruth (Lawrence) Clapp, who migrated to Illinois via North Carolina and Tennessee. It was from there that Elisha came to Texas in 1822. He married Elizabeth Robbins and they settled in Nacogdoches. Elisha's children were Able, John, Elisha II, William, Mary Ann, Sarah, Lucinda, and Lavina.

In 1832, Elisha, along with a small group of some nineteen men, succeeded in expelling Col. Piedras, a tyrannical Mexican government official, from Nacogdoches. He also helped establish the Old Block House in Houston County before 1836 to defend the settlers against the Indians. He received a Spanish Land Grant on October 14, 1834, in the David G. Burnet survey. Elisha enlisted and served in Captain William E. Smith's Company of Cavalry on April 7, 1836. He fought in the Battle of San Jacinto. After the battle, when Santa Anna and his cavalry attempted their escape, Elisha and several other men were instrumental in capturing him and bringing him back to General Houston.

In 1836, Elisha was appointed and confirmed by the Senate as Captain for the County of Nacogdoches in the Regiment of Mounted Gunmen of Texas for the defense of the frontier under Colonel Bennett. Elisha was also a major in the Cherokee Campaign for three months, serving as Quartermaster in 1837 for Montgomery County.

At Mustang Prairie on April 22, 1837, many early settlers of this area created and organized Houston County. Elisha was one of the signers.

This brave Texas patriot died in 1851 and is buried in the Elisha Clapp Cemetery in Houston County on a one-acre plot within his 1834 Spanish Land Grant. A Texas Centennial Marker commemorating his participation in the Battle of San Jacinto is at the head of his grave. In addition, there was recently installed an official Texas Historical Commission marker honoring Elisha. *Submitted by his great-grandson Wilfred Robbins Clapp*

MICAJAH M. CLARK

Micajah M. Clark, born in South Carolina in 1815, came to Texas in 1837 and received a land grant of 640 acres in Harrison County from the Republic. He resided there until 1846, at which time he immigrated to become a founder of a new Henderson County, Texas, settlement south of the towns of Athens and Malakoff called Science Hill. Science Hill, through the founding of Science Hill Academy, was the first community in the area to provide for the adequate educational needs of its people. Mr. Clark also received very early land grants from the state of Texas in Fayette and Henderson counties. Judging from newspaper and other publications, he was active in the civic and political affairs of the area.

In 1862, he married Miss Mary Catherine Russell of the County, and one of their children was Sarah Rosanna Clark. Sarah Rosanna married Stonewall Jackson Riddlesperger in 1886. To this union was born Hobart Clark Riddlesperger, who married Miss Stella Aline Gentry, of Malakoff, in 1930. They had one child, Anthony Gentry Riddlesperger, an attorney who married Miss Jane Johnston of Waco in 1956. The last mentioned couple was the parents of two sons: Johnston Gentry Riddlesperger, a teacher; and Daniel Anthony Riddlesperger, a Certified Public Accountant. Messrs. Anthony, Johnston and Daniel are members of the Sons of the Republic of Texas.

DAVID CLARY

David Clary, progenitor of the Clary family in Texas, was born August, 1787, in Rowan County, North Carolina. When his father, Daniel Clary, died in 1795, David was bound out to learn the blacksmith trade. On May 21, 1804, he married Catherine Pinkston, daughter of Meshack Pinkston and Susannah Coughenour.

David and Catherine were the parents of nine children who lived to maturity: Jesse, born in North Carolina; Meshack Pinkston, John, William, George Washington, and Tresvant DeGraphenread, all born in Georgia; and Francis Marion, David, Jr., and Martha Ann, all born in Alabama.

Shortly after 1810, David left North Carolina, moving first to Jackson County, Georgia, and then to Tuscaloosa County, Alabama, before settling in Washington County, Texas, in January 1835. The family was active in the Texas' quest for independence. Jesse, John, William and George Washington all fought in the Revolutionary Army. David provided horses and provisions for the army. Francis Marion took part in the Somervell Campaign in 1842.

David and Catherine lived on land in Grimes County purchased from Tandy Walker. In 1838, David Clary was granted a League and Labor of land later located in Navarro County. His sons were given smaller grants.

Catherine died on November 6, 1840; David died on November 21, 1849. Shortly before his death, he gave land for a Methodist Church in Grimes County, and it is presumed that he is buried on that property. Four of his sons settled on the Navarro County land grant. *Submitted by Michael J. Vaughn #6064N*

— See Additional David Clary Biography —
On Page 181

JOSEPH CLEGG

Joseph Clegg was born on September 16, 1821, in Chatham County, North Carolina, the son of John Polk Clegg, who was born on October 14, 1792 in Pittsboro, Chatham County, North Carolina, and a farmer and an army veteran of the War of 1812; and his wife, Martha Shurd Boon, who was born on January 25, 1801 in North Carolina.

*Joseph Clegg
Son of John Polk Clegg and
Martha Shurd Boon*

Joseph Clegg married four times (1) first wife, name unknown, before 1837; (2) Martha McGill on November 13, 1844 (3) Grace Mefford, about 1859; and (4) Lucy Forest Harris, November 1, 1863. A daughter was born in Texas in 1838 (census 1850, Upshur County, Texas).

Joseph Clegg claimed 320 acres in Upshur County, Texas in 1850 and title was granted to him in 1855; he also claimed 160 acres in Fisher County, Texas, in 1888, and title was granted to his wife in 1894.

He was a blacksmith in Upshur County, Texas, and was the first blacksmith in Stephenville, Erath County, Texas, in 1856. He was elected Justice of the Peace in Stephenville, Texas, in 1858. In later years, he farmed land in Bell and Fisher counties, Texas.

During the War Between the States, he shoed horses for the Confederate Army. He was also a private in Company A, Rangers for Frontier Protection, Texas State Troops, C.S.A.

He died on July 18, 1889, near Rotan, Fisher County, Texas, and is buried in the Cottonwood Flat Cemetery, Scurry County, Texas. Joseph Clegg was my third great-grandfather. Brian James Boothe #6072

WILLIAM HILL CLEVELAND

William Hill Cleveland was born in Edgefield County, South Carolina, and moved as a child to Clarke County, Alabama. At age twenty-six, he married Caroline Williams. She passed away the following year. Three years later, he married Zilphia Ann Harvey.

In November 1839, he came to Texas. His father-in-law, John Duncan Harvey, was among the group. He settled in Washington County, and there he raised his family.

He and his second wife had three children. One son, Willie, died as a child. The other son, Thomas J., died in Camp Douglas, Illinois, a Union prison camp. Their daughter, Virginia-Ann, married Napolean Bonaparte Rowe.

Cleveland was an ardent Baptist and was a messenger from his church in Independence in 1840 when the Union Baptist Association was formed.

In 1852, he sold land to Baylor University at Independence as additional land for the college. He later sold his home to be used as a girl's dormitory. He lived to be eighty-one and was very highly respected. *Submitted by William Rowe Hugghins*

JEREMIAH CLOUD

Jeremiah Cloud was born in Georgia about 1782-1784, at a time when Georgia was a sparsely settled frontier dominated by hostile Creek and other Indian tribes, in addition to the English. Many members of the Cloud family lived around the Cloud's Creek frontier area by 1750. At this time, it is not known who Jeremiah's parents were. His father was probably one of the nine sons (Ezekiel, Noah, John, Peter and others) of Jeremiah Cloud, Sr., or John Cloud, a cousin. All eleven served in the Revolutionary War.

Jeremiah Cloud and wife Elizabeth lived in what is now Twiggs County, Georgia, moving to Montgomery County, I.T. (Alabama) by 1816-1818.

Jeremiah and Elizabeth joined other family members in the Republic of Texas in 1837, settling on Caney Creek in Austin and Washington counties. Jeremiah, his sons and sons-in-law were planters and stockmen. He was awarded a 3rd-class Headright in Bosque County when it was a frontier.

Jeremiah died in Austin County on March 14, 1861. He was survived by his wife of over 60 years, and many sons, daughters and grandchildren.

Information on his descendants and other Clouds can be obtained from the Cloud Family Association.

Long live Texas!!!

Cloud descendants belonging to the Sons of the Republic of Texas

Leonard G. Cloud	#5014
Jay David Cloud	#5543A
Travis Jay Cloud	#5545A
Byron Leslie Cloud, Jr.	#6149N
T. F. Cloud, Jr.	#6150N
Ronald l. Cloud	#6351J
Wayne Fisher	#5589A
Harris James Huguenard	46812AH

JOHN WURTS CLOUD, SR.

John Wurts Cloud, Sr., was born in Flanders, New York, on February 15, 1797. He attended Yale College (now Yale University) and received a B.A. degree in 1823. He married Sarah Adeline Hull on December 24, 1825. On September 11, 1829 he was ordained to the priesthood of the Episcopal Church of the United States by the Rt. Rev. John Henry Hobart in Onondaga Hill, New York.

He moved to Texas sometime in 1830 or 1831 as part of Stephen F. Austin's colony, and was involved in the Battle of Old Velasco in 1832. He wife, Sarah, died in Brazoria in 1833. He served in the Texas Army in 1836 during the Texas Revolution, and for his service was awarded a league and a labor of land in Brazoria County. He named his homestead Buena Ventura. He taught children and held Sunday school classes in his home; he also did missionary work in the area.

On November 1, 1837, at Morgan's Point, Harris County, he married Rebecca Johnston. John Cloud, Sr., died on September 15, 1850, at the age of 53, in Chappel Hill, Washington County, Texas and is buried there.

In 1962 a stained glass was dedicated in his honor in Christ Church Cathedral of the Episcopal Diocese of Texas (Houston) in recognition of his being the first Episcopal priest known to be in Texas.

JOSHUA BUTLER COCHRAN

Joshua Butler Cochran was born December 8, 1803, in Troy, Montgomery County, North Carolina, the son of David Cochran and Catherine Butler. (See Patrick Jack Cochran biography.) He married first on October 21, 1824, probably in Montgomery County, Sarah Ann "Sally" McNeill. Sally was born May 30, 1802 in Moore County, North Carolina, the daughter of Archibald McNeill and Mary Waddell, who married January 10, 1800, in Randolph County, North Carolina. Archibald died in 1840 in Holly Springs, Mississippi, and Mary died in late 1850 in De Soto County, Mississippi.

Archibald McNeill was the son of Daniel McNeill and Sarah McKay, and Mary Waddell was the daughter of Edmond Waddell and Lucy Birdsong. Daniel McNeill was the son of Archibald McNeill and Janet Bahn, both of Scotland. Sarah McKay was the daughter of Archibald McKay and Ann Gilchrist, both of Scotland.

Joshua Butler Cochran and Sarah Ann McNeill had 12 children: David Archibald, born January 26, 1826; Wincy Ann, born May 25, 1827; Abraham Byron, born June 5, 1828; Mary, born September 2, 1829; Elias Kennedy, born January 17, 1831; Catherine, born December 25, 1832; William A., born July 24, 1834; Sarah, born October 8, 1835; James D., born March 7, 1838; Jane Hannah, born December 29, 1841; Calvin Jones, born May 1, 1843; and Joshua Bee, born October 28, 1844. The first 6 were born in Montgomery County, North Carolina; the next 3 in Tennessee; and the last 3 in Holly Springs, Mississippi.

Wincy Ann Cochran married John Houston Graham on December 10, 1845, in Holly Springs, Mississippi. John Houston Graham was born in 1824 in Tennessee, the son of Rev. George Washington Graham. John died about in about 1870, and Wincy died about 1867, both in Panola County, Texas.

John and Wincy Graham were the parents of nine children: Rosanna, Mary, Catherine, George, Jane, Frances "Fanny," Miriam, Emily Ellen, and Mace. Emily Elen Graham was born June 7, 1861 in Panola County, Texas. (See Patrick Jack Cochran biography for descendants.)

Joshua Butler Cochran arrived in Texas in 1845, and he is found on the 1846 tax list in Nacogdoches County. The area in which he lived became Angelina County that same year. Sarah McNeill Cochran died March 13, 1875, and he married another Sarah before the 1880 census. She died June 3, 1881. Joshua died September 10, 1893 and he and his two wives are buried in the Cochran Cemetery near the Ora community, 11 miles southeast of Huntington, Texas. David Lacey Garrison, Jr. #4745

PATRICK JACK COCHRAN

Patrick Jack Cochran was born April 4, 1815, in Montgomery County, North Carolina, the son of David Cochran and Catherine Butler. David Cochran was born August 9, 1779, in Montgomery County, North Carolina, the son of Abraham Cochran, who was born in 1757 in Brunswick County, Virginia, the son of Jacob and Mary Cochran. He married Tamar Bruton, and had at least three children: David; Mary "Polly," who married a Poer, and died in Alabama; and Elizabeth "Betsy," who married William Coggin.

Patrick Jack Cochran arrived in Texas in March 1840, and received a certificate at Nacogdoches on September 7, 1841, for 320 acres of land.

Patrick Jack Cochran married Mary Elizabeth Thompson on January 12, 1849, probably in Shelby County, Texas. She was born may 15, 1832 in Greene County, Alabama, the daughter of Henry Sewell Thompson and Margaret F. Matthews. Patrick and Mary had six children: Margaret, born 1850, and who never married; Louisa I., born April 16, 1852, and who married William J. Creech; Patrick H., born in1854, and who never married; Sarah Jane, born October 27, 1855, and who married W.T. "Bill" Swanzy; Psalm Jackson, born March 9, 1857, and who married Mary Adella Easter and Nancy Ann Shafner; and David Elias.

Patrick Jack Cochran died December 6, 1862, and is buried in the Cochran Cemetery near the Ora community, 11 miles southeast of Huntington, Texas. Mary Thompson Cochran died between 1870 and 1880 in the Patroon community, Shelby County, Texas.

David Elias Cochran was born November 14, 1858, and on December 26, 1878, married Emily Ellen Graham, who was born June 7, 1861, in Panola County, Texas. She was the daughter of John Houston Graham and Wincy Ann Cochran. David and Emily had 8 children: David Jack, born October 23, 1879; Herbert Edgar, born March 16, 1882; Della, born March 18, 1885; Lura May, born November 1887; Preston Lacy, born March 15, 1890; Harvey, born July 28, 1892; and twins, Macie Louise and Robbie, born February 14.

David Elias Cochran died November 6, 1946 in Teague, Texas, and wife, Emily, died May 14, 1956, in Brazos County. Both are buried in the Greenwood Cemetery in Teague.

Della Cochran was married December 21, 1902 in Angelina County, Texas, to Joseph Devereau Garrison, born 1881 in Garrison, Texas, the son of William Pierce Garrison and Mary Elizabeth Lacey.

Della and Joseph Garrison were the parents of three children: Willie Mae, born July 31, 1904, and who married William Max Harkrider; David Lacey, born October 11, 1908, and who married Marie Bel Gardiner; and Helen, who died at age 21 months. *Submitted by David Lacey Garrison, Jr. #4745*

ROBERT MORRIS COLEMAN

Robert Morris Coleman was born about 1798 in Trigg County, Kentucky, to James and Rebecca (Morris) Coleman. He moved to Marengo County, Alabama, with several of his family and friends in 1820, and was involved in the Indian Wars in that area. Robert M. Coleman married Elizabeth Bounds there in December of 1822, and moved back to Kentucky in about 1825, engaging in planting cotton.

Colonel Coleman's Monument in Velasco

By 1830, the family had determined to relocate to Texas, and arrived in May 1831. They settled near Bastrop where the land was not developed and was available to settlers for the taking. Coleman soon became an outspoken leader of the Bastrop area colonists and was elected alcalde (mayor) of the small group of settlers. He commanded the Mina Volunteer Mounted Rifles and engaged in more Indian fighting and scouting than farming. As the Texian Colonists grew more impatient for independence from Mexico, he became more involved and commanded a company of Volunteers during the siege of Bexar in 1835. He was a delegate to the Constitutional Convention and a signer of the Declaration of Independence in 1836, then served as colonel, aide-de-camp to General Sam Houston at the Battle of San Jacinto. He was described as, "an expert horseman, a skilled axe-man and a sure shot." He was also reported to have given no quarter to adversaries, whether Mexican or Indian.

Col. Coleman drowned at the mouth of the Brazos in July, 1837. His widow and children returned to their farm near Bastrop, where they were attacked by Indians in February of 1839. Mrs. Coleman and the eldest son, Albert, were killed, and little Thomas was carried off into captivity. Son James escaped to warn the settlers. The three girls, Rebecca, Elizabeth and Sarah Ann, survived by hiding under the planks of the cabin floor. Rebecca later married Robert Russell; Elizabeth married William Brown and Sarah Ann married William McClellan.

The city and county of Coleman were named in Robert M. Coleman's honor in 1864. James H. Brown #4155 Michael R. Milam #5343S Tommy A. Milam #5448 John M. Milam #5350S

ELIJAH COLLARD

Elijah Collard was born November 9, 1778 in Washington County, Maryland. He was the son of Joseph and Mary Kennedy Collard. He went with his family to Kentucky, and on May 1, 1801, married Mary Stark in Bullitt County, Kentucky. Mary was the daughter of Jonathan and Margaret Ball Stark.

Elijah served in the War of 1812 from the Louisiana Territory (now Missouri). In 1833, Elijah received a league of land from Coahuia of Texas near the town of Willis. In 1835, he served as a member of the Consultation at San Felipe as a representative from Washington municipality. He was a member of the Board of Land Commissioners for the newly formed county of Montgomery. In 1844, he was Justice of the Peace in Montgomery County. In 1846, when Walker County was formed, he was elected a commissioner.

He died March 13, 1847 of winter fever. He is buried in Gourd Creek Cemetery in Walker County. A Texas State Historical Marker and a War of 1812 Medallion mark his final resting place. Mary Stark Collard died December 24, 1861, and is buried beside Elijah. J.M. Pollard is a third great-grandson of Elijah Collard. *Submitted by Jewel M. Pollard - 4627*

LEMUEL MILLER COLLARD

Lemuel Miller Collard was born in the Missouri Territory on January 3, 1810. He was the fifth of eleven children born to Elijah and Mary Stark Collard. Lemuel came to the Mexican Province of Texas in 1828 to check into the advantages of living in this new land. He told his parents how good Texas was, so in 1832 the family moved to Texas and settled in the town of Danville.

In 1831 Lemuel married Elizabeth Lindley. Her parents were Samuel Washington and Elizabeth Whitley Lindley. Together, they had thirteen children, all born in Texas. After the death of Elizabeth, Lemuel married Sarah Pausel.

Lemuel served in the Texas Army, in Capt. John M. Wade's Company, from June 30 to Sept. 29, 1836 and received bounty warrant #3168 for 320 acres. Lemuel's brothers, Jonathan, Job, and James all fought in the Battle of San Jacinto. One of his wife's brothers, Jonathan Lindley, was one of the "The Immortal Thirty-two Men from Gonzales" who fought and died at the Battle of the Alamo.

Lemuel died on April 22, 1893, and is buried in Gourd Creek Cemetery, Walker County, Texas. Randy D. Pollard is the third great-grandson of Lemuel M. Collard. Randy D. Pollard - 4628 Matthew D. Pollard - 6408 Jonathan M. Pollard - 6407

IVERSON COLLIER

Iverson Collier was born February 9, 1825, in Caswell County, North Carolina. He came to the Republic of Texas in December, 1841, with his parents, Thomas Collier and Susanah Pinson Collier. On December 2, 1844, at Shelbyville, Shelby County, he was issued a fourth-class Headright Certificate for 320 acres of land. He and his parents settled in Upshur County.

Iverson Collier *Farris Glen Collier*

On May 1, 1846, he enlisted as a private in Company D, 2nd Regiment, Texas Mounted Volunteers, during the Mexican War. He served under Col. Woods. He was with the army on the march from Point Isabel, Texas, to Matamores, Camargo, and on to Monterey, where he participated in the Battle of Monterey. He was discharged October 2, 1846, at Monterey due to illness. He served in Company 1, Clark's Regiment, Texas Infantry, C.S.A, during the Civil War.

On October 4, 1853 he married Sarah Elizabeth Dearmore at Coffeeville, Upshur County, Texas. One child, Selena Gilla Ann, died young. Sarah died December 20, 1868. He married Margaret Jane Johnson, April 15, 1870. They had seven children: John, Thomas, Joseph Littleton, Clifton, Martha Lee, Iverson Lewis and Oscar. He moved his family to Franklin County in about 1881. He was a farmer and lay minister. He established Collier's Chapel Methodist Church. He died August 16, 1900 and is buried in Collier's Chapel Cemetery, Franklin County, Texas.

Iverson Collier was my great-grandfather. My father was Farris Littleton Collier, only son of Joseph Littleton Collier. Farris Glen Collier #3487

JOHN P. COLLINS

John P. Collins was born on July 17, 1817 in Robertsau, France, to Anne Marie Dienst and Jean Collin. At the age of 18, he enlisted in the Texian Army to fight for the independence of Texas from Mexico. He enlisted under Major William P. Miller on February 16, 1836. He left New Orleans for Texas on March 4, 1836, on board the schooner, William and Francis. They landed at Copano on March 19, 1836. Later, he was shown on the muster roll of Capt. Teal. John P. was honorably discharged on May 4, 1837, at Camp Bowie in Jackson County, Texas. He signed a pay voucher #1206 for $116.52.

After the war, John settled in Liberty County. He married Mary Secrest from Alabama in 1840. He bought a house in Swartwot, Texas, for $125. He and Mary (Polly) had four children: Alexander Z., Wm. Benjamin Franklin, James and Adaline Rose.

John P. helped organize Trinity Lodge #14 A.F.&A.M. He served as a junior warden.

When Liberty County was divided, John P. and family were on the Polk County, Texas, Census. He was listed as a hotel and tavern keeper.

On May 3, 1841, he was issued Certificate #185 for 320 acres of land in Liberty County by the Land Commission. The document states that he had resided in the republic of Texas for 3 or more years.

After Mary died, John P. married Susan Banks, and they had a daughter named Ida.

John P. Collins died in Houston, Texas, on October 11, 1864.

Eugene Lamar Collins – great-grandson

Ronald Patrick Collins – great-great-grandson

WILLIAM C. COLLINSWORTH

My great-great-grandfather was William C. Collinsworth, son of James and Jane (Jennie) Brown Collinsworth, born Oct 6, 1806, Wilkinson County, Miss. William, a farmer, married Mary Caroline Bonner Jan. 9, 1831 in Warren County, Miss. In 1839, the family was living in Matagorda County, Texas.

William's two brothers fought in the Texas War of Independence. David C. Collinsworth, was killed at the Battle of Goliad, Texas. George Morse Collinsworth has a monument erected to him in Christ Church, Matagorda County, Texas. His gravestone reads: "Major George Morse Collinsworth, commander of Texans at the capture of Goliad, October 9, 1835."

On Aug 7, 1848, the Travis County Board of Land Commissioners gave William a 3rd-class Certificate #102 for coming to Texas prior to Jan 1, 1842.

The children of William and Mary Caroline Collinsworth were: Andrew, James, Mary Caroline, Willis Bonner, Loucinda. They had two sons to serve in the War Between the States: Willis Bonner Collinsworth, a private in Col. Woods' regiment; and James M. Collinsworth, a private in Col. X.B. DeBeay's regiment.

William C. Collinsworth died April 9, 1860, in Smithville, Bastrop County, Texas. His wife, Mary Caroline Bonner Collinsworth, died Oct 16, 1867, in Bastrop County, Texas. *Submitted by Alexander E. Charleston, Sr.*

NICHOLAI CONRAD

The history of the Conrad family in Texas began in 1842. The Nicholai and Anna Conrad family left their home in SarLouis Bas Rhine, Prussia, and departed La Harve, France, on November 2, 1842, sailing on the ship L'Ebro, captained by E. Perry. They were registered on the ship's list: Nicolas - 44, cultivator; wife Anna - 33. Children: Catherine -16, Joseph -13, Pierre - 5, Louis - 3, also Jean - 18, cultivator. They were among the 144 passengers destined for Castro's Colony.

Peter Paul Conrad 1884

The ship arrived in Galveston late in December. They disembarked January 1, 1843. The family lived in Galveston briefly before traveling by wagon to San Antonio. Sadly, en route, Nicholai died and was buried on Buffalo Bayou near Houston. The rest continued and actually lived in the Alamo's ruins for a period, along with other Castro colonists. In 1844, they moved west to help found Castroville. They established their ranch on the Dry Chacon Creek and branded with a CP registered in 1856 in current Medina County. Concurrently, they ranched west of present-day Orange Grove, where they fattened cattle bound for sale in Corpus Christi. In addition to ranching, the family provided much-needed wagoner services to San Antonio and beyond for the community.

Nicholai and Anna's third son, Peter (Pierre), married Elizabeth Vollmer on 11/22/1859. A native of Hanover, Elizabeth emigrated to Castroville with her family, where she lived until her death 12/17/1871. Their son, Peter Paul was born 7/21/1864. On 6/4/1888, he married Mary Ann Etter, the daughter of two more Castroville colonists, Jacob Etter (born 1/28/1842; married 8/13/1866; died 11/25/1929) from Ulmitz, Frieburg, Switzerland, and Katherine Teresa Keller (born 1844, died 8/1911), who was the first white child born in the colony. Peter Paul and Mary Ann's youngest son, Casper Antone, was born November 24, 1908. He wed 8/7/1932 Louise Frances Neumann (born 1/17/1907; died 3/20/1976). One son was born to them, Lamar Joseph Conrad, on July 31, 1944. Lamar married Linda Rektorik on June 14, 1975; two children were born: Elizabeth Louise (1/23/1977) and Lamar Joseph Conrad II (8/16/1979).

JOSEPH THOMAS COOK, SR.

Joseph Thomas Cook, Sr., Texas pioneer, soldier, colonist and founder of Cook's Fort, carved in the eleven short years he was a resident of Texas, a record that still attests to his honor today.

Joseph T. Cook grave at Salem Cemetery *Cook's Fort Monument at Salem*

He was born in 1776 in North Carolina. His father was Benjamin Cook, a Revolutionary War soldier from Wallingford, Connecticut. The Cook's forefathers had settled there after first living near Plymouth, MA, when they first came to America. He was married to Mary (Polly) Moore of South Carolina about 1800.

Joseph T. Cook, Sr., participated in the War of 1812, serving with the 131st Regiment. In 1833, he and his family came to Texas and settled in the San Augustine area, then moved to Nacogdoches, arriving there in March of 1834.

In January of 1835, Cook received a Spanish Land Grant from the Supreme Government of the State of Coahuila and Texas for a league and a labor of land in Cherokee County (about 4,600 acres).

Cook also served the Republic of Texas as a soldier in Captain Michael Costley's Company of Texas Rangers in 1836, and received a land grant for services rendered.

In 1838, Joseph T. Cook, Sr., employed a military company under the command of a certain Captain Black, to build a fort and stockade on his land, three miles south of what is now Rusk, Texas. This became known as Cook's Fort. Joseph T. Cook, Sr., lived at the fort with his sons, William, David, Joseph Jr., James, Samuel, and his sons-in-law, Abaslom and Jesse Gibson. As Cook's Fort was on the main thoroughfare, many prominent figures of the time found refuge there. Despite many printed statements to the contrary, Cook's Fort was never attacked by Indians.

After the stockade was torn down, homesteads were established on adjacent land. At the point where these joined, the Cooks built a store and a blacksmith shop, which proved to be the nucleus of the village of Cook's Fort, said to have attained the population of two-hundred-and-fifty people, including the slaves.

In 1846, a location committee considered Cook's Fort as the site for the new county seat. Family tradition pictures that the Cooks opposed this because it could interfere with their slave-farming interests. After the establishment of Rusk, most of the Cook's Fort inhabitants moved there.

Part of the original grant, including the site of the fort, is still today owned by descendants of Joseph Thomas Cook, Sr. After his death in 1844, Cook's Fort went to his son, Samuel, who in turn left the land to his children: Sloan, Belle, Laura Cook and Alice Petree. After the death of Sloan and his sisters, Cook's Fort was left to Sloan's daughter Dollie Belle Cook Lucas and her husband, Frank Lucas, in 1934. Grandchildren of Frank and Dollie Lucas — including Sloan Lucas of Tyler, Texas; John Lucas of San Leon, Texas; Jeff Lucas of Houston, Texas; Ronnie, Johnnie, Dollie Sue and Scott Lucas of Rusk, Texas — still own parts of the original grant. The Family Land Heritage Program of the Texas Department of Agriculture recognizes that this land has been in continuous agricultural production by the same family since 1835.

On January 21, 1844, Joseph Thomas Cook, Sr., died at Cook's Fort at the age of 68, and is buried there at the family plot in Cook's Cemetery, known now as Salem Cemetery, the land being donated by his family.

A large granite marker was erected at the site by the state of Texas in 1936 in honor of Joseph Thomas Cook and Cook's Fort, which today is owned by John Lucas. *Submitted by great-great-great-grandson John Lucas, SRT #6771*

FRANCIS JARVIS COOKE

Francis Jarvis Cooke, born at Beaufort, Carteret County, North Carolina, on July 13, 1816, was the fifth child born to Henry Marchant Cooke and Frances Buxton Cooke. He died November 11, 1903, at Howth, Waller County, Texas.

Francis Jarvis married Emily Stockton on December 28, 1845, at Brenham, Washington County, Texas. Emily died September 4, 1908, at Howth, Waller County, Texas.

Francis Jarvis Cooke

Francis Jarvis and Emily were parents of eleven children: Hugh, Emily, Francis Jarvis, Sally, Alexander, Mary Frances, Sophia, Harriet Evelina Annie, Ellen, and James Stribling.

In a Christmas letter dated 1892, Francis Jarvis told of his life in Texas: "My father, with all the rest of us, started to Texas early in 1835. He (father) died at Randolph, Tennessee, where we buried him and came on to Texas. We lost nearly everything we had in the September overflow of that year living near Casey's Ferry fifteen miles above Matagorda . . .

"Early in March 1836, my brother Thomas and myself and many of our neighbors started to re-enforce Travis at the Alamo, but at Victoria the place of rendezvous, we heard that the Alamo had fallen. We then reported to Fannin and received orders from him to remain in Victoria until he reached that point. Soon after his surrender, an officer came from Houston's army on the Colorado and detailed nineteen of us to take a wagon load of powder and lead from Dimmitt's Landing to the main army which we succeeded in doing, passing near a part of the Mexican army . . . Brother Thomas and myself joined Captain R.J. Calder's Company in which we remained participating in the Battle of San Jacinto and following the enemy till they were well on their way to the Rio Grande. (We) took honorable discharge from the service, our three months term of enlistment having expired and there being no further call for troops.

". . . In the fall of 1842, my brother and myself enlisted for three months, joined Col. Joseph L. Bennett's Regiment and aided in driving the enemy out of the country. This was called the Woll Campaign and terminated in the Mier Expedition, in which we did not participate but returned home after the enemy crossed the Rio Grande. We returned under Captain Gordon M. Griffin who reported us to General Houston at Washington who came out where we were, expressed himself highly gratified at our return, disclaimed all responsibility as to the Mier Expedition, expressed the deepest concern for those who engaged in it, and seemed to be moved almost to tears in regard to their fate. General Houston must have been something of a prophet. He seemed to anticipate then, what really happened afterwards.

"Next year I left my crop with my brother, went up to the Wilbarger settlement on the Colorado and joined the Texas Rangers to help expel the Comanches but after staying with the Rangers six weeks and failing to get within range of a Comanche I returned home, went from there to Brenham where I sold merchandise several years, married, moved to Houston, sold goods there, but removed back to Chappell Hill where I was successful as a merchant, but the Confederate War broke me up, and since its close my infirm health has kept me out of business."

During the War Between the States, Francis Jarvis was agent for the Cotton Bureau, Department Trans Mississippi, Confederate States of America, in Hempstead, Texas.

Francis Jarvis Cooke was a family man, a civic leader, and a churchman. He was a leader in founding the Episcopal Church in Texas. He served on the Vestry at St. Luke's Church in Chappell Hill and was a founding vestryman at St. Bartholomew's Church in Hempstead. He was active in Masonic work in Chappell Hill and Brenham. He served as Alderman in Chappell Hill in 1856. His businesses in Chappell Hill were a store, Cooke & Woodward, and a partnership in a sawmill with Isaac Applewhite. Another business was called Cooke and Carter.

Frances Jarvis Cooke received three land grants:

Grant #2358, dated February 12, 1838, for 320 acres for service in the Army of the Republic of Texas;

Grant #1226, dated January 12, 1846, for fighting at the Battle of San Jacinto, for 640 acres;

Headright Certificate File #41, dated February 2, 1838, Montgomery County, for 1,476 acres.

Francis Jarvis Cooke and Emily Stockton Cooke are buried at Salem Cemetery, near Hempstead, Texas. The State of Texas caused a Centennial Monument to be erected at their graves in 1936. *Submitted by: Herbert v. Cooke Jr., Tho. Rusk Chapter Richard H. Cooke, Anson Jones Chapter (Great-great-grandsons)*

WILLIAM GORDON COOKE

William Gordon Cooke was born in Fredericksburg, Virginia, on March 26, 1808. Trained in the family drug business, he moved to New Orleans to continue his career and on October 13, 1835, volunteered for the New Orleans Greys. He arrived with the Second Company at Velasco on October 25, 1835, and was elected first lieutenant. After arriving at Bexar on November 8, 1835, Cooke was elected captain of his company and raised volunteers to storm the town. Cooke led the party that captured the priest's house on the main plaza, thus forcing the Mexican capitulation, and received the flag of surrender, which he sent to Col. Francis W. Johnson, commanding officer.

Cooke then volunteered for the Matamoros expedition of 1835-36. As captain, he led the reformed San Antonio Greys to Goliad. After Sam Houston's impassioned speech there, Cooke offered his services to the Texas Army and was sent with his company to Refugio, where they were joined by Col. James Walker Fannin, Jr., and the Georgia Battalion. Fannin ordered Cooke to San Patricio to reinforce Maj. Robert C. Morris. Cooke was left in command there when Morris, Johnson, and Col. William Grant proceeded to the Rio Grande.

Cooke received Grant's letter stating his intentions to join the Mexican Federalists and, after relaying this news to Fannin, was ordered to fall back to Goliad, where he arrived on February 12, 1836. He was then sent with two Mexican prisoners to Washington-on-the-Brazos, where he joined Houston's staff as assistant inspector general. Cooke went with Houston to Gonzales and assisted in organizing troops. At the Battle of San Jacinto, he served on Houston's staff with the rank of major. Cooke was in charge of the prisoners when Antonio López de Santa Anna was captured. Cooke prevented the angry Texans from executing Santa Anna so that he could be brought before General Houston.

While Houston recovered from his wounds in New Orleans, Cooke accompanied him, but soon returned to serve as chief clerk of the War Department. During Houston's first administration, Cooke was appointed stock commissioner (October 1836), acting secretary of war (November 1836), inspector general (January 1837), and signer of the president's name to promissory notes of the Republic (June 1837).

Cooke re-enlisted in the army around October 1838 as quartermaster general. In March 1840, Mirabeau B. Lamar named him commissioner to sign treaties with the Comanches, and he took part in the Council House Fight in San Antonio on March 19, 1840.

On August 18, 1840, Cooke was appointed colonel of the First Regiment of Infantry, assigned to lay out the Military Road from the Little River to the Red River. Fighting Indians and starvation, Cooke explored and mapped much of North Central Texas. He established Fort Johnson and Fort Preston on the Red River, and Cedar Springs Post on the Trinity River. Theirs were the first structures built by white men at the future site of Dallas. The troops were disbanded in 1841, making Cooke the last commander of the regular Texas Army. Cooke's success prompted a grand military ball in his honor in the Senate chamber, and a nomination for vice president of the Republic. He accepted instead an appointment from Lamar in April 1841 as senior commissioner on the Texan Santa Fe Expedition.

Cooke was to have been the chief civil authority in Santa Fe, but on September 17, 1841, he was deceived by the traitor Capt. William G. Lewis and surrendered the Texans' arms. Cooke and his men were marched to Mexico City and imprisoned in Santiago Prison on December 26, 1841. They were released in June, 1842, and returned to Texas in August, 1842.

Ignoring his pledge not to take arms against Mexico under pain of death, he immediately joined Gen. Edward Burleson in expelling the Mexican General Adrián Woll from San Antonio, and was wounded in Capt. John C. Hays's charge on the cannon at Arroyo Hondo. In October, 1842, Houston appointed him quartermaster general and chief of the subsistence department, and Cooke helped organize the infamous Snively Expedition, and the Somervell Expedition, of which he was a member.

Seeking further revenge, Cooke joined Edwin Ward Moore's expedition to the Yucatán aboard the sloop-of-war Austin. Cooke participated in engagements with the Mexican steamships Montezuma and Guadalupe. After the Independencia joined the Texan fleet, he twice accompanied her on raids, resulting in the capture of the Mexican ship Glide. They returned in July, 1843, and Gen. Sidney Sherman appointed Cooke adjutant general of the Texas Militia.

Cooke was elected representative from Bexar County to the House of the Ninth Congress on September 2, 1844, serving as chairman of the Committee on Military Affairs. In December, 1884, President Anson Jones appointed Cooke secretary of war, responsible for raising troops and supplies for the United States Army of occupation under Gen. Zachary Taylor. He served until 1846, when he ran unsuccessfully for Congress of the United States. On April 27, 1846, Cooke was appointed the first adjutant general of the state of Texas by Governor James Pinckney Henderson, and served until his death.

Cooke was a grand royal arch captain of Holland Masonic Lodge No. 36 in Houston. On August 16, 1844, he married Angela María de Jesús Blasa Navarro, daughter of Luciano Navarro and niece of José Antonio Navarro. They had one son, William Navarro Cooke.

Cooke died of tuberculosis on December 24, 1847, at his father-in-law's ranch in Seguin. He was buried in nearby Geronimo, and on March 2, 1937, reinterred in the State Cemetery, Austin. Cooke County, Cooke's Camp near San Antonio, and Cooke Avenue in San Antonio were named for him. SRT members/Cooke descendants: Steven A. Brownrigg #3773 Richard O. Cook #6837AH Carl Greg Cooke #4874 Weldon Charles Cooke #4875

JOHN CARSON COPES III

Born September 6, 1923, Baton Rouge, Louisiana

Married Estelle Givens on March 3, 1944, and has one son (John IV) and grandson (John V.) in Mandeville, LA. He and Estella now live in Baton Rouge, Louisiana, and he is a retired professional engineer.

John C. Copes III

Ancestor: Josiah Hughes Bell, one of "Old 300" — married Mary McKenzie; settled in Austin colony 1821.

Daughter, Elizabeth Lucinda Bell married James Wilson Copes, M.D.,

Son of Dr. Copes: Josiah Bell Copes married Sallie Jane Carson of this marriage a son was born in 1864, John Carson Copes, D.D.S. it was to this distinguished future citizen (Josiah Hughes Bell) of Brazoria County that Austin entrusted affairs of the colony during his trip to Mexico City.

Josiah Hughes Bell died in 1838, and is buried in West Columbia Cemetery. By: John C. Copes

NATHANIEL L. CORBET

Nathaniel L. Corbet — Yankee, Dragoon, pioneer — was born to Daniel and Sarah (Gordon) Corbet at Champlain, New York, on June 13, 1812, and named for his grandfather, an American Revolutionary soldier. In 1833, he joined the Dragoons. The next year, the regiment, led by Gen. Henry Leavenworth and Col. Henry Dodge, marched across Indian Territory to establish contact with Indian tribes. Leavenworth and many of his men died on the expedition.

When Corbet was discharged in 1836, he settled in Arkansas and married Mary A. Price in Van Buren. They moved to the Republic of Texas in 1845, settling in present Delta County. He was a farmer, rancher, store merchant, hotel keeper, deputy sheriff and town marshal. In 1870, he donated part of his farm for half of the Cooper townsite, county seat of newly formed Delta County. Their children were Margaret, Sarah A., Mary A., Louisa, Edward, Henry Gordon, Willie Amma, George and Ethel, born between 1837 and 1859. Mary Corbet died in 1884 and is buried in Minter's Chapel Cemetery in Grapevine, Texas. Nathaniel died about 1901 and is buried in an unidentified cemetery between Atoka and Stringtown, Oklahoma. Nathaniel and Mary Corbet were great-great-grandparents of Weldon Green Cannon #1689 Great-great-great-grandparents of James William Griffith, Jr. #5831A Mark Wayne Moyers #6628M Great-great-great-great-grandparents of Fletcher Christian Freeman #5569A Matthew Wayne Moyers #6657M

NORMAN DALE COX

Norman Dale Cox was born is Harlingen, Cameron County, Texas, on July 4, 1942, and grew up in West Point, Texas, in Fayette County. He is the son of Charles Earl Cox, Sr. and Middie Hart Moore Cox. He graduated from Sam Houston University in Huntsville, Texas, where he studied social studies and theology. He began his career with the state of Texas working in vocational rehabilitation, and then served with the Boy Scouts of America as a professional Scout leader. In 1978, he turned to his creative talents and became the owner and operator of Cox Decorating, a custom picture framing business. In this capacity, he soon distinguished himself by his unique matting techniques. In 1986, he joined a national chain of craft stores as the director of framing. He continued in this position until 1993 when he retired

On December 16, 1967, he married Gloria Crews Cox. They have two daughters, Melissa Cox Hegemeyer and Tara Dale Cox; and two granddaughters, Mandy and Malorie Hegemeyer.

Norman traces his roots back to the earliest settlers in Texas. His ancestors, including great-grandfather James Addison Darby, arrived in Texas as young men with their families in the 1820s and 1830s. Most of them settled in and around the Bastrop area and Fayette County to marry and rear their families.

In 1995, Norman became a member of the Sam Houston Chapter, Sons of the Republic of Texas, where he has served as chaplain. He is also a member of the Albert Sidney Johnston Camp, Sons of Confederate Veterans, and the Albert Sidney Johnston Chapter Military Order of Stars and Bars.

Norman Dale Cox

JOHN ROBERT CRADDOCK

John Robert Craddock was born October 15, 1812, Prince Edward County, Virginia, to John Cross Craddock and Peggy R. Jackson. The family moved in 1820 to Ohio County, Kentucky, where the parents perished in a house fire, leaving John Robert and his sister, Virginia Ann, orphans.

John Robert Craddock   *John Robert Craddock's Marker*

John Robert, Virginia, and her husband, Gabriel Jackson, left Kentucky in October 1832, arriving in Texas in December 1833 and settling in Robertson's Colony. In 1840, he married Amanda Childers, daughter of Goldsby Childers, in Burleson County. They had 13 children; the last two were twins.

He was 23 years old when he fought in the Battle of San Jacinto on April 21, 1836, when Texas won her independence from Mexico. John Robert was one of Sam Houston's personal bodyguards. He was appointed Captain of the Texas Rangers in Red River County by the Texas Senate on May 31, 1837. He was a Notary Public in Lamar County and carried the public mails for the year 1839. He fought many Indians and received many land grants and land donations for his service for the Republic of Texas.

He died on his farm on August 19, 1891, where he is buried, near Rogers, Texas. His grave has granite obelisk marker.

Great-great-grandfather of John William Graham, Jr., #4889

Great-great-grandfather of Dwight Leighman Weathersbee #4923 Great-grandfather of Clarence Austin Rayburn #4910

JOHN CRANE

John Crane, my great-great-great-grandfather, was raised in Virginia, and in 1811 moved with his wife to Hardeman County, Tennessee.

John Crane was a childhood playmate and companion of Sam Houston. Both enlisted with General Jackson's Army in Tennessee and took part in the Battle of Horseshoe Bend.

John Crane, with his wife, Mary (Polly) DeLozier, and seven children, left Hardeman County, Tennessee, and arrived in Texas where they later had two more children, around 1834. He later settled in what is now Huntsville.

He was captain of a company of men who entered Bexar in December 1835, under Ben Milam. Serving in General Rusk's expedition to remove Cherokee Indians from Texas, he was killed July 15, 1839, in the Battle of the Neches. His son-in-law, Jack Robins, and Ben Highsmith buried John about three-and-one-half miles northwest of the town of Chandler.

Frederick J. Reinke, III, in the old Moulton Cemetery Crane Plots

His children were: Elizabeth Ann, who married William Ware; Greenberry, who married Susan Bernice Winters; Eliza, who married Jack Robins; Mary Jane, who married James Elkins, then John Davenport; Andrew Jackson, who married Elizabeth Fairies; Narcissus Emaline, who married William Jones; Newel Walton, who married Elizabeth Tolbert; John Houston, who married Martha Jones; and William Ambrose, who married Sarah Miller, then Jane Watson, and then Jane Powers.

Captain John Crane was the father-in-law of Captain William Ware. Captain Ware founded the town of Waresville, now known as Utopia.

My mother, Rose Marie Crane Reinke, is the daughter of Earl Greenberry Crane; he is the son of James Beal Crane, who is the son of Greenberry Crane, whose father was John Crane. Frederick J. Reinke III SRT #6811

MARSHALL CRAWFORD

Marshall Crawford was born in Kentucky about 1803. He married Rebecca Sinclair who was born in Tennessee in about 1804. He migrated to Arkansas Territory about 1825, settling on the Arkansas River in an area then called Lovely County.

About 1828, the Crawfords were among several hundred families removed from Lovely County when the area was ceded back to the Cherokee Indians. In return, Marshall received a 320-acre land grant from the federal government. He moved his family to Crawford County, Arkansas, where farmed and raised cattle.

Crawford came to Texas in 1843 and located his farm on the headwaters of the Sabine River in present-day Hopkins and Rains County. Crawford was a Mercer colonist. He is listed as the 13th colonist in the Mercer Colony, with a date of introduction of February 23, 1844.

In October 1854, Crawford settled in Bell County, Texas. He died on April 17, 1879, and is buried in the Eulogy Cemetery near Temple. Rebecca died on November 19, 1882.

Marshall Crawford had nine children. Mary married H. Williams. Louisa married T.T. Havens. Harriet married Thomas Deaton, who served as an early sheriff of both Comanche and Hamilton counties. T.B. died in childhood. Martha married E. Allen. Amanda married Thomas Deaton's brother, John Calvin Deaton. Elizabeth married J.A. Clark. Charles Sinclair Crawford, the only surviving son, served in the Confederate Army from Bell County and became a prominent Bell County farmer. Descendants of Marshall Crawford who are members of the Sons of the Republic of Texas *Submitted by Stephen Pate #6930AH*

DAVID CROCKETT

Some of David Crockett's descendants live not far from where his widow, Elizabeth, settled in what is now Hood County, Texas, in 1852. She and her son, Robert, came to claim a grant of 640 acres made to veterans of Texas Independence.

David was born on August 17, 1786, died on March 6, 1836. He was described as a failure as a U.S. Congressman, but he made his mark on Texas history and the United States. David came from Scotch-Irish emigrants who arrived in the early 1700's. No one knows for sure who his great grandparents were. His grandfather, David, and his grandmother were killed by Indians in what is now Eastern Tennessee. He was raised in poor circumstances by his father, John, and mother, Rebecca Hawkins, with nine siblings.

David Crocket

He left home at age 13 because his family needed him to work off a debt. After traveling to Baltimore as a cattle drover, he almost became a sailor, but became homesick and returned to the frontier. He was known as a hunter of wild game, especially bears. He married Polly Finley in 1806. Polly died in 1813, so to find a home for his three small children, he married the widow Elizabeth Patton, who had small children of her own. They farmed, then built a gristmill, which was lost in a flood. They had three children of their own. His house and goods were lost in a fire, so he moved again, and lived by hunting.

He served in the Creek War as a Tennessee scout under General Andrew Jackson. He was elected a colonel in the Tennessee Militia, and to the State Legislature. David served in the Legislature in 1823, and was elected to Congress in 1827, serving three terms. He opposed President Jackson's Indian bill, which sent the eastern tribes westward and took their lands. For that, he was opposed by Jackson forces. He prided his voting independence. After losing the election in 1835, he left for Texas, announcing that "Jackson can go to hell — I am going to Texas."

Arriving at Bexar with several friends in February 1836, he was offered a command by Colonel Travis, but chose to fight and die with his fellow Tennessee sharpshooters.

His motto was: "Be sure you are right, then go ahead.*Submitted by Kenneth W. Hendricks, great-great-grandson of David and Elizabeth Crockett, #6457M*

JAMES CUNNINGHAM (1816-1894)

James Cunningham, solider and Texas Ranger, was born in Warren County, Tennessee, in 1816. In 1835, he married Susannah Tate. He served in the Alabama Mounted Militia in the Florida Indian Wars from October 23, 1837, until his discharge in 1838 at Fort Payne, Alabama. In 1839-40, he immigrated to the Republic of Texas with his wife and two small children, and obtained a land grant in what is now Morris County.

Capt. James Cunningham and Susannah Tate Cunningham

During the 1840s he moved to Bastrop, Travis, and Williamson counties. The Cunninghams moved in 1855 to a wilderness then known as the Upper Leon River Country and settled on Mountain Creek in what is now Comanche County. They were among the first families in that part of Texas, the entering wedge of Anglo-American occupation of the Plains. After coming to Texas, James and Susannah had ten more children. Five of their sons, David, William, James W., George, John, and a son-in-law, T.J. Holmsley served as Texas sheriffs.

Cunningham organized a volunteer company in June 1858 to protect the Comanche County area and reported to Governor Hardin Runnels that the company was in service and that he was elected to its command. Until the cessation of Comanche depredations, he and his sons were involved in virtually every Indian battle in or from Comanche County. In 1861, Cunningham was elected captain of a Comanche County Company of Rangers. In February, he and his men appeared at Camp Colorado in response to Confederate General Henry McCulloch's appeal for state troops to wrest that post from the United States Cavalry. Despite the general evacuation of the Northwest Texas frontier during the Civil War, the Cunninghams remained, and James served as captain of the Comanche County Company of the Second Frontier District, commanded by Maj. George B. Erath. Five of his sons also served as both officers and enlisted men. The Cunninghams participated in Indian fights at Rush Creek, Buffalo Gap, Tater Hill, Blanket Creek, Salt Mountain, Brown Creek, Cow House Creek, and Hog Creek. Captain Cunningham commanded the Comanche County Company at the Battle of Dove Creek in Tom Green County on January 8, 1865.

Cunningham operated a ranch of 9,000 acres in Comanche County until his death at his home in 1894, when he was survived by his wife and all of his twelve children. He was buried at Newburg Cemetery, Comanche County; his grave is designated with a Texas Historical Marker. His home, a Texas Historic Landmark, is the oldest residence in Comanche County.

The reunion of his and Susannah's descendants, the oldest continuous family reunion in Texas, celebrated its centennial in 1989, in recognition of which the Texas Historical Commission placed a marker on the Cunningham family reunion grounds near Newburg.

Susannah Cunningham has been recognized for her deeds in the well-known book by Annie Pickrell, "Pioneer Women in Texas." John Buford Meadows #3018 John Buford Meadows, Jr. #5549 Charles Patrick Meadows #5550 Joshua Stewart Meadows #5386 Thomas Oliver Meadows #6624 Henry Edward Meadows #6625 Daniel E. Lakenmacher #6626 John Buford Meadows III #6640

REV. GOTTLIEB BURCHARD DANGERS

Gottlieb Burchard Dangers was born on October 11, 1811, in Langeragen, Hanover, Germany. He was born to a noble family, and was raised in a life of privilege. Like most boys of the upper class, Gottlieb was well schooled in the classics, literature, and mathematics. He also studied music, and greatly admired the well known composers of the time. His artistic talents included playing the piano and composing original musical scores.

As the younger son of a nobleman, Gottlieb was unable to inherit his father's title, land, and social position. As a result, he was expected to pursue an honorable profession appropriate for a "gentleman." In 1829, he entered the University of Gottingen (Germany) where he continued his studies in the classical arts. Being a devout Christian, Gottlieb enjoyed studying religion, and became inspired to gain a greater understanding of the Bible. He was accepted into the university's divinity school, and, upon completion of his studies, was awarded a Doctorate of Divinity (D.D) degree. Soon afterward, he became an ordained minister in the Evangelical Protestant (Lutheran) religion.

Rev. Gottlieb B. Dangers (1811-1869)

Reverend Dangers was serving as a minister in the German state of Hanover when he met Mathilda Max. Mathilda was born in 1823, and like Dangers, was raised in an upper-class family. She was also well schooled in the classical arts and music. While the details on how the couple met are not known, it was most likely their faith and their love of music that brought them together. Gottlieb and Mathilda were married in Hanover, in the summer of 1845. Soon after their marriage, the Adels Vereins of Mainz (Noble Society of Mainz) commissioned Reverend Dangers to serve as pastor for the newly created German settlements in the Republic of Texas.

On October 10, 1845, Gottlieb and Mathilda Dangers boarded the ship Johan Dethard in Bremen, Germany, and began their journey to Texas. Among their possessions were a grand piano, a leather-bound Bible, hand-written musical scores, and their hope for a happy life together.

On January 12, 1846, the Johan Dethard arrived in Galveston. Here, Reverend Dangers established an open-air parish where he served as a source of spiritual inspiration, conducted religious services, and performed marriages and baptisms. The couple remained in Galveston for six weeks before moving on to the town of Indianola. In Indianola, Reverend Dangers established a congregation of 700 parishioners, where he served as pastor for the next twenty-one weeks.

In July 1846, Reverend Dangers and his wife began their eleven-week journey by ox-wagon to New Braunfels. Here, Gottlieb took a job as a day laborer since the money he had brought with him from Germany had nearly run out. In the spring of 1847, Dangers received his long-awaited salary from the Adels Vereins. He purchased a plot of land along the Guadalupe River, and established a small homestead for his family. The money allowed Reverend Dangers to give up his job as a laborer, and allowed him, once again, to concentrate on his role as pastor. On March 16, 1848, Mathilda gave birth to the couple's first child, a girl named Theodora.

In the summer of 1849, Reverend Dangers was recruited to serve as minister in the town of Fredericksburg. Travel arrangements were secured, and the Dangers family moved to Fredericksburg in November. Upon his arrival, Dangers relieved Reverend Basse as pastor of the "Vereins Kirche." It was here that Reverend Dangers established the Lutheran Church. Among his notable achievements was the creation of written church records. These records closely detail the activities conducted at the church between the years 1849 and 1869, and exist today in published form. It was also here that Reverend Dangers came to realize the true meaning behind his religious calling.

Life was difficult in Fredericksburg during these early years. To help ease the hardship felt by many of the settlers, Reverend Dangers and his wife often entertained the community by performing four-hand piano concerts. These concerts usually consisted of a compliment of familiar classical pieces, and music composed and arranged by Dangers. Reverend Dangers and Mathilda also established a children's choir for the church. These piano and choir concerts greatly contributed to improving the quality of life for the settlers of Fredericksburg.

Life, disease, and death were held in fragile balance on the frontier. During his twenty years as pastor of the Lutheran Church of Fredericksburg, Reverend Dangers married 187 couples, baptized 1,061 infants, confirmed 525 Christians, and buried 256 souls. Sadly, among the individuals receiving last rights from Pastor Dangers were four of his own children: Theodora, Minna, Mathilda, and his only son, Burchard. Historical records show that all four of the Dangers children died within five days of each other, from complications associated with diphtheria. However, two of the Dangers children survived the epidemic. They were Franziska and Augusta.

Gottlieb Burchard Dangers died on November 12, 1869, in Fredericksburg, and is buried in the Old City Cemetery. He was 58 years of age. In 1873, Franziska Dangers married Peter Kraus of Fredericksburg. The couple established a small farm (near the modern-day site of the Gillespie County Fair Grounds) and had two children: a daughter named Mathilda Ann (the former Mrs. A. B. Lange), and a son named Burchard. Sadly, Franziska died on April 29, 1889 from medical complications associated with child birth. She was 34 years of age.

After Franziska's death, life in Texas was no longer tolerable for Mathilda Max Dangers. She had lost her husband and five of her six children while residing in Fredericksburg. She felt it was time to return to Germany. She and Augusta moved to the Galveston, and planned their trip back to Hanover. However, ships destined for Germany were few and far between, and the women were delayed in their departure. During this time, Augusta met and married Mr. Sandlance, editor of The Galveston News. As a result of the marriage, Mathilda remained in Galveston, and lived with her daughter and son-in-law. In 1900, Mathilda Dangers passed away at the age of 77.

Pastor Dangers will always be remembered for his spiritual leadership, inspiration, and his willingness to serve as a pillar of strength in a community plagued with hardship. His memory was honored in 1974 with the placement of several Texas Historical Commission Medallions in and around Fredericksburg, documenting the life and times of this distinguished citizen of Texas.
Robert Tyszkowski # 4466 Great-great-grandson of Reverend G. B. Dangers and Mathilda Max

JAMES L. DANNHEIM
SRT member #6736

Jim Dannheim and his brothers, Dave Al, Bob, and Ernie, were raised primarily in Central Texas. Born in 1935, Jim grew up in the small town of Lometa, outside San Saba.

From Lometa he headed off to Texas A&M, but family circumstances did not permit him to complete his degree at that time.

James L. Danheim

A few years later, Jim settled in Houston and became involved in real estate and developing in the Houston area and at Lake Livingston. His successes eventually permitted him to take off for a few years, and he headed to Kerrville.

During high school, he had excelled in several sports, including tennis, basketball, and football, but tennis became his first love. In his forties, during his Kerrville years, he was able to devote time to the sport of tennis again and succeeded in becoming number six in the state rankings. Tennis is still his most anticipated pastime.

Presently, Jim is involved with child support enforcement in the private sector. He was one of the earliest individuals to see the need and helped to establish a company to meet that need.

Jim is proud of being a sixth-generation Texan. He is also proud of his seventh-generation Texan sons, Mike, Greg, and Eric, and their families.

JAMES ADDISON "ADD" DARBY

James Addison "Add" Darby, great-grandfather of Norman Dale Cox, was born June 11, 1829, in Clark County, Alabama. James Darby was the youngest of four sons born to Benjamin Franklin Darby and Priscilla Ezell Darby. His father died at an early age, and his mother was remarried to Stephen Williams. On October 9, 1837, William brought his new wife and her four sons to the Republic of Texas, where they settled in Washington County. In 1849, the family moved to West Point, Texas, in Fayette County.

James Addison Darby (Great Grandfather of Norman Dale Cox)

In October 1861, Darby joined the Confederate forces and served as a first lieutenant in Colonel Green's Brigade, Company 1, Fifth Regiment, Texas Mounted Volunteers, C.S.A. He was captured by Union forces in 1862, and it is believed that his capture occurred on the New Mexico Campaign. The object of this expedition had been to take and garrison New Mexico and then go on to California. Company 1, organized in LaGrange, Texas, under Captain I. G. Killough, was composed primarily of young men and numbered about 72. The company marched to San Antonio, where they were mustered into the Confederate service and attached to Col. Tom Green's Regiment. The soldiers went through cavalry drill in Camp Manassas near San Antonio for about six weeks. From there, they took up their line of march for Fort Bliss, new El Paso (about 650 miles), and arrived there about the 20th of December 1861. In January, they proceeded up the Rio Grande River to Fort Thorne, where they remained some time recruiting their horses and getting ready for the march to Fort Craig, where they expected to meet the enemy in battle. They came in sight of the fort on February 18. Several battles ensued, and it is thought that Add Darby was captured during one of these.

The campaign underwent indescribable hardships, and in April 1861, a council of war agreed that to avoid further bloodshed, they would abandon the territory and the troops returned to San Antonio. Darby was held in federal prisons until the end of the war. On June 13, 1862, war records show that he was at Fort Riley, but later he was moved to Johnson's Island, Sandusky, Ohio. On February 15, 1865, he was named as one of the prisoners of war who was sent first to New York and ultimately to New Orleans for prisoner exchange.

After returning to West Point, Darby built one of the earliest cotton gins in the area, opened a general mercantile store, and completed several cattle drives to the Kansas railroad. In the early 1890s, when the M.K.& T. Railroad became available, he cut and shipped cordwood by rail. In 1902, he joined with several other businessmen and formed a cannery. Vegetables were raised locally, canned, and distributed to points all over the United States.

Darby married Melissa Frances Hart on October 3, 1869, at Winchester, Fayette County, Texas. His wife died in 1882 during the birth of their only child, Middie Darby. He never remarried, but provided a good home for his daughter as well as for several children of relatives. He died February 22, 1904, and is buried in Woods Prairie Cemetery near West Point.

In 1905, Middie Darby married James Washington Moore, the son of William Cannon Moore. The Moores had five children: Sue Moore Ehlers, Darby Moore Prastik, James Addison Moore, William Cannon Moore, and Middie Moore Cox, the mother of Norman Dale Cox.

SOCRATES DARLING

Socrates Darling was born in Leyden, Massachusetts, on April 24, 1806. He married Julia Ann Woodward in 1823, and arrived in Texas in December, 1834. Until his death thirty-six years later, he distinguished himself as a "Texian" volunteer citizen soldier in pivotal battles of the Texas Revolution, an Indian fighter, a public servant, and a farmer in Fayette County.

Perhaps Socrates was inspired to "get involved" in Texas' battle for independence by the example of his forebears — grandfather, William, and great-great-grandfather, Dennis Darling. William served as a second lieutenant in the Massachusetts 5th, Continental Amy. Dennis lost his home when Wampanoag Indians ravaged Mendon, Massachusetts, during King Philip's War (1675-1678).

Socrates first saw action with Captain Michael Goheen's Company in defeating General Cos at San Antonio de Bexar, December 5-12, 1835. After the fall of the Alamo and the murder of Fannin's force at Goliad in March, 1836, Socrates was among fifty Fayette County men in Captain James Gillaspie's 6th Company, Infantry, 2nd Regiment, Texas Volunteers, when Houston's army defeated Santa Anna at San Jacinto and won Texas' independence on April 21, 1836.

The war won, Socrates Darling was among those who settled in LaGrange after the "Runaway Scrape" within two years of the town's founding. In February 1839, after Comanche Indians attacked Victoria and Linnville, Socrates was with 55 LaGrange volunteers in Colonel John H. Moore's force, which engaged the Comanches on the San Saba River. In September 1840, he was again in Colonel Moore's unit when it attacked and overcame a Comanche encampment on the upper Colorado.

Socrates was elected the first coroner of Fayette County in 1840. Having lost his first wife, he married Mrs. Laurena Jones Lester in LaGrange on February 9, 1845. They had six children.

In 1852, Socrates conveyed 320 acres of the Bastrop County land granted him for service to the Republic, to Baylor University at Independence.

The Darlings moved to Jeddo in 1853. They both died there in 1870 and are buried in the Hallmark Cemetery. Socrates' grave bears a DRT marker honoring his service to the Republic.

Socrates Darling's great-grandsons – fifth-, sixth-, and seventh-generation Texans — are proud of the role be played in helping establish our great state and will always cherish his memory. Jack

Elliott Darling 44933 William Charles Darling #4942 William Charles Darling, Jr. 46634M John Thomas Darling #6635M Kyle David Wilson #4943

ELIJAH P. DECROW

Elijah P. DeCrow was born in Ducktrap, Maine, on February 21, 1799, in a house built by his father, Daniel DeCrow, just prior to his birth. This house still stands and is located on U.S Highway No. 1. His father, Daniel, Sr., was born in Massachusetts on November 17, 1758, and his mother Azubah Gay, was born in Massachusetts on October 19, 1765. From this marriage there were ten children. The names of these children, along with their time and date of births, is in a Bible found in the attic of the old house in Ducktrap, and is the property of the present owner of the home.

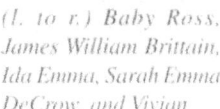

(l. to r.) Baby Ross, James William Brittain, Ida Emma, Sarah Emma DeCrow, and Vivian

Elijah P. DeCrow

The oldest son, Daniel, Jr. Migrated to Texas and was part of Stephen F. Austin's "Old Three Hundred" Colony. He was followed by brothers Thomas, Howard, and Elijah. Part of their land was on the southern tip of Matagorda Peninsula. At DeCrows Point, Elijah had the town site of Port Cavallo surveyed. He and his brother, Thomas, built wharves, warehouses, houses, stores, and sold lots. All of the brothers were men of the sea and served as pilots and boat captains. They also raised cattle, and at one time one of the four brothers was noted for having the largest cattle ranch in the area. The brand of Thomas and Elijah was registered on August 5, 1837 in Matagorda Book A, Page 187.

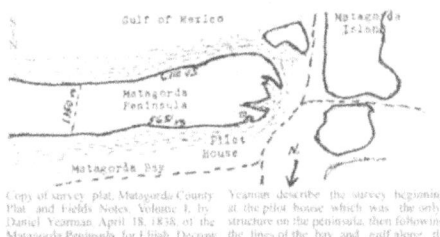

Survey of Port Cavallo requested to be done by Elijah DeCrow in 1838

The townsite of Port Cavallo, along with Thomas's family, were destroyed during the hurricane of 1875. Before the hurricane struck, Elijah, with his new bride, Helen Nellie Givens, moved to Rockport, Texas. Helen Nellie was from Kentucky and was the great-niece of Kentucky Governor John Crittenden. Elijah and Helen Nellie had two children: Sarah Emma, who was the first Anglo-Saxon girl born in Rockport; and Royal.

Charles D. Adams, Jr.

Thomas & Elijah DeCrow 1837 Matagorda Co. Brands

Elijah continued to participate in cattle drives. He died on one of these drives and is buried in an unmarked grave. After Elijah's death, Helen lived with her son, who owned the Fulton Packing Co. in Rockport. Helen Nellie and Sarah are buried in a cemetery in Rockport, Texas. Sarah Emma married James Brittain and had: Ida Emma, Vivian, Ross and Helen.

Ida Emma married Charley Adams, Sr., who was manager of an onion farm in Crestonia, Texas, where she was a teacher. Four children were born: Emma Lee, Katie, Vivian and Charles, Jr. Charley and Ida are buried in Pearsall, Texas, Cemetery. Charles Adams, Jr., #5893 A Charles Adams, III, #5894 A Charles Adams, IV, #5892 A

CHARLES DEMOSS

Charles DeMoss, born circa 1776 in Virginia, and his wife, Martha, lived in Ohio when their first son, Peter, was born in 1796. Seven more children were born in Missouri. They raised corn, flax, and hemp in Cape Girardeau on 640 acres acquired for $41.00 from Spain to induce settlers to populate the upper Louisiana Territory. Pioneers Charles and Peter moved their families to another wild frontier in 1824, when Stephen F. Austin formed a group to colonize Mexico. They were in the first group called Austin's "Old 300." Original Spanish land grants record each received one league of land (4,428.4 acres) in what is now Matagorda County, Texas. Grants also say Stephen F. Austin took each of them by the hand and led them to their tracts, where upon they shouted, pulled grass, and threw stones to celebrate. Charles died there just two years later.

Although Charles and Martha died December 18, 1826, their eight children and numerous grandchildren played an active role in the defense and development of the Republic of Texas. All their sons were veterans of the Texas Revolution. William and Lewis survived the Goliad Massacre when Colonel Fannin sent Horton's Calvary to scout a creek crossing. They united with General Houston's troops at Victoria. Peter and Lewis were judges in Matagorda County. Peter's family is found in "Forerunners of Baylor."

Peter married Susannah Bays; Sarah married Joseph Throckmorton; John married Rebecca Stagner; Lewis married Catherine Tumlinson; William married Susan Williams, whose father, Solomon Williams, was also an Old 300 colonist; Loraharney married Henry Bays; Martha married Caleb Bostic, Thomas Adams, and J.H. Brasher; Elizabeth married Thomas J. Williams.

In the struggle to make Texas a Republic, these brave families endured Indian attacks, catastrophic weather, famine, and myriads other frontier hardships. Charles Fannin DeMoss, III, #5510

CHARLES FANNIN DEMOSS, III

Charles Fannin DeMoss, III, was born November 21, 1932, in Houston, Texas. His parents were Charles Fannin DeMoss, also a native Houstonian, and Pauline Briley DeMoss, born in Nacogdoches County, Texas. He married Cora Sue Rogers, a Houston native, in 1951. They had two sons, Randall Paul DeMoss, and Layne Charles DeMoss, who married Rebecca Sue Long; and two grandsons, Layne Charles DeMoss and Marshall Ray DeMoss.

Charles Fannin DeMoss, III#5510

In 1972, Charles moved his family to Conroe, Texas, where he currently resides. He worked in construction and at Hughes Tool after graduating from Milby High School. His career in the Houston Fire Department began in 1958. Retiring in 2000, after 42 years, he had served 2-1/2 years as assistant chief of the department, and was currently deputy chief/shift commander.

His ancestor, Charles DeMoss, came to Texas in 1824 with Stephen F. Austin's first 300 settlers. All Charles's sons fought in the Texas Revolution. Charles's son, William, is the great-great-grandfather of Charles, III. William and his brother, Lewis, survived the Goliad Massacre.

He is a life member of the SRT, a member of descendants of Austin's "Old 300," and proud of Texas and of those whose courage and sacrifices made it great. Charles Fannin DeMoss, III, #5510

JOHN DENSON

John Denson (1815 Anson Co., NC-1860s Houston Co., TX) came to Texas in 1835 with his parents, Thomas C. and Polly Denson, grandfather Shadrach Denson, and seven siblings. Thomas C. Denson's petition for entry was "accepted in Vehlein" in September 1835. John and his family also joined the Predestination Baptist Church, founded by Reverend Daniel Parker in September 1835. Parker's 9-year-old granddaughter, Cynthia Ann, was taken captive at Fort Parker near Groesbeck in May 1836. She remained with the Comanches 25 years, and her son, Quanah, was the last Comanche chief.

John's brother, O'Conner Denson (1813-1869) served in Captain Henry Reed's Company during the Texas Revolution. In October 1836, 21-year-old John and his grandfather empowered Daniel Parker to locate and survey a one-third league land grant for them along San Pedro Creek, a tributary of the Neches River. In April 1837, three generations of Densons (John, Thomas C., and Shadrach) signed a petition to create Houston County.

In 1839, John C. Denson married a young widow, Mary Ann Crawford Houston (1817 Rowan Co., NC,-1870s Houston Co., TX). Mary came to Texas from Tennessee with her infant daughter, Caroline, and parents (Joseph and Polly Cauble Crawford) to join her first husband, A. Houston. Upon arriving, Mary Ann learned her husband, who was a relative of General Sam Houston, had been slain near Dawson with 16 others in the famous Surveyors Indian Fight against a band of over 150 Kickapoos in October 1838.

John Denson built a fortified log house for protection against Indian attack. Ruins of their axe-hewn home are still visible today. An official Texas Historical Marker is being erected on FM-227 showing the location of his log home 3 miles east of Grapeland and detailing his role in the creation and settlement of Houston County.

John and Mary Ann Denson had two sons and five daughters. Their youngest daughter, Nancy Jane, married a young Confederate veteran, George A. Brimberry, in 1869. George and Nancy were this writer's great-grandparents. Mary Ann's daughter, Caroline Houston, married John's younger brother, Joseph Denson. They also raised a large family and lived out their lives in Houston County.

John C. died during the 1860s, and his wife died between 1872-1879. They are buried in a small family cemetery John established near their home.

This writer also has three other Texas patriot ancestors. Samuel Brimberry (1785 Alamance Co., NC - 1837 Nacogdoches Co., TX) appears on the 1835 Census Roll for Nacogdoches. A lieutenant during the War of 1812 and captain during the Blackhawk Indian War, Samuel "donated guns, a wagon and provisions" to the Republic in 1836, for which his heirs received a league and a labor of land. Samuel Brimberry's brothers-in-law, Joseph P. Jones and Enoch M. Jones, were also slain during the Surveyors Indian Fight. Joseph P. Jones was married to Sara Brimberry.

A collateral ancestor, Michael Ellis "fell with Fannin at Goliad." The son of Hannah and Benjamin Ellis, Jr., Michael was unmarried when he sacrificed his life for the cause of Texas independence. His family also settled in Houston County and received a league and a labor for his service.

A third ancestor, James Hall Moore (1818 Huntsville, AL-1894 Lovelady, TX) also came to Texas when it was a Republic. During the Civil War, he served in Company B, 23rd Regiment, Texas Cavalry. He married Louisa Lemanda Ellis (1829 AL-1867 Houston Co. TX) in 1844 in Houston County. She was the daughter of John Irving Ellis and Elizabeth Ann Goolsby, and a niece of Michael Ellis, who "fell with Fannin at Goliad." Jerry L. Brimberry

Private James Hall Moore

Mary Ann Crawford Houston Denson, wife of John Denson

SIMON DERRICK II

Simon Derrick II, my great-great-grandfather, was born in 1770, Shenandoah County, Virginia, the son of Jacob and grandson of Simon Derk (1) and Catharina Margaretha Stapleton. He was of sturdy German stock, common, hard working, frontiersmen. He made no name for himself, had no education, but he was an experienced "trail blazer." No matter adverse circumstances, he was never too old to start a new life on the frontier. No credit is given them in history books, but it was his type who helped shape the direction this country was to move.

Jacob was baptized on May 17, 1752, in Berks County, Pennsylvania, and moved to Virginia by 1769. While Simon was a boy, Jacob moved to Sevier County, Tennessee, settling at Bird's Crossing, where he established a fort which bears a Tennessee Historical Marker.

Simon moved to Anderson County, Tennessee, and married Lydia Tipton about 1806. Two sons — Caswell B. and William B. were born there before moving to Mississippi Territory, Madison County, where Vincent, my ancestor was born in 1812. Other children were Jefferson J., Washington, and Nancy Ann, who married Thomas F. McBroom.

In 1813, Simon enlisted in the War of 1812, Mississippi Militia, Madison County. He received land grants in Alabama, where Lydia died about 1836, and he signed deed to trustee for his last land in Alabama to be sold to clear debts.

In 1839, at the age of sixty-nine and bankrupt, he began his trek to a new country, the Republic of Texas, to seek his fortune. Many of the family were in the trading and freighting business, and it seems likely that Simon may have been on the trail west as early as the 1820s. Two Derrick stones in Lee Cemetery, Lamar County, Texas, are inscribed with 1831 as the year of death. The monuments were placed there in 1908 by some of Simon's family, who must have known they died in the area.

Simon was in Red River County, Texas, 1839, where he witnessed a deed. Twenty-five days earlier he signed his last deed in Madison County, Alabama. To make that trip so quickly, he had to travel light, probably by horseback, with few companions, and not on the normal trails.

In 1840, he was in Sevier County, Arkansas, and he filed application for a land grant in Titus County, Texas, 1841, a single man, entitled to 320 acres.

At age 74, he built nine miles of the National Road. November 9, 1844, Commissioners certified that, "Simon Derrick was entitled to 999 acres of land for the cutting, opening and hedging nine miles of same National Road at one hundred & eleven acres of land per mile," which Sam Houston had approved. The 999 acres was in Hopkins County, and he bought rights to 960 acres adjoining it.

In 1850, he was in Lamar County. At the age of 90, he was granted his last claim in Lamar County. All but one of his children followed him to Texas. He was in Coryell County with Vincent in 1860, his occupation listed as a herdsman.

When he died, he owned land in Lamar County, and property in Paris, bought in 1854. "History of Lamar County," by Neville, mentions Harland & Diercks, who had a tannery near town, and were making leather for saddles, harnesses, and shoes.

Simon's will was filed for probate in Lamar County, December of 1867. Many family members are buried in Lee Cemetery near his land. No grave has been found for him, but Lee Cemetery seemed the most appropriate location to place a memorial to Simon Derrick. It was erected in September 1999, commemorating his service in the War of 1812, and also bears a Sons of the Republic Medallion. Nearly one hundred fifty years after his death, his legacy has finally been preserved.

(1) Simon Derk arrived on ship, St. Andrew, at the port of Philadelphia on October 27, 1738. Will of Simon Derk, signed 1785 in Shenandoah, Virginia, states payment was to be made to his "two grandsons, sons of Jacob Derk (Viz) Simon Derk & Tobias Derk each the sum of five pounds . . .." E. George Caddel, great-great-grandson of Simon Derrick II

ELIZABETH MENEFEE DEVERS

Elizabeth was born in Knox County, Tennessee, on June 5, 1777. About 1818, Elizabeth and her mother, father, sisters, and brothers moved to Morgan County, Alabama, near Decatur. Before moving to Morgan County, while in Knox County, Tennessee, Elizabeth married James Devers on January 1, 1802. James Devers died on March 27, 1829, in Morgan County, Alabama, before the Alabama settlement moved to Texas in 1830-1831. Elizabeth and James Devers had eight children; however, two died before moving to Texas in 1831. Elizabeth never remarried.

Elizabeth, her mother, Frances Rhodes Menefee, her brothers, and six of her children came to Texas in February, 1831. They came down the Tennessee River to the Mississippi River, and then the Mississippi to New Orleans, where they boarded the Emblem, arriving at the head of Lavaca Bay on February, 12, 1831. These early settlers settled in what is now Jackson County and established the town of Texana at the mouth of the Navidad River. On May 16, 1831, Elizabeth Menefee Devers petitioned the State of Coahuila for a Spanish Land Grant of 4,428 acres in Fayette County, and was awarded the same on June 21, 1831. Elizabeth Menefee Devers died in Jackson County on June 7, 1845. Elizabeth's brother, William Menefee, was a signer of the Texas Declaration of Independence.

Elizabeth's oldest living son, James Henry Devers, born December 29, 1812, was issued a Bounty Grant of 320 acres in June 26, 1838, for service in the Texas Army. On July 17, 1835, James Devers was in Assembly of the Lavaca-Navidad meeting at Milligan's Gin. This meeting is considered "Texas First Declaration of Independence," declared on Jackson County soil. In 1882, James donated 50 acres of land for the present townsite of Ganado in Jackson County. James Devers, my great-grandfather, was born in Knox County, Tennessee, and died in Jackson County, Texas, August 12, 1887. Travis Gerald Dixson #3790 Bryan Douglas Dixson #5196 S.

ELIZABETH "BET" DICKEY

Elizabeth "Bet" Dickey, the first of Moses and Melvina Dickey's children, was born June 29, 1835, in Tennessee. She died December 14, 1924, in Cherokee County and is buried in Mixon Cemetery.

Elizabeth Dickey Dew Swindell

Elizabeth was an infant during her parents' journey from Tennessee to Texas. A story of tradition is that Indians attacked their train of wagons along the trail, and that she was hidden by her parents until the skirmish was over.

Elizabeth married first October 23, 1851, in Cherokee County, William A. Dew, born 1833 in Tennessee. He was killed in 1862 during the Civil War in battle at Pleasant Hill, Louisiana. William A. Dew served in the Army of the Confederacy as 3rd lieutenant in Company C of the 11th Texas Infantry of Col. O.M. Roberts' regiment, organized at Knoxville, Texas, August 1862.

Elizabeth and William A. Dew had five children, all born in Cherokee County Prof. William Bradford Bugg, Life Member

MOSES D. DICKEY

Moses D. Dickey was born in 1804 in Rutherford County, North Carolina, and died about 1870 in Cherokee County, Texas. In about 1833, he married Melvina D. Clark, who was born in June 1814, in Tennessee, and died about 1900 in Cherokee County. Moses and Melvina are buried in Fitch Family Cemetery, formerly known as Community Family Cemetery, near Blackjack in Cherokee County.

Moses and Melvina came from Tennessee to San Augustine County, Texas, prior to December 1835.

Elray Bugg   *Mary Katherine Ayres*

In 1836, the Republic of Texas declared its independence from Mexico, and Moses served in the Texas Army from July until October 1836. Moses Dickey received a Bounty Land Warrant for three hundred and twenty acres for his army service. He also received a Headright Certificate from the Republic of Texas for free land, after proving he was a married man and had arrived before the Declaration of Independence. The parcel of land from the Republic of Texas Headright contained over four thousand acres and was located in Johnson and Tarrant counties. Some of the records of San Augustine County indicate that he sold the Headright land.

In the Texas Census of 1840, Moses Dickey was a resident of San Augustine County, where he owned eleven acres of land with clear title.

From Volume A of the Minutes of the District Court of San Augustine County, dated January Term 1839, Moses Dickey was summoned by the sheriff as one of the thirty six talesmen for the purpose of trying Antonio Manchacca and others imprisoned upon the charge of high treason. Moses was challenged for cause, and the sheriff was ordered by the court to find another talesman to replace him. It is believed that Moses Dickey was challenged for cause because he had served in the Texas Army during the war to gain independence from Mexico.

In the U.S. Population Census of 1850, the Dickey Family was living in Cherokee County, and Moses is listed as a farmer who owned real estate valued at six hundred and fifty dollars. In an 1853 deed record of the county, Moses Dickey received three hundred acres more or less, of land as a gift from his lawful cousin, Robert G. Stadler. The land was located in the Blackjack area of the county. In 1859, Moses sold land in Cherokee County to James S. Upchurch.

When the 1860 census was taken, Moses and Melvina Dickey are believed to have been residents of Tarrant County. There are no 1860 Census Records in existence today for Tarrant County; however, a Moses Dickey is found among deed records of the county about that time.

William Bradford Bugg

In June 1861, Moses Dickey enlisted to serve in a company of Home Guards (Minutemen), which was organized under the Act of Legislature for frontier protection. While in this service, a report filed December 18, 1861, said he killed two Indians and recovered two horses.

During the Civil War, Moses D. Dickey, age fifty-seven, enlisted April 7, 1862, at Dallas. He served in the Army of the Confederacy in Captain John D. Waller's Company D, 31st Regiment Texas Cavalry.

During the 1870s, Melvina Dickey and several of the Dickey children were living in Cherokee County. Among the deed records of Cherokee County in 1874, Melvina as administrator for Moses D. Dickey, deceased, settled a three hundred and twenty acre land purchase made by Moses from O.M. Wheeler for nine hundred dollars. Moses did not pay for the land, so Wheeler sold it to Mary B. Bell, then she sold the land to D.D. Fox. In later years, Robert James Dickey, a grandson of Moses, owned farms very near, if not next to the Fox property. In that vicinity today flows a little stream named Dickey Branch. Only recently, Carl McElroy, a great-great-great-grandson of Moses Dickey, purchased land that is believed to have formerly belonged to his great-great-grandfather, Robert James Dickey.

Melvina D. Dickey was left alone January 7, 1893, when her youngest son, Moses F. "Captain" Dickey was killed when a team of horses ran away with the wagon in which he and his mother were riding. The accident happened a few miles south of Jacksonville. Moses F. was thrown from the wagon, and one of the wheels passed over his body, fatally injuring him. Melvina was thrown to the floor of the wagon and escaped serious injury.

At age eighty-one in 1900, Melvina was living with Elizabeth and Ben Swindell, her daughter and son-in-law.

Over one hundred and fifty years ago, Moses and Melvina Dickey arrived in the wilderness named Texas. They were among the pioneers who lived here when Texas belonged to Mexico, when it was a county known as the Republic of Texas, and when it became one of the United States of America.

Moses and Melvina Dickey had eleven children, all born in Texas, except Elizabeth "Bet," who was born in Tennessee. *Submitted by Prof. William Bradford Bugg - Life Member.*

DICKINSON, BOWMER & SKELTON FAMILY

Amos Dickinson was born 1770, Oyster Bay, Long Island, New York. His will, probated 21 August 1838, named his son, Dr. Samuel Burling Dickinson, and his grandson, Preston Dickinson, Columbia, Texas.

Dr. Samuel Burling Dickinson, born 23 Sept. 1804, Beekman, NY, received his certificate from Fairfield Medical School, Herkimer, NY, in 1829. He went to Natchez, Mississippi, and began his medical practice. He married Caroline Elizabeth Kinnison, 4 June 1835, Jefferson Co. Caroline was the daughter of Nathaniel Kinnison, Jr., plantation owner, Homochitto River.

Caroline E. Dickinson grave marker.

December 9, 1835, Dr. S.B. Dickinson and fourteen Texas Volunteers boarded schooner *Santiago* in New Orleans, bound for Brazoria, Texas. They signed a pact to defend Texas at the peril of their lives, liberties, and fortunes.

They arrived at Velasco, Texas, 23 December 1835. People were excited because a "real" doctor had landed. Texas Commissioners, Stephen F. Austin, W.H. Wharton, and Dr. B.D. Archer met Dr. Dickinson and his friend J.M. Wolfe, and asked them to return to New York and recruit supplies, settlers, and money for Texas. They met Stephen F. Austin and Dr. B.D. Archer in New York.

Dr. Dickinson, Caroline, and son, Preston, (my great-grandfather) settled on 640 acres in Brazoria County October 1836. In 1840, they moved to Austin County next to Groce's Landing. About 1842, they moved to Marshall, Texas. He bought nine original city lots next to the Court House.

He was a founder of the Masonic Lodge. He went to Washington-on-the-Brazos for the Charter. He was the first Master of the Lodge.

They moved in 1847 from Marshall to Sweet Home, Lavaca County, Texas, on 400 acres. He ranched, and practiced medicine. His medical ledger is very interesting.

In 1860, he and Caroline Elizabeth purchased a 510 acre farm at Terryville, south of Yoakum, Texas. They had 11 Methodist children, and owned a large acreage of ranch land.

Dr. S.B. Dickinson died 9 November 1881, at Terryville. He is buried at Hebron Cemetery beside his son, Preston Dickinson, CSA, and brother-in-law, Milton Virgil Kinnison, CSA. Caroline Elizabeth died 29 April 1926, (107 years old). She is buried at County Line Cemetery with her sons, daughters, and their families. All were Texas pioneer children, and direct descendants of John and Elizabeth Howland, pilgrims who landed at Plymouth, MA, in 1620 on the Mayflower.

Jim D. Bowmer, #1315, and Senior Federal Judge Byron Skelton, U.S. Special Appeals Court, Washington, D.C., both residents of Salado, Texas, are great-grandsons of Dr. S.B. Dickinson. *Submitted by Howard Skelton*

JOSEPH DILLARD

Joseph Dillard was born December 16, 1792 in Cooper County, Missouri. He married Susan Beason (August 3, 1797) in Cooper County, Mo., on December 1, 1814. Records in the General Land Office of the State of Texas certify that Joseph Dillard "emigrated with his family to Texas in the year Eighteen Hundred and Thirty Four that he died before the date of the declaration of Independence — but that his family has remained in the Country ever Since."

Joseph Dillard died in Washington County in 1835 in the winter. However, he had been granted "One league and One labor of land" in Gonzales County. In 1836, in the "Runaway Scrape," Susan Beason Dillard took her children Daniel Boone Dillard, Abraham, Eliza A., Jacob W., Henry, William, and M. Jane and went back to Missouri and stayed there until after the Battle of San Jacinto. She then returned to Texas and later married William Burnett.

Joseph and Susan's oldest son, Daniel Boone Dillard, was born in Missouri January 21, 1819. He married Nancy Avant Forrester (March 20, 1827) in 1856. He died April 5, 1877, in Wrightsboro, Texas, the village nearest the old "League and Labor." Their children were Fannie Avant, Nathan, Louisa, Joseph, Eliza, and Priscilla.

Fannie Avant (Aught) Dillard married Francis Marion Buchanan June 18, 1874, in Gonzales County, Texas. They had fourteen children, twelve of whom lived to adulthood. They were Edward Boone Buchanan, Joe Simpson, William Nathan, Henry Lee, Ella Bell, James Melvin, Lela Ann (my grandmother), Maude Grace, Aus Lilly, Hattie Loy, Charles Courtney, Louie Dillard, Morgan, and Polly Wilma. Fannie Dillard Buchanan died February 9, 1952, in Wrightsboro, Texas.

Lela Ann Buchanan married Samuel Cornelius Bozarth February 8, 1908, in Gonzales, Texas. Lela Ann, nicknamed Sally, and Sam Bozarth had five children, one of whom (Haskell Buchanan Bozarth) died in infancy. The other children were Nathan Brown Bozarth, Terrell Hollis Bozarth, Hazel Joy Bozarth, and Marion Cornelius Bozarth. Lela Ann Bozarth died July 30, 1970, in Lockhart, Texas.

The second son of Lela Ann and Sam Bozarth, Terrell Hollis Bozarth, married Eleanor Louise Sanders January 3, 1942, in Lockhart, Texas. They had one son. I am that son. Terrell Hollis Bozarth died June 29, 1992 in Lockhart, Texas. Eleanor Louise Sanders died August 28, 1998 also in Lockhart, Texas.

I am married to the former Cynthia Jane Barnard of Brownsville. I have two sons by a former marriage to Mary Margaret Cameron of Brownsville. They are William Terrell Bozarth, born March 27, 1971, in Bucks County, Pennsylvania, and Thomas Callihan Bozarth, born August 6, 1974, in

Brownsville, Texas. I have two step-children, Jennifer Lynne Cox and Michael Alec Cox.

I am the minister of the First Presbyterian Churches of Lockhart and Luling, Texas. Other of my relatives descended from Joseph and Susan Dillard still live in the Gonzales area. Rev. Dr. John Terrell "Terry" Bozarth #3985

WILLIAM DUNBAR

William Dunbar is listed in Texas Army records, which show that there was a Pvt. William Dunbar in Co. B at San Jacinto, April 21, 1836, in Capt. R(ichard) Roman's Company, per Texas State Archives. It said William Dunbar served in the Texas Army for six months ending July 24, 1836, per the paymaster for the Texas Volunteers, meaning he joined the army January 24, 1836.

He joined what later became known as the Mier Expedition when it formed at La Grange in the fall of 1842. He was at the Battle of Mier on the Rio Grande on Christmas Day 1842. He was captured and all of the P.O.W. lists show William Dunbar of Bastrop.

Marker of William Dunbar (1819-1855)

William, along with 177 others, escaped and was recaptured. In an effort to punish and prevent any further escape, 178 beans were placed in a clay jar —17 of them black. The escapees were forced to draw a bean. The 17 who drew black beans were lined up and shot. William drew white and was taken on to the prison in Perote, Mexico.

William was freed as a result of U.S. efforts on behalf of the Perote prisoners. He was released September 16, 1844, and walked to Vera Cruz, Mexico, where he obtained passage on the schooner Creole, bound for New Orleans. The Creole arrived in New Orleans on October 5, 1844. From New Orleans, William made his way back to Bastrop, where he is found in General Land Office records, obtaining land.

The next record of William Dunbar is in the summer of 1847 in Stewart County, Tennessee, settling his father's estate. While in Stewart County, William met Nancy Rowlett and they were married August 1, 1847. Sometime after October, 1847, William sold his horse and bought a buggy, and with his new bride headed to Texas and Bastrop. October 25, 1848, a son was born, named John Samuel, and August 6, 1851, a daughter, Sarah Arena was born.

William and Nancy set up housekeeping in a cabin near the base hospital on what is now Camp Swift, between Bastrop and Elgin. They lived at that cabin until William was elected county clerk of Bastrop County in 1850. He bought a place about six blocks east of the present courthouse and moved Nancy and little Sam to town. He served as county clerk of Bastrop from his election until his death December 20, 1855.

William Dunbar was 16 when he left home, 17 when he arrived in Texas. He was six days short of his 24th birthday when he was captured at Mier. He was 25 years old when he was released from Perote Prison in Mexico. He was 28 when he married Nancy Rowlett; she was 16 years old. He was 31 when he was elected county clerk and he was 11 days short of his 37th birthday when he died.

John Thomas Lawhon, Jason Scott Dunbar, Kevin James Dunbar, O. Scott Dunbar KSJ past President General Andrew Young Lewis

ALEXANDER DUNLAVY

Alexander Dunlavy, born March 11, 1818, in Virginia, arrived in Texas from Meridianville, Alabama, with his parents, John and Johannah Dunlavy and nine brothers and sisters, around March 1, 1833. His father died a month after the family's Austin Colony arrival.

High tensions and frequent skirmishes arose between the Mexican government and the Texians. Alexander volunteered on October 1, 1835, as a member of Austin's Army in Captain John York's Company. When Austin relinquished his command, Alexander became part of Colonel Ed Burleson's Regiment. Ben Milam asked for volunteers to fight the Mexicans in San Antonio. Alexander and his brother, William Thomas Dunlavy, were two of the volunteers who formed the attack upon San Antonio de Bexar. On December 5, 1835, Alexander helped capture the house of La Garza. While serving in this siege, he lost his black horse. Alexander was discharged by a partial disbandment of the army on December 20, 1835.

After Texas's 1836 Independence Declaration, Alexander served as a corporal in B.F. Ravel's Company from July 1, 1836, to October 1, 1836. For his Republic of Texas Army service, Alexander was awarded a bounty and a donation land grant.

Alexander married Elizabeth Suggs on October 6, 1841, in Colorado County. He farmed and became a San Bernardo Postmaster. About that time, Santa Anna refused to let the war die. Alexander, once again, volunteered to help repel the Mexican invasion and served as a private under General Burleson in 1842.

Alexander and his wife, Elizabeth, had one son, Henry Franklin Dunlavy, born July 31, 1845. Alexander continued with public service responsibilities. On August 4, 1856, he was elected as Colorado County Tax Assessor and Collector. In the years 1862, 1864 and 1866, he was elected to the office of Colorado County Commissioner. During Reconstruction after the Civil War, most of the elected officials, including Alexander, were ousted and replaced.

In the 1860s, Alexander's first wife died. On March 2, 1869, Alexander married Illione C. Mayward and lived in Alleyton. As a surveyor, Alexander wrote and submitted several newspaper articles to the local Columbus paper, The Colorado Citizen. Part of one article, published on June 22, 1877, was even used by T.R. Fehrenbach in his book, "Lone Star."

After an illustrious life of service to his country, county and state, Alexander died in Colorado County on October 27, 1877. Submitted by Robert Vernon Dunlavy Sam Houston Chapter #38

HENRY EARTHMAN

The head of the Earthman clan was Isaac Earthman, a native of Germany. He immigrated to America circa 1740. He had a son, Isaac Jr., who was born in Bucks County, Pennsylvania, in 1749, and later fought in the Revolutionary War. Isaac Jr. had ten children including Isaac Earthman III.

Isaac III and his brother, Lewis, moved to Texas as part of Robertson Colony. The stay of Isaac and Lewis was very short, and they returned to Tennessee in 1828, where they both died, Isaac in 1834.

In 1833, a third brother, Henry, came to Texas with his wife, Tabitha Trammel, and their children. Henry Earthman became a very successful farmer and landowner with property in both Fayette and Gonzales counties. From his log house located eight miles from La Grange, he welcomed his doors to many weary travelers, who could always find food and shelter.

Unfortunately one of his sons, also named Henry, became the last victim to Indian cruelty in Fayette County. In September of 1840, young Henry and brother, Fields, were hunting horses near the Ledbetter Road, at a place now occupied by Matejowsky's store. Indians of the Waco tribe were hiding in a nearby tree. They shot Henry to death, but Fields managed to escape. The Indians then cut off both Henry's hands and the lower part of his heart. Students from nearby Rutersville College searched in vain for the murderers. Fields was soon afflicted with total blindness, which was thought to be caused by the terrible effect of his escape and the killing of his brother.

The elder Henry Earthman died in 1862 at age 90, and is buried in Fayette County. Another son, Isaac Young Earthman (1832-1906), was married to Sarah Mitchell (1841-1899). Isaac served his state during the Civil War. He enlisted at Columbus and joined Captain Wm. G. Webb's Company H, Waller Regiment, Cavalry Unit C.S.A. He and Sarah are buried in Taylor.

One of Isaac Young's sons, James Bradshaw Earthman (1864-1931), was born in Round Top. Through the generations, James' descendants have distinguished themselves in the fields of business, medicine, architecture, law and politics. J.B. Earthman

NICHOLAS WASHINGTON EASTLAND

Nicholas Washington Eastland was born 03 April 1803, at the home of his grandparents, Nicholas Mosby and Susanna Hobson, in Woodford County, Kentucky. His parents were Thomas Butler Eastland and Nancy Mosby.

Nicholas married Frances Bates Moore, daughter of Robert Moore and Ann L. ? 1823 October 1823 in Smith County, Tennessee. Frances died in 1849 in Bastrop County, Texas. In 1834, Nicholas, Frances, and their three surviving children migrated to Fayette County, Texas, where they lived for several years, eventually settling in Bastrop County, Texas, on their plantation, "Paradise". They had seven children.

While in Fayette County, Nicholas participated in several Indian skirmishes under Colonel John H. Moore, his first cousin. He served under Albert C. Horton in the Texas Revolution and was at Goliad with James Fannin the night before Goliad fell. He was a friend and former roommate of Fannin's at West Point.

In 1864, while a member of the 10th Texas Legislature, Nicholas met and married Nancy Harrington Lee, and they had six children.

Nicholas lost a son, Charles Cooper Eastland, in the Mexican war. He also lost a son, Robert Moore Eastland, and his first cousin, Nicholas Dawson, in the Dawson Massacre. His brother, William Mosby Eastland, was in the Mier Expedition, the only officer to draw a black bean and be executed. Jimmie Wynn McGuire, Jimmie Wynn (Micky) McGuire II, Jack Randall McElmurry - #4049 (Life Member) William Mosby McElmurry, Larry Dale McElmurry, Blake Anthony McElmurry, Brady Scott McElmurry, Brett Linden McElmurry.

ABNER ECHOLS

Abner Echols was born about 1800 in Tennessee. He married Sarah Ann ?

They arrived in the Republic of Texas in April 1811. He received a First Class Certificate #87 on February 1, 1838.

He served in the Texas Army for 3 months, from March 7, 1836 to June 7, 1836, as a private in Captain Wyly Martin's company, for which he received Bounty Land Certificate #1177, for 320 acre, signed 12-8-1852 and approved 4-21-1853 (see Travis Bounty Warrant #227).

He purchased 355 acres of land in Fort Rend County in 1838. He served on Road Duty, appearing on Hodge's Bend Road List from 1847 to 1854. He raised horses and cattle in Fort Bend County from 1939 until the time of his death in March 1870. His known children — Rebecca, b 1832; Tennessee, b 1833; Leuisa, b 1834, John G., b 1837; Ann, b 1838; James P., b 1839; Gustavius, b 1842; Abner Jr., b 1845; Eellen B., b 1848; Lewis, b 1849; and Mary — were all born in Texas. David E. LeVrier #4799

DAVID CRAWFORD EDMISTON

Born in Antoine, Arkansas, on March 2, 1825, my grandfather, David Crawford Edmiston, came with his family to Texas in 1835. His parents were Zebulon Brevard and Nancy (Moore) Edmiston.

Young David joined Stephen F. Austin's Frontier Ranger companies and was engaged in several Indian battles during 1845 with Lt. Alexander Coleman's company. During the Mexican War, Governor J. Pickney Henderson appointed David a second lieutenant, Capt. Grumble's company, Bell's Mounted Volunteers of the Texas Rangers.

David Crawford and Rhoda Bowen Edmiston 1856 *R.B. Edmiston*

During the War Between the States, David served in the 33rd Texas Cavalry, Company C, Partisan Rangers of the Confederate Army. In May 1865, he served under Colonel Rip Ford during Battle at Palmito Ranch, in lower Rio Grande Valley.

In later years, David would welcome visitors such as Wilbarger, the Burlesons, and the Hornsbys on the front porch of his frontier home where they would reminisce about their past experiences on the Texas frontier.

David married Rhoda Bowen on July 3, 1856, and they were blessed with eleven children. David died January 18, 1903, and was buried in Manor Cemetery near Webberville, Texas. Rhoda died on May 22, 1924, and was buried next to David. A Texas Historical Marker stands at David's gravesite.

R.B. Edmiston, born 5-22-25, retired. Married Mary Lee Summer on Nov. 10 1957. Daughter, Karen Ann Edmiston, born 7-16-

1958. Married Thomas Jefferson Maddux March 6, 1982. Grandson James Edmiston Maddux, born Oct. 7, 1999. R.B. Edmiston, #3616

JOSHUA NEWTON ELLIS

Joshua Newton Ellis, son-in-law of Ruth Smith Brown, came to Texas and applied for a land grant in September 1833. He returned to Missouri to get his family; but times were so unsettled in Texas that they did not move to Texas until after the Revolution.

Edward Smith Ellis, son of Joshua Newton Ellis

Ruth Smith and her husband, William Brown, had moved from Pendleton District, South Carolina, to Bedford County, Tennessee. Later, she and her husband separated, and Ruth moved, with her children, to the Missouri Territory. The oldest daughter, Artimisa, born February 27, 1809, married Joshua Newton Ellis in about 1830. When they moved to Texas, they were the parents of six children. The seventh child, Merida Green Ellis, was born in April 1847, in Denton County. The Ellis family, with the other children of Ruth Brown, first lived in the Denton County area. The Indians were so hostile that the horses had to be tied to the door post, and Joshua slept by the door, rifle in hand.

Joshua Newton Ellis died in May 1847, when his son, Merida, was only one month old. Artimisa Brown Ellis died in December 1847. It is presumed that both were buried on their home place, three miles east of Denton. The early settlers could not bury their dead in marked cemeteries because the Indians would dig up the graves to mutilate the bodies. Graves would be dug in the middle of a field of grain and covered with rocks to keep the wild animals from digging. The grain would hide the graves from the Indians, but they were also hidden from later descendants, who would like to place a memorial marker in their honor.

In the fall of 1849, the family decided to move to the protection of Fort Worth. They arrived in Fort Worth in December, after soldiers were stationed there in the spring. The seven children of Joshua and Artimisa were divided among their aunts, uncles, and their grandmother.

Ruth Smith Brown is reported to have been one of the first 10 white women in Tarrant County. The hardships and struggles of that day were trying to the pioneer wife and mother, especially with no husband to look to for protection. Ruth's only son died about 1834 in Missouri. Two daughters also died prior to the move to Texas, leaving Ruth with four married daughters: Artimisa Brown, who married Joshua Newton Ellis; Elizabeth Brown, who married Samuel P. Loving; Belinda Brown, who married William Ransom Loving; and Cerena Brown, who married first Francis Knarr, and second L.B. Cresswell.

Merida G. Ellis, youngest son of Joshua Newton and Artimisa Brown Ellis, has been called the "Father of Fort Worth." He was one of the promoters and founders of the original stockyards in north Fort Worth. He was president of the stockyards and a packing house company for more than two years. He then entered the real estate business and was closely identified with the development and progress of Fort Worth. An elementary school in Fort Worth is named in honor of Merida G. Ellis.

Edward Smith Ellis, oldest son of Joshua Newton and Artimisa Brown Ellis, married Julia Ann Howard, daughter of John and Elizabeth Howard. About 1870, Edward and Julia Ellis Moved to Menard County. They lived in that area of Texas about 10 years, when they moved to Tom Green County, near San Angelo. Edward Smith Ellis died on a picnic in Menard County, on July 7, 1882, and was buried in Menard. Julia Ann Ellis and her children decided to move to Snyder, where the oldest married daughter lived with her family. The livestock was rounded up and slowly driven from San Angelo to the Snyder area. Julia Ellis died June 25, 1902, and is buried in Snyder, Scurry County, Texas.

Smith (Doc) Ellis, born April 7, 1875, great-grandson of Ruth Smith Brown, climbed into a cowboy saddle at age 12 and started doing a man's work. In 1892, Smith Ellis came to the Spur Country and began working on the Spur Ranch. He later worked on the S.M.S. Ranch as cowboy, camp man, and foreman. His obituary stated he was "one of those pioneers who climbed into the saddle in boyhood to take a hand in the transformation of the West." Freedom of the trails, the sun-bathed prairies, and an unbounded horizon were a fond heritage.

Smith Ellis married first Martha "Mattie" Jane Pruit, daughter of Samuel Thomas, and Mary Curry Pruit, and they were the parents of one child, Lena Agnes, born May 13, 1903. Lena married Lester Yelma Ericson, descendant of early Swedish settlers, who migrated to Texas in May 1864. Lena and Lester were the parents of Joe Ellis Ericson, past President General of the Sons of the Republic of Texas. Joe Ellis Ericson, KSJ past President General # 2415

JOHN ENGLEDOW

John Engledow was born in 1781, probably in Virginia. Wife Elizabeth and their first two children, Oscar and Creed in 1809 and 1814, born in Wythe County Virginia.

Robert D. and Harriet (Bell) Engledow

The Federal Census of 1820 and 1830 has John Engledow in Warren County, Tennessee. He brought his family, including Robert D, to Nacogdoches, Texas, in 1835. Robert married Harriet Bell. Their daughter, Kate, married Cassius Burks, father of William Loyd Burks, father of Michael Lloyd Burks, #2967.

John's land holdings listed in his will, signed 6-9-1840, totaled more than ten thousand acres in two John Engledow surveys south of Troup in Cherokee County and west of Garrison, partly in Nacogdoches and Rusk counties, and more in Robertson County (Tax List for Republic of Texas 1840, Nacogdoches Public Library). His wife got a receipt for paying for his coffin on July 8, 1840.

John's home place between Nacogdoches and Melrose seems to be bordered on the east by Atascosa Creek. His grave has not been located. But there is what appears to be a very old grave across the road from "the old Hollaman house" on the upper Melrose Road, about two hundred yards from the road among a clump of trees. Large rocks encircle it. This could be John Engledow's grave.

GUSTAVUS ADOLPHUS EVERTS

Gustavus Adolphus Everts, a direct descendant of Captain Myles Standish, was born on August 7, 1797, in Ames, Ohio. In 1823, he was licensed to practice law. In the spring of 1844, he moved with his wife, Achsah (Bingham) and daughter, Eliza Ann, from Platte City, Missouri, to Bonham, Texas. Fannin County elected him to the convention of 1845 to name a Constitution for the state of Texas.

In January 1846, he moved to a farm in the southwest corner of Cooke County. "Deer were abundant, and I loved my gun, a rifle four feet long, twenty balls made a pound. I was a good shot and hunted a great deal; killed hundreds of deer, was healthy until the Civil War broke out." He was opposed to Secession, and in his speeches he told the people "that we were sewing to the wind, and would reap the whirlwind." In 1865, after the close of the war, he was appointed Judge of the 14th District composed of Hill, Navarro, and five or six other counties. He resigned in 1867, went to Sherman, and remained there until the death of his wife. He lived with his daughter, Mrs. Harrison Gill Hendricks in Fort Worth until his death on January 25, 1884. *Submitted by Dorr Huffman Lewright*

SAMUEL G. EVETTS, SR.

Samuel G. Evetts, Sr., brought his family to Texas in 1832, settling at Washington-on-the-Brazos. Samuel Sr. operated a ferry, and his son, James H., was a blacksmith. He and his sons, Samuel Jr. and James, received free land.

Descendants of Samuel Sr. are eligible to join SRT and DRT; through his wife, Susannah Haynie, the SAR or DAR.

In June 1823, to enforce the law, Stephen F. Austin formed the Rangers, whose name was officially changed to the Texas Rangers on 12 June 1835. On 20 July 1835, Captain George W. Barnett formed the Fourth Company of the Texas Rangers, in which Samuel Jr. served. He was paid $15 per month and furnished his own horse and guns. His descendants are eligible to join the Former Texas Rangers Association.

On 12 October 1835, Stephen F. Austin and 300 men arrived in the San Antonio area, including Samuel Jr., who enlisted 25 September 1835.

On 3 December 1835, Col. Ben Milam asked the historic question, "Who will go with old Ben Milam into San Antonio?" Samuel Jr. was among the 200 volunteers who stepped forward. The afternoon of December 7, Ben Milam was shot and killed by a Mexican rifleman. Samuel Jr. was shot in the mouth; the musket ball exited under his right ear. His descendants are eligible to join the Siege of Bexar Descendants.

Honorably discharged from the Texas Army on 4 January 1836, Samuel Jr. returned to Washington-on-the-Brazos to recover from his wounds, later receiving land for his service at the Siege of Bexar.

When news arrived of happenings at the Alamo and Goliad, wounded as he was, Samuel Jr. saddled his horse and rode in search of General Sam Houston. On April 5, 1836, he caught up with Houston's retreating army and re-enlisted.

On 21 April 1836, Samuel Jr. fought along side his brother, James, in the Battle of San Jacinto, for which both received land. Their descendants are eligible to join the San Jacinto Descendants.

Samuel Jr. later lived in Bell and Coryell counties before moving to Wise County to land he patented in 1856. He died August 9, 1884, and is buried at Willow Point Cemetery, located on land he donated for a community cemetery. Harold G. Evetts #2974 George E. Evetts, M.D. #5752

JOHN NEWTON FALL

John Newton Fall was born in Clarke County, Georgia, on January 28, 1810, to John Strader Fall and Fidelia Newton. In his 19th year, he began the study of medicine at Emory University, and in his 21st year, he married Susan Tucker Wilson. Dr. Fall and his family came to Texas in 1837, where he was one of the earliest settlers of the east Texas town of Chireno in Nacogdoches County. In 1840, the birth of his fourth child, Calvin, aroused a great deal of curiosity among the local Indians since tradition says he was the first Anglo child born in Chireno.

John N. Fall

In addition to the practice of medicine, John Newton Fall was a merchant, landowner, and postmaster. He served as Justice of the Peace for Nacogdoches County from 1839 to 1841. He served the State of Texas as a State Senator in 1858, 1861, and 1862. In 1861, he was one of several representatives from Nacogdoches County sent to the secession convention in Austin. Dr. Fall voted to secede from the Union against the wishes of Sam Houston, despite the fact that Houston and Dr. Fall were personal friends.

After the death of his first wife, Dr. Fall married Minerva Hankla Atkinson in 1865. One child, Randolph Hankla, was born to this marriage in 1866. John Newton Fall died November 13, 1866, in Chireno, Texas. *Submitted by Paul Randell Hearn (great-great-grandson of John Newton Fall) Member of Chapters 19 & 38 (dual)*

JUAN FRANCISCO FARIAS

Juan Francisco Farias, rancher and merchant, was an officer of the Laredo Municipal Corporation in 1833, according to a list provided by Mayor Andres Martinez in 1846 to Mirabeau B. Lamar, Laredo Commandant. On January 18, 1840, after a convention of villages and towns near Laredo led by Revolutionary General Antonio Canales, the Republic of the Rio Grande was proclaimed as an independent and sovereign nation. Juan Francisco Farias was elected Secretary of the Republic. The movement, a revolt against Mexico's central government similar to the Texas Revolution, lasted but eleven months. Juan Francisco became a United States citizen on April 29, 1857, and in January 1861, became Laredo's Civil War mayor.

Juan Francisco Farias

Juan Francisco was born January 9, 1807, in San Pedro de las Colonias, Coahuila Mexico. His father, Jose Andres Farias, came from Presidio del Rio Grande de San Juan Bautista in about 1780 to command the Spanish Colonial garrison at Laredo as a member of the Third Flying Cavalry Company of Nuevo Santander. On November 30, 1803, he married Guadalupe Sanchez, a granddaughter of Laredo's founder, Tomas Sanchez.

Juan Francisco married Maria Inocente Benavides on June 15, 1832, a widow whose husband had been killed by Indians, and they had eleven children. Their youngest daughter, Manuelita, became the second wife of Evaristo Madero, an intimate friend and business associate of Juan Francisco, and the grandfather of the future president of Mexico, Francisco Madero.

Juan Francisco Farias, rebel and patriot, died April 9, 1870. Great-great-grandson George Farias # 6231 Great-great great-grandson Michael Fredrick Rollin #6469M

JOHN RUTHERFORD FENN

Fenn: Mr. and Mrs. J.R. Fenn

John Rutherford Fenn (1824-1904), early Texas soldier and settler, was born in Lawrence County, Mississippi, on October 11, 1824, the son of Eli and Sarah Fenn. Sarah was the daughter of David Fitzgerald, one of Austin's "Old 300" settlers.

On June 7, 1833, the family arrived at the area that later became Fort Bend County, Texas. During the Texas Revolution, young Fenn was captured by Mexican soldiers, but escaped to be reunited with his mother and brothers at the William W. Little camp on the Brazos River bottom.

In 1842, Fenn served under Somervell in the continuing Texas Revolution. He served as a lieutenant in the Confederate Army during the Civil War. In 1852, he married Rebecca M. Williams. The couple had four children. Their son, Francis Marion Otis Fenn, (1859-1939) was the founder of the original Sons of the Republic of Texas in 1893. The Fenns settled on a plantation that they called Duke on Oyster Creek, where they lived until 1872 when they moved to Houston. They celebrated their fiftieth wedding anniversary in 1902. An honored guest was Mrs. Anson Jones, widow of the first president of the Republic of Texas.

John R. Fenn died in Houston on November 23, 1904, and was buried in the family cemetery at Duke.

John Rutherford Fenn's direct line descendants are Francis Marion Otis Fenn (son, 1859-1939), Rutherford Benson Fenn (grandson, 1884-1953), Rutherford Hunter Fenn (great-grandson), Randolph Voss Fenn and Bruce Hunter Fenn (great-great-grandsons) and Gordon Hunter Fenn (great-great-great-grandson). All are members of the Sons of the Republic of Texas.

OLLY A. FERGUSON

Olly A. Ferguson and Drucilla Cook married in Mississippi on March 26, 1820. He was 25 years old; she was 18.

After residing in Louisiana, they arrived in Texas in about 1825, settling near Sabinetown. They had 5 children.

In 1826, Ferguson and another man were accused of killing an alleged burglar. As revenge was threatened, the accused pair fled. Upon writing the judge, they returned, stood trial, and were acquitted.

In 1827, Ferguson was awarded a Mexican Land Grant.

The date is unsure; Ferguson accidentally wounded a companion while they hunted in heavy brush. Drucilla provided care while Ferguson journeyed to Louisiana for a doctor. Upon their return, the man had died.

In 1832, Ferguson mysteriously disappeared and was presumed dead. Drucilla later married Eli Low. Eli and his father, Isaac Low operated a ferry on Low's Creek. During the "Runaway Scrape" of 1836, they ferried thousands of Texans to safety when Santa Anna was causing havoc.

The Ferguson's grandson, James E. Ferguson, eventually served in the Civil War as a private in Company C, Eleventh, Ashley Spaight's Texas Battalion. This unit, with others, served courageously along the Texas coast and in Louisiana. Olly A. Ferguson Great-great-great-grandfather to: Jimmie Dale Hays #5795A

JEREMIAH CONRAD FISHER

Jeremiah Conrad Fisher, the son of Samuel Fisher and Mary Rule Roper, was born 11/13/1819, in Opelousas, St. Landry's Parish, Louisiana. He came to Texas in 1830 with his mother and two sisters. They lived on Lawrence's Island near Cove, Chambers County, Texas (then Liberty County).

Jeremiah married Sarah Ann Barrow, daughter of Solomon Barrow and Elizabeth Winfree on August 10, 1841. He received a land grant from the Republic of 640 acres in Hardin County. However, he and Sarah settled on Trinity Bay where Beach City is now. Their house was built facing the bay to take advantage of the cooling breezes. He added large tracts of land to his holdings and became a prominent landowner and rancher. Jeremiah and Sarah had eleven children: Solomon, Henrietta, Amos, Ann Elizabeth, Mary Catherine, Joseph, Benjamin, Martha, Amanda, John and Jeremiah.

Jeremiah Conrad Fisher served the Republic by serving in the Militia with his father-in-law, Solomon Barrow, and other friends and neighbors from Liberty County. Jeremiah was active in the Masonic Lodge and the Methodist Church. He donated money to build the church, and it was called the Fisher Chapel.

Senator James Winwright Flanagan

Jeremiah died 11/10/1899, leaving estates to each of his ten surviving children. The old family home has since eroded into Trinity Bay, the result of many Texas hurricanes.

SENATOR JAMES WINWRIGHT FLANAGAN

James Winwright Flanagan was born in Albemarle County, Virginia, on September 7, 1805, to Charles Flanagan and Elizabeth Saunders. In 1815, his family moved to Kentucky near Boonesboro, where he grew to manhood. He was successful in the merchandise business, operating a flotilla of flatboats on the Ohio River. He served as a Justice of the Peace for 12 years, and from 1833 to 1843 as a member of the Circuit Court of Breckinridge County, Kentucky.

In 1843, he sold his business and migrated to Harrison County, Texas, settling in Henderson, Rusk County, on August 9, 1844. There he combined the practice of law with storekeeping, farming and dealing in land. In the 1850s he edited the "Star Spangled Banner" as one of Henderson's early newspapers. His store, housed in a brick building, was the only structure to survive the fire of 1860. His land holdings near Henderson were quite extensive. He built a reputation for success as a defense lawyer. He served in the Texas House of Representatives, 1851-52, and in the Texas Senate, 1855-56. He served as a presidential elector in 1856 and a delegate to the Peace Congress in 1861. As a legislator, he introduced bills for the first insane asylum in Texas and for the chartering of the Galveston, Houston and Henderson Railway.

James Winwright Flanagan was a Whig and a good friend of General Sam Houston, and like Houston, opposed secession. Houston stayed with the family on several occasions and supposedly he was there on the night one son was born, who was named Samuel Houston Flanagan in his honor. At the outbreak of the Civil War, J.W. retired to his farm, and with his tanyard furnished large quantities of leather to the Confederate government. During Reconstruction, he was a delegate to the Constitutional Conventions of 1866 and 1869. He was elected lieutenant governor in 1869, but resigned to represent Texas in the United States Senate from 1870 to 1875.

James Winwright Flanagan was married three times. His first wife was Miss Polly Moorman in 1826 in Kentucky, and with her had four children. His oldest son, Webster Flanagan, was also a successful businessman and active in politics at the same time. They are sometimes confused or even combined in error in some accounts.

J.W. Flanagan married a second time on January 21, 1845, in the Republic of Texas. His second wife was Elizabeth Susan Lane, daughter of Robert L. Lane, a land surveyor who owned land in Texas since 1839. They had four sons, including Samuel Houston Flanagan.

Twice a widower, he married Elizabeth Vinson, widow of Eli Ware. With her, he had two more sons. During the 1860s, he relocated to Longview and established Flanagan's Mill.

He died on September 19, 1887, in Longview, and was buried in the family plot on the original homestead in Henderson,

In Texas' Sesquicentennial year, 1986, John Covington Flanagan II and his father, Frederick Kittrell Flanagan, joined the Sons of the Republic of Texas. The line was through Fred's father, John Covington Flanagan, Sr., to Samuel Houston Flanagan to Senator James Winwright Flanagan. John Covington Flanagan II, #3798

CAPTAIN SALVADOR FLORES

I am the sixth-generation grandson of Salvadore Flores. He was son of Jose Antonio Toedoro Justo Guadalupe Flores and Maria Antonia Rodriguez.

Family of Capt. Salvador Flores (l. to r.) Sitting: Son Santiago Ignacio Eduardo Flores, granddaughter Margarita Flores, Herminia Flores, and (on lap:) granddaughter Clara, (boy standing:) Grandson Eduardo Flores, Jr., (woman sitting:) Daughter-in-law Saragosa Sequin, (man on far right:) Grandson Jesus J. Flores

Captain Salvador Flores was born about 1810 and died Jan 17, 1855, at his residence, 21 miles from San Antonio. He had five children from his first wife, Clara, and two from second, Concepcion Rojo Seguin.

He was a hero of the Texas Revolution, fighting alongside his brother-in-law, Juan N. Seguin, in the Battle of Concepcion and the Siege of Bexar in San Antonio in 1835. He was highly regarded as a patriot by Stephen F. Austin in a letter to Capt. Juan N. Seguin dated November 24, 1835.

He is a direct descendent of Jose Flores, who in 1996 was accepted by the Sons of the American Revolution as a patriot by providing cattle and horses to General Bernardo de Galvez, a Spaniard fighting the British with 5,000 troops along the Louisiana coastline.

He is listed in the muster rolls of the Texas Revolution as having the rank of lieutenant in Col. Juan N. Seguin's company (Oct. 1835), captain of C Company of Second Regiment of

Cavalry of the Regular Army of Texas 1836, and captain of 1st Regiment of Cavalry 1837. *Submitted by Paul C. Garcia*

LUDEWIG CARL FERDINAND

Ludewig Carl Ferdinand Francke was born in Gustrow, Mecklenburg, on June 28, 1818, of Bishop Peter Francke and his second wife, Helena von Kamptz.

Though he loved music he realized he was not gifted enough to become a musician of first rank, so he entered the University of Jena, where he secured a degree. After practicing law in Mecklenburg, he became dissatisfied with the existing autocratic restrictions of German officialdom. He immigrated to Texas in 1845, landing in Galveston on January 10, 1846.

He lived for a short while at Cat Springs and joined the Texas Volunteers on October 18, 1846, under Captain Shapley P. Ross, later serving with Captain Henry E. McCulloch's company. He is reported to have traveled during this period to Mexico City guarding a shipment of silver, which is believed to have been paid by the U.S. government.

On November 10, 1853, he received his naturalization papers on which his name was spelled Lewis Franke, and this spelling of the family name has been customary since.

He married Bernhardine Romberg in 1853. After the Rombergs moved to the Blackjack Springs community in Fayette County; the Frankes soon followed. Later he taught music at Baylor College in Independence, but left after a few years because of limited financial means, returning to their farm near Blackjack Springs, where he farmed and practiced law on the side.

Though he held some office as guardian of absent soldiers' dependents during the Civil War, he did not take part in active fighting because, like other German-Americans of that time, he was not in sympathy with slavery.

At the close of the Reconstruction period (1872), he was elected a Representative to the Legislature which became known as "The Great Liberator" Legislature in Texas history. At the end of the session, on February 19, 1873, as he was descending the steps of the capitol, he was fatally injured and robbed by unknown assailants.

In the year 2000 he was awarded a medallion as a "Citizen of the Republic of Texas," which will be attached to his tombstone in the burial plot near La Grange, Texas. *Submitted by Paul Hudson*

JOHN FRIES AND JACOB FRIES

John Fries and his wife, Marianna Blatz, immigrated to America with their four children: Adam, Joseph, Jacob, and MariAnna. They left Cadenbach, Nassau, in 1845. They sailed from Antwerp on November 7, 1845, on the ship Riga. The ship arrived in Galveston, Texas, on February 1, 1846. The family continued with colonists to Fredericksburg, Texas. Jacob, their son, remained behind with a doctor, As the doctor advised. The boy was ill and would not be strong enough to survive the journey. En route on the journey to Fredericksberg, the father, John Fries, died, as did many other colonists.

The 1850 United States Census of Gillaspie County, Texas, has a record of the mother, Marianna, married to Wendlin Mittel. The mother and her other children, according to records, were members of the St. Mary's Catholic Church. The mother, Marianna, is buried in St. Mary's Catholic Church Cemetery in Fredericksburg, Texas.

Jacob did not see his family until after the Civil War. The first record we find of him is his marriage license to Emily Catherine Laurence on March 25, 1867, in Chappel Hill, Texas.

After the Civil War, Jacob freighted. On one occasion when driving his wagon down a muddy road, he met another man coming the opposite direction. Neither wanted to give the right-of-way. Each got off his wagon with intention to fight, however. The brother recognized Jacob, who had been left to die in Galveston. The older brother, Adam, brought Jacob at once to see his mother. She immediately recognized him because of a wart over his left eye. Soon Jacob moved to Fredericksburg and bought land in Gillespie County in 1875. Here with his family – Frances, Lee, Edward, Mollie, and Robert — he farmed and ranched in the Crabapple community.

In 1900, he moved to Bandera County so he could buy more land for his sons. After he and his wife. Emily had reach an age where they could no longer live alone, they returned to live at Crabapple with his daughter, Mollie. He died August 24, 1918, and is buried in the Eckert Community Cemetery, Eckert, Texas. A granddaughter, Viola May Gold, attended the funeral and remembers the black coffin placed in the back of a hack, which was drawn by white horses driven by a neighbor, Peter Land. *Submitted by John Frederick Oehler, Jr., #6723*

OSCAR LEON FRITH, JR.

Oscar Leon Frith, Jr. was born August 31, 1932 in Dallas, Texas, the oldest of three sons to Oscar Leon Frith, a Dallas fireman, and Billie Berry.

He graduated from North Dallas High School and married his high school sweetheart, Anne Davis, October 20, 1949. There were two children, David Leon Frith and Candace Anne Frith, born to this unity.

He was employed by the Highland Park Fire Department December 19, 1949 where he served 32 years and retired as Fire Chief January 31, 1984.

Leon and Anne reside in Garland, Texas. Leon was elected president of the Ranger John Beeman Chapter #45 Mesquited, Texas, The Sons of the Republic of Texas for the year 2000. *Submitted by Oscar Leon Frith, Jr. SRT #6724*

GALBA FUQUA

Galba Fuqua, one of the youngest defenders of the Alamo, came to Texas from Alabama and settled in DeWitt's Colony in 1830. Galba Fuqua was born in Alabama to Silas and Sally Young Fuqua in 1820.

Galba was only 16 when he volunteered to go fight at the Alamo in 1936. He was one of the thirty-two from Gonzales who answered William Travis' call for help to defend the Alamo. As the battle entered the final day, Mexican soldiers advanced toward

Jacob and Emily Fries

the walls of the Alamo. During the intense gunfire, both of Galba's jaws were shattered by a bullet. He ran into the church of the Alamo where women and children were hiding and attempted to say something to Susannah Dickinson. After trying again to speak and unable to get her to understand, Galba left the church. He then went back out to the battlefield, and was killed by the Mexican soldiers at the age of 16.

Being so young, Galba was not married, so he left behind no wife or children.

To be 16 years old and volunteer to go fight in a battle that one is almost certain will result in death takes a great amount of courage. Galba Fuqua, my great-great uncle, typified the courage displayed by all the defenders of the Alamo. *Submitted by John C. Fuqua.*

BENJAMIN FERDINAND GAGE

Benjamin Ferdinand Gage was born about 1802-04 in South Carolina. He died near Gilmer, Texas, January 1858. He was married in 1827 or 1828, probably in Alabama, to Sarah Elizabeth Harrell. She was born about 1802-04, in Georgia. Benjamin and Sarah Gage are buried in Hoover Cemetery, Pritchett, Texas.

The Gage Homestead, built in 1845.

Benjamin came to Texas from Indiana. He traveled through Kentucky, on to Tennessee, and from Tennessee to Texas, camping along and scouting about. He was one of the old "Trail Blazers," helping build bridges and such. He camped at Filips Springs, three miles north of Gladewater, Texas. But the location did not suit him, so he scouted around a few days and located on Little White Oak Creek about 12 miles northwest of the springs. There he established a gristmill and a tanning yard. Later, Benjamin, as an heir of James Standefer (a prominent landowner in this area), inherited 640 acres of Texas land.

After statehood (about 1848), the governor of Texas appointed Benjamin Gage, Benjamin Fuller and M.M. Robertson commissioners to select a site for the county seat of the newly created Upshur County. They selected and bought the present site of Gilmer from Matthew Cartwright, famed trader and early Texas landowner.

In 1845, the Gage home was built along White Oak Creek. Alec Marsh and Billy Green were paid $1.00 in gold for each log they hand-hewed for the Gage home. When the men finished hewing the logs, which were hauled from Jefferson, the neighbors joined in a house raising. They constructed a two-story house 17-1/2-x-30-feet, which had a large fireplace at one end and a large porch on the front and on the back. In 1960, this was the oldest house in Upshur County still being used by the same family. In the 115-year-old structure were members of the same family, William Alton Gage, a great-grandson of the builder, and his daughter, Mrs. Judy Holden, the fifth generation to reside in the house. In 1998, the house was still standing.

1. Benjamin Ferdinand Gage 1802-1858, 2. Sara Elizabeth Harrell 1802 – 1874, 3. David Ferdinand Gage 1827-1877?, 4. Nancy Hoover 1829-1892, 5. Leuy Jane Gage 1854-1895, 6. Frances Marion Green 1859-1929, 7. Ada Green 1882-1959, 8. Edmond Luther Oliver 1876-1949, 9. Luther Von Oliver 1914- -, 10. Cathryn Dean 1913 - 1993, 11. Luther Vaughn Oliver 1941 -, 12. Janiece Marie Baker 1947 -, 13. Leniece Irene Oliver 1969 -, 14. Daniel McLennon Fitzgerald 1968 -, 15. Kayla Marie McLennon Fitzgerald 1994 -, 16. Corey Daniel Fitzgerald 1999 - , 17. Robert Vaughn Oliver 1971 - 18. Kathryn Lee Oliver 1976 –

ALBERT GALLATIN

Albert Gallatin was born at Lexington, Kentucky. His parents were Eliza Thompson, born in 1785 in Fayette County, Kentucky (near Lexington), and Abraham Gallatin, born in 1762 in Lancaster County, Pennsylvania. They were married in Lexington, Kentucky, on Oct. 20, 1808. After Albert's birth on Aug. 1. 1809, the family moved to St. Louis, Missouri Territory, where Abraham was a breeder of fine horses. Abraham and Eliza reared six children at their farm, named Marino, near St. Louis. They later moved to Monroe County, Illinois.

In 1832, Albert and his father came to Texas intending to sell a herd of horses. They arrived in Austin's Colony on Dec. 1, 1832. Albert settled in Montgomery County, Texas, where he joined the Texan Army on Nov. 1, 1835. He served in Captain John Crane's Company under Col. Ben Milam at the Siege of Bexar, Dec. 5-10, 1835. He was discharged on Dec. 13, 1835. On March 12, 1836, he re-enlisted in Capt. William Ware's Company, 2nd Regiment, Texas Volunteers. He fought in the Battle of San Jacinto, where he was wounded on April 21. 1836.

Albert Gallatin

Albert married Sarah Louise Jones at Washington County, Texas, on Oct. 23, 1837. Sarah's father, Samuel Jones, was born around 1780 in South Carolina, and lived in Tennessee and Alabama before coming to Texas in 1835. Sarah's mother, Lucinda Fields, was born about 1785. Sarah was born Nov. 20, 1820, in Blount County, Alabama. Both Samuel and Lucinda died before 1850 while living on their Headright Grant in Milam County near Cameron.

Albert and Sarah had 11 children and lived in Milam, Llano, Bell, and Brazos counties, Texas. They also lived in Mexico from 1868 to 1870 after the Civil War. Albert was a farmer by occupation. He also served as the first Postmaster of Cameron, Texas, from 1847-1849. In 1847, he received a commission as colonel in the Texas Militia.

Sarah Gallatin died at the home of her daughter in Hico, Hamilton County, Texas, on Jan. 29, 1889. Albert died at his home in Brazos County near Bryan, Texas, on Feb. 16, 1898. He is buried in the Bickham Cemetery on Cottonwood Prairie, Brazos County, Texas. Albert Reeves Galllatin, (GGS), 2417

SEYMOUR GAREY

Seymour Garey, the third child of Ambrose and Mary Woodruff, was born March 16, 1792, in Lebanon, New London County, Connecticut, but moved while still a boy to Wyoming County, Pennsylvania.

Seymour married Sally Carney on July 21,1814. They had four children. Sally died April 6, 1825, and is buried in Wyoming County, Pennsylvania. About two years later, Seymour married Anna Kingsbury. They also had four children. Seymour migrated to Texas in 1839. Their first home was on the Brazos River in Austin's Colony at San Felipe. On December 28, 1839, Seymour was granted a conditional Headright Certificate to 640 acres in Gonzales County, which was, in 1846, incorporated into DeWitt County. Seymour and Sally's children, all born in Wyoming County were: Amanda, married Truman Courtney; Savanna, died as an infant; Elijah, killed in the Dawson Massacre at Salada Creek in Bexar County on September 18, 1842 (his bones are interred with his comrades in a common grave on Monument Hill, La Grange, Texas). William Carney Garey came to Texas with his family, but went back to Pennsylvania when he was grown.

Seymour and Anna's children were Harriet B., married John Tumlinson in Gonzales County (she was wed five times); Benjamin W., married Mary Criswell in Fayette County; Amanda Susan Seymour Garey, married Henry F.W. Hill; LaFayette, who died young; Royal, married Sicilia Neal in DeWitt County.

Seymour Garey, while on a visit to Pennsylvania, died and is buried in Fasset Cemetery. His grave is marked with a rock with S.G. carved on it.

Seymour's granddaughter, Adeline Prudence Courtney, whose mother was Amanda, married Oliver H. Rice, Sr., at Stratton, Texas. They had five children: William Henry, Orien A., Oliver Jr. (died young), Amanda E. and Mary E. Oliver and his son went to cut down a tree in the pasture. It fell the wrong direction and he was killed. After Oliver Sr. died, Adeline married Abraham Bowen. They had three children: Dora, Daniel and David. The Rice children and the Bowen children were raised as one big happy family. Abraham and Adeline are buried in Alexander Cemetery at Stratton Texas, in a Bowen family plot.

Dora married James Lawrence Bowen, a cousin from Caldwell County. They had Seymour Courtney Bowen, Abraham, Adeline, Rickard, Mahalie, Edna and Andrew Percy (died young).

My father was Seymour Courtney Bowen of Stratton and Cuero, DeWitt County, Texas. He married Bessie Myrtle Phillips of La Vernia and Stockdale, Texas, in Cuero in 1920. They are buried in Hillside Cemetery in Cuero, Texas.

I was the oldest of four children: Justin Ray (died at birth), Wayne Lanier and Shirley Ann are my brothers and sister. Wayne died in 1997 and is buried in Hillside Cemetery, Cuero. Clarence Neal Bowen.

THOMAS B. GARRETT

Thomas B. Garrett, younger brother of Jacob Garrett, was born in 1790 in Williamson County, Tennessee, the son of John and Jane Garrett. He married Levicey Evans who was born in 1802 in Tennessee. He was a grandson of Jacob and Honour Garrett of Virginia, who was an active and material supporter of Colonial efforts during the American Revolution.

Thomas B. Garrett and family emigrated to Texas in the early 1830s. The First Census of Texas 1829-1836 lists Thomas and his family in San Augustine district. During the Texas Revolution he served in the San Augustine Volunteers. His company under Captain William D. Ratcliff reached San Jacinto the day after the battle. The company had been stationed in Nacogdoches to defend it from possible Indian attack. The Mexican military tried to get the Indians to attack the town, but they refused to take sides in the fight. From 1848 to 1850, he served Nacogdoches County as Justice of the Peace. Later he was a plantation owner near Douglass, Texas.

Thomas B. Garrett died 15 October 1868, and Levicey Evans Garrett died in December 1885. Both are buried in the Douglass Cemetery. William Hutchinson Kline #5755, great-great-grandson William Hutchinson Kline, Jr. #6632 William Hutchinson Kline, III #6631 Bradley Edward Kline #6633

ALEXANDER TALEFERIO GAYLE

Alexander Taleferio Gayle was born in Virginia on December 10, 1815 and remained in his native state until the fall of 1836. His father, Bartlett Gayle, was a prominent farmer and a large slave owner, and he was connected with the aristocracy of the Virginia Commonwealth.

Alexander came to Texas in 1836, settling first near where the city of Austin now stands. He later moved his homestead near San Felipe on the Brazos to continue his agricultural pursuits.

He married Frances Agnes Sutherland on December 1, 1843. She was the daughter of Major George and Frances (Menefee) Sutherland, whose family survived the "Runaway Scrape". Major Sutherland fought at the Battle of San Jacinto. Frances Agnes Sutherland's brother, William DePriest Sutherland, died at the Alamo on March 6, 1836.

Family picture of Alexander T. Gayle and his wife, Frances Agnes Gayle and their children: George Sutherland Gayle (Top), Georgia Ann Gayle (Center), Martha Gayle (Left), Virginia Gayle (Bottom), and Alexander Gayle (Right). Circa 1856.

Alexander and Frances (Sutherland) Gayle were blessed with eight children, four of whom lived to maturity. They were George Sutherland Gayle, Georgia Ann Gayle (Mrs. J.D. Rogers), Virginia "Jennie" Gayle (Mrs. S.M. Lesesne), and Bartlett Buckner Gayle.

In 1844, Alexander moved his family to Jackson County, making a permanent home on the Lavaca River, four miles west of Texana, the old county seat. There, he purchased a heavily wooded tract of land. With help of slaves that he brought with him from Virginia, he cleared the land and planted corn. He founded an Episcopal Church in Texana in 1851.

Alexander Gayle's first house was a small cabin, and he was among the first in this area to build a good home from lumber obtained in the area. Settlers were few, and they were widely scattered. The range was free, game was plentiful and stock of all kinds flourished in the area. He became a stock dealer, raising horses and cattle, as well as some sheep. He managed a horse-breeding program using Kentucky thoroughbreds, and he always owned the finest horses in the county. He was a civil engineer, was elected County Commissioner in 1850 and became County Surveyor in 1852. He owned numerous tracts of land throughout Texas.

Early in his time in Texas, Alexander foresaw the demise of slavery, and believing that the liberation of slaves was eminent, he sold a portion of those he owned. His neighbors ridiculed the idea, but he was firm in his convictions. He replied to his critics that he wanted to teach his children to work before the slaves were freed. History proved him a wise teacher.

Like many that settled this area of Texas, Alexander Gayle knew the deprivations and hardships of pioneer life. He helped subdue the Mexicans and Indians who threatened the settlers. And he brought civilized discourse to the area. He was a public-spirited gentleman who, although he did not seek public recognition, was well informed on public matters. He died at his homestead on March 8, 1857. Alexander T. Gayle was my great-great-grandfather. George Shelton Gayle, III #6891AH

Adapted from "A Twentieth Century History of SOUTHWEST TEXAS," Volume II, The Lewis Publishing Company, Chicago, New York and Los Angeles; Published 1907, pp 44-45.

GEORGE SUTHERLAND GAYLE

George Sutherland Gayle was born September 13, 1845, in Jackson County, the son of Alexander T. and Frances Agnes (Sutherland) Gayle, in the waning days of the Republic of Texas.

George Sutherland Gayle seated on the front steps of his home in Edna, Texas surrounded by his family, circa 1910.

In 1863, at the age of eighteen, he volunteered for the Confederate Army in the First Texas Cavalry, serving under Colonel Birchel. He served in the Trans-Mississippi Department and saw action in Louisiana and Texas. His first engagement was the Battle of Mansfield (Louisiana), followed by the Battle of Pleasant Hill. Numerous skirmishes followed, and George was in Corsicana, Texas, when Lee surrendered to Grant at Appomattox, Virginia. Although he saw hard service during his military career, he was never wounded or imprisoned. In later years, he was Adjutant of the United Confederate Veterans, Clark L. Owen Chapter.

At the close of the war, George returned to Chappel Hill, where his mother had temporarily relocated during the war years. He attended school briefly, and then returned to Jackson County in 1866 to take charge of his mother's property. She remained in Chappel Hill, where she died in 1867 of yellow fever. His father had died ten years earlier, in 1857, so George was appointed administrator and guardian for the minor heirs until the settlement of their parents' estate was completed.

George inherited the family's homestead, but after living there for a number of years, he traded that land for land near Edna. With a group of partners, he initially owned 7,000 acres of pastureland that he farmed in cotton and corn. When the cotton crop was finally ruined by the boll weevil in 1898, he turned to rice farming in the early 1900s and was very successful. Simultaneous with his farming, he also raised livestock, including cattle and horses.

George married Miss Regina S. Dill in Goliad on September 1, 1875. In 1884, George moved a portion of the old homestead structure to Edna. He converted it to a lovely, two-story residence that was surrounded by eleven acres planted with shrubbery and evergreens, and a pear orchard nearby. The Gayles were blessed with seven children: Fannie L. Gayle (Mrs. A.R. McDowell), Nannie E. Gayle (Mrs. E.P. Simons), George Shelton Gayle, A.D. Gayle, Gena S. Gayle (Mrs. M.T. Simons), Jennie L. Gayle (Mrs. Hugh L. White) and Lea M. Gayle.

George was a life-long resident of Jackson County, and he served as School Trustee and as County Commissioner on several occasions. He was well regarded for the diligence he displayed in public office; it was said that he gave the same care and attention to the county's business as he did to his own affairs. George was always a strong advocate of public education and good roads throughout the county. In 1876, he joined the Methodist Church, South, and it was a great joy to him that all members of his family became members of the church as well. He served his church on the board of stewards, as a trustee of its property, and as secretary of the Sunday school. These last two positions he held for thirty years or longer, holding both at the time of his death.

George S. Gayle died of heart failure in Edna on February 2, 1914. Friends remembered him as a successful businessman, generous of spirit, and one whose life was deeply entwined with the public good. George Sutherland Gayle was my great-grandfather. George Shelton Gayle, III #6891AH

GEORGE SHELTON GAYLE, III

George Shelton Gayle, III, was born in Houston, Texas on March 24, 1944, to Dr. George Shelton and Velma Jane (Colley) Gayle. The second of three children, George is a sixth-generation Texan. He attended local public schools and completed his BBA degree at the University of Texas in 1968.

Upon graduation, he embarked on his life-long career in real estate development, sales and brokerage. George concentrated in commercial real estate development in the mid-1970's and early 1980's, and he successfully developed several convenience centers in the west and northwest areas of Houston. With his mother, who was also a real estate broker, George became recognized as an expert in farm and ranch properties, primarily in Fort Bend County, west of Houston. He guided the family's personal investments in several ranch properties, first in Clodine and then in the Fulshear and Simonton areas west of Houston, where the expansion of Harris County was booming. The "real estate crunch" of the mid-1980s challenged many successful real estate entrepreneurs, and George worked through the troubles in the Houston economy to emerge with a once-again successful real estate practice.

George followed his father's and forefathers' leads in having an innate love of the land and an appreciation for horse breeding. Dr. George S. Gayle, a successful and admired dentist in Houston for 53 years, acquired and trained several champion Appaloosa stallions. "Son of Snow Cloud" won the World Champion Performance Appaloosa Title in 1965, 1968 and 1969, and the "Mighty Bright" line that Dr. Gayle acquired in 1973 continues on George's ranch in Simonton to this day. George also joined his father as a strong supporter of the Houston Livestock Show and Rodeo, and has been a member of the Appaloosa Horse Show committee for over 30 years, chairing the committee from 1994-96.

George Shelton Gayle, III

George is a member of the Houston Lodge # 1189, AF&AM, and a member of the Scottish Rite and Arabia Temple in Houston, as well as a member of the Royal Order of Jesters. He is a member of the Sons of the Republic of Texas, the San Jacinto Descendants Association, and the Alamo Defenders Descendants Association.

A life-long and charter member of St. Luke's Methodist Church in Houston, George is the father of two children, Ashley Elizabeth Gayle and George Shelton Gayle, IV, who is following in his grandfather's footsteps by also becoming a dentist. George reflects the best of Texas in his honor of our history and his participation in the future of our great state's development. George Shelton Gayle, III #6891AH

JAMES GEORGE

James George and family settled in DeWitt Colony, Gonzales, Texas in 1829. Born in 1802, the son of Robert and Mary Bland George, his youth was spent in Pennsylvania and Ohio, where in 1821 he married Elizabeth Deardruff (Deardoirf). They later moved to Tennessee. James, my great-great-great-grandfather, was a farmer, Baptist, Mason and patriot.

The "History of Gonzales County, Volume I" states: "James George sold three pounds powder, twelve pounds lead, one and three-fourth bushels of peas to the provisional government of Texas and rendered fourteen days service with wagon and two yokes of oxen and two ox bows furnished to San Antonio and La Bahia — for which he was paid $59.50 according to documents in the Texas State Archives." Another document stated: "This to certify that I demanded and received, unto the public service, for halling the the (sic) Gonzales Cannon to San Antonio: one yoke of oxen and all necessary geering; belonging to James George — November 23, 1935, H Neill, Capt."

On February 24, 1836 James George joined Major Williamson's command in Gonzales, as a private, and left for the Alamo where he met his death March 6, 1936. Dan E. Castleberry #6506M

JAMES FREDERICK GOMER

James Frederick Gomer was born 1797 in North Carolina. He died about 1870 in Sabine County, Texas. James and Anna M.B. (?) married around 1821, probably in Tennessee. Anna M.B. was born 1804 in Georgia, and died between 1870 and 1880 in Sabine County. Both are buried in the Gomer Family Cemetery at the site of the old homeplace near Yellowpine.

Amanda F. Gomer

The James Gomer family was living in Giles County, Tennessee, at the time of the 1830 census, and arrived in Texas in time for the third child, Amanda F. Gomer, to be born August 19, 1836. James Gomer qualified for a Second Class Land Grant, which was surveyed in Parker County. He farmed land near Yellowpine in Sabine County. Anna M.B. Gomer kept herbs and was known as a midwife, nurse and "doctor" of the Housen Bayou area of Sabine County. Some descendants believe Anna M.B. was Indian.

James and Anna M.B. Gomer had six children: Augustus C. Gomer married (1) Eliza Minerva Nichols and (2) Margaret Ann Low. Gus served with Capt. J.M. Burroughs Company, Sabine County Volunteer Infantry, Confederate States of America. Mary Ann Gomer married James Ener. Amanda F. Gomer married Vincent Shilling and raised a large family. Leonidas Gomer, unmarried, lost his life when serving with Hood's Texas Brigade during the Civil War. Anna M. Gomer married Mr. Desrisia; Catherine Gomer was unmarried.

The Daughters of the Republic of Texas Chapter in Hemphill, Sabine County, Texas is the James F. Gomer Chapter.

Regan Winslow Smith (great-great-great-great-great-grandson) #5955

MICAJAH GOODWIN

Micajah Goodwin, his wife Elizabeth, and their ten children migrated to Texas from Randolph County, Alabama, in the 1840s. Goodwin was born 20th April 1805, in Georgia, and died 7th May 1870, in Tarrant County, Texas. He came to Texas as a colonist and received a Republic of Texas Land Grant of 620 acres in Peters Colony. The family settled in what is now known as Watson's community in the northwest section of Grand Prairie, Texas. Here he built a cabin for his family of square post oak timbers, secured by the use of the Tennessee notching technique, making the cabin self-supporting without the use of nails or other fasteners. The "Micajah Goodwin Cabin" is a Texas State Historical Site, located in Cottonwood Park in Grand Prairie, Texas.

He was a farmer, but also played an important role in helping to form Dallas County, Texas. He was named Commissioner of the West District. However, when boundary lines were surveyed, his home lay just west of the boundary of the county, making him ineligible to hold the office. During the Hedgecox War, he was

Texas State Historical Site: The Micajah Goodwin Cabin built in 1840, Cottonwood Park, Grand Praire, Texas.

chosen as a delegate to represent Tarrant County to discuss land titles at McKinney, Texas. He was an agent for the Northern Standard Newspaper for many years. The county courts often appointed him to help with the appraisals of the property of the deceased. It is said he is buried in Watson Cemetery along side of his wife, Elizabeth, who was born 20th October 1802, and died 24th of October 1846, in Tarrant County, Texas.

The children of Micajah and Elizabeth were Jesse S., John J., Eliza, Madison L., Nancy, Joel Maulden, Mary Ann, William S., Charles Allen, Martha Rebecca, and Williamson L. Submitted by: Jimmy Woodrow Hendricks, great-great-great-grandson #4763 Jackie Gus Duvall, great-great-great-grandson #4934 Curtis Duvall Anderson, great-great-great-grandson #4929 Gregory Keith Hendricks, great-great-great-great-grandson #4762

JOHN A. GOOLSBY

John A. Goolsby, (born ca 1801, Georgia), arrived in Houston County, Republic of Texas, in December 1839. His wife, Rebecca Thompson Goolsby (born 1798, Kentucky), his mother Margaret N. (born 1783, Virginia), and other relatives, namely a son, Charles Marion Goolsby (born ca 1825, Alabama), came with him. Archive records show John A. Goolsby was granted a 640-acre Conditional Land Certificate in Houston County, Republic of Texas, 1 January 1840. This was converted to an Unconditional Land Certificate 18 February 1950, and 554 acres were later patented.

John A. Goolsby died July 1852. Margaret N. Goolsby died ca 1856-1857.

Rebecca Goolsby died 7 May 1866. All are buried in Houston County, Texas.

Charles Marion Goolsby served in the U.S. Army during the Mexican War and married Martha B.? around 1850-1851 in Houston County, Texas. A daughter, Francis K., (Fannie) Goolsby, was born in Houston County, Texas, in 1853 or 1854. Civil War Militia Records of Houston County dated July 1861 show C. M. Goolsby 2nd Sgt. Probate records of Houston County, Texas, show that Charles Marion Goolsby, administrator, of Rebecca Goolsby Estate, auctioned the land or land certificate for $256.00, 9 February 1871. The 1880 U.S. Census Robertson County Texas lists Marion Goolsby as a farmer, age 57. The exact date and place of his death is unknown.

A Milam County marriage license, signed by a Methodist minister, shows that Francis K. (Fannie) Goolsby married James Albert Cargill 8 March 1876. He was born 1855, Williamson County, Texas, and died 1927, Oklahoma. Fannie Goolsby Cargill died ca 1890-1892 in Milam or Erath County, Texas.

Their son, Thomas Marion Cargill (born 17 December 1876, Milam County, Texas, died 3 September 1957, Brownfield, Terry County, Texas) married Mary Francis (Jay) Rodgers 1 January 1902, in Hardeman County Texas. She was born 27 November 1869 in Texas, died 30 October 1949, Brownfield, Terry County, Texas. Several children were born to his marriage. A son, Henry Marion Cargill was born 7 July 1906, Oklahoma, died 12 November 1978, Brownfield, Terry County, Texas. He was married to Floys Elsie Anderson on 23 January 1927. She was born 14 June 1907, Callahan County, Texas, and died 25 March 1986, Brownfield, Terry County, Texas. Their son, the writer, is the sixth-generation great-grandson of John A. Goolsby. Darwin Leon Cargill #4704

BEVERLY CARTER GREENWOOD

Defender, Beverly Carter Greenwood, (1819-1895), born 1 Nov. 1819, Pendleton District, South Carolina, son of citizen John Greenwood (b. 1797, Georgia, married 1818 Joiney D. Hooper, B. 1796, Georgia). John had Spanish Land Grant 1818, Red River District, Texas. Bev, when 13, migrated with his family and relatives, all from South Carolina, in covered wagons coming to Texas. They lived in Mississippi, Georgia, Tennessee, and Alabama, stopped to raise food for family and livestock, entered Northern Mexico over Old Spanish Trail near Nacogdoches. The family secured land which Indians claimed as theirs, 1832-36, and sought advice of attorney Sam Houston, who persuaded John to return land to Indians after harvest. The family moved to Washington County.

Capt. Beverly Carter Greenwood and wife, Elizabeth Mary Farley Thomas, circa 1868-70.

Gen. Rusk's defeat of the Kickapoos — 1838, Kickapoo Town, in battle fought Tuesday 16 Oct. 1838, Beverly Greenwood lost a bay horse, appraised value $150.00 and saddle $10.00, claim #8776, $160.00, signed J.W. Burton, Wm. B. Lacy, Maj. B.C. Miller, approved, Gen. Thomas L. Rusk and L. Roberts, Qtrmaster Gen. of Texas, also Auditors Office, Houston, 23 Nov. 1838.

John 1837-40, owned and operated a hotel at Washington-on-the-Brazos, and granted 640 acres, Bev 320 acres, Hut 320 acres, 12 December 1839, Washington County; moved 1841 Gonzales County, "La Baca" Precinct, settled between Mustang and Rocky Creek near Sweet Home. John 1843 elected Justice of the Peace "La Baca" Precinct #4, Gonzales County, Land Commissioner, Overseer of Road, Hallettsville to Gephart's, Mustang Creek.

Beverly Carter Greenwood served with Lavacan John Henry Brown, historian/author, "History of Texas from 1685 to 1892," who names himself, B.C. Greenwood and others, March 1842, fought Gen. Vasquez, drove invaders out of Texas, they remained in service of Capt. John C. "Jack" Hays Spy Company 6 weeks on Medina River; Sept. 1842 fought Gen. Adrian Woll at Salado, turned Mexican Army; Nov. 1842 served Gen. Alex Somervell Expedition in Capt. Isaac N. Mitchell's Co., First Regiment of the Southwestern Army, reached Laredo 7 Dec. 1842, brother Hut swam Rio Grande bearing unit flag, Bev, Hut, Brown and others obeyed discharge 7 Jan. 1843, returned to Sweet Home.

Records in the Texas State Archives, Austin, Texas, for B.C. Greenwood, public debt of the late Republic of Texas, claim #1247, 16 June 1851, Service on Somervell Campaign, Private of Capt. Isaac N. Mitchell's Company, enrolled 11 Nov. 1842, First Regiment of the Southwestern Army, 3 months, $67.50; claim #1828, 1 Sept. 1851, service, the Vasquez Campaign in Capt. Hays' Company under General Burleson, $31.50; claim #4893, services on the Woll Campaign, 24 Jan. 1854, $15.75.

Bev married 28 Dec. 1844 Terressa A. Bennett (1822-1851), born 7 April 1822, Greene County, Alabama, daughter of Stephen & Mary Ann Bennett, Sweet Home, married in parents' home by Rufus C. Brown, J.P., Lavaca Precinct, Gonzales Co., (John Henry Brown's brother). Children: Joyce, b.1848; John, B. 1850.

Bev 1846 appointed 1 of 5 commissioners to locate county seat of new Lavaca County; 13 July 1846 helped elect uncle Benjamin Haile Stribling 1st Judge of Lavaca County; Bev 2 Nov. 1846, Lavaca County Land Certificate, 320 acres, established by Wm. Greenwood and Isham Tate; 1851 Bev joined Masonic Lodge A.F.&A.M, initiated 5-3-51 Gonzales Lodge #30, later transferred to Cameron, Brackettville Blue Lodge, Kinney County and Del Rio Lodge as he moved; Bev's wife Terressa died Dec. 1851, Sweet Home.

Bev married 2nd, 18 May 1853, Elizabeth Mary Farley Thomas (1827-1880), born 19 Jan. 1827, Georgia, daughter of Stephen and Matilda Anderson Farley, Jackson Co., Florida, married by Wm. Stapp, J.P., in Clinton, DeWitt County, purchased land on San Antonio River at Charco, adjoining Farley and Greenwood relatives at "Pleasant Hill" & "Mistletoe Ranch" near Goliad, living in late 1860s at Helena and Karnes County; children: Katherine Farley, B. 1854; Robert, B. 1856; Beverly Carter Jr., B. 1857; William H., B. 1860; Frank Sr., B. 1861; Mary, B. 1863; Lee Carter, B. 1866.

Bev enlisted Aug. 1861, Goliad, made Capt. Homeguard Company for Charco Precinct No. 2, Goliad County, 20th Brig., Texas Militia, Hut elected 3rd Lt., to protect county, recruit men & control commerce. Capt. B.C. Greenwood received Confederate orders, Austin, to commandeer all wagons, teams & oxcarts necessary, haul cotton & produce to Mexico, exchange for munitions, food, clothing, medicines, cattle, mules & horses for Southern soldiers. Bev took entire family in these wagontrains on many long trips through San Patricio & Banquete to Mexico border towns, Bagdad and Matamoros, served until end of war.

Bev 1865-69, successful farmer, prominent southwest Texas cattleman, early trail driver; 1867 Bev, Farley, Strickland & other Karnes County families drove their cattle to Rio Grande border, 1870 moved their families & remaining livestock to headwaters of Mud Creek & along Devil's River near Fort Clark at Brackettville, Kinney County; 1868 Bev & 5 sons engage in major stock drives into Mexico, from San Angelo thru Fort Davis & Big Bend to Chihuahua, Mexico, fought Pancho Villa's bandits stealing his cattle; Bev also took herds to Abilene, Kansas, up Chisholm Trail, through Oklahoma Indian Territory, also Pike's Peak & Denver, Colorado. Bev pioneered sheep and goat ranching & the Wool & Mohair Association. Bev's 2nd wife, Elizabeth Mary Farley Thomas, died 18 Feb 1880, Kinney County.

Bev married 3rd, 18 July 1883, Kinney County, Pauline Pafford Allen Strickland (1838-1921), born 1838, Clarksville, DeKalb County, Tennessee, daughter of Randolph Pafford & Mary Phillips; Pauline, widow of Amos Orlando Strickland, moved their family from Gonzales County with Bev, Farley, Kratz, Ragin & other Karnes County families, 1870s relocating in Kinney County; marriage recorded by his 2 son-in-laws, Judge R. Kratz (wife Mary) & W.H. Ragin (wife Katherine), County Clerk, Kinney County; Bev purchased land along San Felipe Springs & Creek, one of pioneer founders of Del Rio; Bev, Pafford, Strickland & others joint owners, SFAM&I Co., 1882 Bev president, R.A. Farley, sec., San Felipe Agricultural, Manufacturing & Irrigation Company that dug "Madre Ditch," "San Felipe Ditch" & others to furnish water, irrigation, electricity & ice for city & area, "Garden Spot of Texas," developed Greenwood Addition, gave land his children later donated for Greenwood Park, Baptist, Presbyterian and Methodist, churches, and Val Verde County Public Library. Mason, banker & promoter, helped create Val Verde County, develop the area, schools, churches & economy, with family & relatives serving in school and county office. Faithful to his God, state, nation and family, died 4 Dec. 1895, buried, Masonic Cemetery section of Westlawn Cemetery, Del Rio, Val Verde County, Texas.

Beverly Carter Greenwood, Jr.	07	P	#6133N
John Murray Greenwood, Sr.	07	P	#6132N
John Murray Greenwood, Jr.	07	L	#3807
John Murray Greenwood, III	07	L	#3806
Robert Henry Yelvington	07	R	#5248S
Bascomb Barry Hayes	07	R	#5289S
Robert Frank Hustin	07	R	#5303S
Allen David Bordelon	07	R	#5362S
Garrison Greenwood Harwell	07	R	#5376S
Myron Thomas Johnston II	07	R	#5377S
William Ryan Hutto	07	J	#5385S

GARRISON GREENWOOD

Garrison Greenwood, son of Fleming Greenwood and Lavina Ann (Gatewood) Greenwood, was born in Franklin County, Georgia, December 19, 1799. His family moved from Georgia, eventually settling in Mount Vernon, Jefferson County, Illinois. There, Garrison married Elizabeth Jordan on September 16. 1819; together they had 14 children. He was an ordained Baptist minister. Hoping to find a better life, Garrison joined the Daniel Parker wagon train, which departed Mount Vernon on August 7, 1833, and immigrated to Texas. He entered Texas at Gaines Ferry on Nov. 12, 1833. Garrison first went to Grimes County, and then moved just west of what is now Palestine, Texas.

Matters with the Indians grew worse as the War with Mexico brewed. Therefore, to secure the inhabitants on the frontiers, the

Texas Consultation organized a defense against both Indians and Mexican soldiers. The General Council made arrangements for raising three companies of Rangers, being the famous Texas Rangers. Garrison Greenwood was selected to head one of the Texas Ranger companies. They fought many a dangerous battle. In 1837, Garrison moved his family to Shelby County, then to his league of land on the Attoyac River in Nacogdoches County, and then to Fort Houston, each time trying to keep his family, safe from the Indians. He moved often, started several churches and was active in politics.

In 1854, Garrison moved his family to Lampasas County, where he remained until his death on October 18,1859. He is buried in Oak Hill Cemetery in Lampasas, Texas. Submitted by: James Buford Briggs, SRT #6552, great-great-great-grandson of Garrison Greenwood Glynn Dwayne Taylor SRT #6856

JOHN ALEXANDER GREER

John Alexander Greer was born July 18, 1802 in Shelbyville, Tennessee. On May 18, 1836, he married Adeline Minerva Orten. Shortly after, they moved to San Augustine County, Texas. Their daughter, Catherine Adeline Greer was born February 2, 1838.

Col. Greer's political career began with his election in 1838 as Senator from San Augustine County. He was re-elected to each succeeding session, serving longer than any other man in the Congress of the Republic. He was elected president pro tempore of the Senate of the Sixth Congress. He was re-elected as long as the Republic lasted, serving as president of the Senate in the Sixth, Seventh. Eighth, and Ninth Congresses. He was the recognized leader of the Houston Party.

In July 1845, Col. Greer succeeded William B. Ochiltree as Secretary of the Treasury, becoming the last officer to hold this position under the Republic.

Col. Greer died on July 4, 1855. Greer County, Texas (now in Oklahoma) was named in his honor.

His daughter, Catherine Adeline Greer, married Dr. W. Bond Dashiell in 1858. They had two children: Anne Ridgeley Dashiell, who married William Abraham; and Alfred Henry Dashiell, who married Adeline Wicks.

John Alexander Greer is my great-great-grandfather. Mark A. Chamber

RICHARD GREGORY, SR.

Richard Gregory, Sr., was born on December 16, 1775, in Fairfield District, South Carolina. He died on February 5, 1872. He is buried in the Gregory Cemetery, Colmesneil, Texas.

Richard Gregory, Sr., was the son of Samuel Gregory and Elizabeth, his wife. They were both born in South Carolina. Samuel was a farmer and was a loyalist to the British. He served in Colonel Clary's Dutch Fork Regiment and Colonel Ballentine's Camden Militia.

Richard Gregory, Sr., moved to Montgomery County, Georgia, in 1799. He married Elizabeth Edwards in 1801. Elizabeth, his wife, was born in North Carolina in 1780. She died on April 25,1856 in Tyler County, Texas.

Four girls and three boys were born and raised in Montgomery County, Georgia, by Richard and Elizabeth Gregory. In 1827, Richard Gregory and family relocated to Thomas County, Georgia. Richard owned and farmed land in the 32nd Land District near the Florida Territory.

In July 1835, John Gregory, Richard Gregory's oldest son, was charged with murder in Thomas County, Georgia. John evaded the law by hiding in the Florida Territory. On June 11, 1836, John Gregory and brother, Richard Gregory, Jr., boarded a schooner in Apalachicola, Florida, for New Orleans, Louisiana. Leaving Louisiana, they came across the Sabine River at what is now Orange, Texas. From there they went to San Augustine, Texas.

Billy R. Gregory, 1997

In 1837, Richard Gregory, Jr., returned to Thomas County, Georgia, and convinced Richard Sr. and all the other Gregory family to relocate in the new Republic of Texas. They moved to San Augustine County in 1837, and in 1839 received land patents from the San Augustine District Land Board.

Richard Gregory, Sr., was born seven months before the Declaration of Independence, and lived to see the United States expand to 37 states. Richard Gregory, Sr., was a citizen of four different nations and a U.S. citizen three different times, all while living in South Carolina, Georgia, Florida and Texas. He saw the United States as a British Colony and a fledgling nation, lived in Florida when it was a United States Territory, came to Texas when it was a Republic and saw it become a state and then a part of the Confederate States of America, and a part of the United States again. Richard Gregory traveled less than one thousand miles from his birthplace. Billy R. Gregory #5058

JACKSON HAWKINS GRIFFIN

A farmer and a city and county Chief Justice, Jackson Hawkins Griffin was born April 3, 1818, Kingston, Adams County, Mississippi, the first son of Absalom Griffin and Scythia Bradley. He moved to Texas age 12, circa 1830, to Liberty Township, and in 1845 married Louisa Martin, born April 2, 1825, in Liberty Texas. They had five children: Mary Ann, born 1846-1865; James Washington, born August 8, 1848-1917; Wilson J., born 1856-1896; Louisa L., born 1857-1865; Randal Coleman, born December 8, 1859 - Dec 1941

Jackson is listed on the muster roll of "Liberty Volunteers" under Captain Andrew Briscoe. This group joined Ben Milam in the Battle of Conception and the Siege of Bexar. Muster roll November 21, 1835, and roll March 6 1836, list him as part of Logan's Troops, which later became 3rd Co. Infantry, 2nd Regiment Texas Volunteers.

On March 5, 1836, Logan's Troops headed for the Alamo; before they reached San Felipe they got word the Alamo had fallen. Word spread of Santa Anna's army murdering women and children, and Jackson was furloughed to see about his family along with a few other men on April 18, 1836, for 8 days. They were to return by Thursday week or send substitutes. San Jacinto Battle was that Thursday, so he probably missed it.

January 25, 1861, Captain J.H. Griffin organized 54 men into a military company killed November 30 1864, Franklin, Tennessee.

Jackson is my great-great-grandfather on my mother side direct. Jay C. Camp #5503

JOSEPH GRIGSBY

Joseph Grigsby was born September 21, 1771 in Loudoun, County, Virginia, and died August 13, 1841 at Grigsby's Bluff, Jefferson County, Texas. He married Sally Mitchell Graham, born June 28, 1782, in Nelson County, Kentucky, and died November 15, 1861, in Jasper County, Texas. They were married June 28, 1798, at Bardstown, Nelson County, Kentucky.

George W. Smyth (1803-1866)   *Frances Grigsby Smyth (1809-1888)*

Joseph and Sally Grigsby and their six children arrived in Jasper County, Texas, in the spring of 1828, coming from near Owensboro, Daviess County, Kentucky. My direct relative, their daughter, Sally Grigsby Glenn, and her three sons lived on a league of land (4,400 acres) nearby. Her married sisters, Susannah and Frances, and bachelor brother, Nathaniel, also were neighbors. All together, the family had about 20,000 acres of land.

Sally Grigsby Glenn Allen (1807-1885)

By the Texas Census of 1830, Joseph and Sally were living in Jefferson County, at a place called Grigsby's Bluff (now known as Port Neches, Texas), where I grew up. With Joseph lived his two sons, Nathaniel and Enoch, and 50 slaves to work the two leagues of land (8,800 acres) he owned. In 1832, Joseph Grigsby, his son-in-law, Duke Glenn, and son-in-law to be, George Washington Smyth, and others went to Anahuac, Texas to get William Barret Travis — a distant relative and later commander of the

James Dudley Parrish, Jr. #1849

Alamo – out of Mexican confinement. Joseph's sons, Nathaniel and Enoch, fought at the Siege of Bexar in December 1835. Then in March 1836, George Washington Smyth signed the Texas Declaration of Independence. After state public service, Joseph died on September 13, 1841. James D. Parrish, Jr., Life Member, SRT # 1849

JESSE GRIMES

Our third- or fourth-great-grandfather was born Feb. 6, 1788, in Duplin County, North Carolina, the third child of Sampson and Bethsheba Winder Grimes. In the War of 1812, he served in Capt. John Looney's Company of Infantry, West Tennessee Militia. In 1813, he married our third- or fourth-great-grandmother, Martha Smith. They moved to Greens County, Georgia, in 1816, and then to Washington County, Alabama, in 1817. Jesse held several public offices in Washington County from 1819 to 1823.

Jesse Grimes

Following the death of wife, Martha, he married Rosana (Ward) Britton. In 1826, they came to Texas, first settling on the San Jacinto River about ten miles above Buffalo Bayou. In 1827, he and his family moved to what is now Grimes County, settling on land which was awarded to him in a Land Grant by the Mexican government in 1831. This place soon became known as Grimes Prairie.

In 1829, Jesse was lieutenant of Militia in Capt. Abner Kuykendall's Company. In 1830, he was elected sindico of Viesca, then regidor in the Ayuntamiento of San Felipe in 1832. He was a delegate to the Convention of 1833. In 1834, Grimes was appointed Judge of the First Instance for the jurisdiction of Austin. He was elected to the Consultation of 1835, and to the Provisional Council; in 1835 he was appointed a colonel in the Army of Texas by Gov. Henry Smith, although there is no record of Jesse Grimes serving in this capacity.

He served as a delegate to the Convention of 1836, at which time he signed the Declaration of Independence and the first Constitution of Texas. While at the Convention, his son, Albert Calvin, perished at the Alamo with William B. Travis. One of the letters Travis sent during the siege of the Alamo was addressed to Jesse Grimes.

Jesse Grimes served the Republic of Texas as Senator in the First, Ninth and Tenth Congress, and was a member of the lower house in the Sixth, Seventh and Eighth Congresses. From 1837-1840, he was Chief Justice of Washington County. After Annexation he was State Senator, and served in every State Legislature until 1861, except the Fifth. In 1857, Jesse ran unsuccessfully for lieutenant governor on the Houston ticket.

Jesse retired from public service in 1861, and returned to his plantation in Grimes County. He died there on March 15, 1866.

In 1929, Jesse and his wife, Rosana were reburied at the State Cemetery in Austin. Fred Averill Burns, Jr. #6079 Ronald Goodwin Burns #6519 Philip Coe Grimes #3623Roy Joseph Grimes #3624 Brian Fred Burns, MD #6261

ERNST GRUENE, SR.

Ernst Gruene, Sr., was born in Netze, district of Binderlohn, Hanover, on 6 July 1819. In 1845, at the age of 26, he departed Bremen, Germany, on the ship Margaretha, accompanied by his bride, Antoinette (Kloepper) and his mother, Engel Gruene. Antoinette was born 9 April 1826, and was a native of Ahdenstadt at Binderlich, Hanover. Engel was born in 1795 in Hanover.

According to tradition, Ernst contracted cholera upon his arrival as a colonist in the Republic of Texas, and recuperated in New Braunfels, the first town to be surveyed and settled by German immigrants in Comal County. The young couple decided to remain here, and Ernst began farming the rich land.

The children of Ernst and Antoinette, all baptized in the Protestant Congregation of New Braunfels, were: (1) Ernst Gruene, Jr., B. 21 Sept. 1847, D. 8 Nov. 1895, md. Wilhelmine Lange, 5 Sept. 1867, great-grandparents of the writer; (2) Henry D. Gruene, B. 25 July 1850; and (3) Antoinette Johanna Gruene, B. 21 Dec. 1852.

In 1872, when land was no longer available in New Braunfels, Ernst and his sons bought 6,000 acres in the community of Goodwin on the northern banks of the Guadalupe River. A mercantile store was built in 1878, and it became a profitable river-crossing store on the stage route between Austin and San Antonio. In the 1880s, the community took the name of its leading citizens and became known as Gruene.

Ernst died 2 April 1914, and Antoinette died 23 march 1917. Both are buried in Comal Cemetery. Preston M. Geren, Jr. SRT #2063 Great-great-grandson

FRANCISCO ANTONIO GUERRA

Francisco Antonio Guerra came to Texas circa 1740, and is listed as one of the original families to colonize what was then called "El Nuevo Santander," or the area from the San Antonio River, south to Tampico, Mexico, west to the Sierra Madre Mountains and bordered on the east by the Gulf of Mexico.

He is listed in the Texas General Land Office as being the original grantee of "Porcion 66," a land grant granted to him by the Spanish Crown confirmed by the "visita General" from Spain in 1767. The "visitador" was Jose De Galvez, who became minister of the Indies. The area had been explored by the "Conde," Jose De Escondor, in 1746. Porcion 66 is located on the north bank of the Rio Grande River of what was the jurisdiction of Mier, Mexico, before 1836.

Francisco was born in Monterey, Mexico, to Antonio Guerra Canamar and Antonia de la Garza Trevino. Francisco married Ana Josepha De La Garza in 1735. Antonio Guerra Canamar was baptized on January 4, 1672, in Monterey, Mexico. His parents were Captain Ignacio Guerra Canamar and Catalina Fernandez T. Gonzalez. Captain Ignacio Guerra Canamar was born in Mexico City in 1636. He was the captain of the "Persidio de la villa de Cerralvo." His father was Captain Antonio Guerra Canamar, who was born in old Castile, Spain. He arrived in Vera Cruz, Mexico, circa 1610, with the annual fleet from Spain.

Francisco Antonio Guerra was granted 4,299.88 acres of land on the north bank of the Rio Grande River, now near the town of Roma, Texas. The land grant was confirmed by the Texas Legislature, Act of February 10, 1852, as recommended by the Bourland and Miller Report.

Francisco Antonio Guerra explored Texas on many occasions from his ranch named "Los Alamos," in what is now Starr County, Texas. The Catholic Church in Mier was built in the late 1700s and attended by the Guerras and other colonists. The later 1700s in colonial Texas was characterized by conflict with area Indians, drought, a lack of military support, and little communication with the outside world. It was a time of exploration, colonization, and the beginning of the Catholic Church in Texas. Luis Guerra, a descendent of Antonio, was under Fannin's command at Goliad. Another descendent, Francisco, 1861, fought with the Union Army.

In 1687, Vicente and Juan Guerra, ancestors of Francisco Antonio, accompanied General Alonso de Leon on his first expedition into Texas in search of La Salle's Fort St. Louis. They made five expeditions into Texas through 1691. Francisco was well aware of the frontier that the Spaniards called "Tejas." Francisco's decedents lived on Porcion 66 during the occupation by Spain through 1821, then Mexico through 1836, then the Republic of Texas through 1845, and then after Annexation by the United States, and for a short period part of the Confederacy between 1860 and 1865. I am the great-grandson of Francisco Antonio Guerra, eighth generation. Benito Figueroa, Jr.

HABY FAMILY

Francis Joseph Haby II and Mary Ann Meyer Haby of Oberentzen, Alsace, had 8 children. Two of those children — Francis Joseph Haby III and Nicholas Haby — came to Texas in 1843 on the ship "Ocean" with the colonizer, Henri Castro. They landed at Port Lavaca and walked to San Antonio and on to Castroville. Nicholas went back to Alsace in 1846 and brought his father and mother and 6 brothers and sisters back to Texas. They came on the ship Duc de Brabant in 1846, and his mother died on the trip over. The land this family received from the Republic of Texas was on the Medina River about 8 miles north of Castroville and on which they formed the little town of "Haby Settlement."

Maria Anna Haby was born to Francis Joseph Haby III and Katherina Koenig Haby on 15 February 1861 in Haby Settlement, Texas. She married Joseph Schorp II in Castroville, Texas on 3 November 1897. The oldest child from that union was Ida Helen Schorp, who married Walter Francis Smith on 27 December 1925, in Laredo, Texas. W.F. Smith was a U.S. Mounted Customs Officer assigned to Company D of the Texas Rangers under Captain Will Wright. From that union came 3 children: Robert Joseph Schorp, Helen Ida and Mary Jo. Robert married Cynthia Lou Bingman, and they have 3 children: Robert Boyd Bingman, Harriett Mandena and Helen Marie. Robert Joseph Schorp Smith

JOSHUA HADLEY

Joshua Hadley, son of Benjamin and Elizabeth King Hadley, was born in North Carolina in about 1794. His grandfather was Captain Thomas Hadley, patriot of the American Revolution and descendant of the Simon Hadley 1 line.

Joshua and his first wife, Obedience Grantham Hadley, settled in Texas in 1831. Obedience bore him five children. After Obedience died, he married a widow, Joyce Bostic Floyd, with two children. This marriage produced three sons: Joshua, William Bostic, and Anthony Drew, all of whom were born in the Republic.

Anthony Drew Hadley (grandson of Joshua Hadley) with wife, lower right holding Dock Hadley and her daughter, Joyce (age 3), standing to her right; Other two women are sisters-in-law with their children

Joshua was a surveyor and surveyed the two leagues of land given to him as land grants on May 17, 1831 and February 25, 1835. These land grants were in what are now Grimes County and Limestone County. He also purchased 15,000,000 varas of land as recorded in Washington County, Texas.

He served as an officer in the Texian Army from June 30, 1836 to September 30, 1836, and for this he received a bonus of 320 acres of land in Grimes County. These large amounts of land served him well, as he had a large herd of cattle. These cattle were grazed and driven as far north as Johnson County, Texas.

In the Convention of 1832 he was a delegate from the District of Viesca. He was elected as the first alcalde of the newly created municipality of Washington on July 18, 1835. He was a charter member of Orphan's Friend Lodge #17, organized April 8, 1842, at Fanthorpe's house in Anderson, Texas.

Joshua had constructed a two-story structure, which served as a house and fort to ward off Indian attacks at Hadley's Prairie. His land grant in Limestone County was located near Parker's Fort, which was attacked by Comanches in 1836, resulting in a massacre of citizens and the capture of Cynthia Ann Parker and others.

Joshua took charge of two of the Parker children (Silas and Orlena) until they could be reunited with members of the Parker family. As a result, Joshua was mentioned in the Parker family probate records on file in Montgomery County.

Marker for Joshua Hadley and others, Grimes Co. Courthouse, Anderson, Texas.

He worked his cattle, horses, and land in close cooperation with his good friend, A.D. Kennard, who lived nearby. In 1843, he served as Justice of the Peace in Precinct 2, Montgomery County. He died at Hadley's Prairie in 1845 as a result of a fall from his horse. His name is presently inscribed on a granite marker located on the lawn of the courthouse in Anderson, Grimes County, Texas. The Zuber-Hadley Chapter of the Daughters of the Republic of Texas was formed in 1910 and named for him.

In tribute to his second wife Joyce Violet Bostic Floyd Hadley proved herself to be a survivor by marrying a third time to Samuel McGuffin, a widower with several children. One of these children was eight years old, Mary E. McGuffin, who lived with them, so with eleven children in various stages of life she managed to carry on, with a lot of trials and tribulations as all frontier women did. Jack Charles Lightfoot (great-great-grandson) #6422J

HENRY H. HAHN

Cooke County's first permanent settler came to the area four years earlier than the currently recognized pioneer family. Martin, Neeley, who established his residence in 1845 on Spring Creek in the southern part of the county was believed by A. Morton Smith in his "The First 100 Years in Cooke County" to have been the first permanent settler.

Henry H. Hahn unknowingly recorded his claim to the honor of being Cooke County's first resident when he regained his citizenship after the Civil War upon signing the Loyalty Oath. Immediately after voting registration opened in 1867, Henry was one of the first county citizens to go to the courthouse and swear his allegiance to the United States. When asked where he was born, he stated Missouri. In the columns asking, "How long in Texas?" "How long in the county?" and "How long in the voting precinct?", Henry said, "26 years" to each question. This places him in the area now known as Cooke County in 1841.

Henry Hahn, the son of Joshua Hahn and Catherine Wise, was born February 13, 1813, in Cape Girardeau, Missouri. Joshua moved his family to Greene County, Illinois, in about 1828. Henry married Patsy Silkwood on January 14, 1836, in Calhoun County, Illinois. Henry and Patsy came to Cooke County in 1841.

In 1843, their son, William J. Hahn, added to the county's list of firsts by becoming the first child of a pioneer family to be born in Cooke County.

Between 1846 and 1850, Henry's father, Joshua, brought his family to Cooke County. Joshua filed the 20th land deed to be recorded in Cooke County, which had just been carved out of Fannin County by the Legislature. Henry and his father bought unfiled land grants of 640 acres each, which were recorded in Cooke County. Henry applied for a 640 acre land grant, which he filed in Collin County, where he is recorded in the 1850 Census. Many residents of North Gainesville are living on the land Joshua had surveyed, then claimed in 1850. Henry's land was north of Gainesville along what is now North Clements, which was earlier known as the Toll Road and the Airport Road. Henry is recorded in the 1860 Census in Cooke County.

In addition to microfilm records, the present generation is blessed with knowledge of Henry Hahn through an oral history begun by Henry's son, John Newton Hahn that has been passed down by his descendants. The current story tellers are Henry Hahn of Portales, New Mexico, and Gwen Brownlee of Dallas.

Henry Hahn came to Texas with Solomon Silkwood, believed to be his brother-in-law. Henry settled in Cooke County. Solomon is recorded in Dallas County, where he was given a 640-acre land grant.

Henry was with the Silkwood family at Bird's Fort on Christmas 1841, when Solomon and several other men left the safety of the fort in 6 inches of snow to explore a proposed supply route. They went 14 miles toward what is now Farmer's Branch. On Christmas morning, they treed a bear; before they could kill it, they were attacked by Indians. One of their party was killed. The rest returned to Bird's Fort and arrived there Dec. 27th. Solomon died Jan 15th from exposure. John Neely Bryant, founder of Dallas, was the executor of his estate. On April 1, 1842, Henry and several other families returned to their homes in north Texas.

Henry was a farmer, gunsmith, trapper and master stone mason, according to the family stories. Until recently, one of the guns created by Henry was still in the Hahn family.

Jim Ned, chief of the Delaware, and Henry made a peace treaty among themselves. They slashed their right wrists, bound them together with rawhide and swore to be blood brothers. The Delaware ranged from around Brownwood to southeastern Oklahoma. When they were in the Cooke County area, they stayed on Henry's place. He would cut out some beef to feed them. Later, Comanche Chief Yellow Wolf put Henry and his family under his protection.

After Patsy Silkwood died, Henry married a neighbor and widow, Martha Jane Wright. Sometime during the Great Hanging in Gainesville, Henry had been tipped off by his friend Bostick that they were going to come after Henry. Bostick did not know just when. Henry and his wife, Martha Wright, kept a constant lookout. Henry's original house, north of Gainesville, was a log cabin, which had become a shed or barn. He had built in front of it a white clapboard house, because Martha thought was that the ideal house. When they saw a large band of riders coming, Henry went into the old log cabin barn. Henry got behind a loophole and trained his gun on the riders. According to the story as handed down in the Hahn family, there were 27 riders.

The leader rode up and yelled for Henry to come out. Martha came out of the house and asked what they wanted.

We have come to hang Henry," the leader said.

What for?" she asked.

They then refered to Henry as a Yankee Sympithizer

Henry is guilty of those things. But if you hang him, Jim Ned will bring the Delaware and Comanche and burn Gainesville to the ground. It that what you want?" she asked. They rode away.

The mob knew Martha was telling them the truth and went back to Gainesville without harming Henry. Several weeks later, the tombstone Henry had made for his father in Fairview Cemetery was smashed to pieces. Henry never replaced it, and until 1998, the grave's location was unknown.

Henry later opened a brickyard southeast of Gainesville. It is believed by his family that he made and laid the bricks for what is now the Morton Museum of Cooke County.

Henry's half sister, Syrena Hahn, married Charles Monroe Leach in 1882. She was the mother of Felix Leach, who was Gainesville's assistant postmaster in the 1940s.

Henry Hahn died April 23, 1889. Martha Hahn died July 31, 1889. They are buried in Union Hill Cemetery, southwest of Callisburg.

ROBERT HALL SR.

Robert Hall, Sr., born April 14, 1814, in the Rocky River District of South Carolina, was one of five children born to James and Rebecca Gassaway Hall. He married Mary Minerva "Polly" King, daughter of famous Texas pioneer, Colonel John Gladden King on June 20, 1837 in Gonzales, Texas. Robert Hall, Sr., died December 19, 1899, in Cotulla, Texas, and is buried in the King Cemetery on Highway 90A, south of Gonzales, Texas, in Oak Forest, along with his wife and several children. He had 13 children, one being my great-grandfather, John Johnson Hall, father to my grandmother, Johanna Hall Handshy.

Robert Hall arrived in Texas in the spring of 1836, and joined the Army of the Republic of Texas on June 1, 1836. He was stationed at Camp Johnson on the Lavaca River. He was a pioneer settler, Indian fighter, Texas Ranger and veteran of three wars. He also fought in the battles of Plum Creek, Medina, Salado and Buena Vista. He was a member of Matthew Caldwell's Ranger Company. While a Ranger under Caldwell, Hall and 33 other Rangers surveyed and laid out the town of Walnut Springs, later changed to Seguin, Texas.

He enlisted in the 36th Texas Cavalry Regiment of the Confederate Army on May 31, 1862, at the age of 48, under Colonel Pete C. Wood.

Space does not permit covering the many interesting events experienced in his life. His biography, "Life of Robert Hall" was published in 1898, mainly for his descendants to have an account of the events of his life. The book was re-published in 1992 by State House Press, Austin, Texas, updated by Stephen L. Hardin, Victoria College.

Robert Hall, Sr., is my great-great-grandfather and I am very proud of this great Texan. Johnny M. Brannan #3986, Wade C. Brannan, William B. Travis Chapter #7

JAMES POWEL HALLFORD

James Powel Hallford was born in South Carolina on June 16, 1812, to Jesse and Rebecca Powel Hallford. He was one of 14 children. The family later moved to Moniteau County, Missouri.

James P. Hallford married Sarah Medlin on October 2, 1834. In early 1844, they joined a large group of families related by blood or marriage, called the Peter's Colony, and left Missouri for Texas. Despite encounters with swollen streams, Indians, and illness, they continued on to their destination. All settled on land later known as Hallford Prairie, northeast of the present town of Grapevine, Texas. This first permanent settlement, made in 1845, was called the Missouri Colony.

On the third Saturday of February 1846, the Lonesome Dove Baptist Church was organized. Among the charter members was James P. Hallford. The first election of the new Tarrant County was held in 1850, and James P. Hallford was elected a Commissioner. In 1854, James P. Hallford followed the call for land to Hays County. He died December 4, 1868, age 56 years and is buried in the Middlebrooks Family Cemetery, Dripping Springs, Texas.

Lineage: John Harrison Hallford, Andrew Jasper Hallford, Chester Irvin Hallford, Chester Arthur Hallford, Joe David Hallford (#2662), Jonathan Andrew Hallford (#5190S).

JOHN WILLIAM HANKAMER

John William Hankamer arrived in Galveston, Texas, in December 1845, with brothers Charles and Frederick, mother Johannette, and step-father John Stengler on the "Harriet," which sailed on October 10, 1845. They were from Prussia and had planned to join the Fisher and Millers colonies, but after hearing of their suffering chose to stay in Galveston until June, 1846, when they moved to Anahuac. None of the family spoke English. In the fall of 184, they moved to what is now Hankamer, to a house formerly owned by Andrew Weaver.

John William Hankamer and his brothers served in the Confederate Army, Company F of Spaights Battalion, Texas Volunteers. Many of their Civil War letters have been published.

John first married Lurinda Smith, daughter of Silas Smith (another citizen of the Republic of Texas) and Lurenda Green, and had eleven children, only three of which survived the smallpox epidemic of 1877, which also took his wife. He then married Mary E. Leger and had six more children.

John served as a Justice of the Peace and County Commissioner for Chambers County. The town of Hankamer, Texas, is named for him. His son, Ira Alvan, my great-grandfather, was the first postmaster. Devin Carr Lindsey

HIRAM HANOVER

Hiram Hanover served in the House of Representatives of the Seventh Congress (called session November 14, 1842 - December 4, 1842; and regular session December 5, 1842 - January 16, 1843), representing Brazos County at Washington-on-the-Brazos during Sam Houston's second administration. Hanover served during a particularly colorful stage of Texas history. Conditions at Washington are described in the Pulitzer Prize-winning biography of Houston, "The Raven," which states, "The president's proposal to commandeer Hatfield's saloon for the meeting-place of the House of Representatives encountered objections, however, in which a majority of the House appeared to concur. The sacrifice, they said, was disproportionate to the emergency. General Houston compromised by persuading a gambling establishment, which occupied rooms above the saloon to surrender its quarters. One entered the legislative chamber by means of a stairway from the barroom. The speaker experienced such difficulty in maintaining a quorum, however, that General Houston removed the steps to the outside of the building. The planks over the opening in the floor were not nailed down, and during a ball one of them slipped from the joists and a stout lady would have fallen through into the bar except for the presence of mind of Congressman Holland, with whom she was dancing. The Senate, smaller in numbers but not in dignity, met in a loft over a grocery whose principle staple was spirits."

Hiram Hanover   *Sarah Ann Sparks (first wife of Hiram Hanover)*

Hiram was born July 8, 1808, in Richmond. Maine, to William Hanover (served as a private in the War of 1812) and Hannah Flitner (daughter of a German degreed physician, Zacharias Flitner, who served as a surgeon in the American Revolution). In an essay he wrote years later in Texas, he referred to Hannah as "a stern, New England mother." During the winter of his sixteenth year, Hiram worked in a Maine logging camp and broke his leg in an ice jam on the Kennebec River. He was in bed for the rest of the winter, and this was the time that he "mastered mathematics," as he told his son many years later. Although his father was a sea captain, from whom Hiram learned navigation and astronomy, he chose a different calling. He was educated at Waterville College (now Colby College) in Waterville, Maine. During the academic year 1833-34, his hometown was listed as Pittston, Maine, south of Augusta.

He then went to Louisville, Kentucky, where he studied law and surveying. All the talk in Louisville was of Texas. After teaching a short time in Kentucky, Hiram left for Texas, traveling to New Orleans and then by ship to Galveston in 1838. He moved up the Brazos River to the area of present-day Brazos and Robertson counties.

Navasota County was formed in January 1841. The county seat, named Boonville for Mordecai Boon, Sr. (nephew of Daniel Boon), was surveyed by Hiram Hanover in 1841. The town plat indicates that he purchased a town lot for $20. Texas Archives show that Hiram was paid $73 in 1841 for assessing taxes in Navasota County. The county was renamed Brazos County in January 1842, and Hiram was appointed its first postmaster on July 1, 1842. He served as postmaster until he was elected to the House of Representatives in late 1842. After his service as a legislator, Hiram Hanover went to the Jacob Snively Expedition to the Red River as a member of Capt. Eli Chandler's company from the Wheelock area. When that expedition broke up, he returned to the Wheelock area and built an academy.

An advertisement in The National Vindicator, November 30, 1844, Washington-on-the-Brazos, entitled "Education," describes Hanover, stating "The Subscriber, having established a permanent institution for the education of youth, in Robertson County, near Kellogg's Post Office, takes this method to inform the public generally, that he will receive such pupils as may be entrusted to his care. Having had six years experience as a teacher, he flatters himself, that by unremitted attention, he may merit the patronage of those who confide their children to his supervision. References could be given, and an egotistical display of recommendations could be made, but he considers that all these weigh but little with men of sense. If, however, any should doubt his qualifications, or his capacity to impart instruction, he invites such to satisfy themselves in either particular by a personal examination of himself and scholars. ... No student will be admitted unless able to spell, at least, in two syllables. Good boarding can be had in the neighborhood at from four to six dollars per month." He was teaching Greek, Latin, algebra, geometry, trigonometry, surveying, the higher branches of mathematics as well as philosophy and chemistry, in addition to "the branches usually taught in a common English school." The academy building is still standing across the road from the Cavitt house on FM 391 in Wheelock.

Hiram married one of his pupils, Sarah Ann Sparks, on December 31, 1848, in Brazos County. He was age 40, and she was 15 years old. Sarah was the daughter of Colonel William Crain Sparks and Sarah Reed, also early settlers in Texas in 1832. They had two sons (William Sparks and Henry Frank) and two daughters (Clara Elizabeth and Mary Ann), all but one son (Henry Frank) living to maturity.

Hiram surveyed for the I. and G.N. Railroad, living in Dresden, Navarro County, in 1850, where their first child, William Sparks, was born. Sarah was cared for by her father and stepmother (Jane Alexander Skelton) in Bell County during her illness and death from consumption in 1857; she is buried near her father in the Volo Cemetery, south of Temple in the Sparks Community.

Hiram was elected County Surveyor of Robertson County on August 2, 1858. He volunteered for the Confederate Army, enlisting at Hempstead as a private in May 1862; he rode his Indian pony, Greybuck, off to war with the 21st Texas Cavalry, Company I, Colonel G.W. Carter commanding. They acted as scouts at the head of the lines between Arkansas and Missouri. His children were boarded with the Armstrong family in Wheelock while he served in the war. Hiram married a second time to Amanda Warren, his housekeeper, in 1867; he was age 59, and she was 23 years old. They had two sons who died young and a daughter (Martha, known as Mattie) who lived to maturity.

A handwritten journal by Hiram, dated December 10, 1870, reads: "For many years past I have employed some portion of my leisure time in solving some of the most difficult geometrical and algebraic problems that chance threw in my way. These solutions have been left on scraps of paper and the blank leaves of old account books, and have become so scattered and jumbled up, and some lost that I have conceived the idea of placing them all together in this book." The book is owned by descendants.

Hiram died on April 19, 1884, and is buried with his second wife at the Arnett Cemetery, near Wheelock, on the old Sparks place. His grave is marked with a stone of Maine granite, erected by his son, William Sparks Hanover. Due to Hiram's mastery of seven foreign languages and reputation, he was given the nickname of "Squire" in the Wheelock community. A 1932 obituary of his daughter-in-law, Mrs. William Sparks Hanover, in *The Bryan Daily Eagle*, reads "...was married to W.S. Hanover, son of Squire Hanover, who established the old Hanover homestead at Wheelock, long before the Civil War."

Hiram Hanover's surveying instruments (compass and Jacob staff, vara chain, and chaining pins) are on display at the Brazos Valley Museum in Bryan, along with the survey of Boonville. Joe G. Hanover, one of Hiram's great-grandsons and a former District Engineer for the Texas Highway Department in Bryan, donated the items in the 1990s for future generations to enjoy. By Walter David Hanover (great-great-grandson) Charles Peter Briggs IV #2658 James Harvey Briggs #2729 Jared Andrew Briggs #5410 Walter David Hanover #6687 Wesley David Hanover #6721 Samuel William Hanover #6722 James Clifton Nance #2676

JOHN MARR HARDEMAN

John Marr Hardeman, son of Constantine and Sarah Marr Hardeman, was born February 2, 1804, in Rutherford County, Tennessee. He married his first cousin, Mary Hardeman, on June 13, 1828, in Hardeman County, Tennessee. In the autumn of 1835, he and his family moved to the municipality of Matagorda, Republic of Mexico. He served in the Texas Army from July to October 1836, and then moved into Washington County, Republic of Texas, sometime in 1837. He was granted a league and a labor of land from Washington County, January 12, 1838. In February 1838, he was issued Certificate of Residency No. 127 that declared, "... he was a resident of Texas at the date of the Declaration of Independence." About 1857, he moved to Ellis County, Texas, where he resided until his death.

Tombstone of John Marr Hardeman and first wife, Mary in the Italy, Texas Cemetery

He married twice. His first wife bore him 12 children — 6 boys and 6 girls. She died in Ellis County, Texas, on September 19, 1857. His second marriage, to Malinda Jennings, in about 1859, endured for about 23 years, but no children were born to that marital union.

As a citizen of Texas, he acquired and sold real estate and was a farmer. John Marr Hardeman died in Ellis County, Texas, on October 15, 1891, at the age of 87 years. In 1936, the State of Texas had his remains reburied in the Italy City Cemetery, Italy, Ellis County, Texas, where a monument was erected in his honor.

John M. Hardeman was the father of James Henry Hardeman (1845-1923), who was the father of James Maxwell Hardeman (1867-1959), who was the father of Mary Ruby Hardeman Smyer (1897-1987), who was the mother of Joe P. Smyer (1931-), 10302 Redlawn, San Antonio, Texas, (210) 696-5809, jsmyer@aol.com, whose Sons of the Republic of Texas member number is 6700 and who is the great-great-grandson of John Marr Hardeman.

WILLIAM KILPATRICK HARGIS

My maternal great-grandfather, William Kilpatrick Hargis, was born in 1815 in South Carolina. His parents were possibly Abraham and Elizabeth Kilpatrick Hargis.

Moving to Texas in the 1830s, he served as a second sergeant in L.P. Cook's Company of Mounted Gunmen in the Santa Fe Expedition of 1837. He also served in the Woll and Vasquez Campaigns. It is thought that he almost went on the Mier Expedition.

Issued to Mr. Hargis on July 6, 1836, was a certificate for 640 acres of land in Gonzales and Kendall counties. His name is in the 1840 list of Gonzales County citizens.

In 1854, he married Elizabeth Floyd, daughter of Dolphin Ward Floyd (who died at the Alamo) and Esther Berry House. Elizabeth died in childbirth. In October 1855, Mr. Hargis married Esther

Jane Glover, daughter of Hinesberry and Emily Lackey Glover. William K. and Esther's children were Elizabeth K., James Edward, Jefferson Davis, Richard Martin, Esther, William Kilpatrick, Jr., Mary, Kenneth and Thomas.

William K. Hargis' name appeared in the May 25, 1878 obituary section of The Gonzales Inquirer.

Kenneth and Sallie (Harvey) Hargis' daughter, Lucill, married Samuel Elvin Isaacks, a descendant of early Texans Elijah Isaacks and William Isaacks. Virgil Kem Isaacks SRT #4401 of Ch. #38

BENJAMIN FRANKLIN HARKNESS, SR.

Benjamin Franklin Harkness, Sr., was born ca. 1810 in Tennessee or Kentucky. He married Ann P. Eakin, daughter of William Eakin of South Carolina.

Benjamin and Ann were in Bedford County, Tennessee, when their first child was born, which was in 1829. The next child was also born in Tennessee. The third child was born in Texas, ca. 1836. The land records places Benjamin Harkness in Shelby County by May 1838.

Benjamin Harkness, Sr., Received three (3) land grants in Shelby County; by all accounts he was a farmer, but when Center became a town, Benjamin Harkness served as postmaster from October, 1866 to July, 1871.

Benjamin and Ann had eight (8) children. Two (2) of their sons fought in the Civil War. It seems that James Harkness was killed in the war, for he wasn't mentioned in the records of Shelby County any more.

Ann Harkness died after 1880. Benjamin Harkness, Sr., died November 16, 1899, leaving a will that is recorded in the Courthouse in Center, Texas. It is thought that Benjamin was buried in the Newburn Cemetery outside Center, Texas. Benjamin Harkness, Sr., is my great-great-great-grandfather. Bobby Joe Fountain, Sr. SRT #4378

DAVID HARRIS

David Harris was born at Harris Ferry, New York, in 1795, the son of John Harris and Mary Richardson Harris. He may have come to Texas in 1823 with his older brother, John Richardson Harris. David Harris received title to a sitio of land in what is now Harris County on August 19, 1824, as one of Stephen F. Austin's "Old 300." He was granted a track of land on the west side of the San Jacinto River on April 7, 1830.

David Harris, along with his two brothers, John Richardson Harris and William Plunkett Harris, established a trading post at Bell's Landing on the Brazos River. Their schooners and sloops sailed between Texas and New Orleans.

Tabitha Kincade, the widow of John Iiams, married David Harris after Christman 1828, and they built a home between Red Bluff and La Porte. They had two sons named after his two brothers.

In 1829, after the death of John R. Harris, David Harris became the administrator of John's estate, operating a sawmill on the property southeast of Brae's Bayou. His attorney was William Barret Travis.

In 1835 Harris advised the men at Harrisburg not to make threats against the Mexican garrison at Anahuac while Stephen F. Austin was in Mexico, for fear of endangering Austin. However, Harris commanded the sloop Ohio in an attack on the garrison later that year.

David Harris died late winter of 1841 at his son's home on Middle Bayou. His home later became a Baptist recreation center.

Winston Arlen McKenzie, Sr. #4427 great-great-grandson Winston Arlen McKenzie, Jr. Maxfield Taylor McKenzie Alexander Harris McKenzie CRT Maxfield Hunter McKenzie CRT Wallace Jackson McKenzie

JAMES HARRIS AND FRANCES WOOLDRIDGE

In 1835, Mexican vessels blockaded the Texas coast. James Harris was involved with the Committee of Safety's action with those vessels and was present at November 1835 disposition of the recaptured Hannah Elizabeth. He later met the main army at Jarred E. Groce's plantation as one of Capt. W. H. Patton's Columbia Volunteers. James and T.F. Corry went with express rider W. Sweeney to Harrisburg and joined the company commanded by Lt. David Murphree. The company was attached to 2nd Regiment, commanded by Col. Sherman. They fought at San Jacinto. James was discharged 7 May 1836, at Camp Buffalo Bayou, with endorsement by Brig. Gen. T.J. Rusk. For this service, he received Donation Certificate No. 676, 12 Dec l838, for land.

James' service to the Republic included Justice of the Peace in Goliad, 1836-38. He was issued Headright Certificate No. 316, 15 Feb 1838, for land in Matagorda County.

South Carolina was probably James' birthplace. He married Frances Wooldridge, and a daughter, Martha Melvina, was born 11 Feb l818, in Abbeyville, South Carolina. The family moved to Mississippi, where Martha wed Edmund Hackney Blake, 24 Feb l834, (SRT members descend from Mary Frances and Cordelia of this marriage). James and the rest of his family, which included three other daughters, Eleanor (married Lewis Goodwin), Louisiana, Eliza Virginia, and a son, Robert W. -who was one of the Mier prisoners to draw a black bean - moved to Texas. Martha and Edmund followed her parents to Texas in 1846, and settled first in Brenham, then Houston.

Wife Frances died at Matagorda 03 Sep 1836, and James died at Goliad 27 June 1838, from wounds received from Mexican bandits. Robert Stuart Koelsch SRT #2998 William Sprong Haddock, Jr. SRT #6759 William Pimlott Haddock SRT #6790 Howard Leon Haddock (number pending)

JOHN WOODS HARRIS

John Woods Harris was born November 1, 1810, in Nelson County Virginia. He attended Washington College, later Washington and Lee University, for two years, and in 1832 he entered the University of Virginia, where he studied for five years, graduating from six departments, including law. In the fall of 1837, he came to Texas and located in Brazoria County, near the mouth of the Brazos River. By January 1, 1838, he was practicing law in partnership with John A. Wharton and Elisha M. Pease. After Wharton's death in 1839, Harris and Pease continued their partnership. The firm, which continued until the election of Pease to the governorship in 1853, was one of the most noteworthy in Texas. When Harris became a member of the Texas bar, there were only four judicial districts. He and Pease divided the work of their office for the sake of greater efficiency and for their own convenience – Pease remaining permanently at Brazoria, while Harris attended the courts of the six counties composing their district. In this way, the firm was enabled to practice in all of the most important cases that came before the courts and before the Supreme Court of Texas as soon as it was organized in 1840.

John Woods Harris

In 1839 Harris was elected to represent Brazoria County in the First Congress, where he advocated and introduced a bill providing for the abolition of the Civil, or Mexican law, and the adoption of the common law as the law of the land. The bill passed in spite of considerable opposition on the ground that the common law was not sufficiently liberal in its provisions regarding the rights of married women — a feature which was incorporated, five years later, in the First Constitution of the state. Harris was appointed the first Attorney General of the state by Governor James Pinkney Henderson, and was reappointed by Governor George T. Wood. He served until 1849, when he resigned and was appointed by the governor as special counsel to represent the interests of the State of Texas before the Supreme Court of the United States.

On July 1, 1852, Harris married Ann Pleasants Fisher (Dallam), the widow of Wilbur Dallam, and the daughter of S. Rhoads Fisher and Ann Pleasants Fisher. They adopted her daughter by the marriage to Dallam, and also had a son, John Woods Harris, Jr., an attorney, who married Minnie Knox Hutchings, and died on June 6, 1918.

Harris regarded the Civil War as entirely unnecessary, but was a strong supporter of the Confederate cause. After the courts were reopened, Harris resumed his law practice in partnership with Marcus F. Mott, and subsequently with Branch T. Masterson. Harris continued to practice law in Galveston until his death there at his home on April 1, 1887.

JOHN M. HARRISON

John M. Harrison, my great-grand father, was born in Alabama, Sept.17, 1822, to Ewel S. Harrison and wife Artemecy Gorman, who were married Sept.11, 1820, in Perry County Alabama. His grandparents were #1 John M. Harrison and Phebery Chism, married in Warren County, Kentucky, in 1802. Phebery; Harrison Tubbs died in Texas 1853, and is at rest in Huntsville Cemetery where Gen. Sam Houston is buried.

John M. Harrison and mother, Artemecy, were in Washington and Walker Counties (paid taxes in 1846). In 1849, he rode a horse back to Huntsville, Texas, and volunteered in Capt. McCown's Company, Texas Mounted Rangers, at Fort Lincoln, near Castroville, 1849-1850. He had two cousins in the same company Hiram and William Harrison also the Tumlinsons of early Ranger fame. He served in the CSA in Capt. John S. Tom's Company.

As per W.M. Shannon "Up the Trail in 1878," with 1,100 two-year-old steers to Abilene, Kansas. In this group were Joe Shannon, Tom Williams, John Harrison, Buck Wright, and myself W.M. Shannon.

John Harrison and Marion Jolly were married in Atascosa County, Texas, on Dec 29, 1857; their certificate was #21 in this new county. They spent most of their married life on a 344-acre farm in the Verdi community northeast of Pleasanton, Texas, about ten miles.

Their son, James (Jim) Harrison, was my grandfather. Waylan D. Harrison

HART-RYAN-BARFIELD

Teddy and Mary Hart, natives of Ireland, were the progenitors of several pioneer Texas families. They were members of the Power and Hewitson colony. Teddy died at sea en route to Texas; Mary obtained a concession as a colonist for a Mexican Land Grant consisting of one league of land in Texas, but she died in Texas prior to November 1834. They were the parents of four children: Felix Hart (married Bridget Carrigan); Bridget Hart (married William Quinn, who died in the Battle of Goliad on March 19, 1836); Timothy Hart (married Mary St. John, daughter of Edmund and Julia St. John); and Mary Hart (married Robert Carlisle of Papalote, Bee County, Texas).

Timothy Hart was one of the signers of the first Texas Declaration of Independence.

Felix and Bridget Hart of Papalote, Bee County, Texas, had three children: Katherine Hart (married David Craven on April 1, 1837, Matamoros, Mexico); Timothy Hart (married Mary Ann Hart), and Ann Hart (married Luke Hart). Mary Ann and Luke Hart were two of the seven children of John Hart and Bridget McCauley, members of the McMullen and McGloin colony, who received Mexican Land Grant sin San Patricio County, Texas.

John Hart died in 1836 in Victoria County. Mary Ann Hart (1834, San Patricio County 1873) and Luke Hart (1829-1883) were the parents of nine children, including Bridget Celie Hart, who married Oliver Franklin West of Bee County, son of Richard Lyons West and Ellen Harriett Moss, daughter of Henry Moss and Ann Ryan, whose brother Isaac Ryan died in the Battle of the Alamo in 1836. Luke Hart West was the only child of Oliver Franklin West and Bridget Celie Hart, and he married Mildred Agnes Lewis, daughter of William B. Lewis and Susan Alice Barfield, daughter of Isham Carroll Barfield and Sarah E. Lattimer. Isham Carroll Barfield was the son of James Barfield (Barefield), who left Yalobusha County, Mississippi, and settled in Leon County, Texas, in 1841. Each of the above families maintained cattle ranches. Dr. Richard D. Culbertson of Fort Worth, Texas, SRT #1841

BLASSINGAME W. HARVEY

Blassingame H. Harvey, was born 1792 in Laurens County, South Carolina, died July 20, 1867, and is buried on his original property in San Augustine County, Texas.

Blassingame W. Harvey (1792-1867)

At an early age, B.W. moved to Catahoula Parish, Louisiana, and served as a private in the Louisiana Militia Tenth Regiment in the War of 1812. He later became a resident of Quachita Parish. He moved to Texas in late summer 1826, where he eventually obtained a Mexican Land Grant on February 20, 1835, of 4,428 acres on the Angelina River in San Augustine County.

His first wife, Eliza Stone, died after giving birth to their first child in 1812. His second wife, Nancy Scoggins Bowie, gave birth to four children until B.W. left for Texas. Records do not reflect so, but B.W. and Nancy must have divorced. Nancy remained in Louisiana with all the children, property and assets until her death in 1833. B.W. married his third wife, Eliza Mary Ann Prather, in Texas, on September 3, 1826. Shortly after giving birth to their tenth child, Eliza died on July 22, 1855. B.W. did not marry again. Eventually, fourteen of his children resided in Texas with him or nearby. One son elected to remain in Louisiana after 1833.

Most of B.W.'s original property was condemned by the government to make Lake Sam Rayburn. Harvey Creek Park is located on the lake. For a more comprehensive review, refer to "Harvey and Allied Families of Louisiana and Texas," written by Shirley Brittain Cawyer. Lynden Edmund Rasch, seventh-generation Texan

REVEREND JOHN HAYNIE

The Reverend John Haynie arrived in Texas on January 8, 1839, and that year was elected Chaplain to the First Congress of the Republic of Texas, an office that he held for several terms. He was one of the group of nine preachers who organized the first Methodist Texas Conference at Rutersville on December 25, 1840. He was assigned to the Austin circuit. He preached the first sermon ever heard in the settlement called Austin. He was the first pastor of the First Methodist Church of Austin, Texas. During his pastorage, he established the Haynie Chapel Methodist Church, about ten miles east of Austin near Garfield, Texas. It is still in operation.

John Haynie

In the fall of 1845, Reverend Haynie served as Chaplain to the first Texas State Legislature, which convened following Texas' Annexation to the United States. At the Texas Methodist Conference in Houston in 1846, John Haynie was appointed missionary to the frontier outpost of Corpus Christi where General Zachary Taylor's army was encamped. Rev. Haynie arrived and preached the first Protestant sermon heard in Corpus Christi, but his stay was short. The Mexican War of 1846 broke out, the army moved south and the reverend returned to his home in Rutersville. His ministry in Texas lasted twenty years. In these pioneer days he traveled by horseback to his appointments with his Bible and sermons, a Mexican blanket, a few articles of clothing and his trusty rifle.

Reverend John Haynie was the son of Spencer and Catherine King Haynie. Spencer was a soldier in the American Revolution and is buried in Tennessee. Catherine accompanied her son to Texas and is buried in Austin. John Haynie was born April 11, 1786 in Botetourt County, Virginia. He married Elizabeth Brooks in Knox County, Tennessee, on May 23, 1805. They had eleven children, nine of whom lived, died and were buried in Texas. John Haynie died in Rutersville, Texas on August 20, 1860, and is buried in the Old City Cemetery in La Grange, Texas. His motto, "Be always ready to preach and always ready to die. All is well," is engraved on his tombstone. Great-great-great-grandson, Donald Holman Gaucher #6304

RICHARD HEATH

Richard Heath was among the original settlers of the DeWitt Colony. He arrived in Texas on October 24, 1828, and obtained a certificate of reception (No. 29) dated Feb. 9th, 1830. Byrd Lockhart surveyed his intended property during 1830 and he was awarded his petition for land on May 23, 1831. As a single person, he received 1/4 sitio of land, which is identified in the DeWitt records as lot No. 74 on the Lavaca River.

In the early years, he was a volunteer "minute man" fighting Indians. In the fight for Texas Independence, he supplied the Texas impromptu Army with 300 canisters of gun powder for the cannon at Gonzales during the first conflict with the Mexican soldiers. In early 1836, he supplied the Texas troops with beef, pork, and corn. The Heaths joined other settlers on the "Chute to Sabine." Their first child was born 1836 in Louisiana. The Heaths and other settlers returned to their land to plant corps in 1837. Later, he was involved in the Texas Volunteer Army in the Medina River Campaign, the Woll Campaign and the Vasques Campaign in repelling Mexican forces attempting to recapture Texas in the early 1840s. Edward Allen Heath, great-great-great-grandson of Richard Heath

MIDDLETON MILLEDGE MEADE HILL

Middleton Milledge Meade Hill, son of Thomas and Sarah McGhee Hill, was born May 13, 1802, in Oglethope County, Georgia. His parents were farmers. He married Julia Foster Walker on November 16, 1825, in Marion County, Alabama. This union produced 8 children, one of which was my grandfather, James Hamilton Hill.

Middleton and two bothers arrived in Bastrop County on July 3, 1835, and later that year purchased the Headright of Edward Burleson in said Bastrop County. At a cost of 50 cents an acre, 4,400 acres were involved in this sale. Thus was founded the community of Hills Prairie and is known today by that name.

Middleton returned to Alabama for his family, returning to Texas to bring wife here with 2 wagons, a hack, 3 teams, 7 field hands and several young Negroes. Within a year, a house was built, 200 acres cleared, and a cotton and mill were built, and they became fairly prosperous and self-sufficient. Twice a year, a trip to Houston was undertaken to sell crops and buy supplies. Teams consisting of six or eight oxen were used for these trips. Cotton, hides, and pecans were sold at market; they returned with coffee, sugar, flour, cloth and other items not available locally.

Middleton died in 1849; Julia died in 1868. Both are buried at Hill's Prairie. Clifton Eugene Hill SRT #6023

JOHN HOBSON

John Hobson was born in Ohio in 1812. He emigrated to the Republic of Texas in November 1835, at the age of 23 years. He was granted a certificate for one-third of one league of land from the Board of Land Commissioners in Milam County, Texas.

He entered the army of Texas on April 8, 1836. He was in the First Regiment of Texas Volunteers. Jesse Billingsly was captain and Micah Andrews was first lieutenant. He fought in the Battle of San Jacinto. He was discharged on July 8, 1836. He joined captain Sterling C. Robertson's company of Texas Rangers on July 18, 1836. He was transferred to Captain Thomas H. Barrow's company on September 14, 1836, and was discharged on October 28, 1836.

He was a farmer, and farmed the land that was granted to him in Milam County Texas.

He was married to Eliza Jane Moore on October 28, 1839 in Milam County, Texas. They had seven children. John Hobson (1846-1939), Tom Hobson (1849), Ann Hobson (married to William Shafer), Perry Hobson (1852), Mary Hobson Culbreth (1856), Texana Hobson Wilson (1858), Luella Hobson (1860-1951, married to George Shafer).

Luella, my grandmother, is buried at Memphis, Hall County, Texas, at the Fairview Cemetery. John Hobson died on August 4, 1862, at age 50, and is buried in the Hobson Cemetery, east of Cameron, Milam County, Texas. Wayne Shafer #2363

VALENTINE HOCH

Valentine Hoch was born October 15, 1808, at Obechonan, Germany. His wife, Johanna, died at some point on the voyage to Galveston, leaving him with number of children. They arrived in Galveston around the middle of December 1845. They took part in the early disposition of land by Prince Carl and traveled to Indianola.

The old Hoch Home has been restored and has a historical marker for the birth place of Molly Hoch.

While there he met and married his second wife, Marie Fleming, and they had four additional children. He migrated to a point that is now known as Hochheim, Texas, and staked his claim. He made lime from the nearby stone and built a stone home for his family. The original home is still standing and in good condition, and has a historical marker.

His youngest daughter, Molly Hoch, married Charles Clark. They had four children, one of which was Joseph Morris Clark, who in turn married Paralee Oaks Fleming; they had one son, Joseph Morris Clark, Jr., born July 5, 1923.

Joseph Morris Clark, Jr." #38 R2879
Son: #38 2969 Joseph Mark Clark
Grandsons: #38 J.50836 Steven Patrick Clark
           #38 J.50845 William Joseph Clark
           #38 J.5118 S Joseph mark Clark IV
           #38 J.5113 S John-Paul Philip Clark
           #38 J.5114 S Dennis Michael Clark

JOHN RICKMAN HOLLAND

John Rickman Holland was born May 8, 1786, in Virginia and died November 10, 1863, in Texas. He is buried in the Old Dublin Cemetery in Erath County with a stone marker.

He married Elizabeth Walker Holland January 16, 1812 in Putnam County, Georgia. (See marriage record, Putnam County, Georgia, Book A Page 62.)

John and Elizabeth lived in Putnam County for some ten years and then moved westward. They were in Jasper, Monroe and Pike, according to land transactions until 1862, and the U.S. Census lists them with their nine children located in Troupe County; ten years later they were in Walker County at Chickamauga, and several of the children were married. Shortly after that time, he left Georgia, stopped to visit his sister in Alabama, and arrived in east Texas by late 1841 in Harri(son) County.

In September 1846, John R. Holland bought from his friend, William Thomas of Harris County, a large tract of land in Milan District, carved from the old Mexican municipality. This land had been an original survey issued by the Board of Land Commissioners, approved by the spring term of Fannin County District Court in 1842 in the Republic of Texas, to William Thomas for one league and one labor of land, attested to by James Goman and Charles Livingston.

This certificate was confirmed by a Land Grant issued by the Honorable P.H. Bell, Governor of Texas, May 19, 1853, Patent #610, Volume 10, Abstract #753, Erath County. He paid $700 cash for the tract situated in Erath County later, when it was formed from the old Milan District.

In December 1854, he divided this into 500 acre portions and deeded them to his children: Mary Burns Holland Bell, Sarah Jane Holland Dobkins, Simruda Catherine Holland Covington, Thomas Walker Holland, William Andrew Holland, and to Moses Holland, husband to Martha Elizabeth Holland. One son, John Benjamin Holland, had died in Burnet County. Samuel Ely was located in Burnet County and Nancy Ann Holland Jackson had died at Gatesville. Eight of the 9 children were in Texas with their father by 1854, coming in three migrations.

Elizabeth Walker Holland remained in Georgia, living with her daughter, Martha Elizabeth Holland Holland, and son-in-law, Moses Holland, on a plantation in Chattooga County. Descendants of this couple in Georgia have told us John Rickman Holland sent generous amounts of money to Elizabeth as long as she lived.

John R. Holland received Certificate No. 115 for land under the Texas Land Grants.

SAMUEL ELY HOLLAND

Samuel Ely Holland was born December 6, 1826, to John Rickman Holland and Elizabeth Walker Holland, on a plantation in Troupe County, Georgia.

In 1846 Samuel, along with some other young Georgians, began their trek to Texas, and by February 1847 had arrived in what was then the village of Austin.

In July 1848, Samuel set out on horseback from Austin to visit his brother-in-law, W.B. Covington, who was with Captain Henry

McCulloch's Rangers, then camped on Hamilton Creek some three miles south of present-day Burnet. On July 3, 1848, Holland purchased 1,280 acres of land, with Captain McCulloch acting attorney for John P. Rozier, owner of the land.

The following week, Holland drove his scantily laden wagon back from Austin to his purchase, pitched camp across Hamilton Creek from the Ranger camp, and began clearing land along the creek bank. At night he worked at assembling a log cabin, which would become the first permanent home and farm in the area. With the coming of the U.S. Dragoons (Cavalry) with plans to establish and build Fort Croghan, Holland protested the fort being located on his land and the location was moved some three miles up the creek, where the town of Burnet was later built.

By 1852, the population had increased, and S.E. Holland helped to circulate a petition that resulted in the Fourth Texas Legislature creating Burnet County on February 5, 1852. He became the first treasurer of the County and set to work inducing other settlers to come into the area. In later years, Holland was elected to the Texas State Legislature from Burnet County.

S.E. Holland was the first home builder in the county, put in the first cultivated farm, strung the first wire fence and built the first all-stone house for his home. He was a veteran of the Mexican War, an Indian fighter, a colonel during the Civil War, and a factor in the Reconstruction period that followed. Holland and Peter Kerr reportedly brought the first white-headed cattle into this section, which later became the famous Hereford strain. He was interested in nearly every major enterprise in Burnet County.

In politics, Holland was a "Greenbacker." He was a Mason, a member of the Church of Christ and a humanitarian. He died November 19, 1917 in Burnet County, and was buried in the Holland Cemetery some three miles south of Burnet, just off the Mormon Mill Road.

Sam Holland was first married October 13, 1852 to Mary Scott, who was born February 28, 1837, in Missouri, and died March 3, 1855, when the horse she was riding threw her and her young infant son, George.

Sam Holland and Mary Scott Holland had one son, George A. Holland.

JAMES SAUNDERS HOLMAN

James Saunders Holman (1804-1867) was a colonist, soldier, public official, entrepreneur. The son of Isaac and Anne (Wiglesworth) Holman, he was born in Kentucky on February 7, 1804, and moved to Tennessee in 1817.

James Saunders Holman

In 1822, Holman married a cousin, Martha Wilson Holman, and they eventually had nine children. A stockholder in The Texas Association, he first came to Texas in 1825, with the Robertson Expedition, exploring the Leftwich Grant. His survey was registered with the Mexican government and ultimately filed in the Texas General Land Office, but title was never perfected. The Expedition returned to Tennessee in 1826. He fought in the Siege of Bexar in 1835, for which he was awarded land by the Republic of Texas, and later by the state.

By 1836, Holman was associated with A.C. and J.K. Allen in founding the town of Houston. In August 1837, as agent for the Houston Town Co., Holman advertised lots and a bank to be located in the new town by the Texas Railroad, Navigation and Banking Company. On August 14, 1837, Holman was elected Houston's first mayor. In his capacity as mayor, Holman wrote Sam Houston on October 2, 1837, telling him of the readiness of the building designed as the first Capital for the use of the Republic of Texas.

Holman was clerk of Harris County and of the District Court until April 1841. He then appointed Thomas M. Bagby his agent, and in the early 1840s, Holman traveled to New York and Washington, advocating annexation of Texas to the United States. For his influence in gaining Texas' annexation to the Union, he was given by the State of Texas a set of silverware made from approximately 2,000 Mexican silver (peso) dollars. During the Civil War, Holman served on the Texas State Military Board from April 1864, until the board ceased to function in 1865.

After the war, while supervising construction of the Houston and Texas Central Railway, Holman succumbed to pneumonia and died near Bryan, Texas, on December 8, 1867. The Houston Daily Telegraph published a brief obituary: "Death of Col. Holman. We heard a few days since that our old friend, Col. James S. Holman, was dead, but could not credit it. He had parted from us but a short time before in full health, having recovered from yellow fever, which had attacked him at Brenham. He went from here to Bryan, took pneumonia, and lived but a short time. He was one of the notable and esteemed citizens of Texas. He fought heroically for her independence from Mexico. He is indissolubly identified with Houston, having laid off the city in the beginning. He was a fast friend and an excellent man." The obituary ended with the sentence: "We shall publish a sketch of his life soon."

References

Land Office Records, State Archives, Austin.

"A Thumbnail History of Houston," by S.O. Young.

"Standard History of Houston," by B.H. Carroll.

"Houston Journal 1837-1841," by Gustav Dresel.

"The Houston Story," by Ed. Bartholomew.

Texas State Archives, April 12, 1864.

The Houston Chronicle - December 13, 1936, January 3-10, 1937

The Houston Post, May 11, 195 8.

The Houston Daily Telegraph, December 14, 1867, P.4, col. 1.

Information compiled by Owen Willis Holman, grandson of James Saunders Holman.

DAVID HOUSTON

David Houston was born May 15, 1802 in Giles County, Tennessee. He is the son of Archibald Houston, who fought in the Revolutionary War with North Carolina troops, and his wife, Rosannah Cunningham. David married Harriet Elizabeth Eleander, circa 1825. Three of David and Harriet's children were born in Tennessee.

In 1833, David, following in the foot steps of his father, chose to continue the colonization in the New World. He and his wife made application for and were granted a league and labor of land in Robertson's Colony, Texas, Republic of Mexico. At the time, Sterling C. Robertson was out of favor with the Mexican government, and his colony was under the control of Stephen F. Austin. David and his family settled in Texas on the original land grant, which is now in the area of Bell, Burleson and Milam counties in Texas. In 1836, when Texas raged the war for independence from Mexico, David assisted those fleeing the armies of Santa Anna in what was known as the "Runaway Scrape."

David and Harriet Houston

After moving to Texas, David and Harriet had five more children. David became a large land holder, and the census showed him in several counties, but it is believed that most of this was due to the formation of counties.

David died on December 5, 1870, and is buried in the Antioch Cemetery near Lovelady, Houston County, Texas. Harriet died August 28, 1890, and is buried next to David. The Sons of the Republic of Texas has provided grave markers of pink granite, the same stone that the capital building in Austin is made of, for both graves. There is a historical marker at the entrance to the cemetery stating that David is the first known burial in that cemetery. Thomas Archie Houston, Jr. #3814 great-great-grandson.

SAM HOUSTON

Sam Houston was born March 2, 1793, at Timber Ridge Plantation near Lexington, Virginia. He was born the fifth of nine children to Samuel and Elizabeth Paxton Houston. Houston married Margaret Lea on May 9, 1840, and to this union eight children were born.

Following his father's death in 1807, Sam Houston migrated with his mother and siblings to Blount County, Tennessee, then a part of North Carolina, where the family had purchased land near Maryville. Not finding life at home to his liking, Houston left to live with a band of Cherokee Indians under the leadership of Chief Oolooteka. From this time until the end of his life, he became a defender of Native American rights.

Houston later joined the Army and was severely wounded at the Battle of Horseshoe Bend against the Creek Indians. His conduct at the battle won him the admiration of General Andrew Jackson, and the two became close personal friends. Jackson assumed the role of Houston's mentor, and in return received young Houston's undying loyalty. Houston later served as congressman and governor of Tennessee prior to coming to Texas in the 1830s.

In Texas, Houston became a leader in the revolution against the abusive Mexican government under General Santa Anna, and was a signer of the Texas Declaration of Independence. On March 2, 1836, he was chosen commander in chief of the Texas Army. With the fall of the Alamo and Goliad, the Texas Army withdrew across Texas, with the Mexican Army in three groups doggedly following, hoping to trap them. At San Jacinto, east of Harrisburg, the two forces met on April 21, 1836, in an epic battle which gave Texas her independence and provided the expansion of the western territory forming the boundaries of the United States as it now exists. Houston served twice as president of the Republic of Texas and later as governor, and United States senator when Texas joined the Union.

Sam Houston

Houston opposed secession and was removed from office for declining to take the oath to the Confederacy. He retired to Huntsville, Texas, where he died of pneumonia on July 26, 1863.

Sam Houston once stated of all the positions he had held — including a leader of an army, governor of two states, and a senator — the job giving him the most enjoyment and satisfaction was that of a school teacher in Maryville, Tennessee.

Ivol Eugene Burnham, #5142
Robert Morris Burnham, #5143
Gary Allen Hannafious, #4753
Roxy Trent Hannafious, #4757
William Dean Hannafious, #4758
Sam Houston IV, #0689
Temple Houston III, #0688
Steven Ray Houston, #3394
Jim Miller, #6623
Henry Claypool Madison, Jr., #4417
William M. Irish V, #2888
Claude John August Rost, Jr., #6861

NOAH E. HUNT

The 1850 Census of Texas lists the household of Noah E. Hunt, a farmer, in Leon County, including Jacob Reinhardt, 76 years of age, born in Pennsylvania; Noah's wife, Ann, the daughter of Jacob; and a daughter, Asalie, born in Leon County, Republic of Texas, July 22, 1844. Noah Hunt, born in North Carolina on October 11, 1812, and Ann Reinhardt, born May 28, 1811, married in North Carolina on February 16, 1832, and emigrated to Texas.

At Nacogdoches, on November 21, 1839, he received a certificate from the Republic for 640 acres of land. Later, he acquired patents from the state of Texas to land in Freestone, Houston and Robertson counties, and deeded land in Leon County.

Asalie Hunt married Elisha Terry, a Methodist minister and Confederate chaplain, in Leon County July 25, 1866. They rode on horseback to Hamilton County, Texas, in the vicinity of the present Jonesboro, where he established a church and they raised their family. Elisha died January 21, 1925, and Asalie died August 15, 1935. Both are buried at Ireland, Texas. A daughter, Andora (Dora), born January 10, 1879, married Joseph D. Jowers. Both taught schools over West Texas from Marfa to May, Brown County. He also served as County Judge of Coke County. Dora was an avid student of Texas history, which she taught to all of her children and students. In 1925, they settled in Gonzales, which she cherished as the birthplace of Texas freedom, and he became the precursor of native pecan improvement. In 1916 their daughter, Garlyn Georgia Jowers, married Jesse B. Bettis at May, where Henry Mike Bettis was born April 15, 1918. The first Bettis to come to Texas, Jesse Richard Bettis, — great-grandfather of Mike — and his family came from Clarke County, Alabama, to a homestead in Brown County between Blanket and Zephyr, in 1881.

On August 27, 1838, Isaac P. Reinhart received an honorable discharge from Thomas J. Rusk for his services as "Assistant Quartermaster of the forces under my command from 9 August to date" (Texas State Archives).

On October 7, 1853, I. P. Reinhardt filed a document in Leon County, conveying his "donation land claim for 640 acres of land No. 517, dated August 26, 1854, for my services in storming Bexar in 1835." (General Land Office). On August 26, 1854, Isaac P. Reinhardt received a certificate of entitlement to 320 acres of land from the State of Texas for his services in the Army of the Republic of Texas from the 4th day of October, 1835, to the 30th day of December, 1835, "having participated in the storming of Bexar." (GLO).

The chronology of events and later appearance of record in Leon County supports the undocumented belief that Isaac Reinhardt was the son of Jacob Reinhardt who came to Texas first and participated in the revolution. Henry Mike Bettis #4500

COL. ALMANZON HUSTON

Colonel Almanzon Huston was Quartermaster General of the Texas Army in 1836. The colonel always signed his name A. Huston.

The Huston family can first be traced to William Huston, who was born in Tyrone County, Ireland. He married Agnes (Nancy) Hinman and came to Voluntown, Connecticut, in 1735. Their youngest child, Thomas Huston, was born in 1767 in Voluntown, Connecticut.

Almanzon Huston

Thomas Huston married Suzannah Campbell in 1795. She was born in 1774 in Voluntown, Connecticut, and was the daughter of Charles Campbell and Patience Kennedy. The young couple shortly thereafter moved to Lebanon, Madison County, New York. Many Campbell families left Voluntown and established the Campbell Settlement in Lebanon, New York, which was one of the largest settlements by a family group at that time.

Almanzon Huston, the only son of Thomas and Suzannah Huston, was born October 26, 1799, in Lebanon, Madison County, New York, about 65 miles southeast of Syracuse. He married Elizabeth Newton in her hometown of Erie, Pennsylvania, in 1819. They had children, who are as follows: Emory F. Huston, Melvina C. Huston, infant Huston, Thomas Melvin Huston, Cordelia A. Huston, Almanzon T. Huston, Elizabeth A. Huston, Ellen & Frances Marion Huston (twins), Mary M. Huston, Newton Huston, Henry M. Huston, Priscilla A. Huston and Alma Z. Huston.

Almanzon Huston as a young man moved to Niles, Michigan, where he had a tavern and inn, and delivered the U.S. mail to Detroit. The first court of Niles was held in this tavern. Almanzon Huston served as a colonel in the Black Hawk War. He served in the Rebellion at the Battle of Nacogdoches, and established permanent residence in East Texas in 1832. Col. Almanzon Huston helped plan the town of Attoyac on the west of Attoyac River.

Col. Almanzon Huston then settled in San Augustine when San Augustine was first established. There he bought and sold city lots for $5 each, having sold one $5 lot to Mirabeau B. Lamar. He also established a hotel called the Mansion House, later called the Huston Hotel. It was a large structure on Montgomery Street. George Crockett, in "Two Centuries in East Texas," described the Mansion House. He said the hotel had large front rooms facing the street. It was wood, very solidly and substantially framed, with large comfortable rooms and a hall in the center. The large front windows opened upon an upper and a lower gallery extending the whole length of the house. Col. Almanzon Huston also had a stagecoach line that went from San Augustine through Nacogdoches to Huntsville and then to Natchitoches, Louisiana, which carried the U.S. mail.

As the difficulties with Mexico increased, in October of 1835, Col. Almanzon Huston and four other members from San Augustine represented San Augustine at San Felipe. When the consultation gathered October 16, 1835, only 31 representatives from Texas — including the four from San Augustine — responded. Low attendance was because most had joined the Army and were on their way to Gonzalez. Col. Almanzon Huston served a few days on the General Council before resigning and joining the Texas Army. He turned over his hotel to a manager while he was away. On February 26, 1836, Col. Almanzon Huston was appointed Quartermaster General of the Texas Army and served until after the Battle of San Jacinto.

Col. Almanzon Huston, while serving as Quartermaster General, forwarded the famous twin sister cannons on the sloop Ohio. These cannons were a gift to Texas from the citizens of Cincinnati for use at the Battle of San Jacinto.

In 1836 while still serving as Quartermaster General, Col. Almanzon Huston wrote a letter to Thomas J. Rusk on 12 July 1836, from Flask, Texas stating: "I sold my riding horse and watch yesterday and bought for the express use of the main Army 2,000 pounds of coffee, which I shall cause to be forwarded with other supplies as soon as possible."

After the defeat of Santa Anna, Col. Almanzon Huston returned to San Augustine and took over the operation of the Mansion House again. He continued to purchase land and lots. Since San Augustine didn't have a courthouse, court was held in the hotel when the first District Court of the new Republic was held in 1937.

In 1837, he purchased about 6,000 acres and several lots. He and Ezekiel Cullen and Sumner Bacon laid out the new town of Lamar, in Jefferson County, on 640 acres. They later took in

Pinckney Henderson as a partner to get the project off the ground, but the town was never successful. Developing town lots was a passion all of Col. Huston's life.

In 1838, Huston was dealing in property and was also doing paralegal work, proving up land titles and assisting in probate and distributing process of estates, since he was a Justice of the Peace. Judge Ochiltree presented him with a license to practice law as an attorney and counselor. The judge ordered his name to be enrolled on the counselors practicing in San Augustine County.

In 1840, Huston sold 5 acres and his home, which he had built in 1838 just east of the city cemetery of San Augustine, to William Anderson. The house was next owned by the Teel family. It is now known as the Anderson-Teel home of San Augustine, and has the State Medallion identifying it as a historical home.

In 1844, the conflict between the regulators and the moderators in Shelby County had spread until it was paralyzing the countryside. President Sam Houston came to San Augustine personally to meet with the contingent of East Texas leaders to develop a plan to put an end to the bloody feud once and for all. At this time, Oran M. Roberts was a young D.A. in San Augustine. The following excerpts from his memoirs, "The Shelby War."

"President Houston arrived at San Augustine bringing with him Gen. Thomas J. Rusk from Nacogdoches, and took lodging at Mr. A. Huston's hotel, a large two-story building with a long, broad piazza in front of it. The next day, he, Rusk, Kaufman from Sabine County, Gens. Berry and Broocks and a number of others, including William B. Ochiltree and District Attorney O.M. Roberts assembled on the piazza for consultation. After some greeting and conversation there, General Houston, getting up, walked through the house, the rest following into the back yard, and crawled up and seated himself on the edge of a scattered pile of firewood, and the others did likewise around him. He engaged intently in whittling a piece of white-pine stick.... Spoke a few words occasionally and heard a few words spoken by the others .... About the all-absorbing topic of stopping this awful war. As an outgrowth of this meeting, the militia from several counties was called together and peace was eventually restored in Shelby County."

Col. Almanzon Huston made certain his children got an education. He paid tuition for six children at the same time to go to the Masonic Institute at San Augustine. He still had four minor children at home when he died August 27, 1861. Col. Almanzon Huston died on the way home from Washington, where he is said to have gone to collect money for delivering the U.S. mail. This was during the Civil War, and there is no record of where he is buried.

The Huston Hotel in San Augustine is now only a memory. It has been gone for years and has been replaced by a series of stores, and eventually replaced by a theater.

The impact of Col. Almanzon Huston's life on San Augustine didn't stop with his death. He had owned more than 42,000 acres in Texas, plus 3 lots in Houston, Texas. Because he had traded so extensively in land certificates and other properties, it took 40 years, even with a will, to settle the estate. During the time it took three different administrators, over $5,000 in administrative costs and more than 70 appearances before probate court.

Col. Almanzon Huston, my great-great-grandfather deserves his place among the great men of our country and state in the struggle for Texas independence, for he was truly the man behind the scenes. By Thomas H. (Tom) Houston

FELIX HUSTON

Felix Huston was a lawyer, military adventurer, and commanding officer of the Army of the Republic of Texas.

Felix Huston was born in 1850 in Breckenridge County, Kentucky. His parents were Joseph Huston and Margaret Allen. Felix was their youngest child; he had a brother, Eli, and a sister, Eliza.

Felix Huston received an excellent academic and legal education. Early in his career, however, involvement in a duel disqualified him from the practice of law in Kentucky. Felix wandered off to Mississippi and soon became prominent in the profession that had been closed to him in Kentucky.

General Felix Huston

On February 10, 1829, at twenty-nine, Felix married Mary Elizabeth Dangerfield in Adams County, Mississippi. Mary Elizabeth was fifteen at the time of their marriage. Together, they had six children: Eliza; Eli; Margaret; Henry; Joseph; and Sidney Hampton.

In the midst of his career, Felix received an offer from Sam Houston (no relation): The supreme command of the Texas Army would be Felix's if he would recruit and equip two regiments for service in Texas. Ambitious for military distinction, Felix arrived in Texas on July 4, 1836, with between 500 and 700 volunteers for the Texas Army. Felix incurred a personal debt of $40,000 in support of this effort. Over six feet tall, and described as a "Hussar", Felix Huston cut a fine figure as a military officer.

Jack Huston Castle

Sam Houston refused to permit the invasion of Mexico, which had been one of the stipulations of Huston's contract. The quarrel between them resulted in Felix being superseded in command. When Sam Houston appointed Albert Sidney Johnston as senior brigadier general, Huston's honor compelled him to challenge Johnston to a duel. On February 7, 1837, the duel took place; Johnston was shot through the right hip. A monument in Jackson County, Texas marks the site of the duel near the Lavaca River. Huston kept his command; but clearly, nothing had changed.

Unable to remove Huston from command of the army, Sam Houston came up with a clever solution: to remove the army from Huston's command. President Sam Houston put his plan into action when Huston left his troops to appeal to Congress for an invasion of Mexico. President Houston sent a message to the troops, praising them for a job well done and awarding them a "deserved vacation". He granted a leave to all but 600 soldiers, instructing them that he would let them know when to return. When Felix Huston returned, he found that most of his army was gone. Although Huston was very angry, he was without a remedy; there was nothing he could do.

Felix Huston is listed in Volume 3, Land Grants of the "1840 Citizens of Texas" and "First Settlers of the Republic of Texas." These records indicate that Felix Huston received a land grant in Harris County, Texas, on December 8, 1838.

On October 5, 1839, Felix was a major general of the Texas Army. In 1840, Felix was in command of the Texas forces against the Comanche in the "Plum Creek Fight." Huston arrived at Plum Creek on the evening of August 11, 1840, and took command of the gathering troops. The next day, Huston formed his troops for battle, dismounted his men, and began random firing. Huston then ordered a charge, at the urging of old Indian fighters, as the Comanches fled with their plunder.

By autumn of 1840, Felix resigned his command and left Texas to open a law firm with S.S. Prentiss in New Orleans, Louisiana. On April 14, 1843, Felix Huston is quoted in The New Orleans Bee: "I have not the least intention of going again to Texas or Yucatan. I am permanently settled here and never intend to fight under any flag than that of the United States."

In 1844, Felix Huston returned to Natchez, Mississippi. He made many speeches in the south in favor of the Annexation of Texas. Felix Huston died in April 1857, and is buried in Adams County, Mississippi.

Felix Huston is listed in "The New Handbook of Texas"; indeed, few books that recount the fascinating and colorful history of Texas' early days do not contain at least the mention of Felix Huston. Whether inspired by Huston's support of Texas independence, his propaganda for the Texas Revolution, his ability to rally volunteers to march across Louisiana with him into Texas, his military maneuvers, or local anecdotes, Felix Huston marked his place in history. A portrait of Felix Huston, as shown in "Texas Lone Star Land," is in the archives division of the Texas State Library.

A newspaper article following the city of Houston's 115th birthday anniversary asked the interesting question of whether the city should be called Huston instead of Houston. The Houston Post's "Texas Heartbeat" section related a story, originally passed down by General Huston's two sons, that the Allen brothers borrowed the $5,000 cash that they used to purchase the land that would become the city of Houston. The family account of the story indicates that the money was borrowed with the natural mention and understanding that the city would be named for Felix Huston. The sale of the muddy lots was so slow that it was difficult to put blame on the Allens for later considering naming the city for President Sam Houston — after all, it helped to sell the lots. Owing to slow sale of the town lots, the $5,000 loan was never repaid.

Felix Huston's two sons were described as "very honorable men." If their account of the transaction is true, then General Felix Huston presented the land to the city and the Allen brothers "put the town on the map of the world". Despite Felix Huston's eventual departure from Texas, he is remembered by historian Eugene C. Barker as a "true friend of Texas."

Dr. Jack Huston Castle of Huston, Texas, is the great-great-grandson of Felix Huston, descended from Felix Huston's son, Henry. From Dr. Castle's marriage to Loretta Arlene McKinney Castle were borne Felix's great-great-great-grandson, Jack H. Castle Jr. (whose children are Trevor Huston Castle, Hayden mills Castle, and Fielding Cullinan Castle; and great-great-great-granddaughter, Lisa Galen Castle Donnell, (whose children are Elizabeth Frances Donnell, Travis Alexander Donnell and Cameron Clayton Donnell). Jack Huston Castle

ANNA RAGUET IRION (1819-1883)

Anna Raguet was born January 25th, 1819, in Newtown, Bucks County, Pennsylvania, to Henry and Marcia Ann Tower Raguet.

A veteran of the War of 1812, Henry Wynkoop Raguet moved his family from Pennsylvania to Ohio in 1820, and 13 years later to Nacogdoches, where he found success as a merchant.

Anna, the oldest of eight Raguet children, became a beautiful, accomplished lady, educated in the best schools in Philadelphia and fluent in several languages. She gave lessons in Spanish to her father's friend, General Sam Houston, and entertained him by playing her gilded French harp. For several years he courted her, always closing his letters to her father with complimentary messages to or about her, calling her "the fairest of the fair," "the peerless Miss Anna," and "the brightest and loveliest star in Texas." He also composed several flowery poems about her,

In June 22, 1961, The San Augustine Tribune reprinted a Houston Chronicle feature story by historian Garland Roark. In the article, Anna is said to have saved Sam Houston's life by throwing herself against an assailant who lurched from the shrubbery with knife in hand.

Later, at Houston's request, Anna helped design the seal of Texas, still in use today. After the victory of San Jacinto, Houston sent Anna a letter and a garland of oak leaves from the tree under which Santa Anna surrendered. Sam Houston often sent his letters to Anna by his friend, Dr. Robert A. Irion, who married Anna on April 9th, 1840.

ROBERT ANDERSON IRION

Robert Anderson Irion, born July 7, 1804, in Paris, Tennessee, received his medical degree from Transylvania University in 1826, and began practice in Vicksburg, Mississippi.

He immigrated to Texas in 1832, and became interested in land speculation and surveying. Moving to Nacogdoches, he engaged in those pursuits, but soon returned to the practice of medicine.

He served as senator from Nacogdoches in the first Senate of the Republic of Texas, until President Houston appointed him in June 1837, to succeed Stephen F. Austin as secretary of state of the Republic. He served until December 1838, when he declined re-appointment.

As a close friend of Sam Houston, he frequently bore messages and letters from him to the lovely Miss Anna Raguet of Nacogdoches, but she rebuffed Houston's advances and instead married the messenger in March 1840.

They had five children. The first, Sam Houston Irion, died in infancy, but the other four — Robert A. Jr., James Raguet, Julia and Harriet — survived to adulthood and left descendants.

Dr. Irion, a charter member of the Philosophical Society of Texas, died March 2, 1861. Irion County was named in his honor. Jos. Irion Worsham S.R.T. 08#1401

HUMPHREY JACKSON

Humphrey Jackson, born in Ireland in 1784, immigrated with his brothers, Alexander and Henry, to Louisiana. There he fought in the Battle of New Orleans, married and buried his first wife, and acquired a plantation. He married Sarah Merriman in 1814. This union produced four children: Letitia, Hugh, John and James.

In 1823, Humphrey joined Austin's "Old 300" and moved his family to Texas, receiving a Mexican land grant for a league and a labor near the San Jacinto River. Part of his land grant is the site of present-day Crosby, Harris County. Humphrey served as alcalda and ex officio militia captain of the San Jacinto neighborhood. In the winter of 1826-1827, he enlisted in Austin's Campaign to quell the Fredonian Rebellion. In 1828, Jackson was selected as regidor of the Muncipality of Austin. Probably his last public service was to help lay out a road from Harrisburg to the San Jacinto River at the present site of the U.S. Highway 90 crossing.

Humphrey was killed in 1833 by a falling tree while clearing land. He is buried beside his wife in Crosby, in a small park with a Texas State Historical Marker. Guy C. Jackson III, great-great-grandson)

JAMES JACKSON

James Jackson, son of Humphrey and Sarah Merriman Jackson, was born near Vermillion, Louisiana, on February 15, 1822. His family moved to Texas in September 1822, and he was raised near present-day Crosby on his father's Mexican land grant. His mother died in 1824, and his father was killed by a falling tree in 1833. James' sister, Letitia moved him and brothers Hugh and John to Double Bayou to be near their mother's cousin.

He married Sarah Cade White, daughter of James Taylor White, I, and Sarah Cade on December 23, 1847. His marriage produced eleven children: Sarah Ellen (1849-1876); Humphrey (1851-1863); Mary (1854-1919); Robert (1859-1923); Edward (1861-1950); Humphrey Hugh (1864-1928); Claude (1867-1944); Ralph (1870-1940); Guy (1872-1941); and Ula Jean (1876-1938).

He bought land in southern Chambers County until he had acquired almost 30,000 acres by 1896. James served Chambers County as judge, sheriff and notary public. Locally, he was doctor, dentist, druggist, postmaster, tax assessor, commissioner, surveyor, cotton ginner, banker, and undertaker. He ran a successful farming-ranching business as well.

James died June 5, 1895, and was buried in the family cemetery in Double Bayou. Guy C. Jackson, III, great-grandson)

PETER JACKSON

Peter Jackson was born March 28, 1807 in Maury County, Tennessee. He was the son of Jeremiah Jackson and wife Ellen Crawley, and died May 4, 1889 in Cameron, Milam, Texas. He married Rhody Holmes on December 20, 1830, in Lauderdale County, Alabama. She died January 10, 1832. Peter Jackson married Susannah Rebecca King on March 30, 1837, in Lauderdale County, Alabama. Susannah was the daughter of Hugh B. King and Rebecca Gill. She was born March 15, 1817, in North Carolina, and died November 8, 1879, in Cameron, Milam, Texas.

Ten children were born to the Jacksons: Gilbert H., William A., Columbus Jeremiah, Hugh Cyrus, Susanna, Rebecca E., Angelina M., Henry Albany, James A., and Auburn H. (Olwin).

After arriving in Texas in 1837, Peter fought in several battles against Indians. One was the Battle Creek Fight, which occurred in 1838 near Dawson, Navarro, Texas. This was a land locating

Peter Jackson
(1807-1889)

expedition under Capt. William M. Love. Peter was issued two Headrights, Number 25 in Navarro County and Number 122 in Blanco County. He served Milam County as county commissioner and county treasurer. He was a Methodist and gave acreage to the Salem Methodist Church. Steven Marshall Jackson

RICHARD RADCLIFF JOEL

Richard Radcliff Joel was born in South Carolina in 1808. His ancestors, the Joels, left Devon, England, in the 1620s and were among the first colonial families in Bermuda. During the late 1600s and early 1700s, they were sea captains and privateers, plundering Spanish ships in the Atlantic.

My 6th great-grandfather, Captain Richard Joel, left Bermuda and settled in Norfolk, Virginia in 1731. My 4th great-grandfather, Ratcliff Joel, moved to South Carolina in 1785. My great-great-grandfather, Richard Radcliff Joel, arrived in the Republic of Texas in 1836. His daughter, Mary Ann, was born in Sabine County in October 1836.

Richard Radcliff Joel was a judge in Cherokee County during the time of the Republic, and operated a sawmill. His name was misspelled by a census taker in the first U.S. Census in 1850, by adding a "w" to his last name. His descendants, Joel and Jowel, reside primarily in East Texas.

BENJAMIN JOHNSON & JACOB HARMON GARNER

Great-great-grandfather Benjamin Johnson, of Danish descent, was born in Calcasieu Parish, Louisiana, in 1815. In 1832 he emigrated to Cow Bayou, Jefferson County, Texas.

After the citizens 1835 meeting in San Felipe, Benjamin enlisted in captain Landrum's Volunteers. In December 1835, he took part in the "Grass Fight de Bexar."

Feeling the war was over, Captain Landrum disbanded his company and sent everyone home. The following February in 1836, Santa Anna reinforced and charged back across the Rio Grande, taking the Alamo. Santa Anna then regrouped and moved across south Texas toward the Sabine River.

Benjamin joined Captain James Gillaspie's Company in Colonel Sidney Sherman's Regiment under General Sam Houston at San Jacinto, where Santa Anna was defeated in April 1836.

Benjamin was discharged in the fall of 1836, received land grants from the Board of Land Commissioners, and settled in Sabine Pass as a farmer and stockman. In 1838, he married Rachel Garner, Bradley Garner's daughter. He died in 1872, a highly respected citizen.

In 1972 a Texas Historical Marker was placed on his grave in the Sabine Pass Cemetery.

Great-great-grandfather Jacob Harmon Garner, son of Bradley Garner, was born in 1814 in Opelousas, Louisiana. Bradley had emigrated from Virginia in about 1800. In 1825, Jacob moved west to Cow Bayou, Texas. Bradley followed a short time later.

In 1835, Jacob fought in the "Grass Fight de Bexar." He was detailed to guard prisoners near San Jacinto, missing the actual battle. He was dismissed from service in 1836; he went back to Cow Bayou.

In 1835, he married Matilda Hayes. In 1848 they moved to Sabine Pass. He farmed and ranched on land grants for his service in the revolution against Mexico, until he died in 1886. He also was a very respected citizen.

In 1995 a Texas Historical Marker was placed on his grave in the Sabine Pass Cemetery, near his brother-in-law Benjamin Johnson's historically marked grave. Rear Admiral Corwin Mendenhall, Retired

CHIEF JUSTICE HUGH B. JOHNSTON

Chief Justice Hugh B. Johnston was born in Georgia in 1794. In 1824, he traveled by wagon train with his wife, the former Martha White, from his home in Liberty, Mississippi, to the Atascosita District in sparsely populated east Texas. The largest number of colonists to arrive prior to the official organization of the Atascosita District government was in 1825, and most were from Mississippi. Subsequent events indicate that the leaders of the 1825 group were Matthew G. White of Amite County, Mississippi, and his son-in-law, Hugh B. Johnston of Wilkinson County, Mississippi, both of whom who were later elected alcaldes of the district.

Hugh B. Johnston

The Atascosita District consisted of a major portion of southeast Texas bounded on the east by the Sabine River, on the west by the San Jacinto River and western shores of Galveston Bay, on the north by the south line of the original Nacogdoches and San Augustine District, and on the south by a line three leagues from shore along the Gulf of Mexico. Atascosita is first shown on the map of Bernardo de Miranda, made in 1757 depicting his inspection of the Trinity River. (the largest river in the Atascosita District, and the state, along which most of the early Anglo colonists settled, including Johnston.)

On March 25, 1825, the sovereign Congress of the state of Coahuila in Texas recited that it desired by every possible means to augment the population of its territory and promote the cultivation of its fertile lands; the raising and multiplication of stock, and progress of the arts and commerce. It enacted a very favorable law for foreign immigrants and those who had already immigrated for settlement. The heads of families who had migrated to Texas and engaged solely in farming were eligible to receive a land grant of one labor (177 acres) and, if engaged also in stock raising, an additional grant amount to constitute one sitio (a league of 4,428 acres). The settlers had to pledge faith to the Catholic Church, agree to support the general and state constitutions, remain domiciled within Texas, and make improvements on the land within six years. Under these conditions, Hugh B. Johnston was awarded a land grant one league north of Liberty on the east side of and abutting the Trinity River.

In January 1827, Captain Hugh B. Johnston, as head of the militia of the Atascosita District, was called upon by Stephen F. Austin to demonstrate loyalty to Mexico by joining him and Mexican soldiers in quelling the "Fredonian Rebellion" in Nacogdoches. The Fredonian Rebellion evolved around an election contest in Nacogdoches, which caused resentment on the part of the settlers. The president of Mexico, without notice or hearing, ordered local Empresario Haden Edwards expelled from Texas. Angered by the controversy with the Mexican authorities, Edwards and thirty followers launched the Fredonian Rebellion on December 16, 1826. Stephen F. Austin was appalled at the conduct of the rebels, wrote a warning and called for action to the various districts including Atascosita. Captain Hugh B. Johnston and his militia company from Atascosita were mustered into service to quell the rebellion on January 16, 1827. Upon the approach of Captain Johnston and his militia on January 31, 1827, the rebels fled across the Sabine River, thus terminating the short-lived Fredonian Rebellion. This service on behalf of Mexico later proved to be very helpful to the Atascosita colonists in obtaining approval of their land grants.

Captain Hugh B. Johnston was the first elected alcalde after the appointment by the Mexican government by Francisco Madero, land commissioner, in 1831. Under alcalde Johnston's watch in 1831, the colonists chose to name their community "Liberty." On May 5, 1831, the first recorded history of Liberty was Hugh B. Johnston's signing two character certificates for the colonists from the "Villa of Liberty."

Later, the settlers of the Atascosita District protested restrictive laws of Mexico designed to limit immigration and trade between the United States and Texas. Mexico feared losing Texas to the United States. The citizens of the Atascosita District were enraged by the unreasonable acts of Colonel Juan Davis Bradburn, a local agent of the Mexican government. Alarm spread after Bradburn unjustly imprisoned several Texans, one of whom was William Barret Travis, later an Alamo hero. Fighting broke out on June 9 and June 12, 1832, between citizens and Bradburn's militia.

Following this, the Texans, under the leadership of Hugh B. Johnston, met at Turtle Bayou to plan future action against the Mexican government. They drew up resolutions censoring violations of Mexico's constitution by President Busta Monte encouraging resistance to his regime and inviting all Texans to uphold the cause of civil liberty. The signers of the "Turtle Bayou Resolutions" — most of whom later served with valor in the 1836 revolution and in the Texas Republic — included Hugh B. Johnston, John Austin, W.H. Jack, Luke Lesassier, Wiley Martin, and R.M. Williamson. The committee of seven drafted four copies of the Turtle Bayou Resolutions, one of which was read to the army, and the most important copy was sent to Colonel Jose Antanio Mexia in Mexico.

Under the leadership of alcalde Johnston, Mexican officials approved an agreement with the colonists that the prisoners who had been taken and incarcerated in Anahuac would be freed and turned over to the civil authorities in the jurisdiction of Liberty; that Bradburn would surrender his command at Anahuac; that Bradburn would be compelled to pay for the property he had appropriated from the colonists; and that the Mexican government would support the establishment of the government in Liberty. These terms were agreed to and signed on June 28, 1832, at Atascosita Creek and were ratified by Mexican Colonel Piedras the following day.

Among his many accomplishments, Chief Justice Johnston was a delegate to consultation in 1835 (declaring Texas a separate state in the Mexican Republic); helped found and lay off the city of Liberty; member of Third Congress of Republic of Texas; and chairman Post Office and Roads Committee. His homestead was prominent outpost and stage coach station; guests included General Sam Houston, William Barret Travis and Patrick C. Jack.

Chief Justice Hugh B. Johnston died in 1850. The State of Texas erected a historical monument, marking his burial site on the Hugh B. Johnston league in Liberty County, Texas, near the town of Hardin, and his portrait is prominently displayed in the 75th District Courtroom in Liberty, Texas.

Chief Justice Johnston's descendants still own and carry on operations in the Hugh B. Johnston league of land their forefather settled over 170 years ago. He had eight children, three of whom were in the Civil War and two killed in battle. Several of his descendants are life members in the Sons of the Republic of Texas.

LOUIS JONES

Louis Jones was born in the Salisbury District of Rowan County, North Carolina, near the forks of Horseshoe Creek and the Yadkin River on June 23, 1790. In 1811, his father, Ebenezer Jones, and mother, Mary Roten Jones, moved to Daviess County, Indiana, along with all fifteen children.

Louis became a skilled wood worker and brick and stone mason. He served one term as representative to the Indiana Legislature, was director of a boys' educational institution, and served as board member of the County Poor Farm. He moved to Texas in 1841 after completing the Washington County Courthouse in 1840.

Louis Jones and members of his family constructed a houseboat on the White River and floated downstream into the Wabash and then the Ohio River. They followed the Mississippi River to Baton Rouge, Louisiana, where they bought a wagon and mules and completed their trip to Texas. After crossing the Sabine at Pendleton's Ferry, all seven of those who had made the trek drank water from the river and declared themselves to be full-fledged Texans.

The Jones family lived in San Augustine County for a year while searching for land to purchase. In 1842, Louis bought a section of land in Shelby County, where he constructed his home and became a farmer. In his later years, Louis carried the mail from Whitehouse, the first post office in Shelby County, to Alexandria, Louisiana. He continued to carry the mail without pay during the Civil War, and his family was eventually paid by the U. S. government after the war ended.

Louis's son, Hardy, served in the Mexican War. Sons Hardy, Pleasant Louis and William Enoch served in the War Between the States on the side of the South. Pleasant Louis was captured by an Illinois Unit. Two of his cousins were serving in the unit, and they made sure Pleasant Louis was well cared for while he was held by their outfit.

Louis died in Shelby County, Texas, June 21, 1865. His wife, Rebecca McDonald Jones, died May 17, 1871. They are buried in the Logan Love Smith Cemetery three miles north of Center, Texas. Most of the land that Louis Jones purchased in 1842 is still owned by members of the family. Joe Louis Jones #0201.

JOHANN ERNST HEINRICH CHRISTIAN FRANZ JORDAN

Johann Ernst Heinrich Christian Franz Jordan was born in Wehrstedt, Lower Saxony, Germany, on June 21, 1821, and died December 23, 1892, in Mason County, Texas.

Ernst arrived in Galveston, Texas, in November 1845, aboard the ship Margarethe as a member of the "Adelsverein," a colonization society. He settled in Fredericksburg in its early days, arriving via Indianola and New Braunfels. Food was very scarce: Acorns provided bread and coffee; friendly Indians provided game. Disease plagued the settlement, and Ernst's black oxen took many cholera victims to the cemetery. He helped build the stone Methodist church in 1855

Johann E. Jordan

Ernst farmed and ranched all his life in Texas, and early was a teamster, hauling supplies to the frontier forts. In 1856, he moved to 640 acres purchased in Mason County in 1858. He helped build a log Methodist church on his land.

During the early years, crops were scarce and ranching unprofitable, so Ernst again began hauling supplies as far as Fort Stockton. The frontier forts closed during the Civil War, so he joined a local frontier guardsman unit. In 1868-70, he served as county commissioner.

Ernst was a spectator at the trial of a cattle thief when the defense attorney declared, "All ranchers steal cattle," Ernst shouted, "And that's a damned lie!"

Land-hungry and frugal, overcoming economic distress, Ernst acquired 7,000 acres of good ranch land, enough to establish each of his seven children in ranching. For one who began adulthood a landless peasant linen weaver, this was equivalent to a principality or feudal manor.

In 1890, Ernst donated 10 acres of land and his sons helped haul, shape and lay the stones of the building which still serves as the Art United Methodist Church. Wesley Norman Schulze # 2193 (great-grandson) John Wesley Schulze #2197 (great-great-grandson)

JOHN JORDAN AND MINERVA (STEWART) JORDAN

John Jordan (pronounced "jerden"), a farmer, was born Tennessee, 1817. He came to Texas as a "Tennessee Volunteer" and served at Fort Houston, 10 September through 27 November 1836, as a private in Capt. Michael Costley's Company of Rangers, under Maj. George W. Jewell. He served next in the Houston Volunteer Guards under a Capt. Smith, 1837-1839, living in Harris County, Texas.

John Jordan took out a 2nd Class Conditional Certificate in Montgomery County, Texas, in 1839, and received a 640-acre Unconditional Certificate in Limestone County, Texas, in 1848. John married Minerva (believed to be "Minerva Stuart"), born 1826 in Alabama. The family was in Limestone County, Texas (which area became Falls County by 1850), but were in Houston County 1860.

Jordan was a private in Company of Volunteers, Houston County, Texas State Troops in the Civil War under Capt. Thomas W. Warren. By 1876, John and Minerva were in Mason County, Texas. They went to McCulloch County in about 1881.

John Jordan died at Camp San Saba, circa 1895, and Minerva died circa 1896 at the Old Davis Ranch that their son-in-law, Josiah Dixon Perry, son of N.B. Perry (see elsewhere) had bought soon after John's death. John and Minerva Jordan are buried in the Camp San Saba Cemetery, McCulloch County, Texas. *Submitted by Patricia McKenna*

HENRY JOURNEAY

Henry Journeay, a descendant of Huguenot ancestors who came to New York in 1663, was born 23 June 1815, on Staten Island. His land grant indicates he came to Texas 21 April 1837. He joined in the Mier Expedition and was imprisoned at Perote, where he made a violin, now in the Texas Archives Building.

Henry Journeay (1815-1870)

He operated a livery stable, mail route and woodworking mill in conjunction with Gilbert Winnie in Galveston. They speculated in buildings and real estate. When their business split in 1852, Journeay took the mill. His mill, employing 16-20 men in 1859, was the largest of it kind in Texas, manufacturing doors, windows, coffins, etc. And his customers included Sam Houston, whom he had to sue to collect his bill. His mill was damaged by cannon during the Civil War, and his business had not fully recovered when he died on 2 July 1870, subsequent to injuries suffered when run over by a street car.

He married Caroline Wetsell, on 11 June 1850. They had ten children. He built a number of buildings in Galveston, including two of the iron-fronts on the Strand that were destroyed in the great fire of 1869. Journeay was twice an alderman in Galveston.

NATHAN (NATHANIEL) JUTSON

Nathan (Nathaniel) Jutson, was born 18 Aug 1798, probably in either New York or Connecticut. Nathan married on 8 Dec 1822 (Sangamon County, Illinois) to Lucinda Brockman. She was born in South Carolina in 1804. The identity of both Nathan's and Lucinda's parents are still a mystery.

Nathan and Lucinda's children included: John Nathan, born 18 Sept 1824; Polly Ann, born May 1823 (perhaps 1830); Mathew (Mack or Mc), born 1833; James Barkly, born 1833; and John David (Jessie or J.D.), born 1839. All were born in Illinois, except for John David, who was born in Jasper County, Texas.

Nathan was listed in the 1830 Illinois Federal Census as living in Vermont Township, Fulton County. Nathan arrived in the Republic of Texas in November 1838, and applied for a third-class land grant which was finally patented on 23 July 1847, in Tyler County.

Nathan was elected Justice of the Peace for Precinct 2, Jasper County, on 21 May 1 842 and 21 Feb 1843. Nathan was living in Robertson County in 1850; however he had moved to Limestone County by 1860. He was a farmer by occupation. He was listed on the Limestone County tax rolls up to 1866, and died in 1880.

Nathan is buried in the McKensie Prairie Cemetery, outside of Oletha, Limestone County, Texas.

GABRIEL KEITH

My great-great-grandfather was born Feb. 25, 1819, in Kentucky, and migrated to Alabama; McNairy County, Tennessee; and Carroll County, Arkansas. He received a land grant from Republic of Texas, Nov. 2, 1839. Gabriel married Synthia Jane Campbell July 15, 1837, probably Red River County, Texas.

Gabriel Keith and wife Synthia Jane Campbell

Land records indicate Stephen and Rebecca Crain-Keith, and sons, Garbriel, William S., and Nichodemus owned land in Franklin County, Texas, in 1849. Stephen Keith donated twenty-four acres for a townsite named Keith, which later became Mount Vernon. Gabriel moved to Hunt County, Texas, where he had a land grant. Hunt County Court Records states involvement in road development around Greenville, Texas. He migrated to Erath County, Texas, ca. 1859, in the Round Grove-Highland, Texas, area.

During Civil War, Gabe served a minimum of two terms with the Texas State Troops (Frontier Guard). His first term was under Capt. J.J. Keith, Aug. 17, 1861 to Feb. 28.1 1862. The second term was under Lieutenant Singleton Gilbert, Feb. 9. 1864 to ?. On Aug. 9, 1864, his son, Leroy Vining (Button) Keith, age 16, was killed by Indians while substituting in the Guard for his ill father.

The 1870 Erath County, Texas Census, indicates Gabriel was living in Alexander, Texas, near lower Greens Creek. In the 1880 Census, he is located at William's Ranch in Brown County (which in 1887 was changed to Mills County). He established a ranch in Santa Anna, Texas, Coleman County.

After Synthia Jane died in 1892, U.S. postal records indicate Gabriel returned to Victor, Texas, serving as postmaster on Oct. 8, 1894. He lived with a daughter, Lydia Waid Keith-McGough, until his death in 1909. He is buried in Victor Cemetery, Erath County, Texas.

Gabriel and Synthia had 15 children. A son, Berry Moore and his wife, Sarah Jane Blair (my great-grandparents) were first couple married in Eastland County, Texas, on July 5, 1863, Blair Fort.

ROBERT KELTON

Robert Kelton, a citizen of the Republic of Texas, was born September 21, 1786, (Bible record). Robert married Catherine, daughter of Samuel and Martha Houston, in 1810, Pendleton district of South Carolina. He served in the South Carolina Militia in the War of 1812. In 1816 they moved to Georgia where he became captain in the Georgia Militia.

After the death of his second wife, he came to Texas. The time of his arrival was before September 16, 1839, which is the date on his Headright Certificate for Texas land. Gifford White's Tax Record of 1840 shows: "312 acres of land, two slaves and a gold watch." Robert Kelton died September 19, 1841, Montgomery County; the location of grave is unknown.

Three of Robert's sons were also citizens or the Republic. Oliver P. arrived before 1835, served as surgeon in the Texas Navy, and saw action against Mexican Navy. Benjamin F. married Rachel, daughter of Samuel W. Lindley, an early Texas

Settler. Samuel's son Jonathan died in defense of the Alamo. Robert Franklin, second great-grandfather, served in the Somervell Campaign against Mexico. He married Eliza Tolbert. Her parents and grandparents; Elijah Collard were citizens of the Republic.

The sacrifices and bravery of our ancestors laid the foundation for the great Texas that we have today.

Robert Kelton is the third great-grandfather of Willard Kelton. Willard Kelton, Life Member #4404.

WILLIAM PRICE KERR

William Price Kerr was born April 6, 1799, in York county, South Carolina. He was the son of Henry Kerr and his first wife, a daughter of James Price who died before 1824 in Giles County, Tenn. Henry Kerr's second wife was Catherine. Henry Kerr died in 1856 in Giles County.

William Price Kerr was married first to Mary Higginbotham, and they are said to have had 9 children, four of whom were William H., Martha J., Thomas M., and Isaac Newton. In April 1839, he migrated to Texas, where on January 11, 1840, he received a certificate for 640 acres of land in present-day Victoria County. His wife was living in early 1840, but she died shortly thereafter.

He returned to Tennessee briefly in 1840-41 and married Rachel Oxley in Haywood County on April 1, 1841. They immediately came to Texas, settling in Bexar County. They had two children. Frances Caroline, born May 5, 1842, married Rev. J.S. Gillett. Mary Jane was born February 17, 1844, and married William Franklin Mitchell on March 16, 1865, in Bexar County.

William Price Kerr died on August 8, 1869, and is buried in the Oak Island Cemetery in Bexar County. Rachel died May 15, 1887, and is buried in Wilson County, Texas. John Gresham Minniece III #6820 John Gresham Minniece IV #6821 Joseph Thomas Minniece #6822

CHARLES AUGUST KESLER (KESSLER)

Charles August Kesler obtained Land Grant # 109 in 1837 from the Republic of Texas. He established Kesler's Arcade and Kesler's Round Tent in Houston in 1838 and later became a well-known winemaker and operated a large vineyard on his land in Alleyton, Colorado County, for many years. He became active in civic affairs, and was a charter member and first president of the Houston Chamber of Commerce, incorporated January 25, 1840.

Charles (Carl) was born on May 16. 1809, in Sagan, Silesia, Germany. At the age of 20, he applied for a pass book as a registered cabinet-maker. The pass book described him as single, of medium build with an oval face, a pouting mouth and black-brown hair and blue-gray eyes. He began his journey on October 27, 1829, to settle in Texas eight years later.

John Franklin Kessler store at 1801 Houston Avenue, Houston, Texas in 1875 with family home on right side.

In the early months of 1837, he met and married Johanna Blaisse in Philadelphia, Pennsylvania. Johanna was born March 10, 1812 in Germany and reared in Philadelphia. Later that same year, she moved with Charles to the booming frontier town of Houston, Texas, to start a family.

Deeds show that Charles signed his name with one "s" and used that during his residence in America. His wanderbook, now in the possession of his descendants, shows that the name was spelled with two "s". That spelling was used by his children, who doubtless took it from that source.

Charles died on December 29, 1884, in Alleyton, Texas, and left behind him a long line of prominent Texas descendants. Charles and Johanna had thirteen children, nine of whom died in infancy. The four surviving were: Hannah, William, John Franklin, and Albert James.

John Kessler, born July 31, 1850, continued his father's business and established the Kessler Grocery at 1801 Houston Avenue in 1875. As this became a leading establishment of the city, John later served two terms as city commissioner.

John married at the age of 22, and had one daughter, Emma Johanna Elizabeth, born August 17, 1873. Emma Kessler married Thomas Kenney "T.K." Dixon from Alum Creek, Texas, and lived with him at 3602 Main in Houston. T.K. partnered with his father-in-law John in the pioneering self-service Kessler-Dixon Grocery, where he invented and patented the first automatic vending machine. He later entered his family into real estate and oil enterprises.

The Texas legacy of Charles August Kesler is further continued through his great-grandson, T.K. Dixon, Jr., great-great-granddaughter, Kenney Marie Dixon, and great-great-great-grandsons, Michael Kenney and John Bryan Pickens. Thomas Kenney Dixon, Jr. Michael Kenney Pickens #5734 John Bryan Pickens #5735

THOMAS WHITE KEY

Thomas White Key was born in St. Mary's County, Maryland, on September 30, 1803. He was the son of Philip Key (1750-1820) and Sophia Hall. His grandfather was Dr. John Key (1730-1755). His great-grandfather was Philip Key (1696-1764), who came to Maryland in 1720 and established the Key family in Southern Maryland. Philip Key, the original settler, was the great-grandfather of Francis Scott Key, who was the author of the "Star Spangled Banner."

John Henry Key holding last pair of spurs made by first cousin Jessie Key (Bill) Brett by spinning horse hair, taught by their grandfather Southern Confederacy Key

Thomas White Key came to Texas in 1835 and settled in what is now Liberty County. After the war for independence, he was the assessor and collector of taxes for the Republic of Texas in 1840 for Liberty County. Offices he held were: City of Liberty City Councilman, 1859 and 1862-1868; Liberty postmaster (1861); and Chambers County Justice of the Peace (1869).

Thomas White Key was a merchant and a farmer. On August 10, 1848, he married Nancy Evelyn Murphy (1834-1889) of Alabama. They had the following children: Francis Heath Key (1849-1909), Cecelia Cook Key (1851-1920), Philip Ross Rey (1856-1920), Southern Confederacy Key (1861-1944), Thomas White Key, Jr., (1865-1960), and Lucrecia Cook Key (1872-1964).

Thomas White Key died in December 1874 and was buried in the Liberty City Cemetery. My grandfather was Southern Confederacy Key. My father was Francis Alvin Key (1890- 1934). John Henry Key (Sept. 5, 1915)

HENRY H. KING

Henry H. King was born in the Republic of Texas October 30, 1841. His father was George W. King, who was born in Tennessee (c1814) and went to Texas sometime between 1829 and 1833. George married Lucy Amanda Lloyd on July 10, 1835, who had gone to Texas with her father about 1823. George and Amanda lived in Lost Prairie, which is now part of Miller County, Arkansas, but at the time was part of Red River County, Texas. George owned a farm, a grocery store on the Red River, and also ran keel boats on the Red River. He served in the Texas Revolution. It is not known what he did specifically, but men from the Red River area arrived at San Jacinto the day after the battle, and Santa Anna was placed in their care on the assumption that they would feel less hostility than those who had friends and relatives executed by the Mexican leader.

Henry was born in that part of Arkansas that was part of Red River County at the time of his birth. At the age of eighteen, he joined the 6th Arkansas Infantry. He served in numerous campaigns of the Army of Tennessee, such as Shiloh, Murfreesboro, and Chickamauga. He was promoted to lieutenant during the Atlanta Campaign, and shortly after received his fourth wound. After several weeks in the hospital, he made use of his knowledge of river navigation skills and served in the Confederate Secret Service. After the war, he returned home to Fouke, Arkansas, where he married Amanda Clementine Echols. He owned a 240-acre farm and served two terms as Justice of the Peace for Miller County, and one term as county coroner.

Henry died January 15, 1925 and is buried at Rocky Mound Cemetery near Fouke.

ROBERT JUSTUS KLEBERG (1803-1888)

Robert Justus Kleberg, was born on September 10, 1803, in Herstelle, Westphalia, and was named Johann Christian Justus Robert. Kleberg attended the University of Göttingen, where he studied law and received a J.D. degree. After graduating, he was appointed a justice of assizes in Nieheim and received several other judicial appointments. He married Rosalie Von Roeder in 1834. They immigrated to Texas that year with their families and settled in Cat Spring in 1836. In the Republic of Texas, Kleberg was associate commissioner and president of the Board of Land Commissioners (1837-38), Justice of the Peace (1841), and chief justice of Austin County (1846). In 1847, the Klebergs moved with the Roeder families to Meyersville, where Kleberg was elected county commissioner in 1848 and chief justice in 1853. He was also a leading Lateiner.

Robert Justus Kleberg Painting by J. Ferdinand McCan 1897

Kleberg fought in the Battle of San Jacinto in Capt. Moseley Baker's Company, and subsequently served as one of the Texas guards around Gen. Antonio López de Santa Anna. After the revolution, he volunteered for six months duty in the Texas Army. In DeWitt County, he was a member of John York's retaliatory campaign against the Indians on Escondido Creek. He is credited with saving German botanist Ferdinand J. Lindheimer's life when Lindheimer was wounded in the Brazos River bottom near Cat Spring. Kleberg was a loyal member of the Democratic Party and supported the cause of the Confederacy. When the Civil War broke out, he raised a company of militia; but because of his advanced age, he was not received into active service. He had no official religious affiliation, but like most Lateiner, had his firm individual moral convictions.

Robert and Rosa's youngest son, Robert Justus Kleberg, became the head of the King Ranch in 1885.

The elder Kleberg died on October 23, 1888, at his daughter's farm near Cuero, and was buried there. He was a longtime member of the Texas Veterans Association, and his grave is marked by a stone monument in the form of a soldier's tent with the words "Remember the Alamo" carved at the base. Kleberg County was named in his honor in 1913; a marker at his homesite near Cuero was erected in 1936. Source: "New Handbook of Texas" Robert Justus Kleberg, I, great-great-grandfather Robert Justus Kleberg, Sr., great-grandfather Robert Justus Kleberg, Jr., great-uncle Richard Mifflin Kleberg, Sr., grandfather Richard Mifflin Kleberg, III, #2270

JOHAN BERNHARD KLEIKAMP

In his emigration permit dated Muenster, Westphalia, Prussia, dated February 13, 1835, it was noted that the "weaver," Johan Bernhard Kleikamp) of Ascheberg was born August 25, 1806, at Ascheberg. It also declared that he refused to give up his plan of emigration to America, having already sold his house, was free of debt and that there no objections on the part of the police. Upon payment of the license of emigration, the permit was granted to Kleikamp, his wife Clara (nee Pauler) and one child.

Three individuals listed as "Klukamp" were on the list of the ship Pilot, arriving June 1, 1835 in New Orleans, with destination listed as Texas. The General Land Office of Texas has records under the name of John Bernard Kleykamp: original title of February 3, 1836; Mexican Title; Headright Certificate #86 dated March, 2, 1838, awarded to Anna Clara Peuler Klekamp, "widow of Bernard Klekamp."

The name of the Klekamp family was listed as being at the Brazos River during the "Runaway Scrape." Family tradition holds that John Bernard Kleykamp was killed by Indians at this time.

The only child of John Bernard Kleykamp, Elisabeth, married Bernard Geistmann in Colorado County at Frelsburg. He arrived in Texas in 1847. Christopher Pierce Krause #5857A Christopher William. Krause #6129N John Bernard Krause #6127N Joseph Daniel Krause #6128N Robert Bernard Krause #5760A Robert Rayner Krause #5761A

JAMES KNIGHT

James Knight was born October 15, 1805, in Columbia County, Georgia. He was the son of Lewis Knight and Elizabeth Bunby. James came to the Atascosita District (later Liberty County), Texas, in 1825, from Mississippi. The Atascosita Census for 1826 shows James as 21 years old, unmarried, with an occupation as wheelwright.

In January 1827, Third Sergeant James Knight marched loyally with militia members from Austin's colonists, the Atascositans, and Mexican officers against the insurgents at Nacogdoches. This was the short-lived Fredonian Rebellion. This service later proved to be very helpful to James in obtaining approval for his Land Grant. He was given a Land Grant in 1831, consisting of one league of land (4,428 acres) on the Trinity River north of Liberty.

The league just south of James' was granted to Amos and Sarah (Hunt) Green. James probably knew the Greens in Mississippi and came to Texas with them. He married their daughter, Eliza, in 1828. James and Eliza had ten children, including twin girls. Their eldest son, Henry, was my great-great-grandfather. The 1840 Texas Census shows James Knight had an additional 177 acres of land, four slaves, 100 cattle, five workhorses, and a wooden clock.

On March 6, 1836, James joined Logan's Company, which became the Third Company Infantry, Second Regiment, Texas Volunteers. They were marching to defend the Alamo when they learned it had fallen. On April 18, James was given eight days furlough, and the company marched into history at San Jacinto on April 21, 1836. He was discharged at Goliad on June 6, 1936, and re-enlisted the next day. On June 3, the Texian Army at Goliad, under General Thomas J. Rust, was burying the victims of the massacre with full military honors. Private James Knight was there with the Second Regiment as part of the funeral and general parade of honor.

Official documents indicate that James Knight was a respected citizen of Texas. He fought for her when he had too, but he also defended her laws as Justice of the Peace of Liberty County in 1839, 1841, 1843 and 1845.

James died November 27, 1846, at the age of 41 years. Death must have been sudden; his youngest boy, Amos, was born nine months later. James Knight is buried on the Amos Green League, Liberty County, Texas. The James Knight League is still an official land designation in Liberty County. Donald L. Wilkinson

LEWIS KNIGHT

Lewis Knight, born 1809 in Granville County, North Carolina. He moved to Bedford County, Tennessee, where in 1831 he married Emilie Crain, daughter of Ambrose Crain and his wife Mary "Polly" Burditt. He came to Texas with the Crains, settling in Nacogdoches County in 1834.

Emilie and her mother Mary were original members of the Old North Church, formed in 1838 and now called Union Baptist Church. Lewis Knight and Ambrose Crain both received Land Grants from the state of Texas, as did Ambrose's sons, Joel Burditt Crain and Newell Crain, both of whom fought at San Jacinto.

In 1852, Lewis Knight moved his family to Travis County, Texas, settling near Austin, on the south side of the Colorado River in an area called Burditt's Prairie. His daughter, Martha, married James Arbuckle Littlepage in 1856. James was the son of James Beverly Littlepage and Susana VanArsdale, who came to Texas from Greenbrier County, Virginia. James B. Littlepage was killed by a runaway mule he had brought from Virginia, which came from the famous breed that George Washington imported from Europe. Martha died in 1868 and Susanna, her mother-in-law, in 1870. Both are buried in a tiny enclosed cemetery located in the middle of the Bergstrom Interchange of U.S. #183 and Texas Highway #71, now a thoroughfare to the new Austin Municipal Airport. An article in October 1965 in "Texas Highways," published by the Texas Highway Department, stated it was believed to be the only cemetery in Texas located within an interchange.

After the death of his daughter, Martha, and her mother-in-law, Susanna Littlepage, Lewis Knight moved to Lampasas County, Texas, where he died in 1871. He is buried in Pitt Creek Cemetery along with his sons, Lewis Walton Knight and John Arthur Knight. Also buried there is his son-in-law, James Arbuckle Littlepage. All have Masonic emblems on their markers.

The son of James Arbuckle Littlepage and his wife, Martha Knight, was James Newel Littlepage, born in Travis County in 1863. In 1884, he married Etta Hunter, daughter of William Dunlap Hunter and his wife, Elliot Smith, who were early settlers from Laurens County, South Carolina. James Newel Littlepage served as chief of police of Austin and was widely known and loved. Police Chief Littlepage was killed in the line of duty on October 9, 1928, in an effort to arrest a man who shot five people that day. He was one of the Texas Peace Officers honored in a special ceremony on May 10, 1999, on the grounds of the state Capitol at the dedication of a new monument honoring the Texas Peace Officers killed in the line of duty.

His granddaughter, Joyce Littlepage Keck (TSDRT #14592) married Ray M. Keck, Jr., of Cotulla, Texas, and is the mother of John Harrison Keck, SRT #4574.

DAVID SMITH KORNEGAY

David Smith Kornegay was born in 1808 to Robert and Lititia Kornegay on their Jones County, North Carolina, plantation. He arrived in Texas in April 1830, with Col. John H. Moore, and settled at Moore's Blockhouse on the Colorado River where La Grange is now located. He was granted 1/3 league of land by Stephen F. Austin. The tract was 14 miles north of La Grange "on the waters of Rabb Creek." When the town of La Grange was laid out, he was among the earliest purchasers of land and lots from the town proprietors. He built his home at 162 South Washington Street. David Kornegay was one of the organizers of Fayette County in 1838, and served as the first county clerk.

David Smith Kornegay (1808-1856)

When the Texas Revolution broke out in the fall of 1835, he fought in the opening campaign under Col. Moore and Capt. Thomas Allee, starting with the Battle of Gonzales and ending with the fall of San Antonio in December. On March 15, 1836, he joined Houston's Army at Burnam's Crossing on the Colorado below La Grange. He retreated east with Sam Houston in what came to be known as the "Runaway Scrape." He served under Capt. William Hill in the First Regiment at the Battle of San Jacinto.

He served during the Republic days in the following campaigns: the Great Comanche Raid of 1840 and the resulting Battle of Plum Creek; Moore's Campaign on the Upper Colorado; the Vasquez Raid on San Antonio in the spring of 1842; and the Battle of Salado Creek or the Dawson Massacre. As a result of this last action on September 18, 1842, he was captured and carried into captivity to the prison of Perote near Vera Cruz, Mexico. On July 2, 1843, he and 15 other men escaped by digging through the walls of Perote. He made his way to Vera Cruz in the company of fellow escapee Richard Barclay, boarded the British steamer "Petrita," and returned to Texas via New Orleans.

On December 22, 1844, he and 18-year-old Elizabeth McGary were married by County Judge James S. Lester. She was the daughter of Bridget Lamb McGary of La Grange and the late Barnard McGary. Their first three children, Edward Dawson, Mary Ellen, and Sarah Elizabeth were born in La Grange. In late 1850, they sold out their Fayette County holdings and moved to McLennen County. They settled on the west bank of the Brazos on a league of land granted to her mother by the Mexican government. Two more daughters — Lititia, and Annie - were born in McLennen County.

It was here that David Kornegay died on April 5, 1856. His grave at the Bosqueville Cemetery has a large granite marker placed by the State of Texas in 1936 during the State Centennial. Doss Kornegay Jr. #6097 Patrick Cullen Kornegay # pending Dowe Sterling Rhodes # 4911

EDWARD DAWSON KORNEGAY

"Doss" was the firstborn child and only son of David S. and Elizabeth McGary Kornegay. He was born at 162 S. Washington St., LaGrange, TX, on December 7, 1845 during the closing days of the Republic of Texas. Statehood was achieved on February 18, 1846, and the fortunes of Texas were forever linked with those of the United States. This Union was challenged fifteen year later when Texas seceded and entered the Confederacy. At fifteen years of age, Doss Kornegay enlisted in the Confederate Army.

Sgt. E.D. "Doss" Kornegay

He spent his earliest years in Fayette County, but moved to McLennen County with his parents and grandmother, Bridget McGary. He attended primary school in McLennen County. His name and that of his sister, Mary Ellen, appear on a scholastic census taken by the state of Texas in 1855-56. The family lived on the McGary Grant, about 10 miles north of Waco on the Brazos at Bosqueville.

Following the 1856 death of his father, his mother sold her McLennen County holdings and moved to Fort Graham in Hill County, where they appear on the 1860 U.S. Census.

Doss joined the Confederate Army at Waco in 1861 as a member of the Texas State Troops. On March 3, 1862, he joined Co. K, Young's 12th Texas Infantry. He served with his cousin, Edward Milton McKissick. He later named a son Edward Milton. He was with the Confederate troops that recaptured Galveston from Union occupation in 1862. In January 1864, he was back in Waco where he joined Waller's Texas Calvary, Co. G. He saw hard action in Louisiana and Mississippi as a Calvaryman.

During the "Red River Campaign" in 1864, he fought in battles at Opelousas and Bayou Boeff, where his mother had spent her girlhood. At 19, he was still a teenager when he surrendered with Waller's Calvary on June 5, 1865 at Marshall, Texas. He rejoined his family in Hill County. In 1868, the family moved to Lavaca County, near Lyons.

On November 6, 1879, he married 19 year old Mullie Lou Williams in Halletsville, Texas. She was the daughter of George and Catherine Coffee Williams, who died during the Civil War. She, her sister, and three brothers were raised by Williams' uncles in Lavaca County.

In 1880, after the death of his mother, the Kornegays left Lavaca County for Coffeyville, in southern Kansas. There, their first child, Robert, was born on their first anniversary. The family soon moved back to Texas where Ruby, Ina May and Clyde were born. The 1890's found them in Oklahoma, first in Pickins County, then in the Atoka Lake area. Milton, Grover, Dolly and Earl were born there.

In 1904, they founded the DK Ranch near Hobbs, New Mexico. They lived in a dugout prior to building a permanent frame home. The ranch is in the hands of their grandson, D.K. Randolph, as of the year 2000.

Edward Dawson Kornegay

On October 17, 1914, after 68 years of good health, Doss died suddenly on his ranch. He was initially buried at Monument Hill, near DK Ranch. September 1960, his son, Earl, had the remains moved to Prairie Haven in Hobbs, to be reinterred next to his wife, who had died in 1957. Their graves are marked by large granite markers. A bronze plaque, supplied by the Veteran's Administration, was place by his grandsons, D.K. Randolph and Doss Kornegay, II. Doss Kornegay, Jr. #6097

ELIZABETH MCGARY KORNEGAY

Elizabeth McGary was the youngest child of Barnard and Bridget Lamb McGary, who were natives of Ireland. She was born in Opelousas, Louisiana, on January 18, 1826, four months after the death of her father. She was christened a week later on January 24th at St. Landry's Catholic Church. She spent her first 8 years in Opelousas.

The widowed Bridget McGary took her family by riverboat to New Orleans in 1834, then across the Gulf of Mexico by schooner to the port of Velasco, Texas, then up the Brazos River by steamer to Washington-on-the-Brazos, arriving in December. There they joined the D.B. Friar family. On March 20, 1836, they all left ahead of the invading Mexican Army. The entire population moved east toward the Trinity and Sabine Rivers in what came to be known as the "Runaway Scrape." The refugees returned to their homes after Houston's victory at San Jacinto. Elizabeth was then 10 years old.

In 1839, they moved to near Clinton (now Cuero) on the Guadalupe River, in the DeWitt Colony, but returned to Washington-on-the-Brazos the following year after the Great Comanche Raid of 1840 and the death of her brother, Edward, killed at the hands of Comanches somewhere between Clinton and the mouth of the San Antonio River. The Friars remained in Clinton, where their descendants live to this day.

By 1843, the family was established in LaGrange, Fayette County. It was here that Elizabeth married David Smith Kornegay on December 22, 1844. Her first three children, Edward Dawson, Mary Ellen, and Sarah Elizabeth were born there. The family lived at 162 South Washington Street.

In November 1848, the family traveled to North Carolina to visit David's family, arriving in New Bern on the 28th aboard the bark Franchiska out of Galveston.

In late 1850, the Kornegay family moved to Milam County, in an area that later became McLennan County. They settled on the Brazos River about 10 miles up from Waco, on a league of land that had been granted to Elizabeth's mother by the Mexican government. Elizabeth's sister, Sarah McKissick, and her family occupied a similar adjacent grant. It was here that the Kornegay's other daughters, Lititia and Annie were born. It was here, also that her husband, David Kornegay, died April 5, 1856, and her mother died in early 1857. Both are buried nearby in the Old Bosqueville Cemetery.

On July 10, 1857, Elizabeth sold her land in McLennan County and moved to Hill County near Fort Graham, in an area now covered by Lake Whitney. It was just across the Brazos River from where the McKissick family had settled in 1850. The 1860 Texas Census shows Elizabeth and her children living in Hill County. Records show she bought a home in 1859 for over $800, way above the average cost of a dwelling in those days.

Elizabeth McGary Kornegay

Elizabeth's son, Edward Dawson (nicknamed "Doss") enlisted in the Confederate Army in Waco in 1861, first serving in Young's 12th Texas Infantry. In January, 1864, he was back in Waco and joined Waller's Texas Cavalry. He saw action in Louisiana and Mississippi. During the Red River Campaign, he fought in battles in the area where Elizabeth had spent her girlhood. After the war, he rejoined his family in Hill County.

The war had meant hard times for Elizabeth and family. On one occasion, she and her daughter, Mary Ellen, drove off a party of Union foragers who had tried to take their last remaining cow.

Elizabeth sold her Hill County home in 1868 and moved with her children to Lavaca County, where her sister lived. She remained there until her death on September 27, 1880. She is buried in Navidad Baptist Cemetery, 3 miles south of Schulenberg, TX. Dowe Sterling Rhodes #4911 Doss Kornegay, Jr. #6097

JOHANN HEINRICH KRAFT

Johann Heinrich Kraft was born on June 2, 1827, in Schletzenrod, Hessen, Germany. He married Katherine Roege on Jan. 22, 1854, in Comal County, New Braunfels, Texas.

Katherine was born Sept. 28, 1837, in Fahren, Hanover, Germany. Katherine's family came to America on the same ship as Heinrich Kraft. They left Bremen, Germany, on board the "Herschel" on September 23, 1844, and arrived at

Galveston, Texas, on Dec. 8, 1844, then boarded a small schooner to the port of Indianola.

They were chosen by Prince Solms of the German Emigration Society to help build a town with total German customs and culture. On Mar. 21, 1845, they arrived at the springs which is now Landa Park, New Braunfels, Texas. The Kraft and Roege families all became founders of the city and founders of the First German Protestant Church of New Braunfels, Texas.

Heinrich & Katherine Kraft home built in 1878, Kraft Ranch, New Braunfels, TX

Heinrich and Katherine became the parents of 12 children. Heinrich died on Jan. 26, 1904, and Katherine died on Mar. 15, 1917. They were buried in the cemetery on the Kraft Ranch, along with two young children. Their beautiful ranch and rock home — still lived in at this time — reveals the diligence and effort these pioneers put forth and prospered during the early years of the Republic of Texas, Charles E. Seiler (great-great-grandson) #6645M Brent L. Seiler (great-great-great-grandson) #6646M Nathan E. Seiler (great-great-great-grandson) 46647M

ROBERT H. KUYKENDALL, SR. (1788-1830)

Robert Hardin (or Hampton) Kuykendall, an early member of the "Old 300," was born in 1788 near Princeton, Kentucky, to Adam and Margaret (Hardin) Kuykendall. After moves through Sumner County, Tennessee, and Henderson County, Kentucky, the family settled in Arkansas near the Cadron Settlement on the Arkansas River around February 15, 1810, in the fall of 1821, having explored west of the Sabine River for some time, Robert joined his brothers Abner, Joseph, and Peter at Nacogdoches. He and Joseph moved with Daniel Gilleland and their families to the east bank of the Colorado River, near the La Bahia crossing, where they established the river's first settlement.

In December 1822, the Baron de Bastrop arrived at the settlement to organize the Austin Colony. The settlers elected Robert Kuykendall captain of the militia for the Mina (Colorado) District and alcalde of the Colorado district. Kuykendall's house was the election site when James Cummins was elected alcalde of the Colorado District.

Kuykendall and his men killed a group of horse thieves and placed their heads on tall poles along the La Bahia Road as a warning to others — a warning that evidently succeeded in deterring lawlessness in the colony. After many Indian depredations in the summer of 1822, Kuykendall headed a party of settlers in an attack on the Karankawas at the mouth of Skull Creek, where the Indians were defeated with considerable loss. In 1824, Kuykendall was involved in further encounters with the Karankawas.

On July 15, 1824, Stephen F. Austin granted Kuykendall two leagues of land, one on the east side and one on the west side of the Colorado River. Kuykendall established his home on the east league near the site of present Glen Flora and named it Pleasant Farm Plantation.

In an Indian fight sometime after the spring of 1826, he received a serious head injury, which gradually led to paralysis, blindness, and eventual death. Between March 20 and 27, 1830, Dr. Robert Peebles performed a successful trepan on Kuykendall, an event that induced Judge Robert M. Williamson, editor of The Texas Gazette at San Felipe, to commend the doctors of the colony. William B. Travis, later turned money over to E. Roddy for Dr. Peebles from the Kuykendall estate for medical expenses.

In 1830, Stephen F. Austin requested that commissioner general Juan Antonio Padilla convey an extra league of land each to two men of particular merit in the early days of the colony: Josiah H. Bell as alcalde, and Robert H. Kuykendall as commander of the militia.

Kuykendall married Sarah Ann Gilleland at Red Hill, Arkansas, in 1814. They had six children. Kuykendall died in the latter part of 1830 and is presumed to have been buried in the Old Matagorda Cemetery. Subsequent hurricanes washed away most of the grave markers, and his headstone has been lost.

Bibliography: Robert H. Kuykendall, Sr., Family Genealogy (MS, Barker Texas History Center, University of Texas at Austin). *Submitted by Marshall E. Kuykendall*

DR. NICHOLAS DESCAMPTES LABADIE

Dr. Nicholas Descamptes Labadie (1802-1867) was born in Windsor, Canada West, on December 5, 1802. He was a son of Antone Louis Labadie and Charlotte Barthe, widow of Lt. Louis Rheaume, both natives of Canada. His ancestors on each side came originally from France, with the line on his father's side having been traced back to Francois Labadie, who was born in the Diocese of Xaintis in 1644 and who as a young man went to Canada where he married and settled.

Antone Louis Labadie, the father of Dr. Nicholas D. Labadie, was twice married and the father of thirty-three (33) children, with Dr. Labadie being the youngest child. Dr. Labadie was reared on the frontier in Canada West by pious parents of meager means who were devout Catholics. At about 21 years of age, he left Canada for the United States, where he initially settled in Missouri. From 1824 to 1828, he attended a Catholic institute at Barrens in Perry County, Missouri, where he studied for the priesthood.

In 1829, he abandoned the ministry to and went to St. Louis, where he studied medicine and defrayed his expenses by clerking in a store. Upon learning from traders of the advantages of the lower Mississippi country, he traveled to Fort Jessup, Louisiana, in 1830. By this time, he had progressed in his medical studies to engage in a limited practice and was dividing his time equally between "calls" and his duties as a store clerk in the post.

At Fort Jessup, Dr. Labadie came to hear a great deal of the Texas frontier and decided that the favorable reports were worth his personal inspection. Mounting his horse, he rode to Nacogdoches, then the chief point between the Louisiana line and San Felipe, the capital of Stephen F. Austin's Colony. He reached Nacogdoches on Christmas Day 1830, where he delivered his letters of introduction to Col. Jose de La Piedras, Commandant. After receiving assurances of good will from the Mexican government, he departed in a few days for Austin's Colony.

At San Felipe, he met Col. Samuel Williams, who accompanied him to Brazoria. A month later, he was in New Orleans accompanied by Captain John Austin and other Texans whom he had met on his earlier inspection of the country. He was persuaded to return.

On March 2, 1831, he landed at Anahuac aboard the schooner "Martha," commanded by Captain James Spillman. He was immediately employed by Colonel Bradburn as surgeon for a military post, which at that time consisted of 300 men and housed a Mexican garrison. Others who settled here during this period were William Barret Travis, Patrick C. Jack, Andrew Briscoe, William B. Slates, William Dobie Dunlap, George M. Patrick, Theodore Dorsett, and William Hardin.

Dr. Labadie wrote two fascinating letters from the hustling town of Anahuac to his nephew, Anthony Lagrave of New Orleans. One letter of March 19, 1831, captures the spirit of the place:

"What few stores we have here are doing very well. I have got me a lot on which I will have a building erected as soon as materials can be had. There will be about 20 houses erected in about 3 or 4 months. I have opened my drugs which have been welcomed by the people as they have been much wanted. The Colonel has employed me to attend on his soldiers. Two or three days after my arrival I got in business and since have not had less than 6 cases daily. I have charged my medical book to yesterday the sum of $115.00, the work of only 16 days."

Dr. Labadie further opened a general merchandise store in partnership with Charles Wilcox, which prospered. He reported that each soldier of the post received twenty-five cents a day, which they then spent readily on liquor, bread, and other such goods.

Shortly thereafter, Dr. Labadie married Miss Mary Norment. His brother-in-law was Thomas Norment, who was a volunteer in the Texas Patriot cause and who shared in the glories of the Battle of San Jacinto with Valentine Ignatius Burch and his brother, James Burch. Major Thomas Norment appears as an officer in command of Valentine and James Burch on page 246 of the Muster Rolls of the Texas Revolution, published by the

Daughters of the Republic of Texas in 1986.

Upon invasion of Texas by the Mexican Army under command of General Santa Anna, Dr. Labadie enlisted on March 11, 1836, in the company of the Second Regiment of Texas Volunteers under command of Captain William M. Logan upon its organization in Liberty County.

He reported with his company to General Sam Houston at Beason's Ferry on the Colorado River on March 20, 1836. He was assigned to scouting duty with a company of volunteers under Captain Karnes when the retreat of San Felipe began. He rejoined the main Army while it was encamped at Groce's Ferry. Subsequently, he was appointed on April 6, 1836, by General Sam Houston as Surgeon to the First Regiment of Regulars, and in this capacity had charge of the medicine chest, which was hauled on ox cart by the retreating Texas Army.

In the subsequent Battle of San Jacinto, Dr. Labadie fought as a volunteer in Captain Logan's Company on the left wing of the Texas Army, commanded by General Sidney Sherman. When the battle ended, he served as a surgeon to the wounded of the Texas Army, and by assignment of General Sam Houston, he further attended wounded prisoners. Dr. Labadie was present when the captured Santa Anna was brought into camp, and being fluent in Spanish, he acted as an interpreter when Santa Anna was presented to General Sam Houston.

In his 1858 memoirs, Dr. Labadie recounted to the press an account of that interview between Santa Anna and General Sam Houston, which was acknowledged as correct by witnesses then in a position to know. Dr. Labadie said:

"While I was engaged in attending the wounded Mexican prisoners, a Mr. Sylvester rode up to the prison square with a prisoner who refused to enter. I was called upon to interpret since neither the sentinel nor Mr. Sylvester could speak Spanish. I told him that this was the place where all prisoners were kept. He replied: 'I want to see General Houston. Is he in camp?' 'Yes,' I replied, 'Mr. Sylvester take this man to yonder oak tree where General Houston lies.' As they departed, the prisoner whose wounds I was dressing, a Mexican Lieutenant, whispered to me, 'Est El Presidente.' (He is the President.) I at once folded up my instruments and followed after them, and met Colonel Hockley who was calling me to come quickly as I was wanted. I found General Houston lying on his back on the ground under the oak tree (he was wounded).

And on his left the prisoner was sitting on a chest. He politely returned my salute and I said to him in Spanish, pointing, 'This is General Houston, do you want anything of him?' He replied, 'Tell General Houston that General Santa Anna stands before him a prisoner.' General Houston hearing this interpreted appeared much surprised and turning on his left side, said, 'General Santa Anna in what condition do you surrender yourself?' 'A prisoner of war,' said he, and continuing, 'Whilst I was in the "camino royal" - the public highway I met two of your soldiers to whom I surrendered myself a prisoner of war.' 'Well,' said General Houston, 'Tell General Santa Anna that so long as he shall remain in the boundaries that I shall allot him I will be responsible for his life.' Upon hearing this Santa Anna's countenance brightened. He said, 'Tell General Houston that I am tired of blood and war and have seen enough of this country to know that the two people cannot live under the same laws, and I am willing to treat with him as to the boundaries of the two countries.' In reply General Houston said, 'Tell him that I cannot treaty with him, but that the cabinet that is in Galveston will make a treaty with him.' Here the crowd pressing against us interfered with the conversations, and the guard had to force them back.

"Colonel Hockley, then appearing with young (De) Zavalla to serve as interpreter, I returned to my wounded who had been taken across the Bayou to the Zavalla place which was thereafter used as a hospital."

A few days after the battle, under orders from the Secretary of War, Thomas J. Rusk, Dr. Labadie started for Galveston, but stopped on the way at his Anahuac home to determine the condition of his wife and family. Dr. Labadie returned to his plantation home at Lake Charlotte to find it vandalized. His pregnant wife, Mary Norment Labadie, had fled to the Neches with their two young children, Nicholas Patrick and Sarah. Unable to cross the river because of the huge crowd, Mary Labadie returned home as soon as word of the San Jacinto victory spread through the refugee camps.

Fortunately, the vandals had somehow overlooked the bacon in the smokehouse and the cows in the field, which afforded the Labadie family some source of food. Troubles rapidly multiplied. Dr. Labadie became ill in May and lost his hearing. Young Nicholas Patrick, only 3 years of age, died on July 7, 1836, of whooping cough, a disease that had run rampant through the refugee camps on the Neches. Later that day, however, Mary gave birth to a daughter, who was named Charlotte in memory of Dr. Labadie's mother. Dr. Labadie spent the remainder of the summer of 1836 inoculating his neighbors and their slaves for smallpox, a disease that had plagued the Gulf Coast area since March 1835.

Dr. Labadie received Bounty Certificate No. 1006 for 320 acres of land for military service between March 6 to June 6, 1836. On Captain Logan's Muster Rolls, he is shown as having been promoted to Assistant Surgeon on April 18, 1836. He received San Jacinto Donation Certificate No. 527 for 640 acres of land issued on August 29, 1838.

In the winter of 1837, Dr. Labadie moved to Galveston from his home on Lake Charlotte in what is now Chambers County. He was one of the first permanent residents of this "tent city" and opened a drug store on the northwest corner of 22nd and Market Street where he also practiced medicine. Dr. Labadie began to treat the fevers and other ills of the island caused by bad sanitary conditions. In 1839, came the first deadly visitation of the fatal "vomito," which caused the death of his beloved wife and companion, Mary Norment.

Dr. Labadie was now a single parent of three little girls, the oldest of which was but six years old and the youngest child only five months old. Dr. Labadie remained on Galveston Island until his death in 1867, where he proved himself worthy of the title of St. Luke, the Apostle, as the "beloved physician."

Prior to his death, Dr. Labadie was active in business and social circles of Galveston. He established a line of steamers between Galveston and Pensacola, Florida, which furnished a considerable quantity of lumber for the early buildings of the city. He built the wharf at the foot of 77th Street, which bears his name and was a popular business under his management. He built the first marine ways, and purchased town lots upon which he constructed substantial buildings, particularly at 2317-2319 Market Street. He was an active leader in establishing the first Catholic Church in Galveston, which was erected on Center Street. Additionally, he was one of he first citizens to respond to a subscription for Charity Hospital built just after the Civil War.

During the Civil War, Dr. Labadie served in the capacity of a Physician Member of the Examining Board of the First Brigade of Texas State Troops from 1861-1865.

After the death of his wife in 1839, Dr. Labadie married Mrs. Agnes Rivera of Galveston on December 9, 1840. The issue of the union was one son, Joseph.

Dr. Labadie's second wife died in 1843, and he married a third time to Ms. Julia Seymeour. There was no issue of this marriage. Dr. Labadie died on March 13, 1867.

The children of Dr. Nicholas D. Labadie and Mary Norment were:

1. Charlotte Labadie, who married Ebenezer Barstow

2. Sarah Labadie, who married my great-great-grandfather, Solomon B. Wallis

3. Mary C. Tucker, born 7/25/1859, and who married Philip C. Tucker II.

The only child of the marriage of Dr. Nicholas D. Labadie and his second wife, Agnes Rivera, was a son, Joseph Labadie.

Bibliography: "Narrative of the Anahuac, or Opening Campaign of the Texas Revolution," by N.D. Labadie, Texas Almanac, 1859; Probate Records of Nicholas D. Labadie, M.D., in Estate No. 673, recorded in Volume 6, P.P 191-194 of Galveston County, Texas; Genealogy Records of the Wallisville Heritage Park, Wallisville, Texas; "Chambers County: A Pictorial History," by Margaret Henson and Kevin Ladd, P.P. 19, 27, 26, 39, 50, 54, 75, 117, 154, 169, and 282, 1988; "The Age," No. 1, Vol. 111, Wallisville Heritage Park, December 1981; Archives of the University of Texas, Barker Texas History Center, Austin, Texas. Jack Reeves Mason, Paul Bateman Mason, Steven Randall Mason, Ronald Alexander Mason and Billy Alexander Mason

WILLIAM DEMETRIS LACEY

William Demetris Lacey was born of English parents in Virginia in 1808. His family moved to Kentucky while he was still a child, and came to Texas at the age of twenty. On March 1, 1831, he was given title to one-fourth of a league of land in Austin's Second Colony, in what is now Fayette County.

In 1832 Mr. Lacy married Sarah Ann Bright, whose father was David Bright, a member of one of Austin's "Old 300." On January 9, 1838, Lacy received Headright Certificate 112 for three-fourths of one league and one labor of land from the Matagorda County Board of Land Commissioners. In the certificate evidencing this fact the name Lacey was changed from Lacey to Lacy.

Mr. Lacy was one of the delegates to the first convention of Texas in Austin on October 1, 1832. In 1836, Mr. Lacy was elected second Judge of the Municipality of Colorado by the General Council of the Provisional Government of Texas. Subsequently, on February 1, 1836, Mr. Lacy was elected delegate to the Constitutional Convention of the Republic of Texas. He was seated at the convention March 1, 1836, and on March 2 he was a signer of the Texas Declaration of Independence.

Having moved his family to Galveston Island, he joined the Army on April 18 until September 17, 1836, and settled on Tres Palacios River in Matagorda County upon discharge. In May 1848, he moved his family back to Paducah, Kentucky, where he died on October 14, 1848. His widow returned to Texas with her children and made Matagorda County her home until her death in 1872. Laurance H. Armour, Jr. William Wharton Chapter #23

EMMANUEL LAGRONE AND RACHEL CLARK LAGRONE

Emmanuel LaGrone was the son of Jacob LaGrone, Sr. and Catherine Riser LaGrone. He was born April 21, 1813 in the Newberry District of South Carolina. After moving with his parents from South Carolina to Georgia in about 1820 and living for a time in Crawford County, Georgia, he came to Texas in 1837 and settled in Harrison County.

Emmanuel LaGrone married Rachel Clark on April 27, 1839 in Harrison County, Texas. Rachel was born June 15, 1823 in Texas, while it was still part of the Mexican State of Coahuila-Texas. To their marriage, the following children were born in:

William Allen LaGrone, born in May 1842.

Cyrus Wilson LaGrone, Sr., born March 4, 1844. He died January 11, 1886 in Harrison County, having been married to Mary Holiday Burton and to Effie Croft.

Mary Frances LaGrone, born September 1847, who married James Allen Reel. She died in 1912.

Jacob Belton LaGrone, born November 17, 1848. He was never married and died in April 1936.

Susan Melvina LaGrone, born September 22, 1851, who married William Henry Reel (Sr.). She died August 29, 1906 in Harrison County, and is buried in the LaGrone Family Cemetery northeast of Longview near LaGrone's Chapel Church in Harrison County.

Rachel Clark LaGrone died October 6, 1893, and Emmanuel LaGrone died February 19, 1905. They are buried in the LaGrone Family Cemetery. Submitted by William M. Huffman, a great-

great-great-grandson of Jacob LaGrone, Sr. and Catherine Riser LaGrone, whose line of decent is as follows:

Emmnnuel LaGrone* and Rachel Clark LaGrone*
Susan Melvina LaGrone and William Henry Reel (Sr.)*
William Henry Reel, Jr. and Janie Ethel Prior Reel
Lois Marie Reel and Perry L. Huffman
William M. Huffman
*Residents of the Republic of Texas

William Henry Reel (Sr.) was the son of Alfred Reel* and Purmelia Norris Reel* and was the grandson of Daniel Reel* and Barbary Reel*

JACOB LAGRONE, SR. AND CATHERINE RISER LAGRONE

Jacob LaGrone, Sr. and Catherine Riser LaGrone, each born in the Newberry district of South Carolina, moved from South Carolina to Georgia in about 1820 and lived for a time in Crawford County, Georgia. They came to Texas in 1837 and settled in Harrison County.

Jacob LaGrone, Sr. was born October 17, 1785, and Catherine (Kate) Riser was born in 1789. They were married in October 1810 in South Carolina. Catherine died January 4, 1860 and Jacob died July 27, 1863 in Harrison County. Each is buried in the LaGrone Family Cemetery northeast of Longview, in Harrison County, near LaGrone's Chapel Church.

The following children were born of the marriage of Jacob LaGrone, Sr. and Katherine Riser LaGrone:

Eva Christine LaGrone, who married Henry M. Robinson on October 29, 1834 in Talladega County, Alabama.

Jacob LaGrone, Jr., who married Mary Ann Randolph on May 26, 1840 in Harrison County, Texas.

Emmanuel LaGrone, who married Rachel Clark on April 27, 1839 in Harrison County, Texas.

Martha LaGrone.
Daniel LaGrone.
Martin LaGrone.

George Washington LaGrone, who married Martha S. Clark August 4, 1857 in Harrison County, Texas.

Elizabeth LaGrone, who married Jacob Hickman Boone January 14, 1847 in Harrison County, Texas.

Mary Frances LaGrone, who married Charles Belton Dickard July 2, 1857 in Harrison County, Texas.

Andrew Jackson LaGrone.

Susan Melinda LaGrone, who married Claiborne Corqham Dickard December 15, 1855 in Harrison County, Texas.

Several children- including Eva Christine LaGrone, Jacob LaGrone, Jr., Emmanuel LaGrone, George Washington LaGrone, Elizabeth LaGrone, Mary Frances LaGrone, and Susan Melinda LaGrone- came to Texas at the same time. Submitted by William M. Huffman, a great-great-great-grandson of Jacob LaGrone, Sr. and Catherine Riser LaGrone, whose line of decent is as follows:

Jacob LaGrone Sr. * and Catherine Riser LaGrone*
Emmannuel LaGrone* and Rachel Clark LaGrone*
Susan Melvina LaGrone and William Henry Reel (Sr.)*
William Henry Reel, Jr. and Janie Ethel Prior Reel,
Lois Marie Reel and Perry L. Huffman
William M. Huffman
*Residents of the Republic of Texas

William Henry Reel (Sr.) was the son of Alfred Reel* and Purmelia Norris Reel* and was the grandson of Daniel Reel* and Barbary Reel*

GEORGE WASHINGTON LANG

In a petition of affidavit for land filed by the children of George Washington Lang on December 25, 1857, in Gonzales County, Texas, the following biographical facts are stated:

1. The surviving children of George Washington Lang (on December 25, 1857) were Daniel P. Lang, James E. Lang, and Sophiah Lang Habermacher.
2. George Washington Lang came to Texas on or about 1835.
3. He participated in the struggle for independence of the Republic of Texas and fought at the Battle of San Jacinto.
4. G.W. Lang died in Perote Castle, Mexico, while in the service of the United States in 1847. (Mexican War)
5. The place of residence for G.W. Lang and his family from 1837 to the time of his death was Texas.

In "The Muster Rolls of the Texas Revolution," published by the Daughters of the Republic of Texas, George W. Lang is listed as a blacksmith under the quartermaster.

All of the above facts were taken from (page 173) the muster roll of Captain Snively's Company "B," 1st Regiment of Infantry, Texas Army, commanded by Lt. Col. A. Turner from the 31st day of October when last mustered to the 31st day of December 1836.

George Washington Lang married Rebekah Priest on December 15, 1819, according to "Williamson County, Tennessee, Marriage Records, 1600-1850," page 157, compiled and published by Wilena Roberts Bejach and Lillian Johnson Gardiner.

A memorial marker stands in the Willowhole Cemetery, Madison County, Texas, in memory of George Washington Lang. The marker is located beside the burial site of his son, Daniel P. Lang. Submitted by Jerry Wilton Fannin, member of William Joel Bryan Chapter, Bryan, Texas Dr. Ralph E. Cole, member of Henderson Yoakum Chapter, Huntsville, Texas

Onie Mack Lang (deceased), member of San Jacinto Chapter, Houston, Texas

ASA LANGFORD

Asa Langford was born September 8, 1820, in Clark County, Arkansas. He was the youngest child of Eli Jr. and Mary Edens Langford. When he was six years old, the family, along with a herd of cattle and two slaves, moved by wagon train to Nacogdoches. At that time Nacogdoches was a part of Mexico.

Mexico promised head-rights of land to families that would settle in Texas. It is not clear whether or not the Eli Jr. Langford family came as colonists or to claim a head-right. Eli Jr. abandoned his family sometime between 1828 and 1830. His wife, Mary Edens Langford, received a Mexican Land Grant for a league of land in Zavalla's Colony in 1835; however, she apparently did not complete the terms of the grant, as she did not receive the title. With the advance of Santa Anna's Army into Tejas in early 1836, Mary took her daughters and joined the rush of colonists to the safety of Louisiana.

In the spring of 1836, Albert C. Horton recruited a cavalry company, and marched to assist Colonel James W. Fannin Jr. in Goliad. Asa Langford joined this cavalry company at age fifteen. They arrived in the Goliad area in early March 1836. With the Mexican Army under General José Urrea closing in, Fannin decided to retreat. Captain Horton's men (thought to number 18) were sent ahead to examine the crossing at Coleto Creek. While Horton and his men were there, Fannin and his troops were surrounded and taken prisoner. Horton did not take his men to aid Fannin, since he feared that the entire party would be lost.

When Texas gained its independence from Mexico, Asa went to Sabine Parish, Louisiana, to join his mother and sisters. While in Louisiana, he married Eliza Lee McDonald, and to this union were born eight children.

Asa Langford

During October of 1854, Asa was awarded 640 acres of land for his service with Captain Horton. In 1855, he moved his entire family, two slaves Sooky and Dudley, and a large herd of cattle to Texas. They made camp in the vicinity of Nacogdoches. Asa left the camp and went west to locate a suitable homesite. He found the land he wanted in a valley surrounded by low hills with an ever-flowing creek in the center. With his Certificate of Donation for 640 acres, he purchased his first land in this valley, and continued to purchase land until he owned 1,120 acres. This area became known as Langford's Cove.

As the population increased, he saw the need for businesses and schools. He built a mercantile store, flour mill, blacksmith shop and saw mill. He sold four acres of land to the community for $1.00, with the proviso that the land be used "forever for educational purposes." It is still in use today by the Evant, Texas School District. The ever-flowing creek is still known as Langford's Branch.

Asa's wife, Eliza Lee, died in 1858, and was buried on a high plain near his store in Langford 's Cove. Since then, many others have joined her, including Sookie and Dudley. This place is known today as Langford's Cemetery.

In January 1859, Asa married Rebecca Ann Morris, of Bennett Creek, near a village that would later be known as Center City. To this union were born ten children. A son, Albert Thompson, was to become my ancestor.

When the Civil War began in 1861, Asa (along with numerous other Texans) was not in favor of secession. He tried to remain neutral, but local sentiment rose against him; and as the war progressed, he came to be known as a "Union man". He hired a young man to go to war in his place. Although this was legal at that time, the distaste in the community for him and his family was not removed. Many of this group of neutrals took to the hills and forests to avoid conscription or bad treatment from the Confederate Army. He hid out in some unknown place, and his wife Rebecca supplied food and other necessities for months.

Rebecca was very close to her family. For many years, when she would be homesick, Rebecca would put one child on the horse behind the saddle, and with another on her lap would ride twenty-five miles to spend a few days with her parents. She was a tough frontierswoman who disliked cooking and housekeeping, and was often to be found digging for Spanish treasure. She was also fond of cock fighting, and therefore her game roosters were moved along with the other prized possessions from place to place as the family relocated.

In the late 1860s a vigilante group was organized to the west of Langford's Cove. Their purpose was to keep law and order in this "no man's land". The vigilantes worked the back roads from Langford 's Cove to William's Ranch some thirty-five miles to the west. Asa was asked to join the vigilante group, and he refused. From that day forward, his life and the lives of his family were in danger. Many men lost their lives because the vigilantes soon turned into a lawless gang. Gangs and feuds became rampant in the area of the Cove during the late 1860s and 1870s, and civil rights and laws were ignored. Ambush was the favorite means of "getting even" and the lives of three of Asa and Rebecca's sons were so claimed.

Asa Langford was a small man, never weighing more than 125 pounds, was quick of speech and step, possessed tireless energy, and seemed always to be in a hurry. He believed strongly in his and his sons' ability to hold their own. Once a neighbor asked Asa why he didn't wear a gun. His answer was, "Don't worry about me and my boys. We can take care of ourselves."

In 1884, the gangs were quelled, and the feud that had risen between the Langford boys and another family was put to rest. Rebecca, Asa, and their six remaining children moved to Center City to be near Rebecca's ailing parents. With them came two of Asa's aging sisters, Juriah and Charollette. Juriah and Charollete were completely blind as a result of laudanum addiction. They were known to sit quite happily on the porch sharing the laudanum pot, which they kept between them.

Asa and Rebecca lived in Center City for the remaining years of their lives. Asa died in 1906, and Rebecca in 1932. Samuel W. Smith 4839 S. *Submitted by Timothy Smith 5153S*

PETER LAUX

Peter Laux (born October 14, 1804) and Rosina Pauli Laux (born November 22, 1797) came to Texas as immigrants with the "Adelsverein" in 1845. They were from Elz, near Limburg on the Lahn River, part of Nassau, Germany, northwest of Frankfurt. The Laux family was aboard the Barque Strabo with their children, Margaretha, Catherine, John and Anna. When they came over, Peter was age 40, Rosina was age 47, Margaretha was age 20, Catherine was age 15, John was age 8 and Anna was age 3. Their ship, the Strabo, left Antwerp on September 11, 1845, and reached Galveston on November 20, 1845, with 169 immigrants aboard, all bound for the Fisher-Miller Grant in central and west Texas. They ended up stopping in the Bluff community of Fayette County, south of La Grange, Texas, not far from Monument Hill.

The Texas State Archives passenger list of the Strabo shows that the Laux family was passengers 68 through 73, and family No. 18. Such list also reflects that Peter Laux was a carpenter and farmer. The "Chronik der Gemeinde Elz," the German history reflects Laux left Elz in 1845 for Texas. Other families on the same ship included the Jacob Roeder family, the John and Margaretha Schumacher family and the Christian Kuehn family.

The Laux children were Margaretha (October 4, 1824-October 8, 1912), who married Christian Munke (March 25, 1825-June 21, 1896); Catherine, who married Joseph G. Fietsam (born February 12, 1825); John Laux; and Anna Laux (February 23, 1842-March 8, 1927), who married Theodore Merrem (February 2, 1833-September 12, 1867).

Peter Laux declared his intention to become a citizen of the U.S. in May 1853. On April 4, 1856, Peter Laux became a citizen of the U.S. in that year. Peter Laux also sold land to his son-in-law, Christian Munke. Peter and Rosina Laux were Roman Catholic and likely worshipped at the cathedral at Limburg on the Lahn River, near Elz, Germany.

Peter Laux died on April 18, 1864, at the age of 59 years. Rosina Laux died on January 12, 1870, at the age of 72 during Reconstruction days. Norman Krischke's history of Williams Creek Cemetery confirms that both Peter and Rosina Laux are buried at Williams Creek Cemetery, which is located approximately 5.5 miles south of La Grange. Rodney C. Koenig 43341 Rear Admiral J. Weldon Koenig #6093

DAVID ERVIN LAWHON

Nacogdoches: One day in November 1835, came, a big, brawny 23-year-old from Tennessee named David E. Lawhon. He was well over six feet tall, heavily built, barrel-chested, with hands like hams and feet to match. He looked like a fighter, and that's what he aimed to be. He promptly took the oath and joined the Texas Army.

Someone discovered that Dave Lawhon had special talents more valuable than his obvious strength. He was a well-trained printer, who had practiced his trade successfully in Tennessee and at nearby Natchitoches, Louisiana. Authorities located an old press and a font of type left when in 1829 The Mexican Citizen had folded. Pvt. Lawhon repaired the press, sorted the type and became printer Lawhon. His was the only paper east of the Brazos. On the front page of the first issue of his paper, The Texian and Emigrant's Guide," he printed the 1824 Mexican Constitution in its entirety, that the people know "the law of the land." David Lawhon set his type, inked his forms and operated his cumbersome little press throughout the war. His played an important role in holding the people together until the final victory.

After the war, he served as a captain in a ranging company, fighting Indians. He was wounded three times, never critically. In 1839, he moved to Jefferson County, and shortly became the Chief Justice of the county. He married Nancy Carr, daughter of William Carr.

In 1858, David Lawhon sold his Jefferson County lands and bought land in the Post Oak Island area of Williamson County. There he died in 1886 and was buried Lawhon Cemetery. John Thomas Lawhon #4589 Great-great-grandson of David

CHARLES LAWRENCE

Charles Lawrence was born February 8, 1789 in Crundisburg, County Suffolk, England, the son of Charles Lawrence and Sarah Block. He married on June 10, 1827, at St. Margaret's Church, Ipswich, County Suffolk to Eliza Fairweather, christened June 23, 1813, at Weybread, County Suffolk, the daughter of Richard Fairweather and Elizabeth Howe.

Charles came to Texas in 1836, before August; his wife died shortly before that in England. He brought at least three of his children with him: William, born April 25, 1832; Eliza, born March 12, 1834; and Hephzibah, born December 31, 1835. All were christened at Stoke Green Baptist Church in Ipswich, County Suffolk. Coming also were his sister, Mary, and her husband, Kingsby Himtly Francis, whom she had married May 2, 1827, at St. Margaret's.

Hephzibah married George Schouller in November 1851, in Houston, Texas. Eliza married Balthasar Shindler on March 2, 1851, in Galveston, Texas. She died December 7, 1875, in Hempstead, Texas. Children of Eliza and Balthasar were Annie Eliza, William Henry, James Thomas, Mary Jane, Franklin Edward, Charles Franklin, Leander, Franklin Edward, Benjamin, and Mary Ella.

Charles received a Class 3 Grant for 320 acres in Galveston County. Charles died in 1847 in Galveston, and his estate was administered by his brother-in-law, Kingsly Frances. Richard Charles Kuriger IV

LEWIS LEVY

Lewis Levy was born August 16, 1799 in Amsterdam, Holland. His parents left Holland for the United States after arranging a marriage between Lewis and Mary Levy in 1817. All arrived in 1818. Lewis and Mary eventually had 20 children. They migrated to Houston, where they settled in 1840.

Lewis A. Levy

Lewis was the first permanent Jewish settler in the city. Other Jews had come earlier, but stayed a short time and moved on.

Lewis was a merchant, and also dealt in land. In 1843, he purchased a tract of land from General Sam Houston, a frequent visitor to the family home and a Masonic Lodge brother.

In 1858, Jacob De Cordova, in his "History of Texas," wrote: "Through the exertions of Lewis A. Levy a Benevolent Association has been formed by the Jewish denomination of Houston." Lewis was the first president of that association. Lewis and his wife were among the first members of Congregation Beth Israel.

He wrote to a newspaper in Europe for persecuted Jews, in 1850, "I would not exchange my fifteen acre lot with the house on it and the garden around it, near the city of Houston, for all the thrones and hereditary dominions of both the Russian Autocrats or the Emperor of Austria."

Lewis died on January 28, 1861. At his death, he was acknowledged as the leader of the young Houston Jewish community. Matthews S. Rubenstein is Lewis's great-great-grandson.

MARTIN BATY LEWIS

Martin Baty Lewis born in Clark County, Indiana, on January 13, 1806, son of Sally (Lemasters) and Samuel S. Lewis. He married Nancy Moore, born March 1, 1817, in Ohio, the daughter of Thomas and Susan Moore. They married in Vermilion County, Indiana, on October 25, 1825. They had eleven children: John Kenny, Samuel Harper, Thomas McFarland, Sarah Ann, William McFarland, Charlotte Harper, Stephen Austin, Malinda H. (married John Pinkney Best Jr.), Benjamin Franklin, Martin Baty, and Elizabeth Lemaster. They immigrated to Texas in January 1830, settling on Ayish Bayou (now San Augustine County), then moved to Indian Creek near Bevil (now Jasper County) in 1832.

In August 1832, Lewis was a sergeant major under Col. James Bullock's command at the Battle of Nacogdoches; in 1835, he was captain of East Texas Volunteers in the Siege of Bexar. In July 1836, he was captain of a company under Gen. Thomas Rusk and marched to join the Army of the Republic of Texas at the Coleto, when a Mexican incursion by Gen. José Urrea was feared. He resigned this command in August 1836. He also fought in the Mexican War from October 1847 to September 1848. He was 1st Sgt. in John Veatch's Co. in Hansbrough Bell's 1st Regiment of Texas Mounted Volunteers.

Lewis was County Surveyor of Jasper County from 1836-1845, and was Chief Justice of Jasper County in 1844. In 1845, he patented title to 2,958 acres of land in Jasper County. He left Texas for the California "gold rush" in 1849. By 1850, he was in Mariposa, California, and in 1863 he settled at Millertown, Fresno County, California, where he died before 1885. David Rolfe Wells (great-great-great-grandson), #6464

SAMUEL S. LEWIS

Samuel S. Lewis, early Texas settler and Congressman, was born to John and Sarah Lewis on July 4, 1784, in Virginia. He married Sarah LeMaster, born March 12, 1785, in Virginia, the daughter of John & Sarah LeMaster. They married in Henry County, Kentucky, on August 7, 1804. They moved to Clark, Orange and Green counties, Indiana, where their seven children were born: Martin Baty (married Nancy Moore), John T., Charlotte, Elizabeth, Ann, William McFarland, and Malinda.

Lewis founded Orleans, Indiana, and served as a lieutenant with the Indiana Militia in the War of 1812. In the mid-1820s the family moved to Ouachita Parish, Louisiana, where Lewis became Justice of the Peace. According to his Certificate of Character for Texas, by March 1832, he and his son, Martin Baty Lewis, had settled their families in the Bevil Municipality (now Jasper County) on Indian Creek in Texas. Lewis served as lieutenant colonel in the Battle of Nacogdoches in 1832 under Col. James Bullock, and participated in the Siege of Bexar in 1835. He was a Bevil delegate to the Consultation of 1835 and represented Jasper County in the First and Second Congresses of the Republic of Texas. He died during the Second Session of Congress on February 10, 1838, at his plantation in Jasper County. David Rolfe Wells (great-great-great-great-grandson) #6464

JOSEPH LINDLEY

Joseph Lindley was born January 7, 1793, in Orange County, North Carolina, and died January 20, 1874, in Limestone County, Texas. He married Nancy Ann Hicks on June 17, 1817, in Bond County, Illinois. She was born May 11, 1801, at Gallatin, Tennessee. She died August 28, 1876, in Limestone County, Texas. Joseph and Ann had seven children. Joseph and his family settled in Montgomery County, Texas in 1827.

Muster rolls indicate Joseph served in Company J, Cavalry, Second Regiment of Texas Volunteers during the Battle of San Jacinto. Joseph's nephew, Jonathan Lindley, was of the famous 32 from Gonzales who died in the Battle of the Alamo.

Joseph Lindley knew Mirabeau Lamar from San Jacinto, and after Lamar became president of Republic of Texas, he appointed Joseph as Indian Agent to the Alabama Coushatta Indians.

In about 1846, Joseph and Ann Lindley and their family moved to Limestone, County, Texas. Joseph and Ann Lindley were reburied Texas State Cemetery in Austin, Texas, on Memorial Day, May 26, 1986, by order of Proclamation #41-2067, by Mark White, Governor of Texas, with full military honors.

Joseph Lindley was my great-great great-grandfather. Dick V. Lindley Jr. #6592 Robert R. Lindley #6591

SAMUEL WASHINGTON LINDLEY

Samuel Washington Lindley was born in Anderson County, South Carolina, in 1788 to John and Sarah (Pyle) Lindley. After his father's death in 1790, his widowed mother moved Samuel and her family to Christian County, Kentucky, where, according to their records, he married Mary (Polly) Hall (d/o John) on June 5, 1809. Together with at least three of his brothers, Samuel W. Lindley and his wife, Polly, moved to Illinois and settled in Moultrie County where she gave birth to a daughter, Sarah. Polly died in 1810 from the effects of childbirth. Samuel W. Lindley then married Elizabeth Whitley, the daughter of a neighboring family in Illinois, and she became the mother of his next twelve children.

Lindley became a member of the Illinois Militia and fought in the only battle of the War of 1812 that occurred on Illinois soil, during the Fort Wisconsin Campaign. He became friends with other militiamen during his service, many of whom became political figures during and after the Illinois' attempt to gain statehood. One of these friends was Governor John Reynolds, who wrote Lindley's letter of recommendation to the Republic of Mexico for his becoming a settler in Texas (Spanish Archives, Texas G.L.O., Vol. R & MC., Pp. 21, 22).

In 1833, Samuel came to Texas with his wife, Elizabeth, and at least ten of their children born in Illinois. He was granted a league and labor of land on the present boundary of Montgomery and Walker counties, where he founded the town of Danville, acquired additional land, and became a well-known planter and cattleman.

During their life together in Texas, they had a daughter, Mahala (b. 1833 and w/o Elijah C. Tolbert), and a son, Elijah (b. 1835), who married Eliza Tolbert Kelton (a widow and sister of Mahala's husband).

His eldest son, Jonathan Lindley (b. 1814), joined with fellow Texians under Ben Milam to defeat General Cos in the Battle of San Antonio in the fall of 1835. He returned to San Antonio around March 1, 1836, to help defend Texas from the Mexican Army led by Santa Anna. Jonathan was killed in the Battle of the Alamo on March 6. 1836. His father, Samuel, became the administrator of his estate and received a Bounty Land Grant from the Republic for his service and sacrifice to the cause of freedom.

Samuel's wife, Elizabeth, died in 1838. In 1839, Samuel married a widow, Margaret Elizabeth Collard Tolbert, and in 1840, they had a daughter, Amanda Marie (w/o W. Thomas Martin). Following the death of Margaret Elizabeth, Samuel married Martha Alphin in 1845 (no issue).

Samuel Washington Lindley died intestate in 1859. The probate and settlement of his estate evolved into a legal dispute between his children and his fourth wife, wherein the children prevailed with their petition (Montgomery Co. Probate Records, V. 11, pp. 47-5 1). Sarah (w/o Thomas Steel of McLennan County, Texas) the daughter of Samuel and Polly, his first wife, was included as one of his heirs, together with the children by Elizabeth. His last child, Amanda Marie, did not participate in the estate distribution.

The other children of Samuel W. and Elizabeth Lindley were Barsheba (b. 1811, d. 1885), wife of John Sadler; Mary Polly (b.

1812, d. 1893), wife of Hiram Little; Elizabeth (b. 1815), wife of Lemuel Miller Collard; William (b. 1817, d. 1870), husband of Martha Jane Hostetter; Martha "Patsy" (b. 1821), wife of (1) John J. Crowson (2) Anthony Gibson; Samuel Washington, Jr., (b. 1832) Rachel (b.1827, d. 1916), wife of Benjamin F. Kelton; John (b. 1829, d. 1911), husband of Eliza Ann Martin; and James (b. 1831, d. 1895, and progenitor of this writer), husband of Mary L. Irvine, daughter of Benjamin F. and Mary Davis (Bellesfelt) Irvine, citizens of The Republic. *Submitted by Richard James Lindley, Jr.*

JOHN HIMES LIVERGOOD

John Himes Livergood was born September 10, 1815, in Lancaster County, Pennsylvania, to John Wilson Livergood and Hannah Himes. In 1829, he migrated to Franklin County, Missouri. He fought in the Battle of San Jacinto as a volunteer from Missouri. On November 11, 1952, Livergood along with other Lavaca County heroes was honored as a San Jacinto veteran at a dedication of the "Heroes Monument" at Memorial Park in Hallettsville, Texas. After the battle, he returned to Missouri before permanently migrating to Texas in September 1837.

He settled in the Zumwalt Settlement on the Lavaca River. Soon after his arrival in Texas, he served with the Minute Men, a local militia organized to protect the settlers from Indian attacks. In 1840, he was one of the men who joined Captain Adam Zumwalt in pursuit of the Indians that attacked Dr. Joel Ponton and Tucker Foley on Ponton Creek. The pursuit ended at the Battle of Plum Creek.

John Himes Livergood

In August 1841, Livergood was active in the Spy Company of the Texas Rangers headed by Jack Hays. He took part in the Vasquez Campaign under General Burleson. In 1842, Livergood served under Colonel Matthew Caldwell at the Battle of Salado. He then joined the Somervell Expedition to Laredo under Captain Isaac Mitchell. When the force disbanded, Livergood was elected Second Sergeant and was transferred to Captain Charles Keller Reese's Company. On December 25, 1842, he fought in the Battle of Mier. He participated in the "Black Bean Incident" and was released from Perote Prison on September 16, 1844.

During the Mexican War of 1846, Livergood served under John Coffee Hays as a scout with the Texas Rangers at Matamoros through intelligence provided by Livergood and fellow scout, Bate Berry, the Rangers discovered the location of Arista's Army and Zachary Taylor stormed their position and defeated Arista.

In 1847, Livergood returned to Missouri and married Sarah Perkins. They returned to Texas where he was elected Chief Justice of Lavaca County in 1850. When the War Between the States broke out he served as a 1st Lieutenant under Captain Spears, Company C, 24th Regiment of the Texas State Troops.

He died October 3, 1893. He is buried in the Mossy Grove Cemetery, Lavaca County Texas. Paul W. Ponton – SRT #6603M (great-grandson) Robert W. Ponton – SRT #6846 AH (2nd great-grandson)

CHARLES LOCKHART

My great-great-grandfather was born December 3, 1790, in Virginia. He was the son of James and Rachel Totten Lockhart.

The National Archives, Washington, D.C., war records of 1812 list Charles' residence at the time of induction into the service as Winchester, Frederick County, Virginia. He and his brothers, Byrd, Andrew and Samuel were all veterans of the Texas (Texas-Mexican) War.

During 1814-1815, Charles and Byrd were appointed surveyors for Madison County, Illinois. He married Catherine Wise Barton on September 20, 1817 in Kaskaskia, Randolph County, Illinois. Evidently the Bartons and Lockharts admired each other, because Byrd married Catherine's sister, Mary, and their sister, Margaret Lockhart, married Catherine and Mary's brother, Kimber W. Barton.

Byrd, who had come to Texas in 1825 with Green DeWitt, made several trips back to encourage all his family to come to the new frontier.

The Charles Lockhart family came to Texas March 2, 1829 to join Byrd and Green DeWitt's Colony. Their brothers and sisters — Andrew, Samuel, Nancy, Sarah Ann, Margaret and Drusilla — also joined the colony by the year 1831.

Charles and Catherine settled at their homestead, Pecan Grove, Texas, located approximately ten miles south of Gonzales, Texas. The family cemetery is here but is in poor condition.

Charles and Catherine, along with five of their children, are listed in "Citizens of the Republic of Texas," published by the Texas State Genealogical Society and Charles and Catherine are also listed in "Founders and Patriots of the Republic of Texas." The listings are on file in the Alamo D.R.T. Library.

Byrd Lockhart, assisted by his brother, Charles, performed all the Colony's surveys after 1826. Byrd was appointed Surveyor General on April 1831 by Jose Antonio Navarro. Surveying was one of the most widespread professions of the frontier. The surveyor was an indispensable functionary within the Empressario System, and prior to the past thirty or forty years had been overlooked by historians.

In 1828, 1829 and 1830, Byrd Lockhart, assisted by Charles, cleared timber and laid out a road via Gonzales from Bexar to Austin — 195 miles — and later on, one from Gonzales to Matagorda. The Bexar to Austin Road was used for present-day paved highway.

The surveyor's world was not always one of mathematics and geometry. On many occasions, they were the first white men in the area and encountered native Indian tribes, which were often hostile. The land survey itself was one of the final steps in processing a clear and valid title.

Catherine's letters to her mother, Elizabeth Barton, in Ohio, often mention the hardships and encounters with the Indians. At least two of her letters are on file in the DRT Alamo Library. So much history was based around their niece, Matilda, who was kidnapped by the Indians.

Under the directions of Colonel John H. Moore, Charles laid out the town of La Grange. He was elected second rigidor of the colony in 1832, and became the first rigidor in 1835.

Charles and Catherine died in 1844. Two of his grandchildren, Margret Lucind Wilson (Mrs. John Bowden Pridgen) and John Patton Wright were living on one of his league of late as 1936 and 1952.

SAMUEL ANDERSON LONG

Samuel Anderson Long was born 16 May 1817, in Marion County, Tennessee. He was the eldest child of Rachel Anderson and Henry Long.

Samuel A. Long was enlisted in New Orleans by Captain Wiehl into the service of Republic of Texas in the 2nd Regiment P Volunteers, January 20, 1837. He was discharged February 20, 1839, at Post West Bernard. He served again in the spring of 1842 to assist in repelling the invasion of Texas by Vasquez. He was a private in the company commanded by Captain W.J. Jones in Colorado County. His third and last time to serve in behalf of the Republic of Texas was in September 1842, when he served with a group of reinforcements who, after the engagement at Salado, joined in the pursuit of the Mexicans.

He was granted a Conditional Land Certificate No. 357 dated September 6, 1838, for 640 acres, and Bounty Warrant 9012 dated March 22, 1839, for 1,280 acres of land for his services to the Republic of Texas.

Just after La Vaca County was created, he was sworn in as Justice of the Peace in August 1846.

Sam Long married Louisa J. McFarlin in Colorado County, Texas, on February 4,

1844. Their seven children, all born in Texas were: William Henry Long, Nov. 18, 1845;

Andrew Jackson Long, Oct. 23, 1848; Julia Ann Long, Sept. 27, 1850; twins Mary Luisa and James Monroe Long, Nov. 4, 1854; Francis Marion, Nov. 20, 1856.

S.A. Long and W.H. Jackson published "The Texas Stock Directory," or Book of Marks and Brands, printed at The Herald office in San Antonio in 1865. It is currently the earliest known work of this type. A second volume was intended, but Sam contracted cholera while in San Antonio during the epidemic. He made his way back home to Medina County and died Sept. 17, 1866. He is buried in the Masonic Cemetery between Hondo and New Fountain.

The maternal grandmother of Walter Beakley Scott, 38 54 R #5579, was Dora A. Long Beakley, daughter of William Henry Long, who was the eldest son of Samuel Anderson Long.

Walter B. Scott, P.O. Box 770, Goliad, Texas 77963, from genealogical research by Tory Crook, 1313 Apache, Richardson, Texas 75080.

JOSEPH C. LOPEZ

My great-grandfather, Joseph C. Lopez, was born in 1820 in Natchitoches Parish, Louisiana to Ygnacio and Mary (Davis) Lopez. Ygnacio was a member of the Flying Company of San Carlos de Alamo, stationed at Mission Valero in 1803. Mission Valero was later to be renamed the Alamo.

Ygnacio Lopez and his family moved to Texas in 1825. He received a Spanish Land Grant in Houston County on 16 May 1865. Ygnacio and his son, Joseph, signed the petition to form Houston County on 22 April 1837. In May 1846, Joseph Lopez joined the 2nd Regiment, Texas Mounted Volunteers from Houston County, for service in the Mexican War. Joseph was given a handwritten discharge signed by Colonel George E. Wood and John L. Hall.

In 1850, Joseph C. Lopez married Minerva Agnes Harrington, a native of Arkansas. Joseph and Minerva attended the ceremony held at Monument Hill near La Grange, Texas, which honored the soldiers from the Mier Expedition. Nine children were born to this union. Many descendants of Joseph and Minerva still live in Victoria County.

Joseph Lopez was a cattle rancher in Inez, Victoria County, Texas.

Joseph, who died in 1881, is buried in Farrer Cemetery, Inez, Victoria County, Texas, beside his wife, Minerva. Robert W. Obsta

GEORGE LORD

George Lord — veteran of the Army of the Republic of Texas, Mier Expedition, Mexican War, Texas Rangers, and Civil War — was born in Saffron Walden, England, on April 21, 1816. His parents were Robert Felstead and Anna Lord.

George Lord

He arrived in Texas on February 14, 1837, and was mustered in the Army of the Republic of Texas at Camp Independence as a private in Captain John J. Holliday's company of the Second Infantry Regiment, Permanent Volunteers, under the command of Colonel H.R.A. Wiggington. Lord was discharged in 1838, and granted 1,280 acres for his service.

During 1839, he served under Colonel Edward Burleson and Captain Nicholas Dawson during the Córdova Rebellion. He also participated in General Antonio Canales' campaigns to preserve the Constitution of 1824.

Harold B. Lord

In 1842, Lord joined Captain Ewen Cameron and fought Mexicans at Lipantitál. He also participated in the Battle of Salado Creek. On November 18, he left San Antonio with the Somervell Expedition. After battles along the Rio Grande, General Alexander Somervell ordered his men to return home on December 19. Six companies (including Lord) disregarded the order and continued their pursuit of the Mexicans as the Mier Expedition under the command of Colonel William Fisher.

At the Battle of Mier, the Texans including Lord were taken prisoner on December 26 and marched 420 miles to Hacienda Salado, where they escaped. They were recaptured and returned to Hacienda Salado, where General Santa Anna ordered 10% of the men executed on March 25, 1843. The victims were selected by drawing beans; a black bean meant death. Lord drew a white bean. The survivors were subjected to Mexican labor camps and held at the Perote Prison until September 16, 1844, when they were freed.

During the Mexican War, Lord served as a private in the First Texas Rangers under Captain Davis (December 1844 to February 1845), and Captain Bell (February to August 1845).

While riding with the first wagon train from San Antonio to the California gold mines in 1849, he met Catherine Meyers, and married her on December 30, 1849. They returned to DeWitt County after three years of gold mining. Using his Land Bounty, Lord started a successful Longhorn cattle ranch near Cheapside. The Lords had eleven children.

Although exempt because of his age, Lord served two years in the Confederate Home Guards during the Civil War.

George Lord died on February 23, 1895, and Kate Lord died on January 19, 1909, both in Cheapside, Texas. They are buried in the Lord Cemetery on the old Lord Ranch.

Harold Beverly Lord, a member of the Sons of the Republic of Texas, is the great-grandson of George Lord.

IRVIN CAPERS LORD

I.C. Lord, sixteenth child of Jacob Nathaniel Lord and Mary Elizabeth Tarbox Lord, was born in Charleston, South Carolina. He married Emeline Seddons in 1848, and their early married life was in Charleston. Yellow fever swept Charleston in 1854, resulting in the deaths of the children of I.C. Lord. Following this tragedy, I.C. and Emeline traveled to Houston to restart their family.

I.C. Lord was a machinist and co-owner of Eagle Iron Works, a prominent early Houston foundry. It was in civic work during the Civil War era, however, that I.C. Lord is best known. For Houston, he served as alderman, city marshal, and mayor (1875) and for Harris County, he was a county commissioner, street commissioner and sheriff.

Irvin C. Lord
Mayor of Houston, 1875 and 1876
The original painting is displayed in the lobby of Houston's City Hall.

Pioneer life in Texas was dangerous. One of the many stories that are told of I.C. Lord's bravery and ingenuity concerns Indians living near Houston. Indians would come into town like lambs but a few drinks of whiskey would transfer them into veritable warriors. Lord, when he was city marshal, faced a belligerent drunk Indian holding a bottle of whiskey. Lord hit on a plan to jail the Indian. He had a friend grab the Indian's bottle and run towards a jail cell. The Indian chased the friend, followed by Marshal Lord. The plan worked. The Indian ran into the jail cell, the friend slipped out and Marshal Lord locked the jail cell door with his prisoner inside.

In 1987, a Texas Historical Commission marker was erected at I.C. Lord's gravesite, honoring his many contributions to Houston and Texas. The following are descendants of I. C. Lord: Ward Noble Adkins, Sr., great-grandson Ward Noble Adkins, Jr., great-great-grandson John August Adkins, great-great-grandson John August Adkins, Jr., great-great-great-grandson

ISAAC LOW

Isaac Low was an early-day settler in what is now Sabine County, Texas. He was born on July 7, 1781, in Tennessee, in probably what is now Knox County. He died August 27, 1857, in Sabine County, Texas, and is buried with other members of his family in the Old Isaac Low Cemetery, located in the El Camino Bay area of Sabine County.

Isaac Low was the son of Aquilla Low, Sr., who died in Knox County, Tennessee, about 1819; his mother is unknown. Isaac Low was married on September 25, 1804, in Anderson County, Tennessee, to Elizabeth Parsons, who was born on February 25, 1787, in Virginia, and died on July 4, 1860, in Sabine County.

Isaac Low enlisted in the War of 1812 at Knoxville, Tennessee, on September 23, 1813 and was discharged on January 1, 1814, with the rank of sergeant. In May 1851, he appeared before the County Clerk of Sabine County, Texas, and stated his age as 69 years, declared he was the same Isaac Low who was a non-commissioned officer in Captain John Chiles Infantry Company, First Regiment of Tennessee Volunteers, commanded by Col. Samuel Wear, East Tennessee Militia. By his declaration in 1851, he made application for bounty land to which the soldiers were entitled under the Act of 1850.

The Low family arrived in Mexico, in what is now Sabine County, Texas, in August 1828. At the time of emigrating to Texas, Isaac Low was 47 years of age and his wife was 41 years of age. They had eleven children between 22 years and 14 months of age. The 12th and youngest child was born in Sabine County; all others were born in Tennessee.

Isaac Low received a Mexican land grant for one league and one labor (4,605.5 acres of land) dated June 20, 1835. The Low land grant covered much land that is now under the waters of Toledo Bend Reservoir. During the "Runaway Scrape" in March and April 1836, Isaac Low and his elder sons operated their ferry at the mouth of Low's Creek and the Sabine River at times for days and nights ferrying the settlers "back to the United States" across the Sabine to Louisiana in the flight from the Mexicans.

Isaac Low is listed in the return of Captain Collins Company, Sabine Volunteers for the date of July 8, 1836. In 1838, he was one of the first Municipal Officers of Sabine Town. James Burnett Low SRT #4044, Alex Debruel Low, Jr. #6780, Loy Kadle Low SRT #6702, Kevin Shae Low SRT #6703

GEORG HEINRICH LUESSMANN

Georg Heinrich Luessmann, our great-great-great-grandfather, and his family set sail from Bremen, Germany, aboard the Weser on September 8, 1845, arriving at the port of Galveston in the Republic of Texas on November 27, 1845. Georg was born May

10, 1809, at Essel, Hanover, Germany. The first of his three marriages produced a son, Heinrich (our great-great-grandfather); his second marriage, to Anna Dorothea Mussmann, produced two children, Louise and Frederick "Fritz." All accompanied him on the trip to Texas.

Shortly after their arrival in Galveston, they made their way to Indianola, where they joined with other Verein immigrants and began their journey inland to New Braunfels. During this trip, tragedy struck. Georg lost his wife on February 26, 1847, in New Braunfels to "Ruher and Wasser" (Bright's disease). It is assumed that Louise died en route to New Braunfels, since there are no records to be found on her.

George Henry Luessmann

Georg received under his colonization contract 640 acres of land located in the community of Twin Wisters, Blanco County. As payment for his transportation from Germany to Texas, he assigned one-half of his acreage back to the German Emigration Company.

Georg's third marriage was to Angelicka "Engel" Carolina Kropp, the young widow of John Conrad Peter. Angelicka was born August 22, 1822 at Netze, Hanover, Germany, and immigrated to Texas at the age of 23 aboard the Margaretha, arriving at the port of Galveston on November 25, 1845. She and Georg were wed in New Braunfels by Pastor Ervendberg on June 18, 1847. Angelicka and Georg were the parents of two children, Conrad Christian and Marie. While living in New Braunfels, Georg and his family were associated with the Protestant Church where his eldest son, Heinrich, was confirmed in 1849.

In 1855, Georg moved his younger family to the newly formed community of Comfort in Kendall County. Georg's eldest son Heinrich stayed at the homestead in Twin Sisters, serving in 1855 with the Texas Rangers under Captain James H. Callahan's Company defending the Texas border from raiding bands of Indians and Mexicans. Georg's second-eldest son, Fritz "Leasman," settled in Wilson County in 1857 and also served with the Texas Rangers under Captain John Sansom during the Indian Wars in the 1870s.

George Luessmann was a farmer and rancher. He had a small herd of cattle and his "HL" brand was recorded in the Kendall County Courthouse on September 19, 1865. He was also a skilled cabinetmaker.

Georg died on April 25, 1871, and was laid to rest in the Comfort Cemetery. Angelicka was blind the last years of her life. She died on August 7, 1901, and was buried beside her husband. The tombstones reflect the change in spelling of our surname, his reading "Luessmann" and hers reading "Liesmann."

Great-great-great-grandsons Randy K. Liesman and Bruce D. Liesman

WILLIAM LOUIS MAGEE

William Louis MacGee (Magee) came to the Republic of Texas at the age of four. He was born on August 12, 1836, in Simpson or Rankin Co., Miss., and died on Nov. 19, 193 in Brookland, Texas. His father was Holton MacGee.

He was a veteran of the War Between the States, and marched with his company out of Jasper amid tears and waving handkerchiefs. They rode to Crockett, and here he met General Sam Houston. "You should have never seceded yet you ought to fight for your rights," General Houston said to his company. Louis Magee had changed his name from the pure Scottish Macgee to Magee. He claimed that his grandfather fought in the Battle of New Orleans, saw LaFayette and possibly Washington.

His stories were many, including knowing John Bevil, the man who first lived upon the site now called Jasper. He was also acquainted with George W. Smith, one of the signers of the Texas Declaration of Independence, and Texas's first Land Commissioner and the first U.S. Congressman from this state.

At the age of 93, he still loved to recall the day he went bear hunting and it was a case of killing the bear or getting killed. He obviously won the fight that day.

He married Armacinda Letney on Feb. 7, 1855, in Jasper County, Texas. They had a daughter, Rebecca Angeline Magee Bell, who married Luther Sidney Bell. From that union there came a son, William Cleveland Bell, who married Maude Mathews Bell. A son, W.C. Bell, Jr., and a daughter, Mildred Pauline Bell Morris, were born. Mildred married Wilford Victor Morris. Both have descendants scattered around Texas. It is interesting to note that his grandson, William Cleveland Bell, received as a gift a glass powderhorn which was a possession of General Santa Anna. This item was taken by General Sam Houston, who later gave it to his "boot black" (servant), who served him at the time of the Battle of San Jacinto. The servant was 9 years of age at the time. In his later years, he was known as "Neptune." He cared for an area known as Robinson Bend Lake for W.C. Bell, Sr. The powderhorn was a gift from "Neptune" to W.C. Bell, Sr., for years of kind treatment. The powderhorn remains in the possession of the descendants of Cleve Bell. Robert Glenn Morris D.D.S. #4246 Wilford Victor Morris, Jr. #3856

ARCHIBALD T. MCCORCLE

My 2nd great-grandfather, Archibald T. McCorcle, a son of James (McCorcle) McCorkel and Rachel was born in Georgia c, 1813, and moved with his family to Monroe County, Alabama, near Fort Claiborne in 1819, where he grew up.

In 1836, he was in Canton, Mississippi where he joined with 500 volunteers as a "bugler" in Captain David M. Fulton's Company, which left for Texas to join in the fight for independence. They left Canton on April 13, 1836, and crossed the Sabine River into Texas in May. Upon arrival, they found that the Mexican Army had been defeated at San Jacinto just a couple of weeks before. He traveled on to Fort Bend where he re-enlisted in Capt. Harreld's Company, Madison County Volunteers of Mississippi Regiment, on May 14, 1836, and was still on the muster roll of that company on September 10, 1836. He received 1/3 league of land for his service on February 17, 1838, and remained in Texas as a citizen of the new Republic.

He served at least two tours as a Texas Ranger from Fort Bend, which delayed his marriage to Caroline in 1839. On one occasion, he enlisted June 9, 1839, as a private in a Texas Ranger Company under Capt. N. Brookshire, which rode to reinforce Capt. Bird's Ranger Company, which had engaged a large Comanche war party at Bird's Creek near present-day Temple, Texas. He returned to Fort Bend and was discharged July 9, 1839.

He married Caroline E.M.C. Allen, the daughter of Martin Allen and Elizabeth Vice (Austin's "Old 300" colonists), on September 5, 1839, in San Felipe, Austin County, Texas, where they bought land and started raising their family: Henry T., born 1840; James A., born 1842; Lavina, born 1844; Ann E., born 1846; and Wipple W., born August 26, 1848.

Archibald served the new Republic as an elected official when he was elected coroner of Austin County on February 6, 1843. While living in San Felipe, Archibald and Caroline witnessed the transition of the Republic into the United States.

In 1849, Archibald traded his property in San Felipe for a wagon and some dry goods, and moved his family first to Bastrop, where they stayed only for a short time. They then moved north to an area which is known today as Belton, Texas, settling first near Childer's Mill, where he became the first merchant to sell goods in the place. He first sold from the wagon box, and later did business in a small store located on the southwest corner of the Belton Courthouse Square on the west side. Later, he built a two-story building there, residing in the second story and keeping his store below.

A.T. McCorcle assisted in laying out the city of Belton, and is credited with building the first "Courthouse," a crude clapboard structure that housed the first blacksmith shop, which was operated by County Judge John Danley and thus did double duty. Archibald served as a trustee for Belton's first Methodist Church, according to deeds filed November 19, 1850.

Another son, William Hudgins McCorcle, was born on August 26, 1853, and Caroline died a few weeks later on September 25, 1853. Archibald remarried to Eliza H. Kneeland on December 27, 1853, in Belton and continued to try to keep his family together.

He was in Company C of the 27th Brigade Texas State Troops CSA, during the War Between the States, and afterwards in 1867, when Texas was suffering through "Reconstruction," he took a stock of goods to Mexico, where he remained two years, then returned to Houston, where he died on February 14, 1869. His family returned to Bell County where they resided on his farm on Owl Creek. Gary Edwin McCorcle SRT #6566

WILLIAM MCCUTCHEON

William McCutcheon lived an interesting life. He came to Texas in 1832, and married Elizabeth Jane Harrell in 1835. This was a turbulent time in Texas, due to oppressive policies from Mexico. He was involved in the "Runaway Scrape" and the Texas Revolution. Later he became a Texas Ranger. His first child, Willis, was born April 14, 1836, during the "Runaway Scrape." This was one week before the Battle of San Jacinto. Thirteen children were born to William and Elizabeth Jane: Willis, Mary, John, Jesse, Joseph, Sarah, George, W.F., Fannie, Elizabeth, James, Beauregard and Jefferson.

After the revolution, William and Elizabeth Jane settled in the Austin-Bastrop area, where William was involved in trading and farming. In 1857, William, with his son Willis, drove the first herd of Texas Longhorns to northern markets. The drive ended in Quincy, Illinois. The McCutcheon's were involved in trail-driving until the mid-1880s.

During the Civil War, William and his son's supported the South and Texas. After the war, William relocated to Williamson County, where he settled and lived out his life in the Brushy Creek area.

Mr. and Mrs. William McCutcheon

William McCutcheon was a husband, parent, patriot, traildriver, Texan and an American. Some of his off-spring still resides on some of the land from granted to him by the Republic of Texas. Alfred Holt McCutcheon Jr., great-great-grandson, SRT #6080 W.B. Travis Chapter, San Antonio, Texas

JUDGE W.C. (COLLIN) MCDANIEL

"Judge Mac," as he was fondly known as in Kleberg County, was born in Hemphill, Sabine County, Texas, on December 5, 1921 to C.A. McDaniel and Mary S. McDaniel, both fourth-generation Texans. He attended public school in Hemphill, where he was a star football player, and graduated from Pineland High School as valedictorian. His first job was delivering ice in the summer and cutting and delivering wood in the winter.

Shortly after graduation, he joined the U.S. Navy, and served in both the North Atlantic and South Pacific theaters during World War II. He was honorably discharged in 1946. In January 1947, he reported to Austin, Texas, for training as a Texas Highway patrolman. After graduation, he was assigned to Kingsville, Kleberg County, Texas for a duty station.

W.C. McDaniel (12/5/1921-6/16/1999)

On November 16, 1948, he married Mattie Olene Evans, a clerk at the District Clerk's office in Nueces County, Texas. After four years as a highway patrolman, he resigned in 1951 to enter then Texas A&I College for pre-law training. He then transferred to Baylor University at Waco, Texas, where he obtained a Juris Doctor Degree in 1954 from Baylor University School of Law, having graduated at the head of his class in law school.

Upon graduation he returned to Kingsville, Kleberg County, Texas and entered into the practice of law. He served as manager and title attorney for a local abstract company for many years. He served as City Attorney for the city of Kingsville, Texas from 1960 to 1970, was elected Kleberg County Democratic Chairman, and in 1970 was elected County Judge, a position he held for 24 years with opposition thereto only one time. He belonged to and was an active member in many social and fraternal organizations, among which are the following: First Baptist Church of Kingsville, Sons of the Republic of Texas, American Legion, Veterans of Foreign Wars, Navy League, Life member of Baylor University Alumni Association, Phi Alpha Delta, State Bar of Texas, Kleberg-Kennedy County Bar Association, Al Almin Shrine Temple, Chamberlain Masonic Lodge, Kingsville Elks Lodge (three terms as Exalted Ruler), South Texas County Judges' and Commissioners' Association (president, 1986), Texas Association of County Judges' and Commissioners' (president, 1991) U.S.S. Savannah Association, U. S. Navy Cruiser Sailors' Association.

Upon his retirement in 1994, he reopened his private law practice. With the addition of a computer, Pro-Doc, and his daughter, he was able to practice law, enjoy traveling, visiting friends, gardening, spending time with their family and the "boys" — Hansel and Fritzel, their schnauzers.

During their travels, they attended the U.S.S. Savannah Association reunions. In August 1998, he was elected Skipper of the U.S.S. Savannah association.

Collin and Mattie Olene celebrated their 50th wedding anniversary on November 16, 1998, with a dinner at Kings Inn in Riviera, Texas. They shared their joyous occasion with their daughter Vickilynn, son-in-law, Steve and their grandson, Collin Evans Stubblefield.

Collin McDaniel passed away at the age of 77 on June 16, 1999. On August 2, 1999, Mattie Olene passed away at the age of 79.

"Daddy was truly one of a kind. His faith, compassion, love, loyalty and humor saw him through his daily decisions. His commitment to helping his country and mankind will be missed by all that knew him. He never forgot where he came from and how hard life was. He taught me that we are all humans, each person should be treated equally and with respect. While he will always live in my heart, I will miss him terribly," his daughter, Vickilynn McDaniel Stubblefield stated.

The Kingsville Record & Bishop News held their presses and reported, "Kleberg County lost one of its most respected and well-liked former public officials today ... He will be missed and his passing is seen by many as the demise of his kind."

BRIDGET LAMB MCGARY

Bridget Lamb was born about 1790 in Ireland. She immigrated to South Carolina as a young girl, probably before 1800. There was a wave of Irish Catholic immigrants, following an insurrection in 1798. Bridget gave her grand daughter, Mary Ellen Kornegay, a green ceramic mug on her 6th birthday (February 16, 1854) that she brought from Ireland as a child. It is now in the possession of Dowe Rhodes, a direct descendant. Sometime about 1810, Bridget married Barnard McGary of London, England. They moved to Milledgeville, GA, where their daughter, Anne, was born on May 19, 1812. By 1817, they had settled in Opelousas, LA where McGary was a retail merchant. According to the 1820 census, he was also engaged in manufacturing and farming. Edward, Sarah, Mary Eleanor and Elizabeth were all born in Opelousas. Their birth and baptism records are at St. Landry's Catholic Church. McGary died in September 1825. Anne McGary married Capt. Daniel Boone Friar on October 19, 1826 at St. Landry's. The couple moved to Tennessee, then to Texas.

The widowed Bridget left Opelousas in 1834 for the Mexican Colony of Texas. They arrived as the historic events of 1835-36 were unfolding. They settled, initially, at Washington-on-the-Brazos. The Mexican government favored Catholics in issuing land grants. Bridget secured a one league (4428 acres) grant. She added to her holdings with a one labor (177 acres) grant from the Republic of Texas. The combined tracts were situated on the west bank of the Brazos near Waco.

On March 20, 1836, Bridget left with her family ahead of the invading Mexican Army. The entire town of Washington fled down river to Groce's Plantation. From there they crossed with Houston's army, then moved east with the Texas force toward the Trinity and Sabine rivers. This came to be known as the "Runaway Scrape." After the victory at San Jacinto, the refugees returned to their homes. There, on November 15, 1837, Sarah married John W. McKissick and on March 22,1839, Mary Eleanor married Joseph E. Lawrence.

Bridget, the Friars, Edward and Elizabeth moved to Clinton (Cuero) on the Guadalupe in 1839, but returned to Washington after the Great Commanche Raid of 1840 and the burning of Linnville. Edward McGary was killed by Commanches in August of 1840 between Clinton and the mouth of the San Antonio River. The Friars remained in Dewit Colony where their descendents live to this day. The Lawrences settled, and descendents still remain, near Hallettsville in Lavaca County.

By 1843, Bridget and her Daughter, Elizabeth, were living in LaGrange. Bridget built a home on the Colorado River. There, in December of 1844, Elizabeth married David Kornegay. Their biography appears elsewhere in this work. In 1850, Bridget and the Kornegays moved to the Waco area and settled on the McGary Grant. The McKissicks occupied the adjacent one league grant, they ultimately settled in Bosque County at Clifton.

Bridget Lamb McGary died in the spring of 1857. She is buried beside her son-in-law, David Smith Kornegay, at the Bosqueville Cemetery near Waco.

HOLDEN MCGEE

Holden McGee was born 12 March 1796, in Richmond County, Georgia, to Jonathan and Rebecca (James) McGee. Around 1808, Jonathan McGee and his family were in Mississippi, and moved into Louisiana settling on the Pearl River. Thus, he and part of his family fought in the Battle of New Orleans.

Holden McGee married Sarah Mary Howell in 1822, and they became the parents of nine children. By 1837, he was issued land grants in Jasper and Newton counties, where the families lived out their lives. Sarah McGee, born 1796, Richmond County, Georgia, died 8 June 1851, and is buried near Farrsville, Newton County.

Most of Holden's children were buried in the McGee family cemetery located in an area known as "McGee Bend." Their remains were relocated to Jasper for reburial due to the construction of the Sam Rayburn Dam and Reservoir.

At the age of 102, Holden was living with his daughter. The family story is that while plowing the garden, Holden unearthed a den of rattlesnakes, resulting in his death. Holden McGee died 12 October 1898, and is interred at Broaddus, San Augustine County, Texas.

Holden McGee was a loyal citizen and patriot. Charles Wayne Benbow # 3762 Evan Thompson Benbow # 3763 Landon Cole Lunz # 5212s

RALPH MCGEE

Ralph McGee was born February 18, 1796, in Alabama, to David McGee and Mary Cook. He was married twice: first to

Lydia Cude in 1816, with whom he had 11 children (Mary, William, Elander, Drusilla, Absolom, James, Martha, Elizabeth, Dorcas, Samuel, and Sarah Ann); and second to Mrs. Eliza Miller (no children).

Ralph and his family entered Texas in 1834, receiving a land grant in Vehlien's Colony dated March 12, 1835. He first settled in Montgomery County, where it is believed that Lydia had family. He then moved to San Jacinto County to what was known as Patrick's Ferry on the Trinity River with titled land in the present day corporate boundaries of Point Blank. Ralph participated in the Storming of Bexar in December 1835, receiving a donation certificate of 640 acres for his service.

He was commissioned postmaster of Walnut Grove, Liberty County, in 1841. Ralph was a merchant by trade, and had a sizable estate when he died on August 19,1851. He is buried in Moscow Cemetery, Polk County, Texas.

Frank Michael Hicks (SRT #6860) is the son of Len Eggleston Hicks (DRT #2128 1), who is the daughter of Artie Leon Eggleston, the son of Martha Green Brown, the daughter of Martha McGee Green (Ralph's daughter). Frank Michael Hicks SRT #6860

JOHN MCGOWN

John McGown was born May 5, 1787, the first of eleven children of Elizabeth, a Cherokee Indian, and Andrew McGown, a Kentucky Magistrate. Andrew was the seventh child of John McGown I, born December 21, 1745, and Rebecca Hammons. Before migrating to Kentucky, they were members of the Highland Scottish Clan MacPherson.

The type of rifle used by John McGown's Cherokee Company at Horseshoe Bend

From 27th January 1814, to 11th April 1814, John McGown was a mounted combatant in the Cherokee Indian Company under command of Captain John McLemore in the regiment commanded by Colonel Gideon Morgan, Jr., under Major General Andrew Jackson. He was the 57th man to enlist in Captain McLemore's Company. According to the Horseshoe Bend National Battlefield's historian, McLemore's Cherokee Company attacked across the river and over the Creek Indians' fortifications, built under British supervision. Family tradition has it that McGown was instrumental in getting the Cherokees to travel from Kentucky to Alabama to join Jackson's forces.

John McGown was married March 16, 1815, to Mary Thompson Floyd, a young widow, whose father, Burrell Thompson, was a teamster in the Revolutionary War at Cowpens and other Carolina battles. As an older man, Thompson moved to Nacogdoches and took part in the Fredonian Rebellion. Four of his letters to Stephen F. Austin appear in "The Austin Papers." After the rebellion's failure, a price was put on Thompson's head and he returned to Tennessee, where his daughter married John McGown.

Chief Menawa of the Creeks, allied with the British agianst General Andrew Jackson.

John McGown was granted First Class Headright Unconditional Land Certificate #181 by San Augustine County Board of Land Commissioners on February 1, 1838, for one league and one labor of Texas land. Through Survey dated April 7, 1850, he received Abstract #238 for 3,481 acres in Fayette County, Patent Volume 8 and Patent Number 438 on April 19, 1850. Near the close of his life, under the same Certificate 181, he surveyed 1,124.44 acres in Navarro County, Abstract #528, for which Texas General Land Office Patent Number 859 in Patent Volume 11 was issued.

The Cherokees crossed the river at Horseshoe Bend from the south in this type of dugout canoe; John Coffee had 1300 troops- half white and half Indian.

Typical fortification of the Creek - British Alliance, scaled by John McGown's Cherokee Company.

The John McGowns had eight children. Their sixth child, William Carroll McGown, received his medical doctorate in the first graduating class from Tulane University in New Orleans. Their oldest child, Andrew Jackson McGown, became a minister in the Cumberland Presbyterian Church. Their seventh child, Burrell Thompson McGown, was a farmer and rancher. And their eighth and last child, Margaret Josephine McGown, married businessman Sylvester Stansbury Munger, who at her urging left the practice of law in LaGrange and Bastrop to export cotton to Mexico in the Civil War, and bring north in his wagons textile machinery to form the Bastrop Manufacturing Company which made blankets

Graves of Judge and Mrs. S.S. Munger in SW corner of M.Y. Stokes lot, Oak Hills Cemetery, Lampasas, Texas.

The S.S. Munger tombstone in the NW corner of M.Y. Stokes lot in Oak Hills Cemetery in Lampasas.

Grave site of Sylvester Stansbury Munger

Grave site of Margaret Josephine McGown Munger.

for the Confederacy. The 1870's Texas Almanacs gave Munger credit for pioneering textile mills in the state. After the Civil War, he built the Eureka Cotton Mills in Houston, and also a sawmill at Conroe. After business failure, he operated a San Saba Hotel and was named Lampasas postmaster by President Arthur.

Applying for Daughters of the Republic of Texas membership from Lampasas on February 15, 1893, Margaret Josephine McGown Munger wrote: "My mother was strongly patriotic and zealous in the cause of Texas, her adopted country. My parents gladly denied themselves, and sent out three sons (Andrew Jackson McGown, Samuel McGown, and William Carroll McGown) to battle for Texas rights and freedom. Two were in the Battle of San Jacinto, 1836, in com. Capt. Billingsly. The two younger went on several later expeditions, continuing in readiness to serve their country, until peace prevailed."

Horseshoe Bend Battlefield

Mary Thompson Floyd McGown was born in 1790, and died June 23, 1845. John McGown died December 15, 1858. Charles Eugene Stokes, Jr. #6574

COL. JOHN HAMILTON MCNAIRY

Col. John Hamilton McNairy, my great-great-grandfather, was born in Guilford County, North Carolina in 1804. He moved to Shelby County, Texas in 1837. He married twice and was the father of 11 children. His first wife was Sallie Leatherman (born Tennessee, died Mississippi in 1836 on the way to Texas). He married his second wife, Susan (Susanah) Runnels (born Tennes-

see 1824) in Shelby County, Texas in 1841. She was the daughter of Henry Runnels and Margaret (Peggy) Smith who came from Tennessee to Texas in 1837.

Col. McNairy was one of the two Regulators who, at the request of Gen. Sam Houston, signed the Peace Treaty for the Regulators to end the Regulator-Moderator War in 1844. Col. McNairy bought acreage in 1847 in the Coffeeville, Harrison County, Upshur County area (all formerly part of Shelby County). He moved there in 1847.

Marker for John Hamilton McNairy

He was instrumental in getting Upshur County created, and was elected the first State representative from Upshur County in 1848. He was one of two State Representatives for Harrison County prior to Upshur County being formed out of Harrison County.

He died at Coffeeville January 7, 1853. A State Historical Marker is located at his grave in the Old Coffeeville Cemetery, Upshur County, Texas.

Col. McNairy's paternal grandfather was Francis McNairy, patriot, of Guilford County, North Carolina. John Hamilton McNairy is named after his maternal grandfather, Gen. John Hamilton, Revolutionary War, Battle of Guilford Courthouse, North Carolina.

JOHANN FRIEDRICH MEINECKE

Johann Friedrich Meinecke was born March 5, 1804 in Werben, Sachsen, Prussia. He married Sophie Dorothea Elisabeth Koyn on March 29, 1829 in Perleberg, Brandenburg, Prussia. As a country, Prussia no longer exists. Much of that land is now in what was East Germany. With the continued revolts, unrest, impending war and oppression, Texas — with its bast undeveloped lands and air of freedom — was especially attractive to the Meineckes.

Meinecke Cemetery, Bellville

The Meineckes (Johann, Sophie, their 4 sons and 2 daughters) came to this country by sailing on the ship Natchez from Bremen, Germany, to Galveston, Texas, in the fall of 1845. The voyage was longer than expected, due to being caught in a "calm" near Havana, Cuba, for two weeks. The trip took 13 weeks, and they almost ran out of food and water.

From Galveston, the immigrants were ferried by boat to the mainland shallow water port of Carlshaven (Indianola) for ox team transportation inland. From there, the Meinecke family made their way to Austin County, where Johann Friedrich purchased 124 acres of land for $8.00 per acre near Kenny, Texas, near what is now Bellville. The cemetery still stands on a hill by the original homesite, with 12 graves, including the immigrants. *Submitted by Tom J. Meinecke*

PETER MERGELE

Peter Mergele (1810-1892) arrived in the Republic of Texas at the port of Galveston, in December 1943, on the ship Jean Key. Traveling with him were his wife, Barbara Schertz Mergele (1812-1886), and their three sons, Jacob, Emil, and Charles. Also included with this group were Peter's in-laws, Joseph Schertz (1781-1863), his wife, Anne Marie (1784-1844), and most of their children. These two families came from the Alsace area of the Haut-Rhin District of France, located on the border of Switzerland and Germany in central Europe. (Schertz, Texas, was founded and named for this Schertz family).

Peter and Barbara (Schertz) Mergele

They had been recruited to immigrate to Texas by Henri Castro. The Jean Key was the second shipload of settlers sent to Texas by Henri Castro. Castro's settlers were required to bring (1) the necessary clothing, (2) farming or other instruments of labor, (3) the means of paying their passage to Texas, and (4) means of subsistence during the first year in Texas.

The Mergeles and Schertzes had brought knocked-down wagons along with them, so upon arriving in Houston, Texas, in January 1844, they merely had to buy oxen to complete their transportation system.

They then traveled overland to San Antonio de Bexar, and, being Catholics, were able to camp on the Old Mission Alamo grounds in their tents and wagons as they awaited Mr. Castro. After his arrival, these two families became dissatisfied with Mr. Castro and his treatment of them. Yellow fever struck about Easter time in 1844, and Barbara Mergele lost her mother, uncle, one sister and one brother. They were buried on the Alamo Mission grounds. Prince Solms contacted these two families later in 1844 while they were camped at the Alamo, and suggested that they join his colony, which was to settle on the Fisher Miller Grant north of present-day Fredericksburg, Texas. The fact that these families were more German than French – besides their displeasure with Henri Castro — probably helped encourage the Mergeles and Schertzes to change their plans. It turned out Solms was short of colonists and wagons, so the Mergeles and Schertzes made ideal colonists for him.

The Mergeles and Schertzes went back to Indianola and began helping to transport Prince Solms' first group of colonists (German Verein), who were camped at that place up the Guadalupe River. Then Solms went back to San Antonio de Bexar and purchased the Comal Tract, later to be New Braunfels, Texas, for a first stop in his colonizing plan.

Jean Jacques Von Coll led the settlers up the Guadalupe River to the site of New Braunfels. Von Coll later became Peter Mergele's brother-in-law by marrying Marguerite Schertz. This small group of first settlers arrived at that site on Good Friday, March 25, 1845. The Mergele and Schertz families thus were among the founders of New Braunfels, and shortly after that, founders of Fredericksburg, Boerne, and Schertz, Texas.

All of the Mergeles in the United States today are descendants of Peter and Barbara Mergele.

Compiled by Edwin Wallace Mergele, Jr. Peter Mergele was my great-great-grandfather, and Joseph Schertz was my great-great-great-grandfather) - L #4606.

ANDREW MILLER

Andrew Miller and family came to Texas in 1824 as Austin Colonists. They settled on Miller's league of land on Doe Run Creek, adjoining the Washington-on-the-Brazos townsite. Miller's league was approved by the Mexican government and title granted in 1831.

Miller was born in North Carolina in 1784, the son of Henry Y. Miller, a Revolutionary War veteran. He came to Texas via Rapides Parish, Louisiana, where he settled in 1815. He married Clia Neal in 1818. Two children were born to them in Rapides Parish: Mary Cecelia in 1820, and Robert T. Miller in 1822. Two additional children were born to them after their relocation to Texas: Lucretia Miller in 1824, and Merideth Neal Miller in 1828.

The Washington Board of Commissioners in 1838 approved Miller's application for his labor of land. The labor was located on Peach Creek in adjoining Brazos County. He was set upon by Indians and killed while on a trip to survey the acquisition,

In 1840 Miller's widow married John Lott, a widower, who arrived at Washington-on-the-Brazos in 1831. Lott was appointed Commissary for the ranging companies of Austin's Colony to protect the settlers against Indian depredations. In the 1836 Revolution against Mexico, Lott was appointed Commissary for the newly declared Republic of Texas.

Lott and Hall's Washington facility furnished supplies to incoming volunteers on their way to join General Sam Houston's Texian army. Lott's facility consisted of a hotel, general store, livery stable and saloon. A document on file with the Texas State Library Archives is a draft from David Crockett for $7.50 to John Lott for furnishing provisions for Crockett and four volunteers on their way to join the Texian army.

Robert T. Miller married Louisa Lott, daughter of John Lott, in 1847. They relocated to McLennan County, where they homesteaded on Tehuacana Creek, near Waco. To this union was born Celia Frances and Sarah Ann Miller.

Robert T. Miller was killed by Indians in 1853. Sarah Ann Miller married Max Lehmann in 1877. Max and Sarah were parents of William Charles Lehmann, my grandfather.

As a descendant of these early Texas settlers, I take pride in their sacrifices and contributions to Texas. Allan O.E. Lehmann #6112N

JACOB (JAKE) MILTON MILLER

Jacob (Jake) Milton Miller was born Christmas Eve, 1844, in Columbus, Colorado County, Republic of Texas. He was the only child of Travis and Diana Miller, who were married January 22,

1841, in Columbus. When Jake was born, his father and mother were 67 and 18 respectively. Before age 3, Jake was deeded two slaves, Travis and Sarah, by his father, who was originally from New York. Jake's mother, Diana Straufschneider, the daughter of Gabriel Straw and Mary Bright Snider, was born 1826. Austin Colony, Texas Territory.

Jake's grandparents, Gabriel and Mary, signed a $10,000 marriage bond before Stephen F. Austin, Judge, Colorado District, Austin Colony, on May 28, 1824. Gabriel and David Bright, Mary's father, were among the original three hundred families of the colony: Each received a Spanish land grant in 1824.

Jake Miller married Susan Virginia Sloneker on June 30, 1865, in Columbus. They were parents of nine children: Travis Burkhart, John Jacob, Mary Miller Wilkerson, Margret (sic), Emer Miller Winkler, William Warren, Henritta Miller Chambliss, Sarah Elizabeth Miller Litzler, and Fredrick Antona.

Jacob Milton was injured while working on a railroad, and died at his Columbus home on September 21, 1894. Susan Sloneker Miller Stephen Peek, owner of the first horseless carriage in Katy, Texas, died October 16, 1926.

Enumerated among Jake's many descendants is great-grandson, Andrew August Litzler, fourth-generation Texan.

DR. SAMUEL REED MILLER

Dr. Samuel Reed Miller, son of Simon Miller and Elizabeth Read, born 1798 in Bedford County, Va., came to Texas with Austin's "Old 300" in 1822, and received one league of land on August 19, 1824. The 1826 Census showed Miller as farmer and stock raiser, aged between 25 and 40, with wife and 3 sons. Wife: Nancy Ann Curby. Children: Thomas, John, James, Samuel L., Louisa Jane, Salina, Henderson, Nancy Ann, Dicey Jane. He was a militia commander June 1826 in the colony. He served in the expedition against Anahuac in 1832 and service of Republic of Texas as a volunteer in Capt. Kirkendoll's Company.

In Bastrop County, he served as county clerk 1838-1839; county treasurer 1838-1846; acting sheriff in San Felipe September-October 1829; 1841 elected to House of Representatives (6th Congress); sergeant-at-arms 1841-1842, and doorkeeper of the Senate 1843. In 1856, the election returned him as a commissioner in Nueces County.

Miller opened a store and operated the Santa Margarita ferry at San Patricio, which was an important factor in bringing food from Mexico to Texas. Endless trains of ox carts carried cotton for exchange. Many distinguished refugees and travelers in buggies, horseback or foot crossed by ferry, the link between San Antonio and Brownsville.

Family tradition says Dr. Miller dressed Sam Houston's wounds after the Battle of San Jacinto. He practiced medicine in Travis County before 1850. Houston was often a guest as they were friends. His big black dog always frightened Miller's daughter, Nan.

Miller died February 12, 1878, in Nueces County, Texas, and is buried in an unmarked grave on the banks of the Nueces River. Charles Motz IV #6415J (great-great-great-great-grandson)

MCGRADY MONTGOMERY

McGrady Montgomery was born in Gibson County, Indiana, in 1812. He was the son of Judge Isaac Montgomery and Martha McClure Montgomery, both from Indiana. The Montgomery family moved from Indiana to Texas and settled in Austin County when McGrady was a young man.

McGrady joined the Texas Army as a private, serving in all campaigns of that eventful period. He fought in the Battle of San Jacinto in 1836, serving in Captain James Polk Price's Company. His name is inscribed on the monument at the San Jacinto Battleground.

McGrady returned to Indiana and married Minerva Lucas on January 14, 1842. McGrady and Minerva had six children, one of whom, Martha, was born in 1843. McGrady, Minerva, and their children returned to Texas in 1852, traveling by train to Houston and by ox cart to Austin County, Texas. The family lived near Sempronius, where McGrady was a successful planter.

McGrady Montgomery

Mr. Montgomery was involved in local politics and development of local education. He was also a member of the Methodist Church.

McGrady died in 1878, at the age of 66, and was buried at the family home. The family obelisk, though damaged, has been restored and moved to the old Masonic Cemetery at Chappell Hill, Texas.

McGrady and his widow were recipients of land grants for his service in the Texas Army.

Martha Montgomery married K.W. Reese in 1870, and they lived on the Reese family farm in Austin County, Texas, not far from the Montgomery place. This land is registered in the Texas Land Heritage Program and has been in the family for six generations. James Reese Jones #3195 SRT, SJD, SAR, SCV Jared Alexander Jones #4031

HAYWOOD MOORE

Haywood Moore was born in Pitt County, N.C., on 5 Jan 1815, a few miles southeast of the current town of Farmville. His parents were William Moore, farmer and magistrate, and Frances Forrest, daughter of William Forrest of Greene County, N.C., who was in the Revolutionary War.

In 1835, William Moore moved his family to Haywood County, Tennessee.

Haywood moved to Texas by 1838 and was granted a conditional certificate on 320 acres in Fayette County, Texas, 22 March 1839.

Haywood served as a private in the expedition commanded by General Edward Burleson in the spring of 1842 to repel the invasion of Texas by General Vasquez (also called the Wall Campaign). On Feb. 7, 1853, Haywood received a Public Debt Receipt from the Late Republic of Texas for $15.75 for his service in the campaign.

Haywood married Mary (Polly) McClure on 14 January 1845, in one of the first marriages in Fayette, Texas, U.S.A. Mary McClure was the daughter of Levi McClure and Elizabeth Archer, who had moved to Texas from Hempstead, Arkansas, about 1841. Haywood lived all his life on his farm in Fayette and Colorado counties. He and wife Mary were Primitive Baptists, who had fourteen children and 57 grandchildren.

Haywood Moore Circa 1870

Haywood died on his farm 18 December 1882, and was buried a day later in the small Black Jack Springs (Pin Oak) Cemetery near Muldoon, Fayette County, Texas, Mary Moore died 20 May 1904, and was buried the next day at Myrtle Cemetery in Rock Island Texas.

The Haywood Moore name has been passed on in each subsequent generation: John Haywood Moore (born 1855); Lit Haywood Moore (born 1884); Merle Haywood Moore (born 1909); Lit Haywood Moore, Jr. (born 1925); Erin Haywood Moore (born 1938); and Daniel Haywood Moore (born 1964).*Submitted by Erin Haywood Moore #5914A*

THOMAS HARRISON MOORE

Thomas Harrison Moore (1790-1842) of Harrison County, Kentucky, settled in Bastrop and Fayette counties, Texas, in 1833. He had migrated from Kentucky with a group of related families, which included his brother, John H. Moore; his cousin, Captain Nicholas Mosby Dawson; the Eastland family; and the McClures.

He and his brother, John, settled on tracts of land on the La Bahia Road near present LaGrange. It is recorded in the actions of the Court of Bastrop County in 1838 that Thomas H. Moore was granted permission to establish a ferry at the La Bahia crossing of the Colorado River, at what is now LaGrange. On March 30, 1839, a land grant confirmed to Thomas H. Moore an additional 640 acres in Bastrop County. He served as a precinct chairman and provided "a permanent voting place" on June 8, 1838, in Bastrop County. In that same year, it is recorded that he purchased slaves. He was taxed in Bastrop in 1840 for land, cattle, and personal property. It is written in the Moore family Bible in Harrison County, Kentucky, owned by the late Judge Richard Menifee Collier, that Thomas H. Moore "died of the fever in Texas during the summer of 1842."

Thomas Harrison Moore was born in 1790 at the Moore homestead in Harrison County, Kentucky, the son of the Revolutionary War Captain Thomas Moore, and his wife, Mary (Harrison). Captain Moore later served in the Illinois regiment commanded by General George Rogers Clark with the rank of major.

On 1 April 1827, Thomas Harrison Moore married in Harrison County, Kentucky, Martha Ann (Webb). It is said that his wife and children were on the journey to join their husband and father when word of her husband's death was received while they were staying in the home of Thomas H. Moore's uncle, Colonel Benjamin Harrison, in New Madrid, Missouri. The family returned to Kentucky without having reached Texas, and the Moore lands in Texas were sold in 1850.

Thomas H. Moore had two sons and one daughter: Moses Webb Moore, Thomas Harrison Moore, Jr., and Mary Ellen Moore, who married Charles Martel Waits of Harrison County, Kentucky.

Submitted by the great-great-grandson of the aforesaid settler in the Republic of Texas, the Reverend Dr. Emmett Moore Waits of Dallas, Texas, member of the Thomas Rusk Chapter, SRT.

WILLIAM WALLACE MOORE

According to a land grant issued on March 7. 1835, colonist John Moore, his wife, Lucy, and one child, settled in Zavala's Colony located in Sabine County. The land is described as being in the neighborhood of Housing Creek and extending to the waters of Bear Creek.

On June 22, 1835, a son, William Wallace, was born to John and Lucy Moore. On July 9, 1857, William married Mary Elizabeth Castleberry, who was born on December 23, 1838. As heirs of John Moore, Lucy (now Lucy M. Caldwell) and William Wallace sold the property to Wright S. Andrews of Galveston on August 30, 1860.

The Texas Census of 1870 lists William W. Moore as a farmer living with his wife, Mary, and two daughters, Cora Ada and Myrtle, in Washington County, Precinct 3, Brenham. Other children were John Wesley, William R. and Mary Emma. He was on the roll of the Baylor Masonic Lodge No. 125 at Gay Hill.

Mary Elizabeth died on January 8, 1892, and is buried in Robeline, La. Moore died ten years later on May 5, 1902, and was buried in Many, La. William Wallace Moore was my great-great-great-grandfather. John F. Woolsey, Jr. #5000 Matagorda Chapter #35

ALFRED W. MORRIS

Alfred W. Morris was born in Georgia on 15 March 1802. He was in the Sabine District of Texas by 1833, emigrating from Franklin County, Georgia. Because his parents are unknown, all attempts to determine earlier ancestry have been to no avail.

The 1835 Sabine Census lists his wife, Sara Ann, and one child, John M., 7 months old, and his occupation as farmer. He received one league and one labor of land in the Sabine District, according to General Land Office Records, Spanish Collection, Box 89, Folder 69. Pension applications show Alfred joining the Texian army to fight for independence against Mexico in 1836. Daniel Fuller, of Earth County, affirmed that both he and Alfred joined Captain Bryant's Company at Milam in Sabine County, and later served in the Battle of San Jacinto. In 1841, he served in Captain J.P.B. January's Company, and in the spring of 1842 he participated in the Vasquez Campaign, helping to drive General Vasquez's army back across the Rio Grande. Alfred also saw service in the U.S. and Mexican War serving in Captain James Chessher's Company of First Texas Foot Riflemen, from 13 June 1846 to 24 August 1846.

In 1858 Alfred, wife Sara Ann, and family were in Gonzales County, where Alfred was Worshipful Master of the DeMolay #199 Lodge, Sandies Chapel, Dewville, Texas.

On 5 March 1881, Alfred Morris passed from this life, and is buried in the Sandies Chapel Cemetery in Dewville, Texas. William Taylor, also a veteran of San Jacinto, lies at rest next to him, along with veterans of the War Between the States.

One of Alfred's grandsons, W.T. "Brack" Morris, sheriff of Karnes County in the year of 1901, was killed by the notorious

Gregorio Cortez on 12 June of that year. The sheriff was questioning Gregorio about some horse thievery when a gun battle started and Sheriff Morris was mortally wounded and subsequently died a short time later. There were over 2,000 mourners at the funeral, and 600 men chased Sheriff Morris's killer all the way to the Rio Grande and brought him back for trial. Sheriff Morris's son, Harper, followed in his father's foot steps and became the sheriff of Karnes County. Gregorio Cortez became a folk hero in song along the border. W.T. "Brack" Morris had joined the Texas Rangers in 1881 and was elected sheriff in 1896. He was well respected by fellow law officers and the community as well.

A real hero died that hot June afternoon in nineteen hundred and one, "when they thought the west had been won." Samuel Franklin Clark Jr. #5235

COL. SAMUEL FOUNTAIN MOSELEY

Col. Samuel Fountain Moseley, born near Huntsville, Alabama, on November 15, 1818, was the son of War of 1812 veteran John Moseley and Elizabeth Wakefield Moseley.

He practiced law before heading for Texas at age 27, and married Eliza Irby Wilkinson. He settled in Cass County in 1845, where first law partner was General Edward Tarrant, for whom Tarrant County would be named. Moseley served in the Mexican War, and was elected to the First and Second Texas Legislatures. He was official escort of Governor George T. Wood during visits to the house.

Samuel F. Moseley
(1818-1858)

Moseley was a dedicated campaigner for his friend Isaac Van Zandt. His diary contains interesting recollections of campaign trips, including a delightful story of a beautiful maid who dropped a handwritten invitation into Van Zandt's hat as he held it in his hand while gesturing during a campaign speech.

Moseley also had successful real estate business and published The Jefferson Herald. He and Eliza owned several thousand acres and lived on a 1,400-acre plantation, "Bonnie Braes," near Texas/Louisiana border. During the Civil War, he headed the Confederate Depository Office in Jefferson.

Eliza died in 1874, and Sam in 1878. Both were buried in the Wilkinson Cemetery near their beloved Bonnie Braes. They had ten children, including Seaborn Wilkinson Moseley, who served as county judge of Marion County for many years, and Eliza Moseley Smith.

Great-great-grandfather of SRT Samuel Ross Moseley and great-great-great-grandfather of SRT Madison Ross Moseley and others. Great-grandfather of SRTs David Madison Smith and Forrest Moseley Smith, Jr. Sam and Kay Moseley

AZARIAH MOSS

Azariah Moss, son of James Peterson Moss and Nancy Abernathy Moss, was born in Tennessee on May 30, 1816. He married Adeline L. Alford on December 20, 1837. Following her death, he married Christiana Watson (born in Alabama on July 18, 1830) on July 3, 1849. Eight children were born to Azariah and Christiana Moss: (in birth order) James Fontaine Moss, Stephen Ellis Moss, Edmond L. Moss, M. Pleasant Moss, Robert L. Moss, Mary Moss (Mrs. J.W. Allen), Ida Moss (Mrs. J.B. Franklin), and Emma Moss (Mrs. Michael Huffman Thomas).

Tombstone of Azariah Moss
(5/30/1816-2/17/1888)
Wheatland Cemetery, South West Dallas Co., Texas

He arrived in the Texas Republic on November 15, 1835, and farmed in Red River County near the Arkansas line. In the early 1850s, he moved his wife and family to a plantation near Wheatland in Dallas County. He engaged in business in Dallas and was one of the founders and directors of Dallas County's first fair, held near Washington Street in the 1870s.

Family tradition speaks of his serving the Confederacy during the War Between the States. He was a member of the Methodist Episcopal Church South. He predeceased his wife, dying (by his own hand) at his Wheatland home on February 17, 1888. Christiana Moss died in Dallas in 1910, and is interred beside her husband in the Wheatland Cemetery. John Mauk Hilliard (great-great-grandson), #6706

MICHAEL (MIKE) MUCKLEROY

Michael (Mike) Muckleroy brought his wife, Elizabeth Ledbetter, and their children, to Texas from Franklin County, Tennessee, in 1840. He brought one half league of land that originally belonged to his brother, Howard, in Colorado County, north of Frelsburg. He farmed this property for fifty-five years before he sold it in 1895. He moved to Terrell, Texas, to retire with his granddaughter, having outlived his wife and children.

Michael was the son of Izack and Sarah Floyd Muckleroy, born September 27, 1808, in Franklin County, Tennessee. His grandfather, Avington (McLeroy) Muckleroy was an American Revolution patriot.

In 1842, Muckleroy joined the campaign to expel General Adrian Woll's Army invasion of Texas from Mexico. Wall, a French mercenary, was an officer in the Mexican Army, who in 1842 led 1,000 troops to recapture San Antonio.

He was elected county commissioner of Colorado County, and served from 1846 until 1852. After the Reconstruction period following the War Between the States, his neighbors persuaded him to seek the office of commissioner again. He served from 1876 to 1878. The people of Colorado County referred to him as "Uncle Mike."

Mike Muckleroy passed away in Kaufman County, Texas, on July 28 1896, and was buried next to his wife in the family cemetery on the Muckleroy plantation in Colorado County. Richard William Muckleroy # 6026

RICHARD WILLIAM MUCKLEROY

Richard William Muckleroy (SRT #6026) was born June 23, 1922, in El Paso, Texas. His parents were Richard Lynn and Georgia Eugenia Love Muckleroy. He received a B.S. degree in chemical engineering from Texas A&M College.

Richard volunteered for service in World War II, was commissioned an officer, and fought in the European Theater, taking part in five battles from Normandy to the surrender of the Germans.

On July 20, 1945, he married Bettie Corrine McKaskle. They had two children, Karen Lee and Sherrel Ann; three grandchildren, Bettie Kristine Parma Donovan, Mandie Lee Parma, and Richard William Barclay; and one great-granddaughter, Kaitlyn Kristine Donovan.

Muckleroy's professional career was in the field of engineering, sales, and management. He retired in 1983 as general manager of the Water Division of the city of Houston.

ARTHUR ALEXANDER MUNCEY

Arthur Alexander Muncey was born on the south fork of the Roanoke River near Christiansburg, Va., in 1823. His parents were Nathaniel Calvin Muncey (Pvt. 75th, Regiment, Virginia Militia, War of 1812) and Elizabeth Muncey nee Vickers; his grandparents were Luke Muncey Sr. (a member of Capt. Joseph Cloyd's Company, Virginia Militia, Revolutionary War) and Mary Muncey nee Britt; his great-grandparents were Nathaniel Muncey (French & Indian War) and Mary Muncey nee Bush.

A.A. Muncey arrived in San Antonio, Texas, at the age of 14 in 1837. He was in the employment of Onesimus Evans, with whom he became a partner in the largest dry good store of that city. Later, Richard A. Howard joined the partnership after marrying the daughter of Onesimus Evans.

Arthur A. Muncey

During the Mexican War in 1846, Major A.A. Muncey commanded a group of Virginians who fought at the Battle of Buena Vista. He was near Archibald Yell, commander of the Arkansas Volunteers at the time of his death at the hands of Mexican lancers. Later, A.A. Muncey commanded a group who kept the communication lines open between the San Antonio Army headquarters and the Mexican border.

After the Mexican War, the Evans-Muncey dry goods company prospered until the untimely death of Onesimus Evans in 1852. His death occurred within a week of the death of his daughter, the wife of Richard A. Howard, and the partnership dissolved in 1852. A.A. Muncey then joined the Alamo Rangers, who became part of the fighting force who accompanied General Walker, the famous filibuster who captured Nicaragua and declared himself president.

In San Antonio, A.A. Muncey married Mary Eliza Sappington, daughter of the recently deceased Dr. Mark Brown Sappington, late of Memphis Tennessee. The wedding occurred on 10 October 1854. The couple were founding, members of St. Mark's Episcopal Church in San Antonio. The father of Dr. Mark Brown Sappington was one of the stockholder-investors in the Robertson Colony, along with the likes of Sam Houston.

Another Virginian, Ben Ficklin, hired A.A. Muncey as his agent for the stage line carrying passengers and the mail through San Angelo and El Paso, and on to California. This was his employment until the Confederacy declared war. The Muncey family removed to Fort Clark with the advent of war, where A.A. Muncey was conscripted into Confederate (Texas Home Guard) service on 10 July 1862.

His duties entailed the movement of cotton from San Antonio through Fort Clark to Eagle Pass, where across the border in Piedras Negras the cotton was ginned and bailed. From Piedras Negras, Mexico, A.A. Muncey accompanied the cotton bails to the Mexican port of Bagdad, below Matamoros, where English interests were paying $1.00/lb gold for the cotton!

After the Civil War, A.A. Muncey continued his work as agent for the Ben Ficklin Stage Company interests until the firm folded with the death of its founder. A.A. Muncey had won the elected office of county weigher, serving in that capacity until his death in 1884.

Arthur Alexander & Mary Eliza Muncey had the following children: Arthur A. Muncey Jr., Mark Edwin Muncey, Walter Muncey, Elizabeth Douglas Muncey, Margaret Sappington Muncey, Stella Bayless Muncey, Benjamin Sappington Muncey

I am a grandson of Mark Edwin Muncey, and a son of James Arthur Muncey. James A. Muncey Jr.

ELIZABETH ANN MYERS

Elizabeth Ann Myers was born October 9, 1829, in Illinois, the youngest of eight to the Samuel Myers family of North Carolina. Samuel with his family started for Texas in 1837, but ill health caused him to settle in Arkansas.

Elizabeth Ann Myers Berry
Circa 1900

After her parents' deaths, Elizabeth arrived in Texas before 1845 in custody of her brother Jessie Myers. She was barley 17 when she married Franklin Davis in Sherman, Texas, on December 15, 1846. After his death, she was left with one son. She married James Edsel Berry of Tennessee in 1857.

James was a farmer and saddler in Kentucky Town in Grayson County, where all seven of their children were born. The youngest was John Berry, born February 7, 1872, my grandfather.

The family moved to Montague County in 1873, where James purchased 160 acres of school land. James died March 6, 1877, when he was struck in the head by a stray bullet. Elizabeth continued on their farm and raised her children. Elizabeth died while visiting her oldest daughter, Mrs. Jane Loving, in Walters, Oklahoma on July 1, 1914.

My great-grandmother is buried next to my great-grandfather, James E. Berry, in Starkey Cemetery, Montague County Texas. Oscar Leon Frith Jr. SRT # 6724 David Leon Frith SRT # 6770

WILLIAM NASH

William Nash, a third great-grandfather of mine, was born 12 August 1809, probably in Williamson County, Tennessee, as that is where his parents, Dempsey and Lucy (Garrett) Nash, were married 17 September 1805, and where Dempsey died.

*William Nash
Circa 1855*

He married Louisa Temple on 21 September 1826, in Davidson County, Tennessee. They were the parents of eight children, one of whom was Lucy (Nash) Gardner, whom I am descended from.

The family arrived in San Augustine County, Texas, in April 1835. Later that year, William was appointed to enlist volunteers for the Texas Army. In 1836, he was a member of the Texas Volunteers, having served in the Captain Thomas S. McFarland Company.

In 1851, the family moved to Kaufman County, Texas. They settled on land two miles west of the present courthouse. William became a prosperous planter, and owned much slave property.

William Nash died 16 August 1865, and is buried in Kaufman Cemetery. A published account states that he was poisoned by two ex-slaves. According to family tradition, he became ill and a young black boy was assigned to keep the flies away from William. The boy, having become bored, ground up some glass and added it to Williams' medicine. Unknowingly, his daughter, Lucy, gave him a dose, which proved fatal. *Submitted by Sam Whitten*

JOSEPH NEWMAN

Joseph Newman, one of Stephen F. Austin's "Old 300," was born about 1787. His parents and his place of birth are unknown. He married Rachel Rabb, daughter of William and Mary Smalley Rabb, on June 10, 1806, in Warren County, Ohio. He served in the War of 1812 under Captain Samuel Judy's Mounted Militia in Illinois.

By 1818, Joseph had moved his family from Illinois to the north side of the Red River. Two years later, they settled in the Jonesboro community on the south side, in Spanish Texas. Due to conditions here, a petition known as the Newman Memorial was signed by 80 citizens of the area and carried by him to San Antonio and presented to the Spanish governor.

On August 10 1825, Joseph received Land Grant #57 from the Mexican government. This grant for one sitio (4,428 acres) and one labor (177 acres) was located in Austin's First Colony near Egypt, in what is now Wharton County.

Joseph died February 15, 1831. His will, signed February 15, 1831, gives the names and ages of his ten children, instruction for the division of this property, and his request to be buried in the "the cemetery near my house."

Details on the Newman/Rabb families can be found in the book, "From the Monengahala to the Colorado," by Coleman and Annabel Newman.

Joseph Newman was my great-great-grandfather. Coleman C. Newman

ROBERT MILTON NEWTON

Robert Milton Newton was born November 30, 1907, in Coryell County, Texas. His parents were Joseph Norwood Newton (whose mother was Mary Virginia Boone Newton) and Nettie Coleman Newton. Robert's father was a farmer, so as a child he experienced the usual chores of that life. He graduated from high school at Clyde, Texas, in 1926, and attended Tarleton Junior College in Stephenville, Texas.

He taught school at Buckholts, Camp Branch (near Hico), then Hays College (Hood County) and Hill City (Hood County), Texas.

On April 20, 1929, he and Dora Carney, a Tarleton student from Hood County, were married in Stephenville. Through the years they had four children: Ann, Nell, Robert Jr., and Donna. In 1999, they celebrated their 70th anniversary.

Robert M. Newton

Robert worked with his father on various farms during the years 1935-40, studied radio and had radio repair shops. After receiving a radio engineer's license in 1941, he worked at KSAM in Huntsville, the radio station in Bryan, and Naval Communications school at Texas A&M College, teaching radio and Morse code to naval recruits.

As World War II was winding down, Robert began working for WBAP (KGKO) in Fort Worth in October 1944. In 1950, the station was sold, so the family moved to Seymour, Texas, where Robert farmed and worked at a new local radio station. A year later, he returned to WBAP, remaining until retirement in 1972.

Robert and Dora moved to Granbury, Hood County, Texas, in 1973 to be near family and old friends. They continue to be active and involved in church and community. Robert M. Newton

THOMAS HENRY NOBLE

No one knows why Thomas Henry Noble came to Texas. Born May 29, 1799, in Kentucky, he grew up in Franklin County, Kentucky, marrying Sarah Jane Patterson in 1820 in Frankfort. In 1828, his parents, William and Hannah Minor Noble, and all his siblings moved to Parke County, Indiana, to start anew. Thomas Henry took a different path, splitting from his large family and heading toward the frontier lands of the future Republic of Texas. He arrived in Red River County around 1836, having first stopped in Missouri and Arkansas.

Tombstone of Thomas Henry Noble near Fairland, Burnet Co., Texas

Both Thomas Henry and son William are found on the Second Class Certificates listed in Red River County, showing settlers who arrived between March, 1836, and October, 1837. Thomas received 1,280 acres and William, 640 acres. In 1841, Thomas served on the grand jury of Lamar County.

The Nobles moved south in 1843 to Victoria, Texas, where they lived until 1851. Four of his children married there. When the family again pulled up roots and moved north to Burnet County, sons William and Henry Noble remained in Victoria.

In Burnet County, Thomas Henry Noble became a successful rancher, raising cattle and breeding horses — especially a quality line of roan horses with white manes and tails for which he became well know in that region. Many of his horses were sold to the government for cavalry use.

His prosperity was short-lived, as Comanche and Kiowa Indian raids depleted Thomas Henry's stock. His son-in-law was scalped, and his young grandson kidnapped. The grandson, James Benson, lived with a Kiowa chief for several years, but was eventually returned to his grieving mother by the U.S. government at Fort Sill, Oklahoma. The Noble descendants were reimbursed for some of their stock losses by the government in 1904.

Thomas Henry and Sarah had thirteen children. Three sons served in the Mexican American War, and two served in the Confederate Army. His son, James Patterson Noble, was successful in re-establishing the excellent ranching operation that Thomas began. Thomas Henry Noble died in 1868. Ervin Ray Miller, M.D. #5937 (great-great-grandson)

JOHN NICHOLS

John Nichols appears on page 109 of Stephen F. Austin's "Register of Families" in 1830. It lists him as a 33-year-old farmer from Sabine. He arrived in Texas in 1827 with his wife, Fanny, and two male and two female children. These were his stepchildren, John and Martha Hutchins, and his children, Thomas and Ellen Nichols.

As described in the book "War of 1812 Veterans in Texas," John served in the U.S. Army during the War of 1812. He was a private in Capt. John R. Goffe's Company of the Louisiana Militia as a substitute for Simon Holden.

According to the Texas General Land Office, John Nichols took an oath on October 20, 1832 to receive 1 league (4428.3 acres) of land in Austin's Second Colony. The land was situated on Piney Creek and joined the Ives and James P. Stevenson Grants. On April 5, 1834, John Nichols sold half his league (2214 acres) to James and Thomas Bell for $200.00. On part of this land, the town of Bellville was established. Later, when Texas became a Republic in 1836, John requested and received a First Class Certificate (#115) for one labor (177 acres) in Austin County.

John Nichols died on March 3, 1864, near Bellville in Austin County. His obituary was published in The Bellville Countryman on March 10, 1864. "A Death – John Nichols, an old citizen and resident of Austin County, died at his home on Piney near the place on the 3rd inst. at the age of near 70 years. He was one of Jackson's men in the Battle of New Orleans in 1815."

In the Texas General Land Office Archives in Austin is a document entitled, "Proof to Procure Land Certificates for Widow of Texas Veterans." It was dated July 6, 1881, and was filed on July 7, 1881 by Mrs. Fannie Nichols, John's widow. She stated that John entered the service of the Republic of Texas military on July 18, 1836, as part of Capt. Cleveland's Company of the Mill Creek Volunteers. No record of a land grant has ever been located. It is uncertain whether or not this certificate was accepted.

Along with his two stepchildren, John and Fannie Nichols had seven children of their own: Thomas, Ellen A., Sarah Jane, James William, Francis "Fannie" Elizabeth, Samuel Houston and Caroline Mary "Carrie" Nichols. Andrew D. Crews #6774

ANDREW J. NORTHINGTON

Andrew J. Northington (born March 99, 1792, Cumberland County, North Carolina; died October 23, 1854, Wharton County, Texas) came to Texas in January 1831, and was granted 1 league (4,428 acres) by the Mexican government on May 28, 1831. The land was located on the east bank San Bernard River (present Fort Bend County, folio # 15007, Colonization Enterprise). For services rendered to the Republic of Texas and the "Runaway Scrape" in 1836, he was awarded 1 league and 1 labor on Feb. 1, 1818 in Medina County (Commissioners Matagorda County Certificate 179); and 1 labor Apr. 5, 1838, in Jones County (Commissioners Fort Bend County Certificate 268).

Photo taken 1890 at Meir Expedition Veteran Reunion with George Lord seated on far left.

Andrew Northington built his first home, "Buffalo Grove," on the trail connecting Richmond/San Felipe and Velasco. A volunteer in Texian Army, he achieved the rank of major. During the "Runaway Scrape," he had charge of fleeing civilians.

An 1837 petition to create Fort Bend County contains Andrew J. Northington's signature. Texas post office papers from 1836-1839 lists payment requests for mail contracts (pgs 83,168,177, 178,182) for Northington; delivery by horseback and by coach. He operated stagecoach between Richmond-Texana, using Mercer's Crossing on the Colorado River near Egypt. After 1840, he relocated to south side of West Bernard Creek on the trail connecting Richmond/Peach Creek/Matagorda, and worked as a surveyor. When Wharton County was created in 1846, he was Road 5 commissioner with Joel Hudgins.

Andrew J. and Pricilla Dawson Northington's daughter, Rachel, married Joel Hudgins on March 4, 1847. Their son, Josiah Dawson Hudgins, established a ranch in Hungerford, Texas, renown for registered Gray Brahmans. His descendants, fifth-generation Texians, operate J.D. Hudgins Ranch Inc. Joe Dawson Hudgins #4213, William H. Wharton Chapter #23

ROBERT W. OBSTA

Robert W. Obsta was born 31 December 1928, to William Lee and Agnes (Prukop) Obsta in Inez, Victoria County, Texas. He graduated Front High School in 1947, and immediately went into the United States Army, and later transferred to the United States Air Force. He served thirty-four months and received an honorable discharge on 29 May 1950.

Robert W. Obsta

He was employed as a locomotive fireman by the Southern Pacific Railroad on 29 June 1950. Robert retired 30 June 1997, after 47 years as a locomotive engineer with Southern Pacific, then Union Pacific Railroad. Robert first worked on steam engines and later diesel locomotives.

On 7 November 1953, Robert married Doris Ann Fischer. They are the parents of Carol Obsta, who married Robert A. Butler; Katherine Obsta, who married Don Schuelke; and Claire Obsta. They are grandparents to Jessica, Sarah, Sam Butler, Katie and Allison Schuelke.

Robert and Doris Obsta are members of the Fellowship Bible Church. Robert and Doris have traveled in the Czech Republic, Poland, Germany, Scotland, Mexico and England, as well as the United States. Through genealogical research, Robert has regained contact with his Polish family roots. He is currently assisting with the Victoria County Family History Project, and ranching even in drought years. Robert W. Obsta

NICHOLAS ORY

Nicholas Ory was born in or about 1703, in the Province of Lorraine, then mostly part of the Holy Roman Empire. He migrated to Philadelphia, the English Colony of Pennsylvania, arriving in 1736 aboard the ship Princess Augusta. He later moved to Frederick County, Maryland Colony, where at least eight children were born to him and his wife, Anna Christina Strasbach. Anna died in Maryland, and he remarried to Christina Michel, who bore at least three children.

The Chapel at the Presidio La Bahia in Goliad, Texas; Nicholas Ory and his family were at the Presidio in 1769.

In January 1769, Nicholas Ory and his family left Maryland on the ship, La Brittania. While at sea, the ship became lost, eventually making landfall on the Texas coast at Espiritu Santo Bay. Found by Spanish soldiers, the passengers and crew were taken overland to the Presidio de Nuestra Senora de Loretto de la Bahia, near present-day Goliad. The Presidio had been at this location since 1749, and had been at different locations in earlier times.

Nicholas Ory and his family lived and worked at La Bahia, a Spanish Texas settlement center of farming, ranching, and missionary work among the Indians. The Presidio, a fortress, contained housing for settlers, clergy, and soldiers, as well as a royal chapel. A mission, Nuestra Señora del Espiritu Santo de Zuñiga, was nearby to the Presidio.

Some, or possibly all, of the members of the Ory family, having determined to seek their fortunes in the Spanish Louisiana Territory, migrated there. In time, the Orys became one of the prominent planter families of Louisiana.

Nicholas Ory is the 6th great-grandfather of Dennis M. Giuffre (#5474), James D. Giuffre (#5743A), and Richard A. Giuffre (#5744A); and is the 7th great-grandfather of Dennis M. Giuffre, Jr. (#5741A), Joseph A. "Alex" Giuffre (#5742A), and Sam G. Giuffre (#6607M).

JOHN WINSTEAD PAINE

John Winstead Paine was born March 15, 1818, the son of Frances Winstead and James Paine of Giles County, Tennessee. James Paine was the son of Prudence Bumpass and William Paine, a patriot in the American Revolution, who was the son of Mary Hardin and Dr. James Paine. Dr. Paine was a physician and early settler in that part of colonial Granville County, North Carolina, that became Person County, where he was a planter, Justice of the Peace, vestryman, sheriff, lieutenant colonel in the Colonial Militia, and member of the Colonial Assembly of North Carolina. The mother of John Winstead Paine was the daughter of John Winstead of Lauderdale County, Alabama.

John Winstead Paine arrived in Texas on February 1, 1838, and by May of 1839 had settled in San Augustine County, where he received a Class 3 Conditional. Certificate for 640 acres of land as a married man. Having met the requirements of three years residency in Texas, he received an Unconditional Certificate in July of 1844, at which time the Land Commissioner's Board of Sabine County issued him Land Grant number 51 for 640 acres of land, which he located in Smith County.

By 1845, John Winstead Paine had settled permanently in Nacogdoches County, where after the death of his first wife, he married a second time on February 26, 1846, to Asenath Morehead Bone, the daughter of Levicey Donnell McMinn and John Houston Bone, at Douglass, where she had resided with her family since 1841. By his first wife, John Winstead Paine had one son, James P. Paine, born August 4, 1842, in Texas. Asenath Morehead Bone and John Winstead Paine had the following five children, all born in Nacogdoches County: Frances Jane Paine, born May 14, 1847; Robert Foster Paine, born May 27, 1849; Mary Ann Helena Paine, born October 2, 1851; John Bone Paine, born November 13, 1853; and George N. Paine, born June 6, 1858, and died October 3, 1859.

John Winstead Paine bought a farm on Bayou Loco near Douglass in Nacogdoches County, where he farmed and reared his family. He was a Mason, a member of Douglass Masonic Lodge Number 43, and he and his family were members of the Cumberland Presbyterian Church.

John Winstead Paine died June 30, 1859, and his widow, Asenath Morehead Bone Paine, died August 25, 1895. They both died at Douglass, and are buried in the Douglass Cemetery.

MARTIN PALMER (PARMER)

Martin Palmer (Parmer) a signer Declaration of Independence of the Republic of Texas in 1836, was born June 2, 1778 in Halifax, Virginia. He was the son of Sgt. Martin Palmer and Mildred Hardwick. In 1798, he bought land in Madison County, KY, and married Sarah Hardwick. They moved to Dickson, TN in 1801, where he became superintendent of Montgomery Bell Lumber.

Martin Palmer

They moved to Ray County, Missouri, in 1817. Martin was elected to the House of Representatives 1820-24, then was elected senator in1824 before moving to Arkansas and awaiting a land grant on east side of Neches River near present-day Alto, Texas.

Sarah died and was buried adjacent to a well dug by Spanish missionaries in 1690. With several small children, Martin decided to settle at San Augustine to be near Americans. In 1827, he led the Fredonian Rebellion at Nacogdoches and was forced to leave Texas.

Martin married Margaret Neal in 1828; she died in Arkansas in 1832. Martin returned to Texas in 1833 and married Lovisa Anderson Lout.

He was elected to represent Teneha and San Augustine at the Consultation of 1835, and attended the meeting for the Declaration of Independence. He was 58 years old, and Sam Houston appointed him to impress horses for the Texas Army. Many of the documents are now on display at Washington on the Brazos Park.

Lovisa died 1839, and Martin married Zina Kelly and had 4 daughters. He died March 2, 1850 in Jasper County, and was reburied in the Texas State Cemetery in Austin in 1936. Dr. Taylor Pendley, great-great-grandson

WILEY PARKER

Wiley Parker is listed in the Texas Army record which shows that there was a Pvt. Wiley Parker in the 2nd Regiment, Texas Army, under Lt. Col. A.L. Bennett, and he was at Harrisburg in Wier's Detachment during the Battle of San Jacinto. His discharge, signed by Lt. Col. A.L. Bennett, shows that he served three months, from March 12, 1836, to June 12, 1836, when he was discharged,

B. Elmer Spradley,
b. Sept. 1907 San Gabriel, Texas
m. Sept. 8, 1931 Houston, Texas

Wiley Parker was born Nails Creek, Franklin County, Georgia, ca. 1803, and he died 10 March 1847, Walker County, Texas. He moved with his parents on a passport signed by governor of Georgia on 30 March 1809, through the Indian Nation to St. Tammany (now Washington) Parish, Louisiana. They then moved across the Sabine River (near where Hemphill is now) in the Mexican state of Texas. They arrived on March 12, 1822, the date given on an application of land grant.

Wiley was the son of Jesse Parker (born ca. 1775, probably North Carolina; died May 27, 1849, Walker County, Texas, and buried of his land), and Sarah (may be) Wiley (born ca. 1777; died early 1828, Hemphill area). They married about 1797, and moved to Nails Creek about 1798-99.

Wiley Parker married Lucindia Fulcher from San Augustine municipality, ca. 1823, and they lived in East Texas until they received their land grant on 11 March 1835 in Walker County. Lucindia was born 1807 in Illinois (see 1860 Census San Angelo, Texas, where she died after 1860). Nine children were born to this union: Jesse J., born 1824; Willis, born ca. 1825; Francis (Frank), born ca. 1827; Matthew, born ca.1829; Nathaniel D., born ca. 1831; Mary Jane, born ca.1833; Erzenia, born ca. 1835; "Betsy" Elizabeth, born 1836; Wiley Jr., born ca.1840. All but three were born in East Texas; the last three were born in Walker County, Texas. B. Elmer Spradley (great-grandson)

WILLIAM WARING PARKER

William Waring Parker, born 1790 in Philadelphia, PA, descended from the Hallowell family. They, along with the Parkers, were Quakers and among William Penn's first colonists. In 1811, he married Hannah Smith, daughter of Griffith Smith, a Revolutionary soldier and a great-nephew of James Smith, a signer of the Declaration of Independence. Parker was an accountant, a bootmaker, and backed the first silk factory in Philadelphia. In the 1837 depression, he lost everything and moved to Texas.

William W. Parker

Marker of Thomas S. Parker

The family arrived in Galveston on the schooner, Venus, just after a hurricane had completely devastated the island. It must have been quite a change from modern Philadelphia. They established the Planters House, at 22nd and Strand. It was the second hotel on the island and the site of the first town meetings. In 1842, Hannah left the island, moved to New Orleans with some of her family and established the Crescent City Hotel.

A daughter, Ann, who married Thomas Penney, remained in Galveston where they operated Penney and Parsons Store. Two of the sons moved in with the Parsons, and a third son, Thomas, moved back to Texas with his wife Rachel, and became the first sheriff of Nueces County in 1846.

MARTIN PARMER

Martin Parmer (originally spelled Palmer) was born in Virginia on June 4, 1778. For a time, he lived in Missouri and in 1820 was elected as a Representative to the Missouri General Assembly. In 1824, he was elected Senator to the Missouri General Assembly.

In 1825, Parmer arrived in Texas, where in 1826 he was a leader of the Fredonian Rebellion. The Fredonian Rebellion was an unsuccessful attempt to liberate Texas from Mexico almost ten years before the Texas Revolution. Martin Parmer was elected as the delegate from Teneha to the Consultation at San Felipe in 1835, where he nominated Henry Smith for governor of the provisional Texas government. Parmer was elected to the General Council of the provisional government. In 1836, Parmer was elected as a delegate from the San Augustine Municipality to the Convention at Washington, where he was a signer of the Texas Declaration of Independence from Mexico. In 1839, President Mirabeau B. Lamar appointed him Chief Justice of Jasper County.

Martin Parmer died in Jasper County, Texas, on March 2, 1850, at the age of 71. He is buried in State Cemetery in Austin. In 1876, Parmer County was established by the Texas Legislature. The county was named for Martin Parmer. For additional reading on Martin Parmer, see Joe E. and Carolyn R. Ericson's "Martin Parmer – The Man and the Legend," Ericson Books, 1999.

Martin Parmer's grave in the Texas State Cemetery in Austin, Texas.

Martin Parmer was married four times and had at least sixteen children. Martin Parmer's youngest son, John Martin Palmer, was born about 1836 in Jasper County, Texas. John Martin Palmer married Eliza P. Shepperd on January 24, 1861, in Walker County, Texas. Eliza Shepperd was born December 22, 1843, in Montgomery County, Texas. Their youngest son, Isom Palmer, was born August 23, 1882, in Walker County, Texas. On June 20, 1905, Isom Palmer married Minnie Lee Redding in San Jacinto County, Texas. They had two children: Isom Palmer (who went by the name Burl Palmer) and Donnie Lee Palmer, who was born September 3, 1908 or 1909 in San Jacinto County, Texas (the 1910 U.S. Census indicates she was 2 years of age).

Donnie Lee Palmer married Harry Kyle Searle, Sr., on August 15, 1934, in Houston, Texas. Their only son, Harry Kyle Searle, Jr., married Mary Elizabeth Thompson in Houston, Texas, on July 9, 1958. They had four children: Harry Kyle Searle III, Kameron Kent Searle, Kristi Arlen Searle and Karla Alise Searle. Kameron Searle and his wife, Marisa Adlong Searle, have two children: Kayla Elizabeth Searle and Kary Ann Searle. Kristi Searle Grove and her husband, Robert Grove, have three children: Kaitlyn Elizabeth Grove, Andrew Knight Grove and Patrick Austin Grove.

The Palmer/Parmer family reunion will be held in 2001 and is held every two years. For more information or to be added to the reunion mailing list, contact Kameron Searle at 21410 Park York, Katy, Texas 77450. Harry Kyle Searle, Jr. Harry Kyle Searle III Kameron Kent Searle

PATTON-WHITE FAMILY

Samuel Boyd Patton was born August 15, 1787, in South Carolina. He moved to Tennessee in 1802, and married Sarah Stephenson, daughter of Revolutionary soldier James Stephenson and Rosanna, in 1809 in Davidson County, Tenn. He fought in the War of 1812 as a captain.

The family moved to Walker County, Alabama, in about 1816, where Samuel served as a clerk in the Walker County Court in 1830. He also served as a State Representative for three consecutive terms 1834-1836. After he lost his first wife in Alabama, he married a widow, Elizabeth Ballard Deas in 1837, and was the father of seventeen children from two marriages.

He was in Texas by January 1837. He was appointed as the president of the Land Commissioners for the Republic of Texas, and served as a representative from Bastrop County on the 4th Republic of Texas Congress. By 1853, he'd settled on Curry's Creek and helped form Blanco County from Comal County. He served as Chief Justice in Blanco County and Kendall County, which was formed from Blanco County.

He died March 20, 1869 in Kendall County. A Texas Historical Marker was dedicated in 1996 marking his grave.

The first born of Samuel and Sarah Patton was James Madison Patton, born March 15, 1811, in Williamson County, Tennessee. He grew to manhood in Alabama. In 1835, he moved to Mississippi for a short time, but by 1836, he'd moved to Texas to help fight for Texas independence from Mexico. He married Sarah Jane Smithson on Dec. 1, 1846, and they had eight children. He was a Red River Ranger in 1840, the pioneer organization of the Texas Rangers. He served in the Mexican-American War in 1851, for which he received a pension, and participated in many Indian skirmishes on the Texas frontier and in the Civil War. He was sheriff of Caldwell County in 1853-1854. He moved to Smithson's Valley, named for his brother-in-law, for a short time, then settled in Kendall County until after his father's death in 1869. He moved his family to Oak Hill, Travis County, Texas in December 1870, where he lived until his death on November 30, 1900. He is buried in the Oak Hill Cemetery. His third son, James Andrew Patton, donated this land.

50th wedding anniversary of James Madison Patton and Sarah Jane Smithson Patton with seven children. (l. to r.) Back: James Andrew, John McMahon, Anson Jackson, Tom Green, and Robert Lee. Front: Cicero Columbus, James Madison, Sarah Jane (Smithson) and William Franklin.

James Andrew Patton was born January 12, 1853 in Caldwell County, Texas. He was a member of the Frontier Rangers, and was in the last Indian battle of Central Texas at Round Mountain, where he saved his brother's life by killing the Indian who had shot his brother, Cicero Columbus Patton. He was a strong believer of education, donating two acres of land for the Oak Hill School and serving as a school board trustee. There was a new school named in his honor, dedicated in 1986 in Oak Hill. He married Virginia Bishop in Travis County, Texas, on January 18, 1875. They ran a general store in Oak Hill, and this building received a Texas Historical Marker in 1970. He was appointed postmaster general of Oak Hill until rural delivery. He died July 11, 1944, and was buried in Oak Hill Cemetery, next to his wife and near his parents.

Their daughter, Rosa Patton, born August 16, 1879, helped run her parents' general store in Oak Hill. On January 10, 1901, Rosa married John Dudley White, Sr., born June 25, 1879, in Travis County, Texas. Dudley was serving as a Texas Ranger in 1918 when he was killed in the line of duty. He was the son of Robert Emmett White, born January 11, 1852, in Maury County, Tennessee, and Caroline Campbell White. Emmett immigrated to Texas in 1871, where he married Margaret Campbell on March 15, 1874, in Austin, Texas. He served as master of the Onion Creek Masonic Lodge #220 in 1884-1886, was elected as sheriff of Travis County from 1888-1899, was elected mayor of Austin, Texas, from 1900-1905, was elected county judge of Travis County from 1909-1912, and was elected county commissioner, for a total of 28 years in public service.

Emmett had three other sons who also went into law work. Thomas Bruce White, 1881-1971, was a Texas Ranger, FBI agent, warden of the federal prison in Leavenworth, Kansas, and warden at La Tuna Prison in Texas, and served on the Board of Pardons and Paroles for Texas, a total of 54 years in law work. Crockett Coleman "Coley" White, 1883-1952, served as a deputy sheriff and later elected as sheriff of Travis County, Texas. The fourth son, James Campbell "Doc" White, 1884-1969, was a mounted patrolman in Austin, Texas, a Texas Ranger, and served as a FBI agent 1924-1947. When he retired, he had served a total of 42 years as a peace officer. "Doc" White was in on the capture of "Machine Gun Kelley," fought in the gun battle, which killed Ma Barker and part of her gang, and was stationed in Chicago during the John Dillinger hunt.

James M. White

Bruce Lamar White was born May 13, 1914, in Ysleta, Texas, while his father, Dudley White, Sr., was serving as a customs agent. He was the second son of Dudley and Rosa Patton White. He was a M.P. in the U.S. Army during World War II, and worked in security at Convair Aircraft plant in San Diego, CA.

James Morris White, born April 12, 1939, in Austin, Texas, was the second son of Bruce and Lena Fuchs White. James was the president of the Sons of the Republic, Moses Austin Chapter, in 1998, and a 6th-generation Texan. He married Annetta Wells White in Austin, Texas, on September 15, 1966. They built, run, and are proud of their business, the Broken Spoke, an Austin tradition and Texas establishment since 1964. James M. White Annetta White

RIGGS PENNINGTON

Riggs Pennington was born 28 Aug 1787, in Tennessee, to Timothy and Susanna (Riggs) Pennington. His uncle, Richard Pennington, married Hannah Boone, sister of Daniel Boone. Riggs married Joanna Osborne in Kentucky in 1810, and moved to Crawford County, Indiana in 1816, then to Illinois in 1819. Riggs and his family resided in Franklin County and were one of the first county commissioners of Knox County. He served as Justice of the Peace in Schuyler County in 1827, and an election judge the year before. Pennington's family were the first white settlers in McDonough County, and from here they departed to Texas. Riggs had first come to Spanish Texas in 1820, and fought in the Blackhawk War in 1832.

The Penningtons left Galesville, Ill., with friends and neighbors in a wagon train of 12, crossing the Mississippi at Quincy Ill., the Arkansas River at Van Buren, and the Red River at Jonesboro and again at Shreveport. They crossed the Brazos at Old Washington in 1836, one week after the Battle of San Jacinto.

*William W. Hackworth
m. Eliza Jane Pennington
(daughter of Riggs Pennington)*

They purchased a tract of 1225 acres from John W. Cole at $3.25 per acre and established the Pennington homestead five miles northeast of Brenham. They reared a family of 11 and lived out their lives in Washington County. Riggs died in 1869 and Joanna died in 1873. Both are buried on the Old Homeplace with other family members.

ALEJO DE LA ENCARNACION PEREZ

Alejo de la Encarnacion Perez, a 5th-generation Bejareño, was born to Juana Navarro and Alejo Perez on March 23, 1835, in the Villa de San Fernando de Bejar. His uncle, Jose Antonio Navarro, was one of the two native-born Texans who signed the Texas Declaration of Independence (the other signer being Francisco Ruiz). Alejo married Maria Antonia Rodriguez in 1853, and they had four children: Corina de Jesus, Lucia, Alejo Guadalupe, and Osvaldo. His second marriage was to Florencia Valdez, and they had seven children.

State of Texas Historical Marker at the grave site of Alejo de la Encarnacion Perez at San Fernando Cemetery No. 1, San Antonio, Texas.

Alejo and his mother were inside the Alamo during the Battle of the Alamo, and were among the nineteen known survivors. By this time, Alejo's father had died and his mother had remarried Horace A. Alsbury. Alejo is recognized as being the youngest survivor of the Battle at the Alamo, and is also recognized as being the last known survivor to have died. He died on October 19, 1918, in San Antonio, Texas, and is buried at San Fernando Cemetery No. 1. In October 1999, a Texas Historical Marker was placed at his grave site.

During his life, Alejo served in the Confederate Army here in Texas. As a citizen of San Antonio, he was a member of the Executive Committee of the Young Democratic Club of Bexar; he served as assistant city marshal, deputy city marshal, and second assistant marshal in the police department; he served in the fire department; and at one time he was ditch commissioner.

Alejo de la Encarnacion Perez

To this date many of Alejo de la Encarnacion Perez's direct descendants still live in San Antonio, Texas, his great-great-grandson, Gilbert I. Patiño, Jr., being one of these descendants. Gilbert I. Patiño, Jr. #3869

JOSIAH DIXON PERRY AND REBECCA PERRY

Josiah Dixon Perry, born circa 1794, in Franklin County, NC, was the son of Solomon Perry and Mary Louisa Crudup. He married his second cousin, Rebecca Perry (born circa 1796, Franklin County, daughter of Joshua Perry and Patty Cheves), according to a marriage bond dated 17 March 1817. He moved his family by 1827 to Montgomery County, Alabama (to the area soon became Lowndes County). Later he moved to Harrison County, Texas, arriving in February 1840.

Josiah Dixon Perry, Port Caddo area, Harrison Co., Texas circa 1867, shortly before his death.

He received a 3rd Class 640-acre Headright, and his 3 oldest sons each received 320-acre 3rd Class Headrights. A prosperous cotton planter, Josiah D. Perry owned over 3,000 acres in Harrison and Marion counties, Texas, and Caddo Parish, La. He loved parties and fox hunts. He raised jacks and owned a sawmill. He paid taxes on 53 slaves in 1861.

In 1862, he and two other men bought half of the Nash Iron Works at Jefferson, turned it into a Confederate munitions factory.

"Capt. Joe," a Mason at Concord Lodge near Blocker, died in 1867. When Capt. Joe was found, he had been hunting. He had suffered a stroke and was propped up against a tree, gun across his lap, his hunting dogs around him. According to his physician and brother, Dr. Harwood Pope Perry, he died March 16th, "Saturday night after supper."

NAPOLEON BONAPARTE PERRY

Napoleon Bonaparte Perry ("Nap," "N.B."), the son of Josiah Dixon Perry and Rebecca Perry, was born Louisburg, N.C., 24 July 1820. His parents moved to today's Lowndes County, Ala.,

Napolean Bonaparte Perry and his second wife Margaret Amanda Burford at North Webb, Texas circa 1901.

by 1827, and then emigrated to Texas, arriving 1840. Nap, as a young adult, claimed his 3rd Class 320 acres close to the Louisiana border in the area of Port Caddo, Harrison County, Texas.

He was overseer to his father's plantation, but was a merchant by 1850 in Port Caddo. He briefly co-owned a steamboat, the "Osceola," on the Red River. He married in 1847 to Sarah Jane Gibson, a local schoolteacher. They had 3 children.

In 1854 he moved his family to Tarrant County, the William Logan survey. His wife, "Sallie," died in 1855, and he married second to Margaret Amanda Melvina Burford in 1857. They moved 1862 to the Webb area (now Arlington). They had 9 more children.

N.B. served in Capt. M.J. Brinson's Cavalry Company, Johnson Station Rangers, Texas State Troops, and in Company A., 15th Texas Cavalry, CSA, at the Battle of Elkhorn Tavern.

He organized drives for new county roads, gave land for the second Loyd School, was an election official at the local poll, and a leader in the Baptist Church. Kicked by a horse in 1903, he contracted pneumonia, died aged 83. Patrick McKenna

DAVID ARTHUR PEVEHOUSE

David Arthur Pevehouse was born in Lawrence County, Arkansas, the son of Jacob Pevehouse and Rachel Kellum, grandson of John Pevehouse and Catherine Smith, on the 31st of December 1811, and died 29th of April 1897, in Navarro County, Texas.

Grave marker of David Pevehouse (1811-1897) at Old Pevehouse Cemetery, Navarro Co., TX

In Lawrence County, Arkansas, he married his first wife, Cynthia Ross, on 14th of October 1830. In January 1834, he and his family emigrated to Texas as part of Austin's Colony, settling in Brazoria County. In 1835, he enlisted in Texas's War with Mexico, in which he fought until hostilities ceased and Texas won her independence. It is thought that he fought in or near San Jacinto.

He moved to Fort Bend County in 1837, where he lived until the death of his wife, Cynthia, on the 6th of June 1841. He then moved to Montgomery County, where he married Malinda Pierce, daughter of Lewis and Alsey Pierce, on 29th of September 1842. She was born 22nd of July 1826, and died 31st of October 1906.

In 1851, he and his family moved to Navarro County, settling near Frost, Texas.

He freighted supplies from Houston, the nearest market at the time, by wagon teams for trade. Active in the Baptist Church, he was ordained a deacon, and was honored as a delegate to the Baptist Association 26 times. He gave liberally to all good enterprises, especially to the schools and churches of his community. At the time of his death in 1987, David Arthur Pevehouse had lived in our great Republic and state 63 years. " He was truly an old Texan."

The children of David and Cynthia were: Mary, Prudence, and Nelson; the children of David and Malinda were: Cynthia, David Arthur Jr., Alice, Rachel, Lewis, Malinda Adelaide, Sarah, John William, James Franklin, and Walter Lavosier. Frank Newburn Scruggs, great-great-grandson 94642, Coy Powell Scruggs, great-great-grandson #4825, Coy Powell Scruggs, Jr., great-great-great-grandson #4827, Roby Andrew Scruggs, great-great-great-grandson #4826, Charles Curtis Shockley, great-great-great-grandson #4645

DR. JAMES AENEAS PHELPS

James Aeneas Phelps was born in Granby, Connecticut, in 1793, the son of James Eno Phelps and Philander Rice Phelps. After college, Dr. Phelps moved to Wilkinson County, Mississippi, where he married Rossette Adeline Yerby on April 18, 1821, and they later had six children.

Dr. Phelps came to Texas aboard the "Lively" as one of Stephen F. Austin's "Old 300." His land grant, called Orozimbo Plantation, was on the Brazos River in Brazoria County. Dr. Phelps was active in the affairs of the community. It is recorded that he was actively treating the ill during the cholera epidemic in San Felipe de Austin in October 1833.

He was attached to the medical staff during the Battle of San Jacinto, where he set up a hospital in the home of Lorenzo de Zavala. After Santa Anna was captured, he was a prisoner at Orozimbo from July through November 1836. Mrs. Phelps once saved his life from attempted assassination, and Dr. Phelps saved Santa Anna's life after he attempted suicide.

In 1845, Dr. Phelps was a member of a Brazoria committee to prepare an address in favor of the Annexation of Texas to the United States. Dr. Phelps' will was probated on November 9, 1847, and he was buried at Orozimbo. In 1936, the state of Texas erected two granite monuments at the site.

Aristide Fredrick Renaud is the great-grandson of Dr. James Aeneas Phelps, through Phelps' daughter, Almira Louise Phelps.

JEAN NICOLAS PICHOT SR.

Jean Nicolas Pichot, Sr. was born 15 Jan 1785, in Nantillois Meuse, France, and died about 1845. He was bitten by a rattlesnake while out gathering straw for the roof of his house only a few months of arriving in Texas. His burial site is unknown (rock pile near the Helotes) Castroville -13th and 14th families on "el ebro" with Capt. Perry in command - "the first ship to come!"

Castro colonists- In 1841, he left France and arrived in Galveston in January 1842. His father, Ogier Pichot, was born 20 May 1740, in Nantillois Meuse, France. His mother was Therese Antoine, born 1747. Ogier was the son of Andre Pichot and Marie Marins.

His wife, Marie Elizabeth Josephine Charpentier, was born 18 April 1785, Grandpre Ardennes, France. She married Jean Nicolas Sr. on 5 May 1807, in Milly Meuse, France, where she died 9 Feb. 1851. She and Jean had 12 children.

Adolph Albert and Minnie Eva (Bendele) Pichot's wedding photo.

Mollie Dawson and Albert Adolph Pichot

Marie stayed in France and never came to Texas because she was afraid of the wild country and animals and to await the birth of a grandchild from their son, Louis born 2 Jan. 1813 Milly, France died 9 May, 1877 Milly, France and Marie Marguerite Gerard Pichot born 1814 France, this third child to be born was Marie Eugenie born 22 Feb. 1843, oldest child was Jean Nicolas Pichot born 13 Aug. 1837, second, Laurent, born 2 June 1839, Jean Baptist born 2 March 1848, and later Marie Josephine, born 20 Dec. 1849, all born in Milly Meuse, France.

Three of Nicolas and Marie's children came along to Texas on the hopes of getting rich and recovering their estate, as it had been confiscated at Napoleon's conquering of France. Marie was of royal blood and now found herself poor and without. Her husband was forced to make rope in order to support the family in Milly. The promises of Castro and Texas were great. Other than Jean Nicolas Jr. were sisters: Marie Jeanne Pichot, born 13 May 1824, Milly Meuse, France, married Gerhard Ihnken 22 Oct. 1846 in Castroville, Texas; and Alexis Pichot, born 24 June 1826, Milly Meuse, France, married Pierre Francois Pingenot 22 Oct. 1846 in Castroville, Texas. Note: shortly after the arrival to Helotes, Texas, Jean Nicolas was bitten by a rattlesnake and died, so the two young girls were married on the same day since there was no way to return to France.

Son Jean Nicolas Pichot, Jr. was born 15 Sept. 1819, in Milly Meuse, France, and died (murdered by a man named Gould, who confessed on his death bed in Del Rio, Texas 28 Feb. 1864. He is buried in Old Cemetery Cross Hill in Castroville, Texas.

He was murdered for his daily receipts in his saloon. He had seen a shadowy figure and had slept over his money. In the morning, he was found with his head chopped off with an ax.

The wife of Jean Nicolas Pichot, Jr. was Regina Haller, born about 1829 in France. They married 24 Nov. 1846 in Castroville. Regina died 12 Feb. 1892, and her burial was near Austin, Travis, Texas, in the Salem Lutheran Church Cemetery under the name of Regina (Rachel) Rich, from her last marriage. She served Castroville and Austin, Texas, as a midwife. After Nicolas was murdered, she moved to Austin where she married a man named Rich and they also had children together.

Regina's father was "4" Paul Haller and her mother was Maria Anne Luttenbacher Haller (it is not clear if Luttenbacher was her maiden name or if she remarried after Paul died) born around 1808; Maria Anne signed a marriage certificate on April 9, 1855 for Josephine Haller to Nicolas Schmitt by the following name Mariane Lutterbacher) They came on the ship *Henrick* in 1843.

The son of Regina and Nicolas was Albert Adolph Pichot, born 7 Aug. 1862 in Castroville. He was married 19 June 1882 in Travis, Texas to Mary (Mollie) Dawson, and he died 6 Jan. 1936. His burial was in Uvalde, Texas, Cemetery. He had a dairy in Uvalde, Texas, and for the large part of his life raised twelve kids and the Jersey cattle that his father-in-law had brought back from the Civil War. Tom Dawson had been a prisoner of war, captured at Shiloh and was released in Chicago, IL, from where he walked home to Austin, Texas. Mollie's sister (Fannie) and her husband (Casey Jones) had come to Uvalde with Albert and Mollie in the early 1900s. They delivered milk to as far away as Hondo (40 miles), with special buggies and blocks of ice and ten-gallon milk cans. His daughter (Myrtle and husband John Hardt) took the dairy industry to Eagle Pass, Texas and continued the tradition. Albert and his family walked to Medina County with their family from Austin when they came. He remarried after the death of Mary a couple of times, and finally died after selling out in Uvalde up in Decatur, Texas. He died from kidney failure in Houston at his son William's (Bill) house. In Decatur, he and his new wife had bought a ranch. When their sons — Leonard, Louis, Jim, and Bill — went up for a portion of their inheritance, they were asked to leave without a cent, as the new wife had persuaded Albert to trust her with the money, and this cut out the kids. The Nicholas Pichot, Jr. and Regina Haller children are Theresa, Catherine, Maria Emily Emma, Louis Nicolas, and Albert Adolph.

Albert's wife is Mary Lucy (Mollie) Dawson (Austin, Texas), was born 16 Sept 1866 in Missouri, and died 18 Jan 1923 from shock from a broken leg. Her burial was in Uvalde, Texas, Cemetery. She was the product of an Irish marriage, her father being Scot-Irish and her mother a Patty Irish. Mollie was the middle child of six.

Adolph Albert Pichot, the son of Albert Adolph Pichot and Mollie Dawson Pichot, was born 29 Aug 1886, in Austin, Texas. He married 24 May 1911 in Hondo, and died 4 Sept. 1943 of cancer. He was buried in the Hondo, Texas, Cemetery. He was a farmer, rancher, wolf hunter, and the father of six children three boys and three girls.

He was the third of twelve children from Albert Adolph Pichot and Mollie Dawson Pichot: Myrtle Matilda, May Theresa, Adolph Albert "Dolph", Louis Henry, John Thomas, Joseph Leopold "Joe", William Fred "Bill or Willie", Antoinette Lucia "Nettie", Leonard Benjamin, James Bets, Dollie Fannie, and Ernest Adkins Pichot.

Dolph's wife was Minnie Eva Bendele, born 28 May 1886 in Hondo. She died 11 Jan. 1985, in Hondo, from natural old age. She was buried in Hondo, Texas Cemetery. After Adolph's death, Minnie married "?" Albert Mumme, native of Medina County, Texas.

Adolph and Minnie's son Charles John Pichot, was born 13 March 1917, and married 24 Nov. 1936, in New Fountain Methodist Church in Medina County and will be buried in Hondo, Texas, Cemetery. The farmer, rancher, and firefighter retired early from a knee injury. He and his wife had four big boys. Charles John was the third son of Adolph and Minnie; other children were George Albert, Homer Louis, Charles John, Myrtle Eva May, Adell Doll, and Ada Belle Pichot.

Charles John's wife, "10" Alice Ruth Saathoff, was born 17 Oct 1913, in Quihi, Medina County. She died 24 Apr 1987 in Hondo, and is buried in Hondo, Texas, Cemetery. She was the youngest of five girls.

The son of Charles John and Alice Ruth is Thomas Earl Pichot, born 1 27 1938. He works as a business owner and has worked in refrigeration, pawnshop and welding. He married Jan 26 1957 in McCamey Texas and will be buried in the Hondo city cemetery He and his wife had two daughters. He was the oldest of four boys, the others being Dennis Leon, Clifton Charles and Perry Lee Pichot

Thomas Earl's wife, Georgia Gwendolyn Partney Pichot operates a pawnshop. She was born 9-5-1937 in Throckmorton, Texas, oldest of seven children.

The daughter of Tom and Georgia, Glynn Rae Pichot Brandt, works as a housewife and business partner in the communications radio business. She was born 9-12-1958 in Hondo, Texas. She married "?" Jim Palmer on 3-14-1981. Glynn Rae was later married 9 Apr. 1988, in Dallas, Texas, to Robert Reed Brandt, an electrical engineer born 8 Sept. 1954 in Brownsville, Texas. They had a son and a daughter before they divorced Dec 2, 1999.

Glynn's daughter is "13" Kayla Larae Pichot Brandt, born Feb. 27 1989, and her son is "14" Russell Reed Pichot Brandt, born Jan. 16, 1992.

Another daughter of Tom and Gwen is Cindee Kay Pichot, a lawyer, born 17 May 1960, in Hondo, Texas. She married 22 Nov. 1984 divorced Nov. 1995, husband

Gerald McBride Link, propane salesperson, born 12 Jan. 1956. She works alone as a lawyer in Norman and Oklahoma City area - no children.

Second son of Charles John and Alice is Dennis Leon born 19 Oct. 1940 married 26 Jan. 1966 to Laura Jane Stricker born 27 Jan. 1945 Bandera, TX, they have a daughter Stephanie Ann Pichot Gualt born 13 July 1966 married 13 June 1992 Arthur Gualt born 24 Jan. 1954 Laredo, TX. They have a son Joshua Thomas Gualt born 28 May 1995 and son Justin Charles Gualt born 8 Jan. 1999. Son of Dennis and Laura is Kenneth Charles Pichot born 12 Aug. 1968, science teacher, who has a son, Kyle Blake Pichot, born 10 March 1998. Third son of Charles John and Alice is Clifton Charles born 3 Sept. 1946, married Maria Guadalupe Barrera Pichot born 12 Dec. 1953 from Falfurrias, TX who had a daughter (Angela) from an earlier marriage. Fourth son of Charles and Alice is Perry Lee, born 12 Nov. 1948, married 8 Sept. 1991 to Suzanne Sterling Fox born 21 Feb. 1953 from Oklahoma City-she had three daughters Christy, Amy and Amanda from an earlier marriage.

From this shaky beginning, the Pichots in this lineage that came from France to Texas now number more than three thousand people. They live all over the world and several groups have returned to the home place in Lorraine, France. A reunion of all is held at the Hondo, Texas, City Park each October or November. Texans and Castro colonists Non Texans Written by Thomas Earl Pichot

JAMES BRADFORD PIER

A native of Circleville, Ohio, J.B. Pier came to Texas in February 1835, at the age of 21, with his wife of one year, Lucy Merry Pier (Jan.27, 1811 -Feb 24, 1897). He was the son of Ira Webster Pier and Sarah Bradford. (Sarah Bradford's ancestors were descendants of the Mayflower).

J.B. and Lucy Pier floated down the Mississippi River on a flat boat to New Orleans. There, they took the required oath to the Catholic Church and were granted a passport into Texas by the Mexican government

They went to Brazosport and walked up the Brazos River to Washington on the Brazos, where Sam Houston was forming his army for the War for Independence. Many of the wives were left near the town of Nacogdoches while the men went to fight.

James Bradford Pier when commissioned as a Texas Veteran. Houston, Texas.

Texas Historical Commission marker of James Bradford Pier.

Because Pier was a pharmacist, during the San Jacinto Battle he was detailed as a rear guard at the medical detachment camp opposite Harrisburg a few miles from the battlefield. For his six months service in the Texas Army, he was given two grants of six hundred forty acres. That early mosquito-infested swampland today is all the area around the Sharpstown Shopping Center in Houston.

After the war, he settled in the early Texas town of Travis in Austin County, where he was a farmer, stock raiser, teacher, and merchant. He served as Justice of the Peace of Austin County, and was the first postmaster of the Travis community. The Piers had five children, three of whom lived to become adults, married and had families of their own: Lucy E. Pier (5/7/1837-10/27/1880); Sarah Charlotte Pier (11/7/1840-8/1921); William Henry Pier (1/23/1843-5/16/1843, died at age 3 months); Samuel Bradford Pier (7/22/1844-3/22/1914); and Julia Louise Pier (6/18/1847-6/23/1847 died at 5 days).

J.B. Pier died February 5, 1888. He, his wife, and family are buried in a family cemetery plot marked by a historical marker, near Kinney, Texas. Donald Gordon Wiley L# 1741, Douglas Wiley L# 1740, Douglas Wiley,II L# 2369, Barney Wiley L# 2609, John Dodge,III L# 2347, David Fersing L# 1779, Steven Fersing L# 1943, Bob Bell L# 1733, Doug Bell L# 1806, Gregg Bell L# 1876

The picture of J.B. Pier taken at a Texas veterans reunion is included. A copy of the Mexican passport is included. (We have the original)

JOHN GOODLOE WARREN PIERSON

John Goodloe Warren Pierson combined his talents of Indian fighter, soldier, surveyor, land developer, judge and lawman during his life in the frontier communities of Arkansas and Texas. Pierson was one of six sons of John and Elizabeth (Warren)

Pierson, born on February 15, 1795, in Person County, North Carolina. He moved in 1805 with his parents to western Kentucky, which later became Union County. Pierson's father served in General George Washington's Continental Army at Valley Forge, Camden and in other actions during the American Revolution.

Pierson married on January 17, 1815, Purity Ruffin Pennington in Union County, Kentucky, and they had three children before her death. In 1818, Pierson moved to the Red River area of Texas, created in 1820 as Miller County, Arkansas Territory. The site where Pierson settled was marked in 1936 as the first Anglo-American settlement of Lamar County, Texas. In Miller County, Pierson was a deputy sheriff (1825), coroner (1826), county surveyor (1828), sheriff (1829), commander of the 9th Militia with the rank of major (1828), and magistrate of the settlement of Pecan Point (1828-29). When the Indian situation worsened in Miller County, Pierson requested on March 22, 1828, that George Izard, governor of the Arkansas Territory, grant him permission to remove the Shawnee Indians with the militia. With the governor's approval, Pierson, commanding 62 volunteers and with the assistance of Colonel William Rector, adjutant general of the militia, Arkansas Territory, forced the troublesome Shawnees to leave the territory peaceably.

Pierson married on December 11, 1826, Elizabeth Montgomery, the daughter of William Montgomery of Miller County. They had three children before her death on September 15, 1833. Pierson moved to Nacogdoches, Texas, about 1830 and joined Stephen F. Austin's colony in October 1831, continuing his surveying activities. He received one league of land in Fayette County through Austin's third empresario contract on November 2, 1832.

Sterling C. Robertson, empresario of the Nashville colony (Robertson's colony), appointed Pierson on December 22, 1833, his "true and lawful attorney" to issue certificates to settlers wishing to settle in the colony and to "do all things relative of said colony." On September 17, 1834, William H. Steele, land commissioner of the colony, appointed Pierson the principal surveyor. Pierson laid out in 1834 the capital of the colony, Sarahville de Viesca, on the west bank at the Falls of the Brazos. To protect the colony, Pierson, Sterling C. Robertson and James W. Parker signed a friendship treaty with twelve Indian chiefs in February 1835.

Pierson married in 1835 Narcissa (Cartwright) Slatter, a daughter of Peter Cartwright. They had three children. Slatter and Pierson each received title to one league of land in the Nashville colony on December 10, 1834.

During the early stages of the Texas Revolution, Pierson became a member of the Committee of Safety and Correspondence of Viesca when it was created on May 17, 1835. Pierson was elected on October 5, 1835, a delegate to represent the municipality of Viesca at the Consultation of 1835 at San Felipe de Austin. At the Consultation, he served on the "Committee of Five," creating the Corps of Texas Rangers on October 17. He was appointed a commissioner to organize the militia at Viesca in the war against Mexico on November 26, and served as secretary of the General Council.

Pierson and Colbert Baker proceeded with their plans to develop the town of Independence in Washington County, Texas, when they purchased on October 30, 1834, contiguous parcels of land from Thomas S. Saul. On November 30, 1835, after surveying and "laying off" the townsite consisting of 78 acres, Pierson and Baker sold one-fourth of their undivided interest in the townsite to Amasa F. Burchard. Pierson, Baker, Burchard, and Robert Stevenson, a fourth proprietor, executed a bond on December 2, 1835, which spelled out their responsibilities as partners in the development of the town.

During the election held in the Nashville colony on February 1, 1836, Pierson was defeated by Sterling C. Robertson and George C. Childress as a delegate to represent the municipality of Milam (Viesca) at the Convention of 1836. The acting governor of the provisional government of Texas, James W. Robinson, commissioned Pierson on February 13, 1836, his aide-de-camp for Milam with the rank of colonel. Pierson was ordered to recruit and equip men for military service in the war against Mexico and to report them to the commander at Gonzales. Pierson informed Robinson that the militia would be ready on March 19 or as soon as arms, ammunition and provisions were procured. Pierson also provided aid to Sterling C. Robertson's company of rangers located at Fort Milam during 1836 and the Texas army in 1836 and 1837 by supplying food and other supplies.

After the defeat of Santa Anna at the Battle of San Jacinto, Pierson moved his family in June 1836 from Milam to an area of Washington County (later partitioned into Montgomery and Grimes counties) that he named Hi Point, located near the present settlement of Stoneham. Pierson built his home at Hi Point where he farmed, operated a general merchandise store, and raised fine horses and other live stock. He built and operated a race track nearby where horse races were held regularly.

Based on reports that the Mexican Congress had repudiated the agreements that Santa Anna had made with the ad interim government of Texas and that General José Urrea was organizing a large Mexican army to invade Texas, ad interim president David G. Burnet issued on June 20, 1836, a proclamation calling for volunteers to meet the enemy. Pierson organized on June 30 in Washington County a militia company consisting of 74 men. He reported his company to Brigadier General Thomas Jefferson Green, whose brigade was located at Cole's Settlement. On the same day, Pierson was commissioned a captain of cavalry, in Green's Brigade, Republic of Texas army, by Green. For his service from June 30 to December 30, 1836, Pierson received on August 22, 1845, a 640-acre land grant in Milam County. Pierson was nominated captain of volunteers of Washington County on May 31, 1837, by President Sam Houston to serve in the Regiment of Mounted Gun Men.

During "Archer's War" in June 1840, after most of the Montgomery County Militia Regiment had abandoned the chase, Pierson led his militia company in hot pursuit of a band of Cherokee and Kickapoo Indians that had murdered J.M. Tidwell and had taken his wife and three children hostage near present Calvert, Texas.

After the capture of San Antonio de Bexar by General Rafael Vásquez and General Adrian Woll in March and September 1842, President Sam Houston ordered Alexander Somervell on October 3, 1842, to organize the militia and volunteers and invade Mexico. Pierson organized a company of volunteers and joined the South Western army at San Antonio de Bexar, later called the Somervell expedition. While on a scouting expedition of the area, Pierson's company skirmished with Comanches on November 9.

After the Texas army had captured Laredo and Guerrero, Mexico, Somervell ordered the army on December 19 to return to Gonzales, Texas, and disband. Pierson, with four other captains and most of the army, ignored the order, organizing the Mier expedition. The reasons given for not obeying the order were presented in a letter written by J.D. Cocke and endorsed by the captains on January 12, 1843.

Pierson and his company reluctantly surrendered to General Pedro de Ampudia on December 26, 1842, at Mier, Mexico, after a battle of 18 hours. In 1845, General Thomas J. Green, in his book on the Mier expedition, gave Pierson and his men "lasting credit" for their united stand against capitulation. On May 20, 1843, Colonel William S. Fisher, commander of the Mier expedition, described the morale of his men immediately prior to surrender. He wrote. "...I found two of the smallest companies under the command of Captain Reese of Brazoria (County) and Captain Pierson of Montgomery (County) united to a man and prepared to fight to the last extremity. The others were in indescribable confusion..."

Pierson was one of the Texas prisoners of war who over powered the Mexican guards at El Rancho Salado, Mexico, on February 11, 1843, making his escape. He was later recaptured, drew a white bean for life at El Rancho Salado on March 25, 1843, and was later released from Santiago Prison at Mexico City on September 16, 1844. Being concerned for the welfare of his fellow soldiers, Pierson served in 1844 on a committee that petitioned the Congress of the Republic of Texas requesting compensation for the men who participated in the Mier expedition.

Pierson served in 1848 as county commissioner of Grimes County. He died at Hi Point, Grimes County, on May 7, 1849, and was buried beside two sons in the Joel Greenwood Cemetery, later called the Saunder's Cemetery, located near Plantersville, Texas. He left an estate of approximately 20,000 acres of land in Texas.

After Texas seceded from the union in 1861, Pierson's five living sons fought in the Confederate Army. During the Sesquicentennial Celebration of Texas Independence, a monument was erected on March 2, 1986, at the Falls County Courthouse, by the Falls County Historical Commission honoring Sterling C. Robertson, Pierson and other Nashville colonists. EGP/jdw Edwin Gray Pierson Jr. #6269

ELIZABETH PLEMMONS TUMLINSON

Elizabeth Plemmons was born in Lincoln, North Carolina, on July 7, 1778, the daughter of John Plemmons and Elizabeth Jane. She married John Jackson Tumlinson, Sr., in Buncombe, Lincoln County, North Carolina, in 1796, and came with him to Texas as part of the "Old 300" original Austin Colony settlers.

Widowed in 1823 when her husband, John, was killed by Indians on a mission to San Antonio to secure ammunition for the Texas Rangers, she stayed on in the colony with her children. On the deed of August 16, 1824, she is granted one league and one labor of land in the Austin 1 Colony in Colorado County.

From 1828, there is a transcription of an article of agreement entered into between her and George Foley, wherein he agrees to do a great deal of specific work on her house and land, the details of each chore laid out. In return, he is sold a piece of the land on which Elizabeth is then living. Some of the details of this agreement include: "George Foley doth bind and obligate himself to do a certin job of work which is to put up a poarch on each side of the house or the two houses and entry that she now lives in and cover them with new boards... Likewise the comers cut down and new sils under the old house and one steeper and the top throne off the chimney and built up in the new... And pourches the pourches is to be eight feet wide and the house is to be boarded on the inside up to the top... The said Foley is if cauled apon six months previous to his doeing it to make two thousand nails haul and put them up for which he is to have fourty dollars... Mrs. Tumlinson is to find team and wagon the said Foley is to haul all the timber for the above mentioned house and likewise the said Foley is to put up poast and rail fence around Mrs. Tumlinsons the yard and house for which he is to have one dollar a pannel...."

Elizabeth died in Colorado County on January 5, 1829. Deed record book G records the distribution of her land, that land which had originally been petitioned for by her husband, John, then granted to Elizabeth after his death. The partitioning among her heirs was drawn up on December 19, 1833, and names those who were to inherit: Jane Tumlinson Ratliff, Peter Tumlinson, Joseph Tumlinson, Catherine Tumlinson DeMorse, John Tumlinson, and Elizabeth Tumlinson Taylor. The land was divided into six sections, and then names were drawn out of a hat to determine who was given each specific section. James L. Dannheim, #6736

DR. JOEL PONTON

Dr. Joel Ponton was born July 3, 1802, in Virginia to William and Isabelle Ponton. Joel acquired some education so that he was equally versed in theology and medicine. He migrated to Boonville, Missouri, where he married Sarah Reavis on January 5, 1827. In 1833, the Pontons left Missouri to join their kin in Texas. Sarah died August 31, 1837. Dr. Joel married four more times, with each wife, except the last, preceding him in death. He married Rhoda Delaney, March 28, 1837; Mary Henderson on July 14, 1850; Mrs. M.A. Beedle in 1869; and Mrs. Harriet W. Koonce on September 5, 1871. From these marriages, Dr. Joel fathered nineteen children.

Dr. Joel Ponton

Dr. Joel and E. M. Benignant served as the principal doctors to the Lavaca community in the period from 1834 to 1840. He enjoyed a large practice in those years, serving his patients on horseback. On August 5, 1840, while en route to Gonzales, Joel and Tucker Foley were attacked by twenty-seven Comanches. Foley was killed and Ponton was left for dead with two arrows in his back. He crawled to the Zumwalt Settlement to receive aid and sound the alarm. This was the first Indian raid of the Indian War, which ended at the Battle of Plum Creek. On October 31, 1841, Parson Joel Ponton organized a congregation of the Church of Christ on the "Rio Navidad." Ponton died September 5, 1871. He is buried on the old home site in Lavaca County. 2nd Great-grandson - Paul W. Ponton #6603M 3rd Great-grandson - Robert W. Ponton SRT# 6846AH

EDWARD B. POWELL

Edward B. Powell was born on February 24, 1816, in South Carolina, the son of Stephen Powell and Patience Bomar.

In 1836, Texas sent out a call to the United States for troops to assist in its fight for independence. In Dalonega, Georgia, a company was being formed. Edward B. Powell, 20 years old, headed for Georgia and joined the volunteers. The company, commanded by Capt. G.A. Parker, arrived in San Augustine, Texas, and was mustered into service on June 12, 1836.

The war had ended at the Battle of San Jacinto on April 21. The Texians there, unlike the forces at the Alamo and Goliad, were mostly residents of Texas, and most returned to their homes. There was still a need of an army. This was met by companies like Capt. Parker's.

When Sam Houston went to New Orleans for treatment of his wound, Gen. Thomas Rusk took command of the army. Capt. Parker's company and similar units moved westward in the wake of the retreating Mexicans. Headquarters was finally established at Victoria. On the way there, the soldiers buried the victims of the massacre at Goliad with full military honors.

Edward Powell received $24 for his three months service and entitlement to 320 acres. He returned to South Carolina, married and had several children. One of these, Y.H.E. Powell, was my maternal grandfather. Chester A. Howell, John R. Howell, Michael Dylan Schafer, Colin Mathew Schafer

HENRY WYNKOOP RAGUET (1796-1877)

Henry Wynkoop Raguet, son of James Michael and Anne Raguet, was born on February 11, 1796, in Bucks County, Pennsylvania. After serving in the War of 1812, Raguet soon moved with his wife, the former Marcia Ann Towers, to Cincinnati, Ohio, where he was in business and elected a director of the Bank of the United States in 1827,

Raguet failed in his business. After his discharge from bankruptcy, probably in February 1833, he made a trip to New Orleans, where he became acquainted with Sam Houston and John Durst, who induced him to make a trip with them into Texas. They reached Nacogdoches some time in March 1833, and Raguet decided to make his home there.

Raguet returned to Ohio by way of Vicksburg, Mississippi, where he made the acquaintance of a struggling young merchant, William C. Logan, who also decided to move to Texas. The firm of Logan and Raguet began its mercantile business in Nacogdoches in November 1833, and was successful from the start. Raguet continued in this business until his retirement in 1852.

In the meantime, on December 10, 1835, Raguet was appointed Treasurer of the Committee of Vigilance and Safety for Nacogdoches; later he was chairman. On February 9, 1837, he was appointed postmaster of Nacogdoches. He continued to live there until 1873, when he moved to Marshall, where he died on December 8, 1877.

ELIJAH RATLIFF (1798 - 1837)

Elijah Ratliff was born in Georgia in 1798. One family story is that he and four brothers came to Texas on horseback, coming through Tennessee and Arkansas. His first child, John, was born in Texas in 1822, and Elijah is not listed as one of the "Old 300" original settlers, so it looks like he actually preceded them.

He had married Jane Tumlinson, daughter of John Tumlinson and Elizabeth Plemmons, who were part of Austin's original colony, and they all did live in the same area. As both Elijah and the Tumlinsons were in Arkansas before coming to Texas, this is likely where he would have met and married Jane, coming on ahead of the rest of the Tumlinsons.

In 1824, a Militia Election was held at the house of James Cummins, alcalde of the River Colorado, on May 15, 1824. James would have replaced John Tumlinson, Sr., Elijah's father-in-law, who was the original alcalde until he was killed by Indians. At this meeting, twenty men were present to vote for their captain and lieutenant. Among those present was Elijah, as well as several Tumlinsons.

The Texas General Land Office has on file a character certificate for Elijah, done in 1834, which certifies that Elijah was a man of good character, industrious, friendly to the Catholic religion and to the laws of the country, and a married man with a family. This character certificate was in Spanish, and was obtained for the purpose of presenting it to the commissioner when applying for a Mexican land grant.

Elijah filed his request for land from the Mexican government out of Nacogdoches on November 15, 1834, stating that he had settled land December 21, 1826, on the Trinity River. He was granted one league of land, obtained through Jose Vehlein's empresario contract with the Mexican state of Coahuila and Texas. The petition section shows that Elijah had a wife and four children at that time. The land covered by this title is located in what is today Polk County.

Elijah died in Colorado, Texas in the winter of 1836-7. His widow, Jane, was left with five children, the youngest only a few months old. James L. Dannheim #6736

RICHARD RATLIFF (1830 - 1904)

Richard Ratliff, son of Elijah Ratliff and Jane Tumlinson Ratliff, was born in Gonzales, Texas, on October 11, 1830. His father died in the winter of 1836-37. He is listed on the Census for Smith County in 1850, living with his mother and siblings in the household headed by his older brother, John.

Shortly after this, he and the other members of his family moved to DeWitt/Karnes to claim land. The Ratliffs's land surveys were completed and approved in 1854, and in 1858 he was issued a preemption certificate for 160 acres of land.

Richard Ratliff, grandson of John J. Tumlinson, son of Jane Tumlinson & Elijah Ratliff, great-grandfather of James L. Dannheim (photo taken in 1862).

He married Hulda Teague before 1861, as they were both listed among his mother's heirs when her land was sold in March 1861. A photo of Richard is included in this book, taken in 1862.

Richard served with the Confederate Army for three years, enlisting on June 14, 1862 at Camp C. Russell at Goliad with Company F, Hobby's regiment Magruder's Command, 8th Texas Infantry. He was serving in Galveston in 1863. In 1864, he was a 5th sergeant, promoted by order of Major Ireland.

By 1880, Richard and Hulda were farming in Llano County. In 1902, Richard and his brother, Elijah, dictated sworn affidavits to be used in proving ownership of their father, Elijah's, original grant from the Mexican government in 1834. These same affidavits were used again in 1951 to investigate claims by the heirs of Elijah in Polk County regarding this land, as there was no record of it having been deeded away, and the question of mineral rights had arisen.

In 1902, Richard applied for and received a Confederate pension. At that time, he was 71 years old, and said he had been living in Bandera County for twenty years. On September 22, 1904, Richard and Hulda went to Brownwood where their daughter, Mary Ratliff, was living. He died there on October 13, 1904 of pneumonia, James L. Dannheim #6736

JOHN MARTIN RAWLINS

My great-grandfather, John Martin Rawlins, was born in Roodhouse, Greene County, Illinois, on July 24, 1825, to William Rawlins Sr., a blacksmith and his wife, Euphamia Martin, a housewife. He left Greene County in the fall of 1845, arriving in December. He came to the Lancaster, Texas, area where he lived for a while with his cousin, Pleasant Taylor. He share-cropped and carted supplies to the other pioneer settlers in that area.

On September 21, 1848, he married Polly Minerva Parks, daughter of Meredith Parks and Malinda Sharp, John and Polly reared a large family of 14 children.

*John Martin Rawlins
Citizen of Republic of Texas,
Lancaster circa 1880.*

John was baptized by Barton W. Stone, well-known Restoration leader of the Church of Christ, before coming to Texas. John and his father, William, were the first ministers of the Church of Christ in Dallas County. John established the first church in Lancaster, and later the Cold Springs Church of Christ, which is the oldest in Dallas County and still in existence. John also was a farmer and blacksmith, like his father.

He left the Lancaster area around 1880 with his family to join Addison and Randolph Clark in establishing the Add-Ran College, later known as the Thorp Spring Christian College in Thorp Spring, Hood, Texas. He preached and taught in that area of Hood County until his death on April 19, 1886.

His father was born on July 5, 1796, in Kentucky, and his mother was born on May 9, 1796, in Kentucky. Both died in the fall of 1850 from drinking polluted water near Lancaster, where they Headrighted a section of land. John is buried in Thorp Spring Cemetery, and parents are buried in Rawlins Cemetery at Lancaster. Billy Joe Denton, Ranger John Beeman Chapter #45, Mesquite, Texas

JOSEPH MARION RAY (1770-1857)

Joseph Marion Ray was born in the Carolina "upcountry" on St. David's Day in 1770. As it turned out, he was aptly named for the sojourning Hebrew patriarch, Joseph, and for the Revolutionary military hero, Francis Marion.

His family moved to Kentucky when he was a child. There he grew up and met and married a "Pennsylvania Dutch" (Palatine German) girl, Mary Phouts, in 1773. The first seven of their eleven children was born in Kentucky. Following the terrible Massacre at Fort Mims, Alabama, he volunteered to fight the Creek Indians in what became the War of 1812. Joseph was a member of Captain Jonathan Owsley's Company of Mitchusson's Regiment of Kentucky Detached Militia. He participated in the Battle at Horseshoe Bend, Alabama, and in the Battle of New Orleans. After the war, Mary and Joseph settled for a while in Warren County, Tennessee, before moving into the rich Coosa River Valley in Alabama.

We do not know when or why they made the long trek to Texas. Joseph owned land here in 1840 ("First Settlers of the Republic of Texas, Vol. 1, p. 186, No. 1243). He and Mary built a house and farmed in Upshur County. They were accompanied in Texas by three of their sons. Leonard, David, and William, and their wives and children. Leonard settled in Upshur County, and David in Wood County. William settled in Smith County. He was a Baptist preacher and the founder of the First Baptist Church in Tyler.

Eventually Joseph and Mary left their Texas children and returned to Alabama, where they lived out their last days with their youngest son, Elijah. Joseph explained their reason for leaving Texas in a poignant letter which he wrote in 1854 to a son, Moses, in Arkansas: " ... For while we were in taxes (sic) it became more sickly every year. We waited on our sick neighbors till we got down ourselves and soon as we got up we left."

Joseph died on 3 September 1857, and Mary on 7 October 1866. They were buried at Mount Pleasant Cemetery in Barbour County, Alabama. A marker was erected in their memory by their Texas descendants at Sand Flat Cemetery near Tyler, Texas. David Lee Veal #2762

ISAAC H. REED

Isaac Reed, my fourth great-grandfather, was born in Pendleton District, South Carolina, on June 6, 1776, the son of Nathan and Hepsibah Bateman Reed. He married Elizabeth Harper on September 17, 1797. Their union would produce eight children.

They moved to Franklin County, Tennessee in 1805, where Isaac was ordained a Baptist minister in 1808. He served the Baptist Church as preacher for 25 years before moving to Texas in 1834.

*Marker of Isaac H. Reed in Panola County
In error on two points:
he was born in South Carolina, not Tennessee
and his son was killed by Indians.*

He and his family first settled in Nacogdoches and moved in 1835 to what is now Panola County. There they established Reed's Settlement, the second-oldest settlement in that area.

Isaac organized the Old North Church near Nacogdoches in 1838; it is thought to be the oldest Baptist church in Texas. Together with Lemuel Herrin, he formed Bethel Church in 1841, Border Church in Harrison County in 1843, and Macedonia Church in 1845.

A dynamic, energetic man with a positive attitude, Isaac traveled over East Texas, preaching in isolated communities. He frequently received strong resistance from the Mexican government, since laws in force prevented religions other than Catholic.

He died November 30, 1848, and is buried in the Old Bethel Cemetery in Panola County. A Texas centennial marker was erected at his gravesite in 1936. Joseph Bryan Howell #4399, Christopher Eric Howell #4767, Matthew Bryan Woolly #4863, Submitted by Joseph B. Howell #4399

JACOB AND MATILDA GAGE REED

Jacob Reed and his wife, Matilda (Gage) Reed, were members of the Austin Colony who received a Mexican First Class Headright land grant. The approval took place in the villa of Stephen F. Austin. They settled on their league and labor of land located south of the San Antonio Road, between the Brazos River and the Yegua Creek (now Burleson County).

L-R: James Reed Clary & wife Saphrona A. West, Stephen Stricklin Clary & wife Mary Dennis, John P. Clary & wife Susan Jane Cate (ancestors of Johnnie Colleen (Ham) Buzusko), Eliz. J. Clary Edens (wife of Elias Edens-deceased), and Jane Wyatt (wife of Ransom Clary-deceased, ancestors of Curtis Younts)

Jacob and Matilda, both 49 years old, arrived from Tennessee on May 9, 1831, with five sons and five daughters: sons - Elijah B. Reed (Texan Army) married Sally West, July 22, 1841; Joseph Reed (Texan Army), killed by Indians; James Reed (Texan Army) married Elizabeth Wick, Sept. 17, 1838; John J. Reed, married Lucinda Hampton in 1852; Thomas J. Reed (possible son); daughters - Sarah (Sally) married John Sumner Clary, July 4, 1852, in Lawrence County, Alabama, (the ancestors of Curtis Younts); Nancy, married Clavin Barker, who was killed by Indians; Mary (Polly) married John H. Harvey, Sept. 15, 1837. As a widow, in 1852 Polly married Avery Ellis; Jane married James W. Harvey, Sept. 15. 1837; Emily married Mr. Ables.

Writer's notes on Jacob Reed include the following: Place and date of birth - Tennessee, 1782. Date he settled in Texas - 1831. Parents unknown. Patriot's craft or profession - farmer/stockman. Date and place of death - 1864, Texas. Author's relationship to ancestor – 4th great-grandson. Curtis Younts (4th great-grandson)

ALFRED REEL AND PURMELIA NORRIS REEL

Alfred Reel, a son of Daniel and Barbary Reel, came to Texas in 1833 with his parents as colonists under David G. Burnet. Alfred Reel was born about 1817, probably in Missouri. Daniel Reel and his family settled just north of Laneville, in Rusk County on land that Daniel and his two oldest sons, Henry and James, received from Mexico. By 1840, Alfred and his father, mother, and most - if not all - of their children, moved to Harrison County.

Alfred Reel was a private in the militia and was called into service October 18, 1838 in Captain George English's Company in the Third Regiment of Mounted Volunteers, commanded by Colonel Willis H. Landrum of the Third Brigade of the Militia of the Republic of Texas and served until his was discharged January 13, 1839. Alfred Reel furnished eighty-nine bushels of corn to Captain Fergerson's Company, also under Colonel Landrum's command.

Alfred Reel, single when he came to Texas, was not eligible to receive a grant from Mexico due to his age, but received a grant from the Republic of Texas on December 11, 1841 for one-third league of land known as the "Alfred Reel Survey" in the southwest part of Harrison County.

Alfred married Purmelia Norris on February 10, 1842 in Harrison County, and died in 1849. Purmelia Norris Reel died in 1852 in Rusk County, leaving as orphans their four young children: Sarah Ann Reel, born about 1843; William Henry Reel, born about 1844; James Allen Reel, born about 1846; and Robert L. Reel, born about 1848.

After living with their mother's brother, Allen Norris, and their maternal grandmother, Judy Norris, about four years, the four children lived with their aunt, Eunity Mason, and her husband, Redin Mason, until they were grown on a league-and-labor of land that Redin Mason received from the Republic of Texas.

Submitted by William M. Huffman, a great-great-great-grandson of Daniel and Barbary Reel, whose line of descent is as follows: Alfred Reel * and Purmelia Norris Reel*, William Henry Reel (Sr.)* and Susan Melvina LaGrone Reel, William Henry Reel, Jr. and Janie Ethel Prior Reel, Lois Marie Reel and Perry L. Huffman, William M. Huffman *Residents of the Republic of Texas . Alfred Reel was the son of Daniel Reel* and Barbary Reel*. Susan Melvina LaGrone was the daughter of Emmanuel LaGrone* and Rachel Clark LaGrone* and the granddaughter of Jacob LaGrone, Sr.* and Katherine Riser LaGrone*.

DANIEL REEL AND BARBARY REEL

Daniel and Barbary Reel came to Texas in 1833, as colonists under David G. Burnet, bringing with them eight children, including Henry Reel (born about 1805, probably in North Carolina), Eunity Reel (born about 1809 in North Carolina), James Reel (born about 1813, probably in Tennessee), Alfred Reel (born about 1817, probably in Missouri), Nancy L. Reel (born about 1818, probably in Missouri), and Elizabeth Reel (born about 1820, probably in Missouri). Daniel was born about 1775, probably in North Carolina, although his Entrance Certificate showed he was a native of Holland, and Barbary was born about 1780.

In May, 1835, Daniel Reel and his two oldest sons, James Reel and Henry Reel, received grants from Mexico of land located just north of Laneville and about eight miles south of Henderson in Rusk County. In 1837-1838, Daniel, James and Henry Reel sold that land, and Daniel and Barbary Reel, and most – if not all– of their children moved to Harrison County, where Henry died in 1840 and Daniel died in 1842. Barbary survived him. Neither the place nor date of her death is known.

One son, Alfred Reel, and two sons-in-law of Daniel and Barbary Reel – M.H. Ussery and Redin Mason – served in the Army of the Republic of Texas in the 1836 War for Independence or during the turbulent years that followed. Another son-in-law, Hezekiah George, served in the Texas Rangers from 1839-1840. Two sons, Henry Reel and Alfred Reel, furnished provisions to the Army of the Republic of Texas.

Eunity Reel married Redin Mason, and they lived west of Hallsville in Harrison County on a league-and-labor of land that Redin Mason received from the Republic of Texas.

James Reel married Mary Jane (Polly) Martin, daughter of Daniel Martin, about 1837, and lived near Tatum, at the boundary of Panola and Rusk counties, where he received a grant from the Republic of Texas.

Nancy L. Reel married Hezekiah George on October 28, 1840 in Harrison County. After he died, Nancy married Jesse Gazaway.

Elizabeth Reel married M.H. Ussery on May 24, 1840 in Harrison County. He had participated in the Battle of Bexar as a member of Captain John M. Bradley's Company. Later, M.H. Ussery and their three children disappeared after leaving their home to grind corn. Believing they had been killed by Indians, Elizabeth Reel married William Inch on January 23, 1851 in Harrison County. After William Inch died, Elizabeth Reel married Edward Taif on September 15, 1857, in Harrison County.

Alfred Reel married Purmelia Norris on February 10, 1842 in Harrison County, and died in 1849. Purmelia Norris Reel died in 1852 in Rusk County, leaving as orphans their four young children: Sarah Ann Reel, born about 1843; William Henry Reel, born about 1844; James Allen Reel, born about 1846; and Robert L. Reel, born about 1848. Submitted by William M. Huffman, a great-great-great-grandson of Daniel and Barbary Reel, whose line of descent is as follows: Daniel and Barbary Reel, Alfred Reel * and Purmelia Norris Reel, William Henry Reel (Sr.) * and Susan Melvina LaGrone Reel, William Henry Reel, Jr. and Janie Ethel Prior Reel, Lois Marie Reel and Perry L. Huffman, William M. Huffman. Residents of the Republic of Texas.

Susan Melvina LaGrone was the daughter of Emmanuel Lagrone* and Rachel Clark LaGrone* and the grand-daughter of Jacob LaGrone, Sr.* and Katherine Riser LaGrone*.

WILLIAM HENRY REEL

William Henry Reel was one of four children of Alfred Reel (son of Daniel Reel and Barbary Reel) and Purmelia Reel Norris (the daughter of Ezekiel and Judy- or Judith- Norris). Alfred Reel came to Texas with his parents in 1833 and married Purmelia Norris February 10, 1842 in Harrison County.

Alfred Reel died in 1849 and Purmelia Norris Reel died in 1852 in Rusk County, leaving as orphans William Henry Reel; his sister, Sarah Ann Reel, born about 1843; and his two brothers, James Allen Reel, born about 1846, and Robert L. Reel, born about 1848.

William Henry Reel did not know how old he was, but the 1860 Census listed his age as 15, thus indicating that he was born in 1844-1845. The 1900 Census showed his age as fifty-seven, indicating he was born about 1843, as did his application for a pension for service in the Confederate Army. Since Texas was a Republic until December 29, 1845, and the 1860 Census was taken earlier in the year, it is clear that William Henry Reel was born while Texas was still a Republic.

After living with his mother's brother, Allen Norris, and his maternal grandmother, Judy Norris, in Rusk County about four years, William Henry Reel, his sister and brothers lived with their aunt, Eunity Mason, and her husband, Redin Mason, until they were grown on a league-and-labor of land that Redin Mason received from the Republic of Texas.

William Henry Reel joined the Confederate Army in April 1862, when he was seventeen to eighteen years old, and returned to Harrison County on April 12, 1865. On January 7, 1869, he married Susan Melvina LaGrone (daughter of Emmanuel LaGrone, who came to Texas in 1837, and Rachel Clark LaGrone, who was born in Texas in 1823). The following children, listed in the order of their birth, were born of the marriage of William Henry Reel and Susan Melvina LaGrone.

Willie A. Reel, who married James Edmond Garner.

Susan Arizona (Zonie) Reel, who married David Needham Moore and later married B.L. (Fate) Palmer.

Alford L. Reel, who married Alice Giles.

Emanuel Franklin Reel, who married Sallie Joe Webb.

Bennie George Reel, who married Sadie Leath.

William Henry Reel, Jr., who married Katie E. Webb and, after she died, married Janie Ethel Prior.

Minnie F. Reel, who married Frank Lafayette Richardson.

Joseph Alonzo Reel, who married Mary Ann (Mollie) Blalock

Ollie Rachel Reel, who married Henry Rouse.

After Susan Melvina LaGrone Reel died in 1906, William Henry Reel married Ada Landers Hudspeth November 27, 1909. She died about 1915-1916, and he died May 13, 1929. Submitted by William M. Huffman, a great-great-great-grandson of Daniel and Barbary Reel, whose line of descent is as follows: William Henry Reel (Sr.) * and Susan Melvina LaGrone Reel, William Henry Reel, Jr. and Janie Ethel Prior Reel, Lois Marie Reel and Perry L. Huffman, William M. Huffman, Residents of the Republic of Texas

William Henry Reel (Sr.)* was the son of Alfred Reel* and Purmelia Norris Reel* and the grandson of Daniel Reel* and Barbary Reel*.

Susan Melvina LaGrone was the daughter of Emmanuel Lagrone* and Rachel Clark LaGrone* and the granddaughter of Jacob LaGrone, Sr.* and Katherine Riser LaGrone*.

JOHN REEVES

My name is John Reeves and I have been a life member of the William Barret Travis Chapter #7 of the SRT since 1986. I am retired now by disability, but am the Lifetime Commander of the All Elks, Fidelity Post #712 of the American Legion since 1989. I have been a volunteer at the NYVMAC since1979, and have put in over 22,000 hours to help our fellow veterans. I have four college degrees: B.A. in cultural anthropology, B.A. in history, B.A. in political science and a B.B.A. in public administration.

My great-grand father Richard Allison, who married Margaret Roberts, daughter of Noel Gill Roberts (born Green County, Ky., on 19 Nov. 1813; died San Augustine, Texas in 1864) married in Green County, Ky., in 1838 to Maria Thomas (born Green County, Ky., in 1814; died San Augustine, Texas).

During the Texas War for Independence and the Mexican War 1846-48, he was the LTC Commandant of the San Augustine Militia.

He was the son of Elisha Roberts (born Holston River, Watauga Settlement, Tennessee in 1775; died San Augustine, Texas on 4 Oct. 1884) and Martha (Patsey) Gill, (born Bedford County, Va., in 1780; died San Augustine, Texas in 1845) who married in 1799.

In 1814, Elisha removed from Kentucky to Washington Parish, Louisiana, and served in the War of 1812, as a first lieutenant in Captain Thomas Bickham's Company, 12th Regiment, Louisiana Militia, commencing on 23 Dec. 1814, and ending on 09 mar 1815 (at the Battle of New Orleans). He removed to Texas 1823 and was a founder of San Augustine County. In 1825 he built the first cotton gin and in 1831 he was elected alcalde of the county. In 1832 he was one of 15 to locate the site for the city of San Augustine. In 1837, the University of San Augustine was incorporated by legislative act of the Texas Republic, and Elisha was one of the 12 trustees.

Elisha was the son of William Robert (born Culpeper (then Orange) County, Va., in 1730; died Washington Parish, Louisiana in 1823) and Sarah, whom he married in Franklin County, Va. He was a soldier in the French and Indian Wars, and road commissioner of Virginia in 1777. During the Revolutionary War he enlisted in the Culpeper Militia. He was with Washington that winter of 1777-78 at Valley Forge, and took part in the Battle of Monmouth; he volunteered to attack Cornwallis at Yorktown, Va., and remained through the siege and surrender.

SAMUEL HUTCHINSON REID

Samuel Hutchinson "Hutch" Reid was born circa 1808, York County, S.C. His parents were Rhoda Hutchison and James Reid Sr. The Reids moved to Tipton County, Tennessee, between 1828 and 1830. By 1837, they had all moved to Texas via Mississippi.

Hutch had come to Texas as early as 1833. He may have returned to Tennessee before finally settling in Texas. He married before 1839 in Bastrop County to Elizabeth Curtis.

The family's Headright was located at "Reed Bend" on the Colorado River. It is noted that the "Reid" name was often spelled "Reed" or "Reede" in early Texas documents and literature.

He was a surveyor for Bastrop County. He served as an Indian Scout under Burleson at the Battle of Plum Creek. He was severely wounded by six arrows.

S.H. Reid amassed thousands of acres of Texas lands through his Headright, public service to the Republic and many purchases. S.H. Reid died at the age of 44 years on 4 December 1852 in Bastrop County, Texas.

At the time of his death he left a pregnant wife and seven children. Most of his estate was divided and/or sold after his death to support his family. He is probably buried at Reid's Bend Burial Ground. Charles Lee Reid is the great-great-grandson of S.H. Reid.

JOHN RILEY RHEA

John Riley Rhea came to Texas in 1826 with Joseph Vehlein's Colony, and received a land grant in 1835. The Atascosita Census of 1826 identifies him as an unmarried male, 29 years of age, from Pennsylvania. The census lists his occupation as house carpenter and cabinet maker.

In c. 1827, John Riley Rhea married Eleanor (Nellie) Smith, who was the daughter of Christian Smith, one of Austin's "Old 300." They settled in Cedar Bayou, Texas, on part of the Christian Smith League. Also in 1827, he joined Captain Hugh B. Johnston's Company of Texas Rangers and helped quell the Fredonian Rebellion. Stephen F. Austin endorsed this company in February 1827, and records regarding the company may be found in the Austin Papers.

The muster rolls of the Texas Revolution indicate that John Riley Rhea served in Colonel Jesse Benton's Regiment of Texas Rangers under the command of Captain E.L.R. Wheelock in May 1836, and in Captain Wheelock's Company under the command of Brigadier General Felix Houston in August 1836.

Headstone of John Riley Rhea in Cedar Bayou United Methodist Cemetery, Cedar Bayou, Texas.

John Riley Rhea lived with his wife and eleven children in Cedar Bayou, Texas. He died there at the age of sixty-seven on August 12, 1864.

John Riley Rhea was my great-great, great-great-grandfather. Paul Thomas Luther SRT #6514

THOMAS MCCLURE RICE

Answering General Sam Houston's call for Americans to come help free Texas from Mexico, Thomas is listed on the August 27, 1836 muster roll of the Texas Army at Velasco (then the capital of Texas).

In 1836 the Alamo fell in March. General Sam Houston won the Battle of San Jacinto in April, and Texas became an independent Republic. The Thomas Rice family lived in Fort Bend County and later in DeWitt County, while the new Republic of Texas continued to be troubled by Mexican invasions. In September 1842, the Mexican Army invaded and captured San Antonio. Answering the call to arms to defend his new nation, on September 16 Thomas Rice joined Captain Nicholas Dawson's company on day and night horseback march from LaGrange toward San Antonio.

Dawson's 53 men encountered 400 Mexican cavalry and artillery near Cibolo and Salado Creek on September 18. Determined not to retreat, the exhausted men prepared for battle. While still out of range of the Texan's rifles, the Mexicans began showering Dawson's men with cannon fire. His cause hopeless against such odds, Dawson raised a white flag and the men put down their arms.

However, the Mexican cavalry charged and decimated the small Texas force. Thomas Rice, Dawson, and 33 others were slain; 15 were taken prisoner; and three escaped. The next day the remains were buried on site.

A newspaper obituary of the event reads, "The details of the fate of the unfortunate company from LaGrange are distressing in the extreme; there is consolation, however, in the recollection that they fought nobly to the last and died like the immortal heroes of the Alamo, bidding defiance to the foe. Their names shall live while the name of Texas endures, illumined with a halo of glory."

In 1848, the remains of Thomas Rice and the other patriots who died in the "Dawson Massacre" were moved to Monument Hill overlooking LaGrange. Interred with them were the remains of the Mier Expedition, who died in the "Black Bean Episode" in Mexico in 1843. The remains of these patriots were given a military funeral in the presence of a large number of Texas dignitaries, including General Houston.

Descendants:

Thomas McClure Rice (1801-1842), son of Nathan and Jemima, married Elizabeth Wilson (1805-1859) of Ireland. A son, Oliver, was born in Steubenville, Ohio.

Oliver H. Rice (1830-), son of Thomas and Elizabeth, married Adeline (name, dates unknown). A son, Oren, was born in DeWitt County.

Oren Aaron Rice (1855-1925), son of Oliver and Adeline, married Mary Alice Hodges (1859-1928). They had ten children, including Mary Adeline, born in DeWitt County.

Mary Adeline ("Addie") Rice (1876-1945), daughter of Oren and Mary Alice, married Marshall Jerone Cooper (1872-1961). While residing in DeWitt and Victoria counties, they had nine children: Amy (married J. Silas Elkins), Effie (married John P. Dodd), Sylvester (married Etta Odom), Earl (married Ida Odom and later marred Imojene Junek), Lee (married May Peterson), Jewel, Newel (married Ludell Duncan), W. Harper (married Ethel Goodson), and E.J. (married Juanita Moody).

References:

Cooper, Norman L., "A Confederate Soldier and His Descendants" (Library of Congress #82-80915). 1982.

Northcutt, Sibyl, research records, Yoakum, Texas, 1985

Rice, H. Craig, "Thomas Rice Killed in Texas Dawson Expedition," "The Rice Family News Journal," about 1976.

Rumsey, Earline (Hodges), research records, Kerrville, Texas, 1983.

Texas Parks and Wildlife Department, "Story of the Dawson Massacre and the Mier Expedition," Austin Texas, 1984. By Norman Lee Cooper, 1999

DANIEL LONG RICHARDSON

Daniel Long Richardson was born ca. 1793 in Hancock County, Ga., and came to Sabine County, Texas about 1835. He settled with his family in the Sabinetown area and became a planter in that region. He had married Mary J. Ponce, also of Georgia, and they had three daughters: Eliza, who married Franklin Barlow Sexton; Jane Baxter Richardson, who married David S. Kaufman, the first representative from Texas to the U.S. Congress; and Anna Maria, who married J. Nash.

He served in the Texas Army from March 17-December 19, 1836, in Captain Teal's Company, and also with Jacob Snively, receiving a bounty warrant for his service at San Jacinto.

He died in February 1849, and is buried with his daughter, Jane Baxter Kaufman, 1825-1852, in the Sabinetown Cemetery, Sabine County, Texas. SRT# 03 R #1613John A. Barton, Jr., great-great-great-grandson

JEREMIAH ROBERTS

Jeremiah Roberts, the son of Nathan Roberts and Abigail Bishop was born 9 January 1801, in Tennessee, and died in Caldwell County, Texas in 1866. Jeremiah's grandfather was Cornelius Roberts, a Revolutionary War soldier, and Mary Benton.

Jeremiah enrolled as a volunteer in the First Regiment of Texas Cavalry on the 18th of March 1837, and was honorably discharged on the 18th of June 1837. He was paid $1.50 per day while serving in the Cavalry.

Jeremiah Roberts was married first to Sarah Sharp and had two children, John Sharp Roberts and Abigail B. Roberts. Jeremiah Roberts was apparently in Washington County, Texas. In a list of taxpayers of Washington County, Texas, for the year 1838 appears the name of Jeremiah Roberts. By 1840, he was in Gonzales County with 1,280 acres of land and 18 town lots in Seguin.

Jeremiah married second, Sarah Nash Bruner 11 May 1845. Sarah, the daughter of Ira Nash, was born 1822 in Missouri and died 1874 in Caldwell County, Texas. They had seven children: Ellen Roberts, Benjamin McCulloch Roberts, Jeremiah Roberts, Joe Roberts, Sarah Elizabeth Roberts, Susan Roberts, and Mathew Roberts.

The following is an excerpt from a letter written by Ben McCulloch Roberts, son of Jeremiah and Sarah Nash Roberts:

"My father came to Texas about the year 1822, from Alabama. He served with Ben McCulloch and they had many fierce engagements with the Indians."

"My father had drawn a single man's part of land in Caldwell County, near where Lockhart is now. He had to go back to Alabama and bring his two children to Texas to prove that he was the head of a family, before he could get more. Afterwards he sold 200 acres to a man to fatten an old Spanish horse on crab grass, and received an old saddle and three plugs of tobacco to boot. He rode this old horse to Alabama to bring his two children. After coming back to Texas with his children, he married his second wife, my mother. Nine children were born in our family. Father built a log cabin and put in a little farm. He made the finest corn crop he had seen. In 1856 and 1857 we had eighteen months drought. I was then thirteen years old. We ran out of breadstuff, and father sent to Illinois for corn to make bread. This corn was sent down the Mississippi river on a steam boat to New Orleans, then on the Indianola, and while on the gulf there was a great storm at sea and the ship could not come into port for three weeks. All this time we were without bread, but we were milking forty longhorn cows, and my mother pressed two big cheese a day. With dried beef and cheese we managed to make out very well until the corn was delivered. When it arrived we found it was hard yellow corn. There was a little water mill on what was called town Branch. This corn was so hard the miller had to throw it back into the hopper to be ground over and then it was made into pretty fair grits."

"With all the hardships we had to undergo, the people were happier than they are now, because there were fewer of them, and a man could rely on another's word. A man's bank in those days was his pocket, and his word was his bond. I have seen my father loan a neighbor as much as $300 at a time without a note or a scratch of a pen, and he was always paid back promptly."

Some of Jeremiah's descendants are: Sarah Elizabeth Roberts, born 26 December 1855 in Caldwell County, Texas, married first William Lee Elwood on 24 December 1873. She married second Henry Wesson Copeland 23 October 1884. They had a daughter, Lura May Copeland, born 15 May 1889, married Thomas House Tumey 31 December 1905, and died 12 May 1973. The fourth child of Lura and Thomas was Wickline Robert Tumey, married Edna Maxine White 23 January 1932. He died 6 November 1998. Their first child, Robert Carl Tumey, Sr., married Barbara June

Ligon 14 February 1953. This union produced five children: Robert Carl Tumey, Jr., Debra June Tumey, Ronald Wickline Tumey, Beverly Jean Tumey, and Sheryl Ann Tumey. Robert Carl Tumey #2681

JOHN S. ROBERTS

John S. Roberts was born in Virginia, July 13, 1796. Of Welsh and Irish extraction, his family had served this country well. His great-grandfather, James Roberts, was a member of a company of regulars for defense of the colonies, and his grandfather, William, and his father, John, Sr., served in the Culpepper, Virginia Militia during the American Revolution.

The Robertses migrated to Tennessee where at age 16, John S. enlisted in Captain James Terrel's troop of cavalry, in Col. John Coffee's Regiment, for service in the War of 1812. He "fought with conspicuous bravery" in the Battle of New Orleans, along with his father.

After discharge, Roberts settled in Natchitoches, Louisiana, and in 1822 was serving as a deputy sheriff. He was also a land speculator.

In early autumn, 1826, he went to the aid of Harriet Fenley Collier, who lived on a ranch with her late husband, Robert Collier. Collier was murdered and Harriet was without friends or family to protect her since they were fairly new to Texas. Roberts brought her and her family to Nacogdoches for safety.

Roberts was a participant in the Fredonian Rebellion led by Hayden Edwards and was a major. During the short rebellion, Roberts and Harriet were married in the Old Stone Fort on December 26, 1826. After the rebellion, he became a merchant and a "man of affairs" in Nacogdoches.

He enlisted as a private under the command of Col. James Bullock of San Augustine, and participated in the short Battle of Nacogdoches. On October 4, 1835, he joined the Nacogdoches Independent Volunteers as a 1st lieutenant (later made captain) and served under Col. Thomas J. Rusk. From December 5th through 10th, he participated in the storming and capture of Bexar. He returned to his family after General Cos went back to Mexico.

In early 1836, he was chosen as one of four delegates representing Nacogdoches at the Constitutional Convention of 1836, and was a signer of the Texas Declaration of Independence. After the Convention, he returned to Nacogdoches to see to his family's safety, planning to join General Houston. Before he could do so, Santa Ana had surrendered.

He returned to the mercantile business, and in 1850 moved into the Old Stone Fort, which had been owned by Harriet since 1839. He was appointed Quartermaster of the Texas Militia by Thomas J. Rusk, a post he held for about 18 months. In the Old Stone fort, he operated a saloon on the first floor along with his business, until his death on August 9, 1871. Harriet died on April 15, 1874. Both are buried, head to head, in Oak Grove Cemetery in Nacogdoches.

The story of his life was recounted in a book, "Spoiling for a Fight," by Joe Ericson, KSJ. Robert Miles White #2527

MOSES FISK ROBERTS

Moses Fisk Roberts (1803-1888) was a soldier and congressman. He was born on July 9, 1803, in Davidson County, Tennessee. He apparently grew up in Davidson County, as did his first wife, Amanda Grant, whom he married before moving to Texas. He and his family arrived in February 19, 1836. It was here that he acquired the name "Dog Roberts" for being a devoted fox hunter and always in the company of a pack of fox hounds.

He joined Capt. James Chesser's Jasper Volunteer Company at San Augustine, and was elected second lieutenant on March 23, 1836. He served in the army until June 22 of that year, when he was discharged because of the loss of his right eye.

Subsequently, he settled in Shelby County, where he was elected to House of the Fourth, Fifth, and Sixth Texas Congresses. During his first term in Congress, his wife died, and in December of 1841 he married Nancy Murray in Travis County.

Upon leaving Congress, he returned to Shelby County and remained until 1853, when he was elected to House of the Fifth Legislature. He also represented Shelby County in the House of the Seventh Legislature.

He died in Shelby County in February 1888. Billy Edward Johnson SRT # 4780

MARY ANN ROBINSON

My great-grandmother, Mary Ann Robinson, was born in Ste. Genevieve, Mo., on July 3, 1837. Her parents, Lasa and Ann Cofer McKenzine, had returned from their ranch near Palestine, Texas, for Mary Ann's birth. The McKenzies had gone to Texas in 1836 to "run cattle on the Brazos."

Mary Ann came to Texas in 1841, and with her family survived several Indian raids by forting up at Fort Houston. A sister, Francis, was born in Fort Houston during an Indian raid.

Family of Joe E. McGuigan in Kernville, CA Sept. 22, 1914. (l. to r.) Gertrude Robinson (cousin), Mary Elvira Robinson (aunt), Rea Johnson (half brother), Mary Ann McKenzie Brewer Robinson (great-grandmother), Joe E. McGuigan, and Robert Erwin Robinson (cousin).

The McKenzie family moved to Fiskville, six miles out of Austin. Later, Mary Ann's father, Lacy McKenzie, was awarded 640 acres just north of Austin for his service in the Texas-Mexican War. Lacy lost an arm after being wounded at the Battle of Kickapoo. The Texans defeated some 900 Kickapoos, Delawares, Ionies, Caddos, Cooshattas, a few Cherokees, and Cordova and his Mexicans.

Mary Ann's second husband was my great-grandfather, Jeremiah Washington Robinson.

My brother and I lived with our great-grandma for many months during 1914-1929. Her tales of early Texas, "Comanche Moons," "Comanche Pincushions," etc. would fill a book. She lived through the last Indian raid on Austin. Joe McGuigan

JOHN ALEXANDER ROGERS

John Alexander Rogers, Jr., a courier, was ordered by President Andrew Jackson in September 1835 to deliver vital dispatches to General Stephen F. Austin, John A. Wharton and Branden T. Archer in Texas. Gen. Austin told John the dispatches pertained to a new government for Texas. In October 1935, General Austin ordered John to Nashville, Tennessee.

John was ordered to Texas in February 1836, to deliver dispatches to General Houston. He arrived March 1836, at Bessoms Crossing on the Colorado. General Houston ordered him to Fort Jessup, Louisiana, with dispatches for Gen. E.P. Gaines. He arrived in April 1836, gravely ill from forging rivers and sleeping on damp ground, almost losing his life.

John Alexander Rogers, Jr.   *Mary Dallas Williams Harlan Rogers*

In May 1836, John returned to Texas and enlisted as a private in Capt. A.B. Switzer's Company and was preparing for a rumored invasion of Texas by Mexico. In August 1836, he was promoted to orderly of Switzer's Company and discharged December 1837.

John re-enlisted in 1840, and fought in the Battle of Plum Creek. In 1840 and 1841, he was with Gen. Morehouse and his expedition of the Upper Brazos and Trinity. In 1842, John served under Col. C.S. Owen. He fought in the Battle of Salado under Caldwell and in the Battle on the Hondo River with Hays. In 1842 and 1843, he was with the Somervell Expedition with Wall and Vasquez. From 1835 till 1845, he was reported of being on various little expeditions against guerrillas and Indians.

John Alexander Rogers, Jr., was born May 14, 1817, in Rogersville, Hawkins County, Tennessee. He was the third of three children born to John A. Rogers, Sr., and Margaret Forgey, who was born February 4, 1794 and died June 2, 1817. Margaret was the daughter of James and Margaret Forgey.

Tennessee salt box house built circa 1889 of cypress lumber hauled by wagon from Center Point, home of John & Mary in Harper, Texas; now owned by Mildred Rogers Allen McElroy, granddaughter.

John A. Rogers, Sr., born July 15, 1789, in Rogersville, Hawkins County, Tennessee. He was the second of fourteen children born to Joseph Rogers (born August 21, 1764 in Cookstown, Ireland, and died November 6, 1833 in Rogersville, Tennessee) and Mary Amis, (born August 22, 1768 in Dublin County, North Carolina, and died November 30, 1833 in Rogersville, Tennessee). Joseph and Mary were married October 24, 1786, in Sullivan County, North Carolina, presently Hawkins County, Tennessee. Joseph Rogers came from Ireland in 1781 and was the founder of Rogersville, Tennessee, in 1786. Also, he was a distiller of fine liquors and postmaster.

John A. Rogers, Sr., in 1807, was captain of the Hawkins County Militia. In 1812, he served in the 24th U.S. Infantry and was commissioned as a captain. He fought in the War of 1812, discharged June 15, 1815. In 1820, he became a member of Masonic Overton Lodge No. 5 in Rogersville, Tennessee. In 1826 he was a trustee of the New Providence Presbyterian Church in Rogersville, Tennessee. In 1827, 1835, 1837, he was elected to the House of Representatives from Hawkins County, Tennessee. On November 28, 1850, the president appointed John A. Rogers, Sr., as Commissioner to the Frontier of Texas to treaty with the Indians.

family of John A. Rogers, Jr. circa 1883, standing L-R: John Hagen, James William, Claudia Harriet, seated center: John Alexander, wife Mary, and Mary Margaret, front: Losson Cook, Eliza Matilda, and Joseph Johnson

Upon retiring, John A. Rogers, Sr., stayed in Texas to be with his three children: Eliza Mary Rogers (born March 23, 1813 in Surgoinsville, Tennessee; married Frederick Cocke); Malvina Margaret Rogers (born February 12, 1816 in Surgoinsville, Tennessee; married John L. Conner); and John Alexander Rogers, Jr. (residing in Harper, Gillespie County, Texas). John A. Rogers, Sr., died 1873 at Center Point, Kerr County, Texas where he lived with Malvina Rogers Conner, his daughter.

John Alexander Rogers, Jr., settled in Texana, Jackson County, Texas. He married Claudia Emily McNutt, January 20, 1853. They had one child, Cornelia. After Claudia's demise, John and Mary Dallas (nee) Williams Harlan were married on January 4, 1871. Mary was the widow of Thomas P. Harlan. She was born August 30, 1845, in Mississippi, the third of four children born to Joseph John Williams and Harriet Atkinson.

John and Mary had seven children. The seventh child, Joseph Johnson Rogers, was born October 24, 1882 in Karnes County, Texas, and died November 5, 1956 in Harper, Gillespie County, Texas. John and Mary lived in Texana, Jackson County; Helena and Riddleville, Karnes County; Harper, Gillespie County, Texas. John received various land grants for his service to the Republic of Texas.

John died January 22, 1886. He was the first person to be buried in the Harper, Gillespie County, Texas, Cemetery. Mary Williams Rogers donated the original land that became the Harper Cemetery. Mary died January 5, 1936.

Mildred Rogers Allen McElroy resides in Harper, Gillespie County, in the Tennessee salt box house built by our grandfather,

John Alexander Rogers, Jr. Some of the land from the original land grants is still in the Rogers family.

John Alexander Rogers, Jr., was my grandfather. Joseph Johnson Rogers was my father. J. Philip Rogers #2757

JAMES JEFFREYS ROSS

James Jeffreys Ross is believed to be the son of the James Ross whose will was recorded in Richland County, South Carolina in 1787, bequeathing all his worldly goods to his infant son, James Ross. Thomas Jeffres and John Bigbea were appointed guardians and executors. There was no other devisee. Colonel William Pettus, a friend and neighbor of Colonel Ross in the Austin Colony said, "Capt. James J. Ross (a South Carolinian by birth, reared an orphan but a fine looking man with little education but very brave) was appointed to protest the Colorado District from depredation of the Indians."

As a Centennial Historical Project, Julia Lee Sinks interviewed many old-timers, including James Talbot Ross, who was born to Col. Ross and his wife, Sinthia, on December 14, 1820, in Clark County, Arkansas. By 1876, he was an old-timer and told Mrs. Sinks:

"My father was six-feet-three-inches in height and very handsome. He brought his State's uniform to Texas. I have seen it many times. He was not only handsome but daring, a man of great force of character, strength of will, broad shouldered hospitality, and afraid of nothing. He was eminently fitted to be the advance guard of a civilization."

Sam (Sammie) Houston Ross Graves (1864-1937), daughter of James Talbot Ross and Martha Mahalia Graham, wife of William Picket Graves, photo taken at time of marriage

"My father organized a company of Creoles and fought in the Battle of New Orleans in 1812, and that after the battle, General Jackson made him a Colonel." Julia Lee Sinks said of James Talbot Ross:

"I look at the gray-haired old man who sat in his father's house amid decayed fortunes and though how full of adventure and adversity his life had been, and bearing about him still the pleasant urbanity of a gentleman."

Colonel Ross and Sinthia (probably Talbot) were divorced in Clark County, Arkansas in 1822. He married Mariah Cummins shortly there after. In 1828, he was divorced from Mariah and married Nancy Cummins, having thus married two of Judge James Cummins three daughters. The old Alcalde and his family moved to the Colorado District of the Austin Colony in 1821 or 1822, probably along with Col. Ross. Both families had last lived in Clark County, Arkansas.

The first record of Colonel Ross in the Austin Colony appears on the list of settlers complied in March 1823 for the Colorado District. His family included Mariah, James Talbot Ross, age three, and six servants (slaves). He received a league of land near present-day Eagle Lake in Colorado County on July 24, 1824 and was appointed Captain of the Militia for the District by Austin on December 5, 1823. In 1828, he purchased the S.A. Anderson League and one-half of an adjoining League in Fayette County and moved there. This land is located on the east bank of the Colorado River, about 10 miles southeast of LaGrange, Texas.

James Talbot Ross (1820-1889) and James Andrew Ross (1849-1864 or 1865) Circa 1858

By his very nature, Col. Ross carried out the objectives of Stephen F. Austin to establish a peaceful, prosperous, law-abiding Colony. Along with John Crier and Judge James Cummins, he established a stage station now known as Fayetteville. Ross Creek and Ross Prairie were named for him. William Barret Travis was his Attorney. He rejected a flattering appeal by B.W. Edwards to join him in the so-called Fredonian Rebellion against Mexico, which he rejected. No instance of personal violence in anger was found. He was a delegate to the Second Convention in San Felipe in April, 1833 and signed the fifteen-page document requesting changes in Mexican governance of the Austin Colony. He spoke Spanish, and was commissioned to go to Mexico to secure the release of Austin from prison in Mexico.

While he attacked marauding Indians, he never used unnecessary force against them. In fact, he was killed by neighbors on January 14th, 1835 for harboring a band of Tonkawa Indians on his land and was buried near his residence in what is known as Ross Cemetery.

Great men are rightly honored, but we should not forget those who remain unsung because they felt no need for recognition or who died before such events as Gonzales, the Alamo, Goliad and San Jacinto had occurred.

James Talbot Ross, also one of the Austin's "Old Three-Hundred", died near Pandora, Wilson County, Texas on February 13th, 1889, thus ending the lives of the writer's maternal great-great and great-grandfather. Orville Graves McClain SRT #4046

THOMAS ROSS

Thomas Ross, sometimes seen as Thomas Smith Hill Ross was born between 1779 and 1781 in Rowan Co., NC to Thomas Hill and Rachel Smith. Little is known about his father except that he died before 1785 at which point Rachel married John Ross of PA. John adopted Thomas and gave him his name.

In 1810, he married Catherine Yost. Her sister, Margaret, married Thomas's half brother, James. In 1825, he filed for divorce in Carroll Co., TN claiming his wife an adulteress. Divorce was granted in 1833 to "Captain" Thomas Ross, implying he may have served in the War of 1812. Shortly after his divorce, he married Elizabeth, born about 1803 in South Carolina (her maiden name not yet known). The couple was in Texas by 1836 as Thomas served in the Texas army from June-October 1836 and was issued a land grant in then Robertson's Colony for the service.

Thomas's half brother, James, also came to Texas, but via Lauderdale Co., AL rather than TN. James arrived after statehood and died in Comanche County in 1868.

On November 14, 1840, Thomas memorialized Captain Sterling "Clack" Robertson before the Congress of the Republic of Texas and made sure his heirs were granted their due.

Thomas's will was probated July of 1841. In it, he mentions "the legitimate children of his first wife, Catherine". He left many descendants including several who to this day reside in Robertson County.

Thomas was a descendant of the Revolutionary War hero, James Smith, who died at Camden, SC and his wife, Clara Anderson, who was said to have hit a British soldier in the head with a frying pan. His Anderson roots can be traced back to the Andries of Holland who settled in New Jersey in the 1600's. Frank Randall Campise #6859AH, Randall Allen Lefevre (junior member), Austin John Colburn (junior member)

ANDREW ROTHERMEL

Andrew Rothermel's first record in Texas was his land grant application December 23, 1839, filed in Harris County. He received a land grant in Robertson County, but it apparently was never patented.

He married Anna Meier, August 23, 1846, in Austin County. They bought a parcel of land, a part of the Ernst land grant, in the Shelby Community in Austin County. Today, an historical marker stands in the Shelby Community listing Andrew Rothermel as one of the first settlers of the area. About 1860, the Rothermel family moved into Bellville and opened the National Hotel. The hotel was noted for its hospitality and the availability of a room, even during the War Between the States.

Rothermel served in the Company A, Infantry, 22nd Brigade, Texas State Troops in the War Between the States. He died December 14, 1866, and is buried in Oak Knoll Cemetery in Bellville, Texas.

He was born October 22, 1818, in Rotenberg, Germany, to Georg Joseph Rothermel and Maria Fellhauer. Andrew and Anna Rothermel's children were: Mary Louisa, born 1847; Magdalena, born 1849; Emilie, born 1851; Johanna, born 1852; Augusta, born 1853; Joseph, born 1855; Andrew, born 1857; Louise, born 1858; Laura, born 1861; Anton, born 1863; Bernhardt, born 1866. Charles J. McDonald, Jr. #6308

JAMES ROWE

James Rowe was born on March 17,1811, in Caswell County, North Carolina. He died December 2, 1868, at his home in or near Carthage, Panola County, Texas. He was the ninth child and the fifth son of Joseph Rowe and his wife, Nancy Ann Murrow Rowe, who were married on November 2, 1792 in Caswell County, North Carolina.

On the August 18, 1836, James Rowe and Myra Tippett were married. They were blessed with twelve children. In 1840, they were in San Augustine County, Texas, and in 1850 in Panola County, Texas. This was his home until death in 1868. His widow, Myra, continued to live there for a number of years after her husband's death. Myra died November 10, 1899. They are at rest about the center of the Old Center Cemetery, a part of which he gave.

In addition to their headstones is a Texas Historical Marker stating their contribution to the Republic of Texas.

James Rowe, my great-great-grandfather, came to Texas before Dec. 3, 1834, for on that date he was issued a certificate of character by Vital Flores, alcalde of Nacogdoches. On the 24 July 1835, James Rowe received a Spanish Land Grant in Empressario Lorenzo de Zavala's Colony. In 1838, he sold this land to Almanzar Houston for $500.00. It stated in the deed record that this land was about three miles from Beaumont, Texas, in Jefferson County.

James Rowe received a bounty Land Grant Certificate #9826 for his service in the Republic of Texas from March 15, 1836 to June 15, 1836. It was for 320, which he sold to H.W.K. Myrick.

He received another Land Grant Certificate #90 for having participated in the Battle of San Jacinto. He was a lieutenant captain in William Kimbro's Company of Texas Volunteers, Second Regiment, Eighth Company Infantry. James Rowe sold certificate #90 (640 acres) to John and Louis V. Greer of San Augustine County for $200.00. This land was located in Woods County. In this transaction, James Rowe stated that he was from Panola County, Texas.

He received his Headright February 1, 1838, for a league and a labor. This Headright was located in Shelby and Panola counties, Texas. It was from this Headright that he deeded to my great-grand-mother, Nancy Rowe Henry, who was his eldest daughter, 640 acres of land.

In the 1978 "History of Panola County," Myra Tippett Rowe's parents are listed as James Tippett and his wife, Catherine Ramsey Tippett. Shortly before Texas won independence from Mexico in 1836, they secured a grant for 6000 acres of land from the Mexican government. in order to obtain the grant, they had to go Mexico City, Mexico, by ox cart. They spent about two years making the trip. This grant is part of Panola County near the Woods community.

James and Myra Rowe's children were: Banard 15-Aug.1837; *Nancy Caroline, 25-June-1839; Emily Missouri-7-Dec.1840; Sarah Virginia-6-March-1843; James Thomas-28-Dec.-1844; Susanah Miry -2-June-1847; Charles Andrew-12-Dec-1848, Elizabeth Catherine-13-Feb-1851; Robert H. -15-Oct-1852; Martha Jane-7-Feb-1855; Joseph-24-Sept-1857; Isaac Newton-17-June-1859.

James Rowe, to me, was many men: He was one of the commissioners to help form Panola County, served as senior warden of Sam Sanford Lodge No. 149 A.F.&Y.M. 1851, an adventurer, a true patriot, soldier. He had many trades: cattle man, farmer, tanner, and a surveyor.

James Rowe served in the Texas Fourth Legislature 12 Dist. Nov-1851-Feb 1852-a special session in 1853 from Panola County.

He was not a well man. In 1866 he said he knew his time was near and he made his will so as to be fair to his beloved wife, Myra, and his family, so as to lift the burdens that his death may cause.

James Rowe served in the Texas fourth legistature 12 Dist. November 1851- February 1852- a special session in 1853 from Panola County. Waylan D. Harrison, a great-great-grandson and thankful to be.

JOSE FRANCISCO RUIZ

Jose Francisco Ruiz was born in San Antonia de Bexar, Mexico, 1-29-1783, where he died 1-20-1840. His father, Jose Manuel Ruiz, was born in Queretaro, Spain, in 1737, and his mother, Manuela de la Peña, came from Saltillo, Mexico.

Jose Francisco Ruiz was the first school master of San Antonio in 1803. He was also a business man. He was one of two native Texans to sign the Texas Declaration of Independence (the other was his nephew, Jose Antonio Navarro, a lawyer).

During the siege of the Alamo, his son, Francisco Antonio Ruiz, was alcalde of San Antonio, and witnessed the fall and identified the bodies of the fallen heroes.

Jim Bowie was related by marriage, having married a niece of Ruiz, Ursula Veramendi, who died along with their two infants and her parents during a cholera epidemic while Bowie was on a mission. Jose Francisco Ruiz was my grandfather 4 times removed. Douglas M. Herrera, SRT #5047 Sam Houston Chapter.

MAJOR JAMES MARTIN RUSH

Major James Martin Rush, born about 1807 in Georgia, first arrived in the Republic of Texas in the spring of 1845 from Pontotoc County, Mississippi, where he had married his second wife, Tennessee Blair Seeton, in about 1844. James M. Rush, the son of Jeptha and Sarah Eaton Rush, had been previously married to Burtha Dunigan in Habersham County, Georgia, on December 31, 1829, where the couple had three children: Henderson C. Rush, born about 1832; Piety Rush, born about 1836; and Arnetta "Ara" Rush, born about 1838.

Maj. James Martin Rush
(1807-1869)

The Rush family lived next door to Col. James Blair, a famous Express Rider, who rode to gather the men for the Battle of King's Mountain. A poem entitled the "Rebel Rider" was written about him, much like the poem about Paul Revere. These men had participated in the Indian Wars of the late 1830s in Georgia, and had received land grants in the land lottery that followed the removal of the Indians from the area.

Both James Rush and his second wife had been previously married, so the couple arrived in Texas with eight children and at least three slaves that Tennessee Blair Seeton Rush had just inherited when her father, John Blair, died September 18, 1844 in Blair's Chapel, Madison County, Tennessee. Tennessee Blair was first married to William M. Seeton on December 9, 1828, in Madison County, Tennessee, and the couple had five children: Rev. James Seeton, born about 1831; Ann Amelia "Anna" Seeton, born about 1833; William M. Seeton, Jr., born about 1834; Martha Rosanna Seeton, born about 1836; and Nancy Parilee Seeton, born about 1838 in Mississippi. Both these families had migrated to the Mississippi Territory after the Treaty of Pontotoc was signed in 1836, which opened the land in this area to the settlers.

Major James M. Rush had purchased a 640-acre land grant from Charles Fenton Mercer who established the Mercer Colony in 1843 located west of Nacogdoches and east of Peter's Colony, which included Dallas, Texas. The Rush family first settled in the Mercer Colony near the community of Alsa, which was located on the Sabine River in what is now northwest Van Zandt, County, Texas. The family built the first toll bridge over the Sabine River on the Clarksville to Austin Road near where the present Lake Towakoni Dam is now located. The toll bridge was a great success, but the women folk did not like living in the "wilderness" and they wanted to move to where there was some "society." So in 1846, James M. Rush went into the newly formed town of Tyler, Texas, to see if he could purchase a town lot. He ended up trading his toll bridge for town lot #2, block #3, owned by Margaret Wiley, and this is where he built the Rush Hotel on the "square" in downtown Tyler in 1847.

The couple had two children of their own: Alanzo Rush, who became a dentist in Kaufman, Texas; and Van Burena Rush, born December 27, 1846, in the portion of Mercer's Colony that was then in Henderson County, Texas.

Vannie Rush, as she was called, married Archibald Cockerell in Tyler, Texas, July 9, 1878. Their son, Dr. Lonnie Lee Cockerell, born June 4, 1879, married Elizabeth Eula Earnest January 2, 1902, at Picken's Spur, Texas; they were my mother's parents. My mother, Melba Dal Cockerell, was born March 28, 1911, in Eustace, Texas, where she married on December 30, 1933, Thomas Bruce Green, Jr., born September 1, 1910, in Athens, Texas.

I was born July 17, 1939, in Athens, Texas, in my grandfather's hospital. I married Margo Irene Oberkampf on June 19, 1961, in New Braunfels, Texas, and we have one daughter, Holly Ann Green. She was born in Key West, Florida, November 27, 1965, and is married to Brian Childs.

Major James Martin Rush obtained a contract for mail route #62333 to deliver the U.S. mail into the Mercer Colony, and he hired Benjamin Wheeler from New Orleans to ride the route on horseback from Tyler to Hamburg, where he appointed my great-great-grandfather, James Coltharp, as post master on April 29, 1852. Ben Wheeler continued on, carrying the mail to Canton, Texas, and finally to Buffalo, then located south of present-day Kemp, Texas, which was the first county seat of Henderson County, Texas. James Rush became the postmaster of Tyler and maintained this mail contract until the Civil War began, as well as operating a stage coach line from Tyler to Shreveport, Louisiana, before his death in 1869 on his farm located one mile north of the Tyler square where he was buried. His wife, Tennessee Blair Rush, died in 1879, also in Tyler, where her son, Rev. James Seeton, became a pastor of the Marvin Methodist Church in which his mother and stepfather were charter members. Thomas Bruce Green, III SRT member #6191

PLASCEE SANCHEZ

Plascee was born May 5, 1840 in Nacogdoches Territory. He died January 9, 1913, and is buried in the Larazine Cemetery located six miles south west of Nacogdoches on Hwy. #7. Plascee Sanchez is known in the family as Placido Sanchez, and lived most of his life in Leon County. He was married in 1865 to Vencenta (Sindy) Y'Barbo.

Plascee had three brothers and one sister. His father, Julian Sanchez, was born in Texas and is listed on school tax rolls and census records for Nacogdoches County in 1836. Julian's wife, Marcissa, was a full-blood Choctaw Indian from Mississippi, whom he married on one of his adventures east.

Plascee was a farmer most of his life. He enlisted in the Confederate Army July 17, 1862, at Centerville, Texas, as a private in Company G, 2nd Regiment, Texas Infantry, CSA. He was captured at the Battle of Vicksburg, Mississippi, and was a prisoner of war for a short time. He was paroled July 7, 1863, and was allowed to return to Texas.

My name is Albert De Leon, and Plascee Sanchez is my great-grandfather. He is the father of my grandmother, Rosa (Rosie) Sanchez, who married my grandfather, Pablo De Leon on January 21, 1887, in Leon County, Texas. Albert De Leon, SRT #2972 Ephraim M. Daggett Chapter #36

EDWARD BENJAMIN SCHOONOVER

Benjamin, his wife, Elizabeth, and their eight young children settled in Lamar County during October 1841. Their youngest son, Henry, was later born in the new Republic of Texas in 1843. Benjamin received a Conditional Land Grant of 640 acres on December 6, 1841, and later received the Unconditional Land Grant on June 2, 1845. Benjamin is listed in the 1842 Lamar County tax roll, the 1846 Republic of Texas poll lists, the Tarrant County census for 1850 (dated November 5) and the Bexar County Census for 1850 (dated November 15).

Manerua (Petty) and James W. Schoonover Married August 4, 1859, Clinton, Texas.

Benjamin is shown in various Texas records as both a farmer and wagoner. A Lamar County recorded bill of sale dated May 9, 1847 shows Benj. Schoonover to Hamilton and Morrison the transfer of one wagon, one yoak of oxen and log chains, $60.

Benjamin was born 1803 in Pennsylvania. He married Elizabeth Wheeler on March 13, 1824, in Scioto County, Ohio. He descends from Dutch colonists who arrived in colonial New Netherlands (New York) between 1630-1640. His father, Christopher, was a wounded Revolutionary War veteran, having served the war with the New York Continental Army.

Today, the many descendants of Benjamin and Elizabeth Schoonover can be found throughout Texas. As the great-great-grandson of these early Texas settlers, I only wish that I could have known them personally. Tony Ray Schoonover # L - 4299

SCHORP FAMILY

The Schorp family in Bieringen, Wurtemberg, Germany, came there originally from Switzerland. The first record is of a Hans Jorg Schorp, who married Anna Maria Sauder. From that union came Thomas Schorp (1735-1801) and his marriage to Marie Heitkorn produced Fidel Schorp (1773-1836). Fidel's marriage to Crescentia Straub (1783-1829) produced a son named Joseph Schorp I on 11 Feb. 1815.

Joseph I came to Texas in November 1843 on the ship "Heinrich," which arrived in Galveston on 1 January 1844. He was a carpenter by trade and settled in Castroville, Texas. He married Marie Louise Tondre there in 1850 and they had 14 children.

Their son Joseph Schorp II was born 28 April 1860 there in Castroville, and married Maria Anna Haby. He and his brother, Louis, who was married to Mary Spettle, came to Pearsall, Texas, in the late 1800s and formed the Schorp and Spettle Ranch.

Joseph Schorp II and Maria Anna Haby Schorp had 3 children. Their oldest child, Ida Helen Schorp, was born on 3 December 1890. She married Walter Francis Smith in Laredo, Texas, on 27 December 1925. W.F. Smith was a U.S. Mounted Customs Officer assigned to Company D of the Texas Rangers under Captain Will Wright. From that union came 3 children: Robert Joseph Schorp, Helen Ida and Mary Jo.

Robert married Cynthia Lou Bingman and they have 3 children: Robert Boyd Bingman, Harriett Mandena and Helen Marie. Robert Joseph Schorp Smith

JOHN ADAM SCHUESSLER

John Adam Schuessler, his wife Eva, and their five children came to Texas in 1845. They sailed from Germany on the ship "Dyle" and landed at Indianola. They received a land grant of 320 acres to farm from the Republic of Texas (Bexar County). They named and settled at Cherry Springs (now, Gillespie County). One child had died, and three more sons were born. While at Cherry Springs, John helped the settlers draft a peace treaty with the Commence Indians — the only peace treaty that was observed and kept by both sides.

The Schuessler family later moved north into Mason County and donated some of their land for a Lutheran church in Mason.

John was born Aug. 24, 1811, in Bonfeld (Wurttenberg Province) in southern Germany to Conrad Schuessler and Eva Bender. John married Eva Katharina Dischinger (born Sept. 5, 1810, at Bonfeld) on Jan. 13, 1835. John died April 7, 1884, and Eva died Jan. 9, 1901. Both are buried in Crosby Cemetery at Mason.

One ancestor, Capsar Schuessler, was instrumental in starting the famous Passion Play at Obermmergau, Germany, after the black plague in 1633.

SRT descendants include Robert Bohmfalk (great-great-grandson) #5810A, Jeff Ullrich (great-great-great-grandson) #5793A, Joe Ullrich (great-great-great-grandson) #5824A, and John Ullrich (great-great-great-grandson) #5823A.

JOHANN VALENTIN SCHULMEYER

Johann Valentin Schulmeyer was born ca. 1798 in Germany. He married in Germany ca. 1829 to Susanne Ackermann. She was born ca. 1812 in Germany.

Johann was a farmer from Menteroda, Sachsen, Gotha, Germany. He and his wife, Susanne, and their children — Faub, Leopold, Wilhelm and Johanna — were immigrants under the colonization contact of the Fisher-Miller Company. Johann and his family departed Germany from the port of Bremen 10 May 1844 aboard the Brig Weser. It arrived in the port of Galveston on 8 July 1844. The family arrived in New Braunfels on 21 March 1845. The First Protestant Church of New Braunfels conducted a dedication ceremony in April of 1845. Johann and his family were present for this celebration.

In 1848, Johann sold his holdings in New Braunfels and moved to Guadalupe County. The 1850 Guadalupe County Census indicates Johann living with his wife, Susanne, and children: Leopold, Wilhelm, Johanne, Fredericka and Henriette. By 1853 he had returned to Comal County and was listed on county tax rolls as farming 300 acres near Cibolo Creek until 1858. He is my 3rd great-grand father. Raymond David Wier, Jr. SRT # 6377

NEHEMIAH SCOTT

Nehemiah Scott was born December 31, 1784, in Sampson County, North Carolina, and died 1878 in Hunt County, Texas. He is believed to be buried in Hope (Sweat Box) Cemetery near Jardin in Hunt County, Texas. He was the son of Nehemiah and Elizabeth Scott of Sampson County, North Carolina. Nehemiah Scott Sr. died in 1801 in Sampson County.

Nehemiah married (1) Christian Williams, daughter of Daniel Williams and Sarah Nixon, ca. 1806 probably in Sampson County, North Carolina. She was born March 26, 1788, in Sampson County, North Carolina, and died May 8, 1826 in Dickson County, Tennessee. They had eleven children.

Joel Marion Crain 1848-1890.
Daguerreotype in open case.

Nehemiah Scott served in the War of 1812 from Dickson County, Tennessee, in the 1st Tennessee Militia, Dyer's Regiment. His unit was Tennessee Volunteer Mounted Gunmen, which was commanded by Captain Joseph Williams, his brother-in-law.

At age 43, Nehemiah married (2) eighteen-year-old Sarah N. "Sally" Williams on September 26, 1827, in Dickson County, Tennessee. Born ca. 1809 in Dickson County, Tennessee, Sally was the daughter of Daniel Hicks Williams and Catherine Spicer and the niece of (1) Christian Williams Scott. Sally died 1860/1870 probably in Hunt County, Texas.

Nehemiah (age 53), Sally Williams Scott, with their four young children and the unmarried children of Nehemiah's first marriage (Williams, Sara Jane, Abraham and Jeanetta Scott, and possibly Richard N. Williams, brother of (1) Christian Williams) emigrated to the Republic of Texas in 1837. One unmarried daughter, Susan Ann Scott, remained in Tennessee.

When Nehemiah Scott received his 3rd Class Land Grant in Lamar County, Texas, he gave his emigration date into Texas as November 24, 1837. One child was born in Red River County, and Nehemiah and his family lived for a number of years in Lamar County (1850 and 1860 census). He sold land in Lamar County in 1861. In 1870, he was listed in Hunt County, Texas, with his son, Williams Scott. Sarah is not listed, but is believed to have died in Hunt County. Nehemiah's age is shown as 97 and born in Tennessee. He was actually age 87 born in North Carolina.

Mary Catharine Scott, born in Dickson County, Tennessee, 13 January 1829, was the first child of Nehemiah and Sally Williams Scott and was eight years old when she arrived in Texas. She married Jasper Newton Crain, son of John and Pheraby Rumley Crain, October 7, 1847, in Lamar County, Texas. Jasper Crain was on the 1844 Lamar County tax list.

The first born child of Jasper and Mary Catherine Scott Crain was Joel Marion Crain who was born August 19, 1848 in Lamar County. He married Nancy Jane Holmes December 21, 1869, daughter of George Thomas Holmes and Nancy Williams Jackson. Joel Marion Crain and Nancy Jane Holmes were the great-grandparents of Mayo D. Dancer, and the great-great-grandparents of Mark Pendley. Mayo Dewayne Dancer 36 L #4001, Mark Austin Pendley 27 L #6041

JESSE THOMAS SCRUGGS, SR.

The third child of Finch and Nancy Thomas Scruggs, was born February 17, 1799 in Buckingham County, Virginia. My great-great-grandfather's line extends from his son, Hamilton McGuire Scruggs born in Texas in 1840, to his son, Hamp Jewel, born in Texas 1884, to my father, James Donece Scruggs born in Texas in 1929.

From Virginia, the family migrated south to Tennessee by 1804 after the death of Nancy's father; Jesse Thomas of Virginia; to Alabama by 1824 then to Iuka, Mississippi where his elder parents remained.

Jesse married first in Tennessee in 1823, but was a widower with five children soon after arriving in Texas in 1834. He married second the daughter of Dr. Lawrence McGuire and Margaret Tolan, MaryAnn Tolan McGuire, April 2, 1835 in Grenada, Mississippi.

He received a Texas Land Grant of 640 acres in 1843, and became a Justice and Judge as his father was and published information may be found; *Elected Officials of the Republic of Texas 1835-46* as Justice of the Peace, *Texas County Sheriffs 1856-60* Sammy Tise, *Judges of the Republic of Texas* Joe E. Ericson, *Sabine County, Texas: 1st 150 years 1836-1986* Robert McDaniel and *The History of McMahan's Chapel 1833-1976* Virgie Scurlock.

He was instrumental in establishing Jackson Masonic Lodge, No. 35, instituted June 23, 1847 and was a Junior Deacon 1857, a Chapter Member and Worshipful Master. His eldest son served in the Texas-Mexican War and five sons served with the Confederate States of America, in which two died.

Two of Jesse's daughters married sons of Elder William Brittain and Rosanna Wright and one son, Hamilton McGuire Scruggs married one of the Elders granddaughters, Sarah Elizabeth Wilburn, the daughter of Elihue Wilburn and Cynthia Brittain.

Jesse died at the home of his eldest daughter, Sarah Arabella Harvey, November 16, 1882 at 83 and he's interred at Harvey Family Cemetery in Sabine County, Texas. James Donece Scruggs, Jimmy Lee Scruggs # 6184, Ricky Don Scruggs, Cody Scruggs

JUAN NEPOMUCENO SEGUIN

Juan Nepomuceno Seguin — Texan, defender at the Alamo and hero of San Jacinto – was born October 27, 1806, in San Fernando de Bejar Tejas, New Spain (present-day San Antonio Texas). His parents were Juan Jose Maria Erasmo de Jesus Seguin and Josefa Augustina Bercerra (Seguin), both Texan, as was his wife, Maria Gertrudis Eusevia Flores (Seguin).

Many events in the lives of Juan and his father Erasmo led to the struggle for the eventual independence of Texas. The Seguin, Flores, and Carvajal families were hard-working and peaceful people. They believed in freedoms that we enjoy today and often take for granted.

Col. Juan N. Sequin

Colonel Juan N. Seguin and his family did not like nor tolerate injustices. Yes, even back then they fought for basic human rights for all native Texans and citizens to be of Texas; thus they were not willing to step aside at the risk of personal ridicule, danger or threats of death.

The colonel was one of the most gallant heroes of the Texas War for Independence. Early on, he sensed the threat of tyranny when the Mexican Constitution of 1824 was disregarded which, among other stipulations, granted all citizens and subjects of Mexico their basic human rights.

In 1835, Juan N. Seguin sought to convene the first revolutionary meeting in protest of the demands and actions of Santa Anna's government. He was the first to sound the alarm of impending danger to the way of life and liberty that Texans had enjoyed."Texas shall be free and independent or we shall die in glorious combat."

The Seguin Family Historical Society Patch

Colonel Seguin was a veteran commander of many battles, defender and courier at the Alamo, hero of San Jacinto, a Republic of Texas senator, savior of San Antonio and namesake for the city of Seguin. He is the only native-born Texan who fought at both the Alamo and at San Jacinto.

A legendary figure as a leader in the Texas Revolution, he was appointed a captain by Stephen F. Austin and later commissioned lieutenant colonel by President Burnet. His life spanned from Spanish rule, Mexico's domination, the Republic of Texas, the Confederacy and Texas as part of the United States of America,

Texas history has often been told without a full representation of the contributions of Tejanos. Both Anglos and Tejanos fought equally against the tyranny of Santa Anna. Had they been unsuccessful, most Anglos could have returned to the United States. The Tejanos would have been subjected to loss of property at best or, most likely, loss of life.

Senator Juan N. Seguin was a Texan by birth who risked his life and property for Texas and all Texans, to do what was right, not to support any particular culture. This is the ultimate contribution that a citizen can offer his or her country. Senator Seguin died 1889. Albert Seguin Carvajal Gonzales #6260. Third great-grandson

PETER SEIDEMANN

Peter Seidemann was born 1813 in Holler, Germany, to Peter Seidemann and Catharine Schlemmer Seidemann. Peter married Anna-Maria Daunt July 10, 1844 in Holler, Germany.

Peter signed German Contract #2082 on August 16, 1845, while in Bremen, Germany. In this contract, he agrees to turn over to the company ("The Society for the Protection of German Immigrants in Texas"), one half of the 640 acres he was to receive from the Republic of Texas, in exchange for passage for him and his family to Texas. Peter and Anna-Maria then sail from Bremen, Germany, along with 137 other immigrants aboard the "Hershel" arriving in Galveston Texas, October 16, 1845.

Of the 640 acres granted to Peter, 513 are in Menard County and 127 in Burnet County. Fisher-Miller transfer #841 is used to transfer one-half of this land to the company. Peter eventually sells the remaining acreage and buys acreage closer to New Braunfels. In the 1860 Texas Agricultural Census, Peter has 28 improved acres and 312 unimproved acres.

Peter and Anna-Maria had seven children all born in Texas. Adam (March 6, 1848), William (October 15,1849), Anna (November 5, 1851), Jacob (September 29, 1853), Helene (May 21, 1856) and Henry (August 1, 1857).

Peter is listed as one of the original builders and contributors to Saints Peter and Paul Catholic Church in New Braunfels.

Peter died August 9, 1860. Lawrence Peter Seidemann Jr., #4455, Lawrence Peter Seidemann, III #4270, Scott Lawrence Seidemann #4269, Mark Burns Seidemann #4828, Jonathan Lawrence Heep #4394

JAMES SHAW

James Shaw was born in Clermont County, Ohio, on August 8, 1808. He settled in present Milam County, Texas, in 1835 and served as a private in Captain William Smith's Cavalry Company at the Battle of San Jacinto. He remained in the Texas Army as a lieutenant until August 1836. As a veteran of San Jacinto, he received a grant of land, which he selected in Burleson (now Lee) County.

After staking out his land, he went to Missouri and married his sweetheart, Nancy Riggs. They returned to Texas and he became a school teacher and surveyor. James and Nancy had three children: 1. Frank, killed in Louisiana while in the Confederate Army; 2. Sophia, married Isaac C. Douglass, a captain in the 17th Texas

Infantry, Confederate States Army; and 3. Travis, who married Elizabeth Ferguson of Virginia.

James Shaw was a member of the Republic of Texas House for the Third and Fifth Congresses and was senator in the Sixth, Seventh and Eighth Congresses. In 1855, he was elected to the Senate of the State Legislature.

He died February 8, 1879 on his farm near Lexington, Lee County, Texas, and is buried in Early Chapel Cemetery. A State Historical Marker was erected at his grave. J Douglass Moore #3853 Great-great-grandson

JESSE SHELTON

Jesse Shelton, a native of Virginia, came west and settled in Miller County, Arkansas Territory, in the early 1820s. In 1837, he moved to Lamar County, Texas. He lived the first two years in a fortification near the present site of Roxton called Shelton's Fort. It served as a way station for travelers and a stronghold for settlers fleeing Indian raids. Shelton's Fort was designated a Republic of Texas post office in 1840, and was also the site of Methodist worship services.

Jesse Shelton served on the committee to select the first Lamar County seat, and was one of the country's first Justices of the Peace.

Texas Historical Marker for Jesse Shelton

The great-grandson of Ralph Shelton, Sr., of Middlesex County, Virginia, he was born on February 22, 1782, and died in Red River County, Texas, on May 25, 1855. On January 22, 1805, he married in Logan County, Kentucky, Rachel Marrs, the daughter of James Marrs and Ann Shannon. Rachel Marrs Shelton died in Red River County, Texas on April 5, 1860. Jesse and Rachel were the parents of the following children: William, who died leaving no heirs; Annie who married William English, and after his death, Andrew S. Young; Miranda, who married James M. Brackeen; Minerva, who married William Yates; Harvey; Eli Jenway who married Martha Ann Elizabeth Yates; Eliza Jane, who was first married to T.C. Forbes, and after his death, to Nathaniel Henderson; Ervin; Lucinda, who married H.R. Latimer; and Marietta who married F.M. Helborn. Edward Milton Bush #3596, Edward Church Bush #3595, Wilson Walter Crook, Jr. #1939

GENERAL SIDNEY SHERMAN

General Sidney Sherman commanded the Second Regiment of the Texas Army. It formed the left wing at the Battle of San Jacinto. It advanced through a fringe of timber that ran along the bluff line on the north side of the battlefield, between the Mexican position and the marsh. Santa Anna had placed 3 companies of infantry (de preferencia) between the north end of their breastwork and the bluff. The 2nd Regiment drove these 3 companies out of the timber and around the end of the brestwork, effectively turning the Mexican right wing.

Sherman, born in Marlboro, Massachusetts, July 23, 1805, moved to Kentucky, owned and operated a cotton bagging plant and a sheet lead plant, and was captain of a company of militia. He organized a company of approximately 55 men and brought them to Texas in 1835, joining the forming army at Gonzales.

When the army was reorganized by act of the Congress of Texas, he was elected major general and held that position until Texas joined the United States. Prior to this, he had served in the Congress of Texas.

He organized and built the first railroad west of the Mississippi, the Buffalo Bayou, Brazos and Colorado, extending from Harrisburg to Alleyton on the Colorado River across from Columbus.

He died August 1, 1873, and is buried in Lakeview Cemetery, Galveston, Texas. Great grandsons: William T. Kendall, Sidney Sherman Kendall, F. Russell Kendall,

OFFA LUNSFORD SHIVERS, M.D.

Offa Lunsford Shivers, M.D., was born 15 February 1815 in Pitt County, N.C., the son of Jesse and Nancy (Briley) Shivers. They moved their family to Greene County (now Hale County), Alabama, near Greensboro in 1818 after his service as a captain in the Indian Wars of Alabama and Florida. In 1835, Dr. Shivers entered medical school at Transylvania University in Lexington, KY. He responded to a speaker who was pleading for men to join Texas colonists in their fight for freedom from Mexico, and traveled by boat down the Mississippi River to New Orleans, then Matagorda Island, Texas, where he arrived on 24 March 1836, just three days after the battle of San Jacinto. He mustered into Captain Love's Company in the 1st Regiment, 1st Brigade of Texas Volunteers on 4 June 1836 as a lieutenant, and served until he was honorably discharged 4 September 1836. A muster roll dated October 1836 shows that Lieutenant Shivers was placed in temporary command on the day he mustered into the army in the absence of Captain Love, who was on leave.

After completing his service in the Texas Volunteer Army, Dr. Shivers returned to Alabama and learned that his family thought that he had died or been killed in Texas. He completed his medical training and married Catherine Obedience Woodfin in Marengo County, Alabama, in 1837. He was a Professor of Materia Medica at Memphis Medical College in the early 1840s, and settled in Marion, Perry County, Alabama, where he died 24 March 1881. He received Pension No. 800, approved 22 Oct. 1874, and Bounty Land Warrant No. 2547 for his service in the Texas Army.

Two of Dr. Shivers' children moved to Texas shortly after the Civil War. Sarah Catherine Shivers (1841-1917) married Rev. John Lee Lattimore, who was a chaplain in the Confederate Army from Mississippi and was captured at Vicksburg. They are buried at Dublin, Texas. One of their sons, Offa Shivers Lattimore (1865-1938) was a Justice of the Court of Criminal Appeals in Austin. Another son, Samuel Harrison Lattimore (born 1881) served on the Oklahoma Supreme Court. A daughter, Mary Catherine (Kate) Lattimore, married Richard Boyd Spencer in Dublin, Texas, in 1886. They were grandparents of the submitter, and she was the first woman trustee at Baylor University in Waco.

Dr. Shivers' daughter, Nannie Elizabeth Shivers (1853-1945), married Albert Boggess, who had been a cadet lieutenant in the

Virginia Military Institute Corps which participated in the Battle of New Market, Virginia, in 1863 as part of the Confederate forces. They met at Baylor University in Waco, where they were both professors.

Submitted by: Richard Thomas Spencer, Jr., SRT #3897, Moses Austin Chapter #12, great-great-grandson of Dr. Offa Lunsford Shivers.

Other descendants of Dr. Shivers: John William Cathey, SRT # 1317, George B. Erath Chapter # 13; Pauline Butte Dawson Zachry, DRT #11648, Alamo Mission Chapter; Elizabeth Lucy Kimball Pratt, DRT #12128, Alamo Mission Chapter

CAPTAIN THOMAS SIMONS

The Simons families of Jackson, Victoria, and surrounding counties are descendants of Captain Thomas Simons who was born on the family estate, Pelaw House, in Durham County, England, on May 26, 1794. His father, Joseph Simons, owner of the Birtley Salt Works, married in 1792 Miss Hannah Vezy, a descendant of Yvo de Vesci, who came to England with William the Conqueror in 1066.

*Thomas Simons
New Orleans prior to 1835*

Captain Simons was the owner of a large sailing vessel, and while having repairs made he settled for a while in Cape Breton, Nova Scotia, where on July 15, 1817, he married Susan Thomas, who was born May 12, 1802 to Thomas Thomas and Elizabeth Haverstock. He and family moved to Halifax, where he was engaged in business and trade, and after six years loaded family and goods aboard his ship "Phoebe" and sailed south, his ultimate destination being South America. He stopped in New Orleans, where two children died of yellow fever. He then sailed for Texas and landed at Dimmit's Point, Jackson Municipality, in 1835.

He and family settled at Texana, where during the Texas Revolution he furnished supplies and drayage to the army both by sea and land. After the war he was a surveyor, preparing a map of Jackson County for the Republic, served two army camps as Counselor for the Republic, served as county clerk, county surveyor and Justice of the Peace. John Gordon Laughter Jr. #5997, Don B. Frels #6914

HARRELLL DOUGLAS SIMPSON

Harrell Douglas Simpson, born Aug. 26, 1931, in Llano, Llano County, Texas, joined George B. Erath Chapter #13 of Waco, Sons of the Republic of Texas, on 21 June, 1995.

He graduated from Brady High School and attended Midwestern University and the University of North Texas. He served in the U.S. Navy from 1951 to 1955. In the Korean Conflict, he was stationed on the U.S.S. Chourre in Japan. He was employed in the office of Roadway Express for over 25 years, retiring in 1988.

Harrell Douglas Simpson holding a photo of his confederate ancestor Capt. David P. Curry, Rockbridge Guards, Va.

He married Gelene Duncan (born 2 Jan. 1937, in Corsicana, Texas, Navarro County), on April 6, 1957, in Gradfield, Tillman County, Oklahoma. They have two children: Darrell Randall Simpson, born 11 Sept. 1959, in Dallas, Texas; and Sarita Carole Simpson, born 2 Aug. 1960, in Dallas, Texas.

His hobby in Irving, Texas was raising racing pigeons, one of his birds having held a national speed record. He is also a member of J.L. Halbert Camp #359, Sons of Confederate Veterans, MOSB, Hubbard City Lodge 530 AF&AM, and is associate patron of Dawson Chapter #1046, O.E.S.

JUDGE JOHN PERKINS SIMPSON (1806-1884)

John Perkins Simpson was born Oct. 17, 1806, in Gibson County, Tennessee. In 1825, he became a Christian at a camp meeting in Rock Spring, Alabama. On June 15, 1831, he married Sina Needham in Madison County, Tennessee. Sina was born Jan. 8, 1814 in Maury County, Tennessee.

Simpson came to the Republic of Texas from Arkansas, with a group of settlers led by Bailey Inglish (1793-1867). Simpson brought his wife Sina, daughter Elizabeth (born 1832), and daughter Martha, (born 1834). The youngest child, Mary Evelyn, was born in 1837 in Fannin County. Inglish was married to Sina's sister, Nancy Needham Crooms.

Simpson was a lieutenant in the Rangers of the Texas Militia during 1838-39. He became the first sheriff of Fannin County and built the first jail in 1839. He also built the first grist mill and helped build the courthouse. He and Inglish donated the land for the courthouse.

Simpson was appointed lieutenant colonel in the militia by President Sam Houston. In 1843, the community's name was changed to Bonham and became the county seat. He was elected judge and served from 1843-1846. He a member of Constantine Lodge #13 AF&AM since 1840, and was Master of the Lodge from 1851-1852.

During the 1870s, Simpson wrote many stories for The Bonham News about the early days of Fannin County. He was a Methodist preacher, although he seldom officiated in that role.

Sina died Feb. 24, 1883, at their home near Ector. Simpson died there on Jan. 13, 1884. They are buried at Willow Wild Cemetery in Bonham, Texas. Simpson Park on North Center Street is named for him The fourth great-grandfather of James Phillips

ROBERT STERLING SIMPSON

Robert Sterling Simpson, great-grandfather of Harrell D. Simpson, was born in Danville, Virginia, March 5, 1822. He was recorded in 1840 Citizens of Texas, but went back to Alabama to marry Rebecca Catherine Henshaw (born 7 Oct. 1823) probably in 1841 in or near Huntsville, Alabama. They had 4 children born in Madison, Alabama, before leaving Jackson County. One child was born in Louisiana on the way back to Texas, where they settled on Simpson's farm land in the part of Milam County that is now Burleson County, and had five more children.

R.S. Simpson died 19 Aug. 1888, and is buried in the Old City Cemetery in Caldwell, Burleson County, Texas. His wife, Rebecca, died 21 Feb. 1905, and is buried in the Masonic Cemetery, Caldwell, Burleson County, Texas.

The family genealogy refers to Robert Sterling sometimes as "Sam Houston" Simpson, probably because he tried so hard to return to Texas. His son, John Tyler Simpson, grandfather of Harrell Simpson, actually named a son "Sam Houston Simpson," and it is difficult to tell whether he was referring to the real Sam Houston or to Robert Sterling Simpson — probably a little of both. Harrell Douglas Simpson #6182

ANTHONY GARNETT SMITH, JR.

Anthony Garnett Smith, Jr. was born January 25, 1809, in Oglethorpe County, Georgia, to the Rev. Anthony Garnett Smith, Sr. and Mary (Polly) Allen Smith. In 1788, the Smith family moved from Cumberland County, Virginia, to Oglethorpe County. The Rev. Anthony G. Smith, a minister in the Methodist Episcopal Church, was ordained deacon by Bishop Francis Asbury in 1811, and was ordained elder by Bishop William McKendree in 1812. In 1820, the Smiths were charter members of the Mount Pleasant Methodist Church in Oglethorpe County. They later built a two-story home in Crawford County around 1830, which still stands.

Anthony G. Smith, Jr.

Anthony Garnett Smith, Jr. was a Georgia Volunteer in the Texas Revolution. He enlisted with the Texas forces at San Felipe in 1836 after making the trip from Georgia on horseback. He later returned to his native state after being incapacitated by wounds to continue in service.

On May 14, 1848, Anthony Garnett Smith, Jr. and Elizabeth Murphey Smith were married in Upson County, Georgia. Elizabeth, the daughter of Charles Lee Smith, Sr. and Martha T. Glenn Smith, was born June 21, 1823, in Talbot County, Georgia. Anthony Garnett Smith, Jr. and Elizabeth M. Smith had the following children: Charles A. Smith, Carey Allen Smith, Mary Elizabeth Smith, Wesley Asbury Smith, M.D., Simeon Hull Smith, M.D., Martha Johanna Smith, Garnett Daniel Smith, Emma Caroline Smith, Robert Lee Smith, Ida Virginia Smith, Eliza Eleanor Smith, Sarah Harriett Smith, and Adelaide Smith.

Anthony Garnett Smith died on February 19, 1891, and Elizabeth Murphey Smith died on February 27, 1902. Both are buried in Glenwood Cemetery in Thomaston, Georgia.

Adelaide Smith was born July 20, 1865, in Talbot County, and married Joshua Calhoun Howell on December 24, 1890, in Upson County. They moved to Hill County, Texas, where Joshua was a schoolmaster and had a cotton farm. Joshua and Adelaide Howell had the following children: Elizabeth (Bessie) Lethella Howell, Mamie Ross Howell, Jewell Howell, Robert Calhoun Howell, and Winnie Davis Howell. The Howells were members of First Methodist Church of West. Many family members are buried in Bell Springs Cemetery near Abbott, Texas. Todd Bradford Willis

FRANCIS SMITH

Francis and Joanna Smith, natives of Dinwiddie County, Va., came to Texas in 1831, from Giles County, Tennessee.

Francis received a league of land on May 7, 1831, in Stephen Austin's Second Colony, in present Burleson County, Texas.

The Mexican government built a log fort on a high bluff on the west side of the Brazos, overlooking the river. Fort Tenoxitlan (t-nots-t-lan) was manned with 100 soldiers under Colonel Ruiz's command on Oct. 17, 1830. It was built to stem the tide of settlers coming from the United States. General Teran had instructed Colonel Ruiz to be careful to get along with both the Indians and Americans who were already citizens of Texas. Ruiz rarely intervened, letting frontier justice prevail.

By July 1831, Francis Smith had a store/fur trading post at Fort Tenoxitlan. He traded merchandise with the Indians and settlers for their furs. In 1833, he established a trading post at the Falls on the Brazos in present Falls County, Texas. He there purchased 2 1/2 leagues of land from Wm. H. Jack for $125.00.

Joanna Smith died Jan. 21, 1846, at her residence in Fayette County, Texas. Francis Smith died Jan. 14, 1846, at his residence in Fayette County, Texas. John Thomas Lawhon #4580. Great-great-great-grandson of Francis and Joanna Smith

GEORGE WASHINGTON SMITH

George Washington Smith, who served Texas at the Battle of San Jacinto, in the Mier Expedition, and in Mexico with Col. John C. Hayes, was born in Wilson County, Tennessee, about 1796. He fought Indians in Tennessee as a teenager under Andrew Jackson, and served in the War of 1812 at the Battle of New Orleans.

Smith was married in Wayne County, Kentucky, to Elizabeth Briggs, who was part Cherokee, in 1817. They had four daughters. The family settled at the head of Bois d'Arc Creek in Red River County, Texas, in 1834 and received a league and a labor of land.

Pay vouchers show Smith's frequent movements for the next decade, from fights for Texas independence back home to put in crops. Reports and family tradition stated that he was with his neighbor, Benjamin R. Milam, at the Siege of Bexar on December 7, 1835, and that the fatally wounded Milam died in Smith's arms.

After the siege, Smith traveled to his home in newly formed Fannin County, then returned to duty with Sam Houston for the fight at San Jacinto. As one of Capt. John G.W. Pierson's men in 1842, Smith was captured with others of the Mier Expedition, but he escaped at the Rio Grande and returned home. After annexation, he again left home, this time to join the First Regiment, Texas Mounted Riflemen, for the campaign to Mexico City in 1847. Smith served as sergeant with Capt. Preston Witt in Company K.

He died at his home in Collin County in about 1876. A Texas Historical Marker placed near the Blue Ridge Cemetery in 1979 marks the place of his original burial, though his daughters had his remains moved to nearby Grounds Graveyard. R.S. Jones, great-great-great-grandson

JOHN WILLIAM (EL COLORADO) SMITH

John William (El Colorado) Smith, early San Antonian, was born March 4, 1792, in Virginia, moved to Missouri where he was married in 1821, and served as sheriff of Ralls County from 1822 to 1826. Migrating to Texas, he settled in Gonzales and lived a short time, going from there to Bexar County. He married Maria Jesua Curbelo, the daughter of Don Patron Juan Curbelo, leader of the Canary Island community. From 1830-35, he conducted a mercantile business in San Antonio, leaving it to join the Texas Army in the Battles of Concepcion and San Antonio. Smith was not in the Alamo slaughter due to his having been elected by Travis to carry his last message to the outside world. From January 1837, to March 9, 1838, Smith served as San Antonio's first mayor; from January 8, 1839, to January 8, 1840, he was an alderman under the Samuel Maverick administration. The 1840 Census of Bexar County and San Antonio includes (4) city lots, (1) gold watch, and 5000 acres. The Republic of Texas granted him the land for his service in the Army. It was bounded by a line from San Pedro Spring, north to a point west of and transit to the headwaters of the San Antonio River, and back along the Camino Real. This was the largest tract owned in all Bexar County, which extended to Colorado at that time.

From January 9, 1841, he served his second term as major; and from April 18, 1842 to March 30, 1844, he again held that position. Meanwhile, at the Seventh, Eighth, and Ninth Congresses, 1842-45, John W. Smith represented Bexar County in the Senate. He was serving in that capacity when he died of a disease similar to influenza, January 13, 1845, at Washington-on-the-Brazos. Congress was in session at the time. This ended the long-held rivalry between Smith and Sam Houston over the decision not to attempt to reinforce the Alamo and prevent the sacrifice of Smith's friends, fellow San Antonians and Texians- see Chabot, "With the Makers Of San Antonio," 274-5; Williams-Barker, "Writings of Sam Houston, III," 278-9; Winkler, "Secret Sessions of the Senate, 1836-45"; Morning Star, January 18, 1845.

WAGER SPEED SMITH

Wager Speed Smith and his wife, Charlotte, were in Texas by 1840. They came from Virginia by way of Tennessee to Rutersville, Fayette County, Texas, where they engaged in farming, buying and selling land, and raising kids.

Wager was a trustee of and established the Rutersville College, the first Protestant college in Texas. The college was founded by the Methodist Church; a charter was obtained along with a grant of four leagues of land from the Republic of Texas. By January 1841, there were sixty students enrolled; by 1850, more than 800 students were educated there. The young men of Rutersville College often spent weeks away from classes, chasing Indians.

Wager Speed Smith died Sept. 11, 1855 age 50 years, 7 months, 16 days. After Wager's death, Charlotte M. C. Smith and James Atkinson were united in marriage on March 26, 1856, by the Rev. H. Baylor.

James Atkinson died Nov. 6, 1865, at Lexington, Texas, and Charlotte Mary Claiborne Payne Smith Atkinson died Nov. 11, 1865, at Lexington, Texas. They are buried at Early Chapel Cemetery in the Woodward Lot, three miles east of Lexington. John Thomas Lawhon #4580, Great-great-grandson of Wager Speed Smith

ABNER BAGBY SPEIR

Abner Bagby Speir was born in 1808 in Jackson County, Georgia, the son of John Speir and Rachel Bagby. Shortly after his birth, the family moved to Jones County, Georgia, then to Conecuh County, Alabama, about 1819, and finally to Pike County, Alabama, before 1830. He married Elizabeth Ann "Betsy" Whatley, the daughter of Seaborn Jones Whatley and his first wife, name unknown. They married about 1831 in Pike County, and came to Texas in February 1835 with her father, and his brother, George W. Speir.

Abner received on December 28, 1835 a league of land in Robertson's Colony in present-day Burnet County, but he first settled in what is now the eastern edge of Travis County, near Webberville. He served in the Texas Army from July 8, 1836 until October 8, 1836. For that service he received 320 acres of bounty land in Fannin County, and later a pension.

About 1842, he moved with his father-in-law to present-day Panola County, Texas, where Seaborn Whatley died about 1845. About 1854, Abner settled on his land in Burnet County. Finally in the 1860s, he moved to Bastrop County, settling in the Coon Neck community, then called Campbell Hill. There he died December 6, 1874, and his wife died July 29, 1879. Both are buried in the Speir Cemetery.

Their children were: Seaborn Jones Speir, Nancy Speir, Rebecca Jane Speir, John Madison Speir, Betsy Ann Speir, Rachael M. Speir, Mahaly Speir, Abner B. Speir, William M. Speir, Emily Speir, Catherine M. "Kate" Speir, and Eliza Speir.

Rebecca Jane Speir was born November 1, 1838, and married Isaac Anderson "Andy" Campbell on September 5, 1856, in Travis County. He was born February 7, 1835 near Huntsville, Alabama, the son of David Campbell and Susannah Pierce. His father was killed in Buena Vista, Mexico in the Mexican War. She died October 21, 1885, and Andy married her niece, Laura Ellen (Speir) Hughes. He died June 16, 1916. All three are buried in the Speir Cemetery. Billy Eugene Russell

ELIJAH STAPP

My great-great-grandfather, Elijah Stapp, was born in Orange County, Virginia, in 1783. He married Nancy Shannon in 1811. He participated in the War of 1812 before starting a family and starting his move toward Texas. Most of his six sons and two daughters were born either in Kentucky or Missouri.

A letter of introduction from Green DeWitt of Missouri tied him in with Stephen F. Austin. After several delays and due to the birth of his sons and daughters, he finally made it to Texas. Elijah received title to his grant of a league of land (4,428 acres) in what is now northern Victoria County. This was in 1831.

Elijah was elected second. Judge in 1835. He was also elected as a delegate to represent Jackson County at the Constitutional Convention the following year. Elijah, being 53 years old at the time, was one of the older Texians to attend, help prepare, and sign the Constitution and the Declaration of Independence at Washington on the Brazos.

Upon returning from the Convention, Elijah learned that his home had been ransacked and burned by Santa Ana's forces. His wife, Nancy, and the younger sons and daughter had joined others in the "Runaway Scrape." Elijah and his two older sons, William Preston and Darwin joined Sam Houston's army and fought at the Battle of San Jacinto.

William Preston Stapp, later (in 1842) took part in the Mier Expedition and was taken prisoner and sent to prison in Perote,

Mexico. After his release he wrote a book about his experiences, "The Prisoners of Perote."

In 1842, Elijah died at his home in Jackson County, Texas, and is buried under a live oak tree about 5 miles outside of Edna, Texas.

My relationship to Elijah is through his oldest daughter, Rebecca Margaret Stapp Stukes, born in Palmyra, Missouri, in 1828, and died in Colorado City, Texas, in 1899.

The information taken for this abbreviated biography is from a book by my sister, Marilouise Chambers Harkins. Lon E. Chambers, Chapter 44

ALFONSO STEELE

Alfonso Steele, born in Kentucky in 1817, left there in 1834, moving to Lake Providence, Louisiana. In November 1835, he joined Daggett's Volunteers and headed for Texas, marching to Washington-on-the-Brazos. Texas had not yet declared independence, so the unit disbanded.

Private Alfonso Steele

He remained in Washington, grinding corn for bread for the men who signed the Declaration of Independence. After independence was signed, he joined Joe Bennett's band and started out to join Travis at the Alamo. At the Colorado River, they learned that the Alamo had fallen. Moving down river, they joined General Sam Houston, and Pvt. Steele was assigned to Company F (6th Company), Second Regiment. Engaging the enemy at San Jacinto, Pvt. Steele was wounded, hospitalized, and recovered. He lived to be the last survivor of the Battle of San Jacinto.

He lived in Limestone County until his death in 1911. He was presented a gold medal by the 31st Legislature in 1909 as one of the two survivors of San Jacinto at that time. A life-size portrait of Alfonso Steele has hung in the state Capitol and at the San Jacinto Monument. Donald Leland Steele #3694, Jimmy Leslie Steele # 3696

GEORGE WASHINGTON STELL

George Washington Stell Chapter, Daughters of the Republic of Texas in Paris, Texas, was named for my great-great-great-grandfather, George Washington Stell.

He was born in Virginia approximately 1780, a son of Jeremiah Stell and Sarah Wynne Stell.

In 1815, he was married to Mary Lewis Wynne. They were the parents of seven children, one, John H.T. Stell, being my great-great grandfather. In 1839, he brought his family along with two widower grandfathers, Jeremiah Stell and John Wynne, and several slaves from Henderson County, Tennessee to Texas. The trip was made in wagons.

He selected for his home six miles southeast of Paris, known today as the Marvin Community. Here he remained the rest of his life.

His rank was that of major in the War of 1812. He served with Jackson at New Orleans and in the din and noise of this battle his hearing was seriously impaired. He never recovered from this as long as he lived.

In early life, he was a minister of the Gospel, but never followed that calling after his sense of hearing was so seriously impaired. He was a farmer, builder, and most importantly, a surveyor.

Major Stell was a very influential and cultured man, rendered much public service in the organizations of Lamar County, and had the contract for constructing the first temporary court house which was built in Paris after it had been selected as the county seat of Lamar County.

He was an earnest advocate of the annexation of Texas to the United States, and never ceased to labor to the end until that consummation was assured. Perhaps no other man who ever lived in Lamar County commanded more esteem and confidence of all his fellow men to a higher degree than George W. Stell.

On February 5, 1844, President Sam Houston approved an act "to open and establish a National Road to be called the Central National Road of the Republic of Texas." George Washington Stell was appointed to survey and measure the road under provisions of this act and directions of the commissioners. They were directed to begin the road on the bank of the Trinity River and extend to the south bank of the Red River opposite the Kiamichi River. In our terms, from central Dallas County to a point approximately 130 miles distance in northwest Red River County. The time-worn field notes in the land office are in Major Stell's own handwriting.

Slightly less than two months after the bill was approved, the surveying crew, headed by Major Stell, began its work at a certain cedar tree on the bank of the Trinity River, and thirty days later the enterprise was concluded in the Red River bottom in the northwest of Red River County opposite the mouth of the Kiamichi River. That designation was practically the head of navigation of Red River. Various supplies of sorts were brought up on boats and cotton, wheat and hides were shipped down the river.

The road provided a route for travelers coming into the Republic from the United States, many taking the route through Arkansas and crossing the Red River at or near the Kiamichi. The records of the General Land Office in Austin show that 27,000 acres of land were given to surveyors, commissioners and contractors on the road. George W. Stell performed the duties required of him by the law. For this service he received 1,280 acres of land. Two sections of the land were in the territory which now belongs to Delta County, but at that time was a part of Lamar County. Papers dated November 1, 1851, show he received from the Commissioners of the Central National Road issued by the Republic of Texas, 2,460 acres of land.

Two markers have been erected in Paris, Texas. One marker is by the Joseph Ligon Chapter, DAR, which is located on Bonham Street. The second marker in the name of George Washington Stell Chapter, Daughters of Republic of Texas, is near the entrance of the Paris Golf and Country Club grounds. These two markers are marking the route of the Central Road.

George Washington Stell Chapter, Daughters of Republic of Texas, held a dedication ceremony for the placing of a bronze historical marker on the grave of George Washington Stell in June 1986. Presiding over the ceremony was Ronald F. Dodson, Ph.D. of Tyler, Texas, a great-great-great-grandson of George W. Stell.

The final resting place for George W. Stell and his wife is Shady Grove Cemetery, located 9.5 miles southeast of Paris. He died December 12, 1870.

WILLIAM STILES, SR.

William Stiles, Sr., was born in Mecklenburg County, Virginia, on March 26, 1769. Hetty Vinson was born on July 4, 1769. They were married on May 24, 1792, in Elbert County, Georgia and are my fifth-great-grandparents. The Stiles had four boys and three girls over a period of eleven years: Robert, Elizabeth, John, William, Solomon, Nancy and Hettie. The family moved west for several years and crossed the Red River to Texas in 1823. They show up on the 1826 Census of the Austin colony.

William Stiles received a land grant in Texas. He died June 2, 1836, before the establishment of the Republic of Texas. Henry Jones, who married Nancy Stiles, was named executor of his estate and saw to the survey of the grant. His will was the first one probated in Fort Bend County, Texas, and he is buried there.

Elizabeth married David Frame in 1809 in Kentucky. They later followed the family to Texas. David signed the Oath of Allegiance to the Mexican government in the Lower Brazos region on May 1, 1824. It was administered to the men in the area by B.H. Bell, under the order of Stephen F. Austin. Elizabeth and David Frame are my fourth-great-grandparents. Elton Lacey #6931

MAXIMILLIAN BUCHANAN STOCKTON

Maximillian Buchanan Stockton was born 1 January 1824 in Lawrenceburg, Lawrence County, Tennessee, to Douglas Hayden Stockton and Emily (Bumpas) Stockton. He was the third of nine children born to this union. Douglas Hayden Stockton was a businessman in Lawrenceburg, owning a mercantile store as well as an iron ore business. He was sheriff of Lawrence County from 1825 until his death. Douglas Hayden Stockton died in Lawrenceburg, Tennessee, on 4 April 1836.

M.B., Siddie and the Stockton Boys: C. 1895. L to R: Augustus Edward, Maximilian Buchanan, Siddie J., Seth Gilbert, Hugh Spurgeon, Robert Arel, Frank Allen, Maximilian Buchanan Jr. and Douglas Hayden. Three youngest children in foreground are grandchildren.

Maximillian Buchanan Stockton was 12 years old when his father died. When he was 15 years old, M.B. accompanied his uncle, Hugh McIntyre (his mother's favorite brother-in-law), to Texas. Records indicate they arrived in the vicinity of Brenham, Texas, on 27 December 1839. His mother and all 8 of his siblings followed later, arriving in 1841.

M.B. Stockton married Henrietta Cooke 20 February 1848, in Montgomery County, Texas. Henrietta was the sister of Francis Jarvis Cooke, said to be the youngest soldier on the Texas side at the Battle of San Jacinto. M.B. and Henrietta had one child, Jarvis Stockton, born 4 January 1849. M.B. Stockton and Henrietta (Cooke) Stockton were divorced in 1855.

Mr. M.B. Stockton and Miss. S.J. Ratliff were issued a marriage license in Clinton, DeWitt County, Texas, on 23 April 1858. J.S. Miles, Justice of the Peace, married them in DeWitt County, Texas, on 25 April 1858. This union produced 13 children, 10 of which reached adulthood.

Census data indicate that M.B. Stockton lived in the Washington, DeWitt, Karnes, and finally Goliad counties of Texas. Records indicate that he owned land and "ranched" in all these counties as well as in Wharton County, Texas.

Maximillian Buchanan Stockton died 12 January 1908 at the age of 84 years and 11 days, and is buried in the Stockton Cemetery just off Highway 239 a few miles west of Charco, Goliad County, Texas.

JOEL WELLS STOWE

Joel Wells Stowe was born in Virginia in 1808. He married Hannah Thompson December 30, 1834, in Noxubee County, Mississippi. She was born in Kentucky in 1815. They came to Texas shortly after the birth of their first child in 1835, and settled in Crockett. After receiving a land grant of 640 acres he gradually acquired more land, totaling 6 1/2 sections. He was a blacksmith as well as a rancher.

After the war, he lost his slaves and a trunk full of Confederate money. He still had his blacksmith shop and about a hundred horses and their foals. He had enough land to give each of his twelve children 160 acres when they married, and he donated land for the cemetery, church and the old school house. Some of his descendants still live on part of his property.

Joel and Hannah Stowe died in Crockett — he on February 10, 1882, and she on December 18, 1893. They are buried in a private cemetery on the old Stowe place in the San Pedro community of Crockett. I am his great-great-grandson. James Edward Wright

SAMUEL STRANG

Samuel Strang (often misspelled) was listed in the Atascosita Census of 1826 as being 30 years of age, unmarried and born in New Jersey in 1796. His occupation was listed as a stock raiser, shoemaker, and farmer in Liberty County, Texas. In the "Manuscript Letters and Documents of Early Texans 1821-45," a document dated September 10, 1826, Samuel Strang's name appears on a list choosing the Nacogdoches group after division from the Stephen F. Austin Colony. Samuel Strang's name (misspelled as Strand) appeared on Captain Hugh B. Johnson's muster roll dated February 17, 1827, as having "marched loyally with the Mexican officers against the insurgents at Nacogdoches" during the Fredonian Rebellion.

In a sworn application for a league of land in 1830, Samuel Strang stated that he arrived in Texas in 1826, and was now married to Elizabeth Lowe Tatman. Their first child, Missouri, was born in 1830. Randolph Strang was born in 1833 and Samuel Strang, Jr., was born in 1834.

Samuel Strang's ("Strong") league of land is listed in the Spanish Land Grant records of 1830-1. The name of Samuel Strang appears in a muster roll book of the Texas General Land Office as being a member of Captain Hardin's Company from July 7 - October 7, 1836. For his service in the Army of the Republic of Texas, Samuel Strang was granted a First-Class Headright for one labor of land in Liberty County. He was listed in the 1838 Republic of Texas Tax List as "Sam'l Stran".

(l. to r.) J. Richard Reese, Charles W. Reese, Jr., J. William Reese, and Robert E. Reese. Dick leads his brothers in an old traditional Christmas song "Men of Harlach" Christmas 1990.

An affidavit by Randolph Strang stated that Samuel Strang, Sr. died in 1855 in Liberty County, and is buried in the family cemetery on what is now the Bill Daniels' Ranch in Liberty County. A formal headstone was placed during the Sesquicentennial Celebration by the Liberty County Historical Society that misspelled his name as Strong.

The townsite of Hardin, Texas, is on part of the original Strang land grant.

The daughter of Randolph Strang, Mary Victorine Strang, married Thaddeus Leullen Palmer on June 25, 1878, and had a daughter Stella Palmer. Stella Palmer married James William Gott on December 30, 1906. Their daughter, Mary Ruth Gott, married Charles Woodrow Reese, Sr., on August 15, 1942. The following are their sons and are all members of the San Jacinto Chapter #1: Charles W. Reese, Jr. #3879, J. Richard Reese #3874, J. William Reese #3875, Robert Edward Reese #3878

JUDGE BENJAMIN HAILE STRIBLING

Benjamin Haile Stribling was born in Pendleton County, South Carolina July 19, 1794. He was the third child of Thomas Stribling III and Elizabeth Haile Stribling. He married Ruth Bradley Greenwood, also of South Carolina, on November 21, 1820. They and their children moved to Texas in 1841, and received a land grant from the Republic of Texas in Washington County. The grant was exchanged for land in Lavaca County in 1844.

Benjamin was sworn in as probate judge of Lavaca County in August 1846, after Texas had become a state. Benjamin and Ruth had 12 children, and lived and farmed their land along Rocky Creek in Lavaca County. He died June 24, 1852 in Lavaca County.

His oldest son was the first divinity student to graduate from Baylor University in Independence and became a Baptist minister. His second son became a lawyer and judge. The third son, our ancestor, was a farmer and elected Justice of the Peace in Lavaca County in 1888. Another son fought in the Civil War in the Texas Cavalry, Confederate Regiment. He also became an ordained Baptist minister.

William B. Wiginton Family

Benjamin Haile Stribling is my great-great grandfather, and the ancestor of my two sons, three grandsons and two granddaughters. Submitted by: William Beckman Wiginton #6509, Matagorda Chapter #35, William Beckman Wiginton #6509, William Kirk Wiginton #6547M, Denton Scott Wiginton #6546M, Phillip Beckman Wiginton #6545M, Connor Burton Wiginton #6544M, Collin James Wiginton #6641M. Cradle of Texas Chapter, Children of the Republic of Texas: Christina Avery Wiginton #7447, Michelle Daley Wiginton #7748

MAJOR GEORGE SUTHERLAND

Major George Sutherland was born in Pittsylvania County, Virginia, on January 8, 1788, to John and Agnes Shelton Sutherland. His father was a soldier in the North Carolina Company of the Revolutionary Army. George left Virginia for Tennessee with his family shortly after the American Revolution.

George was commissioned a major in the Anderson County, Tennessee, Militia, 13th Regiment, in 1809 and was a first lieutenant in the Quartermaster Corps of Col. Edwin E. Booth's 5th Tennessee Regiment during the War of 1812.

George Sutherland

George Sutherland married Frances Menefee in Tennessee on October 10, 1815. He was a state Congressman in the Tennessee Legislature and, when he moved his family to northwest Alabama, he served in the Alabama House as well. In 1830, he moved his family overland to Texas. He signed the contract with Stephen F. Austin to bring a group of settlers to what is now Jackson County. That hardy group of pioneers became known as the "Alabama Settlement."

George was a member of the Texas Convention of 1832 and 1833. He and his son, William, were present at the Lavaca-Navidad Meeting on July 17, 1835, where formal protest was made against the treatment of Texas settlers by the increasingly repressive government of Mexico. As the provisional government took shape, George served on several vital committees. He was also a member of the Congress of the Republic of Texas in 1837.

George Sutherland commanded a company at the Siege of Bexar in 1835. His son, William Depriest Sutherland, and George's brother, John Sutherland, went to Bexar in January 1836 as they were returning to Texas from Mexico. John became a sentry on the west side of town where he saw the approaching Mexican Army. While racing back to the Alamo to report his sighting, John's horse fell on him, injuring his leg. Travis sent John to Gonzales for reinforcements, and William remained at the Alamo where he died fighting on March 6, 1836.

George Sutherland's family joined other residents of the Alabama Settlement in fleeing from Jackson County as the Mexican Army advanced from south Texas. This flight became known as the "Runaway Scrape". George's wife wrote to her sister two months later, describing the terror and confusion of these people: "... I wish you could know how the people did as they kept going about trying to get somewhere, but no person knew where they were trying to get to ..."

After helping his family flee as far as the Brazos River, George Sutherland joined Sam Houston before the Battle of San Jacinto. His horse was shot from under him on April 20, 1836, in a cavalry fight. The following day, he fought bravely in the Battle of San Jacinto. He was a member of Moseley Baker's Company D, 1st Regiment, Texas Volunteers. George was reunited with his family at the mouth of the Sabine River and returned home with them to Jackson County.

Following the Texian's success at the Battle of San Jacinto, George Sutherland organized a militia company at Texana. He received his commission as captain. His company protected the coastal plains from the anticipated re-invasion by the Mexican forces.

George Sutherland was a farmer, a rancher, a large landowner and the owner of a general mercantile business in Jackson County. He and his wife, Frances, had seven children. George's daughter, Frances Agnes Sutherland, married Alexander T. Gayle on November 30, 1843 in Jackson County. Alexander had moved to Texas in 1836 and served in the Army of Texas from 1837-1841. Their marriage was blessed with eight children, one of whom was my great-grandfather, George Sutherland Gayle, born on September 13, 1845, while Texas was still a Republic.

George Sutherland died on April 22, 1853 and was buried at Ganado, Jackson County, Texas. He was a brave man who fought well for the freedom of Texas. He died knowing that his military and political career allowed his family to prosper in peace in the Texas he loved. George Sutherland was my great-great-great-grandfather. George Shelton Gayle, III #6891AH

DAVID NICHOLAS TERHEUN

David Nicholas Terheun was born on 04 April 1776, possibly in Hackensack, New Jersey, probably the son of Captain Jacob Terheun and Elizabeth Nagel. About 1826, David married Elisa Delphine Tottin, probably in New Jersey. Elizabeth was born about 1802 in Orange County, New York. In his early years, David worked as a merchant in Orange County. Their first child, Jasper Tottin, was born on 06 May 1828, in Pittsburgh, Pennsylvania. About 1830, a second child, John, was born in Indiana. A third child, Hasbrook, was born about 1835 in Illinois.

Texas broke from Mexico in 1836 and President Andrew Jackson recognized the Republic of Texas on his last day in office. The state-chartered banks of the Jacksonian Era did not serve the public well, leading to the Panic of 1837, after which Texas lured immigrants by adopting a liberal land policy. Persons en route to Texas took Mississippi riverboats or coastal vessels to New Orleans, Indianola, or Galveston. By 1839, steamers were running between New Orleans and Galveston, where city wharves had been constructed. The port of Galveston shipped cotton and cottonseed oil, sugar, pecans, and hides.

David Terheun and his family arrived in Texas in 1840. According to a family story, he shipped a stock of goods to Galveston, but the vessel went down and everything was lost. He then bought land and cattle on Galveston Island and a number of lots in the city. Three children were born in Texas: Amelia in 1840, Eliza in 1843, and Lydia in 1844.

In Texas, Headright Grants were given in four classes, with the Fourth Class Grants providing land to persons who had arrived in Texas between 01 January 1840 and 01 January 1841. A person desiring land, along with two witnesses attesting to his presence in Texas, appeared before a Board of Land Commissioners in his county of residence. The board issued a certificate to successful applicants stating the amount of land to which they were entitled. Each applicant the found vacant land, often not in his county of residence, and paid the survey and filing fees. A Fourth Class Certificate issued to David Terheun by the Commissioners of Galveston County on 13 May 1844, indicates that he was married and a resident of Texas in 1841. The Texas Land Office later issued a patent for 640 acres in Tyler County.

Population growth in Galveston was slowed by a yellow fever epidemic that struck in 1839, followed by a second in 1844. According to a family tradition, David Nicholas Terheun died in Galveston on 19 July 1845, cause of death unknown. An old map indicates that he was buried in the west half of the Old City Cemetery. The headstone was destroyed by the 1900 hurricane.

The 1850 census enumerated the household of his widow Eliza Terheun, then 47 years of age. Her household included her sons, Jasper, age 23, a carpenter; and Hasbrook, age 15; and her daughters, Amelia, age 10, and Eliza, age seven. John Guy Looney #2528

GEORGE WHITFIELD TERRELL

George Whitfield Terrell, son of James Terrell, was born in Nelson County, Ky. in 1803. As a youth, he moved to Tennessee.

He was admitted to the bar in 1827. During this time he became friends with Andrew Jackson and Sam Houston. In 1828, he was appointed District Attorney by Tennessee Gov. Sam Houston. Terrell later became Houston's Attorney General.

Terrell migrated to Texas in 1839, and made his home in San Augustine County in East Texas. Within months Mirabeau B. Lamar appointed him District Attorney and later the first District Judge in East Texas. Terrell was Secretary of State in Texas under David G. Burnet in 1841. In December of 1841, he was made Attorney General of Texas by Sam Houston. From 1842-1844 Terrell was Indian Commissioner of Texas and negotiated the Indian treaty at Bird's Fort on Sept. 29, 1843. In December of 1844, he was appointed Charge d'Affairs to France, Great Britain, and Spain, and continued in that capacity under Anson Jones.

Terrell remained a close friend of Sam Houston's during Jones' tenure. (General Houston gave Terrell's son, Sam Houston Terrell, a personal flag from the Republic of Texas. This became a family heirloom, but sadly one of Sam Houston Terrell's great-great-granddaughters accidentally threw it out when instructed to clean up her room.)

Upon his return to Texas in 1845, Terrell was again made Indian Commissioner. He was known as an opponent of Texas annexation to the U.S.

He died on May 13, 1846, in Austin. He is buried in an unmarked grave believed to be in Oakwood Cemetery. The Commission of Control for Texas Centennial Celebration had a monument erected in Oakwood Cemetery in his memory. John Paul Loven, Sr. #5520 A

HENRY TEUTSCH

Henry Teutsch, born in Frankfurt, Germany, in 1812, became involved as a young man in a religious mysticism movement led by Count Maximilian Leon Proli, the "Prophet of Offenbach," who inspired a loyal following during his various imprisonments and releases in Germany. Leon's 1830 trial was sidetracked by Grand Duke Ludwig II, on condition that Leon and followers would decamp. After a difficult and lengthy Atlantic crossing, their ship docked at New York in September 1831, and was welcomed by President Jackson's letter, issued that month.

Henry Teutsch

Disorder followed the religious community, resulting in a breakup of the original New Philadelphia in Pennsylvania and a Mississippi voyage to re-establishment as Germantown, eight miles east of Minden, Louisiana. The book, "Fragments of a Dream ... The Story of Germantown," copyright 1962, details Germantown's history, with drawings, recipes, and recollections of various pioneer hardships, including members who were devoured by wolves. These and civil disturbance led to an eventual dissolution off of the community after the countess' death the 1870s.

Many Teutsches were listed community members, but Henry had left long before that stage, and married, in approximately 1843, Louvina Fulcher, Nacogdoches County, born in 1821 to Rebecca Robbins (daughter of a family which owned an early ferry crossing on the Trinity, off of Highway 21 presently), and the wealthy William Fulcher of North Carolina.

Henry and Louvina farmed in Nacogdoches County the remainder of their lives, passing away in 1887 and 1886, respectively, being buried at the Mast/Teutsch Cemetery, between Melrose and Blackjack in Nacogdoches County.

Henry's first wife and a number of children had died from yellow fever in New Orleans, but three surviving sons distinguished themselves in the Confederate Army later: William, Frederick, and August (who lost an arm in the war). Uncle August was a bachelor until his 1928 passing, and my grandfather John Thomas often recounted picking the old man up and giving him a ride over the hills in the Model T from Nacogdoches to Melrose in the early part of the century.

Lewis George Teutsch, the fourth of eight children of Henry and Louvina, married Rebecca Chisum, an orphan of William P. "Cherokee Bill" Chisum and Louisa Brimberry, daughter of Captain Samuel Brimberry, who settled and died near Blackjack after a distinguished career in the Illinois State Militia in the Blackhawk Indian War in the 1830s. (Captain Brimberry's widow, Mary Jones Brimberry, received a pension from the United States government for his service while she resided in the Republic of Texas.)

Lewis and Rebecca's daughter, Ada Lou Teutsch, married John Thomas of San Augustine County, raising their children in the Melrose and Huntington communities, and my mother, Clara Mae Thomas married my father, Dennie C. Cook, of Beulah/Renfro Prairie, Angelina County, in 1940.

My wife, Mary Alice Askins, and I moved to Alaska, where our three sons —Adam, Justin, and William Travis — were born, and where I practice law.

BENJAMIN THOMAS, SR. 1778-1832

Benjamin Thomas, Sr., at age 46, was one of the earliest Texas pioneers, having settled eight miles west of Ayish Bayou, now San Augustine, in 1824. He was born in 1778 in Edgecombe County, North Carolina, the son of Theophilus Thomas, a major in the American Revolution, judge and descendant of John Thomas, who arrived in Jamestown Colony, Virginia from Great Britain at age 16 in 1622.

Accompanying Benjamin Sr., were his wife, Mary Ann Dickerson, and eight children: Shadrack D., Benjamin Jr., Iredel D., Wiley Cary, Theophilus, Jackson, Theresa and Ann. Benjamin Sr. died in 1832 at the age of 54. His children went on to serve the Republic of Texas.

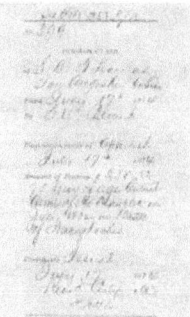

Pension Claim

Shadrack (my great-great-grandfather) was listed among the free males of Ayish Bayou District on June 6, 1826, for the first census of Texas. He entered the Army of the Republic as a 33-year-old private in July 1832, and fought in the Battle of Nacogdoches on August 2, 1832, under Captain James W. Bullock. The Battle of Nacogdoches, sometimes called "The Opening Gun of the Texas Revolution," occurred when a group of Texas settlers defied an order by Colonel Piedras, Commander of the Mexican Battalion at Nacogdoches, to surrender their arms to him. In the battle, Piedras lost forty-seven killed and forty wounded. The remaining 300 Mexican troops were marched to San Antonio by James Bowie, where they were discharged. The Battle of Nacogdoches is an important lesser-known conflict that cleared east Texas of Mexican military rule and allowed the citizens to meet in Convention without military intervention.

Shadrack was listed as 1st sergeant under Captain Thomas Dorsett and 1st lieutenant James Bullock in 1835, and Captain

McFarland's Company in January 1836. At age 75, he received a pension of $250.00 from the state of Texas under an act approved in 1870. He was elected sheriff of San Augustine County in 1847, for a nine-year period. He married Sarah Brown.

Their son, Sam B., was born in Texas in 1831, and served in the Civil War from 1861 to 1865. He was captain of Company F, 13th Texas Cavalry, Walker's Texas Division at war's end. Sam married Mary Garrett, granddaughter of Jacob Garrett, who came to Texas in 1824.

In 1830, Jacob was chosen as alcalde of Ayish Bayou District, and in 1832 was elected delegate to the first Convention at San Felipe. He was also one of the delegates to the Consultation of 1835 in San Felipe. In October 1835, he raised $600.00 and 13 mules for the army. This and a larger sum were the only contributions in money furnished by any town in Texas during the revolution.

Another son of Benjamin Sr., Theophilus, also served at the Battle of Nacogdoches. In November 1835, he enlisted in Captain Bayley Anderson's Company and served as 1st lieutenant in the Grass Fight on November 26, the last engagement in the Siege of San Antonio before the final Texan assault on the town. Erastus (Deaf) Smith had reported that Mexican Cavalry with pack animals, thought to be carrying pay for the Mexican Army, was approaching San Antonio. Colonel Burleson ordered James Bowie and forty cavalry and a hundred infantry under William Jack to seize the supply train. After a prolonged battle, the victorious Texans brought in forty captured pack animals, only to discover that their prizes carried only grass to feed army animals. In December 1835, Thelophilus was granted permission by General Burleson to return home because of ill health. Otherwise, he most likely would have died at the Alamo the following March.

Benjamin Jr., at age 30, fought at San Jacinto under Captain William Kimbro in Sherman's regiment. His discharge on June 15, 1836, was signed by Captain Kimbro and Sam Houston, Commander in Chief. On March 5, 1840, he was issued a donation certificate for having participated in the battle. Benjamin first married Martha Engledow, and following her death, Penelope Wheeler. He died on his ranch north of San Antonio in 1891, while a member of the Texas Veterans Association.

God bless Texas and all those who contributed to her greatness. Terry L. Thomas #6369, Kathy Thomas, Jon Thomas, Cheryl Thomas, Steven Thomas, Charlie Faglie, Brady Faglie, Luke Thomas, Josh Thomas, Maxwell T. Goldsworthy

WILLIAM EVAN THOMAS

William Evan Thomas (3 September 1810 - 6 August 1867) was the seventh of twelve children born to Evan Thomas and his wife, Mary Evans, in Llangunllo, Radnorshire, Wales, a sheep-farming community. He came to America about 1831-33. In an 1848 letter, his mother expresses amazement that he has lost contact with his sister Jane Parlour, living near Niagara Falls, Canada, and his brother James, living near Toledo, Ohio. "It is singular to observe how you lost each other - it is a state of things which we cannot make out."

William received his conditional Texas land grant certificate in 1839; the property was conveyed by unconditional certificate in 1845. He owned the Mustang Stable in Houston, operating a taxi service between Houston and Galveston, and was alderman of the First Ward 1863-1866.

In 1853, at age 42, he married Ann Major, 16, native of Leicester, England, and daughter of foundryman Isaac Major and Mary Tooper. Their children were Lavinia Danish, William, Emily Harrison, Jennie Scollard, Henry, and Gussie. Henry was sheriff of Galveston County for many years. Gussie was my maternal grandmother, wife of Judge John Kirlicks, who is believed to have defined "goo-goo eyes" in court soon after 1905. Gustave Antoine Mistrot III, SRT #6298

HENRY SEWELL THOMPSON

Henry Sewell Thompson was born in Georgia on October 30, 1810, the son of John Nicholas Thompson and Elizabeth Sewell, and the grandson of Henry B. Thompson, who died in 1823 in Jones County, Georgia. John Nicholas Thompson was born December 14, 1786 in North Carolina, married Elizabeth Sewell on February 18, 1807, probably in Robison County, NC, and died March 8, 1856 in Ashley County, Arkansas.

Elizabeth Sewell, the daughter of Thomas Sewell, was born February 4, 1787 in Sampson County, NC, and died June 5, 1860 in Ashley County, Arkansas. They were the parents of 10 children, the oldest of whom was Henry Sewell Thompson.

Henry Sewell Thompson was married first to Margaret F. Matthews on November 5, 1828 in Greene County, Alabama. She was born July 23, 1806 in Georgia, the daughter of John and Lydia Matthews. Henry and Margaret Thompson had 7 children: Joseph B., born November 14, 1829; Mary Elizabeth; Thomas S., born November 7, 1834; James O. A., born November 14, 1836; Isabella F., born February 25, 1839; Wilber F., born January 27, 1841; and John Nicholas, born July 10, 1844.

Mary Elizabeth Thompson was born May 15, 1832, in Greene County, Alabama and married Patrick Jack Cochran on January 21, 1849. They had 6 children, the last of whom was David Elias Cochran, who married Emily Ellen Graham. David and Emily Cochran had 8 children, the fourth of which was Della Cochran, who married Joseph Devereau Garrison, my grandparents.

Margaret Matthews Thompson died September 28, 1845 in Carthage, Texas, and Henry married second on September 10, 1850 in Panola County to Lucinda A. Allsup, born October 10, 1826 in Tennessee, the daughter of Peter P. and Mary Allsup. Henry died April 16, 1855 in Carthage, and Lucinda died September 13, 1872. Henry and Lucinda had two children: Esiah T., born March 27, 1852; and William Ware, born October 27, 1853.

Henry Sewell Thompson is not found on the 1840 tax list, but is in Texas by January 27, 1841 when his son, Wilbur, was born. He is on the 1846 tax list and 1850 Census of Panola County, Texas. David Lacey Garrison, Jr. #4745

JESSE G. THOMPSON

Jesse G. Thompson was born about 1812 in Alabama. The place of birth and his parents's names are unknown. He came to Texas in June 1835. On April 3, 1836, he enlisted in Captain Ware's Company of Texas Volunteers. He participated in the Battle of San Jacinto on April 21, 1836. For this service, he was granted a donation certificate in Houston County, Texas.

He married Margaret Malinda (surname unknown), and was the father of at least 8 children. He and his family resided in several Texas counties before settling in Houston County. These counties included Shelby, Colorado, Lavaca, Jackson and Walker.

He died in Walker County, Texas, in November 1859. His final resting place is unknown, but is believed to be an unmarked grave in Chalk Cemetery, Trinity County, Texas. He was my great-great grandfather. H. Keith Thompson #6567

ALEXANDER S. THOMSON, JR.

Alexander S. Thomson, Jr. was born of Scottish decent in St. Matthew's Parish, South Carolina on August 29, 1785. He was the only son of Alexander and Lucy (Fontaine) Thomson. He was reared by a pious uncle, Thomas Fontaine, in Georgia, with whom he received his education and indoctrination of the Methodist Church. He later moved to Georgia, and in 1805 married Elizabeth Maury Dowsing in Lincoln Country, GA and in 1814 they moved to Giles County, Tennessee.

Alexander S. Thomson

On August 30, 1830, Thomson, who was quite well educated for his time and who had mastered seven different trades, formed a partnership with his son, William Dowsing Thomson, and the Empresario Sterling Clack Robertson, for the colonization of Texas, and loaned Robertson $20,000 to fund the venture. This venture was known as "The Nashville Company" and appointed Thomson and Robertson as managers.

On October 28, 1830, Thomson and his son arrived in Nacogdoches with his son, W.D., and a party of 50 persons, the first group of families bound for the Nashville Colony. However, upon arrival, he was informed of a new law passed on April 6, 1830, barring further colonization without passports. After several meetings with the alcalde at Nacogdoches to plead his case to permit him to proceed without passports, he was granted permission to travel to Austin's Colony to obtain the necessary papers from Austin himself, but the rest of the families were denied entrance until his return.

After two difficult months of travel and having spent a great deal of money, he felt he had no recourse but to continue on to Robertson's Colony. At night, he returned to the colonists' camp located 3 miles from the garrison and decided to go around Nacogdoches by cutting a short road outside the town to connect the two existing roads. Thereafter, the road known as the "Tennesseeans Road" was called "Thomson's Pass," and was used many times by other immigrants lacking the necessary passports.

A few weeks later on November 12, they arrived "at the barracks at Mr. Williams," a site first occupied by Col. Francisco Ruiz, and later known as the site of Fort Tenoxtitlan. The grant began at the west bank of the Navasota crossing of the old San Antonio and Nacogdoches road, west to the divided ridge between the Colorado and Brazos rivers, northwest to the Comanche Trail, further to the Navasota River and south to the river's beginning. It is estimated that the colony's territory was equal to one-sixth of the entire province of Texas, some 40,000 square miles; about the size of Tennessee. It has been said that Thomson and Robertson were instrumental in bringing more families into Texas than any other empresario, save Austin.

Thomson's second trip with colonists was made by steamboat to New Orleans, then by schooner to Harrisburg, now a part of metropolitan Houston. They arrived on April 2, 1831. After hearing that the first group he had brought to Texas in 1830 had been ordered into Austin's Colony, he went immediately to San Felipe, the capital of that colony, to gather information. While there, an order arrived requiring that he and all his families return to the U.S. Austin was in Saltillo at the time, and Thomson wrote to him to intercede with the Mexican authorities to allow the colonists to settle in Austin's Colony. After much negotiating, permission was granted in late September of 1831 for Austin to admit all of the families Robertson and Thomson had brought to Texas.

As surveyors, both Alexander Thomson and his son, William, were prominent in the affairs of the Nashville Colony. Thomson was one of 58 elected delegates to the Texas Convention of 1832 at San Felipe de Austin (October 1-6, 1832), representing the district of Hidalgo, which comprised all or part of the counties of Washington, Burleson, Grimes, Milam and Lee. The delegates petitioned for the repeal of the hated Law of 1830, for tariff exemption and for independent statehood for Texas, or separation from the Mexican state of Coahuila.

Thomson hired a young Viennese immigrant, George B. Erath, to assist he and his son in surveying his own district in late fall of 1834, and chose a section of 25 square miles. As surveyors, no money was earned unless the land was taken by settlers and so Thomson worked as a farmer on his own land. When the call for a General Consultation for all Texas was issued for October 16-17, 1835 at Columbus, Thomson was again elected as a delegate representing the municipality of Viesca. He was one of 55 settlers representing 13 municipalities. The Consultation established the first provisional government composed of a governor, lieutenant governor and an advisory council made up of one member from each municipality. Following the death of Col. Ben Milam during the Siege of Bexar, Thomson introduced the resolution on December 26, 1835, changing the name of the municipality from Viesca to Milam. Thomson remained a member of the General Council, and was the only member of the Provisional Government who was still functioning in San Felipe. In fact, for one fleeting moment, he was the Government de Facto, when all the members left to return to their homes.

Long regarded as the Father of Texas Methodism, Thomson organized early congregations of family and friends on Sundays to read Wesley's sermons. In 1835, he was elected chairman of the quarterly conference of the Methodist Church, and was instrumental in raising $300 for the pastor's salary. This was the first effort in Texas to raise money for a Protestant minister. He helped establish the first Methodist Church in Yellow Prairie, later renamed Chriesman, which still stands today and contains a plaque honoring his efforts.

As the father of 13, children, Thomson finally settled near Caldwell, TX in Yellow Prarie (later renamed Chriesman) and died there on June 1, 1863. He was buried along with his wife in the Thomson Cemetery in Yellow Prairie. His children were active and instrumental in the Texas Revolution and the continued settlement of Texas. One son, Jasper Newton MacDonald Thomson, was captured at Meir, and was one of 17 prisoners who drew a black bean and was executed. William D. Thomson was a 2nd lieutenant in the Volunteer Army of Texas, and served as General Sam Houston's Quartermaster and later served as the first county clerk and county recorder for Milam County in 1837. Later,

W.D. served in the 4th Legislature, from November 3, 1851 to February 1852 representing Milam and Williamson counties.

Alexander Thomson is the ancestor of many noted Texans who have served in various appointed and elected positions in state and national government, including Thaddeus A. Thomson, U.S. Envoy to Colombia and signer of the Thomson-Urrutia Treaty in 1914.

The Texas Historical Survey Committee has erected two historical markers honoring Alexander Thomson. The first, erected in 1968 in Chriesman, Texas, recognizes his settlement of the town known as Yellow Prairie. The second, erected in 1972 near Caldwell, recognizes his leadership in colonizing Texas. Richard Douglas McCrum #5523, Cole Thomson McCrum #5524

CATHERINE OBEDIENCE HILL THORNTON

Catherine Obedience Thornton was born in North Carolina in 1785. Around 1800, she and her family came to Clarke County, Alabama. She met and married Green Hill from Warren County, Georgia in 1807. He died in 1830 in Marengo County, Alabama. After his death, she left Alabama with her unmarried children and two of her sons-in-law.

Thomas Hill Cox, Christmas Day 1995

After several attempts and being beaten back by Indians, on Nov. 28, 1833 she arrived in Texas Territory. For her patriotism from the Republic of Texas, in January 1838 she was given league and labor of land, and on Feb. 6, 1839, another 25 labors. This was in Grimes County, near Richards, Texas.

In 1847, she was granted a league and labor of land by the first governor of Texas. She is buried on her Headright Grant along with some of her family. The land was sold to a Dr. Brown, and has long since been plowed up. A tree marks the plot.

She lived to be 80 years old, and as a medical aid served her community in sickness, as doctors were scarce in this territory. She was small in size, able to ride behind a man on horseback and did this to hasten to the bedside of many sick neighbors and friends. She had been most successful in this area in giving of her time and knowledge in this field. Thomas Hill Cox, Life Member SRT #5709A

HEBRON AND AMANDA BENNETT TOLLESON

Hebron Tolleson (1823-1876) was born in Tennessee, son of William "Grandsire" Tolleson. His mother's maiden name was probably Hitson, but this is not proven. He is known to have been in Texas in Liberty County by 1845. By 1849 or earlier, Tolleson was in Lavaca County, and was almost certainly the first school teacher in Hallettsville. In 1852, he became Lavaca County tax assessor and served in that capacity until 1858, when he became engaged full time in managing his farm near the village of Sweet Home. In 1850, Tolleson became a charter member and the first secretary of Hallettsville's Murchison Masonic Lodge #80.

Amanda Bennett Tolleson (1833-1911), daughter of Stephen and Mary Breazeal Bennett, was born in Alabama. In 1840, she accompanied her parents, who were leading a covered wagon train of about 100 people, into the Republic of Texas. She attended Hebron Tolleson's school in Hallettsville, and married him in 1849.

The couple had ten children, eight of whom survived to adulthood. After Hebron's death, Amanda managed the family farm with the assistance of two sons. Hebron and Amanda are buried in the Bennett Cemetery in Lavaca County near the village of Sweet Home.

Richard L. Berry, (SRT #6188), a 3rd great-grandson of Hebron Tolleson

ASA TOWNSEND

Asa Townsend was born 14 Dec. 1795, Marlboro District, S.C., died 22 Sept. 1876, Colorado County, Texas. He was the first child of Thomas and Elizabeth Stapleton Townsend, and grandson of Light Townsend, Revolutionary War soldier. In 1816, Asa's parents sold their South Carolina land and moved to McIntosh County, GA. There Asa married Rebecca Candacy, daughter of Leonard and Susannah Brothers Harper. When Florida became a U.S. Territory, the Thomas Townsend family moved to (now) Madison and Jefferson counties, Florida. Thomas received a U.S. government military service grant (War of 1812). He died 18 October 1828.

In 1830, his sons, Thomas R. and Stephen, moved to the Texas state of Mexico; the others followed as their lands sold. Asa, the eldest, stayed to care for his mother and settle the estate.

The first five brothers received Spanish Land Grants before 1836. Asa received a grant from the Republic of Texas, February 1838, in Colorado County. Stapleton received land for military service in 1842.

Asa raised cattle, race horses, cotton and food crops. An active Methodist Church member and Mason, he was one of 15 men appointed to draft a preamble and resolution for Texas' annexation to the U.S.A. He was a member of the board of directors, Colorado Navigation Association (1849). The family was politically active.

Asa and Rebecca had 15 children. The last three "died young."

Sarah ("Sallie"), born 29 Jan. 1835, died 9 Sept. 1917, Seymour, Texas, married 22 Aug. 1855, James McDonald Cummins, born 6 Aug. 1826, Overton County, TN, died 24 July 1926, Seymour, Texas.

Samantha Howard Cummins, born 10 Nov. 1866, Colorado County, Texas, married 22 Aug. 1855, Colorado County, Texas, John "Jack" Hays Glasgow, born 17 Dec. 1851, Cape Girardeau, MO, died 12 April 1922, Magnum, OK. They lived in Seymour, Texas. Samantha died 14 Sept. 1938.

Issue: 1) Jim Jack Glasgow, born 9 Oct. 1892, died 17 April 1927, unmarried. (gassed in France-WWI).

2) Kitty Gale Glasgow, born 26 March, 1899, Seymour, Texas, died 22 May 1975, Spartanburg, SC, married 28 May 1917, Seymour, Texas, John Morgan Richards, born Rockwood, Tenn., 31 May 1887, died 23 Jan. 1953, Spartanburg, SC.

Issue: 1) Kitty Gale Richards, born 27 May 1918, Seymour, Texas, married 27 Aug. 1941 to Wm. C. Herbert, born 12 June, 1914.

2) John Mr. Richards, Jr. SRT#2191, born 11 Feb 1921, Seymour, Texas, married 16 May 1947, Valdese, NC, to Mary Lynn Johnson, born 24 March 1925.

TOWNSEND FAMILY

The first documented and accurate knowledge of this Townsend family appears in the Spanish West Florida parishes of Washington and St. Tammany, Louisiana. The progenitors of this Townsend family are thought to be John (uncertain) and Zana (maiden name unknown) Townsend of Washington Parish, Louisiana, and Rankin County, Mississippi. Estate papers in Lawrence County, Mississippi, identify the children of Mrs. Zana Townsend, one of whom was son, Henry J. Townsend, who settled in San Augustine County, Texas.

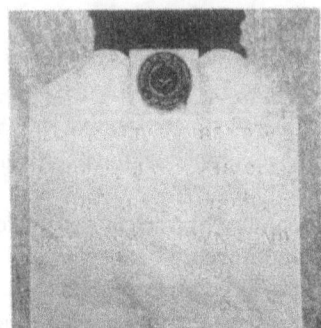

H. J. Townsend tombstone

The Townsend family apparently traveled and resided back and forth between Louisiana and Mississippi, having relatives in both places. Henry J. Townsend, oldest son of Zana, married Rebecca McGee/Magee, daughter of Holden and Sarah (Howell) Magee, also of Louisiana and Mississippi, (ca. 1840), place unknown. Henry J. Townsend first arrived in Texas in 1839 (Jasper County) while Texas was still a Republic. Henry and Rebecca's first two children were born in Louisiana, (so they must have still been traveling and residing back forth, only this time from Texas).

Henry J. Townsend and his family apparently remained in Jasper County until 1851, when they moved to northern San Augustine County on Ayish Bayou and resided there until 1857. They then moved to Baker's Bluff (later Townsend's Bluff), on the Angelina River, thirty-one miles south of the town of San Augustine. On November 26, 1860, Henry purchased six hundred and twenty-six acres from Manning Coleman (out of the Peter Galloway survey filed January 10, 1861, Book J, p. 433) at Lucas Settlement on the Angelina River, seven miles north of Townsend's Bluff in San Augustine County.

Shortly after this move, the Civil War began and Henry and son, George Washington Townsend, enlisted in the Confederate Army. Henry J. Townsend served in Company C, Texas Legion of Cavalry, later known as Whitfield's Legion, C.S.A. It is family legend that while serving, he became ill with rheumatic fever. He returned home with the horses when his regiment became dismounted. A copy of his military discharge gave reason as being over the age of 40. He died July 24, 1864 and is buried in Lucas Cemetery, San Augustine County, Texas. Rebecca (Magee) Townsend, remarried sometime before 1870, to James Bryan, a neighbor and widower, and remained in this area until her death August 5, 1897. She is buried beside her first husband, Henry, and he (James) beside his first wife at Lucas Cemetery

Henry J. Townsend posthumously received a Third Class Headright land grant of 640 acres, No. 14/55 on July 2, 1881. This grant was situated in the southern part of Angelina County, Texas. On May 25, 1986, the Daughters of the Republic of Texas and the descendants of Henry J. and Rebecca (Magee) Townsend performed a sesquicentennial grave dedication ceremony honoring their early Texas ancestors. Clifford Carson Townsend #6028

JOHN LAWRENCE TROTTI

John Lawrence Trotti was born in 1822 in the part of Gadsden County, Florida, which became Leon County on December 29, 1824. His parents were James Francis Trotti of South Carolina and Harriet Harley of Gadsden County, Florida. John Lawrence came to Texas about 1840 to scout out the land along the Sabine River. He returned to Florida and joined with his family and the family of Jacob Horger to go to Texas.

He married Rebecca Ann Booker in Newton County, Texas on November 30, 1847. His father, James Francis Trotti, purchased 640 acres of land for $640 in 1848 at "the survey" in the northern part of Newton County, Texas.

After the death of Rebecca in 1863, John married Elizabeth Frazier Swift, the widow of George Swift. John Lawrence moved his family to a home two miles east of Jasper, Texas. He died on April 3, 1894, at the age of 71 years, five months, and twelve days. He was buried in the Cemetery of Jasper on North Main Street. His grave and the grave of Elizabeth, his second wife, are marked by tombstones. SRT members: #4145 Fitzgerald Paramore Adams, Jr., #4173 Charles Ray Douglas, Ph.D.. #4332 Donald Gilbert Adams, Sr., Edward Aubrey Clark (deceased), Knight of San Jacinto

JANE TUMLINSON RATLIFF (1799 - 1858)

Jane Tumlinson was born in Lincoln, North Carolina, on February 23, 1799, the daughter of John Jackson Tumlinson, Sr., and Elizabeth Plemmons. She married Elijah Ratliff around 1820, and their first child was born in Texas in 1822. The family was living in Colorado County when Jane became a widow in the winter of 1836-37.

In June 1838, Jane received an unconditional certificate from San Augustine County, the requirement for obtaining such being a residence in Texas for three years. She did not work this land, but instead sold her certificate to William Cowlings in 1839, who marked out a plot in Shelby. She sold this for $40, having paid $7 for it originally.

In 1850 Jane was living in Smith County with all of her children and one son-in-law in the household listed under the name of her eldest son, John. The whole family group moved to the DeWitt/Karnes border area in the early 1850s, and each marked out land. Their surveys were approved in 1854, and each one of the adults received a preemption certificate for 160 acres of land in 1858. Adjoining plots were held by Jane and her sons, Richard, John, William, and Elijah, and her son-in-law, Henry Haniff.

Jane died in 1858, and in 1861 we find the heirs of Jane selling her property in DeWitt to F. Wilbur for $250 right after the patent was issued. Her heirs were: John and Alvira Ratliff, William and Mary Ratliff, Richard and Huldah Ratliff, Elijah Ratliff, Henry Harriff and Eliza Jane Harriff, William B. Stockton and Sidey Stockton. *Submitted by James L. Dannheim #6736*

JOHN JACKSON TUMLINSON, SR.

John Jackson Tumlinson, born in Lincoln, North Carolina, around 1776, first heard of Austin's Colony early in 1821 when Moses Austin, passing through Arkansas, announced the grant. Later that same year, John traveled to the Colorado River. He and his wife, Elizabeth, are listed with the "Old 300" original Austin Colony settlers. John was a skilled frontiersman, having made several moves westward from North Carolina to his final destination on the Colorado River.

During the first year, the colony had no authority to govern itself. In late 1822, Governor Trespalacios gave the colonists the right to establish two districts, one on the Colorado and one on the Brazos, and the right to elect their own officials. Residents on the Colorado elected John Tumlinson as alcalde, or civil judge. Thus John became one of the first Anglo-American officials in Texas.

After an expedition to investigate reports of Indian problems, John Tumlinson and Robert Kuykendahl, the military commandant of the district, proposed that a paid military company be enlisted to handle problems with the coastal Indians. Following further provocations, on January 7, 1823, the two men wrote to the governor asking permission to "raise fifteen hardy expert young men who are expert with the rifle by enlistment for the same pay that the troops of the Empire receive." They proposed that the men serve only six to nine months, as they would need to plant crops the following spring. These fifteen men, plus ten regular soldiers from San Antonio, would protect the coast so that vessels could safely land. They would also build blockhouses and small boats and organize a combined land and water expedition against the Indians when the marshes had dried and there was enough grass to support their horses. Governor Trespalacios approved the proposal except that they would not get the same pay as the regular soldiers.

These first Rangers, single and mostly young, were organized under the command of Moses Morrison. They were critically short of gunpowder, which was not available on the Colorado, and they did not have the funds to purchase it in San Antonio. The gunpowder shortage was serious for two reasons, since these Rangers had to depend on their guns for hunting as well as for fighting Indians. Without this, the company could neither fight nor eat. In a report of July 5, 1823, Moses Morrison wrote to the governor that he was sending two men to San Antonio for the vital ammunition, and that the cost of this ammunition could be deducted from the men's pay.

The next day, the two representatives for the Ranger company, John Tumlinson and Joseph Newman, set out for San Antonio to secure the ammunition. On the Guadalupe River near Seguin, they met several Indians, either Wacos or Tawakonis. There are two written accounts of this encounter. One, from Robert Kuykendahl in a report to the governor, states that "after some insolent observations and conduct by the Indians they shot and killed Mr. Tumlinson." Another version, written 55 years after the occurrence by a relative of Joseph Newman's says, "Before the Indians got in reach, Mr. Newman told Mr. Tumbleston to not shake hands with them, but it seems Tumbleston thought it best to be friendly. He gave the Indian his hand. The Indian jerked him off his horse and stabbed and killed him. Newman made his escape on a little pony. The Indians run him six miles."

Thus, in 1823, John Tumlinson became the first white man to die in the service of the Texas Rangers.

GEORGE WASHINGTON VAN VLECK

George Washington Van Vleck was born on October 31, 1814, Lansingburg, New York. He came to Texas in 1839 and settled in the vicinity of where Spurger is located today. He was allotted 640 acres.

George Washington Van Vleck

In the Republic, there was interest in Masonry, and men were waiting for a leader to organize a Lodge. He helped organize, in 1849, the Tyler Lodge #50, Woodville Lodge #62 then later became Magnolia Lodge #495. He was Worshipful Master a total of six times. In 1862, he served as Grandmaster to the Masonic Grand Lodge of Texas.

In years to come, he moved to Woodville, and served as clerk of the District Court for sixteen years. Then, in 1856, Woodville College was incorporated and became one of its trustees. In 1861, he ran for commissioner of the General Land Office.

He was married six times, and out-lived five of his wives. His first wife was a cousin of Gen. Robert E Lee.

On September 7, 1861, he joined the Confederate Army and served as a Brigadier General. His son, Julius Lee Van Vleck, served with the 1st Texas Infantry during the Civil War and was killed at Petersburg, VA, June 20, 1864.

Mr. Van Vleck moved to Houston, Texas, and on October 21, 1890, he died. George Washington Van Vleck was my great-great-grandfather. *Submitted by Ken Mason #6279 SRT Chapter #36*

FRANZ VAN WAMEL AND ANCESTORS

Franz Van Wamel, born 1807, left Shomberg, Germany with wife, Anne, and five children. They boarded the sailing vessel Neptune at Bremen, Germany. They arrived at Galveston on December 3, 1845, and boarded a schooner for a trip to Indianola.

E. A. Wammel age 21

On the way, his wife, Anne, died and was buried at Indianola. Franz and his five children traveled to New Braunfels to claim his land, but due to a land fraud there was no land. While in New

Braunfels, his 4-year-old son died, and was buried on the west bank of the Comal River. Franz and 4 children traveled to the Fisher Colony to settle and farm. Due to hostile Indians, he and his children moved to Austin County, where he started farming and freight hauling.

Franz married Karaline Wilherms in July 1856. One son, Earnest, was born August 8, 1859. Franz died January 18, 1870. Earnest married Augusta Lischka in 1887. He served as Justice of the Peace for 25 years. One son, Fred, born August 10, 1889, married Adele Muery on December 30, 1908. They adopted a nephew, Arthur Hoff, born November 12, 1917. The Wamel land has remained in the family since 1904. Franz Wamel is my great-grandfather. Arthur Hoff Wammel, SRT San Jacinto chapter #1

VAWTER'S FERRY

Although Kentucky-born, David Vawter would spend his final days in Texas. Born in 1800 to Baptist minister and Revolutionary war veteran, Philemon Vawter, and his wife Anna, David possessed an adventurous spirit.

A skillful trader, he knew the value of the frontier highways - rivers. In 1832, his first of several steamboats — the "Bravo" — plied the Red River with freight between Natchitoches and New Orleans.

History marker of the Grand Bluff Cemetery. The land for the cemetery was donated by my great grandfather David Vawter.

Twelve years later, David sold his business and, with his wife and six children, headed for Texas. His fondness for rivers resulted in his purchasing a large tract of land on the banks of the Sabine at Grand Bluff and securing a license to establish and run a ferry there. The ferry became a well-known point on the heavily traveled early pioneer trail between Shreveport and Nacogdoches.

Tragically, David died in 1845 at age 45 without controlling interest in the ferry. His wife, Lucinda (Glover), proved her love for her new homestead by trading their Louisiana property for the ferry and additional land on the Sabine. She died in 1857 at age 52. They both are buried in the Grand Bluff Cemetery located near the ferry landing on land they donated. A state historical marker designates the site. Their children operated the ferry until a bridge was built in 1912.

David is the great-great-grandfather of Lewis Orin Vawter, Jr. (SRT member #6330J), born 5/7/21, who lives in Marshall. Lewis' son, Gary Eugene Vawter (SRT member #5065), born 11/12/44, lives in Dallas.

MARCELINA VIDAURRI

Marcelina Vidaurri was a descendant to one of the first ranching families of Texas. She was born on May 3, 1842 to Francisco Vidaurri and Josefa Salinas in Laredo, Texas. Her father was the grandson of Don Jose Vasquez Borrego, who received a 332,000-acre land grant from the Spanish Viceroy. Her grandmother was Maria Alejandra Sanchez, the granddaughter of Don Tomas Sanchez, the founder of Laredo, Texas.

J. R. "Corky" Rubio

She married Florencio Garza, and had a son, Juan Vidaurri Garza. Marcelina was typical of Tejano women of the period. She was born into a ranching family, where this was a way of life that had been part of her ancestors and descendants for may generations.

Jesus Ramiro Rubio (Corky) is a descendant of Marcelina Vidaurri through his mother, Aurora Garza Rubio. Born in San Antonio and raised in Eagle Pass, Texas, he received his B.B.A. in international business from the University of Texas-Austin and M.B.A. from University of Texas-San Antonio in international economics.

He is founder and CEO of Siderco International, Inc. He married Carla Maria Martinez and they have two daughters: Pauline Aurora and Maria Alexandra, both members of the CRT. They reside in San Antonio and active in civic and historical organizations. J.R. "Corky" Rubio #5056 Bonham Chapter

GEORGE PETER WAGNER

On 13 September 1845, George Peter Wagner and his parents, John Philip and Elizabeth Wagner, members of the German Emigration Company sailed for Texas, arriving 20 November 1845.

It appears that George Peter established residence in Indian Point, Texas while other family members went to New Braunfels for a few months before moving to Fredericksburg. John Philip died prior to the 1850 Texas Census, as Elizabeth was living with a daughter, Josephine and her husband, Joseph Worsham in Montgomery County.

A deed of sale for a lot, a house and all its contents in Indian Point, now known as Indianola, was recorded on the day of George Peter's marriage to Maria Magdelina Hans on 4 October 1848. After the marriage, the couple resided in Victoria. Sixteen children were born to this union.

George Peter Wagner declared his intent for citizenship 8 September 1854, and was granted citizenship in the United States of America 29 July 1857. He was not only a farmer but also a land entrepreneur with holdings in surrounding counties.

Numerous Wagner letters written in old German script were found in the "little tin box." In one letter to Peter from Josephine, dated 17 November 1865, it tells of the death of their mother, Elizabeth, on 3 November 1865 of yellow fever. She asked him to please send either $65 in green backs or $30 in gold to help pay the funeral expenses.

George Peter died in 13 June 1896; Maria died 12 August 1915, and they are buried in Evergreen Cemetery, Victoria, Texas. Gerald Sitterle, great-grandson, SRT #4646 life member

JAMES FRANCIS WALKER

James Francis Walker, Sr., one of Stephen F. Austin's "Old 300" colonists, received title to a site of land in present Washington County on July 21, 1824. The Census of 1826 listed Walker as a farmer and stock raiser, aged over 50. His household included his wife, two sons, a daughter, and four slaves. James Francis Walker, Sr., received Spanish Land Grant No. 109 in July 1824, signed by El Baron de Bastras and Stephen F. Austin. The log cabin that he built in 1826 on this site now serves as a bed-and-breakfast, located on County Road 80, east of Brenham.

James Francis Walker, Jr., (born in Kentucky on October 20, 1793) followed his father to Texas in 1835, by way of boat down the Mississippi River to New Orleans and by sailing boat from New Orleans to Galveston. He was a widower and never remarried. His wife, Abrilla Collette, whom he married in Kentucky on March 20, 1816, died in Kentucky on March 27, 1831.

Both James Francis Walker, Sr., and James Francis Walker, Jr., fought in the Texas War of Independence and were in the Battle of San Jacinto, they received land grants for their services in Washington County and in Milam County, which became McLennan County in 1850. Sterling Henry Smith #4460, Michael Berry Smith #4279, Stacey Lee Smith #5650A

WILLIAM HENDERSON WALLER

William Henderson Waller married Sophia Warren Hardwick when she was fourteen years old and he was twenty-one. When he died at age seventy-one, they had been married over fifty years. They had ten children, nine of whom survived infancy. He served as the first county commissioner of Live Oak County, Texas.

His seventh child, Narcissus, born July 28, 1849, in Houston County, Texas, married John Thomas Curry. One of the Curry children was Sarah Lou Curry, who married John Francis Alexander Custer and had four children: Vella, Elvin, Wiley and Ray. Wiley married Avis Josephine Beedy of Blanconia and they had two children, Mary Lou and Wiley Eldridge Custer.

The following is adapted from Henderson Waller's obituary:

"Near Oakville, Live Oak County, on the 21st day of December 1882, Henderson Waller departed this life after several days suffering from congestive pneumonia. He was born near Sparta, White County, Tennessee, on the 16th day of June 1811. Mr. Waller moved to Texas with his family in the year 1842, then in his 31st year; but for the last 27 years has been a settler of Live Oak County, even before its organization. At the time of his coming, the Nueces River country was subject to incessant Indian raids, and made less desirable as a home for families because it was a sure retreat for the desperado and the fugitive from justice. In addition to all these, the hardships and scarcities of life and the lack of facilities for communication made the country anything but desirable to live in and raise a family of respectability. But all these things were met and overcome with a determined iron will, and today, the large and respectable family he raised and leaves behind to mourn his departure can rejoice, even in their hours of affliction, that all the vicissitudes, ordeals and temptations of a frontier life were passed through, leaving not a blot or blemish nor a blush of neglect.

"Live Oak County itself mourns the loss of one of her oldest, true and tried citizens who saw the county when it was struggling for existence and, when organized, saw and felt her darkest days and then rejoiced in appreciation at her days of prosperity.

"Mr. Waller's hand was always extended to contribute to charity and to aid in building school houses and churches." W.E. Custer

ELISHA HENRY ROBERTS WALLIS

Elisha Henry Roberts (E.H.R.) Wallis (1781 - 1846) was born in Alabama of Scot-Irish-Welsh ancestry. As a young man, he traveled to Tennessee where he became acquainted with the future Texas General Samuel Houston.

Subsequently, Wallis moved to Burke County, Georgia, where he resided until about 1819 when he relocated to Natchitoches Parish, Louisiana. In Louisiana, he met and married his wife, Ms. Sarah "Sally" Barrow on October 17, 1814, in Opelouses.

In the summer of 1822, Wallis made his first trip to Texas, and in his exploration found what he believed to be promising land for a settlement. He returned to Louisiana, but took action to move to Texas with his wife and family.

Accordingly, the first permanent settlers in present-day Chambers County, besides former privateers and adventurers — including Jean Laffite — were my great-great-great grandfather Elisha H. R. Wallis and his brothers-in-law, Solomon Barrow, Benjamin (the Bear Hunter) Barrow, and Reuben Barrow. This small party left Bayou Cocodrie on the border of St. Landry and Rapides parishes on Christmas Day 1824, following the Opelousas Road westward to the Atascosita Crossing on the Trinity River at present-day Liberty. Driving a small herd of cattle, a full compliment of horses and farm implements, they traveled in covered oxen wagons containing my great-great-great-grandmother's favorite rose bushes and vine cuttings to be transplanted at her new home. Upon reaching the Trinity, the party and their eight (8) slaves turned south, possibly following the old road used by the filibusters towards Perry's Point and Bolivar Peninsula.

The only woman among my relatives in the traveling party was Sarah "Sally" Barrow, my great-great-great-grandmother. Solomon's wife, Elizabeth Winfree, had remained behind in Louisiana to await the birth of her second child. My grandmother, who was expecting another child of her own, traveled in one of the ox-drawn wagons with her five children.

Upon reaching the Horseshoe Bend about six miles from the mouth of the Trinity River, Wallis selected a homesite ("Wallis Hill") on a rise above the river's east bank. After leaving Burke County, Georgia, he was now in his mid-thirties, but was thirteen (13) years older than the eldest of the Barrow brothers. Earlier, he had served as a private in the Opelousas Militia formed in December 1814 and was sent to aid Andrew Jackson at the Battle of New Orleans. After the end of the Battle of New Orleans, he and Sally moved to Bayou Cacqdrie. Wallis was trained as an engineer, and he quickly built himself a pioneer home on Wallis Hill, where four more children were born.

In time, Wallis would become one of the leading ranchers in the neighborhood. Like other cattlemen of that day, he would trail his animals to market in Opelousas. After Sally's death in 1841, he married Martha Shelton and had two more sons, Francis Marion "Frank" Wallis and Hansel Roberts.

The Barrow brothers settled in three opposite directions from Wallis Hill. Reuben went south to the area around Bolivar. Benjamin would eventually settle further east. Solomon settled on the west side of the Trinity, locating on a beautiful bluff on the west side of Trinity Bay at what is today called Point Barrow in McCollum Park (1995).

With their leader and brother-in-law, E.H.R. Wallis, the Barrow brothers were to found a Texas family dynasty that met both triumph and tragedy from 1825 until 1966, when most of the town became property of the U. S. Army Corps of Engineers due to construction of the Wallisville Reservoir.

Wallis Hill was one of the first settlements in Joseph Wehlein's grant, and the Wallis home became a principal stopping place for early travelers in the area. In December 1836, after defeat at the Battle of San Jacinto, the visit of the Mexican Commanding General Antonio Lopez de Santa Anna (according to an old legend within the Wallis family) is further documented by the diary maintained by his close aide, Colonel Juan Nepomuceno Almonte, during their trip from the Brazos River to Washington, D.C. Almonte recorded on December 1, 1836, that the party crossed the Trinity River and spent the night at the home of Elisha H. R. Wallis. A total of 18 beeves were slaughtered by the host to feed the Texas troops and Mexican prisoners, who in turn camped under a live oak tree in the Wallis front Yard. (this oak tree and Wallis Hill is now owned by my cousin, Mr. John Middleton, the founder of Wallisville Heritage Park.) Upon leaving the Wallis home, Santa Anna and his escorts moved eastward, stopping the next day at the home of James Taylor White before moving on to the Neches and Sabine rivers in their route to Washington, D.C.

Upon his immigration to Texas in 1824, Wallis became entitled to a league (4,428 acres) and a labor (177 acres) of land. This was in accordance with the Mexican colonization laws that provided for distribution of land to colonists. Although entering Texas under the Mexican government, Wallis did not obtain his land certificates until 1838, when they were issued by the Liberty County Board of Land Commissioners under the Republic of Texas. For the total quantity (26,000,000 square varus), two certificates were issued to him on January 18, 1838, namely No. 69 for 17,724,000 square varus, and No. 70 for 8,276,000 square varus. Both the community known as Wallis Hill, which built up around the home, and the site of the town of Wallisville are located within certificate No. 69.

Elisha H. R. Wallis died on July 31, 1846.

The children of Elisha H. R. Wallis and Sarah "Sally" Barrow are the following:

1. Rachel, who married James Taylor Dunham;
2. Martha, who married John White;
3. Eliza, who married Elisha Stephenson;
4. Julia Letitia, who married Newton Swinney;
5. Sarah Ann, who married John Jackson;
6. Elijah J., who died in childhood;
7. Solomon Barrow, my great-great grandfather, who married Sarah Labadie, the daughter of my great-great-great grandfather, Dr. Nicholas d. Labadie, a surgeon in the Texas Army at the battle of San Jacinto;
8. Elisha, who married Sarah Louisa Stephens; and
9. Daniel B., who married Jerusha L. Kipp.

Following the death of Sally in 1941, Wallis remarried to widow Martha Shelton. He had two other children:

1. Francis Marion, who married Elizabeth Belzora Speights;
2. Hansel Roberts, who married, first Mary Louise Kilgore and, secondly, Sally Ann Wooten.

Bibliography:

"Chambers County: A Pictorial History by Margaret Henson and Kevin Ladd, 1988; Genealogy Records of the Wallisville Heritage Park, Wallisville, Texas; Affidavit of Heirship of H.R. Wallis, dated April 29, 1927, and filed of record on 3/15/1932 at 1:15 p.m. with the county clerk of Chambers County, Texas; Affidavit of Heirship of Philip C. Tucker, dated June 29, 1927, and filed of record on march 15, 1932, at 1:15 p.m. with the county clerk of Chambers County, Texas; Texas Historical Commission Marker for the Site of the Town of Wallisville, Texas. Jack Reeves Mason, Paul Bateman Mason, Steven Randall Mason, Ronald Alexander Mason and Billy Alexander Mason

LEMUEL S. WALTERS SR.

My fourth-great-grandfather Lemuel S. Walters Sr. was born on November 17, 1795, in Person County, N.C. The first record of Lemuel in Texas was a character certificate, dated January 25, 1835, from the municipality of San Augustine. He and his family settled in Jasper County, Texas, in a small trading town known as Bevilport, where he worked as a carpenter. Shortly after coming to Texas, he and his son, Jackson, volunteered to serve in the Texas Revolution with the militia from Snow River. This was not the first war he was a part of. As a young man of 18, he enlisted and served with the 10th Virginia U.S. Infantry in the War of 1812.

After the war, Lemuel became an active member in his new country by being elected and serving as Justice of the Peace from Zavalla in Jasper County, from 1839-1841. After his term was up, and after the death of his wife, Sally, he moved throughout East Texas. Sometime around 1844, he married Delilah Isaacks in Jasper County. This union brought forth the following children: Samuel, Robert, Isabella, Elijah Monroe, and Mary. Delilah and Lemuel set up a blacksmith shop in Moscow, Texas, in the middle 1850s.

Soon thereafter, Delilah died and he was on the move again, selling off his land and moving his family to Grandcane in Liberty County. He was listed there in the 1860 and 1870 Texas Census. He died sometime after the 1870 Census was taken.

The children from his first marriage are as follows: Jackson, Lemuel, Susannah, Henry J., Elizabeth, Eliza Ann, John, Sarah. *Submitted by Brian Scott Walters #6852*

JESSE JERNIGAN WATKINS

Jesse Jernigan Watkins was born in 1776 in "Malborn Hills," Halifax County, Virginia, and the son of a tobacco farmer and was of Scot-Irish parentage. He struck out on his own, traveling through Virginia, and the Clarksville area of north Tennessee. There, he married Mary White McCorkle, daughter of Archibald McCorkle.

In 1833, they moved to Red River County, Texas. Upon the persuasion of close friend, President Sam Houston, they moved to Nacogdoches County in 1835, where Jesse was a miller, farmer and Justice of the Peace.

Watkins' official role was as an agent for the Indian Department, serving as an envoy for the Republic of Texas to many tribal councils. He negotiated many peace treaties and tried to bring peace between the Republic and the Indians, which was a great problem for the Republic in 1837.

Jesse left home on November 21, 1837 to meet with the headmen of the Prairie Tribes and never returned. It is said that Chief Bowles massacred the Kickapoos, the peacekeepers, and drove pine splinters into the flesh of Jesse Watkins and made a human torch of him somewhere between Van Zandt, Ellis and Tarrant counties. He was declared dead in December, 1837. Jeff Austin, III STR # 52-5010

ANDERSON WEBB

Anderson Webb was born in Virginia in 1818. He was in Vicksburg, Mississippi, by the mid-1830s, where he was a wagon maker and slave owner. He removed to Nacogdoches in October 1841, and was granted 640 acres in Henderson County.

Anderson married four times, and had children by each wife. Anderson successfully sued the sheriff of Van Zandt County in May of 1854 for 4,000 acres of land that he had inherited from his second wife, which the sheriff had taken for himself. Anderson then sold the land. He tried farming in Cherokee County, but didn't adapt, and he opened a wagon shop in Tyler, Smith County. His next shop was in Palestine, Anderson County.

By 1863, Anderson and fourth wife, Eliza moved to Fairfield, Freestone County where he became a land agent. The 1870 Agriculture Census of Freestone County, Texas, shows Anderson with 85 acres of land improved, 5 acres wooded, total worth $1200 and having two horses, seven cows and 19 pigs.

The last record found of Anderson Webb, my great-great-grandfather, was a sale of property in 1871. He was deceased by 1873 when his widow, Eliza, remarried Theophalous Webb, a widower from Tennessee. *Submitted by Robert R. Goldsborough, Jr. #2883*

LYDIA ANN DANA HASTING HULL (PAY) WELLS

Lydia Ann Wells, was born September 13, 1818, in Woodville, Mississippi. Her parents were originally from Boston, Mass., or possibly Connecticut. Her father, Mr. Hull, died when she was a small child. Her mother then married a Daniel Willard Smith, who was the American Consul to Mexico.

She received her bilingual education learning Spanish from both mother and step-father. She spoke six languages and was educated in both Boston and in New York. Her knowledge of Spanish would later assist her in translating the Spanish and Mexican land grants into English for her son, Judge James B. Wells. Wells, would later set up District Courts in South Texas so clear title to land could be registered with the courts.

Her first marriage was to Mr. William Pay. They had one child, a son who later was adopted by Capt. Wells after the sudden death of Mr. Pay, in Texas. Mrs. Wells, was 26 when she married Capt. Wells. She and Capt. James B. Wells, were married on June 16, 1844, in Corpus Christi, Texas.

She would find her self once again in political circles as she once grew up with. After their marriage they moved to St. Joseph Island, where they for years were in the cattle business. They had seven children. They would eventually move inland to the town of Lamar. Her youngest child, Frances Verien, was born in Lamar.

Mrs. Wells was a cultural leader and devout Christian. She and her husband suffered many loses, including three of their children during the great epidemic of 1878. She would eventually come down with flu and die while nursing others.

Capt. Wells and Mrs. Wells, are buried in the old Lamar Cemetery with most of their children.

The lighthouse and ship channel at Port Aransas is named for her memory, along with a small island, which we have visited many times with our children. Our eldest is named for her, Lydia M. Jacks; now Mrs. Thomas Osvold. James H.W. Jacks #1571, James Power Chapter #9 Sons of the Republic of Texas

Capt. and Mrs. James B. Wells are our great-great-grandparents.

CAPTAIN JAMES B. WELLS

James B. Wells was born in Macon, Georgia, February 29, 1808. As a boy he was sent to Boston to live with an aunt and uncle, who gave him his education. As a young man he "stowed away" on one of his uncle's ships and went to sea.

Captain Wells had been a river boat pilot on the Mississippi, and had sailed the seven seas as a merchantman before becoming the master of the Brutus. It was at this time that Captain Wells, being a spirited young man, organizes a company of volunteers to fight for Texas in gaining her independence under General Sam Houston. At this time, Capt. Wells was appointed to the Texas Navy as first master of the Texas Navy Yards at Galveston, which position Wells held during Houston's first presidency. During the war, Capt. Wells was the commander of the battle ship of Texas.

In 1837, Captain Wells resigned from the Texas Navy and was given some land near Galveston, under the Republic of Texas, which he traded and ended up settling on St. Joseph's Island. Capt. Wells and his family were among the earliest settlers of St. Joseph's Island, which prior to 1871 was a part of Refugio County. He engaged in the cattle business on a rather large scale, and he soon became a leading political figure in the coastal part of the country, at which time he fell in love and married Lydia Ann Dana Hastings Hull on June 16, 1844, in Corpus Christi, Texas.

During the years 1845 to 1850, he became justice and member of the County Court for St. Joseph's Island. He was again justice in 1865. He finally ended up owner of St. Joseph's Island, a narrow strip of land lying off the Texas coast and comprising some 35,000 acres.

Sometime prior to the Civil War, the Wells family moved to the mainland settling at Lamar. Captain Wells' health failed him while he was in a Confederate prison camp at Gonzalez where he was confined after falsely being accused of being a "Union" man. He spent six months in prison before they found him to be innocent.

Captain Wells died in Lamar, Texas, on February 24, 1880, at seventy-two years of age. James H.W. Jacks #1571 SRT James Power Chapter #9.

Capt. & Mrs. James B. Wells, are our great-great-grandparents.

MARTIN WELLS

In 1826 Martin and Sarah Boyd Wells brought their family to Stephen F. Austin's "Little Colony" in Bastrop. Martin had served in the War of 1812 from Tennessee. His First Class Headright was one of the first in Bastrop.

Son Wayman had fought in the Texas Revolution at the "Siege of Bexar" and was present at San Jacinto, while Martin Jones was with the baggage at Harrisburg.

Martin Jones was a "Texas Ranger," and married Frances Amanda Peyton. They moved to Leander, Williamson County, where his photograph hangs in the Georgetown Courthouse. Their daughter, Sarah Jane, married Charles C. Mason, who had come to Texas from North Carolina in 1851 with his father, Col. C.C. Mason, who settled Bagdad.

Thompson's of Jollyville and their 1930 Model A Ford. L to R: Brit, Mason, Karen, David and Kathy Thompson.

Robert Jentry West

David Loren Thompson (born 1944, Austin) is a great-great-great-grandson of Martin Wells. In 1966, he married Karen Ruth Dannelly (born 1944, Austin), who has eleven ancestors from the Republic of Texas Era, including Johann Phillip Luck, a founder of New Braunfels. They have a daughter, Katherine Howell (born 1969, Austin), son David Mason (born 1971, Austin), and grandson, Cassidy Thompson (born 1990, Austin). David and Karen (noted historical author) have lived in Jollyville since they married. David Loren Thompson #2910, David Mason Thompson #3902, SRT Moses Austin Chapter

MARTIN WELLS JR.

Martin Wells, Jr., was born in North Carolina on December 9, 1774. His father, Martin Wells, Sr., moved to Tennessee in 1796. Martin Jr. bought land in Stewart County in 1896, and married Sarah Boyd in 1807.

He served in the War of 1812 as a mounted Rifleman in Haggard's Company. He moved to Marengo County, Alabama, in 1815, and then in 1829 settled in Stephen F. Austin's Little Colony in Texas. Martin Wells' Headright League received from the Mexican government is on the Colorado River, where his home of log cabins was known as Wells Pyramid. He is mentioned by Jenkins as the earliest settler at Bastrop, Texas; by Smithwick as "old Marty Wells," leader in Indian fights in that area; and by General Burleson in an 1844 letter to Lamar as an "excellent Citizen."

Martin Wells, Jr., died January 4, 1836, leaving "a widow and a large family," one of whom was Wayman Frederick Wells, a scout and a veteran of the Texan Army in the revolution, whose farm north of Austin is now known as the Wells Branch residential Area. John H. Wells, life member The Sons of the Republic of Texas.

ROBERT JENTRY WEST

Robert Jentry West was born in Washington County, Tennessee, January 25, 1809. In 1845, he moved to Peters Colony at Mustang Branch, Texas, later named Farmers Branch, which was part of Nacogdoches County and now Dallas County. He was one of the commissioners appointed by the First Legislature to lay off the city of Dallas and conduct the sale of lots. He was also Dallas County's first treasurer.

Mr. West sold land and shipped meat farther west, under government contract to outlying forts, and operated a tannery and general store. In 1835 Robert Jentry West married Mary Ann Ryland, a teacher in Washington County, Tennessee. She continued to teach after moving to Peters Colony. This union produced six children; one, Robert H. West, became the first Dallas native to serve as County Judge. He received 2104 votes and took office, 15 April 1876.

Another child, Martha Alice West, was born March 25, 1846, in Peters Colony. In September 1865, she married Thomas Henry Floyd in Cochran's Chapel, near what is now Love Field. Her husband, a native of Union County, Kentucky, had served four, years as a cannoneer in the Confederate Army. He operated the Floyd Drugstore in Dallas for a number of years, before moving to Callahan County, where he served forty years as a surveyor; he also held office as Justice of the Peace.

Ret. Tsgt Jack Townsley USN 1941-50, USAF 1957-69

Mr. Floyd's father was a teacher in Kentucky, and at one time had Abraham Lincoln as a student. It was a natural calling that several of the Floyds' ten children chose teaching as their profession. Mr. Floyd died in Abilene, Texas, in 1926, and his wife, Martha Alice West Floyd, one of the first white babies born in Dallas County, died in Abilene on 12 March 1946, just 13 days before her 100th birthday.

One of her sons, J. Douglas Floyd, was an Abilene trolley car motorman for many years. His daughter, Mary West Floyd Townsley, was the mother of Jack Wayne Townsley, great-great grandson of Robert Jentry West. Mr. West died in 1876 and is buried in Farmers Branch. Jack Wayne Townsley SRT #3908

JAMES ALEXANDER WESTMORELAND

My grandfather, James Alexander Westmoreland, was born April 12, 1844, in what later became Panola County, and died March 23, 1932. On December 21, 1865, he married Lucy Caroline Matthews (January 14, 1850, Harrison County - June 30, 1920). There were 14 sons and daughters born of this marriage.

His parents were Joseph Westmoreland (March 16, 1818, McMinn County, Tennessee - Dec. 16,1888, Panola County) and Lucinda

*Pvt. James A. Westmoreland
17th Texas Cavalry
Circa 1861-1862*

Woodley (Mar. 20, 1823, Alabama - Aug. 6, 1885). They were married in Cherokee County, Alabama, Jan. 14, 1841, and moved to the Republic of Texas c. 1843. Joseph was a farmer and licensed preacher.

James enlisted as a private in Capt. Sterling B. Hendrick's Company, later known as Company E, 17th Regiment, Texas Cavalry - Dismounted, on Feb. 22, 1862, Elysian Fields, Harrison County. The name of James A. Westmoreland is found in "This Band of Heroes, Grandbury's Texas Brigade, C.S.A." by James M. McCaffrey. He was present with his command at the surrender at Greensboro, N.C., on April 26, 1865.

James was alert, had a sense of humor, enjoyed music and reading, refused to eat tomatoes and characterized himself as "a farmer, a Democrat and a Methodist." Joseph Robert Madden #4236

MILES WHITLEY

Mills or Miles Whitley was born in Johnston County, North Carolina, in 1792 or 1794. His father was John Saunders Whitley, and his mother was Barsheba Bateman. His father moved to Illinois Territory 1811-1813. Mills married Elizabeth Little of South Carolina on April 2, 1814, in Madison County, Illinois. Their children were Sarah, John, William August, 1819, Josiah, Sharp, Elizabeth, Randolph are all born in Illinois. Their last child, Hiram was born 1837, in Texas.

Mills Whitley and family moved to Texas around 1834-1836 near present-day New Waverly, Walker County.

Mills Whitley shows up in the Sabine District Census 1829-1836, the first Census of Texas. He and his brother Sharpe show up in the 1840 Census of the Republic of Texas. Mills Whitley has five work horses and his brother, Sharpe Whitley, had forty-one neat cattle, both in Montgomery County, which their part becomes Walker County.

In 1846 and October 1849, Mills Whitley sells off his land to his two sons, John and William, and to his brother Sharp and others.

*Tombstone of my great great grandfather
William Whitley, son of Mills Whitley*

He moved to Goliad or Caldwell County with his younger sons, Randolph or Hiram, in the 1850s. He died in the 1860s in South Texas. Philip D. Whitley

SAMUEL WILEY

Samuel Wiley (born Kentucky about 1800) first came to Texas about 1815. On April 25, 1815, his father, Stephen Wiley, Sr., sold his land, located about 17 miles above Campti, Louisiana, and moved with four of his sons — Cornelius, Samuel, Thomas, and Stephen Jr. — to Pecan Point, the site of an ancient Caddo Indian village, on the south side of the Red River in what is now northeastern Red River County, Texas. George W. Wright indicates Stephen Wiley came to the settlement in 1818 with "four sons, three of whom were Indian traders." They were among the first 12 families at the settlement and were constantly in peril of Indian attacks. By 1821, there were some 80 families in these squatter settlements.

Stephen, Sr. left about 1820 and moved to Nacogdoches County, probably near the Cove Spring area near present-day Melrose, nine miles southeast of Nacogdoches. In 1821, Stephen Austin reported only about 36 inhabitants of Nacogdoches, with five houses and a church. He also noted Anglo-American settlers who had built cabins in the forest on Spanish soil.

*Tombstone of Samuel Wiley, a veteran
of San Jacinto, located at Union Valley
Cemetery Wilson County, Texas.*

Stephen's son John, who had sold his land in Louisiana in 1819 and moved to Texas, built a cabin in the same area in 1823. The 1826 muster roll for the District of Ayish Bayou (San Augustine area) lists John Wiley, serving under Lieutenant James Bullock (who commanded the forces that besieged Nacogdoches on August 1, 1832). John sold his land in 1826, the same year Stephen Sr. died. This was also the year of the Fredonian Rebellion, a conflict in the area between the "old" settlers and the new, led by Hayden Edwards.

Stephen's other sons left the Pecan Point area about 1826, when the Indian treaty line forced white settlers to leave. Samuel and his wife Louise Pate had their first son, Stephen just before they left. Samuel returned to Natchitoches to settle the affairs of his brother, Jacob, who died in 1827.

Between 1827 and 1833 (approx.), they lived in the "neutral ground" between Louisiana and Mexican Texas. Samuel's son, William Bennett, was born in Texas about 1833. Thomas also had sons born in Texas about 1827 -1831. Two letters from the Province of Texas dated 1827 make references to sending the mail in care of Mr. Wiley at the Sabine.

According to the Texas General Land Office, an Estephen (Stephen Jr.) Wiley applied for a land grant from Mexico in February 1830, for land in East Texas. On May 5, 1833, Simon B. Wiley (believed to be a brother of Stephen Sr.), was in the province of Texas, state of Coahuila and Texas, municipality of Nacogdoches, where he was recorded as selling his land remaining in Louisiana, also near Campti, for $5,000.

On October 21, 1833, Samuel sold his land at Crow's Ferry on the river at Sabine to Frederick Williams for $350.00. Samuel returned to Louisiana with his wife, Louise Pate, and three children.

Why Samuel moved back to Louisiana in 1833 is uncertain, — perhaps because of the impending war, perhaps because his wife was ill (she died shortly thereafter). Samuel is recorded as one of the first settlers on government land in Sabine Parish (1835), followed by Martha Wiley (1839), Cornelius (1844), and Stephen Jr. (1845).

On June 18, 1835, Samuel and James Tyler purchased land for Bayou Scie Methodist Church, located in Zwolle, La.

On March 1, 1836, Samuel joined Captain James Gillaspie's Company, Second Regiment, Texas Volunteers, Sixth Company, organized in Nacogdoches. He served under Col. Sherman's command at the Battle of San Jacinto, where somewhere between 743 and 900 men defeated Santa Anna's army. According to Gillaspie, he "served his duty faithful as a soldier and honorably discharged." Military Record No. 1367 indicates he received $24.00 for his three months of service.

Stephen Sparks, a veteran of San Jacinto, in a letter he wrote to his pastor, recalled that, "Captain Wiley (note: A.H. Wiley, probably Samuel's uncle) came from Galveston with two pieces of cannon, called the 'Twin Sisters.' We asked the authorities to let us go with Captain Wiley and join Houston's Army. They agreed to let us go, and the next day we took up the line of march, arriving at Houston's Army the following afternoon. They were then at what was known as Groce's Retreat."

On October 19, 1837, Samuel married widow Martha Pate Woods in Natchitoches. Their children were Daniel Levi, Samuel Jackson, and George W. Wiley.

On Sept. 4, 1851, Samuel and John Wiley, as heirs of Stephen Wiley Sr., petitioned the Texas Legislature from the county of Houston for land. Three men, who are also listed as first wave settlers in the Pecan Point area by 1818, witnessed the petition.

The petition states that Stephen Wiley came to Texas in the year 1812, "at a time of imminent peril, that he and his family endured great hardships and sufferings, nevertheless he was ever ready to face danger when necessary and a frontier life in a new country, for the purpose of securing for himself, his family and those that should come before him, the blessings of civil and religious liberty, as well as the temporal comforts desired by all." The writer of the petition, Daniel Daily, concludes, "those who endured the 'heat and burden of day' may remember with grateful emotions the day that they pitched their tents and identified themselves with the then wilderness of Texas."

Although there is no evidence available of the petition being granted, the Wiley family moved to present-day Wilson County in the 1850s. Central Texas was still very much a frontier — San Antonio got its first post office in 1850 and had very few Anglo citizens. Austin was on the edge of the Indian frontier and had a population of only 600.

The Wileys lived in eastern Wilson County near Caddo, Union Valley, and Nockernut. Caddo was probably named after the friendly Caddo Indians they had known near Pecan Point.

Stephen Wiley, Jr., registered a brand January 10, 1853. Stephen, Samuel's son, registered a brand, April 12, 1872. His son, King George registered a brand August 2, 1880. King's son, Garvin Ambus Wiley, and his son, J. D. Wiley, and his son, Larry Ambus Wiley (SRT#4672) have all registered brands in Wilson County. Since county records began, nearly 100 Wileys have registered brands in Wilson County. Larry and his son, Robert Garvin Wiley, continue to raise cattle on their ranch located in northern Waller County.

Eight generations, over 185 years, have made the Lone Star State their home.

Samuel Wiley, hero of San Jacinto, died Christmas Eve 1890, approximately 90 years old. He is buried at Union Valley Cemetery in Wilson County. A Texas Revolutionary War Historical Marker marks his grave.

Note: The above history is based upon research conducted up until the date of publication. Although, all conclusions have been drawn as carefully as possible, research is still underway. *Submitted by Dorothy M. Wiley*

LEONARD G. HOUSTON WILLIAMS

Leonard G. Houston Williams (1802-1854) soldier and Indian agent, was the son of Maria Priscilla and Thomas Williams. Leonard was born in 1802 in Tennessee. The family was in Missouri Territory (now Arkansas) by 1818, and in what is now Red River County in 1819. By 1821, Leonard was in the Nacogdoches District. His first grant of land, a Mexican grant dated March 28, 1829, included the town of Mount Enterprise in future Rusk County. This grant was for services in the Fredonian Rebellion, during which he served under Col. Peter Ellis Bean.

Williams married Nancy Isaacs, the niece of Cherokee Indian Chief Richard Fields; they had nine children. The family professed to be Roman Catholic. Nancy died about 1835. Williams then married Jane Ware; they had three children.

Williams served in the Revolutionary Army at the Siege of Bexar, where he lost the sight in one eye. He was a sergeant in Benton's Regiment of Regular Rangers and enrolled on March 31, 1836, for three months extra duty at Williams Crossing on the Neches River. He served with Thomas J. Rusk and William Goyen during the suppression of the Cordova Rebellion.

On February 3, 1840, Williams was appointed as a commissioner to inspect the land office in Houston County. He was given the title of colonel by Sam Houston, who in 1842 appointed him one of four commissioners to deal or "treat" with the Indians. He participated in the Tehuacana Creek Council and was an Indian agent at Torrey's Trading Post No. 2.

During a trade trip as Indian agent for Houston, Williams came across Cynthia Ann Parker, a captive of the noted attack on Fort Parker by the Comanche Indians. He was later sent as United States agent to try and ransom her. He was considered an intelligent man with knowledge of seven or eight Indian dialects.

He died in April 1854 on his homestead, and was buried in what is now Pitts Cemetery in Limestone County. Williams was recognized for his service to Texas in the United States Congressional Record on April 8, 1965, and by the Texas Legislature in May 1965. A state roadside marker and gravesite marker commemorates his deeds in the service to the Republic of Texas. *Submitted by Clarence Vernon Williams Jr. #6813, Wesley Weeks Williams #6597, John Wesley Williams #6569*

STEPHEN AND SARAH WILLIAMSON

On Friday, April 24, 1863, Stephen Williamson, age 72, and a young neighbor rode out on horseback crossing over the hills of western Coryell County. Upon returning home the following Sunday, they were attacked by marauding Comanches. Stephen's daughter, Sarah, 15, wrote to her sister, Rachael, 21, who was attending school in Burleson Bounty: Coryell County May 1, 1863

Dear Sister: Well, Rachael, I have bad news to tell you. The Indians killed father last Sunday, the 26th of April. John Henderson was going above here after some horses and father went with him. They started Friday and as they were coming back Sunday evening they came upon some Indians. They immediately dismounted and tied their horses. Almost immediately the Indians started towards them. Father threw up his gun to shoot but Mr. Henderson insisted that father not shoot until they were close enough for every shot to count. Father agreed to this and smiled at the remark of Henderson that they were in great danger. Now, Mr. Henderson suggested to father that they had better run for it and they immediately mounted their horses but father's horse didn't get but a few feet before he was shot, and Mr. Henderson says he looked back and saw father jump down and shoot and almost immediately several Indians fell. Mr. Henderson did not know whether the horse was shot or the girt to his saddle broke, but he saw father fire and he saw him fall later. This occurred twelve miles from home. Henderson came on home and secured a number of men and returned at once. Father was shot 17 times with bow and arrows. The Indians took everything he had and then scalped him. The party followed the Indians and recovered some of the horses that the Indians stole from father and Mr. Henderson. Father always said if the Indians got him he would get as many of them as they got of him, and he kept his word.

Brother Joseph came last Sunday. He came to join the Rangers. The last time we heard from brother William he was well. We had a letter from Mike a few days since. He was on his way to Brownsville. Write soon. Your sister, Sarah E. Williamson

Stephen was buried in a wooden coffin with black calico lining at Eliga, in southwestern Coryell. The tragic, gruesome death of Stephen was one of the first recorded and often repeated historical accounts in western Coryell County. Stephen is recognized for founding the community and pioneering civilization the farthest west into Coryell County.

In 1990, 127 years later, while driving down back roads in western Coryell County, Rose Marie, Laura and I stopped to ask directions from two ranchers standing next to the fence line. When directions were sought to several cemeteries, the ranchers asked about our ancestors. Stephen Williamson's name was mentioned and the ranchers surprised us with their knowledge about Stephen's life as a pioneer, founder of the community, Stephen's death and the Williamson family.

Stephen Williamson was born in 1791, South Carolina, and married Sarah Sweeton, born 1805, Mississippi, daughter of Dutton Sweeton, Tippah County, Mississippi. Stephen and Sarah lived in Alabama, Tennessee, Arkansas, the Republic of Texas and the state of Texas. Accounts place Stephen and family in the Republic of Texas, as early as 1833 and 1836.

Stephen and Sarah had twelve children. A public debt of the late Republic of Texas and supporting affidavit indicate that their son, John Williamson, served in captain E.M. Collins' Company, Sabine Volunteers, 1836. By 1842, Stephen, Sarah and their eight children — Joseph, John, Serena, Dutton Sweeton, Daniel Martin, Eli, Nancy and Mary Ann — settled in Panola County, citizens of the Republic of Texas. Later, two children were born in the Republic of Texas: Rachael, 1842, and William Riley, 1845. Sarah Elizabeth was born in the state of Texas, 1848. Sarah Sweeton Williamson died in 1850, Panola County. Thereafter, Stephen and family lived in Rusk, Burleson and Bell counties. By February 1854, Texas created Coryell County from Bell County and Stephen settled the western part of Coryell County, engaging in stock, farming, raising horses and trading with the Indians.

Stephen's and Sarah's son, John Williamson, married September 23, 1847, Terresa Twomey, daughter of William B. Twomey and Nancy Ann Trotter. They had eleven children. John and Terresa's daughter, Julia Ann Williamson, born September 22, 1848, Coryell County, married May 27, 1866, Riley Green Hampton, born January 14, 1841, Arkansas. They had eleven children. Riley Green Hampton and Julia Ann Hampton owned a ranch in western Coryell County. Riley Green Hampton was a rancher, cattle broker and served as a Texas Ranger, 1860.

Their daughter, my grandmother, Ora Bell Hampton, born January 21, 1875, Coryell County, married Hillie Etchison Bennett, April 18, 1893. Ora was widowed in 1897, with a one-year-old daughter, Leta Hillie Bennett, born June 17, 1896. Ora married my grandfather, Thomas Marion Davidson, 1904, Gatesville. Ora was widowed again, in 1928, living 88 years, until 1963.

Ora's daughter, my Aunt Leta, lived 98 years, until 1994. Thomas and Ora's daughter, my Aunt Ora Lee Davidson Reynolds, was also, a family historian and a member of the Daughters of the Republic of Texas (DRT 5154). My grandmother and aunts fostered a love of family history, recalling life and times amidst the blue bonnets and rolling hills of Coryell County, along the Leon River.

Thomas and Ora's son, my father, Riley Green Davidson, born June 8, 1913, Gatesville, received a B.B.A. at Baylor, and enjoyed adventurous work with the Texas Company, later Texaco, in the late 1930s in Colombia, South America. Riley Green Davidson's service during World War II with the 449th Bomber Group of the Army of the United States was distinguished by his participation in air combat in the Balkans, Rhineland, Naples-Foggia, Rome-Arno, southern France, northern France, Po Valley, north Apennines, Central Europe, Air Offensive Europe and Normandy. He was awarded the European African Middle East Campaign Medal, eleven Bronze Stars, the Good Conduct Medal, and Distinguished Unit Badge with one Oak Leaf Cluster. My father said he prayed to return home to Coryell County. He returned home and married my mother. He owned Davidson Insurance Agency in Gatesville until his death, October 27, 1962, in Waco.

My mother, Aba Laura Mitchell Davidson, born August 13, 1919, Hubbard, Navarro County, Texas, was a member of the Daughters of the American Revolution. (DAR 767961). My mother was a descendant of William Paist of the Pennsylvania Militia, a patriot who fought in the American Revolution.

I was born October 29, 1947, Gatesville. My sister, Sally Bennett Davidson, was born October 17, 1954, Gatesville. My mother died May 17, 1998, in Austin. Sally lives in New York City. Sally's son, Alexis William Bull (CRT 3721) is in the United States Air Force in Aviano, Italy, with his wife, Tina and son, Reece.

On March 3, 1973, in Austin, I married Rose Marie Grimm, born October 4, 1947, Montgomery, West Virginia, daughter of Clayford Thomas Grimm and Elide Lucia Medone. I have practiced law since 1973, in Houston, Texas. Our daughter, Laura Catherine Davidson, born October 14, 1978, is a member of the Children of the Republic of Texas and Children of the American Revolution. (CRT 3653) (CAR 135384) Laura has graduated from the University of Texas, Austin, and will attend law school. Rose Marie, Laura and I live in Houston, and enjoy frequent visits to

Lake Belton, Bell County, and Gatesville, Coryell County, in the heart of Texas. I am honored to be a member and past president of the San Jacinto Chapter No. 1, Sons of the Republic of Texas, and a member and past president of the Paul Carrington Chapter No. 5, National Society and Texas Society, Sons of the American Revolution, Houston, Texas.

Joe Riley Davidson (SRT 2806) (NSSAR 134356) (TXSSAR 6439)Great-great-great-grandson of Stephen and Sarah Williamson, Great-great-grandson of John and Terresa Williamson, Great-grandson of Riley Green and Julia Ann Hampton, Grandson of Thomas Marion and Ora Bell Davidson, Son of Riley Green and Aba Laura Davidson

DEMETRIUS WILLIS

Demetrius Willis came to San Augustine County from Talladega County, Alabama, about 1843 to live with his uncle, Isaac W. Hall. He had been orphaned as a child when his parents died of yellow fever in 1835-1836. Demetrius was born on January 14, 1825 in Florence, Lauderdale County, Alabama to Joshua Willis and Martha Hall. Joshua Willis was a tailor and mercantile store owner in Triana. Demetrius worked as a mercantile clerk, and at age 21 years he registered to vote in 1846 in Henderson County.

Demetrius volunteered in San Augustine for the Mexican War on May 16, 1846. He served as a private in Captain Wheeler's Company, 2nd Texas Mounted Volunteers, commanded by Colonel (Governor) George T. Wood. His company was engaged at the Battle of Monterey.

Upon discharge, he returned to Gonzales, Texas, where he became active in civic and business affairs. He served as Gonzales city secretary, district clerk of Gonzales County, president of Gonzales Lyceum Society, and was a founder of Gonzales College. He also owned a mercantile store, "Matthews & Willis," which sold staples and fancy goods.

On April 8, 1849, he married Margaret Elizabeth Brown, daughter of Dr. Hugh H. Brown and Lucinda Johnson. They had six children: Emma Cornelia, Persia, Walter Demetrius, Hugh Joshua, Charles and William Leonidas.

Demetrius Willis, State Representive, 9th Texas Legislature, circa 1861.

In March 1858, Demetrius moved to Livingston, Polk County, and started another mercantile store, as well as continuing his Masonic affiliation rising, to Worshipful Master in the lodge. He was elected State Representative from the Second District to the 9th Texas Legislature from 1861-1865. During this time he also saw Confederate Service in the Civil War at Galveston as a private in Company E, 20th Texas Infantry, Elmore's Regiment, and was appointed clerk of the General Court Martial.

On October 15, 1865, his wife died in childbirth. Demetrius remarried on May 15, 1866 to Anna Brown McKean and had two children. They were Felix Henry Willis and Anna Elizabeth Octavia Willis.

Demetrius Willis died of tuberculosis in Livingston on August 12, 1872, and was buried in the Old City Cemetery. His white marble headstone reflects his Mexican War service and an SRT medallion shows he was a "Citizen of the Republic of Texas." It was placed there by his great-great-grandson, Colonel Cannon H. Pritchard. *Submitted by Cannon H. Pritchard #5974*

WILLIAM WOODERSON

William Wooderson was born in Pennsylvania in 1811. He was apprenticed to a master furniture maker. When William Barret Travis sent an open letter for help to American newspapers, William left for Texas. He served in the Texas Army as a private, between May 18, 1836, and August 18, 1836, under Captain Van Norman, serving the majority of his service at Velasco, Texas.

Following the Texas Revolution, in 1839 or 1840, William married his first wife, Elizabeth. The Texas Poll List Census of 1840 lists William Wooderson (misspelled as Woodison) living in Walker County, Texas.

In the 1840s and 1850s, William earned his living as a cabinetmaker, farmer and owner/operator of a steam-operated lumber mill. William Wooderson's craftsmanship has been recognized in Taylor and Warren's "Texas Furniture: The Cabinetmakers and their work, 1840-1880."

The 1860 United States Census reveals that William lost wife Elizabeth and his four children between 1850 and 1860. It is not known what tragedy befell the Wooderson family, but the 1850s and 1860s in the south and in Texas brought yellow fever epidemics, and this may be what happened.

In 1866, William Wooderson married his second wife, Eliza Stark. Four children were born of the marriage. William was a farmer and cabinetmaker during the 1860s and 1870s. He was rewarded in 1881 with a Veteran Land Grant of 1,280 acres for his service during the Texas Revolution. William Wooderson lived out the remainder of his life in Walker and Grimes counties.

ZADOCK WOODS

Zadock Woods is documented as a member of Stephen F. Austin's First Colony in "The Old Three Hundred," by Lester G. Bugbee. The Bugbee research was printed in the "Quarterly of the Texas State Historical Association" in October of 1897. When Austin established the first Anglo colony of Texas in the early 1820s, Zadock Woods presented his character certificate and petition for land. He received title to a league of land in Matagorda County. However, the land on which Woods finally settled was a few miles above LaGrange in the Colorado River Valley — Indian country.

A Texas Centennial Historical Marker has been placed near the site of the Woods Fort that Zadock built. It stands 1.5 miles west of West Point on Texas Highway 71. The fort was built in an area that only a few years earlier had been a buffalo trail. Settlers in the area used the fort as protection against Indian attacks.

Zadock was already 52 years of age when he began to move his family to Texas. The son of Jonathan Jr. and Keziah Keith Woods, he was born September 18, 1773 in Brookfield, Massachusetts. Early accounts connect him with the western part of Massachusetts, Connecticut and Vermont. In Woodstock, Vermont, the

Woods Fort as it appeared in this photo taken in 1910. The Moore family of LaGrange, Texas provided the photo. Moore occupied the house and land after the death of Zadock Woods.

year 1796, Woods met Minerva Cottle, the daughter of Joseph Cottle. They were married in 1797. In 1800, the National Census recorded the Zadock Woods family in Litchfield County, Connecticut. Minerva taught school and Zadock dug wells and helped in construction projects.

They soon moved to Missouri. In 1802, Zadock Woods and Joseph Cottle had adjoining land grants in the St. Charles District, Missouri, across the river from St. Louis. Among other enterprises, Woods invested in a lead mine with Moses and Stephen Austin. Through this business venture, Zadock learned of the dream that Austin had for an Anglo colony in Texas.

The children of Zadock and Minerva Cottle Woods and their spouses are as follows: Minerva, 1798-1897, married William Harrell 1796-1891; Ardelia, born in 1804, only lived seven months; Norman, 1805-1843, married Jane Boyd Wells, 1809-1866; Montraville, 1806-1857, married Isabella Gonzales; Leander 1809-1832; and Henry Gonsalvo, 1816-1869, also married Jane Boyd Wells Woods.

A historic marker has been placed at the actual site of the Woods Fort. The fort burned down in 1920. A Texas Centennial marker is also placed on Hwy. 71 north of LaGrange, about 2 miles from the actual site.

By 1829, the homesteads in the area of Woods Fort were called Woods Prairie. Over the following years, the men of the Woods family would fight the Indians, and fight against the Mexican government for Texas independence. One of Zadock's sons, Leander, was killed in the Battle of Velasco. This battle in 1832 was a prelude to the Texas Revolution. The Woods' son Gonzalvo joined his father at Gonzales in the famous "Come and Take It" incident. The Woods family had even survived the famous "Runaway Scrape," when Texans fled east to escape Santa Anna.

Six years after Texas became independent from Mexico, on September 11, 1842 a Mexican Army led by General Woll invaded San Antonio. When news of the invasion spread, Captain Dawson of LaGrange called for volunteers to face General Woll in San Antonio. When Zadock's sons, Norman and Gonzalvo, heard the call for battle, they hid their father's horse. They pleaded with Zadock not to take the ride to San Antonio and risk going into battle. Zadock was almost 69 years of age, and the sons thought he was to old to fight. Zadock announced he would ride with them or he would walk without them. With his mare saddled, Zadock mounted, and holding his rifle above his head, spurred twice around the old fort at great speed. He declared, "I fought with Andrew Jackson at New Orleans, and with old Sam Houston at San Jacinto, and I'll give the enemy one more crack at old Zadock."

Zadock Woods and his sons, Norman and Henry Gonzalvo, and their 18-year-old nephew, Milvern Harrell, would join Captain Dawson and his troops at Muldoon on the way to San Antonio. On Sept. 18th, the 54 men from the LaGrange area, led by Dawson, approached San Antonio from the east. Their intent was to join the 225 Texans led by Mathew Caldwell from Gonzales. Caldwell and his men were outnumbered when they engaged in battle with a Mexican force of about 900 men. The fierce battle took place on the Salado Creek six miles east of old San Antonio. Caldwell would eventually repel the Mexican charge.

As Dawson's men came within a half-mile of Caldwell's men, they were surrounded by a secondary Mexican force that had been held in reserve. The men dismounted and took cover behind a small cluster of mesquite trees. The Texans began to fire with pistol and rifle. The Mexican cannon and musket barrage overcame the Texans within minutes. On his 69thth birthday, Zadock Woods was one of the first to die as he ran to the aid of his son, Norman.

Norman Woods suffered severe shrapnel wounds that sliced through his hip. Also, he received head wounds from Mexican swords as the battle was ending. Norman's brother, Gonsalvo, escaped by taking away the spear of a Mexican soldier that was on horseback. Gonsalvo knocked the man from his horse and then killed him with his own spear. As Gonsalvo Woods escaped, he carried the spear with him. That spear is now on display at the Alamo. Norman's nephew, Milvern Harrell, was not seriously injured. When the massacre was over, 36 Texans were killed, 15 were taken prisoner, and 3 escaped. In 1848, the remains of the fallen Texans were disinterred and entombed in the old Rock Tomb on Monument Hill south of LaGrange, overlooking the wide sweep of the Colorado River Valley.

Norman Woods and Milvern Harrell were taken as prisoners to San Carlos Prison near Perote, Mexico. On December 16, 1843, Norman died from his wounds and was buried in the moat of the prison. Milvern was eventually released and returned to Texas.

So went the original Woods line. Brave and hardy heroes. Their hardships gave birth to a nation. They suffered with little reward, so we might inherit our freedoms. Andrew David Durham #5154S, David Ross Durham #4728, Marshall P. Durham Jr. #6073

WILLIAM RICHARD WORNELL

William Richard Wornell was born near Crab Orchard, Lincoln County, KY, on 15 February 1790. His parents were Richard Wornell and Mary Jane (Polly) Gore Wornell. His father, Richard Wornell, a veteran of the American Revolution, was killed by Indians the August preceding William Richard's birth. After spending several years in Lincoln and Green counties, he moved to Tennessee. The exact place is not known, nor is the date of his first marriage to a Miss Wilson, although it was ca. 1814. Lucy and William Wilson Wornell were born to this union.

His first wife died prior to 1818. On 7 May 1818, William Richard Wornell married Judith Middleton, (daughter of John and Rebecca Middleton), and together they had ten children: Mary Ann, Nancy Jane, Amanda Adaline, Elizabeth M., John M., Rebecca, Fletcher Mark, David Crockett, Martha Isabelle, and Emily M.

William Richard Wornell served in Col. Steele's West Tennessee Militia in the War of 1812. In 1836, after living in various Tennessee counties, Wornell and his brother, Notley Gore Wornell, and a group of friends departed by wagon train from Wayne County, Tennessee, for Texas. The Wornell's stopped in Marshall County, Mississippi, near Holly Springs for about 18 months between early spring of 1836 and fall of 1837 before continuing their trek to Texas. David Crockett Wornell was born in Marshall County, Mississippi.

W. R. Wornell arrived in San Augustine County, Texas, 25 Sept 1837. By 1840, he was living in Shelby County, Texas, from whence he went to Rusk County, where he settled about one mile southeast of the future community of New Salem. In 1855, on June 9th, he and his family arrived in Hill County, Texas. He died on 8 Dec. 1865, and is buried in Hickey Cemetery in Hill County. He married twice more after Judith died, and had at least one more daughter, Eller, by his fourth wife, Martha.

Two of his sons served in the Confederate Cavalry: John Middleton, who was killed at the Battle of Yellow Bayou in Louisiana; and David Crockett, who survived the war and served several terms in various elected positions in Hill County. Another son, William Wilson, was hanged in the Great Gainsville (Texas) Hanging in October 1862.

One of his daughters, Rebecca, who emigrated to Texas with her family in 1837, married Andrew Jackson Kellam, through whom this author descended. *Submitted by Bobby Joe Mitchell (#3524)*

COLONEL NAHOR BIGGS YARD

Colonel Nahor Biggs Yard, born at Trenton, New Jersey, in 1916, died at Galveston in 1889. He was the husband of Caroline Nichols; the son of Joseph Yard (1785-1872) of Trenton; grandson of Nahor Yard (1752-1791); great-grandson of Benjamin Yard (1714-1808); great-great-grandson of William Yard (1674-1744), whose father, Joseph Yard (1647-1716), emigrated from Churston Ferrers, Devon, England, to Philadelphia before 1687. Joseph, heir of the Yard Coat of Arms, was a mason. William, a carpenter, was first clerk of the Hunterdon Court, and owner of the Black Horse Tavern. Benjamin built a plating mill and arms factory that supplied guns for General Washington. Joseph, publisher of "The True American," was a member of the Jersey Blues, the first company to enlist in the War of 1812. Of 89 men, he was the only survivor.

Colonel Nahor Biggs Yard arrived in Galveston, on a ship he built, in 1838, and joined the Galveston Guards as first lieutenant. Elected alderman, he participated in the formation of city government, but after a year, resigned to join the First Company of Texas Rangers under John C. Hayes. They fought the Comanches — 14 men against 70 Indians, of whom they killed 40. The following years at Bandera Pass they killed or wounded 60. In the Kearnes Expedition, only two of Nahor's group were lost.

He operated a clothing store for many years, organized the Galveston Rifles, and when it grew to regimental size, he became colonel. He commanded a battery at Pelican Spit, and was second-in-command of the General Rush at the time of the Major Sibley surrender of Federal troops. He was active in the recruitment of the First Regiment of Texas State Troops, but lost his

Colonel Nahor Biggs Yard, William B. Nichols, Edward Jacob Yard, and Howard Nahor Yard.

command and personal property with the close of the war. He organized the funding of the Gulf, Colorado and Santa Fe railroad, and numerous services for the city, and rose in Masonic affairs to thirty-third degree, and was Grand Commander for Texas.

Edward Jacob Yard, son of Colonel Yard, (1860-1907) was the chief engineer for the J. Gould Denver and Rio Grande and Rio Grande Western Railroad systems, laying track from Galveston to Sacramento. He was my grandfather.

FRANCIS MARION YOAST

Francis Marion Yoast was probably born about 1795 in Pennsylvania. He died in 1847, suffering from wounds incurred in the Mexican War. He was discharged and died in Goliad on the way to his family and home in Bastrop. No record of his burial place has been established to date. He married Nancy Owen, daughter of Anthony Owen. Anthony Owen was a wealthy planter of Wyeth County, Virginia.

Francis and Nancy left Virginia about 1833, stopping in Bibb County, Alabama, after losing their wagon while crossing a swollen stream. He became a cotton ginner and saved enough money to make their way to Bastrop about 1837-38.

Bonham J. Sparks Jr. G.G.G. Grandson of Francis Marion Yoast

In 1846, Francis went with the Texas Army to Saltillo to fight the Mexican Army. He served with Company H, July 5, 1846-September 9, 1946; with Company I, June 21, 1847-May 1, 1848; with David Cady's Company, Texas Rangers, October 1845-December 1845, as fourth sergeant (first service); with David Cady's Texas Mounted Rangers as fourth sergeant (second service); and with Cady's Mounted Rangers April 1846-July 1847.

In the Daughters of the Republic of Texas Museum in Austin, there is a large iron pot this family brought from Virginia. The author of this biography is shown holding the pot. The author is a great-great-great-great-grandchild of Francis Marion Yoast. *Submitted by Bonham J. Sparks, Jr. #5060 - author, Alan Jaime #5789A, Thomas Jay #5803A, Kenneth Sparks #5414*

"RED" ZUMWALT SR.

"Red" Adam Zumwalt, Sr., was born February 1790 in Virginia. He owned property in Femme Osage and Darst's Bottom, Missouri. He married Nancy Elizabeth Caton (1795-1886) on 6 May 1813 in St. Charles County, Missouri. The family of nine arrived in the DeWitt Colony via New Orleans in 1829-1830. Land grant records indicated that Adam Zumwalt, married with nine persons (seven children, two males), arrived in the DeWitt Colony 20 May 1829, and was granted a league and labor of land on 28 Jan 1830. He was 40 years old.

On 15 Nov. 1831, Adam Zumwalt as a breeder of stock petitioned for title to his league of 4,428 acres in Gonzales County. On 3 Oct. 1834, he was deeded Lots 5 and 6 in Block II of Gonzales. In 1841, Adam received a land certificate for 320 acres from the Republic of Texas for service from June to September of 1836.

By 1836, "Red" Adam Zumwalt had established a residence and business in Gonzales. His residence was the hotel and restaurant of the period. It was one of the prominent 32 structures in Gonzales in early March 1836. On 29 February 1836, following instructions from his father, Andrew Kent, David Boyd Kent moved his mother, Elizabeth Zumwalt Kent, and his 9 brothers and sisters into Gonzales. The family stayed with Elizabeth's first cousin "Red" Adam. On 6 March the Alamo fell. On 13 Mar. General Houston ordered the evacuation of Gonzales, and the town was put to the torch. On 14 Mar., only Adam Zumwalt's kitchen and Andrew Ponton's smokehouse were the only structures standing of the over 32 structures that were present a week earlier. Adam assisted in the evacuation of Gonzales towards the Sabine River. This became known as the "Runaway Scrape." He was 46 at the time of the Texas Revolution. Adam and his family returned to Gonzales in 1837 to rebuild their lives in the Republic of Texas. He and Nancy provided housing and meals for numerous settlers while they rebuilt after the burning of Gonzales.

Adam died on March 9, 1853. He was 63 years old. Adam and Nancy are buried in the Zumwalt Family Cemetery in Slaton near their homestead. Thomas L. Zumwalt #6316

DAVID CLARY

David Clary (1787-1849) came to Texas from Alabama in the 1800s and settled in Grimes County, receiving a League and Labor in 1845, the year of our annexation to the United States. David was the father of Francis Marion Clary, who at the age of 20 years served as a Texas soldier in the Somervell Campaign. Jesse Clary, a brother to Francis Marion, also served in these early campaigns and was in Captain Bird's company in 1835 at the age of 18 years. There were four other sons of David: Meschack Pinkston Clary, my great-great-grandfather, born in 1811 and died in Navarro County in 1887; George Washington Clary; Tressant Clary; and David Jr., who at the reading of David's will in 1857 had gone to California in search for gold. In 1849, cattle were selling for two dollars a head, a casket cost seven dollars, and a good horse $35.00. 1151 1/4 acres were valued at $760.00, or $1.51 an acre.

Elizabeth Catherine Clary, our great-grandmother and daughter of Meschack Clary was born 5th of March 1845, in a log cabin in Grimes County. She kept a diary and recorded that her father had given her gifts, including a new horse, saddle and enough money to purchase a bolt of calico for a new dress. On August 20th 1872, Elizabeth married Captain Asa Grism Freeman, C.S.A., who served in the 1st Tennessee Cavalry, Company F, from July 5th 1861, until the war was over. Freeman was in the saddle for

Capt. Asa G. Freeman   *Mrs. Elizabeth Catherine Clary-Freeman*

over four years and traveled over 2,000 miles, and was three times wounded in the war. Some of Capt. Freeman's exploits are documented in the book *Company Aych*, written by his nephew, Pvt. Sam Watkins, also from Maury County, Tennessee. Captain Freeman and Elizabeth established one of the first cotton gins in Corsicana, Texas. Among the six children of Asa and Elizabeth Freeman was a daughter, Maggie Freeman, our grandmother.

Maggie married Edgar Barry Church. Their daughter, Hazel Church, married Jere Charles Showalter in Houston in 1924, at the Heights Baptist Temple in Houston. Showalter, orphaned at an early age, later found out through inquiries as to his place and date of birth in a newspaper classified that he was a descendant of Major John Burleson and has "several Texas relatives that had done well." "One founded some Baptist college in Waco and another was noted for his talent in protecting early settlers from the Indians after fighting at the Battle of San Jacinto," as was written in a letter from one of his aunts in Illinois. The college was Baylor and the cousin was Rufos Burleson and the Indian fighter was another cousin, Gen. Edward Burleson.

We apologize for sounding like a "Texas Bragger," but we were unaware of all the history until we dabbled in some genealogy. Our father, Jere C. Showalter, held numerous patents while working as a research specialist for the Humble Oil and Refinery Co. Showalter, enlisting in the Marine Corps on the first day war was declared in 1917, tried to re-enlist for the Second World War at about the time that a *Life* magazine cover showed dead marines on the beach at Guadalcanal. These were difficult times during World War II and the Marines told him he could be of a greater service to his country by contributing his talent as a chemist. He did just that by developing a detergent with steam to clean the tanks of oil tankers as they came into the Humble docks. He cut cleaning time of tankers and enabled switching of cargo to be done far quicker. The U.S. Navy, Standard Oil Co. and the U.S. Bureau of Standards soon adopted this process. Showalter also contributed his talent to the production of toluene which was crucial during the war since one of the final products is TNT. 75% of the toluene production in the U.S. was at the Baytown refinery. Consulting with researchers from M.I.T., Showalter solved a critical problem in the production of toluene and helped to end World War II through doubling the Humble Company output of this explosive product for the war effort.

Jere C. Showalter Jr., #6758, attended Baylor University and graduated in 1951 with a B.B.A. degree in marketing. Later, he graduated from the University of Texas School of Dentistry class of 1959. Dr. Showalter Jr. married Vernille Winkler on the 20th of February, 1960, and practiced dentistry for 38 years in Liberty, Texas, before retirement. Jere and Vernille have two children, a daughter, Sharon, and a son, Jere III.

Index

A

Abernathy 128
Ables 144
Abraham 85
Ackermann 153
Adair 26
Adams 33, 41, 43, 67, 68
Adamson 42
Addelsey 21
Adkins 119
Adlong 134
Alcorn 44
Alford 128
Alister 46
Allee 108
Allen 13, 28, 39, 63, 96, 99, 100, 121
Allison 28, 29, 145
Allsup 165
Almonte 12, 172
Alphin 116
Alsbury 136
Alsworth 33
Alvarez 52
Amette 32
Amis 149
Amsler 29
Anderson 48, 83, 99, 118, 165
Andrews 35, 95, 127
Applewhite 60
Archer 71, 126, 148
Arguelles 18
Ariola 30
Armour 112
Arnold 26, 29, 49
Arocha 29
Arriola 29
Arthur 124
Ashe 13, 16

Askins 164
Aston 50
Atkinson 75, 149, 159
Austin 7, 8, 13, 14, 22, 23, 28, 29, 31, 32, 36, 38, 51, 52, 53, 56, 67, 68, 71, 73, 75, 77, 92, 97, 100, 102, 107, 108, 110, 112, 123, 126, 130, 131, 137, 140, 144, 146, 148, 150, 158, 159, 161, 162, 163, 169, 171, 173, 174, 178, 179
Awalt 23, 30

B

Bachman 30
Bacon 99
Bagby 96, 159
Bahn 56
Baker 46, 79, 107, 140, 163
Ball 57
Ballentine 85
Banks 12, 18, 26, 58
Banta 31
Barclay 108, 129
Barefield 93
Barfield 93
Barker 26, 31, 50, 100, 144, 159
Barnard 71
Barnes 38
Barnett 31, 75
Barrera 19, 26, 139
Barrow 77, 95, 171
Barstow 112
Barth 31, 32
Bartholomew 96
Barton 31, 32, 117, 147

Basse 65
Bateman 175
Bates 26, 42
Bavoux 19, 20, 32
Bays 67
Beakley 118
Bean 176
Beason 71
Beckham 37
Bee 12
Beedy 171
Beeman 22
Beene 37
Bejach 113
Bell 26, 28, 32, 33, 62, 70, 73, 75, 95, 110, 116, 119, 120, 131, 133, 139
Bellesfelt 117
Bellows 26
Belt 28
Benavides 76
Benbow 122
Bendele 138
Bender 153
Benecke 30
Benignant 141
Bennett 33, 34, 55, 60, 84, 133, 160, 167, 177
Benson 131
Benton 146, 147, 176
Bercerra 155
Beretta 26
Berry 78, 99, 129, 130, 167
Bettis 98
Bevil 120
Bickham 146
Billings 21, 22, 26, 37
Billingsley 34, 35, 36, 37
Billingsly 95, 124

Bingham 43, 75
Bingman 88, 153
Binion 39
Birchel 81
Bird 38, 89, 121, 163
Birdsong 56
Birdwell 42, 43
Bishop 135, 147
Bizzell 41
Black 59
Blair 39, 105, 152
Blaisse 105
Blake 92
Blakey 35
Blalock 145
Bland 82
Blanto 26
Blanton 17, 19, 26, 39, 40
Blatz 78
Block 115
Blount 14
Boggess 157
Boggs 41
Bohmfalk 153
Bolton 51
Bomar 141
Bone 133
Bonesio 33
Bonham 21
Bonner 58, 59
Booker 168
Boom 41
Boon 55, 90
Boone 41, 48, 49, 113, 130, 135
Booth 41, 42, 43, 162
Boothe 56
Bordelon 84
Borden 52
Bostic 68

182

Boston 43
Bounds 57
Bowen 73, 80
Bowie 35, 44, 94, 164
Bowman 44
Bowmer 71
Box 44
Boyd 173, 174
Bozarth 71, 72
Brackeen 156
Bradburn 102, 111
Bradford 139
Bradley 44, 85, 145
Brae 92
Branch 13
Brandon 14
Brandt 139
Brannan 89
Brantley 39
Brasher 68
Breazeal 34
Brewer 51
Briant 51
Brigance 44
Briggs 26, 85, 91, 158
Bright 112
Briley 68
Brimberry 68, 69, 164
Brinkley 36
Brinson 137
Briscoe 11, 26, 85, 111
Brittain 44, 45, 67, 155
Britton 26, 86
Brockius 37
Brockman 104
Broocks 99
Brooks 45, 94
Brookshire 121
Brown 18, 26, 37, 49, 57, 74, 84, 123, 165, 167, 178
Brownrigg 61
Bruner 147
Brush 45
Bruton 57
Bryan 13, 14, 26, 168
Bryant 45, 46, 47, 48, 89, 127
Buchanan 71
Bugbee 178
Bugg 70
Bull 177
Bullock 36, 37, 116, 164, 175
Bumpas 161
Bunby 107
Burch 111
Burchard 140
Burditt 107
Burford 137
Burk 44
Burket 48
Burks 75

Burleson 12, 34, 35, 38, 48, 50, 72, 84, 94, 118, 126, 146, 165, 174
Burnam 108
Burnet 17, 35, 45, 50, 54, 140, 144, 155, 163
Burnett 30, 71
Burnham 97
Burns 87
Burrell 51
Burress 48, 49
Burris 49
Burroughs 82
Burton 37, 83, 112
Busby 49
Bush 20, 23, 26, 156
Buster 49
Butler 26, 39, 56, 57
Buxton 60
Byrd 117
Byrn 44

C

Caddel 69
Cade 101
Cady 180
Calder 50, 60
Caldwell 35, 50, 89, 117, 127, 149, 179
Callahan 120
Cameron 71, 118
Camp 86, 157
Campbell 22, 50, 98, 104, 135, 159
Campise 151
Canales 118
Canamar 87
Candacy 167
Cannon 62
Canole 51
Caperton 30
Capps 51
Cargill 83
Carl 23
Carlisle 93
Carlos 19
Carnes 51
Carney 80, 130
Carr 14, 51
Carrigan 93
Carroll 96
Carson 51, 52, 62
Carter 52, 60, 91
Cartwright 26, 140
Caruthers 52
Carvajal 26, 155
Castle 100
Castleberry 82, 127
Castro 125

Cate 52
Cathey 157
Cathriner 29
Caton 181
Cavalier 6
Cawyer 94
Cellum 53
Chabot 159
Chamber 85
Chamberlain 48
Chambers 50, 160
Chambliss 126
Chandler 53, 90
Chapin 45
Chappell 53
Charleston 59
Charlton 17, 26
Charpentier 138
Chesser 148
Chessher 127
Cheves 136
Childer 121
Childers 62
Childress 140
Childs 152
Chiles 53, 54
Chirino 54
Chisum 164
Chrisman 25
Clapp 30, 54
Clark 18, 26, 55, 58, 63, 70, 95, 112, 113, 127, 128, 143, 145
Clary 85, 144
Claunch 52
Clegg 55
Clements 51
Cleveland 56
Cloud 56
Cochran 56, 57, 165
Cocke 140
Cockerell 152
Coffee 148
Coggin 57
Colbert 16
Colburn 151
Cole 113
Coleman 28, 57
Collard 57, 58, 105, 117
Collette 171
Colley 81
Collier 58, 127, 148
Collins 58, 119, 177
Collinsworth 58, 59
Coltharp 152
Cone 29
Conger 26
Connally 15
Conner 149
Conrad 59

Cook 39, 59, 60, 61, 76, 91, 122, 164
Cooke 60, 61, 161
Cooper 147
Copeland 147
Copes 33, 52
Corbet 62
Corodova 35
Corry 92
Cortez 128
Cos 66, 116
Costley 59, 104
Cottle 179
Courtney 80
Covert 48
Covington 95, 96
Cox 53, 62, 66, 72, 167
Craddock 11, 62
Craig 15, 21, 26
Crain 105, 107, 154
Crane 63, 79
Craven 93
Crawford 63, 68
Crawley 101
Creech 57
Cresswell 50, 74
Crews 62, 131
Crier 150
Criswell 80
Crittenden 67
Crockett 18, 22, 30, 34, 63, 98
Crook 118, 156
Crooms 157
Crow 176
Crowson 117
Crudup 136
Cude 123
Culbertson 93
Cullen 26, 99
Cummins 110, 150, 167
Cunningham 64, 96
Curbelo 29, 159
Curry 171
Custer 171
Cutrer 37

D

Daggett 21
Daily 176
Daingerfield 24, 25
Dallam 93
Damon 11
Dancer 154
Dangerfield 16, 99
Dangers 64, 65
Daniel 17, 18, 26
Daniels 162
Daniley 41
Danish 165

183

Danley 121
Dannelly 174
Dannheim 65, 141, 142, 143, 169
Darby 37, 62, 66
Darling 66
Darst 11
Dashiell 85
Daunt 155
Davenport 63
Davidson 50, 177, 178
Davis 11, 37, 38, 53, 118, 119, 129
Dawson 73, 118, 127, 138, 146, 179
Day 26, 30, 37
De Ampudia 141
De Bastras 171
De Cordova 115
De Coronado 6
De Cos 9
De Escondor 87
De Galvez 19, 87
De La Garza 87
De la Peña 151
De La Piedras 110
De la Salle 6
De Leon 87, 153
De Pineda 6
De Santa Anna 8, 15, 21, 61, 97, 101, 107, 111, 113, 119, 120, 137, 156, 172
De Soto 6
De St. Denis 6
De Vesci 157
De Zavala 13, 17, 151
De Zavalla 111
Deal 39
Dealey 26
Dean 79
Deardoirf 82
Dearduff 82
Dearmore 58
Deas 134
Deaton 63
DeBeay 59
DeBray 32
DeCrow 67
Delaney 141
DeLozier 63
DeMorse 141
DeMoss 67, 68
Denson 68
Denton 38, 143
Derk 69
Derrick 69
Desrisia 82
Devers 69
Dew 70
DeWitt 8, 50, 117, 159

Dickard 113
Dickens 54
Dickerson 164
Dickey 69, 70, 71
Dickinson 71, 79
Dienst 58
Dikes 37
Dill 81
Dillard 11, 71, 72
Dillinger 135
Dilworth 26
Dimmitt 45
Dischinger 153
Dixon 37, 50, 53, 106
Dixson 69
Dobbs 33
Dobkins 95
Dodd 147
Dodge 62
Dodson 161
Donnell 100
Donovan 129
Dorsett 111, 164
Doscher 21
Dougan 33
Douglass 50, 156
Dowsing 166
Doyle 19
Dresel 96
Drury 26
Duke 52
Dumble 13
Dunbar 23, 26, 72
Duncan 147, 157
Dunham 172
Dunigan 152
Dunlap 111
Dunlavy 72
Durham 179
Durst 142
Duvall 83
Dyer 44, 154

E

Eakin 92
Earthman 72
Easter 57
Eastland 35, 73
Echols 73, 106
Edens 113
Edmiston 73, 74
Edwards 8, 40, 54, 85, 102, 148, 150, 175
Eggleston 123
Ehlers 66
Eisenhower 18
Eleander 96
Elkins 63, 147
Elliot 25

Ellis 26, 68, 74
Elmore 50, 178
Elwood 147
Engledow 74, 165
English 156
Equis 29
Erath 64, 166
Ericson 6, 21, 26, 54, 74, 134, 148, 154
Estes 50
Etter 59
Evans 80, 121, 129, 165
Eve 25
Everts 75
Evetts 22, 75

F

Faglie 165
Fairies 63
Fairweather 115
Fall 75
Fannin 9, 28, 29, 34, 54, 60, 61, 67, 69, 73, 113
Farias 76
Farley 84
Farnham 45
Fate 145
Fehrenbach 26, 72
Fellhauer 151
Felstead 118
Fenn 11, 12, 76
Fentress 35
Ferguson 14, 76, 156
Ferguson 30
Fersing 139
Ficklin 129
Fields 79, 176
Fietsam 115
Figueroa 87
Finley 63
Fischer 132
Fisher 20, 26, 56, 76, 77, 93, 118, 141
Fitch 70
Fitzgerald 76, 79
Flanagan 77
Fleming 95
Fletcher 41
Flitner 90
Flores 77, 151, 155
Flournoy 31
Floyd 88, 91, 123, 174
Foley 117, 141
Fontaine 166
Forbes 156
Ford 22, 73
Forgey 149
Forrest 126
Forrester 71

Fountain 92
Fox 70
Frame 161
Francis 115
Francke 78
Frank 17, 18, 26
Franke 78
Franklin 50
Frantz 26
Fraser 26
Fraussereau 32
Frazer 49
Freeman 62
Frels 157
Friar 109, 122
Friedrich 125
Fries 78
Frith 78, 130
Fuchs 135
Fulcher 11, 133, 164
Fuller 79
Fulton 120
Fuqua 28, 45, 78

G

Gage 79, 144
Gaines 38, 149
Gallatin 79, 80
Galvez 78
Gambrell 18, 26
Gammage 26
Gantt 21
Garcia 78
Gardiner 57, 113
Gardner 130
Garey 80
Garner 22, 26, 44, 102
Garrett 49, 80, 130, 165
Garrison 57, 165
Garza 170
Gatewood 84
Gaucher 94
Gay 67
Gayle 80, 81, 82, 163
Geistmann 107
Gentry 55
George 82, 145
Geren 87
Gibson 117, 137
Gilbert 16, 26, 105
Gilchrist 56
Giles 145
Gill 101, 146
Gillaspie 66, 101, 176
Gilleland 35, 110
Gillett 105
Gilmer 16
Ginn 20, 21, 22, 23, 26, 32
Giuffre 132

Givens 61, 67
Glasgow 167
Glenn 86, 158
Glover 92, 170
Goffe 131
Goheen 66
Gold 78
Goldsborough 173
Goldsworthy 165
Gomer 82
Gonzales 155
Gonzalez 87
Gonzalvo 179
Goodbread 38
Goodson 147
Goodwin 82, 92
Goolsby 69, 83
Gordon 62
Gore 179
Gossett 14, 15, 16, 26
Gott 162
Goyen 176
Graham 56, 57, 62, 86, 165
Gran 31
Grant 61, 148
Grantham 88
Grantom 43
Grasmeyer 41
Grayson 8
Greaser 37
Green 31, 50, 66, 79, 90, 107, 123, 140, 152
Greenhill 40
Greenwood 83, 84, 162
Greer 85, 151
Gregory 17, 26, 85
Griffin 34, 60, 85
Griffith 62
Grigsby 86
Grimes 86
Grimm 177
Grissom 44
Groce 92, 111, 122, 176
Groces 46, 47
Grove 134
Gruene 87
Grumble 73
Gualt 139
Guerra 26, 87
Guittard 26
Gutiérrez 7
Guzman 29

H

Habermacher 113
Haby 87, 153
Haddock 92
Hadley 88
Haggard 174
Hahn 88
Haley 26
Hall 89, 116, 118, 125, 178
Haller 138
Hallford 89
Hamilton 30, 42, 124
Hampton 144, 177, 178
Handshy 89
Haniff 168
Hankamer 90
Hannafious 97
Hanover 90, 91
Hardeman 26, 91
Hardin 37, 89, 110, 111, 132, 162
Hardt 138
Hardwick 133
Hargis 91
Harkness 92
Harkrider 57
Harlan 149
Harper 143, 167
Harreld 120
Harrell 79, 179
Harrington 118
Harris 51, 55, 92
Harrison 28, 93, 127, 151, 165
Hart 66, 93
Hartman 17
Harvey 56, 92, 94, 144, 155
Harwell 84
Hastings 173
Hatfield 90
Hatley 49
Haverstock 157
Hawkins 63
Hay 21, 26
Hayes 84, 102, 158, 180
Haynes 48
Haynie 75, 94
Hays 19, 26, 35, 61, 76, 84, 117
Hearn 75
Heath 16, 94
Heep 156
Hegemeyer 62
Heitkorn 153
Helborn 156
Helm 53
Henderson 11, 35, 61, 73, 93, 99, 156, 177
Hendrick 175
Hendricks 64, 83
Henry 151
Henshaw 158
Hensley 31
Henson 37, 172
Herbert 168
Herrera 152
Hicks 116, 123
Higginbotham 105
Highsmith 63
Hill 13, 16, 17, 19, 21, 26, 80, 94, 108
Hilliard 128
Himes 117
Hinman 98
Hitchcock 54
Hitson 167
Hobart 56
Hobby 15, 142
Hoblitzelle 26
Hobson 73, 95
Hoch 95
Hockley 111
Hodges 11, 147
Hoff 170
Holden 79
Holland 90, 95
Holliday 118
Holman 96
Holmes 101, 154
Holmsley 64
Holt 33
Homeguard 84
Hooper 83
Hoove 79
Hopkins 49, 51
Hornbuckle 26
Hornsby 31
Horton 20, 23, 73, 113
Hostetter 117
Houston 9, 10, 12, 13, 14, 15, 17, 19, 20, 21, 22, 24, 25, 26, 30, 31, 33, 34, 36, 37, 38, 42, 44, 45, 46, 47, 50, 54, 57, 60, 61, 62, 63, 68, 69, 75, 77, 83, 90, 93, 96, 97, 99, 100, 103, 104, 105, 108, 111, 115, 120, 122, 124, 125, 126, 133, 140, 142, 146, 151, 157, 159, 160, 163, 165, 166, 171, 172, 173, 176, 181
Howard 26, 74, 129
Howe 13, 115
Howell 122, 144, 158, 174
Howland 71
Hudgins 132
Hudson 78
Hudspeth 145
Huebner 26
Huffman 112, 113, 144, 145
Hugghins 56
Hughes 32, 159
Huguenard 56
Hull 56, 173
Hunt 45, 97, 107
Hunter 37, 108
Huson 12, 26
Hustin 84
Huston 13, 98, 99
Hutchings 93
Hutchins 131
Hutchison 146
Hutto 84

I

Iiams 92
Inch 145
Inglish 157
Ireland 33
Irion 100
Irish 97
Irvine 117
Isaacks 92, 172
Isaacs 176
Izard 140

J

Jack 8, 102, 103, 111, 158
Jacks 173
Jackson 57, 62, 63, 95, 97, 101, 118, 123, 148, 150, 154, 158, 163, 164, 171, 172, 179
Jacobs 30
Jaime 181
James 21, 122
January 127
Jay 181
Jenkins 37, 174
Jennings 91
Jewell 104
Joel 101
John 13
Johnson 9, 35, 50, 58, 61, 101, 102, 148, 162, 168, 178
Johnston 21, 52, 55, 56, 84, 99, 102, 146
Jones 10, 11, 13, 14, 16, 21, 26, 38, 40, 51, 53, 61, 63, 68, 76, 79, 103, 118, 126, 138, 159, 161, 163
Jordan 20, 84, 103, 104
Journeay 104
Jowel 101
Jowers 98
Judy 130
Junek 147
Junemann 32
Jutson 104

K

Karstendiek 52
Kaufman 99, 147
Keck 108
Keith 31, 105
Kellam 180

Keller 59
Kellum 137
Kelly 133
Kelton 105, 116, 117
Kemp 16, 26, 36, 37, 50
Kendall 13, 14, 17, 20, 23, 26, 43, 156
Kennard 88
Kennedy 51, 57, 98
Kenny 40
Kent 23, 181
Kerr 45, 96, 105
Kesler 105
Kesselus 37
Kessler 105
Key 106
Kiest 47
Kilgore 172
Killough 66
Kimble 38
Kimbro 53, 151, 165
Kincade 92
King 13, 88, 89, 94, 101, 106
Kingsbury 80
Kinnison 71
Kipp 172
Kirkendoll 126
Kirlicks 165
Kitterer 47
Kleberg 12, 106, 107
Kleikamp 107
Klekamp 107
Kleykamp 107
Kline 80
Kloepper 87
Klukamp 107
Knapp 39
Knarr 74
Kneeland 121
Knight 107
Knowles 46
Knox 28
Koelsch 92
Koenig 88, 115
Kornegay 108, 109, 122
Koyn 124
Kraft 109
Kratz 84
Kraus 65
Krause 107
Krischke 115
Kropp 120
Kuriger 115
Kuykendahl 169
Kuykendall 12, 50, 86, 110

L

Labadie 36, 110, 111, 172
Lacey 57, 112, 161
Lacy 83
Ladd 172
LaFayette 120
LaGrone 112, 113, 144, 145
Lakenmacher 64
Lamar 9, 10, 35, 50, 61, 76, 98, 116, 134, 163
Lamb 108, 122
Lancaster 12
Landrum 101, 144
Lane 77
Lang 113
Langford 113, 114
Latimer 156
Lattimer 93
Lattimore 157
Laughter 157
Laux 114, 115
Lawhon 72, 115, 158, 159
Lawrence 115, 122
Lawshe 32
Le Moyne 6
Lea 97
Leach 51, 89
Leath 145
Leatherman 42, 124
Ledbetter 128
Lee 51, 73, 169
Lefevre 151
Leftwich 8
Leger 90
Lehmann 125
LeMaster 116
Lemasters 115
Lenz 18, 26
Lesassier 102
Lesesne 80
Lester 18, 66, 108
Letney 120
LeVrier 73
Levy 115
Lewis 50, 61, 115, 116
Lewright 75
Liesman 120
Liesmann 120
Ligett 41
Lightfoot 88
Ligon 148, 161
Lincoln 39
Lindheimer 107
Lindley 58, 105, 116
Lindsey 41, 90
Link 139
Linn 37
Lischka 170
Liston 43
Little 45, 76, 117
Littlepage 107, 108
Litzler 126
Livergood 117
Liverman 31
Lloyd 106
Lobit 21
Lockhart 52, 94, 117
Loftin 45
Logan 111, 112, 142
Long 7, 26, 68, 118
Looney 86, 163
Lopez 118
Lord 118, 119
Lott 37, 125
Love 26, 101, 156
Loven 164
Loving 74, 130
Low 76, 82, 119
Lucas 60
Luck 174
Ludwig 164
Luessmann 119, 120
Lunz 122
Luther 146
Luttenbacher 138

M

MacDonald 37
MacGee 120
MacPherson 123
Madden 175
Maddux 74
Madeley 19, 26
Madero 76, 102
Madison 97
Magee 120, 168
Maguire 26
Mahan 48
Main 26
Major 165
Malone 23, 26
Malsch 18, 26
Manchacca 70
Marins 138
Marion 143
Marrs 156
Marsh 79
Marshall 26, 53
Marsters 30
Martel 19, 26
Martin 45, 85, 102, 116, 117, 143, 145
Martinez 76, 170
Mason 112, 144, 145, 169, 172, 173, 174
Mast 164
Masterson 26, 93
Mathis 26
Matthews 57, 165, 174
Maverick 26
Max 64
Mayfield 20, 35
Mayward 72
McBroom 69
McCaffrey 175
McCall 29, 49
McCarthy 17
McCarty 43
McCauley 93
McClain 150
McClellan 57
McClenon 52
McClure 126
McCombs 26
McCorcle 120, 121
McCorkel 120
McCorkle 172
McCown 93
McCrum 167
McCulloch 64, 78, 96, 147
McCutcheon 121
McDaniel 121, 154
McDonald 103, 114, 151
McDowell 81
McElmurry 73
McElroy 70, 149
McFarland 130, 165
McFarlin 118
McGary 108, 109, 122
McGee 7, 122, 168
McGhee 94
McGill 30, 55
McGinnis 35
McGough 105
McGown 123
McGuffin 88
McGuigan 148
McGuire 73, 154
McIntyre 161
McKaskle 129
McKay 56
McKean 178
McKendree 158
McKenna 104, 137
McKenzie 32, 33, 62, 92
McKenzine 148
McKinney 26, 100
McKinzie 53
McKissick 109, 122
McLane 23, 26
McLaughlin 40, 51
McLean 26
McLemore 123
McLeroy 128
McMinn 133
McNabb 11
McNairy 42, 43, 124
McNeill 56
McNutt 149
McVea 15, 16, 26
Meadows 64
Medlin 89

Medone 177
Mefford 55
Megarity 17, 18
Meier 151
Meinecke 124
Mendenhall 102
Menefee 69, 80, 162
Mercer 152
Mergele 125
Merrem 115
Merriman 101
Meusebach 22
Mexia 103
Meyer 31, 87
Meyers 119
Middleton 172, 180
Milam 9, 19, 26, 29, 57, 75, 79, 85, 116, 166
Mill 77
Miller 26, 58, 63, 83, 97, 123, 125, 126, 131
Minniece 105
Minter 52
Mistrot 165
Mitchell 13, 73, 84, 105, 117, 177, 180
Mittel 78
Monigold 43
Montalbo 26
Monte 102
Montgomery 126, 140
Moody 13, 14, 16, 147
Moore 16, 18, 26, 61, 62, 66, 68, 73, 95, 105, 108, 116, 117, 126, 127, 145, 156
Moorman 77
Morehouse 149
Morgan 45
Morris 15, 16, 26, 57, 61, 114, 120, 127, 128
Morrison 169
Morrow 26
Mosby 73
Moseley 128
Moss 93, 128
Mott 93
Motz 126
Moyers 62
Muckleroy 128, 129
Muery 170
Muncey 129
Munger 123
Munke 115
Murphey 158
Murphree 92
Murphy 52, 106
Murray 148
Murrow 151
Mussmann 120
Myers 21, 129
Myrick 151

N

Nance 26, 91
Nash 130, 147
Navarro 12, 61, 117, 136
Neal 80, 125
Ned 89
Neff 14, 46
Nelson 53
Neumann 59
Neville 69
Newell 37
Newman 130, 169
Newton 32, 41, 44, 75, 98, 130
Nichols 82, 131
Nimitz 16, 26
Nixon 26
Noble 131
Nolan 7
Norment 111, 112
Norris 144, 145
Northington 131, 132

O

Oberkampf 152
Oberste 26
Obsta 118, 132
Ochiltree 85, 99
O'Connor 18, 19, 26
Odom 26, 147
Oehler 78
Oliver 79
O'Neal 26
Orton 50
Ory 132
Osborne 135
Osvold 173
Owen 81, 149, 180
Owsley 143
Oxley 105

P

Padilla 110
Paine 132
Paist 177
Palacios 30
Palmer 133, 134, 145, 162
Parker 45, 68, 84, 88, 133, 134, 140, 142, 176
Parks 143
Parma 129
Parmer 133, 134
Parrish 86
Parsons 119, 134
Parten 21
Partin 32
Partlow 21
Partney 139

Pate 63, 176
Patrick 111, 123
Patsey 146
Patterson 39, 131
Patton 31, 54, 63, 92, 134, 135
Pausel 58
Paxton 97
Pay 173
Pearson 29, 52
Pease 92
Peebles 110
Peek 126
Pendleton 103
Pendley 133, 154
Penn 134
Penney 134
Pennington 26, 135
Perez 30, 136
Perkins 117
Perry 19, 20, 104, 136
Peter 120
Peterson 147
Pettus 29, 150
Peuler 107
Pevehouse 137
Peyton 173
Phelps 137
Phillips 80, 84, 158
Phouts 143
Pichot 137, 138, 139
Pickens 106
Pickrell 64
Piedras 54, 103
Pier 139
Pierce 137
Pierson 139, 140, 141, 159
Pingenot 138
Pinson 58
Pleasants 11, 93
Plemmons 141, 142, 168
Polk 10
Pollard 58
Ponce 147
Ponton 117, 141, 181
Powel 89
Powell 141, 142
Powers 63
Prastik 66
Prather 94
Price 23, 45, 47, 62, 105, 126
Pridgen 118
Priest 113
Prior 144, 145
Pritchard 178
Procter 26
Proli 164
Pruit 74
Prukop 132
Putnam 40
Pyle 116

Q

Quinn 93

R

Rabb 130
Raguet 100, 142
Randolph 109, 113
Rasch 94
Rash 20
Ratcliff 80
Ratliff 141, 142, 161, 168
Ravel 72
Rawlins 143
Ray 143
Rayburn 63, 94, 122
Read 126
Reavis 141
Rector 140
Red 26
Redding 134
Redwine 51
Reed 30, 68, 91, 143, 144
Reel 112, 113, 144, 145
Reese 117, 126, 162
Reeves 145
Reid 146
Reinhardt 97
Reinhart 98
Reinke 63
Rektorik 59
Revere 152
Reynolds 116, 177
Rhea 146
Rheaume 110
Rhodes 108, 109, 122
Rice 39, 50, 80, 146, 147
Rich 138
Richards 167
Richardson 26, 92, 145, 147
Riddlesperger 55
Riggs 49, 135, 156
Rios 30
Riser 112, 113
Ritchie 19, 20, 23, 26, 37
Rivera 112
Roan 44
Roark 100
Robbins 54
Robert 105, 106, 146
Roberts 17, 20, 21, 26, 70, 99, 145, 146, 147, 148
Robertson 79, 95, 97, 140, 141, 151, 159, 166
Robins 63
Robinson 11, 17, 26, 113, 140, 148
Roddy 110
Rodriguez 77, 136

Roege 109
Rogers 23, 26, 53, 68, 80, 148, 149
Rollin 76
Roman 72
Romberg 78
Romero 30
Roper 76
Rose 51
Ross 48, 78, 137, 150
Rost 97
Roten 103
Rothermel 151
Rouse 145
Rowe 56, 151
Rowlett 72
Rozier 96
Rubenstein 115
Rubio 170
Ruckman 31
Ruiz 151, 158
Runnels 42, 64, 124
Rush 152, 180
Rusk 30, 35, 63, 83, 92, 98, 111, 116, 142, 148, 176
Russell 45, 55, 57, 159
Rust 107
Ryan 93
Ryland 174

S

Saathoff 139
Sadler 116
Salinas 170
San Miguel 20, 26
Sanches 54
Sanchez 76, 152, 170
Sanders 71
Sandlance 65
Sansom 120
Santa Anna 9
Sappington 129
Sartwelle 26
Satel 41
Sauder 153
Saul 140
Saunders 77
Schafer 142
Schertz 125
Schiwetz 26
Schlemmer 155
Schoonover 153
Schorp 88, 153
Schouller 115
Schuelke 132
Schuessler 153
Schulmeyer 153
Schulze 104
Schumacher 21, 115

Scobee 41
Scoggins 94
Scollard 165
Scott 11, 32, 53, 54, 96, 118, 154
Scruggs 137, 154
Scurlock 21, 40, 154
Searle 134
Sears 26
Seaton 48
Secrest 58
Seddons 119
Seeligson 19, 26
Seeton 152
Seguin 29, 77, 78, 155
Seidemann 155
Seiler 110
Seitzler 31
Sewell 165
Sexton 147
Seymeour 112
Shafer 95
Shafner 57
Shannon 93, 156, 159
Sharp 143, 147
Shartle 19
Shaw 156
Shelton 156, 172
Shepherd 26
Shepperd 26, 134
Sherman 13, 15, 19, 34, 36, 46, 47, 61, 92, 111, 156, 176
Shilling 82
Shivers 26, 156
Shockley 137
Shuffler 26
Sibley 180
Silkwood 88, 89
Simes 30
Simons 81, 157
Simpson 19, 157, 158
Sinclair 63
Sinks 150
Sitterle 171
Skelton 71, 91
Slates 111
Slatter 140
Sloneker 126
Smith 20, 21, 22, 24, 25, 26, 28, 29, 36, 38, 42, 54, 86, 88, 90, 104, 108, 114, 120, 124, 128, 134, 137, 146, 151, 153, 156, 158, 159, 165, 171, 173
Smithson 135
Smithwick 23, 174
Smyer 91
Smyt 86
Snider 126
Snively 90, 113, 147

Solms 125
Somervell 12, 76, 84, 118
Sonnichsen 37
Spaight 76
Spaights 90
Sparks 91, 176, 181
Spears 117
Speights 172
Speir 159
Spellman 26
Spencer 157
Spettle 153
Spicer 154
Spiller 31
Spoonemore 42
Spradley 133
St. John 93
Stadler 70
Stagner 67
Stallings 44
Stallones 44
Stalnaker 26
Standefer 79
Standish 75
Stapleton 69, 167
Stapp 84, 159
Stark 57, 178
Steel 116
Steele 140, 160, 180
Steen 26
Stell 160, 161
Stephens 172
Stephenson 134, 172
Sterling 14, 15
Sterne 19, 23
Stevenson 131
Stewart 44
Stiles 161
Stockton 60, 161, 169
Stokes 51, 124
Stone 26, 94, 143
Stowe 161
Strake 26
Strang 161
Strasbach 132
Straufschneider 126
Straw 126
Stribling 84, 162
Stricker 139
Strickland 84
Stripling 18, 26
Strong 41, 49
Stuart 104
Stubblefield 122
Stukes 160
Suggs 72
Summer 74
Sutherland 80, 162, 163
Swanzy 57
Sweeney 92

Sweeton 177
Swindell 70
Swinney 172
Switzer 149
Sylvester 111

T

Taif 145
Tannehill 48
Tarrant 39, 44, 128
Tarver 26
Tate 64, 84
Tatman 162
Taylor 61, 85, 94, 117, 127, 141
Teague 142
Teal 58, 147
Teel 99
Temple 130
Tennelle 37
Terheun 163
Terrell 163
Terry 50, 97
Teutsch 164
Thomas 74, 84, 95, 128, 145, 157, 164, 165
Thompson 4, 57, 79, 83, 114, 123, 134, 161, 165, 166, 174
Thomson 166, 167
Thorn 8
Thornton 167
Thrall 37, 50
Throckmorton 67
Thurmond 21
Tidwell 39, 140
Tindall 23, 26, 30
Tinkle 26
Tippett 151
Tips 26
Tipton 69
Tise 154
Todd 34
Tolan 154
Tolbert 63, 105, 116
Tolleson 167
Tom 93
Tondre 153
Tooper 165
Totten 117
Towers 142
Townes 26
Townsend 33, 167, 168
Townsley 174
Trammel 73
Travis 21, 22, 28, 30, 38, 64, 79, 86, 87, 92, 102, 103, 110, 111, 150, 159, 163, 178
Trespalacios 169

Trevino 87
Trinkle 14
Tritico 17, 18, 19, 20, 26
Trotter 177
Trotti 168
Tucker 112, 172
Tumbleston 169
Tumey 147
Tumlinson 67, 80, 141, 142, 168, 169
Turner 4, 113
Twomey 177
Tyler 11
Tyszkowski 65

U

Ullrich 153
Underwood 52
Upchurch 70
Urrea 9, 113, 116, 140
Ussery 145

V

Valdez 136
Van Norman 178
Van Vleck 169
Van Wamel 169
Van Zandi, 25
Van Zandt 128
VanArsdale 107
Vandiver 26
Vasquez 31, 127, 140
Vaughan 49
Vaughn 52
Vawter 170
Veal 143
Veatch 116
Veazey 39
Vehlein 49, 142, 146
Vehlien 123
Veramendi 152
Vice 28
Vidaurri 170

Vinson 77
Vogelsang 32
Vollmer 59
Von Coll 125
Von Roeder 106

W

Waddell 56
Wade 16, 18, 26, 43, 58
Wagner 170
Waits 127
Wakefield 128
Wales 31
Walker 31, 94, 95, 129, 165, 171
Wallace 26
Waller 70, 109, 171
Wallis 112, 171, 172
Walter 11
Walters 35, 172
Wamel 170
Wammel 170
Ward 54, 86
Ware 63, 77, 79, 165, 176
Warren 91, 104, 139
Washington 58, 107, 117, 120
Watkins 172
Watson 30, 63, 128
Watts 17, 26, 48
Wear 119
Wearden 17, 18, 26
Weathersbee 62
Weaver 90
Webb 50, 73, 127, 145, 173
Weeks 31
Wehlein 172
Welborn 53
Wells 26, 40, 116, 135, 173, 174
Wesley 166
West 93, 144, 174
Westmoreland 174
Weston 50
Westover 45
Wetsell 104

Wharton 14, 37, 50, 71, 92, 148
Whatley 159
Wheeler 51, 70, 152, 153, 178
Wheelock 146
Whitaker 35
White 20, 26, 48, 51, 54, 81, 101, 102, 105, 116, 135, 148, 172
Whitfield 168
Whiting 45
Whitley 51, 116, 175
Whitten 130
Wick 144
Wicks 85
Wiehl 118
Wier 52, 133, 154
Wiggington 118
Wiginton 162
Wiglesworth 96
Wilbarger 37
Wilbur 168
Wilburn 155
Wilcox 111
Wiley 19, 23, 26, 133, 152, 175, 176
Wilkerson 126
Wilkinson 107, 128
William 11, 105
Williams 13, 14, 15, 18, 21, 26, 48, 50, 53, 56, 66, 67, 68, 76, 93, 109, 110, 154, 159, 166, 176
Williamson 82, 102, 110, 176, 177, 178
Willis 26, 158, 178
Wilson 17, 67, 75, 118, 147, 180
Winder 86
Winfree 77, 171
Winfrey 26, 37
Winkler 126, 159
Winnans 35
Winnie 104
Winston 11

Winters 63
Wise 26, 88
Witt 159
Woliver 28
Woll 35, 61, 84, 128, 140, 179
Wolters 13, 14
Wood 21, 89, 93, 118, 128, 178
Wooderson 178
Woodfin 156
Woodruff 80
Woods 58, 176, 178, 179
Woodward 26, 66
Wool 32
Wooldridge 92
Woolly 144
Woolsey 127
Wooten 172
Wornell 179
Worsham 101
Wright 22, 26, 31, 44, 88, 89, 93, 153, 155, 161, 175
Wynne 160

Y

Yarborough 26
Yard 180
Yates 156
Y'Barbo 7, 54, 152
Yelvington 84
Yoast 180
York 72, 107
Yost 150
Young 45, 96, 156
Younts 144

Z

Zaboly 37
Zachry 157
Zavalla 113
Zonie 145
Zuber 88
Zumwalt 37, 48, 117, 181

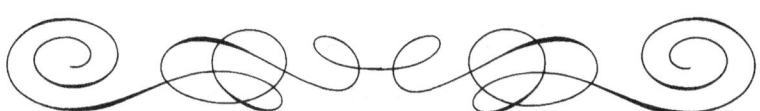

Family Tree

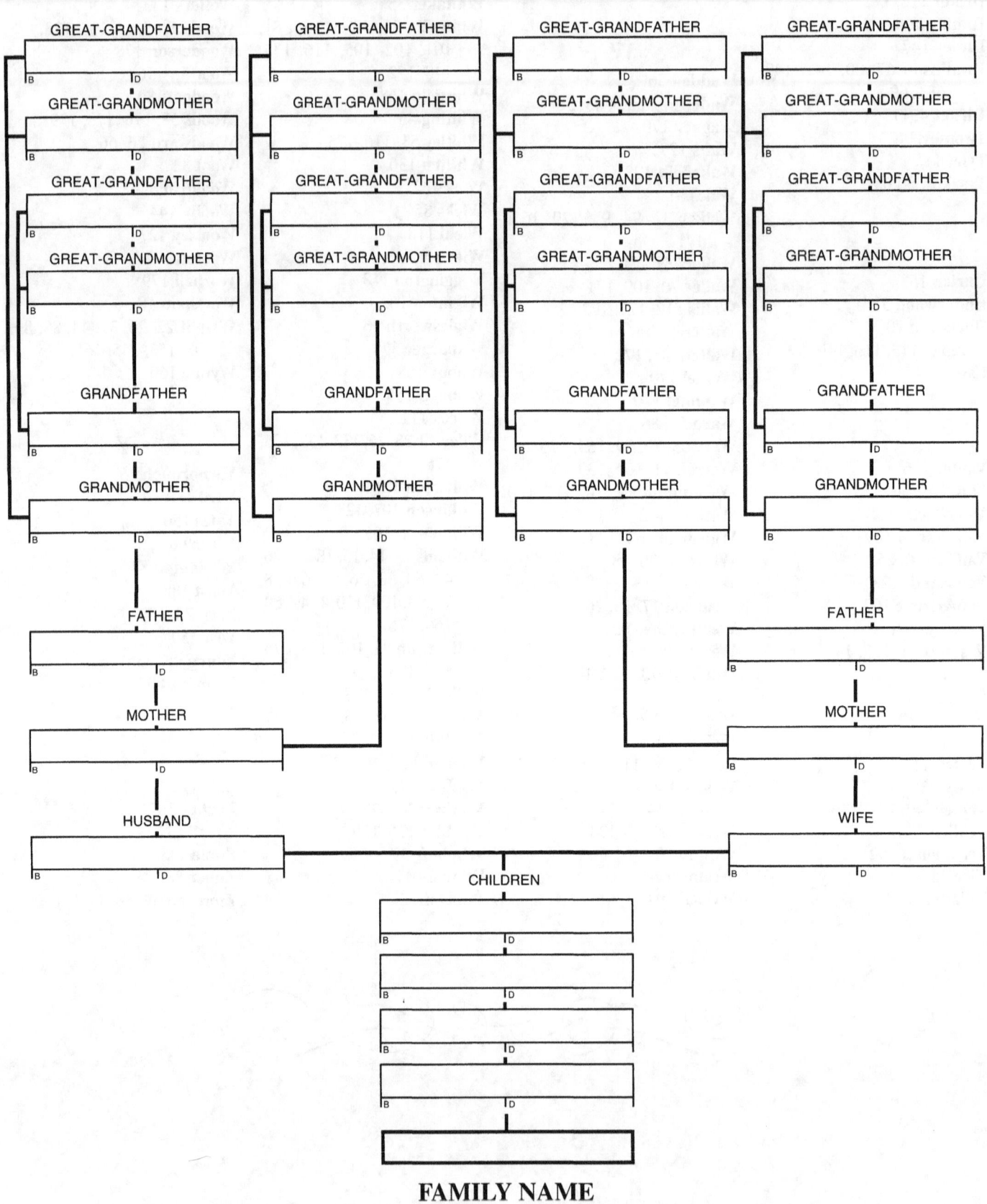

FAMILY NAME

FAMILY RECORD

NAME	BIRTH	DEATH

Notes

www.ingramcontent.com/pod-product-compliance
Lightning Source LLC
Chambersburg PA
CBHW082044300426
44117CB00015B/2604